The Middle Classes in Latin America

As a collective effort, this volume locates the formation of the middle classes at the core of the histories of Latin America in the last two centuries. Featuring scholars from different places across the Americas, it is an interdisciplinary contribution to the world histories of the middle classes, histories of Latin America, and intersectional studies. It also engages a larger audience about the importance of the middle classes to understand modernity, democracy, neoliberalism, and decoloniality. By including research produced from a variety of Latin American, North American, and other audiences, the volume incorporates trends in social history, cultural studies, and discursive theory. It situates analytical categories of race and gender at the core of class formation. This volume seeks to initiate a critical and global conversation concerning the ways in which the analysis of the middle classes provides crucial re-readings of how Latin America, as a region, has historically been understood.

Mario Barbosa Cruz is Professor in the Humanities Department at Universidad Autónoma Metropolitana.

A. Ricardo López-Pedreros is Professor of History at Western Washington University.

Claudia Stern is Research Associate at The Latin American Centre for the History of Housing CEIHVAL at the Architecture, Design and Urban Studies Faculty at Universidad de Buenos Aires, FADU-UBA.

Routledge Studies in the History of the Americas

American Divergences in the Great Recession
Daniele Pompejano

Social and Political Transitions During the Left Turn in Latin America
Edited by Karen Silva-Torres, Carolina Rozo-Higuera and Daniel S. Leon

A New Struggle for Independence in Modern Latin America
Edited by Pablo A. Baisotti

Problems and Alternatives in the Modern Americas
Edited by Pablo A. Baisotti

Setbacks and Advances in the Modern Latin American Economy
Edited by Pablo A. Baisotti

Social, Political, and Religious Movements in the Modern Americas
Edited by Pablo A. Baisotti

The Policy of the Ford Administration Toward Cuba
Carrot and Stick
Håkan Karlsson and Tomás Diez Acosta

The New Pan-Americanism and the Structuring of Inter-American Relations
Edited by Juan Pablo Scarfi and David M. K. Sheinin

The Middle Classes in Latin America
Subjectivities, Practices, and Genealogies
Edited by Mario Barbosa Cruz, A. Ricardo López-Pedreros, and Claudia Stern

For more information about this series, please visit: https://www.routledge.com/Routledge-Studies-in-the-History-of-the-Americas/book-series/RSHAM

The Middle Classes in Latin America

Subjectivities, Practices, and Genealogies

Edited by Mario Barbosa Cruz, A. Ricardo López-Pedreros, and Claudia Stern

Routledge
Taylor & Francis Group
NEW YORK AND LONDON

First published 2022
by Routledge
605 Third Avenue, New York, NY 10158

and by Routledge
4 Park Square, Milton Park, Abingdon, Oxon, OX14 4RN

Routledge is an imprint of the Taylor & Francis Group, an informa business

Library of Congress Cataloging-in-Publication Data
A catalog record for this title has been requested

ISBN: 978-0-367-46530-8 (hbk)
ISBN: 978-1-032-28513-9 (pbk)
ISBN: 978-1-003-02931-1 (ebk)

DOI: 10.4324/9781003029311

Typeset in Sabon
by SPi Technologies India Pvt Ltd (Straive)

Contents

Figures

Tables

Acknowledgments

The idea for this volume was born in 2018. The first iteration of what we now share in book form was an international conference titled *Clases medias en Latinoamérica: subjetividades e historias* that the editors of this volume organized in El Colegio de México in Mexico City in April 2019. Both the conference and this volume have been the product of a collective effort. They have also been the result of multiple transnational discussions about the meanings, practices, and ideas about the middle classes in Latin America. Just as the formation of the middle classes have been a transnational experience, so has the ongoing knowledge production about such formation.

The conference was made possible thanks to the support of the Programa de Ciencia Básica SEP CONACyT and project CB2015/258106 *"Condiciones de vida, prácticas socioculturales y rasgos de identidad. Los sectores medios en la ciudad de México, 1855–1931"*; the Humanities and Social Sciences Division at the Universidad Autónoma Metropolitana, Cuajimalpa Campus; the seminar on Social History at El Colegio de México, IIH UNAM and UAM Cuajimalpa; and the Department of History and the Office of Research and Sponsored Programs at Western Washington University. We thank Gerardo Romero Medrano and Luis Hernández Huerta for their invaluable work in organizing and coordinating the conference.

This peer-reviewed volume was supported by funds from the Programa de Ciencia Básica SEP CONACyT and project CB2015/258106 *"Condiciones de vida, prácticas socioculturales y rasgos de identidad. Los sectores medios en la ciudad de México, 1855–1931"*; the Humanities and Social Sciences Division at Universidad Autónoma Metropolitana, Cuajimalpa Campus; and the Department of History and the Office of Research and Sponsored Programs at Western Washington University. Our deepest gratitude goes to the chapter reviewers and to Samia Saliba for her work organizing and editing the text. We are also grateful to Quentin Pope for his professionalism and committed work on the volume. We are indebted to Gilbert Joseph and Brian Owensby, who selflessly undertook the challenge of writing the Foreword and Epilogue to the volume.

We would like to express our deep appreciation to all the contributors whose commitment, enthusiasm, and attentive responsiveness have made this a smooth and especially enjoyable process. For the three of us as a collective, this was a challenge that we undertook with conviction and enthusiasm, and we learned a great deal from our countless and fruitful dialogues. The process has been an absolute inspiration. Finally, this volume would not have been possible without the interest, support, and guidance of Max Novick, editor of the Routledge Studies in the History of the Americas series. We are grateful for the trust he placed in us and for the opportunity to offer a contribution to the study of the middle classes in Latin America.

The Editors

Abbreviations

ANAPO	Alianza Nacional Popular
APRA	Alianza Popular Revolucionaria Americana
BANOBRAS	Banco Nacional de Obras y Servicios Públicos
BIMSA	Buró de Investigación de Mercado, S.A.
BNHOUOPSA	Banco Nacional Hipotecario Urbano y de Obras Públicas
CAA	Centro de Alumnos
CCM	Confederación de la Clase Media
CC-ARI	Coalición Cívica-Afirmación para una República Igualitaria
CCSS	Costa Rican Social Security Fund
CECH	Comité Permanente de la Conferencia Episcopal
CEPAL	Comisión Especial para América Latina
CEREN	Centro de Estudios de la Realidad Nacional
CESO	Centro de Estudios Socioeconómicos
CONASUPO	Compañía Distribuidora de Subsistencias Populares
CRCP	Costa Rican Communist Party
CSNP	Center for the Study of National Problems
CTC	Confederación de Trabajadores de Colombia
CTM	Confederación de Trabajadores de México
CUPA	Centro Urbano Presidente Alemán
DAPP	Departamento Autónomo de Prensa y Publicidad
DC	Democracia Cristiana
DDF	Departamento del Distrito Federal
DINA	Dirección de Inteligencia Nacional
DNT	Departamento Nacional del Trabajo
DOP	The Municipal Works Department
ECLAC	Economic Commission for Latin American and the Caribbean
ENP	Escuela Nacional Preparatoria
ENS	Escuela Normal Superior
ENU	Escuela Nacional Unificada
FARC	Fuerzas Armadas Revolucionarias de Colombia

FEC	Federación de Empleados de Comercio
FLACSO	Facultad Latinoamericana de Ciencias Sociales
FPMR	Frente Patriótico Manuel Rodríguez
MAPU	Movimiento de Acción Popular Unitaria
MAPU/OC	MAPU Obrero campesino
MAS	Movimiento al Socialismo
MPST	Ministerio de Previsión Social y Trabajo
NAFTA	North American Free Trade Agreement
ODS	Observatorio de la Deuda Social
PAC	Programa de Aceleração do Crescimento
PD	Partido Democrático
PNR	Partido Nacional Revolucionario
PC	Partido Comunista
PCC-ML	Partido Comunista Colombiano–Marxista Leninista
PRM	Partido de la Revolución Mexicana
PRP	Partido Republicano Paulista
PT	Partido dos Trabalhadores
SENAI	Serviço Nacional de Aprendizagem Industrial
SESI	Serviço Social da Indústria
UC	Pontificia Universidad Católica de Chile
UDI	Unidades de Inversión para Préstamos Hipotecarios
UNAM	Universidad Nacional Autónoma de México
UNESCO	United Nations Educational, Scientific and Cultural Organization
UP	Unidad Popular
TEC	Instituto Tecnológico de Monterrey

Notes on the Contributors

Mario Barbosa Cruz is Professor in the Humanities Department at Universidad Autónoma Metropolitana. His research focuses on the social history of Mexico since the nineteenth century. His most recent book is *La paz, un largo proceso. Relato autobiográfico de Alberto Rojas Puyo* (Universidad del Rosario/Siglo del Hombre Editores, 2018). He received a PhD in History from the Colegio de México in 2005.

Azun Candina Polomer received her PhD in history from the University of Chile. She is Professor at the Department of Philosophy and Humanities and coordinator of the Magister in Latin American Studies at the same institution. She has researched and published on identities and social memories, authoritarianism and conflicts in Chile and the Southern Cone.

Valeria Coronel received a PhD in history from New York University. She obtained a Master's Degree at Facultad Latinoamericana de Ciencias Sociales (FLACSO). Her research addresses the transition from the oligarchic state to the national social state in the Andean region, as well as forms of mobilization and integration of the indigenous peasantry in political parties during the nineteenth and twentieth centuries. She has published essays on the relationship between corporatism and the democratic process in Ecuador.

Terioska Gámez is a PhD candidate in anthropology at Universidad Autónoma Metropolitana. He obtained a master's degree in anthropology at the Escuela Nacional de Antropología e Historia. He majored in chemical engineering at the Universidad Autónoma de México. He has held visiting positions at University of Texas, Austin, UDELAR in Uruguay and CIS in Argentina.

George I. García-Quesada is Professor and Director of the *Journal of Philosophy* at the University of Costa Rica. Among other publications, he has written books about Henri Lefebvre's critique of everyday life, about Karl Marx's philosophy of history, and about the history of the middle class in Costa Rica.

Enrique Garguin received an MA from SUNY-SB and is a professor of history at Universidad Nacional de La Plata. He has co-edited, with Sergio Visacovsky, *Moralidades, economías e identidades de clase media. Estudios históricos y etnográficos* (Antropofagia, 2009) and *Argentina y sus clases medias. Panoramas de la investigación empírica en ciencias sociales* (Biblos, 2020)

Gilbert M. Joseph is Farnam Professor Emeritus of History and International Studies at Yale University. During 2015-2016 he was the President of the Latin American Studies Association (LASA). Among the books he has authored are *Revolution from Without: Yucatán, Mexico, and the United States, 1880-1924* (Cambridge 1982; rev. ed., Duke, 1988); and (with Jürgen Buchenau) *Mexico's Once and Future Revolution: Social Upheaval and the Challenge of Rule since the Late Nineteenth Century* (Duke, 2013). He is editor or co-editor of *Everyday Forms of State Formation: Revolution and the Challenge of Rule in Modern Mexico* (Duke, 1994); *Close Encounters of Empire: Writing the Cultural History of U.S.-Latin American Relations* (Duke, 1998); *Fragments of a Golden Age: The Politics of Culture in Mexico Since 1940* (Duke, 2001); *Crime and Punishment in Latin America: Law and Society Since Late Colonial Times* (Duke 2001); *Reclaiming the Political in Latin American History (Duke, 2001); The Mexico Reader: History, Culture, Politics* (Duke, 2002; rev. ed, 2022); *In from the Cold: Latin America's New Encounter with the Cold War* (Duke, 2008); and *A Century of Revolution: Insurgent and Counterinsurgent Violence during Latin America's Long Cold War* (Duke, 2010). He is the co-editor of the Duke University Press' book series American Encounters/Global Interactions.

A. Ricardo López-Pedreros is Professor of History at Western Washington University. He is the author of *Makers of Democracy. A Transnational History of the Middle Class in Colombia* (Duke, 2019) and the co-editor of *The Making of the Middle Class: Toward a Transnational History* (Duke, 2012). He is the editor of *Social Movements in the Americas* (Rowman & Littlefield/Lexington Books) and is currently writing a biography of the Colombian sociologist Gabriel Restrepo. He is also working on a history of domination in Colombia during the second half of the twentieth century.

Sara Minerva Luna Elizarrarás received a Master's and a Ph.D. in history at the Universidad Nacional Autónoma de México (UNAM), and a bachelor degree in psychology. Currently, she is a Lecturer at Centro de Investigaciones y Estudios en Antropología Social (CIESAS, Ciudad de México).

Moisés Kopper is a Marie Curie Postdoctoral Fellow at the Laboratoire d'Anthropologie des Mondes Contemporains, Université Libre de Bruxelles. His project explores the technopolitics of Brazil's inequality measures and its powers to fashion images of national futurity. His forthcoming book, *Architectures of Hope*, charts the effects of first-time homeownership among once-socially-ascendant Brazilians.

María Graciela León Matamoros received a PhD in history at El Colegio de México, a Master's Degree in history at ICSyH- BUAP, and a Master's Degree at UJI de Castellón. The Academia Mexicana de Ciencias gave her an award for the best dissertation in 2017. She was the manager of the Centro Histórico y Patrimonio Cultural del Ayuntamiento in Puebla, México.

Brian Owensby is Professor of History in the Corcoran Department of History at the University of Virginia. His scholarly work has ranged from social and political history in nineteenth- and twentieth-century Brazil to legal and imperial history in seventeenth-century Mexico. He is the author of *Intimate Ironies: Modernity and the Making of Middle-Class Lives in Brazil* (Stanford, 1999); *Empire of Law and Indian Justice in Colonial Mexico* (Stanford, 2008; paperback 2011); and *Gain and Global Transformation in the "Land without Evil." Settlers, Guaraní and Jesuits in Early-Modern Paraguay* (Stanford, 2022). He served as chair of the Corcoran Department of History from 2009 to 2012.

David S. Parker is Professor of History at Queen's University, Canada. He is author of *The Idea of the Middle Class* (Penn State, 1998) and *The Pen, the Sword and the Law: Dueling and Democracy in Uruguay* (McGill-Queen's, 2022), and the co-editor of *Latin America's Middle Class* (Rowman and Littlefield, 2013).

Susie S. Porter is Professor in History and Gender Studies, and Chair, Gender Studies Division at the University of Utah. She is also the author of *From Angel to Office Worker: Middle- Class Identity and Female Consciousness in Mexico, 1890-1950* (2018), winner of the McGann Award for Best Publication in Latin American Studies, Rocky Mountain Conference on Latin American Studies Association, 2019; *Working Women in Mexico City: public discourses and material conditions, 1879-1931* (2003), winner of the Outstanding Book Award, Latin American Studies Association, Labor and Class Relations Studies Section, 2004; and the co-editor of *Mexican History: A Primary Source Reader*, with Nora Jaffray and Ed Osowski (2009); *Orden social e identidad de género. México siglos XIX y XX*, with María Teresa Fernández Aceves and Carmen Ramos Escandón (2006); and *Género en la encrucijada de la historia social y cultural*, edited with María Teresa Fernández Aceves (2015).

Graciela Queirolo received a PhD in history at Universidad de Buenos Aires (UBA), and a Master's Degree in history from Universidad Torcuato Di Tella. Currently, she is Professor at the Universidad

Nacional de La Plata (UNLP). She is also a Research Fellow at CONICET - Instituto de Investigaciones en Humanidades y Ciencias Sociales (UNLP). She is the main editor of *Descentrada*. Her doctoral dissertation received an honorable mention from the Asociación Latinoamericana e Ibérica de Historia Social (ALIHS). This dissertation later appeared as *Mujeres en las oficinas* (Biblos, 2018). Her research addresses question of gender and labor.

Sebastián Rivera Mir is a Professor and researcher at El Colegio Mexiquense, and received a PhD in History from the Colegio de México. He is also a member of the National System of Researchers of CONACYT, Level I. He has published articles in specialized magazines and books in Mexico, Argentina, Colombia, Chile and Germany, and is currently researching the academic exchange between Mexico and Latin America during the government of Lázaro Cárdenas.

Cristina Sánchez Parra received her Master's Degree and PhD in history from El Colegio de México. She majored in education, with an emphasis on social sciences at the Universidad Pedagógica Nacional de Colombia. She is currently Professor at Universidad Nacional Autónoma de México. Her research interests are social history and the realm of luxury consumption.

Miriam Shakow is Professor of Anthropology at The College of New Jersey. She is the author of *Along the Bolivian Highway: Social Mobility and Political Culture in a New Middle Class* (UPenn Press, 2014). She earned a PhD in Cultural Anthropology from Harvard University in 2008.

Claudia Stern is Research Associate at The Latin American Centre for the History of Housing CEIHVAL and lecturer at the MEUVAL at the Architecture, Design and Urban Studies Faculty at Universidad de Buenos Aires, FADU-UBA. She is also the author of *Entre el cielo y el suelo: las identidades elásticas de las clases medias* (*Santiago de Chile, 1932–1962*) (Santiago: RiL editores 2021). She received an MA in Cultural Research (2008) and PhD in History (2016) from Tel Aviv University.

Celso M. Villegas received his PhD in sociology from Brown University. His research interests lie in the nexus between political economy, culture and democracy in the developing world, particularly in Latin America and Southeast Asia. Villegas has published work on comparative-historical methodology and comparative middle-class formation in the Philippines, South Korea, Ecuador, and Venezuela. He is currently working on a book manuscript tentatively titled "Social Origins of Distinction and Democracy: Revolutions 'from the Middle' in the Philippines and Latin America."

Sergio E. Visacovsky is Director and Researcher of the Centro de Investigaciones Sociales (Instituto de Desarrollo Económico and Consejo nacional de Investigaciones Científicas y Técnicas), and Postgraduate Professor at the Escuela Interdisciplinaria de Altos Estudios Sociales, Universidad Nacional de San Martín and Universidad Nacional de General Sarmiento. Visacovsky received a PhD in Cultural Anthropology from the University of Utrecht, Netherlands in 2001, and graduated in Anthropological Sciences from the Universidad de Buenos Aires in 1987.

Mara Viveros-Vigoya is Professor of the Escuela de Estudios de Género, Facultad de Ciencias Humanas de la Universidad Nacional de Colombia. She is the author of *Les Couleurs de la masculinité* (París: La découverte. 2018) and editor of Angela Davis and Gina Dent, *Black Feminism. Teoría crítica, violencias y racismo* (Bogotá: UNAL, 2019).

Barbara Weinstein is Silver Professor of History at New York University and author of *For Social Peace in Brazil: Industrialists and the Remaking of the Working Class in São Paulo* and *The Color of Modernity: São Paulo and the Making of Race and Nation in Brazil.* Her current project is an intellectual biography of the Latin Americanist Frank Tannenbaum.

Claudia Zamorano obtained a doctorate degree in Social Sciences from the École des Hautes Études en Sciences Sociales in 1999, with a specialty in urban studies. Since 2000, she has been a Professor-Researcher at the Center for Research and Higher Studies in Social Anthropology, Mexico City. Urban questions are her main research interest, focusing on the residential practices of different social sectors, the right to the city and the impact of the privatization of security in metropolitan spaces.

Foreword

Gilbert M. Joseph

This sprawling and ambitious volume on Latin America's middle classes powerfully reshapes the way we think about the region's past, present, and future. It also contributes insights to timely global discussions of the middle class that should facilitate similarly critical re-readings of the historical trajectories of other regions of the Global South. Harnessing the methods and perspectives of a growing intergenerational cohort of historians, anthropologists, sociologists, and literary scholars writing from Latin America, the United States, and Canada, and synthesizing the major trends in historical and theoretical scholarship of the last several decades, *The Middle Classes in Latin America* promotes expansive thinking about the formation of the middle classes. This newly emergent discursive community of scholars approaches middle-class identities, practices, and genealogies within an eclectic conceptual framework that sheds light on both their local histories as well as their broader connective, comparative, and transnational dimensions.

This is, to put it mildly, an ambitious agenda, one that prompted the editors to set out a sumptuous buffet of offerings on the diverse and complex roles of middle-class women and men in Argentina, Bolivia, Brazil, Colombia, Chile, Costa Rica, Ecuador, Mexico, and Peru. At the same time, the collection calls for careful engagement by its readers. It is organized thematically and roughly chronologically across four broad sections, which effectively turn on larger historical inquiries about modern Latin America. These might be summarized as 1) liberalism, citizenship, and the idea of race during a *long* nineteenth century (which in some essays extends liberalism into the contemporary period of neoliberalism); 2) the multivalent dynamics of labor, consumption, and the political disparities reflected therein, with principal focus on the late nineteenth and early twentieth centuries; 3) populist radicalization and revolutionary politics, experience, and memory during the twentieth century, culminating in the Cold War decades; and 4) the question of social mobility amidst the ascendance of neoliberal discourses and the left-leaning movements (the so-called "Pink Tide") that challenged them at the turn of the twenty-first century. In short there is substantial chronological overlap,

DOI: 10.4324/9781003029311-1

and certain themes, like neoliberalism, range across sections; moreover, several essays might well be accommodated in more than one section. The editors' organizational scheme risks a bit of whiplash at times; on the other hand, it compensates by promoting a satisfying resonance and intertextuality across the thematic divisions. The complex interplay of agency, contingency, and structure, and an attempt to integrate local, regional, national, and transnational fields distinguishes each of the sections. So do two other important leitmotifs: the dynamics and inequalities of gender relations and a dynamic understanding of class. The essays underscore that race, ethnicity, sexuality, and occupation is not the same for men and women; moreover, many of the contributors effectively show that class, contrary to earlier orthodox materialist formulations, is not a fixed category, but must be understood relationally in a manner that does not sideline ethno-racial, gendered, regional, or generational identities, though it may speak through them with important consequences for collective political action. (In this regard, among many relevant contributions, see the masterful essays by Mara Viveros-Vigoya and Barbara Weinstein.) Each of the volume's sections is jam-packed with local case studies, though these detailed micro studies are usually inflected by conceptual introductions and codas, and the book is interspersed with a few more explicitly theoretical essays. In addition, the editors provide handy section introductions that highlight cross-cutting themes. Most importantly, A. Ricardo López-Pedreros' far-ranging theoretical and historiographical introduction showcases the volume's cutting-edge project and stakes, and Brian Owensby's epilogue effectively puts the two dozen essays into a global historical perspective that includes a pithy reflection on the particularly fraught current moment for the world's middle classes.

Indeed, the timing of the volume, in terms of both hemispheric and global events, as well as prevailing scholarly trends, could not be more propitious. As Owensby aptly observes, it has been "the best and worst of times" for the world's middle classes. Less than five years ago, according to criteria provided by leading development organizations, "for the first time ever," more than 50% of the earth's population had crossed the "tipping point" to being "middle class or wealthier." Neoliberals crowed about the milestone, empirical proof, they argued, of the profound revolution wrought by their market-driven doctrines. Nevertheless, although middling folk were said to be surging in Latin America and elsewhere in the Global South, many researchers, journalists, and pundits raised worrisome red flags: not only were their gains so fragile that many in the expanded global middle class were at risk of slipping back into poverty; its members often seemed reluctant to assume the role they have typically been assigned as a modern, democratic "force for change." In fact, as this volume amply documents for Latin America, too many times the middle classes have expressed anti-democratic sentiments, suggesting that their natural tendency was—and remains—as autocratic as democratic. In recent years, in Latin America and elsewhere, in the face of jarring economic fluctuations, the application of "shock treatments," and now, a rampaging pandemic, many have begun to debate whether, rather than coming into its heyday, the end of the middle class might be just as imminent. In the current moment, which Owensby sees as a "simultaneous celebration and hand-wringing," the middle class remains that broad, variegated, Janus-faced swath of society that political contenders invariably recruit to legitimate their projects, whether they themselves are middle class or not. Take, for example, the popular rebellion that has broken out with such force in Colombia in May 2021. Not only did the boisterous popular movement in Cali and other regions include middle-sector adherents—storekeepers, housewives, plot holders, students, artists, intellectuals, and local officials—but the middle class and its "modern," entrepreneurial values were claimed by embattled Colombian President Iván Duque to be the principal beneficiary and rationale of his government's policies. This discourse resonated with right-wing members of the Colombian middle classes who have formed armed militias to defend their "way of life" (much the same rationale that broad sectors of the Chilean middle class initially voiced in supporting General Augusto Pinochet's bloody coup that toppled Allende's *Via Chilena* almost a half century earlier). At the present moment, similar political scenarios could be invoked elsewhere in Andes, the Southern Cone, Mexico, and Central America, and they pervade the historical cases analyzed in the present volume. In sum, the middle class and its allies, its political prospects and practices, and the manner in which it has constructed its social identities—or the way that others have—could not be more relevant.

It is significant that co-editor A. Ricardo López-Pedreros has entitled the volume's introduction "For the First Time Ever." In one sense, he is drawing attention to the optimistic language that celebrated the "tipping point" for a middle-class majority in a 2013 study issued by the World Bank. At the same time, he is sardonically puncturing the latest of many roseate forecasts that have accompanied the definitive arrival of a middle class—robust, expansive, and democratic—forecasts that have rarely panned out in a region that has always ranked as one of the most unequal in the world. The consolidation of such a middle class has therefore been more mirage than reality: the construction of a "fundamental rupture with the past that... locates the middle classes in the fragile present and above all, in an idealized future." No doubt it was owing to this "unanimist fantasy"—the middle class's image as a cherished future aspiration, reflecting a post-class society stripped of unremitting social division and conflict, rather than as an empirical reality—that over time led to the discrediting of successive iterations of "modernization theory," and propelled the region's area specialists, North and South, in other more progressive directions. Dependency theory, neo-Marxian analyses of capitalism and imperialism, subalternist readings of domination and hegemony, and critical theories of post-colonial society—while rather distinct, all based their historical explanations of power and domination on asymmetrical relationships between the ruling classes and masses that relegated the role of the region's diverse, typically collaborationist middle classes, thereby effectively marginalizing their influence in histories of Latin America. My own scholarly career, which began in the early 1970s, as I cut my teeth on dissident paradigms of development like dependency theory, and then evolved increasingly in the direction of subalternist perspectives of twentieth-century social and revolutionary movements, provides a clear illustration of the marginal explanatory role accorded to the middle classes in the work of my generational cohort. Like so many middle-class scholars and activists in the North—and like many of our middle-class counterparts in Latin America who are insightfully treated in the essays of López-Pedreros, Claudia Stern, and Celso Villegas in the third section of this volume—I sought to radicalize and transcend my class position in solidarity with the campesino and popular movements I was studying, especially during the intensely polarizing Cold War years. No doubt this radicalizing political stance accentuated my elision of the middle class as a historical subject.

In another sense, then, the title of A. Ricardo López-Pedreros' introductory essay also signals the volume's intention to move in a radically new direction. Rather than marginalizing or isolating the middle class, he insists on

> locating the formation of the middle classes—the structural conditions of their social (re)-production, their multilayered economic interests, their ample repertoire of political roles, their classed subjectivities, their contradictory political discourses, their multidimensional racial categorizations [and] identities, and their [gender and] sexual politics—at the *center* of the heterogeneous histories of Latin America.

This portends an important new problematization of the middle classes, a bold attempt to rethink society as a whole, not because, as Owensby stresses, "the middle class is more central to some autonomous force or project than other social groups but because middle-class people, perhaps more self-consciously than others, have lived the contrarieties of modern economic, social, and political regimes." The task, then, that the contributors have set for themselves, is not to "reclaim" the historical existence of Latin America's middling sectors, but rather to think about the often motley, occasionally messy, and contingent roles they have played in shaping relations of power at different junctures of Latin America's modern past.

In considering the collection's new currency in scholarly terms, it must be emphasized that scholars have wrestled with the middle classes since at least the late 1940s. It was then, as we learn from David Parker's contribution, that the Pan American Union sponsored a series of publications that sought to empirically define and delimit the inchoate middle class and assess it various roles as a force for modernization. This project was very much a product of its times, the early years of the Cold War in the wake of World War II. Not surprisingly, in the late 1950s and early 60s, the most influential (and best-selling) volume on the region's middle classes was John J. Johnson's *Political Change in Latin America: The Emergence of the Middle* Sectors, which epitomized American-centric modernization theory and saw the middle sectors as the ineluctable force for political change. From the 2010s forward, led in great part by the editors of this volume—A. Ricardo López-Pedreros, Mario Barbosa Cruz, and Claudia Stern—as well as by more senior historians and social scientists such as Barbara Weinstein, David Parker, Ezequiel Adamovsky, Carla Freeman, and Louise Walker, the first two of whom have also contributed essays here—we have witnessed a second wave of studies on the "making of the middle class," the transnational, local, and regional determinants that shape its multiple and elastic identities, and on the new debates that characterize its political and socio-economic agency, cultural habitus, and global formation. It is obvious from the essays gathered in this landmark volume that these scholars, the majority of whom write in Latin America, have formed a vital collegial network and shared their cross-disciplinary research at a series of conferences and panels that they have organized in Argentina, Mexico, and the United States. The exchanges at these events in recent years have effectively refined the questions and *inquietudes* that lie at the core of this synoptic collection.

As I have suggested above, in many ways this collection synthesizes and deepens many of the sensibilities and insights of several decades of broader scholarship on modern Latin America. I have already mentioned the volume's contributions to newer, more open-ended understandings of gender and class as categories of analysis. The collection also contributes to the exploding scholarship on Latin America's "long Cold War," which frees Latin America from reductionist bipolar, grand strategy narratives of the conflict, and advances a more robust analysis of the regional Cold War's cultural phenomena, including struggles around memory. Also liberating is the contributors' fundamental insistence that the origins of Latin America's middle class (like those of other regions of the Global South) need not be conceived according to templates derived from the "more advanced" societies of the U.S. or Western Europe. Congruent with a raft of new studies from the Global South, it makes more sense to conceive of the formation and practice of Latin America's middle class in a mutual and reciprocal manner constituted at a variety of global locations. In this framework, particularly well-illustrated in one of the volume's signature essays on São Paulo, Brazil by Barbara Weinstein, regional identities and discourses can nestle uneasily with national and transnational ones, with race intersecting with notions of class privilege and status anxiety to produce political alliances that at first glance might appear counterintuitive.

In a more general sense, this volume on Latin America's middle classes provides a good barometer on the progress of what many since the 1990s have termed "the new cultural history." The volume combines diverse research strategies, including archival research, oral history, ethnographic participant observation, quantitative analysis, and discourse analysis. By effectively integrating materialist analysis with interrogations of consciousness, constructions of political language, meanings, and authority—for powerholders, subordinate groups, and the dynamic middle sectors who mediate, support, or oppose their interactions—this collection advances the best work on politics as cultural formation. As co-editor Claudia Stern observes, while work on the middle class has now reached a critical mass, the present group of contributors have taken the research on Latin America "to another level." Mindful that their work is often exploratory and that many substantial lacunae remain, several of the authors interpolate questions for future research in their essays. But without question, *The Middle Classes in Latin America* marks out an innovative and exciting agenda, one that historians of the region's modern past can no longer afford to ignore.

1 Introduction

"For the First Time Ever"*

A. Ricardo López-Pedreros

The middle classes continue to be the common currency in conflicting definitions of how globalized societies should be organized. By mobilizing modernization theories, developmentalist philosophies, liberal discourses, and neoliberal rationalities, developmental offices across the Americas have proclaimed that, after decades of economic stagnation, the size of the middle classes in Latin America has finally expanded "to the point where, for the first time ever, the number of people in poverty is equal to the size of the middle classes."[1] Although different organizations uses dissimilar socio-economic indicators, most of these developmental offices conclude that, in the last fifteen years, close to 50 million people in Latin America,

> "have worked their way up the social and income ladder ... [a]lmost one third of Latin American families are now considered to be middle class, a development that has also helped shrink the region's share of the poor to almost exact same proportion (or 30% of the population)."[2]

Indeed, some scholars celebrate that "Latin Americans are ... less poor, less unequal ... more middle class than ever before."[3] And because this expansion is economically fragile and socially reversible, particularly in a context of a global pandemic, scholars and policymakers alike continue to argue that the ultimate task is to ensure that societies across the region include as many people as possible into a middle class. It is the ultimate task, the argument goes, because "the essence of democracy [is] the advancement of middle-class interests."[4]

Decolonial theories, while critically unpacking the colonial matrix of power at the core of Western modernity, endorse this belief. They imagine a middle-class existence—one that, it is important to say, has historically been linked with a "Western modernity"—as a source of political inspiration for a decolonial future. Take, for instance, Walter Mignolo, who, as he critically describes the political differences between modernization/development theories, de-westernization ventures, and decoloniality options, finds it significant to clarify that, in a decolonial non-capitalist

DOI: 10.4324/9781003029311-2

economy, the question "is not that de-colonization rejects modernization," defined, following Kishore Mahbubani's characterization, as a comfortable middle-class existence: "rule of law, stable politics, personal safety, infrastructure, communications, a good education system, and basic standards of living." The issue and the challenge, he continues, are "to have that level of comfort in a noncapitalist economy, that is ... to modernize without reproducing coloniality in such a way that not only the middle class enjoys certain basic standards of living, but also the entire planet."[5] A decolonial future, Mignolo infers, would have to be universalized after—or according to—a middle-class existence.

The very possibility of materializing a middle class seems to ignite a consensus among otherwise markedly different political positions, dissimilar disciplinary traditions, and divergent theoretical approaches. Policymakers and scholars alike concur to imagine the middle classes as the embodiment of what is perceived as a *more* democratic future.[6] In the present, such omnipresent consensus often translates into a trivial question. As neoliberal policies dismantle democracy, and expand material inequalities, the assumption goes, who would *not* want to have a robust, expansive, and presumably all-inclusive middle class in the region that, according to the Economic Commission for Latin American and the Caribbean (ECLAC), is one of the most unequal in the world?[7] The unison response is offered as an obvious reality: the consolidation of a middle class could create a *post-class* future—in a capitalist and non-capitalist economy—to a present society characterized by a class conflict between a shrinking oligarchy and an expansive poor, which simultaneously produces political instability, ideological radicalization, economic inequality, and "autocratic populist politics."[8] Following the neoliberal algorithm of the present, this response assumes social classes could at long last cease to exist because this future would transform a two-class struggle—the putative past of Latin America—into a presumably one-class society with neither elites nor working classes but just with an ever-expanding middle class.[9] Thus, the consolidation of a middle class is often explained as a fundamental, if teleological, rupture with a Latin America past, a rupture that often locates the middle classes in fragile present and, above all, on an idealized, desirable future.[10]

Thus, the middle classes in Latin America, the assumption goes, have no histories to criticize but only democratic futures to homage. If history textbooks are any indication, it is telling that the middle classes appear, on the one hand, as a "fond aspiration for the future" rather than a reality of a past, and, on the other, as a historically timid social group that, due its precarious material positions, social fragility, and occupational heterogeneity, "has not been a strong voice in the political arena." Only as of late, such social group has emerged in "most of the continents' large cities ... a more sustained and consistent actor in many emerging democracies."[11] In short, the emergence of the middle classes is the main feature of a "new" Latin America.[12]

This is an "unanimist fantasy" that conditions, if not actively coerces, the historical analyses of the middle classes in Latin America.[13] It has led scholars to locate the historical explanations of power, exploitation, and domination elsewhere: at the class struggle between rich and poor, the conflict between ruling classes and masses, oligarchies and popular classes, the hegemonic relationships between subaltern and elites, the perennial binary between colonizer and colonized: what is perceived as "the old conflict[s] at the heart of Latin American history."[14] Along the way, the study of the middle classes is usually professed either as vestigial because it would presumably distract scholars away from what is considered the canonical manifestation of class domination and simultaneously the only cause for material inequalities. The middle classes, the assumption goes, are merely a camouflage that preclude scholars from studying what Latin America has historically been *really* about.[15]

This volume proposes to break away from this prevalent framework by locating the formation of the middle classes—the structural conditions of their social (re)production, their multilayered economic interests, their ample repertoire of political roles, their classed subjectivities, their contradictory gendered discourses, their multidimensional racial categorizations/identities, and their sexual politics—at the center of the histories of Latin America. It draws upon an increasing number of interdisciplinary studies critically committed to the analysis of the middle classes.[16] In so doing, it brings together multiple historiographies, anthropological methodologies, sociological approaches, intersectional analyses, and ethnographic studies produced in Latin America, Canada, and the United States in order to elucidate the historical formation of the middle classes in Argentina, Bolivia, Brazil, Colombia, Chile, Costa Rica, Ecuador, and Mexico. It delves into how middle-class people—bureaucrats, professionals, white-collar workers/employees, managers, teachers, and youth—struggled against and negotiated with other social groups their place in society in different historical moments. The volume locates middle-class women and men at the center of the numerous struggles over the legitimacy of vast material disparities that have historically shaped the structuring of competing hierarchical class regimes in Latin America during the last two centuries. To that end, it proposes that the study of the middle classes shed light on *universal questions* about power relations and systems of domination that are important beyond Latin America, even if Latin America remains the historically and geographically situated case of the volume.

The Middle Class and its Discontents: Theoretical Problematizations

No matter how sophisticated the analyses about the middle classes have become, there is always a sense that something is amiss because, the argument goes, the middle classes cannot be located in an exact sociological description of society. Scholars continue to deem the middle class too heterogeneous and elusive— "a gray zone in the social structure"—to constitute a category for rigorous historical analysis.[17] Indeed, the assumption is that the middle class defies categorical certitude because, unlike presumably homogenous, objective, and common interests of the working classes and elites, it is too heterogenous.[18] In these explanations, there seems to be an academic fixation to find a fully constituted—stable, meta-sociological, and transcendental—definition of the middle classes that can be applicable or translatable across different historical moments and geographical locations. This fixation invites scholars to consider class formation as crystalline objective reflection of economic developments and structural changes. In this context, scholars continue to ask what is presumably the most important, if not totemic, question: *what is the middle class, really?* Or, alternatively, *does the middle class—in singular—exist at all as an empirical reality?* Thus, scholars have thus sought to erect an index of certain assignations, attributions, and characteristics that must be found in given historical contexts in order to evaluate how homogenous, inadequate, exotic, or illusory the middle class, as a concept or as a practice, actually is.[19] It is a class absolutism of sorts that works on the supposition that "real social classes" must be empirical totalities with rigidly demarcated distinctions from other classes, composed by willful agents speaking with a politically unified voice and joining forces together to produce an united class consciousness. Anything short of this measure is seen either as the empirical evidence of the inexistence of a middle class as a class or, conversely, as the manifestation of an illusion incongruent with any a real social formation. The empirical value of class as a concept and as a practice, it seems, is in its putative homogenous unity. It is such absolutism that partially leads scholars to, on the one hand, disregard the middle classes as a non-topic to understand class formation and, on the other, perhaps unconsciously, to exonerate the middle classes from their participation in the consolidation of multifaceted forms of domination in Latin American societies.

Although in critical dialogue with these approaches, the chapters in this volume take a different route. They argue that it is when we follow an "academic imperative to impose order" that the heterogeneity of the middle classes become a theoretical obstacle at all.[20] This volume proposes the middle class as a meaningful analytical category to historicize—and question—power relations, technologies of domination, experiences of subordination, practices of classism, and multiple manifestations of resistance at the center of the histories of Latin America. It invites readers to see the formation of the middle classes simultaneously as historically contingent discourse, politically polysemic concept, socially motley practice, collectively heterogenous identity, and economically polyphonic conditions through which class hierarchies have been sedimented, gendered distinctions constituted, and racial exclusions legitimized.[21]

The volume also understands the porosity and heterogeneity of the middle classes as an entry point for class analysis. It argues that, paraphrasing Ann Stoler, the historical creation of porous class boundaries at the core of class formations are by no means phantom ones.[22] To that end, it brings up the indeterminacy of the middle class belonging as a historical question—and the contributors to this volume pursue such an effort in numerous, if conflicting, ways—in order to elucidate the very struggles and negotiations through which Latin American societies have historically become hierarchized. The task is not just to say whether the middle classes have historically been "real classes" but rather how multiple forms of classism get naturalized. In so doing, the volume pays close attention to what we might call the thick texture of "boundary making."[23] That is to say, the volume seeks to historicize the edges of class belonging, the racialized coordinates of class hierarchies, the gendered distinctions of class demarcations, the exclusionary imaginaries shaping stratified social orders, and the perpetual, if changing, reverberations of all these practices. It shows how structural/material circumstances—macro-conditions of possibility—shaped middle class relational, messy, and molecular subjectivities at the micro-level through which many actors engaged in struggles and negotiations with other social groups and among themselves to define conflicting meanings, competing political projects, and everyday practices of middle-classness. It is by unraveling such struggles and negotiations at the tick texture of boundary making that the middle class, as a category of historical analysis, offers a powerful way to see how vast material disparities have become sanctioned realities, hierarchies have been sedimented, and inequalities get reconfigured themselves across time and space.

Thus, the chapters featured in here propose to understand the formation of the middle classes as a historical—again, collective, contradictory, heterogenous—*assemblage*.[24] Taken together, they argue for no overdetermination or supremacy between structural positionality over agency or a simple teleology traveling from autonomous economic conditions to crystal class consciousness, no unidirectionality from lived experiences to discourse or vice versa, no univocal causality between structural societal position and class subjectivities. They demonstrate how these conditions of possibility intimately interweave with each other—sometimes through contradictions particularly in context of economic crisis, often through congruence in moments of material affluence, at times through negation predominately in moments of political upheavals—in an assemblage to materialize the hierarchical boundaries, material, figurative, and unconscious, of what it meant to be part of a middle class in specific historical conjunctures.

Beyond the Elision Hypothesis: Narrative Problematizations

Who *owns* the historical origins of the middle classes? The formation of the middle classes has long been associated exclusively with "North Atlantic societies," with the middle classes seen as originating first in Europe and the United States and then moving out to the rest of the world.[25] This depiction has perpetuated a teleological narrative of a Western and universal democracy against which other regions are found wanting.[26] The universalization of these particular experiences has naturalized the notion that divergent historical middle-class realities can only be understood as failures, deviations, or derivatives.

To be sure, the model of a fully modern and democratic middle class overcoming the feudal and authoritarian conditions of pre-modern Europe has been questioned by scholars of both Europe and its colonial projects.[27] They have shown how, for the United States, a powerful, robust and unified middle class has been the exception rather than the rule during the second half of the twentieth century, as it has historically faced constant economic crisis, internal divisions, and political challenges.[28] Furthermore, recent scholarship has sought to detach the origins of the middle class away from Europe and the United States in order to historicize how the formation of the middle classes were mutually—and coevally—constituted across the globe.[29]

Nevertheless, Europe and the United States, as it were, keep fighting for the original ownership of the histories of the middle classes. In a context of revival of the role of the Western cannon, such scholarly arguments have gained renewed traction. The resistance comes in two mutually contradictory narratives. On the one hand, the arguments are presented as an obvious historical reality that is impossible, if not unthinkable, to question. Thus, some scholars argue that, modernity, and its intimate relation with the constitution of a middle class, "may be a less than perfect reflection of the realities of Western societies but Western priority and non-Western imitation seem hard to deny."[30] Others concur to say that at least at the discursive level "the European origins of the middle class … is undeniable," thereby suggesting that the studies of the middle class outside Europe should limit themselves to "reconfigure this myth in order to make it more inclusive and less Eurocentric."[31] As a result, some scholars reinstate that the formation of the middle classes must be historically explained as originating first in the West and then spreading out to other societies that are anxiously waiting to appropriate this irresistible gift.[32]

On the other hand, more complex, multilayered historical analyses are presented. For instance, in their work on the formation of the global bourgeoisie and the rise of the middle classes in the age of empire, Christof Dejung, David Motadel and Jürgen Osterhammel argue that, from the very beginning of the nineteenth century, the middle classes, far from an exclusive historical reality to Europe, were the product of international connections. In so doing, they seek to avoid a teleological understanding of the middle classes by offering entangled social histories of the middle classes and comparative understanding of the making of the global bourgeoisie. And yet, despite, or precisely because of, an impressive geographical coverage the editors of this book still locate a binary, if hierarchically categorized, distinction between the middle-class experiences in the

Western world and those of the non-Western realm. By rehabilitating major tropes of modernization theory of the 1960s, they call on scholars to engage with comparative and entangled histories in order to examine different meanings and connotations of middle classness, as it is important to acknowledge, they argue, "the problems of using a European term as a category to analyze non-European societies."[33] Indeed, they continue,

> when we turn to the non-western world, the problem of terminology gets even more complex. It should be obvious that the sociological-historical concepts of European origin, such as the bourgeoisie or the middle class, cannot be smoothly applied to non-European history.[34]

Similarly, this invitation seeks to rescue the agency of the middle classes outside the Western world because it is imperative to include other cases of middle class formation across the world: "the applications of models that are at the heart of Western historicism to non-Western societies result in seeing the history of most of the world in terms of 'lack' ... reinforce the othering of non-Western societies and abet their exoticism."[35] Yet again, they contend, it is vital to recognize the historical, sociological, cultural differences between the Western and the non-Western world because, after all, "the formation of the middle classes around the world was the result of the global spread of European bourgeois cultural standards lifestyles among economically and socially independent groups."[36]

The subtle contradictions in these arguments suggest the main question. The so-called Western World model—imagined as a hyper-real Europe—is understood as simultaneously universal, unique, and exceptional. Thus, as important as these arguments are, the analysis of the middle classes tend to be reduced to comparative global histories that often seek to recuperate a singular point of origin/ownership which concurrently imagine the middle classes in the Western world—in this case Western European societies—as a locality that can be truly globalized whereas the non-Western world(s) are the products of, and are produced by, a variation of the middle classes, a local version, a provincialized, and hybrid experience in perpetual comparison to what is seen as the authentic Western experience. In this politically powerful narrative, the histories of a "global middle class" are spatially understood as a differential and sequential process moving from what is considered *global* (frequently coupled with an original consolidation of a middle class at the epistemological and practical levels in the "North Atlantic societies") and the *local* (usually associated with praxis, alternative contexts, vernacular formations, and hybridization). Such narratives, now professed as global and inclusionary histories, solidify the very hierarchical dichotomy that for so long have reduced those middle-class worlds considered outside Europe and United States to a counter-essence—fractured, fragmented, hybrid, incomplete or non-existent.[37]

It is indeed tempting to omit these discussions and, instead, focuses on the empirical realities of the middle classes in Latin America. But, as Claudia Stern argues, these discussions continue to reproduce the dichotomy between Eurocentric origin and alternative reception/translation elsewhere.[38] These narratives shape and, in some cases, exhaust how the historical formation of the middle classes should at all be discussed. They compel scholars to analogize the middle class in Latin America, to argue for or against the historical existence of a middle class in tacit or explicit comparison to Europe or the United States, even when those places are not part of the discussion. As a result, we keep asking how translatable, exotic, or commensurable the middle classes—as a concept or as a practice—could be into Latin American realities.[39]

These narratives also work on the assumptions that the discussion of the middle classes in Latin America is a new endeavor. Since the late 1990s, scholarly works have legitimized their historical inquiries by arguing that, in contrast to North Atlantic societies, Latin American middle classes have been elided from scholars' agenda. Take, for example, the foundational work of Michael Jiménez that inspired several reinterpretations of the middle classes. Writing in the late 1990s, Jiménez contended that developmental studies neglected or at best marginalized the historical inquiry into the nature and the role of the middle classes outside the "North Atlantic basin." As modernization theories became dominant, the middle classes as historical topic "receded ever further into the background." Then with *dependentistas* and their structural analysis, Jiménez argued, the analyses did not translate into a "new light being cast on the middle classes."[40] And, concluded this historian, poststructuralist critique did not "discern any historical agency for the middle classes ..." as postmodern, subaltern, and new social movements studies had no space for it.[41] This was what Jiménez named the elision of the middle classes in Latin America.

But, as this volume shows, since the second half of the nineteenth century, the role of the middle classes have been endlessly discussed. Indeed, after World War II, contested discussions about the middle class materialized a field of knowledge through which scholars, policymakers, and spokespersons for developmental institutions across the Americas engaged in what Ann Stoler defines as politics of disregard.[42] It was not that the middle classes were merely elided or simply neglected, as Jiménez argued. Rather, in a context where the horror of Nazi racism was still fresh and where populist experiences in Latin America were understood as the root metaphor describing everything that was evil about democracy as it promoted political radicalization and social polarization, academic books, articles, policies, and conferences papers proliferated to examine, in a comparatist framework, the potential democratic role of the middle classes. Why, scholars, policymakers, and politicians asked, was the middle class and its axiomatic relationship to democracy so "alien" to Latin American traditions? What was so "Latin American" about the Latin American middle class? The contested answers to these questions erected an *elision hypothesis* through which the middle classes in Latin America became understood as a chimera, as a failure, as an ontological absence, as an indecipherable—or alternative—reality in comparison to an apparently "real," empirical, and "universal" middle class historically located in the United States and Europe.

As I have argued elsewhere, this elision hypothesis has trapped historical analyses of the middle classes in Latin America in an epistemological quandary: either the middle classes are too Europeanized or US-influenced and thus presumably not exotic enough to be worthy topic to understand the perceived radical alterity of Latin America, or the middle class is depicted as diverging from Europe and the United States and thus closer to a "subaltern" position, which, by implication, means the consolidation of a two-class society where the middle classes as social or political realities become omnipresent yet unthinkable to historicize power relations in Latin America.[43] Such analysis has been further solidified in critical decolonial theorizations because in what is considered local spaces (i.e., Latin America) the middle classes are non-existent, not because there is no social reality, an identity or a class consciousness one could describe as middle class, but rather because such reality is explained away as an alien product of a transcendental—indeed perennial—Western colonial matrix of power. Middle-class people, the argument goes, have lived in "parallel universe of meaning" incongruent with certain Latin American realities.[44]

Decolonial approaches, as critical as they have been to challenge the triumphalist of an exclusively Western modernity as the putative model for the world, reproduce one of its central tenets that has allowed the West, as a political project, to claim universal/imperial legitimacy: the middle class is a reality only for what is seen as proper, if superior, Westernized societies. What is considered "local"—outside a hyper-real Europe and the United States—is often subsumed into a transhistorical unpolluted, glorified, and authentic subalternity positioned against a prevailing Western colonial matrix of power.[45] In this framework, the elites in Latin America are a mimicry of global superpowers and their colonial matrix of power. The middle classes are simultaneously defined as pawns of the Latin American elites which, by implication, assumes these middle classes are also reproducing the colonial matrix of power. Thus, Latin America would be globalized insofar as the future, decolonial or otherwise, could materialize a middle-class existence already experienced in those geographical places considered "global."[46] As a result, in a regime of knowledge which is rapidly becoming hegemonic, the middle classes in Latin America or Latin American middle classes are perceived—or, more accurately, disregard—at best, as inauthentic, Americanized or Europeanized realities, and, at worst, as a fundamental contradiction to, a deviation from, an exotic reality for, a "proper" Latin American subalternity. Taking these arguments to their logical conclusion, one has no option but conclude that the very reality of *Latin American middle classes*, however defined or experienced, is, in fact, an oxymoron.

A Middle Class Worthy of its Name: Historical Problematizations

This raises a fundamental question: How can we study the middle classes in Latin America when the very notion of a middle class is deemed irremediably outside—or beyond—a putative Latin American ontology? Certainly, the task is not to reclaim—or acclaim—the historical existence of a homogenous Latin American middle class. Nor is it to redeem an essential "LatinAmericanness" of the middle classes in the region to make up for their alleged historical incapacity to exist in comparison to other parts of the world. Rather, this volume invites the reader to think about the motley roles the middle classes have played in shaping the multiple power relations and forms of domination at the core of the histories of Latin America.[47]

The volume is thus divided into four overlapping parts which highlight historical process of *longue durée*: Liberalism, the Idea of Race, and Neoliberalism; Labor, Consumption, and Political Disparities; The State, Social Movements, and the Cold War; and Social Mobility, Neoliberal Discourses, and the "Pink Tide." As these titles suggest, the main purpose of this organization is to understand the histories of the middle classes in Latin America along three specific axes: subjectivities, practices, and genealogies. Each section proceeds thematically and chronologically. The volume simultaneously presents brief introductions for each section that draws transnational commonalities across the region while emphasizing national differences/conditions in the constitution of the middle classes. In so doing, the volume discusses the multiple ways in which middle-class women and men critically shaped—and were shaped by—interlocking and overlapping historical problematizations: the relationship between liberalism, republicanism, and meanings of citizenship since the second half of the nineteenth century; revolutionary politics, nation-state formation, cultural practices, and populist experiences during the first half of the twentieth century; rapid population growth, urbanization, industrialization, developmental programs, professionalization, and the growth of public and private service sectors since the early twentieth century, along with the financialization of the economy in more recent decades; the experiences of political radicalization and (counter) revolutionary politics during the long Cold War; the contradictory social foundations of neoliberal rule since the 1970s; and a political consent—and dissent—to the consolidation of Left-leaning governments since the turn of the twentieth first century.

Although the historiographical significance of these problematizations will be discussed in the introduction for each part, it is important to briefly outline them here. Unlike most studies that assume the middle classes as a non-existent reality during the nineteenth century, several contributors show how, during the consolidation of a liberal republicanism, the ideal of a middle class—defined through knowledge, concepts of ownership rights, practices of love and politics of sexuality—shaped who could speak in the public sphere in the name of democratic harmony, gendered notions of citizenship, the very hierarchical boundaries of the public and private spheres and racialized definitions of nation belonging. Middle-class women and men entered in negotiations with elites and popular groups over the meanings of liberal ideas/practices—from freedom to popular sovereignty to equality. Such process produced competing notions of liberalism in which, in a perpetual, if uneven transnational dialogue with Europe and the United States, the middle classes were seen—and defined themselves—as the future of national republics.

Across Latin America, the worldwide economic crisis of the late 1920s and 1930s accelerated a transition from a primary-export economy to an expansion of industrial capitalism, along with the dramatic and rapid growth of the service sector, particularly commerce, government bureaucracy, and transportation. The volume locates what feminist theories have called immaterial labor at the core of these structural changes.[48] In so doing, it questions long-held conceptualizations in which middle classness and labor relations appear as a contradiction in terms precisely because scholars tend to assume the working classes only labor while the middle classes only consume.[49] A number of contributors show how the growth of the service sector and the expansion of the state produced profound transformations in capitalist social relations, as they reconfigured a new gendered divisions of labor and shaped a novel classed organization of work in office spaces, households, and union halls. They demonstrate how the middle classes—in intimate dialogue with contradictory notions of *mestizaje* that linked ideas about class unity and racial harmony as well as heterogenous discourses about regional "superiority"—were mobilized in legitimizing racialized and gendered hierarchizations of who could be part of a service economy. All of these changes consolidated the practice of what it was supposed to be a middle-class worker: a central historical figure through which the industrialized and service sector driven capitalism, as a system of exploitation, was often legitimized and contested.

Because the middle classes have been linked with the process of democratization, scholars have for a long time tried to determine whether middle-class groups have politically embraced—or opposed—reform or social transformation.[50] Although in dialogue with these arguments, contributors propose to critically expand the very notion of political agency since the second half of the nineteenth century: from the participation in populist practices and revolutionary/counter-revolutionary politics to everyday practices of consumption and cultural performativity in the public sphere to the reconfiguration of a sexual division of labor in domestic spaces. Such redefinition of agency allows the readers to see how the middle-class women and men—far from being merely emissaries who support or reject somebody else's political project, either joining the elites in a reactionary/conservative project or following popular groups in search for revolutionary change—shaped the disputes, demands, and negotiations over the meanings and practices of land, justice, education, gendered moralities/desires, the struggles for the ownership of urban spaces, politics of decency, as well as the conflicts/negotiations between state and society over economic resources/rights in multiple nation-states during the last two centuries.

Scholars often see neoliberalism as a monolithic historical process ineluctably leaving behind a middle-class society. In contrast, the volume historicizes how the contradictory meanings and practices of multiculturalism, individualized upward mobility, racialized meritocracy, and economic debt conduced to a forced consent for a hierarchical neoliberal rule—partial, fragmented, tenuous—in exchange for a political recognition as a black, white, and mestizo middle class. Similarly, the volume shows how, despite what decolonial theories would have us believe, the middle classes, as contested discourse and as competing practice, played an important role in the consolidation of left-leaning governments since the beginning of the twentieth century. In some cases, it became the very justification of the state policies. In others, this notion of middle class, unlike a neoliberal definition, was linked with pluriverse practices of interculturality and delineations of economic progress and social justice as a collective endeavor. Yet, both neoliberal and left-leaning governments shared the notion that a middle-class existence as the sine qua non condition for the materialization of democracy, however defined.

In conclusion, by grounding the historical analysis on interdisciplinary approaches and intersectional questions, the volume invites the reader to think that the middle classes, far from being ornamental to the multiple struggles for power, played a foundational role in challenging but also rigidifying multiple class stratifications, perpetuating various forms of material inequalities, building contradictory gender hierarchies, and structuring a series of racial categorizations in Latin American societies. The volume as a whole is an effort to question the binary understanding—perpetuated in modernization conceptualizations, naturalized by dependency theories, disregarded by subalternist perspectives, and reproduced in decolonial approaches—scholars have canonized to understand class formation. The volume works on the assumption that the arguments presented here are neither a particular regional example lacking universal relevance outside Latin America nor a singular version of a universal case; rather, they are a planetary problematization. It is an invitation to critically understand—and question—how systems of domination, supported by a diversity of hierarchies and vast disparities in wealth, have historically become common sense.

Notes

* I want to thank the co-editors of this volume for their critiques of this introduction.

1 Ferreira, Francisco H.G.; Messina, Julian; Rigolini, Jamele; López-Calva, Luis-Felipe; Lugo, Maria Ana; Vakis, Renos. *Economic Mobility and the Rise of the Latin American Middle Class* (Washington, DC: World Bank, 2013). https://openknowledge.worldbank.org/handle/10986/11858.

2 World Bank, "Latin America: Middle Class hits Historic High." https://www.worldbank.org/en/news/feature/2012/11/13/crecimiento-clase-media-america-latina, accessed, December 2020. The World Bank considers those households that receive 10–50 dollars per capita per day part of the middle class. For comparison see Cecilia Güemes, "Auras mediocritas: Crecimiento, características y papel de las nuevas clases medias en Latinoamérica," in *Las nuevas clases medias latinoamericanas: ascencso e incertidumbre*, Ludolfo Paramio and Cecilia Güemes (Madrid: CEPC, 2017), 17; ECLAC argues that by 2017 41.1% of the population in Latin America was part of a middle class; ECLAC, *Social Panorama of Latin America* (New York: ECLAC, 2019), 26.

3 Michael Raid, *The Forgotten Continent. A History of the New Latin America* (New Haven: Yale University Press, 2017), 13, 242, 264.

4 Tarben Iversen and David Soskice, *Democracy and Prosperity: Reinventing Capitalism Through a Turbulent Century* (Princeton: Princeton University Press, 2020), 20.

5 Walter Mignolo, *The Darker Side of Western Modernity: Global Futures, Decolonial Options* (Durham, NC: Duke University Press, 2011), 47; Kishore Mahbubani, "Peeling Away the Western Veneer," http://www.digitalnpq.org/archive/2008_spring/02_mahbubani.html.

6 OECD, *Under Pressure: The Squeezed Middle Class* (Paris: OECD Publishing, 2019), 4. Daron Acemoglu and James A. Robinson, *The Narrow Corridor: States, Societies, and the Fate of Liberty* (London: Penguin Books, 2020).

7 ECLAC, *Social Panorama of Latin America.*

8 Raid, *The Forgotten Continent*, 9,10,265.

9 Christophe Guilluy, *No society: El fin de la clase media occidental* (Barcelona: Taurus, 2019).

10 David De Ferranti et al., *Inequality in Latin America: Breaking with History?* (Washington, DC: World Bank, 2004).

11 Teresa A. Meade, *A History of Modern Latin America*, (New York: Wiley-Blackwell, 2010), 8.

12 Raid, *The Forgotten Continent.*

13 Paul Gilroy, *Against Race: Imagining Political Culture Beyond the Color Line* (Cambridge, MA: Harvard University Press, 2000), 7.

14 John Charles Chasteen, *Born in Blood and Fire: A Concise History of Latin America* (New York: W.W. Norton, 2016), 9.

15 Silvia Rivera Cusicanqui, *Ch'ixinakak utxiwa. On practices and Discourse of Decolonization* (Cambridge: Polity, 2020).

16 Ezequiel Adamovsky, *Historia de la clase media argentina: Apogeo y decadencia de una ilusión (1919–2003)* (Buenos Aires: Planeta, 2009); Mario Barbosa, "Los empleados públicos, 1903–1931," in *Los trabajadores de la ciudad de México, 1860–1950. Textos en homenaje a Clara E. Lida*, eds Carlos Illades and Mario Barbosa (México: El Colegio de México, 2013), 117–154; D. S. Parker, *The Idea of the Middle Class: White-Collar Workers and Peruvian Society, 1900–1950* (University Park: Pennsylvania State University Press,

1998); Patrick Barr-Melej, *Reforming Chile: Cultural Politics, Nationalism, and the Rise of the Middle Class* (Chapel Hill: University of North Carolina Press, 2001); Maureen O'Dougherty, *Consumption Intensified: The Politics of Middle-Class Daily Life in Brazil* (Durham: Duke University Press, 2002); Dennis Gilbert, *Mexico's Middle Class in the Neoliberal Era* (Tucson: University of Arizona Press, 2007); Brian P. Owensby, *Intimate Ironies: Modernity and the Making of Middle-Class Lives in Brazil* (Stanford: Stanford University Press, 1999); Louise Walker, *Waking from the Dream: Mexico's Middle Class after 1968* (Stanford: Stanford University Press, 2013); A. Ricardo López-Pedreros and Barbara Weinstein, eds., *The Making of the Middle Class: Toward a Transnational History* (Durham: Duke University Press, 2012); A. Ricardo López-Pedreros, *Makers of Democracy: A Transnational History of the Middle Classes in Colombia*, (Durham: Duke University Press, 2019); David S. Parker and Louise E. Walker, eds., *Latin America's Middle Class: Unsettled Debates and New Histories* (Lanham: Lexington Books, 2012); Sebastián Carassai, *The Argentine Silent Majority: Middle Classes, Politics, Violence, and Memory in the Seventies* (Durham: Duke University Press, 2014); Sergio Visacovsky and Enrique Garguin, eds., *Moralidades, economías e identidades de clase media: Estudios históricos y etnográficos* (Buenos Aires: Antropofagia, 2009); Isabella Cosse, *Mafalda: A Social and Political History of Latin America's Global Comic* (Durham: Duke University Press, 2019); Claudia Stern *Entre el cielo y el suelo: las identidades elásticas de las clases medias (Santiago de Chile, 1932–1962)* (Santiago: RiL editores, 2021); Graciela Queirolo, *Mujeres en las oficinas: Trabajo, género y clase en el sector administrativo (Buenos Aires, 1910–1950)* (Buenos Aires: Biblos, 2018); Heather Vrana, *This City Belongs to You: A History of Student Activism in Guatemala, 1944–1996* (Berkeley: University of California Press, 2017); Mara Viveros Vigoya. *El Oximoron de las clases medias negras: Movilidad social e interseccionalidad en Colombia.* (Guadalajara: Universidad de Guadalajara. Collección CALAS, 2021) Sergio Visacovsky and Enrique Garguin, eds., *Argentina y sus clases medias. Panoramas de la investigación empírica en ciencias sociales* (Buenos Aires: Biblos, 2021).

17 Camilo Sémbler, *Estratificación social y clases sociales: Una revisión analítica de los sectores medios* (Santiago de Chile: ONU, 2006), 8; Göran Therborn, "Dreams and Nightmares of the World's Middle Classes" in *New Left Review*, 124 (July–August, 2020), 63–87; Klaus-Peter Sick, "El concepto de clases medias," in *Clases Medias: Nuevos enfoques desde la sociología, la historia y la antropología*, eds. Ezequiel Adamovsky, Sergio E. Visacovsky, and Patricia Vargas (Buenos Aires: Ariel, 2014), 21–54; Sarah Maza, *The Myth of the French Bourgeoisie* (Cambridge, MA: Harvard University Press, 2003), 4.

18 Adamovsky, "'Clase Media:' Mitos, usos y realidades" in *Nueva Sociedad*, No. 285 (February 2020), 36–37.

19 Göran Therborn, "Dreams and Nightmares;" Amaru Villanueva Rance "Bolivia: La clase media imaginada." In *Nueva Sociedad* No. 285 (February 2020), 122–138.

20 Robin D.G. Kelley, *Africa Speaks, America Answers: Modern Jazz in Revolutionary Times* (Cambridge: Harvard University Press, 2012), 10.

21 René Zavaleta Mercado, *Towards a History of the National-Popular in Bolivia, 1879–1980* (London: Seagull Books, 2018); Achille Mbembe. *Out of the Dark Night: Essays on Decolonization* (New York: Columbia University Press, 2021), 13.

22 Ann Stoler, "Intimidation of Empire: Predicament of the Tactile and Unseen," in *Haunted by Empire: Geographies of Intimacy in North American History*, ed. Ann Stoler (Durham: Duke University Press, 2006), 8.

23 This point finds inspiration on Carola Lentz, "Elites or middle classes? Lessons from transnational research for the study of social stratification in Africa" (Working Papers of the Department of Anthropology and African Studies of the Johannes Gutenberg University Mainz, 161, 2015).
24 Félix Guattari, *Chaosmosis: An Ethico-Aesthetic Paradigm* (Bloomington: University Press, 1995).
25 Dipesh Chakrabarty, *Provincializing Europe: Postcolonial Thought and Historical Difference* (Princeton: Princeton University Press), 2007.
26 A. Ricardo López-Pedreros with Barbara Weinstein, "We Shall Be All: Towards a Transnational History of the Middle Class," introduction to *The Making of the Middle Class*, eds. López Pedreros and Weinstein, 1–11.
27 As an example, see Christof Dejung, David Motadel and Jürgen Osterhammel, eds., *Global Bourgeoisie: The Rise of the Middle Classes in the Age of Empire* (Princeton: Princeton University Press, 2019); Simon Gunn, "Between and Backwardness: The Case of the English Middle Class," in *The Making of the Middle Class*, eds. López-Pedreros and Weinstein, 58–74.
28 Samuel Lawrence, *American Middle Class: A Cultural History* (New York: Routledge, 2013).
29 Rachel Heiman, Carla Freeman, and Mark Liechty, eds., *The Global Middle Classes: Theorizing Through Ethnography* (Santa Fe: SAR Press, 2012); López-Pedreros and Weinstein, *The Making of the Middle Class.*
30 Dennis Gilbert, review of *The Making of the Middle Class: Toward a Transnational History*, by A. Ricardo López-Pedreros and Barbara Weinstein, *Reviews in History*, review no. 1297 (August 2012).
31 Markus Daechsel, review of *The Making of the Middle Class: Toward a Transnational History*, by A. Ricardo López-Pedreros and Barbara Weinstein, *Journal of Global History* 8, no. 3 (November 2013): 509.
32 For other examples, see Thomas Piketty, *Capital in the Twenty-First Century* (Cambridge, MA: Harvard University Press, 2013), 21–22; Michael Raid, *Forgotten Continent*, 23.
33 Christof Dejung, David Motadel and Jürgen Osterhammel, "Worlds of the Bourgeoisie," in *The Global Bourgeoisie*, eds. Dejung, Motadel, and Osterhammel, 13.
34 Dejung, Motadel, and Osterhammel, "Worlds of the Bourgeoisie," 14.
35 Dejung, Motadel, and Osterhammel, "Worlds of the Bourgeoisie," 14.
36 Dejung, Motadel, and Osterhammel, "Worlds of the Bourgeoisie," 15; See also Ammara Maqsood, *The New Pakistani Middle Class* (Cambridge, MA: Harvard University Press, 2017), 3.
37 Gayatri Spivak, "General Introduction," to *Towards a History*, René Zavaleta Mercado, vii–xv.
38 Stern, *Entre el cielo y el suelo*, 35.
39 Ezequiel Adamovsky, "Clase media:" in *Clases Medias*, eds. Adamovsky, Visacovsky, and Vargas, 115–138.
40 Michael Jiménez, "The Elision of the Middle Classes and Beyond: History, Politics and Development Studies in Latin America's 'Short Twentieth Century,'" in *Colonial Legacies: The Problem of Persistence in Latin American History*, ed. Jeremy Adelman (New York: Routledge, 1999), 211, 213.
41 Jiménez, "The Elision of the Middle Class," 216.
42 Ann Stoler, *Duress: Colonial Durabilities in our Times* (Durham: Duke University Press, 2016).
43 López-Pedreros, *Makers of Democracy.*
44 Walter Mignolo, *The Politics of Decolonial Investigation* (Durham: Duke University Press, 2021), 241, 316.

45 Walter Mignolo and Catherine E. Walsh, *On Decoloniality. Concepts, Analytics, Praxis* (Durham: Duke University Press, 2018); For a critical reading see Gaya Makaran, Pierre Gaussens, coords., *Piel blanca, máscaras negras: Crítica de la razón decolonial* (México: UNAM, 2020).
46 Mignolo, *The Darker Side*, 47.
47 Mercado, *Towards a History*.
48 Rachel Heiman, Mark Liechty, and Carla Freeman, "Charting an Anthropology of the Middle Classes," introduction to *The Global Middle Classes*, eds. Heiman, Freeman, and Liechty, 21.
49 Some exceptions are Parker, *The Idea of the Middle Class*; López-Pedreros, "It is not Something You Can Be or Come to Be Overnight," in *Latin America's Middle Class*, eds. Parker and Walker; Susie S. Porter, *From Angel to Office Worker*; Barbosa, "Los empleados públicos"; Queirolo, *Mujeres en las oficinas*; López-Pedreros, *Makers of Democracy*, 86–107.
50 For a historiographical description, see David S. Parker, "The Making and Endless Remaking of the Middle Class," introduction to *Latin America's Middle Class*, eds. Parker and Walker, 7–10.

Part I

Liberalism, the Idea of Race, and Neoliberalism

Introduction to Part I

Claudia Stern

Figure I.1 "Dry goods store in San José, Costa Rica (Photograph shows men and boys standing in a store selling umbrellas, machetes, fabric, clocks, and other articles)," between 1880 and 1990. Library of Congress Prints and Photographs Division Washington, LC-DIG-ds-11613.

Source: Retrieved from the Library of Congress, www.loc.gov/item/2017652264/.

Eurocentric and Northern imperialist perspectives have often formed the basis of widespread myths and definitions of the middle classes in Latin America. These views have displaced more incisive studies concerning a transnational dialogue that recognizes specific regional circumstances as something other than mere reproductions of a unique original. Such myths have borne little resemblance to the genuine Latin American class experience, since the copies have generally been reductionist or, worse still, responded to the interests of foreign agency over and above the individual features of each local reality. In the past thirty years, however, there has been a shift in focus in the study of the middle classes.[1] The

DOI: 10.4324/9781003029311-3

chapters in this section reflect the change that has inspired the authors' interest in taking their research on Latin America to another level. Underestimation of the possibilities of research into the middle classes has also been a tonic, unlike the case of the upper or popular classes, whose legitimacies as objects of historiographical study can seem unassailable.

The series of chapters in this part of the book do away with the aforementioned myths, underestimations, and reductionisms, focusing on specific issues that offer new perspectives in the study of identities and national histories, and increasing our understanding of the role played by various middle-class sectors in historical events. The idea of race, pigmentocracy, *mestizaje*, gender distinctions, heteronormativity, and their connection to institutional rhetoric and regulatory discourses published in the press have shaped the region's major cities and spurred on the evolution of urban modernity. These contributions boost the visibility of the middle classes from other perspectives, including local regionalism and intersectionality.

The five chapters—on Brazil, Colombia, Costa Rica, and Mexico—tackle everything from class commonalities to the particular features of each local reality. These aspects are crucial when considering the evolution of Latin American societies from the dawn of liberalism to their expressions in the neoliberal era.

The political structures of liberalism, such as elections, representative legislatures, fixed-term presidencies, and guarantees of civil rights, were established across the region in the wake of independence processes.[2] The ideology of liberalism spread rapidly throughout Latin America in the 1800s; however, further revolutions were required in the following century, as illustrated by the Mexican Revolution, which led to renewed versions of liberalism. As a system of government, liberal democracy took shape between liberalism and neoliberalism during the twentieth century. Constitutionalism, parliamentary representation, and citizenship lie at the core of the system,[3] which emerged at different times across Latin America, revealing deeply entrenched differences between nation-states.

That also contributed to the rise of diverse versions of middle class through which men and women themselves developed their own bound to nationhood nurtured by public symbols, sense of belonging, and resulting also in experiences and conditions that enabled them.[4]

In this context, the precariousness of the middle classes became a recurring theme that was internally differentiated within their sectors, as well as in those sectors that were their staunch defenders. Different expressions of this narrative existed during the period, and neoliberalism undoubtedly gave it a new appearance, exposing the deep inequality perpetuated over time by this economic model that also framed the repercussions in societies that have embraced left- and right-wing populist movements. As such, the specter of precariousness also extended to forms of distinction to which the middle classes appealed in order to maintain their political clout.

Differentiated, gender-based expressions of precariousness also exist among the middle classes. The phenomenon arose in Mexico during the early nineteenth century, and the evolution of press treatment of the middle classes lowered women's status in terms of both their gender and their class. In Colombia, multiculturalism possessed its own distinctions: social mobility among the black middle classes was perceived as a process of whitening, neoliberalism simply emphasized the individualist path, and sectors that managed to get ahead did not represent a collective phenomenon whatsoever. Meanwhile, the precariousness of the middle classes in Brazil was seen as a regional issue—a gap that was even harder to close and that proves definitive in the racial experience of class, which combines deeply entrenched colonial notions of civilization and barbarianism. Disputes over the legitimacy of Costa Rica's middle classes, meanwhile, were marked by the agency shown by its different sectors, with capitalism as a backdrop, along with the structural transformation between small and medium-sized rural landowners and salaried employees that was not immune to ideologies and contradictions. In the mid-1900s, Mexico City's geography developed a cartography of heteronormative decency that the middle classes raised as their banner as they strove to achieve their imagined and much-desired cosmopolitan identity. Taken together, these various texts bring into focus various snapshots of daily life and social imaginaries in the region.

The following five texts can be understood from the perspective of "*ciudadanismo*" (citizenism) both as a form of democratic fundamentalism proposed by modernity and as a cultural project that takes the political view that democracy is a way of life and an ethical community.[5] As such, urban development and the middle classes' embodiment of modernity was an enduring binomial during the mid-1900s, in which the overarching narrative was also male-dominated and personified society's hopes and ideals.[6] The abstract notion of democratic values applied through an expansion of state capabilities was put forward in different dimensions in Latin America. Since what the state offered was segmented, it led to further contradictions within different sectors of society as well as deep structural differences rather than coping with the latter as contingencies that may have been treated to ethically improve the domination system,[7] in the long run. Together, the chapters in this part provide new perspectives on the political conditions of the urban experience and their mutations, and highlight tensions and contradictions regarding interdependency between public and private space for middle-class men and women, and for society in general. This interdependency emerges from the intersections between gender, class, and the idea of race, which, in turn, is dependent on positions in government and power structures. The liberalism that frames the beginning of this part soon reveals issues to be sidelined—otherness in all of its expressions, starting with gender and ethnicity. The non-inclusive nature of Latin American democracies can be interpreted through the lens of their weaknesses and strengths, while the two faces of neoliberalism make it possible to understand the perpetuation of long-standing inequality on the one hand, and on the other to recognize historically marginalized sectors. Championing equality in societies as unequal as those in Latin America is a collective challenge that still defies consensus within Latin America's diverse realities.

Notes

1 Sergio Visacovsky and Enrique Garguin, "Introducción," *Moralidades, economías e identidades de clase media; Estudios históricos y etnográficos* (Buenos Aires: Antropofagia, 2009), 11–59, 14–16.
2 John Charles Chasteen, *Americanos: Latin America's Struggle for Independence* (New York: Oxford University Press, 2008), 183.
3 Antonino Palumbo, "Liberalism," in *Understanding Democratic Politics*, R. Axmann (ed.) (London: Sage, 2003), pp. 231–240, 235.
4 Yi-Fu Tuan, *Space and Place: The Perspective of Experience* (Minneapolis: University of Minnesota Press, eighth printing, 2001), 149, 159.
5 Manuel Delgado, *El espacio como ideología* (Madrid: Catarata, 2011), 21.
6 George L. Mosse, *The Image of Man: The Creation of Modern Masculinity* (New York; Oxford: Oxford University Press, 1996), 12.
7 Delgado, *El espacio como ideología*, 22.

2 "São Paulo is Modernity"

Middle-Class Identity and Narratives of Exceptionalism in Brazil

Barbara Weinstein

In 2012 the eminent urbanist Teresa Caldeira published an article in the journal *Public Culture* on graffiti, tagging, and public space in the city of São Paulo.[1] As I read the essay, I appreciated the author's keen insights into these forms of cultural expression by residents of the urban periphery, which she depicted as a challenge to the elites' monopolization of public space, but I found myself repeatedly distracted by her use of the term "elites." In Caldeira's depiction of "Grande São Paulo," the metropolitan area consisted almost entirely of the poor of the periphery and the elites who controlled the "espaços nobres" of the city. There were, to be sure, occasional references to the middle class but typically embedded in the phrase "middle and upper classes." Nowhere in this representation of the city was there mention of a middle-class milieu, even though the Brazilian government just a few years earlier had triumphantly announced that a majority of the nation's population had risen into the middle class—including a vast lower middle-class population that had very little in common with those classified as upper class. However dubious the government's yardstick of middle-classness might seem, the erasure of the middle class in Caldeira's article struck me as a quintessential example of what historian Michael Jiménez described, in a 1999 essay, as the "elision of the middle class" in Latin American scholarship.[2] More than a decade after the publication of that essay, it was still difficult for even an astute observer of urban life in contemporary Brazil such as Caldeira to shift from talking about elites and the poor to discussing a social and cultural landscape that included a sizable and distinct middle class.

This minimizing of the middle class is made all the more striking when we consider that São Paulo, city and state, has in absolute terms the largest middle class in Brazil, and perhaps in Latin America. Far from constituting a small minority of the population, the *modal paulistano*—resident of the city/município of São Paulo—is someone who self-identifies as middle class.[3] Furthermore, the regional identity of São Paulo has long been associated with a proclivity for "modern" middle-class virtues and values. Travelers arriving in the newest terminal of São Paulo's international airport are greeted by an illuminated billboard of the city's skyline

DOI: 10.4324/9781003029311-4

proclaiming in three languages that "São Paulo is Modernity." Indeed, I will argue in what follows that modernity and middle-class identity in São Paulo, premised on the reputed whiteness of the state's population, have to be analyzed primarily from a regional and transnational perspective (regional here referring to a subnational, not a continental, space). Not only is there ample room for the (implicitly white) middle class in *paulista* identity, but I would argue that middle-classness is *constitutive* of that identity and of ongoing claims to regional exceptionalism.[4] At the same time, this has made it problematic, even misleading, to speak historically of a *national* middle class even as people who self-identify as middle class have become an ever larger portion of the Brazilian population.

Regionalism, Transnationalism, and Middle-Class Identity in São Paulo

Prior to the cultural and discursive turns that emerged in the late 1980s, scholars who explored the question of the middle class in Brazil adopted sociological and structuralist approaches that typically resulted in the conclusion that the middle class barely existed or if it did, it had no independent identity or socio-political agency. Even as recently as 2004 (the 450th anniversary of the founding of São Paulo city), *História da Cidade de São Paulo*, a massive volume issued by a major paulista publisher and counting on the collaboration of over a dozen leading paulista historians, didn't include a single entry in the table of contents that referred to the middle class.[5] The 16 chapter headings and 92 chapter subheadings refer repeatedly to workers or the laboring classes, or the plebeian sectors, on the one hand, and the elites or the rich on the other, but one would search in vain for a reference to those "in between."[6] Why, then, this ongoing elision of the middle class? At least with regard to the aforementioned volume, it may reflect an inclination to deny the paulista "elites" any claim to being progressive and enlightened, or to representing social sectors that earned their relatively privileged positions through something that could be defined as "merit." And it fits with the well-known (and well-deserved) image of Brazil as a land of extreme social inequalities. It also reflects an assumption that a "truly modern" middle class would have played a more consistently progressive political role than can be attributed to the middling sorts in São Paulo.[7] In other words, middle-class qualities are seen as having legitimating effects that critically-minded historians seek to deny the more privileged members of the regional population.

Although I recognize, even sympathize with, the political impulse behind this elision of the middle class, I think it is an increasingly untenable and ineffectual way to think about Brazilian (and Latin American) history. First, it is crucial to undo the normative assumptions about the middle class and politics that underlie the refusal to acknowledge the millions of middle-class-identified paulistas. Among other things, it reproduces a certain narrative of Brazilian (or Latin American) political "backwardness" that rests on an unfavorable comparison of São Paulo/Brazil with more "fully modern" societies (especially Britain and the United States), as well as on a notion of Brazil as a nation where liberal ideas are intrinsically out of place or "*fora do lugar*," and where a "true" middle class cannot thrive.[8]

To date the most influential study that challenges this normative conceptualization of the middle class and shifts historical analysis away from the positivist conception of the middle class as an objectively identifiable thing is Brian Owensby's 1999 monograph *Intimate Ironies: Modernity and the Making of Middle-Class Lives in Brazil.* Owensby focused on the tension between the middle class as a cultural construct and the daily social and political practices of people who self-identified as middle class in urban Brazil, particularly Rio de Janeiro and São Paulo. In the pages of *Intimate Ironies*, he seeks to demonstrate that a modern middle-class sensibility could form and coexist with patronage networks and other features of Latin American social life understood as traditional, and could be meaningful as an identity even absent a specific middle-class political project. Thus, it made perfect sense for Owensby to choose "middle-class lives" in Rio de Janeiro and São Paulo as his object of study, and it also made sense to privilege national processes and trends over regional particularities. But by combining and homogenizing these two urban centers, Owensby not only downplayed regional divergences in middle-class cultures, but also assumed that we can speak of a national/Brazilian middle class, a premise that diminishes the significance of both transnational and regional circuits of influence and aspiration.[9]

Despite my debt to Owensby, in my own work on modernity, whiteness, and the middle class in São Paulo I take a different approach: I consider the way in which paulista professionals, civic leaders, journalists, writers, historians, industrialists, businessmen, and politicians in the early decades of the twentieth century infused an emerging regional identity with elements of "middle-classness" and crafted a set of norms for middle-class identity in São Paulo that were not only distinct from other regions of Brazil, but were constructed *in explicit contrast to* class and racial stereotypes associated with other regions. In other words, these shapers of public opinion asserted a paulista middle-class identity that was not just a *variation* of other Brazilian middle-class identities; rather, this identity was based on a notion of paulista exceptionalism, and of the paulista middle sectors as forming the only genuinely modern middle-class culture in early twentieth-century Brazil—one that situated São Paulo within the transnational circuits of liberal modernity.[10] Hence, they represented the paulista middle class as the bearers of modernity, and the middle class elsewhere in Brazil as either non-existent (the Nordeste) or incompletely modern (Rio).[11] Or to quote a functionary of the Rockefeller Foundation who visited Brazil in 1920: "The northern boundary of the State of São Paulo divides Brazil into two sections presenting contrasts, with respect to populations, as sharp as those between Mexico and the United States."[12]

What I sought to do in my own research was to explore the multiple ways in which paulistas of a variety of social and cultural backgrounds constructed and reconstructed a regional identity that distinguished *paulistanidade* from other Brazilian regional identities, indeed, invented a sort of paulista exceptionalism that had as its foundation a narrative that situated São Paulo as different from the patriarchal and seigneurial order of the (northeastern) plantation and the courtly culture of the national capital, then located in Rio de Janeiro. In effect, it projected São Paulo as the white, modern, progressive Brazil, the Brazil that could follow the historical trajectory of those (middle-class) societies abroad that were widely regarded as fully "cultured and policed," to quote modernist writer Menotti del Picchia.[13] And I argue that, as a regional identity, its middle-class qualities could be extended upward to segments of the elite and downward to portions of the working classes.[14] The examples I will use as evidence for this argument—a rehabilitated historical figure, the contested meaning of a political epithet, a new generation of industrialists, a regional uprising—may seem analytically unrelated—but they all reflect an emerging paulista identity that had at its core a particular transnational conception of what it meant to be middle class that deliberately set paulistas apart from the middling sectors elsewhere in Brazil.

First, the Rehabilitated Historical Figure: The Bandeirante as Middle-Class Striver

Wickliffe Rose, the Rockefeller Foundation representative cited above, not only extolled the virtues of Brazilians located below the northern border of São Paulo, but also ventured an explanation for the contrast he was drawing. According to Rose, "South Brazil, beginning with the State of São Paulo, was settled by adventurous, self-reliant Portugese [sic], who from the beginning crossed with the native Indians, [and] developed a sturdy Brazilian stock..."[15] He then goes on to acknowledge the more recent "contribution" of European immigrants to this "hearty Brazilian breed," but ultimately insists that its roots could be traced back to the earliest colonial settlers and the emblematic paulista colonial figure, the *bandeirante*.

It is beyond the scope of this chapter to delve into the long and contested history of the *bandeiras*—seventeenth-century expeditions that originated in the village of São Paulo and explored the interior of Brazil to map its territory, prospect for precious minerals and, above all, search for indigenous peoples to enslave. Their slaving activities, which devastated the native populations of the surrounding regions, incited the ire of the Jesuits, who vehemently denounced the bandeirantes and publicized their brutal massacres and abuses of indigenous cultures.[16] Far from being unanimously celebrated as heroic figures, the expeditionaries who became known as bandeirantes were often portrayed in colonial accounts as bloodthirsty and uncouth.

The first generation of paulista genealogist/scholars to try to rehabilitate the bandeiras' reputation—writing in the eighteenth century—claimed that the leading bandeirante figures were actually men of noble Portuguese descent, and had performed inestimable services for the Portuguese Crown despite their neglect by the colonial authorities.[17] But when Afonso de Taunay, Alcântara Machado, Alfredo Ellis Júnior, and others, revisited the bandeirante saga in the 1920s and '30s, a substantially different image emerged. The bandeiras were still celebrated for their service to the Crown and the future Brazilian nation, but now the emphasis was on their spirit of initiative and enterprise, their risk-taking ventures, and their roughly egalitarian practices, including their ability to absorb the best traits of the native population. Alcântara Machado's canonical *Vida e Morte do Bandeirante*, based on seventeenth-century wills and inventories, portrayed them as respectable, civic-minded men of modest means and moderate habits.[18] With their home base on the interior plateau, rather than the coastal lowlands, they forged a way of life that demanded hard work and initiative.

By the time São Paulo took up arms against the government of Getúlio Vargas in 1932 (an episode I will discuss below), the phrase "o povo bandeirante" (the bandeirante people) had become synonymous with the "o povo paulista" and it had become conventional wisdom that São Paulo's exceptional progress and industry could be traced back to its bandeirante origins. The saga of the bandeirantes created an identity that was peculiar to São Paulo but permeable to new groups (such as European immigrants) that adopted the bandeirante spirit of hard work and innovation;[19] it emphasized the bandeirantes' contribution to the Brazilian nation (expanding borders, discovering gold, domesticating the "savages") but also differentiated São Paulo from the rest of Brazil.[20] Ultimately, it implied that in São Paulo—unlike in Rio de Janeiro or the Nordeste—success and respectablity came from one's efforts, initiative, and expertise, rather than from a distinguished family name or good connections.

Next, the Contested Meaning of a Political Epithet, Or... Who Are You Calling an Oligarch?

Despite all the intellectual and cultural production that contributed to crafting this image of the "povo bandeirante," by no means would I argue that images of the more privileged portion of paulista society had become thoroughly bourgeois, much less middle class, by the early twentieth century. The frequent use of phrases such as "coffee barons" and "Italian counts" to refer to the big planters and nouveau-riche-immigrant industrialists indicates that a certain patriarchal/aristocratic image continued to cling to those with wealth and standing, even when the wealth was derived from investments in the "modern" manufacturing sectors. But it was also evident that such phrases had increasingly negative connotations, especially as the rapidly growing rural and urban workforces began to organize, protest, and strike, and as dissident political factions, both within and outside São Paulo, began to denounce the political dominance of the "paulista oligarchy" at the federal level.[21]

Historians have long understood the "oligarchic rule" referenced in such denunciations as the overlapping power of political and economic elites.[22] Yet a 2009 study of paulista politics under the Old Republic by James Woodard demonstrates that the term "oligarchy" had a very different meaning, and was typically wielded in a very different way in São Paulo in the 1910s and 20s. According to Woodard,

> literate paulistas of the early 20th century would have found the [historians'] usage puzzling. Indeed, when many complained of 'oligarchy' or 'professional politicians,' they were not bemoaning the marriage of public and private power, but rather their divorce: they found it galling that political power should be exercised by men who lacked the customary trappings of sociocultural status and socioeconomic success.[23]

This "complaint" might appear to be a call for rule by an enlightened elite, a political position that seems at odds with an incipient middle-class identity. But instead I would argue that their critiques reflected a germinating bourgeois sensibility that rejected politics for political power's sake, and the attendant patrimonial machinations of traditional politicians. Instead, they sought to invest greater political/administrative power in those whose "authority" stemmed from practical knowledge and achievements in the private sector and for whom politics meant "public service," rather than political muscle.[24]

This line of criticism culminated in 1926 with the formation of the Partido Democrático (Democratic Party, PD) the first mainstream opposition party to challenge the monopoly on political power of the Partido Republicano Paulist (Paulista Republican Party, PRP). For years historians struggled to find the sociological key to the PD's founding, first asserting that its leadership reflected new industrial and commercial interests, then traditional and declining agrarian interests, then generational differences. But each time closer inspection revealed the alleged socio-economic bases for the schism to be statistically insignificant. Finally, historian Maria Lígia Prado—starting with the premise that there were no significant differences in the social profiles of the PRP and PD leaderships—argued that the PD should be analyzed as an attempt to forge a more inclusive and reformist political project, though still within the confines of mainstream paulista politics.[25]

Building on Prado's insights, I would argue that the PD project, despite references to laboring men and workers' rights, was fashioned around the figure of the middle-class citizen-voter. The PD's calls for moderate reforms and the secret ballot reflected not so much an incipient populism as an antidote to what the *democráticos* saw as the degradation of politics resulting from the patronage-based participation of uncultured and incompetent voters. And as one might expect, this campaign not only drew on class-based imagery, but on racial distinctions as well. Thus the "ignorant [and] truly beastlike multitude," who allegedly crowded out cultured and thinking Brazilians at the polls, were implicitly nonwhite in print, and explicitly so in posters and cartoons advocating the secret ballot.[26]

Similarly, paulista pundits such as publisher and author Monteiro Lobato couched their demands for the secret ballot in appeals to transnational modernity. In a 1924 letter to President Artur Bernardes, Monteiro Lobato claimed that secret balloting "has already been adopted by *all cultured peoples with one single exception*." Here the dividing line between those who favor the secret ballot and those who oppose it was culture. But he also goes on to equate support for the *voto secreto* with modern (middle-class) consumerism: "Can we play the part of a people that forbids the entry of a marvelous invention into its territory? Can one imagine a country that has resisted the adoption of the telephone, of the 'Ford,' of cinematography?"[27] Monteiro Lobato and other paulistas also proposed the adoption of the secret ballot first in São Paulo—the natural entry point for modern political practices—with the hope that it would then spread, like a benevolent contagion, to the rest of Brazil.[28]

Bourgeois Industrialists in an Age of Italian Counts Or... Knowledge as Power (I)

If we conceptualize the middle class (or the bourgeoisie—terms that were and are often used interchangeably) as literally being "in the middle" of the social scale, it makes it difficult to imagine a group of leading industrialists adopting elements of a middle-class identity. But if we take seriously Ricardo López-Pedreros' argument, in his historical study of professionals and office workers in Cold War Colombia, that the middle class sought to place itself above both workers *and* elites, then the discourses of these emerging industrialists seem much more intelligible.[29] They may not have been middle class, but they were furthering their own public position by advancing a critique of a world where inherited wealth and/or social standing, alone, were sufficient to guarantee prestige or authority.

In my study of paulista industrialists, *For Social Peace in Brazil*, I argued that an emerging circle of industrialists and industrial managers, whose leading light was the businessman, engineer, and economic historian Roberto Simonsen, adopted in the 1920s and '30s what I have called a "technocratic discourse." Subtly distinguishing themselves from the "Italian Counts," whose leading light was the immigrant industrial magnate Francisco Matarazzo, these promoters of industrialization foregrounded their training as engineers, managers, sanitationists, and psychologists, and their familiarity with rational methods of production and organization, to claim authority to oversee the vast project of creating a more industrialized and productive Brazilian nation. While this was, to some degree, a response to growing labor militancy, and the need to reduce the authority and power of skilled workers on the shopfloor, I would argue that our tendency to think of class struggles strictly in terms of capitalists and workers obscures concerns and tensions that may have been, at that particular moment, even more pressing than the need to discipline the labor force.[30]

Specifically, paulista industrialists in the 1910s and '20s faced a host of criticisms from intellectual and professional sectors that, given their appreciation for modern, transnational trends, could normally have been counted on to be allies in the crusade for industrialization. But these critics accused manufacturers of running "artificial industries" that produced shoddy, over-priced goods and depended upon government protection to earn a profit.[31] And employers' inflexible responses to workers' protests in the general strikes of 1917 and 1919 were widely regarded as fueling the intensifying atmosphere of class conflict and social tension. If an unreserved enthusiast for modern innovation such as Monteiro Lobato, who translated and published Henry Ford's *My Philosophy of Industry*, could claim that industrialization in Brazil had created "magnates in return for the perpetuation or aggravation of human misery," it was time for substantial damage control.[32]

In response to this and other criticisms, Simonsen and his acolytes—many of whom had done advanced studies overseas—stressed their technical expertise and their familiarity with the most modern forms of industrial organization, rather than their prerogatives as capitalists. What they could offer São Paulo, and then Brazil in general, was social peace through greater productivity. Moreover, their efforts in this regard would require a small army of trained professionals ranging from engineers, supervisors, and technicians to efficiency experts, industrial psychologists, and factory physicians, and thus would greatly expand the middle class so widely associated with modern industrial society. It is significant that Simonsen, in his first major publication (1918), referred to "engineers and managers" as those who had to confront the problem of the "economical utilization of labor," and then urged "today's industrialists" to "abandon the old patterns, recognize the worker's discontent, and firmly offer him fair remuneration."[33]

This vision of rational and reasonable industrial relations (though not the actual fair remuneration) would reach its fruition in the 1940s when Simonsen spearheaded the founding of the Serviço Nacional de Aprendizagem Industrial (National Service for Industrial Training, SENAI) and the Serviço Social da Indústria (Industrial Social Service, SESI), industrialist-funded agencies that provided a wide range of vocational programs and social-welfare services to urban workers and their families. Working closely with technicians, educators, social workers, psychologists, and other professionals, and using the latest pedagogical materials from abroad, the founders of SENAI and SESI institutionalized a project predicated on the idea that an essentially middle-class cohort of urban professionals would teach industrial operatives how to work productively, how to raise proper, hygienic families, and how to be good citizens.[34] Long before the developmentalist and modernizing programs implemented under the US-funded Alliance for Progress (1961), Brazilian industrialists and their allies had initiated their own program to transform the popular classes through the guidance of middle-class technocrats and professionals.

And Now, the Urban Planner as Maker of the Middle Class: Knowledge as Power (II)

Although coffee and manufacturing are usually seen as the keys to São Paulo's economic ascent, Cristina Mehrtens' recently published study of urban space and modernity in early twentieth-century São Paulo shows that a major source of enterprise, innovation, employment, financial gain, and social mobility was the explosive urban growth of São Paulo itself. The number of construction projects and public works generated by an urban center that went from under 50,000 inhabitants to several million in the space of a half-century was vast, as were the opportunities that such growth offered to those who could provide the needed capital, connections, and expertise. Mehrtens' study illuminates the rise of particular middle-class sectors by examining three entities that played central roles in the remaking of São Paulo city: the Municipal Works Department (Departamento de Obras Públicas DOP), the City of São Paulo Improvements and Freehold Land Company Limited, and the F.P. Ramos de Azevedo Technical Firm.[35]

Francisco de Paula Ramos de Azevedo was arguably the most important figure in urban planning and development in São Paulo during the early decades of the twentieth century. Born in 1851 in Campinas, the son of a modest family—on his mother's side, it is possible that some of his ancestors were African slaves—his early work as an apprentice on the construction of a regional railway drew the attention of the Barão de Parnaíba, who made Ramos de Azevedo his protégé, and sponsored his studies in architecture and engineering at a university in Belgium.[36] A few years after his return to Brazil, Ramos de Azevedo founded the architectural and engineering firm that would establish him as one of the leading figures in the expansion of metropolitan São Paulo. His career, as Mehrtens notes, is a stellar example of the intersection of established patronage networks and new professional opportunities created by technical innovation and urbanization.

Despite his extensive ties to the paulista "aristocracy," Ramos de Azevedo (like Simonsen) cultivated a non-aristocratic image—he always had himself painted or photographed seated at his desk in his office, engaged in his work, surrounded by symbols of his professional success. And he played a central role in the founding of the Escola Politécnica (1894) and the Liceu de Artes e Ofícios, two institutions that would be "factories" of middle-class professionals and technicians. In 1911 the newly formed "Sociedade dos Arquitetos e Engenheiros de São Paulo" sponsored an event honoring Ramos de Azevedo in the recently inaugurated Theatro Municipal.[37] Their esteem for him was hardly surprising; his architectural firm, plus various other enterprises that his firm had spawned (a sawmill, a ceramics factory), provided employment for a phalanx of freshly minted architects, draftsmen, and engineers educated at the "Poli" and the Liceu. Not only did Ramos de Azevedo carefully cultivate a bourgeois/middle-class image, and provide large numbers of "middle-class professionals" with highly remunerative employment, but his firm also designed whole neighborhoods (such as the Cidade Jardim) specifically conceptualized as housing for an emerging upper middle class.[38]

And Finally, the Uprising against Vargas: 1932: The Middle Class in Arms

Discourses of regional exceptionalism had been circulating in São Paulo since the final years of the Empire. To cite just one example of emerging regional chauvinism, Republican Party leader Alberto Salles, in an 1880 essay on "how the climate of São Paulo influences its inhabitants," concluded: "Thus [we have] the proverbial energy of the paulistas, manifested ever since colonial times. Men of energetic disposition … incapable of living in indolence, they felt compelled to give free rein to their enterprising spirit…"[39] But the most intense moment of regional chauvinism undoubtedly came in the early 1930s, when the state of São Paulo declared itself at war with the unconstitutional regime of Getúlio Vargas. Although paulistas of all social backgrounds supported the 1932 "Constitutionalist Revolution," as it came to be known, the key contemporary representations of the uprising consistently portrayed it as a revolt of the (white) middle class.[40] Much of the actual fighting for the paulista side seems to have been done by the state's Força Pública, whose troops, except for the officers, were not likely to be middle class. But eyewitness accounts and retrospective chronicles of this brief conflict overwhelmingly highlight the contributions, sacrifices, and experiences of the middle class on the battlefield (whether political or literal), and sharply contrast these middle-class "voluntários" with the "wretched hordes" recruited to fight for the federal government.[41]

Even a quick survey of the various speeches, radio addresses, and newspaper articles presented by those rallying the paulista "troops" confirms that the speaker or writer's interlocutor was a putative member of the paulista middle class. Public orations frequently referred to the urgent need to prove to the rest of Brazil that the paulistas had not become "soft" or "unmanly" as a result of their prosperity, surely not anxieties associated with manual workers, urban or rural.[42] And most of the published personal accounts of this three-month civil war contain the recollections of law students, journalists, or engineers who emphasized the unaccustomed daily hardships of life in the trenches, and who apparently had never expected to find themselves engaged in armed combat (and, not surprisingly, performed rather incompetently on the field of battle).[43]

Paulista media coverage of the uprising routinely highlighted the dramatic class differences between the rude, thuggish federal troops—virtually always portrayed as semi-savage conscripts from the impoverished interior of the Brazilian Nordeste—and the cultured, educated professionals who populated São Paulo's battalions. An excellent example is the following description of the Vargas regime's efforts to crush the Constitutionalist Revolution, from the newspaper *O Estado de São Paulo*: "Against the youth of São Paulo, against the students, the doctors, the lawyers, the engineers, the merchants, the landowners, the men of industry and intelligence, [the government is] throwing a band of thugs [jagunçada] gathered and herded together in the backlands... Against a civilized people, they hurl battalions of hoodlums."[44]

Similarly, a headline in *A Gazeta* informed São Paulo's citizenry that "The Dictatorship Makes Use of Fanatical Jagunços Against the Conscious Army of Liberty."[45]

If the paulistas portrayed the federal troops as virtually sub-human, the supporters of the federal government portrayed the paulista leadership as a band of reactionary oligarchs. In the words of a typical anti-paulista and pro-Vargas manifesto:

> All of Brazil, unified and cohesive, repudiates this criminal assault to gain power, undertaken by those professional politicos [*politiqueiros*] who have always, whether in the factory or on the coffee estate, kept the working masses enslaved to their low and nefarious interests and ambitions ...

In light of such accusations, it became crucial to obscure the "political" character of the uprising, and to highlight the mass nature of the movement, and provide evidence that "todo São Paulo" had risen up against the Vargas regime, even while invoking the modern, civilized, middle-class character of the combatants and their supporters. Thus José M. Whitaker, president of the Commercial Association of São Paulo, responded to *getulista* critics by insisting that "this is not a political revolution, but rather a human explosion; it is not a rebellion of political parties but rather a reaction fueled by sentiments, a general insurrection..."[46]

Ultimately, the most effective discursive strategy for asserting the non-oligarchic character of the Constitutionalist movement was to foreground its nearly universal support from the "povo bandeirante," and especially from groups defined in such a way (i.e., by profession) as to situate them outside of the political arena. Most prominent of all were the repeated invocations of the role of women, or, more specifically, "A Mulher Paulista" (The Paulista Woman).[47] As with the "povo bandeirante," The Paulista Woman was not an identity explicitly represented as middle class, but the many commentaries regarding the contributions of the Mulher Paulista to the struggle implicitly defined her as a respectable, middle-class housewife. Thus, texts praising the Mulher Paulista always noted how, during normal times, she was attached to home and hearth, and that only extraordinary circumstances, and her modern sense of civic duty, could move her to appear in public and become involved in the affairs of the nation. Her enthusiastic support for the "causa paulista" was the most persuasive evidence that this was a moral, not a partisan-political, crusade. Even a woman as cosmopolitan and sophisticated as the very upper-class Olívia Guedes Penteado opened her radio address to the Mulher Brasileira in behalf of the causa paulista with the following statement: "Never have I ventured a word in public, ladies. Never have I thought to make myself heard by anyone at all, beyond the intimate circle in which I live, as the simple mother of a family…"[48] The many photographs and articles depicting the labor donated by the Mulher Paulista, whether sewing uniforms, preparing food, or visiting families in need, also presented women's efforts in such a way as to make clear that toiling in sewing shops or soup kitchens was not a part of their usual routine. One widely reproduced photo of paulista women seated at the sewing machines in a clothing factory shows them dressed in a way that heightens the message that this was not a space they were accustomed to inhabiting, and that this work was a sacrifice that they were making for the cause. There were also many references to their "delicate hands" and their unprecedented willingness to perform "even the most repulsive tasks."[49]

To be sure, this portrayal of the Mulher Paulista as "normally" a contented housewife confined to the private sphere was not even accurate for much of the population that defined themselves as middle class.[50] A newspaper article entitled "Mobilisação Feminina" reported that women office-workers (bookkeepers, typists, stenographers, and translators) had called upon their female colleagues to sign up with the Liga de Defesa Paulista to offer their temporary services to firms whose male employees had taken up arms. Surely these women regarded themselves as part of the "povo bandeirante," and probably as middle class, and for them work outside the home was definitely part of their *normal* routine.[51]

Despite these tensions between the identities constructed in Constitutionalist discourses and the details of paulistas' daily lives, I would argue that the 1932 uprising was a crucial moment that consolidated a specifically paulista middle-class identity. Furthermore, there is evidence that it continued to be a constitutive element of middle-class identity well beyond the three-month span of the civil war. The short-lived "welfare state" created to address the significant social problems generated by wartime mobilization provided opportunities for educated paulista women to go beyond traditional forms of Catholic charity, with their implications of noblesse oblige, and refashion themselves as social-work professionals. Several women who ran dispensaries and other social services during the uprising later collaborated to found São Paulo's first school of social work, which then became an important source of professional employees for the industrialist-funded "SESI."[52]

Even more striking is the role that the 1932 uprising played in certain patterns of middle-class male employment that ostensibly relied on "merit." According to Cristina Mehrtens, who has studied hiring patterns in the municipality of São Paulo during the 1930s and '40s, the "spirit of 1932" created a common bond among local government officials and aspirants to municipal employment; for the latter, military service in the "guerra paulista" could serve as a major source of social capital. Constitutionalist leaders such as Paulo Duarte openly acknowledged bringing to the prefecture "all [his] soldiers … who needed employment." And this pattern was particularly pronounced among young men with engineering degrees who had used their technical expertise in the war effort. Mehrtens not only argues that the veterans of 1932 clustered around the "social middle," but also that those of more modest backgrounds could enjoy a certain degree of upward mobility as a result of the connections forged by the Constitutionalist experience.[53]

The Rule of Law = Democracy?

If we consider the central role of the 1932 uprising in the formation of middle-class identity in São Paulo, we can more easily see why a national framework might be inadequate, even misleading, as a way to approach the question of middle-class identity in Brazil. To be sure, during the 1932 civil war there were some demonstrations of solidarity with São Paulo by medical and law school students in urban centers such as Rio, Recife, and Belém, which generated a fleeting expectation that there could be a broader, transregional middle-class politics. But the paulistas' insistence on the exceptionalism of their region, and the backwardness of other regions, ultimately made them more likely to identify with a transnational image of modern middle-class life and culture than acknowledge the middle-classness of Brazilians in other, "less modern" regions. This was even the position articulated by paulistas, such as the modernist writer Mário de Andrade, who eventually adopted a critical posture toward the decision to revolt against Vargas. According to Mário's unpublished manuscript on the "Guerra de São Paulo":

> The paulistas constituted a blatant aberration within the race and the nation. São Paulo had become too great for Brazil. Brazil had not yet become a civilization, [whereas] São Paulo was a European Christian civilization, with the mentality, the climate, the cosmopolitanism, the resources of a European Christian civilization.[54]

The paulistas' frequent invidious comparisons of São Paulo's modernity and progress with the lassitude and frivolity of Rio de Janeiro and the decadence and even backwardness of the Nordeste, created a sense that the only truly middle-class Brazilians were the paulistas, and that the only true paulistas were the middle class. This helps to explain a peculiar silence, or near silence, in the rhetoric of the "causa paulista" in the early 1930s. One might expect a movement that claimed *liberal constitutionalism* as its defining ideology and that was rallying the masses against a *dictatorship* to make extensive use of the term *democracy*, and yet there were remarkably few references to the need for democratization in the writings and speeches produced by the insurgents. There were innumerable declarations of the need for a constitution, for the restoration of order and the rule of law but, for the most part, the paulistas were silent on the matter of democracy. On the rare occasions when the question of democracy did appear, it was primarily as an object of skepticism. Thus we have the particularly blunt assertion by journalist Vivaldo Coaracy who, in *O Caso de São Paulo*, wrote: "The difference in their evolutionary rhythms unavoidably establishes a hierarchy among the Brazilian States … Democracy proclaims civil equality for all citizens and tends to concede them political equality. But it is incapable of creating natural equality."[55] Or this similar remark by Partido Democrático militant Leven Vampré: "We [Brazilians] are an immense democracy of illiterates. Democracy, under such conditions, inevitably assumes the appearance of dictatorship."[56] Such sentiments, far from being restricted to a reactionary oligarchy, profoundly informed the worldview of an emerging middle class in what was widely regarded as the most modern and cosmopolitan region of Brazil. It was the middle-class paulista's self-identification with a "superior" transnational modernity that produced a highly illiberal worldview in the putative stronghold of Brazilian liberalism. And it was this same aversion to a more egalitarian order that fueled massive middle-class paulista support for the 1964 military seizure of power, a moment when the lead editorial in the daily *O Estado de São Paulo* declared "São Paulo Repeats'32," and went on to inform its readers that "as if one man, today São Paulo finds itself in full mobilization, and with the same spirit from three decades ago, it rises up in defense of the existing constitution."[57]

The Middle Class: Makers of Fascism?

This brings us to the question of the middle classes and their role in Brazil's current, and possibly sharpest, turn to the right. It is widely acknowledged that the greatly enlarged twenty-first-century middle class was heavily responsible for the election of extreme-right-wing politician Jair Bolsonaro by a margin of some 11 million votes in the 2018 presidential race. Even in several Brazilian states where a preponderance of the ballots went to Bolsonaro's center-left opponent, Fernando Haddad of the Partido dos Trabalhadores (Workers' Party, PT), in the more middle-class state capitals a majority of the votes went to Bolsonaro. This has generated a great deal of consternation and discussion since, despite all prior evidence to the contrary (in Brazil and outside of Brazil), many observers still imagined that a more middle-class Brazil would be both more economically stable and more politically democratic.[58] Politicians across the political spectrum, including former presidents Luiz Inácio Lula da Silva and Dilma Rousseff, showed themselves eager to define larger and larger portions of the Brazilian population as "middle class" to provide convenient markers of the success of their economic projects—it meant both rising incomes and declining income inequalities. And Lula and Dilma surely hoped that this new and improved middle class, which owed much of its prosperity to policies implemented by the Partido dos Trabalhadores, would become loyal political supporters of the PT even as they distanced themselves from any imaginable version of working-class identity.

Clearly, those hopes were not fulfilled.[59] There are many different researchers and commentators trying to explain what happened—especially with regard to the middle class—but here I will focus on two schools of thought. One is the claim by two economists associated with the World Bank that Brazil under Lula and Dilma (2002–2016) witnessed what they call "a middle-class squeeze." In other words, they argue that middle-class Brazilians had a real, concrete, and material basis for feeling that the PT governments favored the very rich and the very poor over the middle class, and were thus acting rationally when they cast their ballots for the non-PT candidate.[60]

The graph that is the centerpiece of their argument shows that between 2002 and 2014, the income of the poorest Brazilians grew faster than that of middle-class Brazilians (but of course, the top 1% grew much faster than everybody else in terms of income, in line with global trends). These economists apparently think that the numbers speak for themselves, but such a claim assumes that socio-economic groups are acutely aware of how they stand vis-à-vis other segments of the income pyramid, and that the conclusion to be drawn from such numbers is singular and evident. Yet even if we take these numbers at face value, there are multiple ways to question the implication that middle-class Brazilians were "rationally" responding by voting against a government that was giving preference to the poor over the middle class.

What these economists' argument ignores is, first, that people rarely have a precise sense of who is getting what and how much, and therefore it takes a great deal of ideological work to get people to read their circumstances in one way and not another. These statistics are of no use to us in understanding why those allegedly being "squeezed" are more inclined to blame the very poor rather than the top one percent. Secondly, the graph is, in effect, a series of snapshots and therefore does not reflect the fact that many members of the middle class actually *became* middle class during this period. It ignores the painfully obvious insight that the middle class is not a stable entity with fixed boundaries or sharp definitions.

Then there is the equally obvious point that given how extremely poor a segment of Brazil's population was, surely even a significant increase did not allow them to escape poverty (it just moved them out of the grim category of "absolute misery").[61] While they experienced a relatively greater improvement than those classified as middle class, it was only because their incomes were so miniscule at the outset. Thus, if you look at the graph, what you can see is that, overall, middle-class purchasing power was increasing (and probably most steadily toward the end of this period, since the real boom was 2008–2014), and only the very upper end of the middle class suffered an actual decline in its purchasing power. Given that we are talking about a comparatively small portion of the middle class, and one that enjoys vastly greater comforts and privileges than the average Brazilian, the fairly gentle "squeeze" portrayed in the graph seems an inadequate explanation for a massive and dramatic shift in voter preference. Rather, I would argue that it took a steady stream of propaganda—of corruption investigations, evangelical church sermons, WhatsApp messages, media exposés, racist and homophobic tropes, all aided by an economic downturn and increased insecurity due to rising crime, to make middle-class Brazilians see the poor and those who championed the poor as primarily responsible for their "troubles." It also is essential to note that electoral trends in the more middle-class regions of southeastern and southern Brazil were already turning against the Workers' Party long before the economic recession or the Lava Jato corruption scandals erupted.[62] Later in the article the authors turn their attention to the role of PT-related corruption scandals in swinging middle-class voters to the right, but they ignore the much earlier, pre-Lava Jato evidence of this trend.

The other, and more compelling, explanation that centers on the middle class is the one offered by André Singer in his 2018 book *O Lulismo em Crise*. Different from other authors, Singer starts with the assumption that the middle class is not a natural ally of the Workers' Party, and maybe not even of democracy. To reduce his argument to the simplest terms, Singer faults both the Lula and Dilma presidencies for their frequent celebrations of the expansion of the middle class (which, by implication, disparaged the "massa trabalhadora"), and for not making it clear enough to the new middle class that they owed their newfound prosperity to PT policies.[63]

I agree that using middle-classness as a measure of success for an administration led by the PT was not necessarily an inspired idea, politically speaking. And it seems a truism to say that a chief of state should claim as much credit as possible for positive developments during his or her tenure. But the problem with Singer's argument is that it treats the Brazilian middle class as if it were a strictly national phenomenon, that could be defined within the context of Brazilian politics and culture, and thus all Lula and Dilma had to do was adjust their language and voilá!, the new middle class would have seen themselves instead as workers, and not just that, but also as workers who attributed their enhanced standards of living to the policies emanating from the political sphere. But the Brazilian middle class is inextricably part of a transnational phenomenon and actively participates in global religious, ideological, and mediatic trends.[64] In an age of neoliberalism, consumerism, and de-industrialization (including in Brazil), how likely is it that Brazilians who for the first time find themselves able to buy a car or a washing machine, or hire someone to clean their house, or have a son or daughter attend university, will opt for a working-class identity?[65] How likely are they to attribute their upward mobility to state policies rather than to their own hard work and sacrifices (a story that is reinforced by church sermons, telenovelas, and advertisements of all sorts). Moreover, if they find themselves in danger of falling back into the "massa trabalhadora," how likely is the middle class to forgive politicians for their alleged sins? In other words, in a neoliberal world, the state gets little credit for upward mobility but it does get the blame for downward mobility.

Again, I think Singer's analysis has much to recommend it, especially his assumption that the middle class is not necessarily the key to a more egalitarian or progressive future for Brazil. But he still fails to consider the transnational processes that produce middle-class identities and that severely limit the rhetorical power of even a very popular political figure like Lula. And his national perspective also occludes the role of regional affinities, reflected in electoral maps since the 2006 national elections that depict a deeply divided Brazil, with the southern states becoming ever more conservative, and the north and northeast emerging as the bastions of PT support. Thus politicians in the more populous south can draw on longstanding tropes about nordestino backwardness and paulista modernity to consolidate the image of right-wing candidates as the champions of the middle class, including someone as racist, sexist, homophobic, and unsavory as President Jair Bolsonaro.

Notes

1 Teresa P.R. Caldeira, "Imprinting and Moving Around: New Visibilities and Configurations of Public Space in São Paulo," *Public Culture* 24, no. 2 (2012): 385–419.
2 Michael Jiménez, "The Elision of the Middle Classes and Beyond: History, Politics and Development Studies in Latin America's 'Short Twentieth Century,'" in *Colonial Legacies: The Problem of Persistence in Latin American History*, ed. Jeremy Adelman (New York: Routledge, 1999).

3 "Greater São Paulo," which includes peripheral areas that are quite poor, would be less heavily middle-class than the municipality. "Paulistano" refers to a city resident; "paulista" refers to a resident of the state.

4 Barbara Weinstein, *The Color of Modernity: São Paulo and the Making of Race and Nation in Brazil* (Durham, NC: Duke University Press, 2015), chap. 3.

5 Paula Porta, (ed.), *História da cidade de São Paulo: A cidade na primeira metade do século, 1890–1954* (São Paulo: Paz e Terra, 2004).

6 Though even the Argentine historiography has little to say about that country's middle classes. For recent works that start the process of undoing that neglect, see Ezequiel Adamovsky, *Historia de la clase media argentina: apogeo y decadencia de una ilusión, 1919–2003* (Buenos Aires: Planeta, 2009); Enrique Garguin, "'Los argentinos descendemos de los barcos': The Racial Articulation of Middle-Class Identity in Argentina, 1920–1960," in *The Making of the Middle Class: Toward a Transnational History*, eds. A. Ricardo López and Barbara Weinstein (Durham, NC: Duke University Press, 2012).

7 Maureen O'Dougherty encountered this scholarly disdain for the middle class when she was doing research in São Paulo for her dissertation and later book, *Consumption Intensified: The Politics of Middle-Class Daily Life in Brazil* (Durham, NC: Duke University Press, 2002). The paulista academics she interviewed, to a person, insisted that they were not "middle class." In a different but related vein, James Woodard argues that well-off paulistas have eschewed a middle-class identity throughout much of the twentieth century, associating it with a lack of culture and social connections—hence, the preference for the terms "Classe A" and "Classe B" in the world of marketing and public relations. James P. Woodard, *Brazil's Revolution in Commerce: Creating Consumer Capitalism in the American Century* (Chapel Hill, NC: University of North Carolina Press, 2020), xv-xvi.

8 On liberal ideas being "out of place" in Brazil, see Roberto Schwarz, *Misplaced Ideas: Essays on Brazilian Culture* (London: Verso, 1992).

9 Brian P. Owensby, *Intimate Ironies: Modernity and the Making of Middle-Class Lives in Brazil* (Stanford, CA: Stanford University Press, 1999).

10 Many paulistas of means spent considerable amounts of time in the federal capital and had extensive ties to intellectuals and politicians in Rio de Janeiro. However, one can easily detect the emergence of stereotypes about the two cities that identify São Paulo as a place to work and Rio as a place to have fun—and the latter image is particularly difficult to square with a transnational middle-class identity. See, for example, Assis Chateaubriand, "Renovação Paulista," Arquivo Aureliano Leite, Instituto Histórico e Geográfico de São Paulo, Pacote 13. According to this media magnate (Brazil's version of W.R. Hearst), in the past when one spoke of a "moço de São Paulo," it meant a "a spoiled young man, who didn't work…" But Chatô claimed that the 1929 crash and the 1932 uprising had toughened up paulista youth, whereas in Rio the young men continued to show an aversion to work.

11 For an excellent study of race and modernity in Rio, see Rafael Cardoso, *Modernity in Black and White: Art and Image, Race and Identity in Brazil, 1890–1945* (Cambridge: Cambridge University Press, 2020).

12 Wickliffe Rose, "Public Health Situation and Work of the International Health Board in Brazil," Rockefeller Foundation Archive, Record Group 5, Series 2, Folder 153, 1920.

13 Paulo Menotti del Picchia, *A Revolução Paulista* (São Paulo: n.p., 1932), 26–7.

14 Weinstein, *The Color of Modernity*, especially chap. 3.

15 Rose, "Public Health Situation," 8.

16 Justo Mansilla and Simón Maceta, "Atrocities of the Bandeirantes," in *The Bandeirantes*, ed. Richard Morse (New York: Alfred Knopf, 1965). The crucial study of Indian slavery in colonial São Paulo is John M. Monteiro, *Blacks of the Land: Indian Slavery, Settler Society and the Portuguese Colonial Enterprise in South America*, ed. and trans. J.P. Woodard and B. Weinstein (Cambridge: Cambridge University Press, 2018).

17 Kátia Maria Abud, "O Sangue Intimorato e as Nobilíssimas Tradições: A Construção de um Símbolo Paulista—O Bandeirante," (PhD diss., Universidade de São Paulo, 1985); Antonio Celso Ferreira, *A Epopéia Bandeirante: Letrados, Instituições, Invenção Histórica, 1870–1940* (São Paulo: Editora UNESP, 2002). Laura de Mello e Souza, "Vícios, virtudes e sentimento regional: São Paulo da lenda negra à lenda áurea," *Revista da História-USP* 142–3 (2000): 262–276.

18 On the controversies regarding captured Indians, see Monteiro, *Blacks of the Land*.

19 Starting in the 1920s (though with some ambivalence), paulista intellectuals began referring to Italian immigrants as the "novos mamelucos"—a reference to the colonial mestiço in whom (allegedly) who blended the best of indigenous culture with the dominant Portuguese qualities. Ferreira, *A Epopéia Bandeirante*, 105.

20 On the crafting of paulista exceptionalism, see Tania Regina de Luca, *A* Revista do Brasil*: Diagnóstico para N(ação)* (São Paulo: Editora Unesp,1999), 108.

21 On the regional alliances and conflicts during the Old Republic, see Joseph L. Love, *São Paulo in the Brazilian Federation, 1889–1937* (Stanford, CA: Stanford University Press, 1980).

22 I myself defined oligarchy as "the monopolization of power by a small group of families and their clients." Weinstein, *For Social Peace in Brazil: Industrialists and the Remaking of the Working Class in São Paulo, 1920–1964* (Chapel Hill, NC: University of North Carolina Press, 1996), 361, n. 1. Implicit in this definition was the monopolization of both economic and political power.

23 James P. Woodard, *A Place in Politics: São Paulo, Brazil, from Seigneurial Republicanism to Regionalist Revolt* (Durham, NC: Duke University Press, 2009), 58.

24 On the legitimating effect of "public service," especially for the generation of the 1920s–30s, see Cristina Peixoto Mehrtens, *Urban Space and National Identity in Early Twentieth-Century São Paulo, Brazil: Crafting Modernity* (New York: Palgrave, 2010), 96.

25 Maria Lígia Coelho Prado, *A democracia ilustrada: O Partido Democrático de São Paulo, 1926–1934* (São Paulo: Ática, 1986).

26 My discussion here comes almost entirely from James P. Woodard, *A Place in Politics*, chapter 5. The quote is on p. 126. Monteiro Lobato specifically laments that those whom the law gives the "artificial ability to vote" were crowding out the "elite," but in an electoral context, one can presume a somewhat expansive conceptualization of that category, and the regional "modernist" perspective implies an elite distinct from traditional wielders of power and influence.

27 Woodard, *A Place in Politics*, 126–127. Monteiro Lobato also expressed a sentiment that would be echoed by various supporters of the "Paulista Cause" of the early 1930s to the effect that elections were being delegitimized by ignorant voters who had only been given the "artificial ability" to cast a ballot by the law, an ability that he described as "a vulgar lie with terrible consequences."

28 Even Antonio Baptista Pereira, an anti-racist paulista intellectual, declared that São Paulo would always be in the "forefront" of Brazil's march to modernity. *Pelo Brasil Maior* (São Paulo: n.p., 1934), 347.

29 A. Ricardo López-Pedreros, *Makers of Democracy: A Transnational History of the Middle Classes in Colombia* (Durham, NC: Duke University Press, 2019).
30 Weinstein, *For Social Peace in Brazil*, 3; "The Discourse of Technical Competence: Strategies of Authority and Power in Industrializing Brazil," *Political Power and Social Theory* 12 (1998): 137–175.
31 A pioneering study of the dispute over industrialization in Brazil is Nícia Vilela Luz, *A Luta pela Industrialização do Brasil* 2nd ed. (São Paulo: Alfa-Omega, 1975).
32 Weinstein, *For Social Peace in Brazil*, 20–22.
33 Weinstein, *For Social Peace in Brazil*, 18. The Simonsen circle included Morvan Dias de Figueiredo, Mariano Ferraz, Armando de Arruda Pereira, José Ermírio de Moraes, Antonio Noschese, and Antonio Devisate, among others.
34 Weinstein, *For Social Peace in Brazil*, chap. 4.
35 Mehrtens, *Urban Space and National Identity*, 14.
36 Mehrtens, *Urban Space and National Identity*, 19.
37 Carlos A.C. Lemos, *Ramos de Azevedo e seu Escritório Técnico* (São Paulo: Editora PINI, 1998); a somewhat analogous figure was Roberto Simonsen's maternal grandfather, Inácio Wallace da Gama Cochrane, a civil engineer who devoted much of his career to public works. Weinstein, *For Social Peace in Brazil*, 17.
38 There are contexts in which it may be useful to distinguish between "bourgeois" and "middle-class," but here they can be used interchangeably, as they were in practice. For Marx, writing in 1850, the distinction between the bourgeoisie and the middle classes was crucial since he saw the latter as temporary allies of the proletariat, but that alliance was increasingly irrelevant in the context of early twentieth-century São Paulo. Karl Marx, *The Class Struggles in France, 1848–1850* (New York: International Publishers, 1964).
39 The essay appeared in the *Almanach Literário de São Paulo*, Vol. V (1880); cited in Ferreira, *A Epopéia Bandeirante*, 76.
40 Within 24 hours of the outbreak of hostilities (July 9, 1932), the Liga de Defesa Paulista (The Paulista Defense League) had signed up 30 medical doctors, 30 engineers, 35 pharmacists, 29 typists, 10 telegraphers, 106 drivers and mechanics, 207 workers [operários], and 46 "diversos" (unspecified). Instituto Histórico e Geográfico de S. Paulo, Coleção Rev. Const. de 1932, Recortes de jornais, 7.
41 Weinstein, *The Color of Modernity*, 87–97.
42 For descriptions of these mass protests, see Paulo Nogueira Filho, *A Guerra Cívica 1932* (Rio de Janeiro: José Olympio Editora, 1965), Vol. I, 422–26.
43 This incompetence, however, should not be interpreted as synonymous with cowardice (a frequent charge by the *getulistas* against well-off paulistas). However questionable their motives, many young men (and some women) put their lives at risk in fighting for São Paulo, and the record of those killed includes many combatants who likely regarded themselves as middle class. Benedito Montenegro, org., *Cruzes Paulistas: os que tombaram em 32 pela glória de servir São Paulo* (São Paulo: Campanha Pro-Monumento, 1932).
44 *O Estado de São Paulo*, July 19, 1932.
45 *A Gazeta* (São Paulo), Aug. 7, 1932.
46 Museu Paulista, Coleção Revolução de 32, Doc. 2.777, 25/8/32.
47 It is noteworthy that the phrase generally appeared this way, with the words capitalized, which reinforces the archetyping implications. On the figure of the Mulher Paulista, see Barbara Weinstein, "Inventing the *Mulher Paulista*: Politics, Rebellion, and the Gendering of Brazilian Regional Identities," *Journal of Women's History* 18, no. 1 (Winter 2006): 22-49, and Weinstein, *The Color of Modernity*, chap. 4.

48 Text of radio address reproduced in J. Rodrigues, *A Mulher Paulista no Movimento Pro-Constituinte* (São Paulo: Revista dos Tribunaes, 1933), 58.
49 US National Archives and Records Administration, RG59, M1472, Political Report no. 48, July 30, 1932.
50 See, for example, *A Gazeta*, August 7, 1932.
51 A draft of an "appreciation" of the movement of 1932, likely written by Carlota Pereira de Queiróz, who coordinated the movement's social services, has a line that is crossed out referring to women who had to sew uniforms at night because they worked during the day. Arquivo do Estado de São Paulo, Coleção '32, Pasta 385, Doc. 2.034.
52 Mônica Raisa Schpun, "Carlota Pereira de Queiroz: Uma Mulher na Política," *Revista Brasileira de História* 17, no. 33 (1997): 167–200.
53 Mehrtens, *Urban Space and National Identity*, 95.
54 Mário de Andrade, "Guerra de São Paulo," unpublished manuscript, Coleção Mário de Andrade, Caixa l, Instituto de Estudos Brasileiros, Universidade de São Paulo.
55 Vivaldo Coaracy, *O Caso de São Paulo* (São Paulo: Ferraz, 1932), 18.
56 Leven Vampré, *São Paulo, terra conquistada* (São Paulo: Editora Paulista, 1932), 13. As López-Pedreros cogently argued in *Makers of Democracy*, the embrace of democracy by the middle class certainly does not imply a rejection of hierarchies. But in the specific context of mid-century Brazil, the refusal to identify liberalism with democracy meant that the paulistas had a limited capacity to effectively criticize the Vargas regime; it also enabled an anti-populist politics that portrayed the military men who seized power in 1964 as defenders of "democracy."
57 "S. Paulo repete 32," *O Estado de S. Paulo*, Apr. 1, 1964, p. 4.
58 Soon after Dilma Rousseff succeeded Lula as president, distinguished social scientist Emir Sader wrote that Dilma had "inherited not just a country in much better shape than Lula did eight years ago, but also a weakened, demoralized, and defeated right-wing." Clearly, this assessment would soon prove to have been wildly inaccurate. Emir Sader, "Dilma as Lula's Successor: The First 100 Days," *NACLA Report on the Americas* 44, no. 2 (2011): 31–33.
59 Not only did Bolsonaro win a clear electoral majority in the states with the largest middle classes, but even in the Norte and Nordeste—the stronghold of the PT—Bolsonaro won a majority of the vote in the urban centers (generally assumed to be more middle-class) of Belém, Maceió, Natal, and João Pessoa. In the state of São Paulo, 68% of the vote went to Bolsonaro, vs. 60% of the vote in the state capital, and a similar pattern can be seen in Santa Catarina and Rio Grande do Sul, which may indicate that portions of the urban middle class hewed to a more progressive position. https://especiais.gazetadopovo.com.br/eleicoes/2018/resultados/mapa-eleitoral-de-presidente-por-estados-2turno/
60 Amory Gethin and Marc Morgan, "Brazil Divided: Hindsights on the Growing Politicisation of Inequality," World Inequality Lab, WID.world, Issue Brief 2018/3, Oct. 2018. Chart is on p. 4. https://wid.world/document/divided-brazil-hindsights-on-the-growing-politicization-of-inequality-wid-world-issue-brief-2018-3/
61 The sociologist Hélio Jaguaribe first used the formal category of "miséria absoluta" in the Brasil 2000 report that he prepared for President José Sarney in 1986. http://almanaque.folha.uol.com.br/brasil_09abr1986.htm
62 For maps of Brazilian elections (showing which candidate in the second round won a majority of the votes in each state) from 1945 to 2014, see https://sites.google.com/site/atlaseleicoespresidenciais/mapas-eleitorais-de-1945-a-2010

63 André Singer, *O lulismo em crise: Um quebra-cabeça do período Dilma, 2011–2016* (São Paulo: Companhia das Letras, 2018).

64 For a discussion of ties between the right-wing in Brazil and US-based neo-conservatives, see Benjamin A. Cowan, "Holy Ghosts of Brazil's Past," *NACLA Report on the Americas* 48, no. 4 (2016): 346–52. Cowan expands on these arguments in *Moral Majorities Across the Americas: Brazil, the United States, and the Creation of the Religious Right* (Chapel Hill, NC: University of North Carolina Press, 2021).

65 On consumerism, education, and the markers of middle-class identity in São Paulo, see O'Dougherty, *Consumption Intensified*.

3 Uneven Development and the Concept of the Middle Class

Costa Rica, 1890–1950[1]

George I. García-Quesada

In 1944, two sociologists from the United States, John and Mavis Biesanz, published a book with their analysis of the Costa Rican society, where they had lived for a couple of years by then. From their observations, they concluded that "the [Costa Rican] middle class thinks about itself as the spine of the country, and is proud of its own virtues: respectability, morality, aspiration to education, participation in the church and in public charity."[2]

The concept of a widespread middle class has played indeed a fundamental role in Costa Rican national identity and politics since the mid-twentieth century. In this country, as in many other countries at the time, the expansion of the state, redistributive measures through stronger taxation, and an open support for the development of local industries after 1949, during the so-called *Second Republic*, were based on an ideology of egalitarianism (*middleness*) and upwards social mobility.

However, far from emerging organically from a consensus, the concept of the *middle class* and the role in society assigned to it came from discursive agents with specific interests in the struggle to hegemonize the language about social differentiation and, in consequence, to promote a particular socio-economic project. The examination of the Costa Rican social structure and its conflicts in the time period between 1890 and 1950 hence throws light on the conditions that made the emergence of this myth of the *middle class* possible.

This chapter proposes a historicization of the discussions about social differentiation in Costa Rica that led to the concept of the *middle class*, by relating the changes in the discursive struggles about social differentiation, on the one hand, with those in the state and the economic structure, on the other. This historicization aims to analyze the crucial political role of this concept during this period as part of the development of capitalism in Costa Rica, and hence to better describe the process of class struggle in that context.

In this sense, an analysis based on classes in the properly Marxian sense helps us to reveal the underlying social contradictions in the development of capitalism in Costa Rica, which the emergence of the concept of *middle class* sought to obfuscate. In that context, for instance, salaried

DOI: 10.4324/9781003029311-5

workers such as professionals and bureaucrats had a different relation to the dynamics of capital accumulation than peasants or urban small proprietors – the proper petty-bourgeoisie. Indeed, as we will see, these social sectors went in quite different directions in the development of capitalism during the first half of the twentieth century. In this chapter, *middle class* ("clase media") is thus not a class defined in terms of the social relations of production, but a social concept – a specific kind of *ideologeme*, in Jameson's sense[3] – which conceals a plurality of social agents whose interests are often mutually contradictory.

Thus, besides censuses and analyses of the Costa Rican social structure of this period, the main sources for this chapter are articles from the everyday press, which show the struggles between different social agents trying to impose their vision of society and classes, and hence to legitimize their particular interests. These discussions were especially vivid during the presidential election periods, not only in the press from the parties but also in the working-class newspapers; these periods and agents have been hence fundamental in order to reveal the discursive agents that invented and made use of the concept of the *middle class* in Costa Rica.

A Prehistory of the Costa Rican *Middle Class:* 1890–1930

The myth of Costa Rican middleness – according to which its past of poverty, hard peasant labor and small property guaranteed the democratic and pacific character of its people – was already well spread in the first years of the Independence. "The Costa Rican People are made up in their totality from proprietors in a small or a large scale,", assured a local newspaper in 1834, while Felipe Molina – the author of the first book about the history of Costa Rica – affirmed in 1851 that in Costa Rica "everybody has some goods and everybody works, while proletarians and large-scale capitalists are unknown [...] This absolute absence of castes and social classes prove that Costa Rica is an eminently republican country."[4]

Some years later, in 1877, President Tomás Guardia Gutiérrez described Costa Rica as a country consisting of an "homogeneous population" of "proprietors in a larger or a lesser scale," and lacking "opposite interests."[5] From then on, this commonplace ritually reappears in official discourses – and especially in the annual Presidential Message to the National Congress.

But numerous local intellectuals, under a positive or a bad light, from official or critical perspectives, also reproduced this myth. For example, in 1938, the essayist and novel writer Yolanda Oreamuno described the contempt for excellence – which she argued was the real motivation behind the Costa Rican middleness – as the cause of what she considered her country's mediocre social and cultural environment.[6]

This myth also played an important role in the popular classes as a symbolic strategy of class conflict containment; it offered them – and especially to the peasants – a privileged place as the foundations of the Costa Rican nationality. As the Communist writer Fabián Dobles assessed in 1950:

> In the [Central] Plateau, the tone of the civil life was rural and democratic. It was difficult to find a family of peasants that thought about themselves as lesser than any other. Although the educated, the rich man or the priest were more highly respected, the conscience of equality was well trenched in their spirits, since all of them, on the top or in the bottom, had in equal measure built the country.[7]

In spite of this myth of Costa Rican exceptionalism based on an assumed agrarian small-sized -property egalitarianism, the socio-economical structure in this country developed in a similar direction as the rest of the capitalist world-system. By the early 1900s, the expansion of the so-called "new middle classes" – the salaried non-manual workers – in the metropolitan countries was notorious. Eric Hobsbawm has indicated that the employment in management and trade had increased almost three times during the *Belle époque* in the United Kingdom, while in Germany the percentage of white-collar workers and public servants rose from 10.3% to 17.3% between 1907 and 1925, and the self-employed population decreased from 19.6% to 15.6%.[8]

In the periphery of the world-system, Latin American countries, witnessed these social process as well. [9] The emergence of the Costa Rican *middle class* takes place during a period characterized for the tendency to the concentration of capitals and the decline of the rural small- and medium-sized property. Although the urban middle sectors that gained political power across the twentieth century identified themselves with the rural independent producers as part of the *middle class*, they were a product of the structural process towards the prevalence of waged labor over independent peasant labor.

The censuses show, indeed, a growth in the amount of day laborers (*jornaleros*): from 33.8% in 1883 to 36.4% in 1892, and 40% in 1927.[10] However, as Víctor Hugo Acuña has pointed out, this relatively slow growth may conceal a qualitatively more important transformation: the condition of a day laborer in 1927 was probably more precarious than in 1883 due to the former's impossibility to grow their own goods for subsistence.[11] As the percentage of independent rural workers decreased, so did also that of properly liberal professionals – like accountants and lawyers – who tended to become employees working for a salary.

In regard to rural labor, this tendency towards salarification was decelerated by the availability of land, albeit the agrarian frontier moved further as the time passed. In this manner, the simple commodity production could, with growing difficulty, delay its absorption into salaried labor. In particular, the threats to small- and medium-scale producers of coffee – the main product from the Central Valley for exportation – generated their energetic response: before the Great Depression, they had repeatedly mobilized against the processors/exporters of their bean – who also lent credit to the producers before the harvest season. The fundamental conflict was in how the prices were set by the latter, who acted as an oligopsony, especially when defining the quality of the different varieties of this fruit. These conflicts were not bound by specific economic conjunctures, but were of a structural kind:[12] as Acuña indicates, even between 1922 and 1928, a period of prosperity for coffee trade, small- and medium-scale producers attempted or founded around ten forms of organization representing their interests.[13]

But the structural problems of rural simple commodity production came also from their demography. The division of the inheritance left the parents in the dilemma of fragmenting the family land property – which made it less profitable – or leaving it to one of their children – thus depriving the rest of their children from their livelihood.[14] Those left out of the family resources could – as mentioned above – wander into the periphery of the country in search for new land to colonize;[15] besides this, there was the opportunity for the younger children to go through formal studies,[16] among which teaching was the most usual means to work stability. Since teachers were needed all across the country, the government sponsored studentships for talented children from families with limited economic resources who were interested in pursuing a career in education.[17]

Not surprisingly, the percentage of public servants, educators, and professionals in general rose during this period: while the 1892 Census counted 2.7% of these occupations (all in the same category) from the total economically productive population, in 1927 they accounted for 7.4% (4.8% public servants, 1.2% professionals, and 1.4% educators).[18] A career was also a good option for the children of the bourgeoisie who did not inherit the family's assets, increasing the ranks of the military, the clergy, lawyers, and physicians (who had to study abroad due to the lack of a Medicine Faculty at the time in Costa Rica), among other professions. However, more than a quantitative importance, these professionals – with their love–hate attitude to their wealthy relatives – had a crucial political weight in the first half of the twentieth century Costa Rica; they were, for instance, the social base for the Center for the Study of National Problems[19] – whose importance in the 1940s we will describe below.

The expansion of the Costa Rican state also allowed an important upwards social mobility for people from subaltern classes; as Palmer has argued, the formation of the *middle class* in Costa Rica has been strongly related to the institutions of social control and the civilizing process of the popular classes.[20] In this direction, the government directly and indirectly contributed to the formation of the *middle class* in the country: directly, by generating employment for the educated, the vanguard in its civilizational project; as in the rest of Latin America, the Costa Rican *middle class* has been a child of Leviathan.[21] In addition to the *clientelar* structure of the electoral politics in the country, the efficient operation of the nation-state implied an increase in the number of civil servants dedicated to public administration and education, as well as their distribution across the territory of the country. Bureaucracy and social control thus mutually reinforced, in spite of the constant economic crises and payment problems to these servants.

On the other hand, the state indirectly promoted the emergence of the salaried *middle class* through the education of the professional and managerial staff needed by the local capitalists. Hence, the intellectual workers were the most thriving group in the rise of the *middle class*; the Liberal model originally formed them as mediators between the oligarchic project and the popular classes, but with time they developed their own interests and political struggles. These workers could identify themselves with the modernizing project of capitalism, but were also able to negotiate their own different orientation – one where they played the main role in the narrative of the progress of the Costa Rican nation – into it.

Hence, this process formed socio-occupational groups with spaces, behaviors, and expectations clearly differentiated from those of manual workers and from the bourgeoisie,[22] but most of the time they were discursively included within the ranks of the working class. *Middle class* was a recognizable concept that appeared every once in a while in the press, but did not have a significative recurrence or an ideological development to turn it into a political interpellation. In contrast, *worker* ("obrero") and *capitalist* ("capitalista"; "burgués," on the other hand, was a derogatory term) were used in newspapers as signifiers that called for specific groups who identified with them.

The 1923 presidential campaign, for example, would have been a timely moment for the electoral use of discourses in praise of a *middle class*: while the Reformist Party self-identified with the interests of the *proletariat*, and the Agrarian Party was defined by its adversaries as an elitist group, Ricardo Jiménez's Republican Party had the possibility to identify as an intermediate option – and to thus take advantage from the traditional myth of Costa Rican middleness. In spite of a couple of isolated derogatory commentaries from the Reformist side in that direction,[23] Jiménez's party did not seize the opportunity to become a third – a *middle* – option in class struggle at the electoral level.

The point of view of the elites tended to use two approaches when they symbolized social differentiations: the first, which Spanish historian Juan Francisco Fuentes calls a *minimalist* approach, designates classes in reference to socio-occupational groups or strata within them.[24] For example, President Cleto González Víquez mentions the *military class* and the *clerical class* ("clase sacerdotal") in his 1907 and 1910 messages to the National Congress, while in 1913 the newspaper of his party affirmed that the *working class* ("clase obrera") and the *magisterial national class* ("clase del magisterio nacional") were the largest among the *working classes* ("clases trabajadoras") in the country. The second approach was the plain denial of the existence of classes. Unsurprisingly, this line of argument, which emphasized the possibility of individual social mobility, was very common in the press of parties that downplayed popular demands. Congressman Luis Cruz Mesa in 1913 and former president Ricardo Jiménez in 1919, for instance, argued in that direction.[25]

The working-class press had a very different stance on this matter. The narrative in such publications is tragic, and calls for transformations in the prevailing relations of production. Their protagonist is a morally superior collective agent who faces an adverse social environment, and typically glimpses a solution to the opposing class interests through the mediation of the government, or ultimately through a revolution. These discourses functioned as denunciations for the public opinion in general as well as for the mobilization of the struggling working class. Their attack on the ideologeme of the *middleness* was hence permanent.

The logic of this narrative about class interests is thus clearly dichotomic, and is perhaps most importantly expressed through the colloquial opposition between *jackets* and *frock coats* ("chaquetas" and "levitas"). As for the latter, Miguel Ángel Quesada Pacheco refers to Gagini's 1892 definition in the *Dictionary of Costa Ricanisms*, where it is described as "a derogatory term by which the people ['el pueblo'] call those who wear a frock coat," while the 1938 version of this dictionary defines it, more succinctly, as "rich, in a derogatory manner."[26] Thus, during the 1906 elections, an allegedly neutral bystander indicated that

> as I walked down a street in the capital city, some people at a rally mistakenly assumed I was a supporter of Cleto González Víquez, and raising his voice, one of those in the center of the street said: 'Cleto's crowd will only consist of four miserable *frock coats*.'[27]

In a similar manner, in 1928 the Reformist Party through their news outlet, *La Prensa* – directed by the anarchist Ricardo Falcó Mayor – explicitly related the situation of the *frock coat* to the opposition between proletarian -and bourgeois.[28] However, traditional political groups like the Republican Party also used the agonistic narrative when they faced more established candidates – as in the case of Máximo Fernández in his various electoral campaigns, and Carlos María Jiménez in 1932. The meaning of the terms utilized to characterize collective social agents are often ambiguous, depending on the social place and the conjuncture where the specific discourses emerge. The use of such terms should thus be understood as a relation within which each one of them, more than belonging a univocal definition, is a range of definitions that vary according to the ideology from which the signifier is enunciated.

Depending on the context and the speaker, in Costa Rica the opposition could refer to conflicts such as rural/urban, manual/intellectual labor, common citizen/politician, etc. Different contents were assigned to signifiers like "chaqueta" and "levita." [29] We should in any case emphasize that *discursive forms are ideological and have a history of their own*, and thus the formal analysis of the discourses should relate them to the concrete conflicts that generate them. Agonistic discourses seek to interpellate specific groups in order to engage in social conflict, and in order to do this they attribute symbolic places of identity and alterity. Working-class publications were explicit about the socio-economic character of the conflict, while those directed to a wider audience were more ambiguous about their criteria for social differentiation. Non-classist political parties that followed agonistic narratives most of the time affirmed that the problems of the poor were due to the action of specific powerful groups. Criticism was thus aimed at some of the hegemonic social agents, not as representatives of a system that produces inequality, but merely as corrupt individuals.

The Emergence of the *Middle Class*: 1930–1940

While the 1920s were for Costa Rica a decade of prosperity due to the rise in the prices of coffee in the world market, the Crisis of 1929 had devastating effects on the economy of this country. The contraction of the national market caused by the fall in the prices of coffee led to a fiscal crisis because the greatest part of the government income came from customs duties; this, in turn, led to a monetary crisis. There was thus a reduction of money supply, a massive withdrawal of bank deposits, a restriction on credits and an urgent demand on the payment of contracted debts.[30] Unemployment and commercial crisis were then inevitable.

Each of these aspects negatively affected the middle sectors. The first group damaged by the fall in the price of coffee were the small- and medium-scale producers of these beans, though the most severe effects of the fall were not immediate. By the end of 1929 the coffee processors suspended their advances to small-scale producers and demanded that they settle their debts. The processors tried to put the burden of the international fall in the prices of coffee on the shoulders of the small-scale producers; probably, as Clorito Picado affirmed, these capitalists disproportionally decreased the price paid to the producers, in order to keep their own levels of profit. Similarly, the independent banana growers in the Caribbean coast had to accept "enormously decreased" prices from the United Fruit Company for their product.[31]

Between 1930 and 1931, as unemployment soared, the income from commercial activities dropped around 60%, leading numerous venues into bankruptcy or – following a vicious circle – into massive firing of employees; only traders who counted with considerable capitals could resist the crisis.[32] Furthermore, the government deficit caused cuts on wages and the dismissal of workers – a measure soon emulated by the private employers.[33]

Professionals, government and commercial employees, small-scale merchants, and owners of small artisanal workshops were, along with small- and medium-scale rural producers were victims of this contraction of the national economy. But also, due to their level of consumption – conspicuous consumption, in good measure[34] –, the crisis was an existential threat to socio-occupational sectors such as these. Several public figures have written about how their families lost their *middle-class* livelihood during the 1930s, thus enduring very difficult conditions at the time.[35]

Following policies from other latitudes, the government responded to the economic hardship by investing in infrastructure, but also by accentuating its intervention on social conflicts. During the 1930s, before the creation of the Costa Rican Social Security Fund (CCSS) in 1941 and the Labor Code in 1943, the government enacted a series of laws and institutions that increased the quantity of public servants at the same time as legitimizing them as mediators in different aspects of class struggle and tacitly established a model where the middle sectors functioned as the keepers of social stability.[36]

The Crisis accelerated the process of concentration of capitals. While the 1927 Census showed a 59.8% of salaried workers in the economically productive population, by 1950, the corresponding percentage surged to 66.54%. This tendency was stronger for professionals and managers, who passed in this same period from 68.1% to a surprising 87.82%, mainly composed of women – especially teachers and nurses.[37]

The economic crisis thus broke the ideological certainties of the Liberal era. The promise of a better future was no longer plausible, and in the midst of the world-scale Depression there was no possible way to argue for the efficacy of an unrestrained capitalism. In this reconfiguration of the ideological field, different social agents tried to seize control over the increasingly important signifier *middle class* and use it for their interests; even though its meaning was basically the same for every ideology, its place within each one of them – its function as an ideologeme – changed according with the different socio-political narratives of the conjuncture.

There were two fundamental narratives in regard to the role of the *middle class*: its integration with one of the opposite classes (whether with the dominant or with the subaltern classes) and as a third, autonomous class, economically and politically well separated from the polar opposites in the social hierarchy. In other words, the alternatives in the ideological conflict for the signifier *middle class* were narratives of class struggle or of class conciliation. As in the pre-Depression conjuncture, the concept of middleness was under dispute; however, with the emergence of the discussions about the *middle class* additional social sectors came into this dispute.

As mentioned, the small- and medium-scale producers of coffee considered themselves as the incarnation of the Costa Rican middleness, a sort of Aristotelian social right balance. However, they had a very clear conscience of their immediate interests and did not think of administrative officers and professionals as their allies; on the contrary, they systematically expressed their animosity against bureaucracy and government intervention.[38] These small-scale proprietors had no interest in inventing a *middle class* for their political purposes. They assumed they were the right balance for the country.

The first attempts to mobilize the *middle class* came from the left-wing side of the political specter. Already in 1931, the Costa Rican Communist Party (CRCP) observed the tendency of this "class" towards proletarization,[39] and repeatedly tried to attract small-scale proprietors to their ranks. The struggles of small-scale coffee and banana producers, or those of small storekeepers were not new, but the CRCP provided a new explanation to them: from then on, the Communists considered small-scale proprietors as non-proletarian allies to the working and the peasant classes against capital.

In their search for an alliance between subaltern classes, the discourses of the Communists insisted on such a bloc:

> at a purely human level, we Communists see exploiters of men and exploited men. [...] Workers from city and country, small-scale proprietors, small-scale producers, students and revolutionary intellectuals who are also workers, can all be members of the Communist Party with identical rights.[40]

Hence, the Costa Rican Communists differentiated the *middle class*, while also subsuming it into the whole of the exploited people. The radicalization of the professionals who founded the CRCP took place during the 1929 crisis, which was particularly harsh on the Costa Rican middle sectors, especially in the case of the public servants, whose reduced incomes led to a sensitive decline in their quality of life. The *middle-class* Communists, besides being impoverished by the crisis, lacked the social capital that in the 1940s the also *middle-class* members of the Center for the Study of National Problems (most of whose leaders were family-related to the economic élite) did have.

The CPCR also used the term *petty-bourgeoisie* – which in nineteenth-century Marxism referred to small-scale proprietors – as a synonym of *middle class*, albeit with a pejorative connotation. Thus, in 1936 they disqualified the Socialist Party for its alleged distance from the popular classes: "what Mr. Vicente Sáenz [the leader of the Party] wants is to organize the petty-bourgeoisie: professors, teachers, lawyers and physicians with left-wing ideas, bookkeepers and badly-paid bureaucrats."[41]

Although the syntagm *middle class* appeared occasionally in the press for decades before the foundation of the CPCR in 1931, their conception was probably rooted in the anti-imperialist circles frequented by Manuel Mora Valverde, Jaime Cerdas, and Ricardo Coto Conde, founders of the Party, as well as Carmen Lyra, who was a member of the Costa Rican section of the Alianza Popular Revolucionaria Americana (American Popular Revolutionary Alliance, APRA, founded by Peruvian activist Raúl Haya de la Torre) in the late 1920s.[42] This organization called for the radicalization of the Latin American middle classes, which should in their view unite with the popular classes and with the progressive local bourgeoisies in the struggle against large landlords (*latifundistas*) and against imperialism.[43] Hence, the *middle class* serves two functions: uniting the popular classes in each country, and as an avant-garde against the enemies of the nation – imperialism and the *latifundista* oligarchy.

APRA's positions were evidently not completely shared by the Communists, but its specific conception of the *middle class* could have influenced theirs. The Communists coincided with APRA about the socio-occupational composition of the *middle class* as well as about the subalternity of this "class," but did not conceive it as the avant-garde of social change, nor – at least until they assumed the popular front strategy – the position of supporting the national bourgeoisie against imperialism.

Broadly speaking, the Socialist Party directly adopted APRA´s political positions. For the 1936 presidential campaign, for example, Carlos Fernández Mora, one of the founders of this party, praised their own politics for promoting the *middle class*, while their most prolific writer, Vicente Sáenz, called for the union between intellectual and manual workers with the mediation of the Costa Rican *middle class*. [44] Like the Communists, Sáenz insisted that this "class" was in a process of impoverishment with the rest of the popular classes. This party's interpellation to the *middle class* was not done in the name of the latter's particular interests, but as part of the social classes put in disadvantage by the capitalist system.[45]

An Anti-Communist *Middle Class*: The 1940s

Nonetheless, the political role of the *middle class* in these agonistic ideologies was not to prevail. In the early 1940s, the young professionals from the Center for the Study of National Problems (CSNP), from a reformist standpoint, formulated their conception of the *middle class* not only as a leading avant-garde, but as the majority of the Costa Rican population:

> What we find in Costa Rica is a large middle class that practically encompasses all of the Costa Rican people. [...] The way to help this society to evolve is therefore not to promote class struggle – which does not actually exist – but, on the contrary, to try to form a single front representing manual workers, peasants, middle class, small-scale capitalists, etc., in order to engage in a common fight against the common enemy: imperialism. The small-scale capitalist proprietor, the small-scale shopkeeper, intellectuals and employees form that large middle class in Costa Rica, whose interests are under attack from imperialism. [...] As of this moment, there are only a rising

> proletariat and a rising bourgeoisie in the borders of the large middle class that forms the majority of our nationality. The peasants in Costa Rica also have a middle-class mentality, because they don't live as miserably as those in other countries.[46]

Their ideology was opposed to the conceptions of social differentiation of both the Liberal elite and the recently founded left-wing parties. The CSNP adapted Haya de la Torre's positions to their interests, but soon left the antagonism against imperialism for a functional vision, whose aim was to remove the ill tissues from the otherwise healthy body of the Costa Rican nationality. They kept the notion of the *middle class* as the social avant-garde, and affirmed that the obstacle for the development of the country – rather than a *latifundista* oligarchy – were "monopolistic or speculative capital, [...] the exploitative activity of foreign capital and [...] the civil oligarchies who defend them."[47]

While APRA maintained a tragic vision of history, the CSNP promoted a comical conception, according to which the solution to the social problems was already there, and a due technocracy was responsible for solving the disfunctions of the system. In APRA's narrative, the social world was something to be conquered; for the Centrists, the task was to simply go back to the path of their grandparents, from which their fathers had diverted.[48] Where APRA said *revolution*, the CSNP said *restoration*; the latter sought their poetry from their (imagined) past.

These positions were quite original for the early 1940s Costa Rica. In a survey sent in 1943 by Surco (the CSNP's outlet) to diverse personalities, only they referred to the *middle class* and justified its importance in their social project. Moreover, during the 1930s neither the syntagm *middle class* nor any other synonym were, except for the left-wing parties, used in an electoral campaign; the established parties tended to reproduce pre-1929 narratives of social differentiation.

The Centrists – championing a sort of anti-communist reformism – thus took the signifier *middle class* from Communists and Socialists, giving it a new meaning in their reformist political ideology and project. In order to gain a place for this project, however, they had to be allies with less progressive sectors who did have economic resources and political experience, and whose expectations did not fully coincide with those of these young intellectuals. In a country with a political culture profoundly rooted in the electoral processes,[49] this was the price that the Centrists had to pay in order for their ideology to eventually become hegemonic.

With the slow economic recovery, the pattern of uneven development favored petty-bourgeois activities like retail sales in the cities – in San José in particular –, as well as salaried occupations in the secondary and tertiary sectors. In this case, the surplus value produced by rural labor migrated into the cities; as Harvey indicates, the accumulation of capital is inherently spatial, and its circulation implies a geographical movement in time.[50] The permanent crisis of rural small-scale property (leading to the proletarization of its workforce) contrasted with the concentration of capital in the cities, expressed in the growth of urban employment and infrastructure.

Small-scale employers hence flourished in the 1940s Costa Rican cities, as a result of the investment, especially due to the governmental expansion, in the secondary and tertiary circuits (not to be confused for sectors) of capital accumulation: adequate assets and infrastructure for more productivity and better circulation, investment in health and education, among others. Furthermore, the opportunities of work in the government increased for those who earned their secondary education or university diploma (the university reopened in 1941, after more than fifty years). At the same time, the agricultural processors and exporters also used some of their profits in luxury consumption and personal services, activities whose importance becomes apparent when we see the increase of the tertiary sector between the 1927 and the 1950 Censuses.[51]

The better situation of the petty-bourgeoisie and the salaried professionals led them away from the left-wing parties. Throughout the 1940s, as the opposition to the populist government of Rafael Ángel Calderón Guardia – by then allied with the Catholic Church and the Communist Party (rebaptized as Popular Vanguard Party) – took possession over the concept of the *middle class*, both Communists and *Calderonistas* grew increasingly suspicious of it. The alliance of the Communists with the government led them to moderate their discourses about class struggle, and to assume a rhetoric more similar to that from the official reforms. Hence, in the 1944 electoral campaign, the Communist outlet, *Trabajo*, affirmed that the "negative tendency" in the Costa Rican social forces was no longer constituted by the whole bourgeoisie, but by reactionary sectors within every class: between them, "the ignorant wealthy people,", the exploitative companies, and "the cowardly sectors of our middle class who, in spite of having the permanent threat of poverty over their heads – like the sword of Damocles – are afraid of any kind of social change."[52]

The rhetoric of the Calderón and Picado campaigns in 1944 and 1948 avoided the theme of the *middle class*, opting instead for discourses based on a vague "understanding between classes" and emphasizing the qualities of Dr. Calderón as a redeemer of the country. Such discourses were more religious or moral than political or sociological, and thus the *Calderonistas* yielded the concept of the *middle class* to their opponents by not incorporating it in their usual language. Moreover, when they mentioned this concept, they assumed that such "class" was part of the coalition against their government. In early 1948, for example, a government sympathizer argued that

> in order to face the social legislation of Calderón Guardia, an opposition candidacy should have been a candidacy of capitalists with a capitalist candidate. But they presented a middle-class candidacy that, at

> this moment, has no support from the working class [...] nor from the strongest capitalists.[53]

The day after this interview, the same analyst asked:

> did you notice that in his most recent discourse Otilio [Ulate, the opposition presidential candidate] said that his Party is not from the rich or from the workers, but from the middle class? [...] When he wrote his discourse he already felt he lacked the support from the large capital.[54]

The *Diario de Costa Rica* newspaper, owned and directed precisely by Otilio Ulate, was the first major outlet to adopt the social conception proposed by the Centrists. In August 1943, its pages attacked Calderón's government for allegedly not protecting the *middle-class* citizen, the urban and the rural workers,[55] and some months later characterized Costa Rica as a "new country, of middle classes."[56] During the next two presidential campaigns, the anti-Communist and anti-Calderonista reformism of the CSNP was appropriated by several wealthy businessmen – José Figueres Ferrer among them – who were against the government and promoted a right-wing version of social democracy.[57]

In August 1949, almost a year and a half after defeating the *Calderonista* government and their communist allies in a civil war, Figueres (later to become two times president of the Republic) praised the role of the *middle class* in the new hegemonic project:

> Our country, like a car, is marching over all these hardships [produced by the 1948 War], which are holes and rocks in the path of progress. There is a whole generation of studious and honest young people who are exercising now in the duties of the Public Administration. It will be a new homeland. There is a numerous middle class of cultured people without economic resources that will increase as the working people and the peasants have the means of material and educational progress that they desire and deserve so much within their reach. This middle class is the seed supplier for the new Costa Rica. It is now assuming positions in organizations that were once forbidden to them. It is the consumer of most of our products and services. It should cultivate the art of producing them abundantly for everyone.[58]

He continues:

> now the ideal to be achieved is that all the social classes, promoted by the economic technique, eventually melt into a huge middle class that widely enjoys the advantages and cultural opportunities of the era. The real spiritual values will arise from this huge class, which will become the humankind.[59]

In the discourse of the leader of the armed rebellion, in this manner, the idea of the *middle class* is overwhelmingly Utopian: the *middle class* is no longer just representative of the Costa Rican nationality, but of the future of the whole of Humankind.

Economic structural violence, through the dispossession of the main producers of wealth in the country, and a more apparent political violence through legal and illegal actions (such as threats, exile and extra-judicial killings) against the defeated – the Communists in particular – were hence the foundations for the *middle-class* Utopia that officially guided most of the second half of the last century in Costa Rica.

Epilogue

Although the classical approaches to the middle classes in Latin America, such as John J. Johnson's, have emphasized the democratizing and modernizing capacities of such social groups, a closer and disaggregated approach to them shows the contradictions that have underpinned the emergence of the concept and identity of the *middle class*. As Marx had observed in a methodological statement that aptly describes the case of this concept, "these imaginary expressions arise, nevertheless, from the relations of production themselves. They are categories for the forms of appearance of essential relations."[60]

In this sense, the rise of the salaried sectors contrasted strongly with the decline of the small- and medium-scale rural property – where the largest part of the wealth of the country was produced. In Costa Rica – as part of a general tendency of capitalism in the twentieth century – the *middle class* was, in this sense, a concept, an *idea*; however, it was deeply rooted in the development of the class struggles in a context where middleness and egalitarianism were privileged topics of national identity.

Indeed, the concept of the *middle class*, as developed by the Center for the Study of National Problems in the early 1940s, helped to consolidate the place of the salaried intellectual workers – especially in the acceleratedly-growing government – and the urban small-scale proprietors, while undermining the ascending political and discursive leadership of the Communists, and filling the ideological void left by the power élite of the pre-Great Depression Costa Rica.

In the nascent order of the post-World War II world-system, the prevailing narrative in Costa Rica around the concept of the *middle class* helped to reinforce the alliance between these emerging social sectors and the renewed capitalist project. In this light, the *middle class* in Costa Rica, in spite of its claims, was not a neutral concept, external to class struggle, but a cornerstone of the reconfigured ideology of capitalism for the Cold War context.

Notes

1 This chapter summarizes some of the arguments presented in George García-Quesada, *Formación de la clase media en Costa Rica. Economía, sociabilidades y discursos políticos (1890–1950)* (San José: Arlekín, 2014).
2 John and Mavis Biesanz, *La vida en Costa Rica* (San José: Ministerio de Cultura, Juventud y Deportes, 1975), 56.
3 "The ideologeme is an amphibious formation, whose essential structural characteristic may be described as its possibility to manifest itself either as a pseudoidea – a conceptual or belief system, an abstract value, an opinion or prejudice – or as a protonarrative, a kind of ultimate class fantasy about the 'collective characters' which are the classes in opposition." Fredric Jameson, *The Political Unconscious. Narrative as a Socially Symbolic Act* (London and New York: Routledge, 1983), 73.
4 Quoted in Víctor Hugo Acuña "La invención de la diferencia costarricense (1810–1870)," *Revista de Historia*, 45 (January-June 2002): 204–205; also Iván Molina Jiménez, *Costarricense por dicha. Identidad nacional y cambio cultural en Costa Rica durante los siglos XIX y XX* (San José: EUCR, 2002), 69.
5 Quoted in Víctor Hugo Acuña, "Historia del vocabulario político en Costa Rica: Estado, república, nación y democracia (1821–1949)" in *Identidades nacionales y Estado moderno en Centroamérica*, comp. Jean Piel and Arturo Taracena (San José: EUCR, 1995): 68–69.
6 Yolanda Oreamuno, *A lo largo del corto camino* (San José: Ed. Costa Rica, 1961), 17.
7 Quoted in Margarita Rojas et al., *La casa paterna. Escritura y nación en Costa Rica* (San José: EUCR, 1993), 230.
8 Eric Hobsbawm, *La era del imperio (1875–1914)* (Barcelona: Crítica, 1998), 62; Detlev Peukert, *The Weimar Republic: The Crisis of Classical Modernity* (New York: Hill & Wang, 1993), 10.
9 For the cases of Argentina and Brazil, see: Ezequiel Adamovsky, *Historia de la clase media argentina: Apogeo y decadencia de una ilusión (1919–2003)* (Buenos Aires: Planeta, 2009); Brian P. Owensby, *Intimate Ironies. Modernity and the Making of Middle-Class Lives in Brazil* (Stanford, CA: Stanford University Press, 1999).
10 Mario Samper, *Evolución de la estructura socio-ocupacional costarricense: labradores, artesanos y jornaleros (1864–1935)* (San José: Universidad de Costa Rica, 1979), 117, 143.
11 Víctor Hugo Acuña and Iván Molina, *Historia económica y social de Costa Rica (1750–1950)* (San José: Porvenir, 1991), 140; also, Samper, *Evolución de la estructura socio-ocupacional*, 146.
12 Víctor Hugo Acuña, "Clases sociales y conflicto social en la economía cafetalera costarricense: productores contra beneficiadores (1932–1936)," *Revista de Historia*, Costa Rica Special Issue (1985).
13 Víctor Hugo Acuña, "Patrones del conflicto social en la economía cafetalera costarricense (1900–1948)," *Revista de Ciencias Sociales* 31 (1986): 117.
14 Lowell Gudmundson, "Campesino, granjero, proletario: formación de clase en una economía cafetalera de pequeños propietarios (1850–1950)," *Revista de Historia* 21–22 (January-December 1990): 169–171.
15 Ana María Botey, *Costa Rica entreguerras (1914–1940)* (San José, EUCR, 2007), 12–28.
16 Iván Molina, "Clase, género y etnia van a la escuela: El alfabetismo en Costa Rica y Nicaragua (1880–1950)" in *Educando a Costa Rica: Alfabetización popular, formación docente y género (1880–1950)*, eds. Iván Molina and Steven Palmer (San José: Porvenir, 2000), 28.

17 Iván Molina Jiménez, *El que quiera divertirse. Libros y sociedad en Costa Rica (1750–1914)* (San José: EUCR, 1995), 73–74.
18 Samper, "Evolución de la estructura," 117, 143.
19 Samuel Stone, *La dinastía de los conquistadores. La crisis del poder en la Costa Rica contemporánea* (San José: EDUCA, 1982), 280, 283.
20 Steven Palmer, "Adiós *laissez-faire*: la política social en Costa Rica (1880-1940)," *Revista de Historia de América* 124 (January-June 1, 1999): 116.
21 Michael Jiménez, "The Elision of the Middle Classes and Beyond: History, Politics and Development Studies in Latin America's 'Short Twentieth Century,'" in *Colonial Legacies: The Problem of Persistence in Latin American History*, ed. Jeremy Adelman (Abingdon: Routledge, 1999), 218–220.
22 García Quesada, *Formación de la clase media*, 191–312.
23 Luis Badilla Castro, "A los obreros y campesinos," *La Prensa*, Oct. 15, 1923, 4; Luis Badilla Castro, "A los obreros y campesinos," *La Prensa*, Sept. 19, 1923, 4.
24 Juan Francisco Fuentes, "Clase," in *Diccionario político y social del siglo XIX español*, dir. Javier Fernández Sebastián and Juan Francisco Fuentes (Madrid: Alianza, 2002), 156.
25 García Quesada, *Formación de la clase media*, 336–339.
26 Miguel Ángel Quesada Pacheco, *Diccionario histórico del español de Costa Rica* (San José: EUNED, 1995), 93.
27 "Cuatro levas miserables," *El Combate. Órgano de la Juventud Nacionalista*, Aug. 5, 1905, 1.
28 Juan Verdades, "Delito, condena, libertad," La Prensa, Jul. 21, 1928.
29 Around 1900, the prominent diplomat and writer Ricardo Fernández Guardia observed that "peasants think that any person who wears a frock coat is rich." Ricardo Fernández Guardia, *Cuentos ticos*. San José: EUNED, 2004), 95.
30 Ana María Botey and Rodolfo Cisneros, *La crisis de 1929 y la fundación del Partido Comunista de Costa Rica* (San José: Ed. Costa Rica, 1984), 84.
31 Acuña and Molina, *Historia económica y social*, 164–165; Viales, *Después del enclave (1927–1950): Un estudio de la región atlántica costarricense* (San José: EUCR, 1998), 82.
32 Botey and Cisneros, *La crisis de 1929*, 89–90.
33 Victor Bulmer-Thomas, "La crisis de la economía de agroexportación (1930–1945)" in *Historia general de Centroamérica 4: Las repúblicas agroexportadoras, 1870–1945*, ed. Víctor Hugo Acuña Ortega (Madrid: FLACSO-Sociedad Estatal Quinto Centenario, 1993), 352–353; Botey, *Costa Rica entreguerras*, 61.
34 García-Quesada, *Formación de la clase media*, 250–266.
35 Óscar Barahona Streber, *Memorias y opiniones* (San José: Editorama, 1996), 4; Alberto Cañas, *80 años no es nada* (San José: EUCR, 2006), 4, 8, 14; Manuel Solís Avendaño, *La institucionalidad ajena. Los años cuarenta y el fin de siglo* (San José: EUCR, 2006), 170.
36 García-Quesada, *Formación de la clase media*, 151–152.
37 García-Quesada, *Formación de la clase media*, 167–168.
38 V. H. Acuña, "La ideología de los pequeños y medianos productores cafetaleros costarricenses (1900–1961)," *Revista de Historia* 16 (July-December, 1987).
39 Comité Ejecutivo del PCCR, "A los trabajadores del Guanacaste," *Trabajo*, August 5, 1931, 2.
40 "El intelectual en la lucha revolucionaria," *Trabajo*, Jan. 19, 1936, 1.
41 Quoted in José Manuel Cerdas Albertazzi and Gerardo Contreras, *La política de alianzas del Partido Comunista de Costa Rica: Vanguardia Popular en los años cuarenta* (San José: Universidad de Costa Rica, 1984), 47.
42 Iván Molina Jiménez, ed., *Ensayos políticos: Carmen Lyra y Carlos Luis Fallas* (San José: EUCR, 2000), 32.

43 Víctor Raúl Haya de la Torre, *Por la emancipación de América Latina. Artículos, mensajes, discursos (1923–1927)* (Buenos Aires: Gleizer, 1927), 74, 87, 121, 194.
44 Fernández Mora, Carlos. "No le cité a don Carlos…," *La Tribuna*, Jan. 10, 1936, 5.
45 Vicente Sáenz, *Obras escogidas* (San José: Editorial Costa Rica, 1985), 85.
46 Eugenio Rodríguez Vega, "Clases y lucha social en Costa Rica," *Surco* 42 (December 1943), 12–13.
47 Ottón Acosta Jiménez et al., "Respuesta de los señores Ottón Acosta Jiménez, Isaac Felipe Azofeifa et al." in *Ideario costarricense: Respuesta a una encuesta nacional*, comp. Editorial Surco (San José: EUNED, 2002), 127.
48 Manuel Solís, *Costa Rica: ¿Reformismo socialdemócrata o liberal?* (San José: CLACSO, 1992), 139–140.
49 Iván Molina Jiménez, *Demoperfectocracia: La democracia pre-reformada en Costa Rica (1885–1948)* (Heredia: EUNA, 2005).
50 David Harvey, *The Urban Experience* (Baltimore and London: Johns Hopkins University,1989), 19.
51 Fernando Herrero and Leonardo Garnier, *El desarrollo de la industria en Costa Rica* (Heredia: EUNA, 1982), 32-33; Samper, *Evolución de la estructura*, 258–59.
52 "Teodoro Picado y don León Cortés no son en estos momentos dos simples hombres, sino dos símbolos," *Trabajo*, Oct. 23, 1943, 3.
53 "Por qué el Dr. Calderón Guardia tiene el triunfo en la bolsa?," *La Tribuna*, Jan. 6, 1948, 4.
54 "Prosigue entrevista con 'El viejo abogado,'" *La Tribuna*, Jan. 7, 1948, 5.
55 Quoted in Eugenio Rodríguez Vega, *Voces del 43* (San José: EUCR, 1995), 210.
56 "Reaccionarios," *Diario de Costa Rica*, Dec. 14, 1943, 3.
57 Solís, *Costa Rica: ¿Reformismo socialdemócrata o liberal?*, 223–47.
58 Quoted in Arturo Castro Esquivel, *José Figueres Ferrer, el hombre y su obra (ensayo de una biografía)* (San José: Imprenta Tormo, 1955), 235-36.
59 Castro Esquivel, *José Figueres Ferrer*, 237.
60 Karl Marx, *Capital* volume 1 (London: Penguin Books, 1976), 677.

4 The Ordeal of Decency

A Perspective on Mexico City's Urban Space and Middle Classes (1952–1966)[1]

Sara Minerva Luna Elizarrarás

Introduction

In 1958, a newspaper article pointed to the need to encourage the working class to understand the importance of living "decently." With this aim in mind, it suggested giving them the opportunity to have "decent, ventilated, well-lit" apartments with enough bedrooms to ensure rectitude in the family: "sons and daughters need separate bedrooms. And parents need their own one."[2] The author of the piece assumed that this lifestyle was uncommon among the factory workers who suffered "a nightmare of returning home to just one room and a tiny kitchen."[3] This text hints at how decency differentiated social classes in at least two ways. In one sense, it implied having functional living spaces with furnishings to facilitate daily life; not only clean but comfortable, this ideal home would be equipped with consumer goods, and white goods in particular, similarly to other countries around the world in the post-war period.[4] The emphasis on the separate bedrooms reflected the other aspect of living decently, embodied in an ideal of a nuclear family where sexual relations were restricted to the parents' bedrooms and promiscuity was not supposed to enter the picture.

These decency-related distinctions applied equally to the interior of the domestic sphere as well as outside it. For example, a resident on Yácatas street in the Narvarte neighborhood complained about brothels near his house, saying that "decent families" lived in his neighborhood, and therefore it was "improper" for such places "to exist alongside those of us who have our homes there."[5]

These examples show how the notion of decency demarcated borders and social hierarchies at a time Mexico City was undergoing significant changes,[6] owing to a multitude of factors. In around 1940, the capital entered one of its most critical phases of urbanization, rapid population growth, important technological developments, and expanding consumer and leisure markets. New ideas about the family, sexuality, and child-raising were also beginning to spread. The combination of these processes sparked a moral panic; some sectors of the city feared that the wave of

DOI: 10.4324/9781003029311-6

transformations was undermining the traditional values of family and society.[7] These anxieties revealed, and gave importance to, the possibility of defining oneself as a "decent person." This could improve one's position within a shifting social context, and confirm a set of aspirations, demands, and representations about family and sexuality.

This chapter sets out to explore these references to "decency" as a marker of hierarchy referred to in newspaper articles, letters from local residents, and government files following expressions of moral panic. My contention is that decency was a discursive trope that articulated a specific set of urban meanings, representations, and practices,[8] combined with normative and aspirational prescriptions about sexual and family morality. This trope—the cause of some tension—constituted one of the most important markers during the period; it established a dynamic border between those who sought to differentiate themselves, particularly from the popular sectors, and instead to self-identify as members of the "middle class."

The analysis covers the 1952–1966 period when Sonoran politician Ernesto P. Uruchurtu was head of Departamento del Distrito Federal (Federal District Department, DDF), as the capital's administrative office was known at the time.[9] These years are particularly interesting because of the city government's major infrastructure projects and its response to the moral panic: raids, establishment closures, and evictions, earning Uruchurtu his nickname as the "Iron Mayor."[10]

The chapter highlights how, during this period, certain areas of Mexico City such as the Del Valle, Narvarte, Roma, Condesa, and Nápoles, and their resident populations, established a reputation as typically middle-class, "decent" neighborhoods. This contrasted sharply to popular areas, such as the "horseshoe of slums" ("herradura de tugurios") to the north and east of the capital's historic center. Although not quite the exact opposite, these parts of the city were perceived, represented, and experienced at the minimum as threats to decency on account of their dilapidation and living arrangements that made promiscuity, overcrowding, and lack of privacy a part of everyday life. This text also suggests that, despite the contrast between the areas inhabited by the middle class and the popular sectors of society, the "decent neighborhoods" were not homogenous. These neighborhoods' places of ill-repute considered offensive to the mores of family and sexual decency shows the importance of demands in the process of social stratification, over and above the material conditions of that sociospatial order.

French sociologist Pierre Bourdieu's ideas about social stratification processes provide the theoretical underpinnings of this chapter. Instead of seeing social classes as specific entities in their own right, Bourdieu analyzes the mechanisms that produce and reproduce differentiated and hierarchical social conditions. As such, subjects in specific positions and living under relatively homogenous conditions share ingrained habits, demands, aspirations, and dispositions or "habitus" that help reproduce practices and systems of social classification that in turn allow them to retain that position and its economic, social, and cultural capital.[11] Bourdieu warns that these structures of social differences and their embodied dispositions (habitus) can become objectified in physical space, leading to the situation in which people in socially advantageous positions conceive the place of inhabitation as "naturally" belonging to them, and conversely perceive those who are "socially distant" as alien and threatening.[12]

The Belgian-Canadian philosopher Marc Angenot, for his part, highlights the importance of discourses in the understanding of society and its hierarchies. He emphasizes the possibility of identifying linguistic tricks, tropes, and norms with hegemonic meanings establishing "pre-eminences, legitimacies, interests, and values" that favor those "better placed" in society. [13]

This analysis uses these ideas as a platform to contribute to the history of the middle classes in Mexico's capital during a period marked by large-scale demographic, social, and urban transformations. Instead of attempting to define "objectively" those who constitute the middle class, this text aims to explore how certain subjects used methods of stratification to identify themselves as members of this class and to differentiate them from the working classes whom they feared and distrusted. This argument recognizes the heterogeneity within the middle classes, and considers that the classificatory methods of differentiating them from other classes gives visibility to shared practices and discourses within that diversity.

Decency: Socio-spatial Order and Consumption

Using the concept of decency as a means of social differentiation was not new in the mid-twentieth century. At least one century earlier, it had become a common theme in Western cultures, although its meanings were specific to the time and space in which it was employed. Generally, it was linked to the idea of "civilization" understood as the self-control of body and thought.[14] Its shades of meaning differed by area, as the antithesis of the "unruliness" of the lower-classes, intertwined with ethnic and residual aspects of class society or as a mark of non-manual labor.[15]

In Mexico, decency as a badge of distinction existed since the early nineteenth century. It became more deeply entrenched during Porfirio Díaz's regime following the modernizing redefinition of the class-based notion of honor that acquired a universal legal meaning centered on maintaining social prestige.[16] As part of this shift at the end of the 1800s, decency developed into a differentiating trope, incorporating marks of distinction coupled with incipient urban development: consumption, personal hygiene, and the cleanliness of clothing and homes.[17]

Decency-related practices, representations, and discourses took on a specific hue with Mexico City's increasing urbanization in the 1940s. The rapid transformation of the urban infrastructure and landscape changed how people perceived, inhabited, and represented their city; it also altered self-perception among the capital's swelling population—which tripled in size between 1940 and 1970, from 1,757,530 to 6,874,165, largely due to rural migration.[18]

Industrialization and import substitution in the context of World War II caused the city's expansion and transformation. This trend continued after the war with certain similarities to other Western cities.[19] Uruchurtu's city administration oversaw an intensive expansion of public utilities such as mains water systems, electrification, sewerage networks, and street lighting. Covering up rivers also helped improve the hygiene in many neighborhoods and to open up new thoroughfares.[20]

During this period of change, new consumer habits and ways of inhabiting the city became visible; a functional division of spaces sought to improve hygiene, widen the everyday use of technology, and safeguard privacy.[21] The diversification of employment, increased school enrollments, the expansion of television broadcasting, and the proliferation of recreational spaces in the capital heightened the importance of discussions about norms of the nuclear family and sexuality. Through the trope of "decency," these factors combined to create a series of material and embodied aspirations, practices, and demands that were instrumental in the social classification systems that distinguished those socio-spatial orders identifiable as middle-class neighborhoods.[22]

These areas in the west and south of the city received government investments in infrastructure and utilities, and also benefitted from public and private housing projects. This was the case with the Roma and Condesa neighborhoods, originally founded in the early twentieth century for the elites,[23] who subsequently moved out to the new enclaves for wealthy families (in Lomas de Chapultepec, Pedregal de San Ángel). This altered the demographic profile of the Roma and Condesa, a trend that accelerated when the government ordered a rent freeze in 1942.[24] The Multifamiliar Juárez housing complex—a state-backed project inaugurated in 1955 to provide accommodation for mid-level bureaucrats—along with numerous condominiums built in the 1950s and 1960s, cemented Roma's middle-class status.[25]

Del Valle was another neighborhood that consolidated its reputation as a middle-class area after the 1949 inauguration of another housing project, the Centro Urbano Presidente Alemán (President Alemán Urban Center, CUPA).[26] This development, also built for public-sector employees, was a major landmark for the Del Valle and adjacent neighborhoods such as Nápoles, Narvarte, Vértiz-Narvarte, and San José Insurgentes that became symbols of the city's modernization (see Figure 4.1). Despite a certain social and material heterogeneity, these neighborhoods became equipped to allow their residents to adopt or aspire to the aforesaid modern living standards: functional separation of spaces, new domestic technologies (white goods), and the possibility to lead most of their lives inside the home.[27]

Figure 4.1 A map by the state-operated agency for subsidized food, clothing, and other essential items, subsidiary of Compañía Exportadora e Importadora (Exporting and Importing Company, CEIMSA) that depicted various areas in the city. The central region left blank consisted of middle- and upper-class neighborhoods, while CEIMSA's mobile stores and routes operated mainly in the working-class districts. In: *Últimas Noticias*, July 7, 1961, 7.

Source: Courtesy of the Miguel Lerdo de Tejada Library of the Ministry of Finance and Public Credit (S HCP).

A 1959 study to help "understand the middle class" reflected how these residential spaces were considered typical of middle-income groups.[28] Among the families interviewed, 38.5% lived in an apartment and 58.8% in a single-family dwelling or a detached house. Most of these homes had a functional separation of spaces, except for 2.3% that lacked separate bedrooms, 4.6% that did not have a kitchen, and 6.2% that were without a bathroom.[29] The geographical location, spatial distribution, and practices involved in inhabiting housing therefore became a badge of class distinction at that time.[30]

The articulated distinction to the socio-spatial order was more obvious by comparing "decent neighborhoods" to other parts of the capital. For example, around the center and the north of the Mexico City was the so-called "horseshoe of slums," an area mainly consisting of *vecindades*—housing complexes with single-room dwellings—and shacks made of recycled or flimsy materials, and mostly without basic public services. In the 1940s, these areas started noticeably going downhill: the rent freeze meant that the buildings received little or no maintenance, while at the same time population density increased by people seeking cheap rents.[31] Public utilities took a long time to reach the working-class neighborhoods in the city's east, north, and south, areas where residents mostly built their own homes.[32] According to census data from that period, houses in these neighborhoods tended to lack bathrooms and running water.[33] To compound these material deficiencies, the popular sectors supposedly did not know how to inhabit modern homes—an idea clearly expressed in the local government's Unidad Santa Cruz Meyehualco. This social housing project was designed to "rehabilitate" the families of waste pickers (*pepenadores*) who toiled on the garbage heaps in the east of the city, by providing them homes boasting "excellent standards of hygiene, with running water, drainage, electricity, and everything necessary for a healthy and civilized life."[34] Unlike similar developments for middle-class occupants, the complex for the *pepenadores* was located on the outskirts and the authorities saw fit to educate its future residents on how to use the space "properly."[35]

The middle-class concept of decent living not only included the functional division of spaces, but also various practices and aspirations about jobs, education, and consumption.[36] Consumption was particularly connected to ways of urban living, so that the purchase of cars, televisions, radios, gas stoves, and refrigerators were part of the aspirational norms and requirements related to the trope of decency.[37] Their inclusion for the first time in the 1960 census reflects the importance of these domestic goods, though actually acquiring them could pose significant difficulties.

Household income was a relevant factor for the purchase of these products, but the social status they gave—more than their actual usefulness—proved a strong incentive for buyers to make the necessary sacrifices. Televisions provide a case in point. Figures from 1963 show that almost half of the families in the Federal District earned less than $1,500 pesos per month, and only 27% of them had a car, refrigerator, or television.[38] At the opposite extreme, 16.8% of families earned $4,501 pesos or more, and 65% of this segment owned these goods. On average, less than half of those families with incomes of between $1,500 and $4,500 pesos owned a car or refrigerator, reflecting their limited purchasing power. Nevertheless, 56% of them had televisions, revealing a distinction associated with these consumer goods.[39]

The price of televisions was a significant barrier. In 1953, Sears Roebuck advertised a 17-inch television for $2,595 pesos and a refrigerator for $2,426 pesos.[40] Families could forego the distinction of buying a television at a department store by finding a cheaper set elsewhere, or they could even acquire one second-hand. However, the investment still represented between one and four months of income for more than half of the capital's population in 1956; this proportion remained the same in the following decade.[41] The fact that many families preferred to own a television set instead of a refrigerator reveals its high symbolic value.

The geographical distribution of television sets reflected the capital's different socio-spatial orders. In 1960, 62.6% of sets belonged to families who mostly lived in *cuarteles* or quarters consisting of "decent neighborhoods." For example, between 40% and 60% of homes had sets in the *cuarteles* nos. VII, VIII, X, and XII comprised by the Juárez, San Rafael, Condesa, Hipódromo, Eugenia, Narvarte, Del Valle, Nochebuena, Nápoles and Vértiz Narvarte neighborhoods. By contrast, only 11.8% of homes had them in working-class neighborhoods such as Gómez Farías, Balbuena, Magdalena Mixhuca, Jamaica and Tránsito (in *cuartel* no. II).[42] Elsewhere in the city, less than 34% of homes had sets. The gap began to close in the late 1960s thanks to processes of social mobility and wider access to credit.[43]

Such consumer habits and lifestyles were not only social markers connected to decency, they also indicated the social status of subjects who could buy, rent, and furnish "modern" accommodation. Furthermore, they marked a distinction related to the trope of decency associated to the idea that these living spaces were free from promiscuity and unhygienic conditions deemed typical of working-class *vecindades*.[44] The overlapping of sexuality and the family with the trope of decency was complex and sometimes contradictory, as we will see below.

Decency, Sexuality, and Discontinuities of the Sociospatial Order

Social and cultural transformations after the Second World War gave greater importance in the West to the upholding of sexual and family norms. Geographer Phil Hubbard suggests that debates about sexual morality at the time largely defined what it meant to be a good citizen, and this was reflected in the ordering of public space. In his analysis of London's urban development, Hubbard shows the influence of "the naturalization of heterosexual norms" in promoting reproductive sexuality as the only morally acceptable possibility, especially for women.[45] He points to the actions of the "decent" citizen to hide from view, displace, and isolate places, subjects, behaviors, and practices outside marital norms into "spaces of confinement"; in parallel, this naturalized male desire and stigmatized women who transgressed these boundaries in their sexual activities.[46]

In the case of Mexico, the overlapping of sexuality, decency, and spatial order followed a similar path. Fears about the increasing female presence in public spaces used by the middle classes and the cultural shifts relating to marriage, courtship, and raising children made an impact on middle-income sectors, especially those closest to the prescriptions of the Catholic Church.[47] The ensuing moral panic left a strong mark on norms governing family and sexuality in the trope of decency and its differentiating uses, albeit asymmetrically for men and women.

Decency was articulated at that time with a normative model of the nuclear family legitimized by civil and religious authorities. This model prescribed a hierarchical and differentiated relationship between man and wife: the man held authority and preferably was the sole breadwinner, whereas women did the housework and raised the children. This marital ideal became entrenched in the post-war period in most Western countries as a means of restoring order after the "chaos" of the war.[48] In Mexico, the model was interweaved with the discourse of post-revolutionary governments that extolled feminine domesticity and motherhood as lying at the heart of the country's identity.[49] Therefore, during this period middle-class women were lectured on the importance of ensuring their husbands' happiness and devoting themselves to domestic chores, even at the expense of their own happiness.[50] Wives were also responsible for upholding the family's good moral standing, as one editorial piece suggests:

> when the man errs and fails in his duty, the paternal home is shaken, but remains standing, because there is the mother, a granite column who sustains the household through her abnegation and virtue; but if the woman relinquishes her maternal obligations, then the home comes crashing down.[51]

In terms of sexuality, this model exemplifies Hubbard's differentiated concept. In Mexico, this naturalization of men's extra-marital sexual behaviors was nothing new; until 1940 there was a zone of official tolerance and the Civil Code even established differentiated norms relating to children born out of wedlock.[52] The abolition of regulated prostitution hardly circumscribed men's (largely unrestricted) sexual activities—womanizing was even a badge of honor provided men were discreet about their alternate relationships and "casas chicas."[53] In contrast, women's sexuality was only considered acceptable within marriage; pre-marital relationships and infidelity were severely censured by society. Transgressing this norm would lead to the loss of dignity, propriety, honor, and decency—for the women themselves as well as their whole family.[54] As Elvira Bermúdez noted, for "many middle-class women, virtue is like capital invested in the bank of marriage."[55] This demand could feel like a burden, as revealed in an article written in 1955 in which various young middle-class women recounted their frustration, and agreed that "it was impossible to swim against the current" of these conventions and that "you cannot overstep the mark without facing dire consequences."[56] Such demands marked a sharp social contrast to the situation facing working-class women, whose supposed promiscuity and material deprivations led to their sexual corruption at a young age.[57]

This double standard for sexual behavior was at odds with the prevailing diversity in material conditions and practices in the middle classes' socio-spatial orders. The complaints people made against those places, subjects, and practices considered at odds with their socio-spatial order reveal the importance of the sexual norms and demands related to the trope of decency.[58] Those making these complaints—mainly residents in the Roma, Condesa, Del Valle, Narvarte, and Nápoles neighborhoods—show an interest in differentiating themselves socially from the subject of their criticisms, directly or indirectly referring to decency.[59]

Complaints generally focused on "hoteles de paso" or love motels, cabarets, bars, clandestine brothels, and the presence of prostitutes on the streets, as these were seen as brazen affronts to morality and decency. This was not the first time that such dens of iniquity ("sitios de gozo y retozo") had irked local residents.[60] However, it was during this period of moral panic and changes to the sociocultural and urban space that the issue of decency became particularly visible given the number of complaints and how the grievances were addressed. Signatories often identified themselves as belonging to "decent families" and being "decent people," "decent neighbors," people of "good moral standing," or "not very hard-up." In their desire to differentiate themselves, they described the subjects of their complaints as belonging to different socio-spatial orders, specifically *barriadas*—the word used to describe the city's overcrowded "horseshoe of slums comprising the Merced, the Lagunilla and the *barriadas* of Tepito and Jamaica," places littered with "derelict houses," "slums," and "dive bars."[61] In describing such places, press reports highlighted the lack of modern public services: street lighting, "drinking water, no drainage, no means of transport, no police officers, no public transport…"[62] Compounding these material deprivations, complaints also referred to the local residents' supposed criminality; these areas were described as "nests of drug dealers, criminals and petty thieves."[63] This stigmatizing discourse fed into the moral panic of the middle class, adding legitimacy to the local government's hounding of people and commercial premises with police dragnets, closures of premises, and evictions.[64]

At the same time, a kind of metonymic association existed between the idea of a *barriada* and that of a red-light district, both the subject of complaints by "decent residents." One female resident in the Condesa neighborhood lamented the presence of "streetwalkers" on her road, considering this "such a shameful sight, more appropriate for a toleration zone."[65] This connection reflected that, in the trope of "decency," alcohol consumption, unrestrained base instincts, and sexual abandon were all characteristics of the lower-class populations.[66]

This reveals the idea that the sexual behavior of decent, middle-class citizens was somehow different to that of the working class, without forgetting the asymmetrical boundaries for men and women. Men from middle-income sectors (the clients of the women and places of disrepute) were criticized for their drunken behavior and talking loudly in vulgar language, but this in itself only posed a threat if directed toward "decent women" passing by who could be mistaken for "those who work in those houses."[67] In a similar vein, complaints against prostitutes touting for business on the streets described the situation as "a denigrating and shameful spectacle that decent families have to put up with," an offence derived from the corrupting "bad influence" of women and children in the area.[68] In contrast, the only danger these women posed to men was essentially about money; several articles referred to these women stealing from their clients.[69]

In complaints filed against the love motels—places frequented for sexual activities outside the realm of the model family—tensions clearly existed between such locations considered to exist outside the socio-spatial order and beyond the unequal boundaries relating to sexual behavior connected to the idea of decency. But these "hoteles de paso" differed from brothels in that they were not the preserve of prostitutes; *señoritas* (young ladies), employees, and even married women also frequented them. One resident of the San José Insurgentes neighborhood complained about the Hermes love motel because it was visited "even by girls from honorable families, who waltz into such places accompanied their boyfriends, knowing the depravity of their behavior yet ignoring the danger, misfortunes, and likelihood of abuse."[70] The perceived danger of these motels was found in the blurring of the social line inscribed in the trope of decent behavior for middle-class women, since these were spaces of marital infidelity and premarital sex. For a woman from a "good family," entering such a place was enough to cause a scandal. One member of Mexico's Supreme Court of Justice expressed this in the following terms: "in a place like the Federal District, a woman who is honest would not spend the night in a love motel with her boyfriend," even if she came from a "proper family."[71] By visiting such places, a middle-class woman risked being mistaken for a prostitute, according to the requirements of "decency." She could be classified as belonging to a lower social stratum or lose her and her family's social capital by no longer being able to claim to be "decent."

Conclusions

This analysis has shown the frequent use of decency in the mid-twentieth century as a discursive trope to differentiate social classes, as in the description of middle-class socio-spatial orders as "decent neighborhoods." This trope also revealed practices, places, and subjects considered extraneous or heterotopian—either for material reasons or for transgressing the prescribed mores of family life or sexuality.[72] The same trope of decency allowed Mexico City's middle-income sectors to grasp the changes to urban space, and they contributed to producing and reproducing discourses and practices that legitimized deep social inequalities through the stigmatization of spaces inhabited by the lower classes, known as *barriadas*, at the same time that they navigated their way through the moral panic triggered by the sociocultural changes of the time. The country's capital was not the only place where the urban spatial order overlapped with norms on decency, as shown in Hubbard's work. However, it is important to consider how specifically the trope formed a part of differentiated discourses about male desire, domesticity, and motherhood promoted by the post-revolutionary regime and the Catholic Church, driving the "rehabilitation" and the displacement of sectors of the population who gained less from modernization.

The research also revealed that the trope of decency did not imply a fixed social order, in the way as honor once did. In contrast, it revealed a dynamic and porous border that reflected social mobility experienced by various groups at this time. In this regard, a person or neighbor could "become decent" by changing their living conditions or practices.[73] But they could also move in the opposite direction, and although individuals or families may not have lost their class status, they could lose some of their social capital. Self-identifying as a decent person could represent an ordeal due to the demands for consumption and norms imposed on family life and sexual behaviors. This applied particularly to young women, who had increasing educational and professional opportunities at the same time as having to comply with axiomatic family and sexual conventions.[74]

The particular aspects of decency in relation to practices, norms, demands, and representations of city life does not imply that the middle classes of the time constituted a uniform, homogenous group. Instead, this chapter shows that among the many strata of Mexico City's middle classes, the trope of decency articulated shared aspirations and norms that went beyond their heterogeneity. It also reveals the importance of appearances in processes of social stratification.

This text certainly leaves further avenues to explore, such as the tensions and contradictions between cosmopolitan recreational activities and the desire to self-identify as being decent. However, it does provide a starting point to consider in more detail how people conceive, classify, and recognize themselves in specific historical social hierarchies.

Notes

1 Chapter written as part of PhD project, "Cartografía de la decencia: ansiedad moral, espacio urbano e intervención del Estado en la Ciudad de México, 1952–1963," funded by CONACYT and assigned to CIESAS, Mexico City.

2 Joaquín Torres, "Mensajes humanos: el departamento familiar," *Últimas Noticias*, February 4, 1958, 5.

3 Torres, "Mensajes humanos," 5.

4 Anahí Ballent, "El arte de saber vivir: Modernización del habitar doméstico y cambio urbano, 1940–1970," in *Cultura y comunicación en la ciudad de México*, vol. 1, ed. Néstor García Canclini (Mexico City: Grijalbo; UAM-Iztapalapa, 1998), 65–131.

5 "La voz del ágora: piden desterrar la prostitución," *Últimas Noticias*, November 9, 1960, 5.

6 At this time, Mexico City consisted of 12 areas or *cuarteles*, that combined with the boroughs to form the Federal District.

7 Moral panic is a concept that refers to the episodes in which people, groups, and conditions considered as threats to social values and interests, becoming folk devils—fears stoked by sensationalist articles in the press. Jeffrey Weeks has indicated that it is a useful conceptual tool to analyze the reactions generated by changes in sexual regimes. Stanley Cohen, *Folk Devils and Moral Panics* (Abingdon: Routledge, 2002), 1; Jeffrey Weeks, *Sex, Politics and Society: The Regulation of Society Since 1800* (Abingdon: Routledge, 2012), 20.

8 "To inhabit" is the process in which subjects appropriate or give meaning to the spaces where they have extended interactions, through practices, objects, and norms. Angela Giglia, *El habitar y la cultura; Perspectivas teóricas y de investigación* (Barcelona/ Mexico City: Anthropos; UAM-Iztapalapa, 2012), 13, 57.

9 The Mexican president directly appointed the head of the Mexico City government.

10 A succession of presidents (Adolfo Ruiz Cortines, Adolfo López Mateos, and Gustavo Díaz Ordaz) all appointed Uruchurtu, a lawyer by training, as head of the Mexico City government. His clashes with Díaz Ordaz, and the scandal caused by an eviction, forced him to resign in September 1966. Publications on Uruchurtu's period in office include Rachel Kram, *Gladiolas for the Children of Sánchez: Ernesto P. Uruchurtu's Mexico City, 1950–1968* (PhD diss., University of Arizona: 2008), and Sara Luna, *Modernización, género, ciudadanía, y clase media en la ciudad de México: Debates sobre la moralización y la decencia, 1952–1966* (PhD diss., Mexico City: UNAM, 2017).

11 Pierre Bourdieu, *La distinción, criterio y bases sociales del gusto* (Buenos Aires: Taurus, 1998), 100.

12 Pierre Bourdieu, "Los efectos del lugar," in *La miseria del mundo* (Madrid: Akal, 1999), 123.

13 Marc Angenot, *El discurso social: Los límites históricos de lo pensable y lo decible* (Buenos Aires: Siglo XXI, 2012), 37.

14 Norbert Elías, *El proceso de la civilización. Investigaciones sociogenéticas y psicogenéticas* (Mexico City: FCE, 2016), 41

15 Ezequiel Adamovsky, *Historia de la clase media en Argentina: Apogeo y decadencia de una ilusión.* (Buenos Aires: Planeta, 2012), 85–86; David Parker, *The Idea of the Middle Class: White-Collar Workers and Peruvian Society, 1900–1950* (Pennsylvania: State University Press, 1998), 24–29.

16 Pablo Piccato, *La tiranía de la opinión: El honor en la construcción de la esfera pública en México* (Mexico City: COLMICH; Instituto Mora, 2015), 35, 288.

17 Julio Moreno, *Yankees Don't Go Home! Mexican Nationalism, American Business Culture and the Shaping of Modern Mexico, 1920–1950* (Chapel Hill, NC: University of North Carolina Press, 2003), 86, 210; Piccato, *La tiranía de la opinión*, 245; Ernesto Aréchiga, "Lucha de clases en la ciudad: La disputa por el espacio urbano. *ca.* 1890–1930," in *Los trabajadores de la ciudad de México 1860–1950: Textos en homenaje a Clara E. Lida*, eds. Mario Barbosa and Carlos Illades (Mexico City: COLMEX; UAM-Cuajimalpa, 2013), 29; Mario Barbosa, "Insalubres e inmorales: Alojamientos temporales en la Ciudad de México (1900–1920)," *Scripta Nova: Revista electrónica de geografía y ciencias sociales* 7 (2003): n.p.
18 Luna, *Modernización*, 394.
19 David Harvey indicates the state's strong support for public housing in Fordist and Keynesian terms, referring to it as a current of "universal modernism." David Harvey, *La condición de la posmodernidad* (Argentina: Amorrortu, 1998), 52, 87–88.
20 Luna, *Modernización*, 29–42; *La ciudad de México, Departamento del Distrito Federal 1952–1964* (Mexico City: DDF, 1964), 36–82, 135–153.
21 Ballent, "El arte de saber vivir," 103.
22 The socio-spatial order is a concept consisting of a set of practices, discourses, and representations of space that structure and reproduce social and cultural norms on what is permissible and desirable, affecting how we perceive and experience such spaces. Emilio Duhau and Ángela Giglia, *Las reglas del desorden: Habitar la metrópoli* (Mexico City: Siglo XXI; UAM-Azcapotzalco, 2008), 28–29.
23 Aréchiga, "Lucha de clases," 27.; Manuel Perló Cohen, "Historias de la Roma: Microhistoria de la Ciudad de México," *Historias* 19 (1987–1988): 160, 164.
24 Ballent, "El arte de saber vivir," 68.
25 Perló Cohen, "Historias de la Roma," 164; Ana María Durán, "Notas sobre los efectos de los sismos en la colonia Roma," in *Sociológica* 2, no. 4 (1987): n.p.
26 Although the subdivision of Del Valle neighborhood began in 1910, 70% of its residents still lacked access to utilities in 1930. This situation changed from 1940, when it became one of the main beneficiaries of urbanization. Aréchiga, 30. Sobre el CUPA: Graciela De Garay, *Rumores y retratos de un lugar de la modernidad, Historia oral del multifamiliar Miguel Alemán, 1949–1999* (Mexico City: Instituto Mora, 2002).
27 Ballent, "El arte de saber vivir," 91–92.
28 The survey included between 442 and 521 homes. José Gómez Robleda and Ada D'Aloja, *La familia y la casa* (Mexico City: UNAM; IIS, 1959), 77.
29 Gómez Robleda and D'Aloja, *La familia y la casa*, 81.
30 Susana Sosenski and Sergio Miranda, "La ciudad anhelada: espacio urbano, emociones y segregación social en la publicidad inmobiliaria de la ciudad de México, 1940–1970," *Urbana* 11, no. 1 (2019): 172–204.
31 Sergio Miranda, "La vivienda popular del milagro mexicano en la ciudad de México (1940–1970)," in *Aproximaciones a la historia del urbanismo popular: Una mirada desde México*, comp. Héctor Quiroz (Mexico City: UNAM, 2014), 115.
32 Working-class neighborhoods developed from land plotted and built upon by trade union and neighborhood associations. They legalized the properties through clientelist and corporativist networks so that the state would give them access to services. Cristina Sánchez Mejorada, *Rezagos de la modernidad, memorias de una ciudad presente* (Mexico City: UAM, 2005), 209–215.

33 The area called "Cuartel I" in the east of the capital included neighborhoods such as Romero Rubio, Morelos, Moctezuma, Pensador Mexicano, and Valle Gómez. In 1950, barely 35% of its homes had running water, a percentage that rose to 53% ten years later. Up until 1960, surveys continued to include figures on whether homes had bathrooms or not. Luna, *Modernización*, 395–396.

34 The housing project included 3,000 single-family dwellings with a bathroom, kitchen, living room and from two to four bedrooms. "Información general del Departamento del Distrito Federal," *Gaceta Oficial del DDF* 801 (September 20, 1963), 1.

35 "Información general del Departamento del Distrito Federal," *Gaceta Oficial del DDF* 800 (September 10, 1963) 1; "Construcción de una guardería para hijos de pepenadores," *Últimas Noticias*, August 19, 1963, 1, 13.

36 Taking vocational courses and working in white-collar jobs were aspirational activities, connected to the material aspect of decency and to the possibility of earning higher salaries. Luna, *Modernización*, 55–59.

37 Eric Zolov, *Rebeldes con causa: La contracultura mexicana y la crisis del Estado patriarcal* (Mexico City: Norma, 2002), XIX; Louise Walker, *Waking from the Dream: Mexico's Middle Class after 1968* (Stanford, CA: Stanford University Press, 2013), 8; Lilia Bayardo, *Historia del consumo moderno en la ciudad de México durante los años 1909–1970 a través de las encuestas de gastos familiares y de la publicidad en prensa* (PhD diss., Mexico City: COLMEX, 2013).

38 *Ingresos y Gastos Familiares en México, 1963* (Mexico City: Banco de México, Investigaciones Industriales, 1966), 372.

39 *Ingresos y Gastos Familiares*, 372.

40 *El Universal*, Aug. 4, 1953.

41 The classified advertisements included refrigerators for $1,500 pesos. *El Universal*, October 17, 1952, 6; In 1957, television sets cost from $3,000 and even up to $5,000. In 1964, refrigerators were on sale for $2,188 up to $5,488. "Sears Roebuck" advertisement, *Excélsior*, July 21, 1957, 27ª; "Sears: Madrecita mexicana" advertisement, *Últimas Noticias*, May 8, 1964, 7.

42 Luna, *Modernización*, 65–66, 398.

43 Luna, *Modernización*, 65–66, 398.

44 Miranda, "La vivienda popular," 115; Moisés Quiroz, *Las vecindades del centro de la ciudad de México frente al crecimiento de la ciudad, 1940–1970* (Bachelor's diss., Mexico City: UNAM, 2014), 84–91.

45 Phil Hubbard, "Sex Zones: Intimacy, Citizenship and Public Space," in *Sexualities* 4, no. 1 (2001): 51.

46 Hubbard, "Sex Zones," 58.

47 Valentina Torres Septién, ""Bendita sea tu pureza": Relaciones amorosas de los jóvenes católicos en México (1940–1960) in Pilar Gonzalbo and Milada Bazant, *Tradiciones y conflictos: Historias de la vida cotidiana en México e Hispanoamérica* (Mexico City: COLMEX; El Colegio Mexiquense, 2007), 385–413.

48 Stephanie Coontz, *Historia del matrimonio: Cómo el amor conquistó el matrimonio* (Barcelona: Gedisa, 2006), 291.

49 Martha Santillán, "El discurso tradicionalista sobre la maternidad: Excélsior y las madres prolíficas durante el avilacamachismo," *Secuencia* 77 (2010): 89–110.

50 Alfredo Vicent, "Lo que la novia debe saber del matrimonio," *Madame* 52 (December 1955): 35–38.

51 Rafael Rojas Loa, "La niñez y la juventud," *Últimas Noticias*, July 16, 1954, 8.

52 Katherine Bliss, *Compromised Positions: Prostitution, Public Health and Gender Politics in Revolutionary Mexico City* (University Park, PA: Pennsylvania State University Press, 2001); Sara Luna, "Familia y retórica revolucionaria: apuntes en torno a las reformas al Código Civil en México, 1953–1954," *Nuevo Mundo, Mundos Nuevos* [online edition] (December 14, 2018): http://journals.openedition.org/nuevomundo/73760.

53 "Casa chica" is a term that referred to the families or extramarital relations that gave the men involved reputation for financial prestige and virility, provided that their concealment preserved the decency and respectability of the legitimate family. Arthur Corwin, *Contemporary Mexican Attitudes Toward Population, Poverty and Public Opinion* (Gainesville: University of Florida Press, 1963), 28.

54 Torres Septién, ""Bendita sea tu pureza,"" 385.

55 Elvira Bermúdez, "Gente decente," in *La vida familiar del mexicano* (Mexico City: Antigua Librería Robredo, 1955), 60.

56 "Hasta qué punto puede una mujer traspasar los convencionalismos sociales," *Madame* 53 (December 1955): 52–53.

57 "Dos millones de personas viven en promiscuidad en el Distrito Federal," *Últimas Noticias*, June 12, 1964, 1, 3.

58 My research of newspapers and official records revealed almost 120 complaints by local residents.

59 Others came from other established middle-class neighborhoods of the 1960s: Portales, Narvarte, San José Insurgentes, San Rafael, Santa María la Ribera, and Álamos.

60 Bliss, *Compromised Positions*, 66–67, 145–46.

61 "Perifonemas: Centros de vicio," *Últimas Noticias*, Mar. 24, 1953, 5; Perifonemas," *Últimas Noticias*, Oct. 23, 1953, 5; Julián Carlos and Jiménez, "Guerra al jacal, habrá casas decorosas y baratas," *Últimas Noticias*, April 11, 1957, 1, 7; "9,000 tabernas con apariencia de misceláneas," *Últimas Noticias*, June 29, 1960, 1, 10.

62 "Perifonemas," *Últimas noticias*, October 23, 1953, 5.

63 "El vicio ha ganado la lucha en la metrópoli," *La Extra, Últimas Noticias 2ª edición*, Mar. 17, 1955, 1; "Perifonemas," *Últimas Noticias*, March 5, 1960, 5.

64 Further research could explore the overlap between expressions of moral panic, the stigmatization of subjects, and what in recent decades has come to be known as a sense of insecurity. Gabriel Kessler, *El sentimiento de inseguridad: sociología del temor al delito* (Buenos Aires: Siglo XXI, 2009).

65 "La voz del ágora: SOS a la policía," *Últimas Noticias*, October 6 1954, 5.

66 "La voz del ágora: que muera el vicio," *Últimas Noticias*, October 29, 1955, 5.

67 "La voz del ágora: Protestan por un lenocinio," *Últimas Noticias*, January 23, 1963, 4; "La voz del Ágora: una súplica a la Dirección de Gobernación," *Últimas Noticias*, May 8, 1963, 4; La voz del ágora: protesta contra el vicio," *Últimas Noticias*, May 22, 1954; "La voz del Ágora: Contra los centros de vicio," *Últimas Noticias*, April 23, 1964, 4.

68 "Clamor contra un hotelucho," *Últimas Noticias*, October 25 1963, 2. In complaints and newspaper articles, the narrative was usually about women of "humble backgrounds" forced into prostitution due to financial necessity, promiscuous surroundings, or a man's "deceit."

69 The second page of *Últimas Noticias* carried at least one story a day about such thefts, for example "Lo robó una cabaretera," *Últimas Noticias*, January 26, 1956, 2; "Una cabaretera le birló 300 dólares," *Últimas Noticias*, July 11, 1957, 2.

70 AGN/ARC/425.3, Letter from Georgina S. to Ernesto P. Uruchurtu and Adolfo Ruiz Cortines, October 20, 1953.
71 AHSCJN, Exp. Amparo directo 1172/1951, Sentencia sobre amparo directo promovido por Julio V., ponencia de Teófilo Olea, Primera Sala, August 14, 1956, f. 4
72 Heterotopia: a place without a geographical reference, a "no-man's land" where the unsaid has a place: male sexual initiation, "deflowering." Michel Foucault, "Los espacios otros" *Astrágalo* (September 7, 1997): 83–91.
73 Joaquín Torres, "Mensajes humanos: disciplina juvenil," *Últimas Noticias*, June 25, 1958, 5; "Perifonemas: Las Fuentes de la ciudad," *Últimas Noticias*, November 14, 1953, 5–6.
74 Bermúdez, "Gente decente," 52.

5 Gender, Race, and the Evolution of Middle-Class Identity in the Mexico City Press, 1820–1900

Susie S. Porter

Introduction

While scholars engage in instructive debates over how to define "middle class," it is also worth asking how historical actors themselves have done so.[1] Confronted with an overwhelming variety of definitions of the middle class, scholar Klaus-Peter Sick examined how historical actors themselves utilized the phrase "middle class" as a political slogan, rooted in Aristotelian ideals, that circulated throughout France, Germany, and Belgium to different ends and according to context.[2] For Mexico, Mario Barbosa Cruz raises questions about the cultural resonances of a term, middle class, that is often narrowly defined using objective criteria such as occupation and income.[3] Focusing on Mexico City newspapers contained in the Mexican National Digital Newspaper Archive, this chapter explores how over time historical actors invoked the precise phrase "middle class," with reference to whom, to what ends, and the cultural resonances of the phrase. As the nature and distribution of the Mexico City press evolved, from low levels of production by political pamphleteers to a prolific news press in the mid-nineteenth century, mentions of the middle class grew significantly, from about 20 times a year prior to 1870, and to over 40 times a year during the subsequent thirty years. The increase in mentions of "middle class" corresponded with expanding newspaper production and the shifting content of reporting. Furthermore, over the course of the period from 1820 to 1900, invocations of the "middle class" evolved from being tied to discussions of political philosophy to practices of class distinction and as a means to make demands on the state.

When the phrase "middle class" first appeared in press reports on foreign affairs in the 1820s, it did so within a constellation of ways of talking about class. The term "buen tono" (good taste) marked status differences without using the word "class" and had appeared in the Mexican press as early as the first decade of the 1800s.[4] The press did not make mention of "la burguesía" (the bourgeoisie) until the early 1870s, even though historians have dated the origins of the Mexican bourgeoisie to the seventeenth century. (An 1884 article in *El Siglo XIX* interpreted

DOI: 10.4324/9781003029311-7

the term "bourgeoisie" for its readers to mean middle class.)[5] With Mexican Independence (1821) and through the 1830s, explicit reference to the middle class appeared most frequently in reports on events in Europe. Such references defined "middle class" in European terms—property owners, merchants, and artisans, terms that did not fully correspond to Mexican reality. In the decade of the 1840s the press turned to focus on Mexico-specific ways of talking about class distinction. As a part of the Mexicanization of "middle class," in the 1860s intellectuals concerned with national economic development employed racial metaphors and wrote of "la clase mestiza" as the middle class between a white upper class and a popular "Indian" class. Within the context of a public sphere grounded in conceptions of masculine honor, writers in the mid-nineteenth century invoked middle-class women primarily as a rhetorical tool to attribute meaning to "middle class" identity or to critique class relations.[6] It was not until the last third of the nineteenth century that the Mexico City press discussed middle-class women as such to any significant degree. While such discussions reflected a changing socio-economic reality for middle-class women who increasingly sought work outside of the home, explicit reference to the plight of "middle-class women" was significant for the ways it allowed the press to critique government neglect of the middle class and to make demands on the state for resources.

Imagining "Middle Class" in Post-Independence Mexico

Prior to 1870, the phrase "middle class" did not appear more than roughly 20 times annually. The relatively low frequency of mentions was due in part to the limited size of the middle class in the first half of the nineteenth century. Scholars argue that, on the eve of Independence, no significant middle class existed and that it would be a mistake to identify mestizos as a middle class in socio-economic terms.[7] What middle class did exist was, in fact, a fairly privileged group, perhaps more appropriately described as upper-middle class. Furthermore, during the first half of the nineteenth century, Mexicans were less likely to use the word "class," and more likely to use the phrases "gente de bien," "gente de orden," "gente decente," and "gente de frac" (people who are "well-off," "orderly," "respectable," or "suit and tie").[8] Early mentions of "buen tono" (good taste) include an 1826 article in *Aguila Mexicana* describing a tertulia attended by "the distinguished classes of society," held by Joel Roberts Poinsett, first United States minister to Mexico.[9] The term "buen tono" also appeared in etiquette manuals that likely circulated in Mexico.[10]

The limited frequency of mentions of "middle class" was also due in part to the nature of the press at the time, what historians have described as "prensa política." According to Elías J. Palti, early nineteenth-century pamphleteers, many trained as lawyers, wrote, printed, and distributed their own newspapers.[11] The cost and labor involved limited production and distribution. Nevertheless, Laurence Coudart finds that between 1821 and 1855 some 188 papers appeared in Mexico City.[12] Despite limited circulation and readership, the collection of historical actors who made up the press played an important role in politics and, with their interventions in public opinion, sought to influence class formation.[13] An association emerged between the press, public opinion, and the middle class as early as the 1820s. An 1828 article in *El Correo de la Federación Mexicana* expressed it thusly:

> [there exists] a difference between public opinion and popular opinion, the latter being the foolish clamor of the riotous plebs, and the former, that which follows the spirit of the middle class, the only one capable of common sense, and of the judgment required to comprehend … public things.[14]

Such opinions came from writers who themselves could be identified as middle class, those whom Coudart describes as "between the public and the masses."[15]

During the period immediately following Mexican independence, three newspapers rose to the top in terms of the frequency of references to the middle class: *El Fanal del Imperio*, *El Sol*, and *El Correo de la Federación*. While the former two papers represented a conservative Catholic position (including supporting a constitutional monarchy in Mexico), the latter took a more liberal viewpoint. The earliest mentions of the phrase "middle class" in the 1820s appeared in reports on international politics. When writers used the phrase "middle class," the subject was assumed to be a male individual, implicitly white, endowed with universal rights, and representative of the possibility of democratic forms of government. The middle class loomed large as a conceptual possibility that existed outside of Mexico and, it was hoped, served as a model for national development. For example, an 1822 article about land redistribution in England highlighted the role of the middle-class male head of household who, as the owner of modest-sized landholdings, served as the foundation of democratic institutions.[16]

As in Europe at this time, the Mexican press wrote about the middle class in Aristotelian terms, that is to say as a class known for its reason and moderation.[17] The middle class demonstrated such qualities, one Mexican pamphleteer wrote in 1826, through the courtesy it showed to people of other social classes. The article, on the equality and rights of men, characterized the middle class as a moderating social force, neither "confrontational" with the lower classes nor "belittling" itself with the aristocracy. When conflict arose over the presence of Spaniards in the former colony, the Mexican press praised the middle class for its mediating influence. According to *El Correo de la Federación*, while "the masses" called for the expulsion of Spaniards, the "middle class" was the only sector of society showing any "common sense" or tolerance.[18] Newspapers also made explicit mention of middle-class status as a means of marking male public virtue. In an era of political strongmen, narratives of individual virtue characterized political figures as exercising legitimate public power. *El Correo de la Federación*, for example, published articles about public figures, making explicit mention of their middle-class status, and whom it identified by the probity of their actions, loyalty, and disinterest in social climbing.[19]

Conservative opinions about the Mexican middle class were not always positive. In the estimation of *El Fénix de la Libertad*, the middle class was replete with ne'er-do-wells. Might not they serve some useful purpose, one journalist asked in an 1834 article titled "Vagrants"? [20] Concerned with United States westward expansion and the growing number of Anglo-American settlers in Mexican territory, the journalist expressed his regret that the Mexican middle class did not make itself useful to the nation by moving to the regions of California and Texas. Unfortunately, he lamented, such men were useless: they were boastful, considered themselves better than artisans, and showed little inclination for work. If during the colonial era men of status avoided non-manual labor, masculinity was increasingly associated with productivity.[21] The article also made a veiled critique of *empleomanía*, a term coined by Lorenzo de Zavala in 1828 to describe an over-reliance on government jobs as a source of employment. Zavala used the term to both criticize Federal policy that inhibited economic development and what he considered a lack of individual (male) productivity.[22] The journalist further impugned middle-class masculinity when he pitied the woman who married such a man, as "they are merely scavenging for income."

During the late 1830s through the 1850s, reports on events in Europe served as a means to debate the role of the middle class in contributing nation-building.[23] The "Foreign news" section reported on political conflicts in France and Spain and, in so doing, debated whether the middle class demonstrated democratic tendencies. Reporting on France, *El Sol* wrote,

> Recent events in Paris have unequivocally determined the power of the respective parties, with the constitutional [party] completely dominating, it being the one which includes men of reason, property, business, commerce, and manufacturing, the one that, in sum, is called the middle class, the heart and life force of all nations.[24]

Such reports reiterated a narrative of the historical importance of the middle class as political actor across national boundaries. They also defined the middle class in European terms: artisans and owners of property, commercial interests, and manufactories. However, very few middle-class Mexico City residents owned property; they were as likely to be employees as owners of commercial or industrial interests; and many were government employees.[25] Whether Mexico City artisans could be categorized as, or called themselves, middle class has changed over time depending on the theoretical framework within which scholars have worked. Drawing on

European scholarship, Mexican sociologists in the 1950s referred to artisans as middle class; however, since at least the 1990s, scholars have included artisans in histories of the Mexican working class.[26] The diversity of artisans' relationships both to production and identity claims further complicates efforts to assign them a class identity. Carlos Illades finds that by the mid-nineteenth century some artisans owned their own workshops while others hired themselves out; some artisans referred to themselves as working class and others claimed middle-class attributes.[27]

Mexicanization of "Middle Class," 1840-1870

In an 1841 speech published in *El Siglo XIX*, jurist and politician Mariano Otero contributed to a narrative of the role of the middle class in Mexican history.[28] His project was anti-colonial and favored the liberal position. Countering the celebratory narrative of Spanish colonization, Otero held harsh judgement for Spain: "It's inhabitants practiced pure and simple customs, the habit of submission and blind obedience, superstitious respect for power, intolerant fanaticism, and the stupid credulity of the majority of the inferior and middle classes in Spain." His characterization implicitly discredited Conservative Party respect for religious authority and monarchical forms of government. In contrast, he described the Mexican middle class as "wherein reside education, morality, the desire for progress, and humanitarian sentiments." According to Otero, in Mexico the middle and exploited classes had been the life force of the independence movement. They were "the last to be considered by the government, and the first in social importance, [that] alone threw themselves into the revolution and left a profound imprint on its character."[29] Thus, Otero fashioned a central role for the middle class, distinct from that of its former colonial power, at the heart of the founding of an independent nation, allied with the exploited classes, and central to democratic forms of government.[30]

Alongside political philosophy and international news, the press reported widely on the customs of the Mexico City middle class. New media content, echoing the *costumbrista* tradition of descriptions of daily life, appeared in a new section of the newspaper: "Variety. Customs."[31] While the dimensions of the Mexico City middle class are not fully understood, by 1849, 38 percent of households were composed of skilled workers and 26 percent upper middle-class households, with the extremes composed of 23 percent unskilled worker households and 13 percent elite.[32] *El Siglo XIX*, in particular, delighted in descriptions of uniquely Mexican middle-class cultural practices. For example, multiple articles praised middle-class posadas festivities, the Mexican Christmas tradition of travelling from the home of one neighbor to the next, in honor of the journey that Mary and Joseph made from Nazareth to Bethlehem.[33] While the aristocracy locked itself up in their private homes, it was, according to *El Siglo XIX*, thanks to the middle class that uniquely Mexican forms of sociability continued.

The press also defined the middle class through its association with certain neighborhoods and geographies. Weekend outings to Tlalpam, for example.[34] In reports on how city residents spent leisure time, the press praised the middle class as modest, cultured, and uniquely Mexican. The press also pointed out how the middle class struggled to maintain cultural practices. *El Siglo XIX* noted how the middle class skimped and saved so as to be able to attend the theater. Middle-class men, dressed in suits, were forced to economize and sweat it out in the un-shaded seats at bullfights.[35] The accumulation of class-associated cultural markers contributed to define the middle class in national terms, as keepers of tradition, and in distinction from a privileged, inward-looking elite.[36]

During the Reform Era (1855-1861), liberal politicians and intellectuals envisioned a future with a small-land-owning middle class as the basis of Jeffersonian agrarian democracy.[37] Contributors to the press drew on racial metaphors to analyze economy and society, and in the process created conceptions of class specific to the Mexican reality. Drawing on racial formations that construed white at the top of a hierarchy and "Indian" at the bottom, intellectuals referred to the "mestiza class" that, like the middle class, drew from above and below. To be clear, the relationship between mestizos (as a possible demographic group) and the middle class (as a quantifiable sector) remains in doubt and understudied.[38] Quite aside from demographics, ideologies of race served as metaphor to conceptualize class identity. For example, in 1861, statesman and author León Alejo Torre published an article responding to criticisms of Benito Juárez in which he performed a translation of terms for the reader by equating "mestiza class" with "middle class."[39] In his defense of Juárez, whom he identified as "indio," Torre faulted middle-class prejudice.

> The truth is that the majority of Indians lay submerged in ignorance and indifference, because of the criminal indifference and unjustifiable disregard with which the middle, or mestiza class, and the descendants of their first conquerors, has held them. But is there anyone who doubts their inclination for work in the fields, in war, and even in the arts and sciences?[40]

Almost fifty years later, Andrés Molina Enríquez, in *Los grandes problemas nacionales* (1909), also understood the middle class within the framework of racial ideologies and as drawing from above (criollo or white) and below (Indian).[41]

Female Vulnerability as Middle-Class Precariousness

In the mid-nineteenth century, mainstream journalist, many of whom could be identified as (male) middle class themselves, invoked middle-class women as a rhetorical device in the service of a masculine public sphere, and only infrequently as historical actors. As Pablo Piccato writes, "masculine honor was the keystone in the building of a modern public sphere."[42] Most reporting focused on formal politics, a realm in which women did not engage.[43] Even when journalists appropriated a female voice, as shown by Edward Wright-Ríos, they did so within the logic of masculine honor.[44] Within the context of restrictions on freedom of the press, reports of affronts to female sexual honor served as a veiled political critique.[45] Such was the case when, in 1858, several papers reported the rape of "women from middle-class families" in Oaxaca.[46] The reference to "middle-class families" heightened the sense of offense not only against said women, but to middle-class patriarchal norms. The centrality of heteronormative marriage to middle-class identity was also reinforced by reports of what was construed as scandalous behavior, as with an 1868 case of a "middle-class man" who, mistakenly thinking that his wife had died, married again and in so doing became a bigamist.[47]

The practice of invoking middle-class women as a rhetorical device in the service of social critique is clear in the writing of Juan Díaz Covarrubias (1837-1859), whose novel *Las clases medias* (1850) was advertised in the newspapers regularly for eight years following its publication.[48] The novel tells a tale of aristocratic youth (male) enjoying their privileges, free time, travel, and hours spent drinking champagne in the cafes of Mexico City. One such young man, Isidoro, is smitten with a Señorita Amparo, who gives in to his gallantries. Isidro quickly tires of Amparo and, after cheating on her, abandons her. In commenting on this tragedy, Díaz Covarrubias criticized class relations in Mexico: "has not the middle class been raised to be victim to the pleasures of the aristocracy?"[49] *Las clases medias* is not centrally concerned with Amparo, but with the aristocracy's victimization of the middle class, in this case underlined by the violation of the sexual honor of a middle-class woman. Later, friends see Amparo at Church, alone in the corner, praying. Díaz Covarrubias, an adherent of the Liberal Party, thus discrediting the Catholic Church as an institution and religiosity as a poor salve for aristocratic abuse of the middle class. A modest middle-class youth, Roman, challenges Isidro to a duel. That Roman perishes in the duel further underscores the injustice of aristocratic abuse of the middle class. The press would soon denounce the middle class's continued engagement in duels as tragically outdated.[50]

While we still have much to learn about the history of the Mexican middle class, data suggest this sector grew in the last third of the century.[51] The well-being of that middle class, however, is another question. Press reports increased about the financial challenges its members faced. In 1878, one journalist fretted that "misery has spilled over the boundaries of the lower classes and has, with terrifying swiftness, invaded the middle class."[52] Journalists who feared political retaliation could report on the travails of middle-class women as a means to criticize government.[53] The 1870s saw a significant increase in frequency of mentions of the phrase "middle class" in the Mexico City press, approximately 40 times a year, an uptick that coincided with increased references to "middle-class women." The phrase "middle class" appeared in conjunction with the word "woman" half a dozen times annually during the 1870s, and then increased to 20 mentions a year between 1883 and 1886. As of 1886 "woman" and "middle class" appeared together some 30 times a year. At the same time, references to "la clase mestiza" in the Mexico City press waned.[54] While women played an increasing role in the production of the press after 1870, women's periodicals infrequently made explicit use of the phrase "middle class."[55] Even contributors to mainstream papers who, like journalist Juvenal (Enrique Chávarri), directed their column to middle-class women, rarely, if ever, explicitly referred to women's class identity. The male-dominated mainstream press, however, began to dedicate entire articles to the subject of middle-class women and the economic well-being of the middle class.

The press reported on the significant number of female-headed households, limited employment options for women, and female poverty and, in so doing, criticized government ineffectiveness in creating the conditions for middle-class prosperity.[56] In an editorial that appeared in *El Ferrocarril* in 1870, J.P. de los Ríos described widespread begging in the city, the sight of "a woman over-burdened or accompanied by one or two small children; a woman who by all appearances is decent; a young girl who enters a dangerous age."[57] In identifying the causes of such misfortune, de los Ríos shifted to focus on the difficulties faced by the middle class: "Public upheavals on the one hand, and on the other the general unhingedness of society, have inhibited so many sources of work, that today the majority live in misery. Yes. The majority, which is the middle class."[58] De los Ríos blamed "political instability, the hardship of excessive taxes on industry, the military conscription system (*leva*), the shortage of manufactory and industrial establishments, and many other circumstances of a similar nature." He also blamed middle-class stubborn adherence to female domesticity which, he argued, kept them from maintaining a decent standard of living. As evidence, he related the story of a woman who, out of a desire to protect her respectability, would not venture beyond her house to find work, and so was unable to feed her family. "If you lock her in the house, you will leave that family without bread and, as a result, numerous children will be on the street begging." De los Ríos thus challenged the centrality of female domesticity for middle-class practices of class distinction.

While patriarchal authority within the family was expected, including control of female labor and sexuality, press reports of the abuse of that authority allowed journalists to signal the fragility of the middle class.[59] Several articles fretted over the precariousness of middle-class well-being, which had led to the practice of fathers, motivated by economic self-interest, to marry off their daughters to the highest bidder. And not only were middle-class women exploited by their own families, they were also exploited by society at large. Author, journalist, and former mining administrator Pedro Castera, for example, mounted an early critique against the commodification of women's sexual virtue.[60] Writing for the "Literary section" of the liberal paper *El Radical*, Castera painted a picture of the widespread poverty into which middle-class women had fallen.[61] The situation was so dire, he argued, that middle-class women had to turn to prostitution in order to survive. In other reports, experts suggested the need for special hospital wards for middle-class women who, while suffering from illnesses contracted while engaging in prostitution, were too embarrassed to seek help in hospitals that treated the general population.[62]

Public conversations about women's vulnerability, both economic and moral, opened space for debates over middle-class women's education. In the last third of the nineteenth century, social commentators began to support women's education that would prepare them not only to be better mothers, but also to be able to work outside of the home.[63] While such conversations addressed women's concrete need for income and professional fulfillment, they were also a means to make claims on the government for resources for the middle class. Early debates over the education of middle-class women first appeared in news from abroad. In 1871, the Spanish-born, Paris-resident Baroness Wilson (an occasional visitor to Mexico) advocated for middle-class women's education.[64] The following year *El Ferrocarril* published a debate over the purpose of education for women. A report of a speech by Dr. Meier de Lubeck, director of a girls' school in Germany, underscored the distinction between an education that prepared women for employment outside of the home and, on the other hand, one that prepared them for their domestic responsibilities. Meier de Lubeck favored the latter.[65] The newspaper report not only disagreed with such a limited vision of women's education but gave a degree of agency to women by quoting a Miss Augusta Wegrowitz of Berlin, who argued women should be educated so they could be economically independent. "Idleness," Miss Wegrowitz stated, "… dominates high society, despite its apparent occupation, and in the middle class, annoyance and ignorance fill the abyss that, too often, emerges between men and women." In a section titled "Other news," *El Monitor Republicano* reported that in England middle-class women had access to an education equal to that offered to men. *La Bandera Nacional* reported that in Saint Petersburg women could study to become doctors.[66]

Such debates served as an opportunity to advocate for women as well as to critique the Mexican government for its lack of support for the middle class. In 1881, the Mexican Chamber of Deputies debated women's right to professional titles. *La Patria*, edited at the time by Ireneo Paz, criticized government indifference to the plight of the middle class. An unidentified contributor (who may have been Paz himself, as he frequently wrote unsigned articles for *La Patria*) argued for men and women's equality before the law.

Paz pointed to the Constitution of 1857 as the basis of his argument in favor of women's right to work in respectable occupations outside of the home. "Of course, women enjoy the same rights and prerogatives as granted to men, not just to the citizen but to every man in general."[67] Specifically, he noted, Article 4 of the Constitution stated that "all men are free to embrace the profession, industry, or occupation that suits them as long as it is useful and honest, and we must understand that this right also extends to women." Echoing earlier concerns about middle-class women and prostitution, the article asked why the government would deny women professional titles when it already regulated the activity to which women would resort (prostitution) if they had no means to support themselves honestly.

Journalistic reports on the middle class engaged in debate over the causes of its precarious status. Who was responsible: the government, individual behavior, or women? Those who opposed the expansion of work and educational opportunities for middle-class women characterized women as frivolous. Frivolity, claimed *El Nacional*, had become a "dreadful plague," especially among middle-class women.[68] A debate emerged in the press about how to understand the causes and cures of female frivolity, a debate that also served to police the boundaries of middle-class desires more generally. For some, middle-class women fell victim to imitation, the desire for a lifestyle above one's means. Drawing on Friedrich Froëbel, the Catholic newspaper *El Nacional* divided middle-class women into three categories which echoed the tripartite model of class relations: those born and bred as such; those from a higher social class who experienced misfortune and descended into the middle class; and those from a lower social class who ascended into the middle class. Froëbel believed that middle-class women's love of luxury and desire to imitate upper-class women made them vulnerable to in fact descend in class status.[69] *El Nacional* lamented middle-class women's "immoderate desire" for luxury that led to their fall. More than a decade later, Dr. Luis Lara y Pardo, in his study *La Prostitución en México*, elaborated on the concept of "imitation" as a manifestation of class envy.[70] *El Siglo XIX* scolded *El Nacional* for its criticism of women's behavior and argued that the weak Mexican economy had had a punishing impact on the middle class. This middle class was the heart and soul of the country, the journalist affirmed, and therefore the problem demanded solution.[71]

Conclusion

How and when people have invoked the precise phrase "middle class" forms part of the warp and weft of class identity. Alongside objective criteria (income, property holding patterns, etc.), political engagement, or cultural activities, the language historical actors have used to categorize or describe status mattered. Words and phrases accrue meaning as they are used over time. Taking the newspapers at the Mexican National Digital

Newspaper Archive as a sample, we can trace some of these meanings. Whereas prior to the mid-nineteenth century Mexicans characterized people of middle- and upper-class status by using the phrases "de buen tono," "gente de bien," and "gente decente," over the course of the nineteenth century they increasingly used the phrase "middle class," representing a subtle shift from terms. From the establishment of the nation in 1821 and through the 1840s, press reports on international affairs invoked the middle class as a central actor in political struggles. Thus, the reader of the Mexican press might have imagined themselves a part of a middle class that transcended national boundaries, even when such privileges and attributes were defined in ways that did not fully correspond to Mexican reality. In the press, the middle class, implicitly white and most often male, enjoyed certain privileges (ownership of property and individual rights) and possessed attributes construed as both inherent (reason, moderation, and selflessness) and acquired (culture and education). And yet, many Mexico City residents who scholars identify as middle class were not property owners, rented their home, and struggled to pay for cultural activities. The question of how historical actors self-identified seems all the more relevant when we consider that scholars have not agreed on who pertains to the middle class or not, as has been the case with artisans.

During the 1840s, various authors contributed to grounding the "middle class," as both a noun and a descriptive phrase, within the specificity of Mexican reality. In 1841 Mariano Otero placed the middle class within a national historical narrative. In his retelling, the middle class allied with the "popular class" against Spain, playing a crucial role in forming the nation. The press also participated in defining the middle class in uniquely Mexican terms by identifying that class with specific customs and attributes: posadas, outings to Tlalpam, and suffering in their unshaded seats at the bullfights. These reports construed the middle class as the preserver of Mexican culture and, unlike the elite, socially minded. So, when in the last quarter of the nineteenth century, journalists made claims on the state on behalf of the middle class, the concept of "middle class" had already come to be associated with national history, traditions, and customs.

Intellectuals, statemen, and journalists often used the phrase "middle class" as a rhetorical device or metaphor. The tripartite model of class—upper, middle, and lower—served to explain racial formations specific to the Mexican context (mestizaje). Journalists and intellectuals likened the "mestizo class" to the middle class, in that both drew individuals from "above" and "below." Upper class and lower class were replaced by the categories white and Indian. Journalists and intellectuals who drew such false equivalencies reified racial categories and hierarchies. By implicitly asserting the possibility of social mobility and decline, the press thus contributed to the myth of racial democracy.[72] This essay, focusing as it does only on the Mexico City press, offers only initial observations on the role of race in middle-class identity.

Mid-century press reports on political events referred to middle-class women less as historical actors than as a rhetorical device to shore up male honor in the public sphere. Reports of violations of middle-class female virtue, for example, served as a means to critique the aristocracy. As the frequency of reports on the middle class increased, so too did discussion of middle-class women. By 1870, journalists expressed their growing concern with the material conditions of the middle class through reports on female poverty. While some journalists criticized middle-class domesticity, or women themselves, others used the opportunity to make demands on the state. Their concern for female virtue was less likely to incite government censure than an outright critique of state policy. Journalists often slid from discussion of women's issues into a critique of government lack of support for middle-class prosperity. While the press rarely opened space for women to speak for themselves, journalists nevertheless placed middle-class women in the center of important political debates, thus shifting the relative position of middle-class female identity within the public sphere.

Notes

1 Scholarship on the history of the Mexican middle class takes on a series of important questions. On practices of class distinction, see, for example, William E. French, "Prostitutes and Guardian Angels: Women, Work, and the Family in Porfirian Mexico," *Hispanic American Historical Review* 72, no. 4 (1992): 529–53; Susanne Karin Eineigel, "Distinction, Culture, and Politics in Mexico City's Middle Class, 1890–1940" (PhD diss., University of Maryland, 2011). On professions that scholars have categorized as middle class, see Michael E. Ervin, "The Formation of the Revolutionary Middle Class during the Mexican Revolution" in *The Making of the Middle Class: Toward a Transnational History*, eds. A. Ricardo López and Barbara Weinstein (Durham, NC: Duke University Press, 2012); Mario Barbosa Cruz, "Profesionalización, capacitación e identidades de los empleados públicos de la ciudad de México a comienzos del siglo XX," *Historia Mexicana* 270 (October–December 2018): 749–85; and Susie S. Porter, *From Angel to Office Worker: Middle-Class Identity and Female Consciousness in Mexico, 1890–1950* (Lincoln: University of Nebraska Press, 2018). On middle-class political participation, see Soledad Loaeza, *Clases medias y política en México: La querella escolar, 1959–1963 (*Mexico City: El Colegio de México, 1988); Tiziana Bertaccini, *El régimen priísta frente a las clases medias, 1943–1964* (Mexico City: Consejo Nacional para la Cultura y las Artes, Dirección General de Publicaciones, 2009); and Andrés Reyes Rodríguez, *Clases medias y poder político en Aguascalientes* (Aguascalientes: Universidad Autónoma de Aguascalientes, 2016). On the middle class since 1968, see Louise E. Walker, *Waking from the Dream: Mexico's Middle Class after 1968* (Stanford, CA: Stanford University Press, 2013).

2 Klaus-Peter Sick, "Le concept de classes moyennes. Notion sociologique ou slogan politique?," *Vinghtieme Siecle. Revue d'Histoire* 37 (1993): 13–34.

3 Mario Barbosa Cruz "La clase media en la Ciudad de México entre el porfiriato y la Revolución," *Revista de Historia e Interdisciplina* 10 (January–June 2020): 9-23.

4 Don Mariano de Rementería y Fica, trans., *El hombre fino al gusto del día ó manual completo de urbanidad, cortesía y buen tono* (Madrid: Imprenta de Moreno, 1829); María del Pilar Sinués de Marco, *La dama elegante: manual práctico y completísimo del buen tono y del buen orden doméstico* (Madrid: Impr. de los hijos de J.A. García, 1892). Sinués de Marco's work circulated in Mexico City.

5 The unidentified author translated the term thusly: "la clase media de la sociedad (bourgeoisie)," see "Revista," *El Siglo XIX*, July 10, 1884, 1. For a discussion of the literature on the historical evolution of the bourgeoisie, see Brígida Von Mentz, *Movilidad social de sectores medios: Una retrospectiva histórica (siglos* XVII *al* XX*)* (Mexico City: Centro de Investigaciónes y Estudios Superiores en Antropología Social; Miguel Ángel Porrúa, 2003), 28.

6 Several authors have debated the degree to which the nineteenth-century public sphere was a masculine construct, see, for example, Susie S. Porter, *Working Women in Mexico City: Public Discourses and Material Conditions, 1879–1931* (Tucson: University of Arizona Press, 2003), xviii-xx, 121-32; Erika Pani, "¿Ciudadana y muy ciudadana,?: Women and the State in Independent Mexico," *Gender and History* 18, no. 1 (2006): 5–19; and, Pablo Piccato, *The Tyrrany of Opinion: Honor in the Construction of the Mexican Public Sphere* (Durham, NC: Duke University Press, 2010), 4.

7 David Brading, *Merchants and Miners in Bourbon Mexico 1763–1810* (Cambridge: Cambridge University Press, 1971), 23–24.

8 Michael P. Costeloe, *The Central Republic in Mexico, 1835–1846: 'Hombres de Bien' in the Age of Santa Anna* (Cambridge: Cambridge University Press, 1993), 17. For early reference to "gente de bien," see "Los muy leales habitantes de la ciudad de Havana," *Diario de México*, October 29, 1808, 500. For early reference to "gente de orden" as part of the "clase alta," see "Ley electoral: artículo 11," *El Siglo XIX*, April 24, 1853, 1. This article also refers to the "mal apreciada clase media" as "those who had been suffering (*abatidos*) and were able to rise up, and with time and under the sway of the freedom of institutions, has come into being."

9 "Pasatiempo," *Aguila Mexicana*, March 18, 1826, 1; and, "Aniversario," July 7, 1826, 1. Lorenzo de Zavala, Juan Nepomuceno Gómez de Navarrete, and José Ignacio Esteva served as owners of *Aguila Mexicana* which, at the time of the article cited here, was published by a Mexico City press by the same name and directed by José Ximeno. The earliest reference to *buen tono* in the Mexico City press held in the HNDM archive was in a story about English royalty: "La Coquetilla," *Diario de México*, January 8, 1808, 1–2.

10 Rementería y Fica, *El hombre fino*.

11 Elías J. Palti, "Tres etapas de la prensa política Mexicana del siglo XIX: el publicista y los orígenes del intelectual moderno," in *Historia de los intelectuales en América Latina*, vol. 1, eds. Carlos Altamirano and Jorge Myers (Madrid: Editorial Katz, 2008), 227–241.

12 Laurence Coudart, "Los orígenes de la era mediática de la prensa periódica," in *Dimensiones de la cultura literaria en México (1800–1850): modelos de sociabilidad, materialidades, géneros y tradiciones intelectuales*, ed. Esther Martínez Luna (Mexico: Universidad Nacional Autónoma de México, 2018), 21–28.

13 Víctor Villavicencio Navarro, "Cuando la prensa incomoda al sistema político: la libertad de imprenta frente a la propuesta de José María Gutiérrez de Estrada de 1840," *Historia Mexicana*, LXIX: 1 (2019): 160.

14 "Noticias nacionales," *El Correo de la Federación Mexicana*, February 7, 1828, 1. *Correo de la Federación* was a four-page daily produced by Lorenzo de Zavala and Isidro Rafael Gondra and distributed throughout the country.

The paper was associated with liberals, York Rite Freemasons, and Federalists; it supported the expulsion of Spaniards and countered Scottish Rite Freemasons and Centralists. For more, see Miguel Castro Medina, *Publicaciones periódicas mexicanas del siglo XIX: 1822–1855* (México: Universidad Nacional Autónoma de México, 2000), 92–95.

15 "Noticias nacionales," *Correo de la federación mexicana*, February 7, 1828, 1.

16 *El Fanal del Imperio Mexicano*, May 15, 1822, 407-10. Founded and directed by Francisco Severo Maldonado, *El Fanal* was a short-lived monthly publication of 48–50 pages. Catholic and heterodox contributors supported a proposal for a constitutional monarchy. See Castro Medina, *Publicaciones periódicas*, 182–83. *El Sol* was a conservative daily or at times bi-weekly newspaper and was the object of critique by *El Correo de la Federación Mexicana*. For more on *El Sol*, see Castro Medina, *Publicaciones periódicas*, 413–419.

17 Klaus-Peter Sick, "Le concept de classes moyennes," 13–34; Ezequiel Adamovsky, "Aristotle, Diderot, Liberalism, and the Idea of the Middle Class: A Comparison of Two Contexts of Emergence of a Metaphorical Formation," *History of Political Thought* 26, no. 2 (2005): 303–333.

18 "Noticias nacionales," *El Correo de la Federación Mexicana*, February 7, 1828, 1. Timo H. Schaefer characterizes the initiative to expel Spaniards as an example of class conflict, in *Liberalism as Utopia: The Rise and Fall of Legal Rule in Post-Colonial Mexico, 1820–1900* (Cambridge: Cambridge University Press, 2017), 23–24. On the moderating force of the middle class in Gran Colombia, see "Mexico de 21 de mayo de 1830," *El Sol*, May 21, 1830, 4; *El Sol*, Nov. 14, 1830, 2; and *Águila Mexicana* October 15, 1826, 2. On *Águila Mexicana*, see Castro Medina, *Publicaciones periódicas*, 3–6.

19 Andrés Zenteno, "Comunicados," *El Correo de la Federación Mexicana*, July 18, 1827, 2.

20 "Vagos," *El Fénix de la Libertad*, February 23, 1834, 4. On *El Fénix*, see Castro Medina, *Publicaciones periódicas*, 190–192.

21 Sonya Lipsett-Rivera, *The Origins of Macho: Men and Masculinity in Colonial Mexico* (Albuquerque: University of New Mexico Press, 2019), 85–87; and, Schaefer, *Liberalism as Utopia*, 16, 23–24.

22 Felipe Aguilar Hernández, *Moral pública en los procesos de buen gobierno*, (Mexico: Universidad Autónoma del Estado de México/ Instituto de Administración Pública de Estado de México/Plaza y Valdés, 2000), 121; and, Jose María Luis Mora, "Discurso sobre los perniciosos efectos de la *empleomanía*," in *Obras sueltas de Jose María Luis Mora, ciudadano mejicano*, vol. 2 (Paris: Librería de Rosa, 1837), 122–133. The association between the middle class and government bureaucrats dates to early use of the term "middle class" in France, see Adamovsky, "Aristotle, Diderot, Liberalism," 327–328.

23 Elías J. Palti argues that newspaper reporting on theatrical performances served as a means to debate monarchical forms of government, in "La Sociedad Filarmónica del Pito. Ópera, prensa y politica en la República restaurada (México, 1867–1876)," *Historia Mexicana* 52, no. 4 (April–June 2003): 941–978.

24 "Esterior. Nueva York, octubre 2," *El Sol*, November 14, 1830, 2. On events in Spain, see "Toma de Morella y sus consecuencias," *La Hesperia*, September 9, 1840, 1.

25 Von Mentz, *Movilidad social de sectores medios*, 27–29. On middle-class living standards and property-owning patterns, see Marie Francois, *A Culture of Everyday Credit: Housekeeping, Pawnbroking, and Governance in Mexico City, 1750–1920* (University of Nebraska Press, 2006), 162–163.

26 For a comparative analysis of artisan identity, see Meglio, Gabriel Di, Guzmán, Tomás, & Katz, Mariana, "Artesanos hispanoamericanos del siglo XIX: identidades, organizaciones y acción política," *Almanack* 23 (2019): 275–315. For Mexico, see, for example, Carlos Illades, *Hacia la república del trabajo: la organización artesanal en la Ciudad de México, 1853–1876* (Mexico: El Colegio de México, 1996), 105; Sonia Pérez Toledo, *Los hijos del trabajo: Los artesanos de la ciudad de México* (Mexico: El Colegio de México, 1996), 17–19, 52. Von Mentz associates artisans in Mexico with the "poorest sectors," see Von Mentz, *Movilidad social de sectores medios,* 7. Sociologists Mendieta y Nuñez and Iturriaga included artisans in the middle class, see Lucio Mendieta y Nuñez, "La clase media en México," *Revista Mexicana de Sociología*, 17, 2/3 (May–December, 1955): 521; and José E. Iturriaga, *La estructura social de México* (Mexico: Fondo de Cultura Económcia, 1951), 28, 43, 57, 60.

27 Illades, *Hacia la república del trabajo*, 22, 39. In the late nineteenth century, artisan parents hoped their sons could ascend to middle-class status through a government office job, see Mario Barbosa Cruz "La clase media en la Ciudad de México entre el porfiriato y la Revolución," *Revista de Historia e Interdisciplina* 10 (January–June 2020): 17. By the late nineteenth century, some artisans simultaneously claimed a working-class identity while also engaging in the politics of respectability associated with middle-class identity, see Porter, *Working Women*, 60–71.

28 "Discurso que en la solemnidad del 16 de Septiembre de 1841 pronunció en la ciudad de Guadalajara el Lic. Mariano Otero," *El Siglo XIX*, October 22, 1841, 1–2. For more on *El Siglo XIX*, see Castro Medina, *Publicaciones periódicas*, 397–412. Ricaurte Soler, "El pensamiento sociológico de Mariano Otero," *Cuadernos Americanos* 1, (January–February 1960): 15–31.

29 "Discurso que en la solemnidad del 16 de Septiembre de 1841 pronunció en la ciudad de Guadalajara el Lic. Mariano Otero," *El Siglo XIX*, October 22, 1841, 1–2.

30 For Otero, the middle class included lower-level priests and military. Mariano Otero, *Ensayo sobre el verdadero estado de la cuestión social y política que se agita en la república* (Mexico City: Impreso por Ignacio Cumplido, 1842), 52.

31 Gerardo Francisco Bobadilla Encinas, "Apuntes de poética narrativa. El primer costumbrismo en México (1843–1850)," in *Imágenes de México y el mexicano en dos momentos de su historia: Representaciones culturales y literarias*, coords. Daniel Avechuco Cabrera y Gerardo Francisco Bobadilla Encinas (Mexico: Universidad de Sonora, 2019), 24–25.

32 Francois, *A Culture of Everyday Credit*, 81, 90.

33 Fidel, *El Siglo XIX*, December 30, 1842, 1. The press continued to associate posadas with the middle class well into the 1880s, see *El Tiempo*, December 30, 1884, 3; and, *La Libertad*, December 28, 1884, 3.

34 "Recuerdos de un Paseo a Tlalpam," *El Siglo XIX*, Jan. 31, 1842, 2; "Recuerdos de un Paseo a Tlalpam," *El Siglo XIX*, July 3, 1842, 3.

35 *El Siglo XIX*, January 31, 1842, 3.

36 Enrique Chávarri (Juvenal) also characterized the aristocracy as self-absorbed and the middle class as the keeper of national traditions, see, for example, "Charlas de los domingos," *El Monitor Republicano*, December 6, 1885, 1.

37 David A. Brading, "Creole Nationalism and Mexican Liberalism," *Journal of Interamerican Studies and World Affairs* 15, no. 2 (May 1973): 139–90.

38 Brading, *Merchants and Miners*, 23–24; Francois, *A Culture of Everyday Credit*, 78–80; Guillermo Zermeño-Padilla, "Del mestizo al mestizaje: arqueología de un concepto," *Mem. soc.* 12, no. 24 (2008): 79–95. In the modern period, census takers did not record ethnicity until 1921.

39 Alonso de Regil y Peón, Manuel Sánchez Mármol, Rubén Reyes Ramírez, *Poetas yucatecos y tabasqueños: colección de sus mejores producciones* (Villahermosa, Tab.: Universidad Juárez Autónoma de Tabasco; Universidad Autónoma de Yucatán; Compañía Editorial de la Peninsula, S.A. de C.V., 2005), 227–228.
40 León Alejo Torre, "Espíritu de la oposición contra el Sr. Juárez.---!Abajo los falsos demócratas!," *El Siglo XIX*, July 5, 1861, 1.
41 Andrés Molina Enríquez, *Los grandes problemas nacionales* (Mexico: Imprenta de A. Carranza e hijos, 1909), 31, 40–43, 218–221.
42 Piccato, *The Tyrrany of Opinion*, 4.
43 Silvia Arrom, *The Women of Mexico City, 1790–1857* (Stanford, CA: Stanford University Press, 1983); Erika Pani, "Ciudadana y muy ciudadana"?: Women and the State in Independent Mexico," *Gender and History* 18, no. 1 (2006): 5–19.
44 Edward Wright-Ríos, "La Madre Matiana: Prophetess and Nation in Mexican Satire," *The Americas* 68, no. 2 (2011): 241–274.
45 Laurence Coudart, "La regulación de la libertad de prensa (1863–1867)," *Historia Mexicana* 65, no. 2 (October–December 2015): 629–687.
46 "Más sobre Oajaca," *La Sociedad*, April 20, 1858, 3; "Más sobre Oajaca," *Diario Oficial del Supremo Gobierno*, April 22, 1858, 4. *La Sociedad* was a conservative paper run by F.V. Sánchez, Francisco Vera, F. Escalante, and José Maria Bárcena (1857–1867). On *La Sociedad*, see *Publicaciones periódicas mexicanas del siglo XIX, parte 2, 1856–1876: Fondo Antiguo de la Hemeroteca Nacional de México*, Curiel, Guadalupe, Miguel Ángel Castro y Vicente Quiriarte (coords.), (México: Universidad Nacional Autónoma de México, 2019), 551.
47 "Acontecimiento notable," *La Constitución Social*, August 14, 1868, 3. See also *El Siglo XIX*, July 6, 1842, 2. The press frequently characterized the middle class as the only class that respected the practices of marriage and monogamy, see for example "Jurisprudencia Criminal. Adulterio," *El Foro*, July 24, 1873, 2; Pedro Castera, "Sección Literaria. La Mujer. El Matrimonio," *El Radical*, April 19, 1874, 2. On bigamy in colonial New Spain, see Richard E. Boyer, *The Lives of Bigamists: Marriage, Family, and Community in Colonial Mexico* (Albuquerque: University of New Mexico Press, 1995).
48 "Avisos. Libros," *La Sociedad*, July 6, 1858, 4; "Miscelania. El C. Juan Díaz Covarrubias," *El Ferrocarril*, September 7, 1870.
49 Juan Díaz Covarrubias, *La clase media: novela de costumbres mexicanas*, (Mexico City: Tipografía de Manuel Castro, 1859), 10–11.
50 "El Duelo," *La Constitución Social*, October 29, 1868, 1. Literature printed in series also circulated ideas about the middle class. See, for example, "Señora Venus" y "Las Grandes Señoras," *El Monitor Republicano*, April 17, 1869, 3.
51 Fernando Rosenweig, "La evolución económica de México, 1870–1940," *El Trimestre económico* vol. 56, no. 221 (1) (January–March 1989): 11–56; Francois, *A Culture of Everday Credit*, 95.
52 "Boletín del Monitor," *El Monitor Republicano*, February 14, 1878, 1.
53 Fausta Gantús argues that journalists used cartoons to criticize the government in ways that might allow them to avoid retaliation, see *Caricatura y poder político. Crítica, censura y represión en la Ciudad de México, 1876–1888* (México: El Colegio de México; Instituto Mora, 2009), 179, 221.
54 Some observers continued to use racial categories as a metaphor for class identity, see for example "El expediente para el porvenir," *El Tiempo*, October 6, 1885, 2; Enrique Zamudio, "El porvenir de la mujer mexicana," *La Patria*, March 1, 1896, 2.

55 Lucrecia Infante Vargas, "De la escritura personal a la redacción de revistas femeninas. Mujeres y cultura escrita en México durante el siglo XIX," *Relaciones* 113 (2008): 69–105.

56 Arrom, *The Women of Mexico City*, 154–58, 161, 165; Ana Lidia García Peña, "Madres solteras, pobres y abandonadas: ciudad de México, siglo XIX," *Historia Mexicana* 53, no. 3 (January–March 2004): 647–692.

57 J.P. de los Ríos, "Editorial: La Mendicidad," *El Ferrocarril*, September 29, 1870, 1–2.

58 de los Ríos, "Editorial," 1–2.

59 On male authority within the family, see Lipsett-Rivera, *The Origins of Macho* 90–91. On women's education, see Ana Laura Zavala Díaz, "La política y la discordia huyeron luego al aspecto agradable de la fraternidad:" El discurso doméstico familiar en las veladas literarias de 1867–1868," in *Aproximaciones a una historia intelectual: revistas y asociaciones literarias mexicanas del siglo XIX*, coords. Guadalupe Curiel Defossé and Belem Clark de Lara (Mexico: Universidad Nacional Autónoma de México, 2016), 59–78.

60 Pedro Castera Cortés (1846–1906) was a miner, journalist, and author. See, Clementina Díaz y de Ovando, "Pedro Castera, novelista y minero," *Mexican Studies/Estudios Mexicanos* 7, no. 2 (Summer 1991): 203–23.

61 Pedro Castera, "Sección Literaria. La Mujer. La Miseria," *El Radical*, April 4, 1874, 2. *El Radical* was edited by Vicente Riva Palacio, a liberal novelist, journalist, and military leader. Some commentators denied the practice of marrying off middle-class daughters for economic benefit occurred in Mexico, see for example Francisco Sosa, "Teatros. Ambición y coquetismo," *El Bien Público*, August 13, 1876, 2–3. Literature also portrayed women's sacrifices to maintain middle class lifestyles, see Francois, *A Culture of Everyday Credit*, 162.

62 "Higiene Pública," *Anales de la Asociación Larrey*, January 1, 1876, 10–11; Higiene Pública," *Anales de la Asociación Larrey*, February 1, 1876, 24–25. According to Luis Lara y Pardo, middle-class women suffered "abandonment" and "seduction," but did not engage in prostitution, see Luis Lara y Pardo, *La Prostitución en México* (Mexico: Librería de la Viuda Ch. Bouret, 1908), 115–116. Middle-class women's engagement in prostitution does not appear in the several excellent studies of prostitution in Mexico City. See, for example, Fernanda Núñez Becerra, *La prostitución y su represión en la ciudad de México (siglo XIX)* (Barcelona: Gedia, 2002).

63 María del Carmen Berdejo Bravo, *Regir y formar: Institucionalización jurídica y educativa de las mujeres mexicanas (1880–1884)*. (México: Universidad Autónoma Metropolitana, 2011), 89; French, "Prostitutes and Guardian Angels."

64 "Editorial. La Educación," *El Ferrocarril*, May 3, 1871, 1–2. Emilia Serrano García, Baronesa de Wilson (1834?–1923) was a born in Spain, raised in Paris, and occasionally resided in Mexico, see Janet W. Pérez and Maureen Ihrie, eds., *The Feminist Encyclopedia of Spanish Literature, N–Z* (Westport, CT: Greenwood Press, 2002), 553–555.

65 P.P. de P., "Editorial. Sobre educación," *El Ferrocarril*, May 3, 1871, 2. Editor and editor in chief, J. Rivera y Rio; see also, "La educación superior de la mujer en Inglaterra," *El Monitor Republicano*, January 28, 1872, 1.

66 "La educacción de la mujer en Inglaterra," *El Monitor Republicano*, January 28, 1872, 2. Newspapers reported that women in Saint Petersburg could study medicine, see *La Bandera Nacional*, November 7, 1877, 3.

67 "Los títulos profesionales y las mujeres," *La Patria*, June 24, 1881, 1.

68 "Frivolidad," *El Monitor Republicano*, January 8, 1882, 1; "El Nacional," *La Patria*, November 30, 1894, 2.

69 "Cuestión Social: la educación de la mujer," *El Siglo XIX*, December 5, 1894, 1.
70 Dr. Luis Lara y Pardo, *La Prostitución en México* (Paris: Librería de la Viuda de Ch. Bouret, 1908), 115–119.
71 La Redacción, "Cuestión social. La educación de la mujer," *El Siglo XIX*, December 5, 1894, 1.
72 José E. Iturriaga, *La estructura social de México* (Mexico: Fondo de Cultura Económcia, 1951), 60.

6 Escaping the *Carimbas*

An Intersectional Analysis of "Black" Middle-Class Trajectories in Colombia[1]

Mara Viveros-Vigoya

Introduction

For Black Colombians, upward social mobility is more complex than for the rest of the population, requiring an intersectional analysis that considers class as an experience bound up with race (and gender) and that introduces subjective and objective, micro- and macro-social aspects to relationships. As Fernando Henrique Cardoso said:

> for Black people, upward social mobility—apart from success in terms of greater social recognition, respectability, [...] financial security (and all that goes with it), and a higher social status—also means, in their eyes, losing their alienated condition inflicted upon them by society's discrimination against them because of their skin color.[2]

This infliction derives from racialization—a process of "producing bodies, social groups, culture, and ethnicities as if they were fixed categories of subjects, in racial terms."[3] We could say, keeping historical perspective and proportions, that racialization exists today no longer as a brand scorched onto a slave's skin as an indelible reminder of a painful and dishonorable socioracial situation, but as an internalized mark. Those inflicted with these marks wish to erase them, and to escape them through upward social mobility, avoiding, resisting, and fighting against the social discrimination against Black people in Colombian society. However, can upward mobility prevent racialization? Is it possible to continue being Black without being poor? Do class and race always mean the same thing in Colombia—for both men and women, at different historical moments, and in the country's various cultural regions?

For this study, we collected 18 family stories that included 54 biographies of men and women who identify as Black or Afro-Colombians from the middle-income sectors, and who belong to three generations of one of these families from the Pacífico and Caribe regions but who have lived in Bogotá at some point in their lives.[4] Although calculating the size of this sector is very difficult due to the lack of specific studies on this issue, according to the

DOI: 10.4324/9781003029311-8

ENDS (*Encuesta Nacional de Demografía y Salud*) survey on population and health (2015), 17% of Afro-Colombians were in the median quintile of income, representing 33% of the total if we joined together the top and median quintiles; at the same time, this same population is over-represented in the lower and bottom income quintile, reaching 55%.[5]

In this chapter, I intend to make an intersectional analysis of the upward social mobility of Colombia's Black population in the transition from the ideology of *mestizaje* to state multiculturalism, and the scope and limitations of these two "racial regimes,"[6] in order to eliminate the social inequalities suffered by Afro-Colombians. My aim is to explore the connections between individual paths of upward social mobility and the socio-historical processes linked to their insertion in Bogotá's middle classes.

I will refer to the process of upward social mobility of a small layer of the population of African descent that began in the 1930s, a time when the country was forced to find new forms of economic and industrial modernization and adopted a celebratory discourse about racial *mestizaje* as the essence of the Colombian identity.[7] The economic model in force since then entered a period of crisis in the 1980s, when Colombia embarked on a political and economic project that has since mixed multicultural and neoliberal policies and reforms. This has created a greater recognition of ethnic differences at the same time as a highly precarious job market. All of these changes have affected what we could call the "configuration" of the Black middle classes in contemporary Colombia, understood as an articulation of structures and social and individual dynamics that produce narratives related to racialization and class issues.

The Configuration of Colombia's Black Middle Classes: When, Where, and How?

Researchers focusing on the middle classes acknowledge the heterogeneity of this social group as an inescapable fact, and many studies on this issue point to the complexity of this category and propose an ad hoc definition of these sectors and their nomenclature.[8] In this research, the "middle classes" are understood as sectors occupying an intermediate position in society, whose members have university degrees and incomes that allow them a certain level of material comfort and a lifestyle that evokes symbolic universes and values related to modernity.

From a historical perspective, we can say that, in Colombia's case, society's structure began to change in the early twentieth century for various reasons: industrialization, wider access to formal education, the growth of urban populations, demographic changes, and women's increasing presence in the workforce. By the middle of the twentieth century, using employment information from the 1951 population survey, Louis Lebret estimated that "the middle class, consisting of owners of mid-sized stores, civil servants, and employees, owners of small and industrial firms, and owners of mid-sized farms, accounted for between 15% and 20% of all workers."[9] However, as Ezequiel Adamovsky points out,[10] the mere presence of these new worker categories does not necessarily imply the empirical presence of a middle class, which requires an identity that glues it together and differentiates it from other sectors of society defined as the upper or lower classes.

This chapter analyzes whether the process described also applied to Afro-Colombians, and, if so, when, where, and how did this population appear in sectors of society associated with an intermediate status in the social hierarchy, and acquire an awareness of itself in this position?

Some early examples of social mobility of people of African descent existed in eighteenth-century Colombia. After studying the wills of slaveowners in the Chocó region, the historian Sergio Mosquera registered the presence, in the city of Quibdó, of a tiny, slave-owning "Black elite" who "desired the lifestyle and refinement of the White elite and sought to mimic its customs."[11] Although the majority of the Black population was poor and lacked education, this select minority continued to exist well into. the twentieth century in the racially segregated city of Quibdó, with business interests in mining, agriculture, and small-sized enterprises. Their social standing enabled them to send their children to study in Cartagena and Medellín and to organize their own clubs, cultural events, and social gatherings.[12] In Cartagena, a sector of society consisting of artisans of mixed descent began to develop in the eighteenth and nineteenth centuries, and in several cases their children were able to attend universities, enter professions such as medicine and law, and obtain high-level jobs in government.[13]

Given these precursors, in the mid-twentieth century a generation of Black professionals from regions such as the Chocó, Norte del Cauca, and Caribe participated in national politics to defend the interests of the Black population in their regions. But it was only in the 1990s that it became possible to use "race" as a category to support political mobilization and to create independent political organizations; previously, social relationships were viewed through the prism of an ideology of *mestizaje* that precluded the possibility of framing the problems facing Black people in racial terms, and politics was carried out within political parties and traditional union organizations.[14]

Since then, a project of social and racial identity has begun to take shape and Colombia is seeing the emergence of a small sector of the Afro-Colombian population identifying as Black but aspiring to sever links from its traditional identification with poverty and marginalization. However, if we accept their objective position in labor relations, we can identify a significant increase in the proportion of the middle classes in employment during the period of the import-substitution policy.[15] This also benefitted this small population of Afro-Colombian employees, professionals, and technically qualified workers through social policies, welfare programs, and mortgages.[16] The consolidation of their incorporation into the class system—understood as the appropriation of certain attributes and capital to mark a social distinction and position—only became possible at the time of the import-substitution model's crisis and the implementation of structural reforms. The advent of the neoliberal regime had one of the strongest and most negative impacts of all on the Afro-Colombian population.

Fresneda writes that the middle classes has not seen a tendency of relative growth since the 1990s,[17] although its share of employment has fluctuated. The resulting social-class structure has perpetuated social segmentation and the unequal distribution of income by maintaining the proportion of working-class employees but without any increase in the middle-income sectors. For Afro-Colombians, the limitations of this context and the devastating impact of Colombia's armed conflict in Afro-Colombian regions have affected the development of this population's middle-income sectors to a greater extent.

Below I will undertake an intersectional (gender, class, generational, and regional) analysis of social mobility among Colombia's Black middle classes since the 1930s. I propose a period-based approach to the accounts gathered during the aforesaid research, based on the years when the interviewees were in their youth—which we defined as beginning at the age of 20, often a time when the interviewed young men and women migrated to a large city to continue their studies or to obtain a better job. These periods comprise two or three decades, and they are organized chronologically and marked by different historical events in Colombia that had an impact on its class structure. The themes and ideas do not necessarily disappear from one period to the next since many of them develop out of preceding events and extend over time. Each one of them enables a documentation this simultaneous process of racialization and class positioning.

The Promises of the Liberal Republic: 1930–1950

At the beginning of this period, the coffee industry was flourishing; industrialization was expanding; and the Liberal Party was in power, implementing social and political projects for education and universal suffrage. These combined circumstances promised a new opportunity for modernization, despite the global crisis.[18] Nevertheless, at the end of president Alfonso López's Pumarejo's first term in office and in the late 1930s, 57% of Colombian society consisted of campesinos and agricultural workers linked to social relations of production and forms of land ownership connected to historical processes and stark regional contrasts.[19] In this context, and given the country's racial and ethnic mix, some politicians, such as Miguel Jiménez López and Luis López de Mesa, considered it impossible to plan national progress centered on the country's middle classes. Instead, they drafted various draft laws to encourage European immigration to Colombia, though this plan failed to deliver results.[20]

A number of factors were instrumental in strengthening these intermediate sectors of society: the gradual decline of agriculture; growing urbanization; the emergence and expansion of services in trade, the public sector, and transport; and the creation of government departments, ministries, banks, postal offices and schools. Although these developments fell short of creating a middle-class identity, this social group's creation also required new class identities nourished by other imaginaries of gender to interpret these recent conditions of social existence. In particular, a new antagonism between the industrial and service sectors on the grounds of gender and class proved important to launch the social project of these middle classes.[21]

Ricardo López Pedreros described how industrialization and the expansion of the service sector—two economic processes that developed in parallel during this period—created conflicting meanings for those who were supposed to work in the industrial sectors and others who were supposed to be public-sector employees or have a job in the service sector.[22] In turn, this formed a landscape inhabited by two gendered subjects, the male employee and the office angel, who not only experienced these structural shifts in labor relations but also helped produce new social identities, defined outside the conflict between capital and labor. These identities not only arose from these new social experiences but were also the corollary of the meaning they acquired in a new discursive formation.

Although the liberal governments' promotion of education mainly benefitted the early generations of predominantly male, Black professionals during the 1930–1950 period, women also began to be allowed to enroll at Colombian universities following laws passed during these years.[23] Within this context of economic and cultural modernization that allowed women to participate more actively in society, the figure of Delia Zapata Olivella—a woman from the Caribe region—stood out as the first Black woman to enroll at a university in the 1940s, initially in Cartagena, and then in Bogotá.[24]

The few Black families who managed to save up enough money during this period migrated to the main provincial towns or large cities such as Bogotá, Medellín, and Cali. They wanted to give their children access to education, discovering that liberal professions and teaching provided the best opportunities for upward social mobility.[25] In the second half of the 1930s, the newly created teacher-training colleges (Escuelas Normales) gave young students unable to leave their regions the chance to receive training for them to participate in regional leadership processes as teachers. In other cases, the experience in training institutions such as the Escuela Normal Superior (Higher teacher training college, ENS)—a pioneering institution for the teaching of social sciences, founded in 1936 by President López Pumarejo—provided an opportunity for academic study. One notable beneficiary was Aquiles Escalante Polo (1923–2002), who came from Baranoa in the Atlántico region. In 1941, during Eduardo

Santos's liberal government, Escalante chose to study the new discipline of anthropology following the creation of the National Ethnological Institute (Instituto Etnológico Nacional), one of the three ENS institutes. Throughout his life, Escalante became both a ground-breaking researcher and teacher of ethnological studies on Colombia's Black populations. Despite his prolific and innovative work, he gained greater recognition abroad than within Colombia.[26]

As part of these economic, social, and axiological shifts taking place in Colombia, a group of university students from the Norte del Cauca and Caribe regions founded, in 1943, in Bogotá, the country's first ever "Black" movement. The historian Pietro Pisano considered that the Día del Negro and the Club Negro de Colombia set up by these young students represented the first attempts to acknowledge "Blackness" as a racial identity and to give the word a political meaning hitherto denied to it.[27] In regards to the middle classes, it is worth emphasizing that the Club Negro wanted Colombia's Black population to integrate more fully within Colombian society by extolling how "Black values" had influenced society, and rejecting this sector of society's "sense of inferiority," though without referring to social inequality or discrimination.

The Club Negro's discourse lay outside the dynamics of racism, understood by its founders as a phenomenon neither specific to Colombia nor a contemporary issue, but one that belonged to a past of slavery and related to countries such as the United States with their segregationist laws, and Colombian regions such as Norte del Cauca, where Black people were excluded from political and economic life and education. This group played a pioneering role by saying that it was not a contradiction to ask for the acknowledgement of specific values and to belong to the nation,[28] breaking away from the hypothesis that a country needed a homogenous society and culture to exist. After the Club Negro disappeared, several of its former members—who had already embarked on careers by then—set up another organization in 1947, the Centro de Estudios Afrocolombianos.[29]

The existence of Normales (teacher training colleges) for female students gave Black women an opportunity to gain an education and receive social recognition. One of our interviewees, a teacher called Ezequiela Urrutia who was born in the Chocó region in 1921, told us that she wanted to become a teacher because "I wanted to learn something! Something different from housework." She went to live with a brother who lived in the nearest large town and told him that she "was not there to serve him like a maid but to study. She enrolled at school and then at the Normal." So many women studied to become teachers that there ended up being an oversupply. School and university infrastructure could not cope with the numbers and many of the women teachers had to move to inland cities to seek job opportunities in schools—the only source of employment for women at the time, and one that offered plenty of work that was both legitimate and prestigious. The regional and national growth of the teaching profession led to a new social category for Afro-Colombians. This was different to the prevailing position of laborers and campesinos at that time, but also obviously distinct from the (White or mestizo) elite. It promised an escape from a fate that predestined manual labor in the fields and factories for men, and housework for women. Put differently, it helped draw gender and class distinctions by developing skills associated with mental work and moral attributes such as honesty and the sense of responsibility.

Carmen Serna Velásquez—a teacher from the Chocó who came to Bogotá to study at the Liceo Femenino de Cundinamarca "Mercedes Nariño" and later enrolled at the aforementioned Escuela Normal Superior—gives the following description:

> [...] It was hard when I first arrived at the Normal Superior. People were shocked [because] I was the first Black woman they had seen at the college: this was in early February 1947. I enrolled on a social studies course [...] and I worked really hard during the first year to get a good grade point average and in the second year I received a grant and my whole life changed [...].[30]

This new group of women teachers aspired for a better life than most of their peers and began to self-identify as members of an intermediate space in society and yearned for more than their social milieu allowed after working hard to open up new intellectual horizons. In turn, these teachers passed on to their children a worldview that prioritized learning. Our interviewees reveal that behind their various success stories was the presence of a mother-teacher who instilled in them the importance of studying and who conveyed the expectations of upward social mobility through educational achievements.[31]

For these women, becoming a teacher implied employment that, albeit modest, challenged the stereotype of gender and race that associated Black women with domestic service. The aim was to attain a more important and highly prized objective: social progress, "to do our duty for the country," in the words of one of our interviewees, who talked about opening up the way for "her people" to access formal education and to educate citizens, as part of a mestizo and modern nation that paradoxically excluded their ethnic group from its narrative. Unlike male teachers who saw their employment as a stepping-stone toward a wider world of politics and regional political leadership, their female counterparts generally worked as part of a social and solidary mission to challenge discrimination against those on the margins of society, striving to ensure the ethical values of the younger generations. In terms of their relation to the middle classes, it is worth pointing out that through the teaching profession, female teachers in particular embodied the moral discourse of the happy medium and assumed a role as intermediaries between the public and private realms, an important nucleus of meaning in defining the middle classes.

At the end of this period—in a country battered by violent clashes between liberals and conservatives following the assassination of the Liberal Party's leader Jorge Eliecer Gaitán on April 9, 1948—Black female teachers began to participate, prompted by the need to stand up to state-sponsored violence and to guarantee the survival and integrity of their families and communities. During this period of increasing discussions about domesticity and about women's identification with the mother figure, Black women teachers could aspire to a new social class.

Urban Dynamics and Intellectual Influences: 1950–1975

Gaitán's assassination and the criminalization of protests led to restrictions on collective and political movements that had developed over the previous decade in some sectors of Afro-Colombian society.[32] Within this context, there was a new influx of men and (in smaller numbers) women from the Pacífico and Caribe regions to the capital, seeking to start or finish their higher education in order to qualify for public-sector employment. Although medicine and the law continued to be the most requested career options by these migrants, they also chose disciplines that were non-existent in their regions of origin.[33] This cohort actively integrated into various social circles in Bogotá and as part of different support networks set up for Afro-Colombian migrants; in parallel, this group produced new interpretations of their experiences at a time of widespread economic growth.[34] The ability to find stable jobs with labor rights gave them considerable upward social mobility, facilitating their children's access to higher education.[35]

The Frente Nacional period had several consequences for the Afro-Colombian population. On the one hand, Black Colombians' political leadership lost its ability to attract popular support in a context dominated by pro-government nationalists and radical left-wing organizations; moreover, the influx of vast numbers of migrants stoked the circulation of "Afro-Colombian cultural counter-discourses through national networks and the Afro-diaspora of Black intellectuals and artists."[36] The city of Bogotá was a hub for the Afro-Colombians' working, political, and family lives, and for their ethnic and racial identity, perceived and described up until then in regional rather than racial or ethnic terms. Their experience in the country's capital gave them a chance to discover themselves as "Black," in communion with other migrants and in contrast to the predominantly mestizo or White citizens of Bogotá, who were culturally Andean.

Such was the case of Cicerón Flórez, a well-known journalist, whose studies in Law in Bogotá placed him contact with various Afro-Colombian intellectuals keen to champion Black people's contribution to the country's cultural life, or to make race an issue within the class struggle. Many people of this generation actively supported the Liberal Party, a historic reference point for this ethnic and racial group as the party that, when in power, implemented political, economic, and educational reforms that enabled them to play a more active role in national affairs.[37] Others, such as Flórez, were connected to left-wing parties, such as the Communist Party, which supported popular cultures.

Here are his memories:

> I joined the Dance group set up by Delia Zapata Olivella, sister of my great friend Manuel Zapata Olivella, as well as a television program called "Verbo y ritmo de América," in which Leonor González Mina, "la Negra grande de Colombia," also participated [...] We gave importance to Black culture, spoke about Nicolás Guillén and the folklore of the Caribe and the Pacífico regions. We also used to read all the literature by Black authors and poets: works by Colombian, African, and Cuban writers filled the libraries. [...] I joined the Communist youth that opposed the Rojas Pinilla's government and [...] the La Voz and Nuevo Mundo broadcasters by producing a series on Colombian history that ended up censored by that government.

His experience is fairly typical of the changes crystallizing in new identity discourses about ethnic and racial issues between the late 1970s and the late 1980s. And it also shows the genesis of "cultural and political projects that led to organizations and collectives of national importance in the 1970s."[38]

Tensions Between Class Identity and Ethno-Racial Identity: 1975–1985

After 1975, many Afro-Colombian men and women migrated to the capital due to the dismantling of the campesino economies in the Pacífico and Caribe regions; they also arrived from other cities and smaller provincial towns. Many of these internal migrants were women, due to the large number of female teachers; these new arrivals, both men and women, were seeking not only to study at university but also to fill teaching posts in primary and secondary schools, or else to work as national teaching supervisors and inspectors in Bogotá. They became a visible presence in the public-education system in Bogotá and around the country, and made a considerable impact. One notable aspect of this generation of Black men and women, who mainly came from the Chocó region, was their active involvement in the teaching profession's union movement, through the national teacher's organization called the Federación Colombiana de Educadores, and regional teacher associations such as the Asociación Distrital de Educadores, which also connected them to left-wing movements in the country's main cities.[39]

Thanks to their urban experiences, they could

> transfer to their new surroundings an incorporated sense of territorialities that produces a dynamic and tense relationship with the city [...], aware that they come from another part of the country with which they maintain emotional bonds, yet also conscious of their right to live fully their present lives in the capital.[40]

Accordingly, they began to call for an intermediate space in society based on their knowledge, hard work, experience, and training, but from the perspective of their ethnic and racial identity that connected them to other marginalized sectors. Knowing that they lived in a "colorist" society, they realized that whatever their social strata, they were identified as members of the popular classes, since they saw the ruling elites as "White" and hence as their oppressors. Upward social mobility was therefore often interpreted as a form of "Whitening" that distanced Black people from their backgrounds, making them feel that they no longer "needed solidarity with their home communities,"[41] given that assuming their Black identity meant appropriating—at least ideologically—a different social status than that associated with the middle classes.

This period saw an intensification of the dynamic that "Negritude had acquired in 1970s Colombia: in research, activism, and political groupings."[42] This reached a climax at the First Congress of Black Culture in the Americas, from August 24 to 28, 1977, an event organized by the Fundación Colombiana de Investigación Folclórica and the Centro de Estudios Afrocolombianos, led by Manuel Zapata Olivella, and the Asociación Cultural de la Juventud Negra Peruana. Participants at this Congress included some of the founders of the Club Negro of 1943 and various intellectuals and artists from America, Europe, and Africa, who had gathered for the first time in Latin America to discuss issues such as Negritude and racism. The establishment continued to oppose such initiatives, considering them to represent a challenge to Colombia's republicanism.

Discussions about linkages between class and race emerged during this first Congress and continued during the second Congress held in Panama in March 1980, revealing racial discriminations hidden behind the discourse that subsumed all distinctions in class differences.[43] Furthermore, these conversations connected the debate about ethnic and racial issues with social and economic inequalities affecting Afro-Colombians in their regions; and for the first time they explicitly recognized not only Black women's historical role in the various social struggles within their communities, but also the twofold oppression facing them on account of being Black and being women.[44] This same period saw a partial and contradictory questioning of White canons of beauty established over the years, and a relative "democratization" of the aesthetic ideals that opened up space for the acceptance of "Belleza negra" or Black beauty. This opening-up also reflects the unusual status given to the Afro-Colombian population and their participation in "modernity," a concept that encompasses issues such as their involvement in urban life and in the middle classes.[45]

Social tensions continued to exist between class and race, a topic addressed at this first Congress. In the 1980s, a remarkable statistic reveals that at least 15% of the teachers on the Distrito Capital's payroll came from the Chocó region.[46] It also shows that the teaching profession continued to be, particularly in the case of male teachers, a stepping-stone for future political careers in the capital in which they sought to resolve these conflicts. Such motivations explains why many decided on a political career. But it was also a matter of prestige, since politics promised a higher status and upward social mobility.[47]

Although Black men and women from the Caribe and Pacífico regions became eligible to join in the capital's intellectual and political life, Bogotá society continued to exclude them from the social imaginary about the middle classes, who were typically seen as being White or mestizo female office workers or secretaries, or employees in the service sector. Middle-class men were said to possess "mental and professional skills, personal independence and autonomy," and women "the ability to turn the office into an extension of the home."[48] Such characteristics were not generally attributed to Black men and women, who continued to be weighed down by the stereotypes that pigeon-holed them into forms of manual labor work that required physical strength, thus excluding them from jobs that required mental agility, intellectual specialization, and autonomy.

A variety of initiatives during this period sought to make a nationwide impact: the Centro para la Investigación y Desarrollo de la Cultura Negra; the *Negritud* and *Presencia Negra* magazines; seminars to train teachers about Black culture between 1978 and 1983; Juan Zapata Olivella's ephemeral presidential candidacy representing the Black political party called the Movimiento de las Negritudes y el Mestizaje de Colombia, built on a variety of ideological and organizational foundations. Some developed out of student groupings from the country's Buenaventura, Chocó, and Caribe regions, while others were planned as political organizations or platforms to promote critical thought.[49] They helped raise awareness about Black identity, racism, and the "colorism" in a Colombian society that confined Black people—whatever their social position—to a lower-class identity since the elite sectors were perceived as being "White" and therefore as oppressors.

At the end of this period, the policies and programs that gave the state a central role in planning and managing economic growth began to fall apart. The economic downturn, the adoption of liberalization models in other countries in the region, and external pressures to dismantle protectionism all combined to create a consensus about the need for a new development model that drastically reduced the state's role in the economy and imposed neoliberal, free-market reforms with disastrous consequences for most Afro-Colombians, as discussed below.

Neoliberal Multiculturalism, Opening and Closing Doors: 1985–2000

A new, politically based Afro-Colombian identity began to emerge along with the social movement of so-called Black communities following the implementation of new government policies promoting development in the Pacífico region, and the reappraisal of local and regional issues, ethnic identities, and environmental protection measures. The novelty of this situation was that paradoxically the Pacífico region began to modernize without going through a phase of urbanization but thanks to the acknowledgement and invention—in an anthropological sense—of ethnic particularism and a focus on ancestry.[50] Applying the concept of an ethnic group to the Black population, formerly the preserve of indigenous groups and entailing special legal safeguards, and the use of the "Black community" as a category, resulted in many urban Afro-Colombians not recognizing themselves in these changes since they referred to "ideas based on communities, traditions, and rural environments [that] were more (though not entirely) relevant to the realities of the Pacífico region."[51]

At the same time, the various agreements, peace processes, and negotiations underway in the second half of the 1980s, followed by the 1991 Constitution, opened up opportunities for various Afro-Colombian groups to join in the national discussion. Zulia Mena's political career provides a case in point. Mena was a member of the Committee that helped enact Law 70 of 1993 that regulated collective property ownership of Black communities and gave Afro-Colombians access to two seats in the Chamber of Representatives. In 1994, she was the first female congresswoman elected by the Circunscripción Especial de Comunidades Negras—an electoral constituency specially created to ensure electoral representation for Afro-Colombians—following a large-scale national vote; in this position she worked to prevent the forced displacement of Black populations.

From that point on, Afro-Colombian politics began to diversify and become more complex with the incorporation of various right-wing, left-wing, centrist, and even independent agendas, compared to any pre-existing ideology.[52] At the same time, the economy began to open up, based on neoliberal principles: from the 1990s onward, the state reversed the industrialization process, put the brakes on the creation of salaried manufacturing jobs, and incentivized independent employment in the service sector.[53] The social class structure shifted due to the increasing numbers of skilled workers and professionals, flexible working conditions, and the expansion of the self-employed population working in precarious conditions.[54] Within this new context, Black people did not have to blend into the culture of the mestizo and White population in order to be accepted; instead, they could defend their ethnic differences without the perception that these were a sign of social inferiority.

A small percentage of this population, descendants of the generation that arrived in Bogotá in the 1950s and 1960s, had been born and later studied in the Colombian capital, and in some cases undertook postgraduate studies abroad. Their positions as directors, highly skilled employees, professionals, and technically qualified workers, and their types of career, all indicate a change from the preceding generations. No longer limited to being lawyers or teachers, members of this new generation have become engineers (mainly working in systems), economists, business administrators, accountants, communications specialists, and scientists. Furthermore, they are not restricted to public-sector jobs, and some even work for foreign, private-sector firms. Within this cohort, many women have enjoyed successful careers and remained unmarried, asserting their independence and autonomy as distinctive aspects of the social experience of Black women, though on some occasions as an unwelcome corollary of their success.[55] Their careers have furthered the process begun by the office clerks in the service sector, who changed Colombian society's binary vision that put the country's oligarchy in opposition to the people, and who helped redefine gender models. They now identify with, and seamlessly fit into, this new economic, political, and social situation, one that also includes the middle-income sectors of society.

Another sector of this social group work in state agencies or in national and international NGOs that have implemented multicultural policies, negotiating and voicing the demands of Black communities. The wide participation of women in this section of the job market— particularly as "etnoeducadoras," teachers of ethnic issues—has boosted and given greater stability to their household incomes, swelling the ranks of the so-called middle classes. Nevertheless, despite these new spaces of social participation and successful careers, the vast majority of Afro-Colombians still suffer the same poverty and marginalization as ever, and the gender-based segmentation of the labor market continues to discriminate against women.[56]

Where Are the Black Middle Classes Headed in the New Millennium? By Way of a Conclusion

For the Afro-Colombian population's political agenda, one of the most important events of the twenty-first century was the third World Conference Against Racism, held in Durban, South Africa, in 2001. This event opened up a space of recognition for African descendants and supported their political project; it also reinforced changes brought about by multiculturalism and provided a pedagogical space for the fight against racism. However, this process has had paradoxical effects on Afro-Colombians' social mobility.

Some of the successful professionals whom we interviewed explained to us that their employment possibilities provided "the freedom to express their personality." They explained how their improved social status was the result of hard work and personal intellectual and professional merits. Neoliberal multiculturalism appears to have offered them the opportunity to join the "global middle class," making it possible to bridge the age-old gaps between capital and labor and to be rid of preference, discrimination, and both sexual and racial discrimination.[57] This was also President Uribe Vélez's political message when in 2007 he appointed a young Afro-Colombian woman to his cabinet as Minister of Culture. Paula Marcela Moreno's background—she was born in Bogotá to parents originally from the Cauca region who worked as public-sector civil servants—and her degree in Industrial Engineering followed by a postgraduate program abroad in Management Studies, makes her the personification of the "post-racial" image that Álvaro Uribe Vélez wanted to portray in his government.

Interestingly, few of these successful Afro-Colombians, regardless of their gender, take part in ethnicity-based organizations or movements, and in some cases they even question their legitimacy, perceiving them to exist for the benefit their leaders rather than for helping the Afro-Colombian population as a whole to get ahead. Such a generalization often conceals their unwillingness to validate the need of a specific job with Black populations to address their particular needs. Although some feel drawn to certain expressions of Afro-Colombian cultures, they consider it a private matter and that their position in society and in the workplace should be seen solely on the basis of merit and values associated with individual ability or competitiveness, removing any identity-based issue from the equation.

Other Afro-Colombian men and women, on the other hand, have sought to take full advantage of, and extend, the spaces opened up by this new recognition of their communities' "unique" contributions; some of them have even set up firms that focus on anti-racist ideas, discourses, and practices. Such is the case of some women owners of micro-enterprises supplying alternative natural products for Afro hair, one very specific means of reinforcing processes of subjective empowerment for Black women and to combat racist and sexist stereotypes about their physical appearance.[58] However, it is important to consider the effects of such projects. Despite their economic, political/pedagogic, and symbolic achievements, they leave open questions about their impact on the struggle against structural racism and on the degree of independence from the ruling elites and neoliberal capitalism.

In terms of the ethnic and racial identity of those who now self-identify with the middle class, we find that some express their desire to anchor their sense of belonging in attributes unrelated to ethnic or racial issues, or at least as characteristics that operate in a plural system of differences; others choose to explore their ancestry and aim to appropriate that culturalized difference fundamentally through food and music. Another, smaller group adopt, support, or defend expressions that seek to bring into view aesthetics, cultural, or religious customs linked to this ancestry. All of these contrasts and apparent contradictions reveal the ambiguities generated by the multiculturalist discourse, which has both opened and closed doors, within a neoliberal context.

Today we can argue that "education" about Black culture, generalized multiculturalism, or personal convictions have helped create an "Afro-Colombian" identity; we can either shun ethnic identification or apply a regional definition, such as "Caribeña," to avoid negative stereotypes and the position of radical otherness attributed to people from the Pacífico region, the area that received most attention during the 1990s. Similarly, there is now a greater public focus on structural and everyday racism, and on the struggles against racial discrimination. These problems are now being related to other issues such as the defense of lands, environmental protection initiatives, affirmative action in schools and in the workplace, guarantees for the peace process, or to tackle urban and police violence. These various ways of articulating Negritude are not incompatible with belonging to the middle classes,[59] but they do define the regional, generational, and sexual specificity of each intersectional experience of race and class.

In any case, the only Afro-Colombians now in a position to enjoy social recognition, respect, financial stability, and prestige, as indicated by Cardoso, are those who adapted most successfully to a development model that promotes individual entrepreneurship and discourages the possibility of creating a collective path leading to social progress. We cannot overlook the widening gulf between this relatively privileged sector and the majority of the Afro-Colombian population, expelled from their lands and driven to the cities due to political and economic violence. As such, we can assert that neither universalist republicanism with its ideology of *mestizaje*, nor neoliberal multiculturalism, with its rhetorical support of diversity, have managed to erase the enduring marks left by the *carimbas* on Colombia's Black population as a long-lasting remnant of their status as "non-beings"[60] that has been so hard to remove.

Notes

1 I carried out the bibliographical research for this chapter while supported by a grant from the Center of Advanced Latin American Studies (Centro de Estudios Avanzados Latinoamericanos CALAS) to carry out the research entitled "Las clases medias 'negras' en Colombia: desigualdades sociales, identidades étnico-raciales y experiencias de interseccionalidad," between August 2019 and February 2020. A preliminary version of this chapter was presented as a lecture at the Universidad de la Habana during the seminar called "Republicanismo popular y racialización en los Andes y el Caribe," on January 8, 2020, and at the Biblioteca Iberoamericana Octavio Paz de Guadalajara on January 24, 2020. *Carimbas* were brands applied with hot irons on African slaves, certifying their legal introduction to the New World and ownership by slave owners.

2 Cardoso 1960, 584, quoted in Daisy Macedo de Barcellos, "Família e ascensão social de Negros em Porto Alegre," (PhD diss., Museu Nacional da Universidade Federal do Rio de Janeiro, 1996), 112.

3 Alejandro Campos García, "Racialización, racialismo y racismo: un discernimiento necesario," *Universidad de La Habana* 273 (January–June 2012): 184–199, 185.

4 For an analysis of the differences in trajectories in Medellín or Cali, cities which were also destinations for migrants, see Peter Wade, *Blackness and Race Mixture: The Dynamics of Racial Identity in Colombia* (Baltimore, MD: JHU, 1993) and Fernando Urrea Giraldo, "La conformación paulatina de clases medias negras en Cali y Bogotá a lo largo del siglo XX y la primera década del XXI," *Revista de Estudios Sociales* 39 (2011): 24–41.

5 Mara Viveros Vigoya, Franklin Gil Hernández, Pietro Pisano, and Klara Hellebrandová, "Grandes Esperanzas. Memorias de raza, género y clase en familias afrodescendientes del siglo XX," Manuscrito Convocatoria de Investigación Orlando Fals Borda – 2017 Apoyo a Proyectos de investigación docentes, 2019.

6 By "racial regimes" I refer to forms of governance that involve a form of racialization of populations and subjects without always explicitly using the category of race.

7 George Reid Andrews, *Afro-Latin America, 1800–2000* (New York: Oxford University Press, 2004); Wade, *Blackness*.

8 Klaus-Peter Sick, "El concepto de clases medias: ¿Noción sociológica o eslogan político?" in *Clases medias; nuevos conceptos y estudios comparativos en Europa y América Latina*, eds. Ezequiel Adamovsky, Sergio Visacovsky, and Patricia Vargas (Buenos Aires: Ariel, 2014).

9 Lebret 1958 quoted in Oscar Fresneda, "Evolución de la estructura de clases sociales en Colombia, 1938–2010. ¿Han crecido las clases medias?," *Sociedad y Economía* 33 (2017): 225.

10 Ezequiel Adamovsky, "'Clase media': reflexiones sobre los (malos) usos académicos de una categoría," *Nueva Sociedad* (October 2013): 49.

11 Sergio Antonio Mosquera, *Quibdó: un sueño en construcción* (Quibdó: Alcaldía Municipal de Quibdó, 2012), 34.

12 Carlos Arturo Caicedo Licona, *El Chocó por dentro* (Medellín: Lealón, 1980); Mosquera, *Quibdó*; Pietro Pisano, *Liderazgo político 'negro' en Colombia, 1943–1964* (Bogotá: Universidad Nacional de Colombia, 2012); Peter Wade, "La relación Chocó-Antioquia: Un caso del colonialismo interno?" in *Colombia Pacífico*, vol. 2, ed. Pablo Leyva (Bogotá: Fondo para la Protección del Medio Ambiente 'Jose Celestino Mutis' – FEN Colombia, 1993).

13 Sergio Paolo Solano, "Los sectores sociales medios en la historia social colombiana del siglo XIX," *Memorias: Revista digital de Historia y Arqueología desde el Caribe colombiano* 7, no. 13 (November 2010): 1–38.

14 Agustín Laó-Montes, *Contrapunteos diaspóricos. Cartografías políticas de Nuestra AfroAmérica* (Bogotá: Universidad Externado de Colombia, 2020); Pisano, *Liderazgo político 'negro.'*

15 Fresneda, "Evolución."

16 Fernando Urrea Giraldo, "Dinámica de reestructuración productiva, cambios institucionales y políticos y procesos de desregulación de las relaciones asalariadas: el caso colombiano," in *Trabajo y modelos productivos en América Latina*, eds. Enrique de la Garza Toledo and Julio César Neffa (Buenos Aires: CLACSO, 2010).

17 Fresneda, "Evolución"; Oscar Fresneda, "Regímenes de acumulación, estructura de clases sociales y desigualdad en Colombia 1810–2010" (PhD diss., Universidad Nacional de Colombia, 2016).

18 Daniel Pécaut, *L'Ordre et la violence: évolution socio-politique de la Colombie entre1930 et 1953* (Paris: Éd.de l'École des hautes études en sciences sociales, 1986).
19 Fresneda, "Evolución," 217.
20 A. Ricardo López-Pedreros, "'We have everything and we have nothing': Empleados and Middle-Class Identities in Bogota: 1930–1955" (Master's thesis, Virginia Tech, 2001); Pisano, *Liderazgo político*; Fernando Urrea Giraldo, Carlos Viáfara López, and Mara Viveros-Vigoya, "Del mestizaje blanco al multiculturalismo triétnico. Raza y etnicidad en Colombia," in *Pigmentocracias. Color, etnicidad y raza en América Latina*, eds. Edward Telles and Regina Martínez (Mexico City: FCE, 2019).
21 A. Ricardo López-Pedreros, "Empleados, mujeres de oficina y la construcción de las identidades de clase media en Bogotá, 1930–1950," *Anuario Colombiano de Historia Social y de la Cultura* 30 (2003): 257–279.
22 López-Pedreros, "Empleados"; A. Ricardo López-Pedreros, "'Nosotros también somos parte del pueblo': gaitanismo, empleados y la formación histórica de la clase media en Bogotá, 1936–1948," *Revista de Estudios Sociales* 41 (2011): 84–105.
23 In Lucy Cohen, *Colombianas en La Vanguardia* (Medellín: Editorial Universidad de Antioquía, 2001), xiv.
24 Massa 2008 and Ortega 2002 quoted in Urrea Giraldo, "La conformación," 30.
25 Mara Viveros Vigoya and Franklin Gil Hernández, "Género y generación en las experiencias de ascenso social de personas negras en Bogotá," *Maguaré* 24 (January 1, 2010): 99–130.
26 Rudy Amanda Hurtado-Garcés, "'Quítate de mi escalera, no me hagás oscuridad': imágenes de lo 'negro' en la antropología colombiana 1930–1970," *Revista CS* 30 (January–April 2020): 141–172.
27 Pisano, *Liderazgo político*.
28 Pietro Pisano, "Movilidad social e identidad 'negra' en la segunda mitad del siglo XX," *Anuario Colombiano de Historia Social y de la Cultura* 41, no. 1 (2014): 179–199.
29 Pisano, *Liderazgo político*; Carlos A. Valderrama, "La diferencia cultural negra en Colombia. Contrapúblicos afrocolombianos," *Revista CS* 29 (September 12, 2019): 209–242.
30 Interviewed by Mercedes Angola in Julia Mercedes Angola Rossi and Maguemati Wabgou W., *Llegamos a Bogotá: Décadas 1940–1950–1960* (Bogotá: Universidad Nacional de Colombia, 2015), 21.
31 Viveros Vigoya and Gil Hernández, "Género y generación."
32 Valderrama, "La diferencia."
33 Rossi and Wabgou W., *Llegamos*.
34 Fresneda, "Regímenes de acumulación."
35 Viveros Vigoya and Gil Hernández, "Género y generación."
36 Valderrama, "La diferencia," 219–220.
37 Pisano, *Liderazgo político*.
38 Valderrama, "La diferencia," 225.
39 Urrea Giraldo, "La conformación."
40 Santiago Arboleda, *Le han florecido nuevas estrellas al cielo. Suficiencias íntimas y clandestinización del pensamiento afrocolombiano* (Cali: Poemia, 2016), 202.
41 As expressed by Marino Viveros, quoted in Silvia Valero, "*Los negros se toman la palabra.*" *Primer Congreso de la Cultura Negra de las Américas: debates al interior de las comisiones y plenarias* (Bogotá: Editorial Pontificia Universidad Javeriana, 2020), 124.
42 Valero, "*Los negros se toman la palabra,*" 55.

43 Valero, "*Los negros se toman la palabra*," 55.
44 Valderrama, "La diferencia," 228.
45 Pietro Pisano, "Blancos, no blancos, casi blancos. Cuerpo, color y belleza en Colombia," (PhD diss., Universidad Nacional de Colombia, 2019), https://repositorio.unal.edu.co/handle/unal/75792.
46 Urrea Giraldo, "La conformación," 34.
47 Wade, *Blackness*, 315, 324.
48 López-Pedreros, "Empleados."
49 Pisano, "Movilidad social"; Arboleda, *Le han florecido*; Valderrama, "La diferencia."
50 Odile Hoffmann, "Sociedades y Espacios en el Litoral Pacífico Sur Colombiano (Siglos XVIII–XX)," in *Tumaco: haciendo ciudad. Historia, identidad y cultura*, eds. Manuela Álvarez, Michel Agier, Odile Hoffmann, and Eduardo Restrepo (Bogotá: ICAN/IRD/Universidad del Valle, 1999), 19.
51 Pedro J. Velandia and Eduardo Restrepo, "Estudios afrocolombianos: balances de un campo heterogéneo," *Tabula Rasa* 27 (July–December 2017), 174.
52 Andrews, *Afro-Latin America*; Laó-Montes, *Contrapunteos*.
53 Fresneda, "Evolución."
54 Fresneda, "Evolución."
55 Mara Viveros Vigoya, "Social Mobility, Whiteness, and Whitening in Colombia," *The Journal of Latin American and Caribbean Anthropology* 20, no. 3 (2015): 496–512.
56 Urrea Giraldo, Viáfara López and Viveros-Vigoya, "Del mestizaje."
57 López-Pedreros, "'Nosotros."
58 Mara Viveros Vigoya and Krisna Ruette-Orihuela, "Care, Aesthetic Creation, and Anti-Racist Reparations," in *Care and Care Workers – A Latin American Perspective*, eds. Nadya Araujo Guimares and Helena Hirata (New York: Springer, forthcoming).
59 Eduardo Restrepo, "Articulaciones de negridad: políticas y tecnologías de la diferencia en Colombia," in *Hegemonía cultural y políticas de la diferencia*, eds. Alejandro Grimson and Karina Bidaseca (Buenos Aires: CLACSO, 2013)
60 Frantz Fanon, *Peau noire masques blancs* (Paris: Éditions du Seuil, 1952).

Part II

Labor, Consumption, and Political Disparities

Introduction to Part II

Claudia Stern

Figure II.2 Family portrait, Concepción, Chile, 1958. Private collection.

DOI: 10.4324/9781003029311-9

In the early 1900s, as the countries of Latin America were preparing to celebrate their independence centenaries, although the prevailing social narrative still connected the middle classes to the oligarchy, deeper issues such as the Social Question were arising and awakening new sensibilities across different societies. The repercussions for social and occupational identities (sustained by rights and duties) were generating new forms of consumption and distinctions between men and women within the embryonic sectors in the middle, affecting their evolution during the first half of the twentieth century. As such, a study of the period offers insights into the region's social, cultural, and labor history and helps to disentangle its complex labor structures within broader historical issues that transcend dichotomous positions.

The realities of countries in the north and south of the region developed at differing paces. Mexico's middle classes evolved at an early stage and the Revolution, in turn, led to new expressions of middle-classness; further south, Peronism was key to the differentiation of the various sectors of the Argentinian middle classes some years later. The chapters in this part of the book also reveal a convergence in the symbolic universe of class, transcending *a priori* interpretations and taking into account the essential differences of gender when examining certain issues. By taking this approach, the texts propose new meanings, making the middle class a subject of study that creates new perspectives on historical problems inherent to modernity, on the development of power structures, and on the nationalist capitalism being forged at the time.

The five chapters in this part share a view of class as a subjective expression of modernity and highlight the struggle for differentiation that was a constant part of the class experience. In turn, differentiation pointed to individualism, a particular aspect of the middle-class ethos that we can observe variously in this sector of society among public-sector employees in Mexico, among store clerks in both Argentina and Mexico, within middle-class marital aspirations in Mexico, and as part of efforts by members of the middle class to differentiate themselves, as expressed by Tango lyrics in Argentina.

Differentiation, often an intrinsic part of middle-class existence, is axiomatic in the study of social class in general. As such, the differentiation revealed in the well-researched, original, and suggestive examination conducted by the authors in this section highlights the particular aspects of the inter-class, inter-gender, and intra-class experience. Decency, morality, and modesty, together with job-related knowledge and skills, are common aspects of individuals' aspirations to join a desired class or to maintain their place within the social hierarchy. As subjectivities, these differentiations are more imaginary than quantifiable, and are by no means exclusive to the middle classes: rather, they are inherent to the very concept of class itself. This is crucial to the suitability of the middle classes as an object of study and highlights their peculiarities, interrelations, and their shared similarities with other social groups.

In addition to aspirations for differentiation, material stability is central to the various middle-class struggles analyzed in this part. As seen broadly in this section, the aim to materialize their class position encompassed from social tasks as marriage in Mexico, to structural aspects related to the role they played on the labor structures in general, and in Mexican bureaucracy in particular. In Argentina, the limitations and precariousness of the working conditions of public clerks shed light on other aspects that actually contributed to their material instability which deepen according to gender, contrasting with the imaginary of the public clerks in Mexico and the skills needed to be materialized to get access and keep their jobs, elements that constantly juxtapose with the embodiment of the us and the Others, as seen from a different viewpoint also across the Tango imaginary. The link to material stability can prove instrumental in broader identifications of social processes in "classless" or "class-bound" societies,[1] and the political developments contextualized here are suggestive in this regard. The authors historicize the classes in question, thus proposing ways of producing a conceptually plural history.[2]

The five chapters debunk myths linked to specific sectors commonly equated to the middle classes, including the culture of salaried store clerks among the Argentinian middle classes, and modern complaints such as *surmenage* or stress; subjective narratives on the border between the popular classes and the "bourgeoisie," identified by analysis of Tango from the inter-war period (again in Argentina); the consolidation of love as a form of modern, middle-class consumption in Mexico; the particular skills and everyday life of male store clerks working in Mexico City's clothing emporia; and the development of the bureaucratic apparatus that gave structure to employment within the Mexican state. The various chapters help elucidate political processes that combine both agency and contingency,[3] as well as the narratives of inclusion and exclusion developed by the middle classes themselves.

The contributions in this part of the book also define the class experience in its connection to particular locales—experience that leads to tensions that highlight not only the inequalities between men and women in similar employment, but also how masculinity and class overlapped as an idealized model in the public sphere,[4] along with the inherent tensions in their connection to space. Hence we have women employees, women with professional ambitions, women who wrote music under male pseudonyms, women "in love with love" who were disparaged and discounted—women with unequal rights and/or blamed for a lack of taste from a class perspective. Ultimately, they embodied the image of the modern woman in an advancing world that inspired dreams and hopes of inclusion, yet it was the image of the modern, urban man and his smart appearance that determined the capitalist democratic experience. The labor structure that over the decades gradually transformed access, rights, and duties ultimately benefited men more than women. Perpetuating the man's perspective, the same official narratives also point to an analysis of agency developed by these sectors that prevailed throughout most of the twentieth century.

Notes

1 Neville Kirk, "Decline and Fall, Resilience and Regeneration: A Review Essay on Social Class," *International Labor and Working-Class History*, No. 57 (Spring 2000), pp. 88–102, 98.
2 Geoff Eley and Keith Neild, *El futuro de la clase en la Historia ¿Qué queda de lo social?* Translation by Mónica Burguera (Valencia: PUV, 2010), 230.
3 Dror Wahrman, *Imagining the Middle Class: The Political Representation of Class in Britain, c. 1780–1840* (New York: Cambridge University Press, 1995), 10.
4 José Olavarría, *Sobre hombres y masculinidades: "Ponerse los pantalones"* (Santiago de Chile: Ediciones Universidad Academia Humanismo Cristiano, 2017), 21.

7 Sales Knowledge, Labor Mobility, and Working-Class Identity

Store Clerks (Argentina, 1900–1940)[1]

Graciela Queirolo

In 1937, Academias Pitman published one of its many advertisements promoting training courses for store clerks (Figure 7.1). This was one of the training institute's frequent strategies in the early 1930s to take advantage of the flourishing trade press and the population's increasing literacy.

In this advertisement, Academias Pitman invited women and men to undertake one of its training courses for store clerks to make them eligible for "skilled employment." It depicted manual labor as a gloomy world of physical effort, personified by men carrying heavy loads or pushing wheelbarrows, or by the dexterity of a woman sitting behind the sewing machine. On the other hand, white-collar work—represented by draftsmen, bookkeepers, and women typists—was a brightly lit realm where skills learned through study shone through. The illustration shows an interesting abstraction of the division of labor, according to trade and gender, in the urban job market.

I am interested in more detailed research into the different meanings given to training, in particular the shift from manual labor to white-collar employment or, to be more precise, the consequences of the transition from unskilled to skilled jobs. Leaving to one side how the labor market exactly defines skilled employment, while acknowledging the fact that every job requires a learning process of varying degrees of complexity, I seek to understand perceptions of this labor mobility, and the significance of this phenomenon for society.

The period of economic growth catalyzed by Argentina's capitalist modernization in the late nineteenth century was one of the many drivers of the expanding private bureaucratic structures that became essential for the economy's proper functioning. In the cities, a proliferation of new workplaces such as offices and large stores required a skilled workforce represented by male and female employees. These skilled jobs called for a mastery of certain administrative, literacy-based competences such as shorthand, typing, and basic accounting. Along with these areas of expertise, the "modern" aspects of these new jobs necessitated an understanding of how to use mechanical devices such as telephones, typewriters,

DOI: 10.4324/9781003029311-10

Figure 7.1 Mundo Argentino, 10 November 1937.

Source: Courtesy of the Hemeroteca de la BNMM.

calculating machines, and cash registers. The market distinguished between "provisional" employees, who lacked the required skills, and their "specialized" counterparts, who had training and aspirations for a career that would bring them material comforts. Therefore, the issue of upward labor mobility has the world of the employees as a social background.

Argentinian historiographical studies have largely overlooked this sector of society, due to its complexities. Instead, labor historiography has focused on factory workers, although it has explored employees' union organizations, especially in analyzing the origins of Peronism.[2] For its part, the historiography of the middle classes has directed its gaze toward employees, while Women's History—in common with gender studies, and reviving an interest in women as protagonists—has sparked debates about the conceptualization of work and given visibility to female employees.[3] Finally, the issue is further complicated by the differences between employees working in private-sector offices and stores, and those who held public-sector government jobs. Despite similarities between the two groups in terms of their skill sets, political clientelism was influential in the case of public-sector employees, unlike in the private sector. Although this subject is on the radar of academic study, further research remains pending.[4]

Employees and the middle class are closely linked. I will mention studies on certain Latin American societies in the first half of the twentieth century. Employees in Peru, Colombia, and Mexico (either in the public or private sector, depending on each research project) defined themselves as members of the middle class. Various historical studies exist on these self-perceptions, which evolved from specific national circumstances, clearly seeking to reject any purely theoretical conceptual approaches. In these three cases, I will emphasize how employees constructed their middle-class identity by differentiating themselves in the labor market by working in white-collar jobs that required "intellectual" or "mental" skills as opposed to manual duties. They also set themselves apart in their attire and lifestyles as evidenced in their housing and children's education.[5] In the case of Chile, public-sector employees (known as *funcionarios*) also assumed a middle-class identity and the concepts of "dignity" and "sacrifice" helped them resolve the contradiction between their situation as wage earners (something they had in common with the working class) and their consumer habits (which overlapped to some extent with the upper classes).[6] Analyses of private-sector employees also connected them to the middle class.[7]

In Argentina, public- and private-sector employees also had connections to the middle class, albeit of different kinds. In his pioneering studies, Gino Germani defined employees (people who used "mental faculties even while doing automatic, routine jobs") as belonging to a "dependent middle class" developed thanks to their own and their families' "upward mobility."[8] In this regard, José Luis Romero argued that "the growth and transmutation of the middle classes was the most surprising and significant urban phenomenon to evolve in the wake of economic transformations in cities," and they numbered among "those who worked as clerks in stores and offices."[9] According to both authors, the upward social mobility of some white-collar employees, who had more intellectually demanding duties, ushered them into the middle class. In other words, labor mobility led to social mobility. Leandro Gutiérrez and Luis Alberto Romero took this interpretation further by connecting employees to the popular sectors of society benefitting from an upward social mobility.[10] More recently, analyses by Enrique Garguin and Ezequiel Adamovsky criticized previous interpretations by contending that a middle-class identity only developed as late as the 1940s as a result of the profound socio-cultural changes brought about by Peronism. In particular, Adamovsky emphasized how upward labor mobility was not necessarily a precursor for social mobility that redefined the person's social background.[11] Furthermore, although "middle class" existed as an expression in the first decades of the twentieth century in Argentina, male and female employees did not see themselves (nor were they perceived by their contemporaries) as belonging to the middle class but as members of the working class. As I mentioned previously, training institutes such as Academias Pitman targeted their courses at "those who lived off their wages," while the federation of store clerks (Federación de Empleados de Comercio, FEC), a union organization that defended the rights of private-sector employees since the 1920s, classified them as all belonging to the working class engaged in a struggle against employers' abuses.[12]

In the following pages, I will begin by analyzing the state's perspective on employees' characteristic labor mobility. For that purpose, I will concentrate on private-sector employees by analyzing the Code of Commerce reforms that culminated in the approval of Law 11.729 (1934). These legal debates strengthened the working-class identity of store clerks because it highlighted their vulnerabilities and justified their protection under law. Secondly, I will explore gender relations within the world of the wage-earning store clerk (known in Spanish at the time as an "asalariado comercial") to indicate the state's support for androcentrism, prioritizing the identity of the breadwinning male. As a result, although legislators acknowledged that women worked in stores and offices, they overlooked their particular needs and endorsed labor inequality.

Who Were the Store Clerks?

By analyzing censuses we can reconstruct certain estimates about the number of Argentinians employed both in shops as store clerks ("empleados de mostrador") and in private-sector businesses as office workers ("empleados de escritorio"): surveys recorded 28,859 employees in 1895, rising to 161,694 in 1914, and reaching 854,966 by 1947 (Table 7.1). We can confirm this increase in absolute numbers by comparing it to the total of the salary-earning population aged over 14: employees accounted for 1.75% of this population in 1895, 5% in 1914, and 13.64% in 1947. Although these employees were predominantly male, there was also a sharp proportional rise of women in these jobs, despite being fewer in total. Legislators were clearly aware both about this workforce's growth and gender configuration: in 1929, the socialist deputy referred to the "tens of thousands of men and women working in all kinds of activities related to the vast and complex world of commerce."[13]

Table 7.1 Argentine Republic (AR). Employees (private sector): Women and men, 1895–1947

AR	*Total*	*Women*	*Men*	*Total (%)*	*Women (%)*	*Men (%)*
1895	28,859	981	27,878	100	3	97
1914	161,694	12,536	148,958	100	8	92
1947	854,966	107,354	747,612	100	13	87

Data retrieved from the *Segundo Censo de la República Argentina. Mayo 10 de 1895. Tomo II. Población* (Buenos Aires: Taller Tipográfico de la Penitenciaría Nacional, 1898), CXCI; *Tercer Censo Nacional. Levantado el 1 de junio de 1914. Tomo IV. Población* (Buenos Aires: Talleres Gráficos de L. J. Rosso y Cía., 1916), 390 and 393; Presidencia de la Nación. Ministerio de Asuntos Técnicos. *IV Censo General de la Nación, Tomo I: Censo de Población* (Buenos Aires: Dirección Nacional del Servicio Estadístico, 1952), 31.

The labor market's new areas of specialization clearly distinguished between the type of work for male and female employees compared to their counterparts in manual jobs. Instead of activities mainly requiring physical or motor skills, they carried out more mentally demanding work that required literacy. Contractual terms also varied between employees (on monthly contracts) and manual laborers (hired on a daily or weekly basis), and this affected how they received their pay: employees received a monthly salary whereas laborers earned a weekly or sometimes daily wage. The regularity of a monthly salary, as opposed to laborers' intermittent weekly pay packet, also enhanced the status of employees.

Many training institutes for salespersons drew attention to both of these characteristics by calling for "men and women who have endured physically exhausting, or poorly paid, dead-end jobs, and who seek a comfortable, dignified, and well-remunerated occupation."[14] These "physically exhausting," "poorly paid," and "dead-end" jobs were generally synonymous with manual labor, although in the 1930s this category of employment included work described as "improvisada" that did not require prior training. In contrast, "comfortable," "well remunerated," and "dignified" occupations referred to work in sales which did need qualifications.

A gender division existed among office and store clerks in the labor market. In the large stores that opened in Argentina's largest cities, men and women worked as sales clerks or "empleados de mostrador," although it was possible for members of both sexes to have a career (starting out as "cadetes" before rising up the ranks to become a "primer vendedor"), men continued to hold the most senior positions. Moreover, women earned lower salaries despite working in the same category of sales job.[15] And while men generally carried out accountancy work in offices (as bookkeepers, for example), women had more administrative roles (such as typists). In this sphere, some workers enjoyed a smoother climb up the social ladder. But whereas men could rise to become directors, women ended up as secretaries. In short, there was salary inequality between men and women in offices.[16] We can explain this gender division in jobs by analyzing the social meanings given to masculine and feminine identities: men constructed their masculinity around the figure of the breadwinning male, while women developed their femininity in the role of the wife and mother. Within the working class, this translated into a situation in which salaried employment became a core activity for men, enabling them to earn a salary that made them providers for their families. By contrast, for women, earning a salary was something exceptional because their presence in the job market implied an addition to, or actual competition with, schedules and jobs that were impossible to carry out. The wife and mother had to take care of domestic chores and the children; women took jobs to meet pressing material needs in the absence of the provider; it was a temporary situation, a phase in their lives, complementing or "helping out" the family to make ends meet. For all these reasons, the labor market propagated androcentric ideas about salaried employment, providing the basis for the aforementioned unequal relationships that were detrimental to women.

Promises of "comfortable," well-remunerated," and "dignified" occupations, as well as possible professional careers for women and men who worked as employees, had their own difficulties that inevitably put them on a par with the financial dependency of manual laborers. Firstly, they faced the expense of purchasing suitable clothing for their jobs. A smart appearance ("buena presencia") was essential and consumed a large part of their earnings. The following article appeared in *La Prensa* in 1901:

> The employees of those stores [earn] an income on a scale ranging from $60 to $100 pesos. [...] We must bear in mind that these store workers must be dressed decently and this implies an expense [...] that eats into their wage [...] Even for those store clerks who earn [...] $150 pesos, life is hard; the majority of those who attain this relatively well-paid employment are men who are married and have children; families who must be provided for, and given clothes and shoes.[17]

This reveals that the cost of dressing decently made such an impact, even on a relatively generous salary, that it threatened the husband and father's role of provider. Some 20 years later, typists and cashiers in the city of Buenos Aires admitted spending between 25% and 28% of their monthly income on clothes, shoes, and accessories.[18]

There were also voices claiming that working in stores and offices was harmful; they challenged the view that this kind of work was "comfortable" and caused less wear and tear to the body in comparison to other more physical forms of labor. In the 1910s, advertisements appeared for tonics that warned of the exhaustion produced by the mental activity ("trabajo mental") that had the undesirable effect of causing premature aging. One such notice, published in the weekly magazine *Caras y Caretas*, posed the question: "Did you know that three hours of continuous mental activity destroys more tissues and consumes more energy than an entire day of manual labor?" The text referred to office clerks as workers who used their mental faculties ("obreros del cerebro") and portrayed the gender division of office jobs—the bookkeeper and the typist (Figure 7.2).

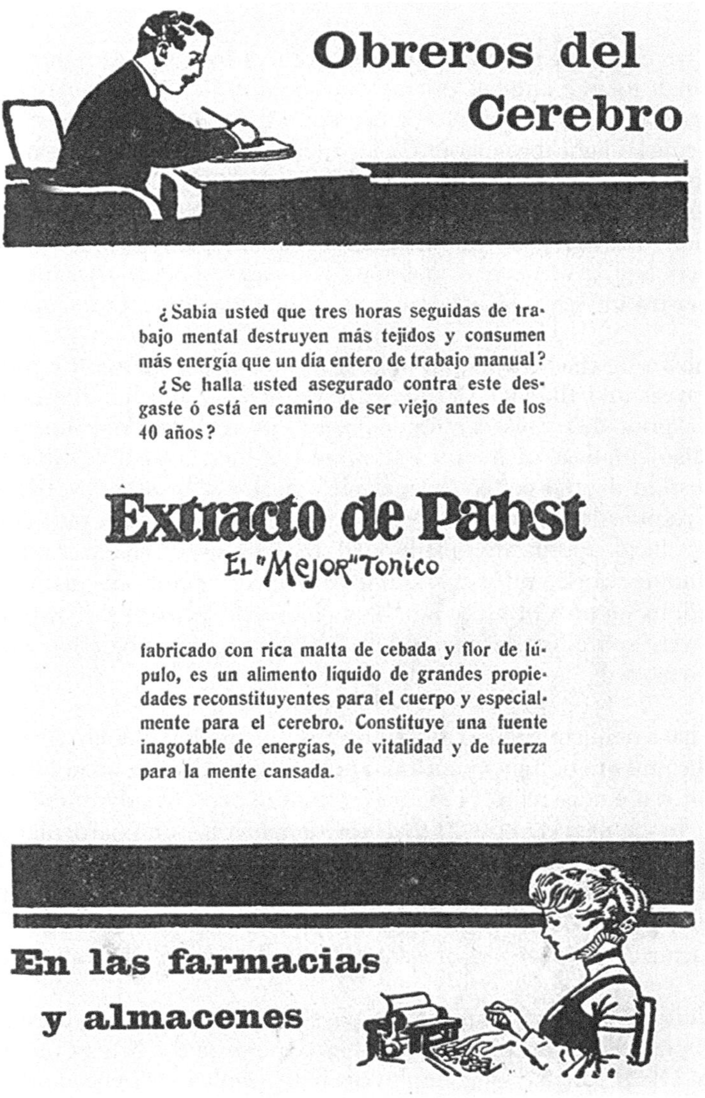

Figure 7.2 *Caras y Caretas*, 26 March 1910.

Source: Courtesy of the Hemeroteca de la BNMM.

In the 1930s, these ideas were still prevalent and advertisements for tonics promised to treat physical and mental impairments ("debilidad cerebral y física") as well as depression ("depresión nerviosa") that affected employees in particular with neurasthenia.[19]

In between announcements, Leopoldo Bard, a deputy for the Unión Cívica Radical party, submitted a draft law in 1923 to regulate the poor working conditions faced by salespersons:

> Overcrowding is a problem in most offices because the premises are too small for the number of employees and visitors, leading to a lack of fresh air; daylight does not penetrate the interiors thus necessitating artificial light throughout the day. Hapless employees must also spend long hours hunched over books, engaged in mentally exhausting duties. Office clerks are victims of "surmenage" [stress] in insalubrious conditions and lack proper nourishment—circumstances that contribute to a very high percentage of pulmonary diseases, tuberculosis, and asthma. Gastro-intestinal illnesses are also common among office employees.[20]

As shown by this extract, an unhealthy workplace caused by too many employees and the lack of adequate ventilation and lighting combined with a poor diet caused pulmonary and gastro-intestinal illnesses. The text also emphasized the mental strain ("esfuerzo mental") that caused exhaustion diagnosed as "surmenage" or stress. In other words, offices were responsible for causing employees to fall sick with particular ailments. Bard specifically mentioned the illnesses related to mentally demanding work and careers, underlining the emotional damage they caused; in support of his views, he included the accounts of two doctors who were specialists in mental health ("clínica neurológica"), whom he had consulted:

> I have frequently found that store clerks or employees who have risen up the ranks to occupy more senior positions, heads of households who are often about to retire, present clear signs of nervous exhaustion.
>
> In my medical notes, I find store employees—and particularly managers and accountants working in banks—exhausted by their duties and anxieties, revealing that they had all suffered neurasthenia when they started out in their jobs, under pressure to work harder and harder, facing every greater worries to make up for lack of experience.[21]

In addition to these fears about physical and emotional harm, other threats were also lurking and called into question the benefit of having a career. Older, long-serving employees with ample experience and knowledge were replaceable by someone much younger, eager for promotion and on a far lower salary. The dismissed employees—known as a "cesante" at that time—would find it hard to step straight into another job (if he could find one at all) on the same salary as they earned in the position just lost. Therefore, he could not fulfil his responsibilities as husband and father who provided for the family. In 1928, Víctor Juan Guillot, another deputy who represented the Unión Cívica Radical, described this situation:

> Older employees with higher salaries systematically face substitution by others who are more efficient and earn less. Old employees with 20 or 25 years of service are dismissed from their jobs overnight [...] They have formed households and reached an age at which they cannot restart their lives or embark on a new career; but their dismissal plunges them into a new struggle in adverse conditions with depleted reserves of energy and without a financial cushion to help them cope with the new situation forced upon them by circumstances.[22]

To sum up, in response to the question posed at the beginning of this section, in early-1900s Argentina store clerks were men and women who worked in sales and office jobs in salaried positions. They needed to be literate and have sales training to qualify for these jobs. This opened the door to careers in which men could reach higher positions than women, creating an unequal gender relationship, as I will discuss in the following section.

Labor-related identity was unique for two reasons. On the one hand, professional knowledge, upward labor mobility, and smart attire differentiated male and female employees as members of a more advantaged sector than those in the working class. In other words, they could earn higher salaries and enjoy a better quality of life. Yet, on the other hand, this privileged status was in permanent tension with their arduous working conditions, the intensity of demanding jobs that led to emotional distress and were performed under the constant threat of dismissal ("cesantía"), revealing the precariousness of their salaried status.

All of these issues discussed in the Chamber of Deputies in the 1920s resurfaced in the following decade within the context of a financial crisis that exacerbated the social contradiction between employees' privileged status and the possibility of "cesantía." In this period the conflict between the upper and lower classes came to the fore during debates about Law 11.729, which reformed the Code of Commerce, assigning employees an unambiguously working-class identity.

Law 11.729 and the Consolidation of a Working-class Identity for Employees

The Great Depression triggered a recession in Argentina between 1930 and 1935, leading to job losses, a reduction in salaries' purchasing power, and deteriorating working conditions. Unemployment and the threat of dismissal was a cloud constantly hanging over the entire working class. In this context, the aforesaid contradictions inherent in the work of store clerks between having a career and dismissal, became more pronounced. The federation of store clerks (Federación de Empleados de Comercio, FEC), under the leadership of Ángel Gabriel Borlenghi, a member of the Socialist Party and a former accountant, put intense pressure on legislators to reform the Code of Commerce, culminating in the approval of Law 11.729 in 1934—a piece of legislation designed to improve the job security of both male and female employees, based on a compensation for dismissal calculated according to the number of years worked. This gave recognition to the employee's career within a business establishment.

I have analyzed the twists and turns of this FEC campaign in other articles.[23] For the purposes of this text, I am interested in exploring two particular aspects. Firstly, I look at how business sectors opposed this reform through a concerted lobbying of the legislative and judicial branches. Such a reaction lays bare the social conflict between business owners and salaried employees, and reveals the working-class identity of employees, a constant claim of the FEC. The second important aspect is that as the Chamber of Deputies debated the draft reform, one of the most fiercely contested issues was the identity of those to whom the bill would apply: Only to store clerks? Or to store clerks *and* manual workers in stores?[24] The debate also referred to the situation of public-sector employees who were "victims of political fervor," but ultimately this reform excluded them on the grounds of unfeasibility.[25]

Finally, Law 11.729 extended the categories of workers included as store employees because it referred to business agents ("factores"), clerks ("dependientes"), traveling salespersons ("viajantes"), supervisors ("encargados"), and laborers ("obreros"), unlike the nineteenth-century code approved in 1869 that only comprised business agents and clerks. The bill defined the store employee as "anyone, man or women, of any age or nationality, who works for someone else in any aspect of the business, at any level of seniority."[26] The legislative text prioritized the store's business activity above the jobs carried out by its workers. In other words, it glossed over the differences between the blue- and white-collar jobs and focused instead on business establishments' inherent activities. As explained by Alejandro Unsain, a former director of the national labor office (Departamento Nacional del Trabajo, DNT) and an expert on labor issues, in his analysis of the law, the complexity of the economic activities involved various duties, and therefore required personnel with different skills to carry them out:

> The legal precept therefore developed in parallel, in both its broadest and narrowest sense, to the business activity itself, objectively externalized in the economic unit known generically as a "store." It has expanded its operations, activities, action, personnel and categories thereof.[27]

In brief, the law defined as working-class ("asalariados comerciales") everyone who worked in stores, regardless of their particular duty. In the second half of the 1930s, personnel dismissed from various establishments filed a number of lawsuits in order to benefit from the new legislation, alleging that their employer was engaged in sales, even though their business establishment was not strictly a store.[28]

Law 11.729 regulated private employment contracts; it established types of definitive termination for both justified and unjustified causes, or in case of voluntary redundancies. The same legislation applied to temporary interruptions such as diseases, accidents, or military service. The law also established compensations in case of unfair dismissal ("cesantía"), paid leave in case of diseases or accidents, as well as obligatory, paid annual vacations.[29]

Commercial regulations in force in the nineteenth century already established compensation for unfair dismissal and paid leave in case of sickness or accidents. These required employers to give one month's notice before terminating the employment contract of an employee, who had the right to receive the salary corresponding to that month. That payment was the dismissed employee's only legally entitled compensation. In case of sickness or accidents (the most common risk facing workers), store employees had the right to a maximum of three months' paid leave. However, the legislation on workplace accidents (Law 9.688, 1915) applying to compensation in case of workplace accidents or sickness notably excluded this group in its provisions.[30] It fell on employers to decide whether to give their employees annual vacations, and whether these should be paid.

Law 11.729 established that seniority (the number of years in employment) should be the basis for calculating payments for severance, sickness, and vacations. As such, workplace seniority gave men and women employees recognition and support in stores. The reformed code established that dismissed employees had the right to receive 50% of their salaries for every year, or fraction thereof, longer than three months' service in the business establishment. It also gave sick employees three months of paid leave if they had worked for more than 10 years in the business, and up to six months if they were more senior. In both cases employees had the right to a year's unpaid leave.

As Borlenghi noted, the new Code included "diseases in general that prevent employees from going about their work [...] Any common sickness (flu, pneumonia, diphtheria) affecting the employee through no fault of their own, is included within the scope of this article."[31] This marked a clear difference compared to Law 9.688 on accidents in the workplace and work-related sicknesses.

Seniority also defined the number of days' of annual vacation allowance: 10 days for up to 5 years of work, 15 days for up to 10 years, 20 days for up to 20 years, and 30 days for those with more than 30 years of service. But the number of years worked for a firm was definitely a way to protect store workers from arbitrary dismissals or health-related emergencies, because unjustified dismissals required employees to compensate the employee concerned and the payment guaranteed them a financial cushion until they found a new job.

Law 11.729 contained many new provisions, and for reasons of space I will simply list them: prior notification of dismissal; employment certificate after termination; payments in case of the damage or loss of personal items during work hours following the suspension of labor, salary cuts, or changes in business ownership; and compensation in case of the employee's death (calculated using the same formula as in the case of dismissals). It also specified the procedure for employees' resignations (prior notification given to the employer) and the causes for justified dismissal (fraud, incompetence, conducting business for personal benefit).[32]

These regulations were not free of gender inequality. Although the law established unpaid leave for men carrying out their compulsory military service, it omitted any reference to maternity leave, because it was subject firstly to the provisions of Law 11.317 (1924) and then Law 11.933 (1934). In August 1932, while the Chamber of Deputies debated the law that reformed the Code of Commerce, Law 11.317 was in force, regulating unpaid leave for 45 days before childbirth, and 45 days afterward, for "women working in factories or stores."[33] Law 11.729 was passed on September 21, 1934. Some weeks later, on October 15, the same happened with Law 11.933, which established compulsory maternity insurance. With this legislation, pregnant workers kept their job during their maternity leave that would now, with the application of the new law, apply for 30 days before childbirth and 45 days afterward. Although this was unpaid leave, they received an allowance equivalent to their salary, up to a maximum of $200 pesos—though such a high wage was infrequent in those days. Free medical care was available in addition to the leave and allowance.

In line with the above, Law 11.729 covered women store workers in the case of sickness; Law 11.933 in the case of maternity. Unsain underscored the benefits of these differential laws when analyzing the situation for female employees that earned even more than $200 pesos per month, because they all received the additional bonus of free medical care:

> The female employee in the throes of maternity is at a disadvantage compared to her sick male counterpart who receives his full salary, whatever its amount. But that disadvantage is lesser or counterbalanced if we consider that the pregnant woman does not only receive this allowance as part of this special law. She must also receive—free of charge—medical care from a doctor or midwife.[34]

The allowance would come from money paid in each quarter by salaried female employees aged between 15 and 45 years old, employers, and by the state. However, the lack of government agencies fit for purpose delayed the implementation. The Caja de Maternidad only began to administer the allowance as recently as 1936.[35] Up until that point, pregnant store clerks had no access to maternity allowance or sick leave. This stark reality did not dent the optimism of Unsain, who pointed out how Law 11.933 addressed the shortcomings of the Code of Commerce and of Law 11.729:

> The Code of Commerce reflected its time and failed to consider women's maternity. This is easily explained by considering that women only gained access to employment in stores at a much later date. Its provisions relating to illness did not refer to maternity. Law 11.729 did not remedy this situation, therefore reference was only made to pregnant employees with the advent of this new legislation [Law 11.933], whose regulations remain pending.[36]

To sum up, Law 11.729 considered every store worker, male or female, whose number had increased since the beginning of the twentieth century. One of its key achievements was the recognition of seniority, acknowledging employees' careers and mitigating the contradiction between distinction and dismissal, at the same time as reinforcing their working-class identity. One of its weaknesses was the legislation's implicitly androcentric focus: it considered men's work experience while ignoring the particular qualities of salaried women's experience. The protection of working mothers legitimized the notion that women employees were the exception to the rule, hence the failure to question the mechanisms of labor discrimination against women.

Conclusions

One aspect of the "experience of modernity" has been mobility understood as being open to all kinds of horizons: geographical, labor-related, and social.[37] People's legal freedom, despite the restrictions affecting some of them, including women, a counterpart of their financial dependency enabled such an experience that soon made an impact on the workforce. From this perspective, horizontal and vertical labor mobility was a form of upward social mobility, referred to at the time as *dignidad* ("dignity") and *bienestar* ("well-being").

Training courses in sales skills gave labor mobility to male and female employees in Argentina, even helping them reach a higher rung on the social ladder compared to some manual laborers. Nevertheless, salaried employees were still in a precarious situation and upward social mobility was counteracted by adverse working conditions, emotional distress, and the ever-present threat of dismissal after working for the same firm for many years. Employees' working-class identity resolved the tension between being a manual labor and having a salaried position. The state reinforced these meanings through legislation (Law 11.729). This working-class identity also suffused the androcentric meanings that made male employees the breadwinners and their female counterparts an exception, generally born of some financial need but always to make ends meet with an *ayuda* for the family. This was the particular situation facing store clerks in Argentina during Latin America's modernization during the first half of the twentieth century.

Notes

1 I presented a preliminary version of this chapter at the international conference "Clases medias en Latinoamérica: subjetividades e historias" [Middle Classes in Latin America: Subjectivities and Histories] (Mexico City, April 2019). I wish to express my gratitude to Mario Barbosa Cruz, A. Ricardo López Pedreros, and Claudia Stern, coordinators of the event and this book, both for inviting me to participate and encouraging me to write this article. I am also grateful for having had the opportunity to share thoughts and ideas with—and to receive feedback from—the other participants at the conference during those days of intense activity. Additionally, I benefitted enormously from the comments made by the participants at the seminar (La Plata, February 2020) to discuss the project "Modernización en clave de género (Argentina, 1880–1970)" (Proyecto H 846, Programa de Incentivos, Facultad de Humanidades y Ciencias de la Educación, Universidad Nacional de La Plata, 2018–2021).

2 Hugo del Campo, *Sindicalismo y peronismo: Los comienzos de un vínculo perdurable* (Buenos Aires: CLACSO, 1983); Joel Horowitz, *Los sindicatos, el Estado y el surgimiento de Perón, 1930–1946* (Buenos Aires: EDUNTREF, 2004); Torcuato S. Di Tella, *Perón y los sindicatos: El inicio de una relación conflictiva* (Buenos Aires: Ariel, 2003).

3 Graciela Amalia Queirolo, *Mujeres en las oficinas: trabajo, género y clase en el sector administrativo, Buenos Aires, 1910–1950* (Buenos Aires: Editorial Biblos, 2018).

4 David Rock, *El radicalismo argentino, 1890–1930* (Buenos Aires: Amorrortu editores, 1977), 13–35; Silvana Palermo and Jeremías Silva, "Expertos, burocracias y política de masas en Argentina," *Estudios Sociales del Estado* 2, no. 3 (2016): 6–21.

5 Abel Ricardo López Pedreros, "Empleados, mujeres de oficina y la construcción de las identidades de clase media en Bogotá, 1930–1950," *Anuario Colombiano de Historia Social y de la Cultura* 30 (2003): 257–279; Mario Barbosa, "Capacitación y posición social de los empleados públicos de la ciudad de México a comienzos del siglo XX," *Historia Mexicana* 68, no. 2 (2018): 747–783; David S. Parker, "Movilización de clase media y el lenguaje de estamentos: de "casta" a "categoría" en la Lima de principios del siglo XX," in *Moralidades, economías e identidades de clase media: Estudios históricos y etnográficos*, comps. Sergio Eduardo Visacovsky and Enrique Garguin (Buenos Aires: Antropofagia, 2009), 195–216; Susie S. Porter, *From Angel to Office Worker: Middle-Class Identity and Female Consciousness in Mexico, 1890–1950* (Lincoln: University of Nebraska Press, 2018); J. Cristina Sánchez Parra, "Detrás del mostrador": espacios de trabajo y lugares de sociabilidad de los empleados de comercio en la ciudad de México a inicios del siglo XX, *Estudios del ISHiR*, 26 (2020): 1–19.

6 Azun Candina, *Por una vida digna y decorosa: Clase media y empleados públicos en el siglo XX chileno* (Santiago: Frasis, 2009); Azun Candina Polomer, *Clase media, Estado y sacrificio: la Agrupación Nacional de Empleados Fiscales en Chile contemporáneo (1943–1983)* (Santiago: LOM, 2013).

7 Jacqueline Dussaillant Christie, *Las reinas de Estado: Consumo, grandes tiendas y mujeres en la modernización del comercio de Santiago (1880–1930)* (Santiago: Ediciones Universidad Católica de Chile, 2011); J. Pablo Silva, "Repensando aspectos de las relaciones de clase en el Chile del siglo XX," in *Moralidades, economías e identidades de clase media*, comps. Visacovsky and Garguin, 123–159.

8 Gino Germani, "La clase media en la Argentina con especial referencia a sus sectores urbano," in *La clase media en Argentina y Uruguay: Cuatro colaboraciones*, ed. and comp. Theo R. Crevenna (Unión Panamericana, 1950), 1–33; Gino Germani, *Estructura social de la Argentina: Análisis estadístico* (Buenos Aires: Solar, 1987 [1955]).

9 José Luis Romero, *Latinoamérica: Las ciudades y las ideas* (Buenos Aires: Siglo XXI, 1986), 273–274.

10 Leandro H. Gutiérrez and Luis Alberto Romero, *Sectores populares, cultura y política: Buenos Aires en la entreguerra* (Buenos Aires: Sudamericana, 1995).

11 Enrique Garguin, "El tardío descubrimiento de la clase media en Argentina," *Novo Topo* 4 (2007): 85–108; Ezequiel Adamovsky, *Historia de la clase media argentina: Apogeo y decadencia de una ilusión, 1919–2003* (Buenos Aires: Planeta, 2009).

12 Queirolo, *Mujeres en las oficinas*.

13 Congreso Nacional, *Diario de Sesiones de la Cámara de Diputados, año 1929, tomo 1* (Buenos Aires: Imprenta y Encuadernación de la Cámara de Diputados, 1929), 237.

14 Academias Pitman, *El libro del éxito: Cómo prepararse para el comercio* (Buenos Aires: Academias Pitman, 1950), 1.

15 Graciela Queirolo, "Vendedoras: género y trabajo en el sector comercial (Buenos Aires, 1910–1950)," *Estudos Feministas* 22, no. 1 (2014): 29–50.

16 Queirolo, *Mujeres en las oficinas*.

17 Diario *La Prensa*, September 4, 1901.

18 Queirolo, *Mujeres en las oficinas*, 53.

19 *Mundo Argentino*, March 10, 1937; May 5, 1935; August 11, 1937.

20 Congreso Nacional, *Diario de Sesiones de la Cámara de Diputados, año 1923, tomo 2* (Buenos Aires: Imprenta y encuadernación de la Cámara de Diputados, 1923), 184.

21 Congreso Nacional, *Diario de Sesiones, año 1923, tomo 2*, 194–195.

22 Congreso Nacional, *Diario de Sesiones de la Cámara de Diputados, año 1928, tomo 2* (Buenos Aires: Imprenta y encuadernación de la Cámara de Diputados, 1928), 611.

23 Queirolo, *Mujeres en las oficinas*; Graciela Queirolo, "Indemnizaciones, enfermedades y antigüedad entre los empleados de comercio: Alcances y límites de la ley 11.729 (Argentina, 1934–1945)," *Estudios Sociales* 50 (2016): 145–169; Joel Horowitz, *Los sindicatos*.

24 Congreso Nacional, *Diario de Sesiones de la Cámara de Diputados, año 1932, tomo V* (Buenos Aires: Imprenta del Congreso Nacional, 1933), 194–197; Alejandro Unsain, *Empleados de comercio: Exposición y comentario a la ley no. 11.729 (reformando los artículos 154 a 160 del Código de Comercio)* (Buenos Aires: Valerio Abeledo Editor, 1935), 45–71.

25 Unsain, *Empleados de comercio*, 61

26 Ángel Borlenghi, *Beneficios del nuevo artículo 157 del Código de Comercio* (Buenos Aires: Confederación General de Empleados de Comercio, 1934), 24.
27 Unsain, *Empleados de comercio*, 74.
28 In fact, this aspect is undefined in the legislative texts and was left to jurisprudence. "Aplicaciones de la ley 11.729. Tienen acción las reformas al Código de Comercio en las relaciones entre las empresas ferroviarias y sus empleados," in *CGT*, May 21, 1937; "Aplicaciones de la ley 11.729. Está amparado por esta ley el obrero de la industria con tareas a domicilio," *CGT*, Mar. 3, 1939.
29 Unsain, *Empleados de comercio*.
30 Karina Ramacciotti, "De la culpa al seguro: La Ley de Accidentes de Trabajo, Argentina (1915–1955)," *Revista Mundos do Trabalho* 3, no. 5 (2011): 266–284.
31 Borlenghi, *Beneficios*, 36.
32 Borlenghi, *Beneficios*; Unsain, *Empleados de comercio*.
33 *Boletín Oficial de la República Argentina*, November 19, 1924, 530.
34 Unsain, *Empleados de comercio*, 116.
35 The Caja de Maternidad did not work smoothly due to bureaucratic hurdles that discouraged women from joining and claiming their allowance. Carolina Biernat and Karina Ramacciotti, *Crecer y multiplicarse: La política sanitaria materno infantil argentina 1900–1960* (Buenos Aires: Editorial Biblos, 2013).
36 Unsain, *Empleados de comercio*, 121.
37 Marshall Berman, *Todo lo sólido se desvanece en el aire: La experiencia de la modernidad* (Spain: Siglo XXI Editores, 1989 [1982]).

8 The Cost of Love

Middle Classes, Consumption, and Sentimentalism in Mexico (1880–1920)

María Graciela León Matamoros

In 1880, one of Mexico City's leading newspapers published an announcement about a new marriage agency teaming up with a recently announced publication called *El Correo del amor*. This joint venture promised to be the perfect combination to counteract the decline in the number of marriages in Mexico. A business concept of "Sres. Valle, Robert y Compañía," the plan was to receive portraits of anyone eager to marry and to publish them in their newspaper. The agency undertook to keep a discreet register of "all the special qualities of every young lady or gentleman," while the newspaper would include a spread with love letters inserted for a "modest fee." The rest of the publication would publish reports on social issues and customs to promote the values of marriage and the "noble" aspirations of domestic life.

After the readers initially interacted through the newspaper, the marriage agency would take over, and organize get-togethers where they would not be guests "but young people with honest amorous relations with the chance to form a relationship." As an additional service, it would also offer the assistance of agents who—with the utmost discretion—would take care of writing the love letters, ensuring the dispatch of prudent missives and messages as required.[1]

Some days later, *El Monitor Republicano* published a criticism of this service. Despite concurring that marriage was declining at an alarming rate due to increasing moral laxity, it did not consider that marriage agencies provided a solution, essentially because "marriage should be born of love, and love is not something to be sought or found through a small ad, because it is not an item for sale [...], but the spark in two hearts that lights a sacred fire."[2]

This forms part of a (frequently contradictory) discourse in which love played a leading role. Various authors have suggested that the nineteenth century was notable as a period when love matches became the norm,[3] and there were even discussions of love originating with the unrestricted choice of one's partner. Nevertheless, these increasing freedoms went hand-in-hand with social rules on the right unions that delineated the acceptable types of love. As Peter Gay writes, "the eternal, interminable contest between freedom and control is the critical issue in all civilizations, not least in love."[4]

DOI: 10.4324/9781003029311-11

As part of this rivalry, consumerism began playing a central role in the commercialization of romance associated directly with the middle class; the products and rituals of exchange that emerged in late-nineteenth-century Mexico focused on that sector of society. As Eva Illouz writes, "once romance broke free from certain social controls, money tied it to the market through multiple [...] acts of consumption."[5] The expanding "love market" introduced many discourses about dating, choosing partners, marriage, and permissible romance among members of the middle class. Mario Barbosa has already established that historiographical studies in Mexico have largely overlooked the complexity of discussing the middle class. But we can still explore the contemporary perspectives and descriptions as discussed in this chapter through the lens of consumption.[6] Here we analyze these discourses through newspaper publications of the time, in order to observe the portrayal of a sentimental education based on consumption practices identified with the middle classes.

Loving Advice: Rituals of Romance, Letters, and Gifts

By analyzing love as a social and cultural construct open to historicization, we can see various codes come into play during courtship. For Rosario Esteinou, romantic love[7] appeared as a series of norms and beliefs that spread through sectors of middle- and upper-class Mexico at the end of the nineteenth century.[8] Many prohibitions and taboos applied to these norms, but incentives also marked individuals' love lives.[9]

Such incentives existed particularly during courtship, when passions were strongest and the relationship-forming rituals had links to products and services imbued with romantic meaning. These were vital because they did not simply represent a commercial transaction but allowed lovers to know whether their love was reciprocated,[10] all within the framework of behavioral codes during the different phases of courtship. These codes almost exclusively targeted the urban middle class.

For the romantic ideal to exist and then to flourish, various aspects needed to come together. Firstly, courtship required a certain amount of capital and free time; the recommended strategy was a slow conquest during which both parties could express their feelings and make their honorable intentions clear. The man initiated contact, while the woman had to observe a series of subtle gestures and rules that could reveal her interest to her suitor.

> When a young man comes across a young lady on the street, he begins to follow her, without daring to address a single word to her until she reaches her home, even if this process takes the whole day. The suitor stays for several hours on the street looking up at the windows or balconies. If the young lady leans out, this is a sign that she is not entirely indifferent, and from that day onward he will

> spend all his free time, and even when he should be at work, beneath the window or outside the house of his future sweetheart.
>
> After four or five days, when the young man appears, the girl appears on the balcony, [...] and after ten or twelve days she consents to set her eyes on the youth [...] The smiles and greetings now begin, followed by gifts of flowers with symbolic colors sent with the water or coal deliverers, until a month has passed and a perfumed letter, written on pink-colored paper with elaborately cursive handwriting reaches the girl's hands, hidden amidst the most artistically arranged bouquet of flowers that the young man could find in the market in front of the cathedral.[11]

This shows how a set of very specific and elaborate codes applied to the courtship ritual, and although it is difficult to gauge their scope, a number of sources help us see the methods of encouraging certain practices. Newspapers of the time began publishing advice columns for people with anxieties about love to express their concerns anonymously (mostly using pseudonyms) and obtain guidance on matters of the heart.[12]

Newspapers had begun printing questions and answers on general topics since the mid-nineteenth century, sometimes including worries about sentimental matters. But it was only in 1910 when *El Imparcial*, Mexico's top-selling broadsheet, introduced its column called "Amor y buenas formas" (Love and good manners), included in its section entitled "Para las damas" (For the ladies).[13] More than an education in love, the tips signed by Silvia Setalla gave tips on the social aspects of romance, and although the letters sent were not published, the information in the replies revealed plenty of information about their contents.[14]

In this series of replies, we can see the types of courtship allowed, the moral parameters and, of relevance to this chapter, the commercialization of rituals that gave legitimacy to middle-class romance. Of the 280 consultations we found, the most common issue—appearing in 70% of responses—related to the exchange of gifts and similar tokens of affection between the courting couple, revealing this to be the young lovers' most pressing concern.

The code of romantic love detailed a precise order for the exchange of these love tokens, hence the constant questions about the right gift in order to avoid confusion and to communicate the message properly. Gifts were a faux-pas during courtship. For example, in her answer to a question by "Leo K," Silvia Setalla considered a bracelet a good choice, although she thought it inappropriate to make the gift before there was reciprocation. She told "Paganini" that without any relations, even of a friendly nature, it was improper to give any present to the young lady in question.[15] Setalla explained that, one month after making the acquaintance of a young lady, the ideal gift for a special occasion, such as on her saint's day, was a simple bunch of flowers.[16]

A letter expressing amorous intent was necessary before the gift of any love token. Letter-writing had long played a crucial role in cultivating a romance. Letters often implied a certain cultural standing, because the writer needed to be versed in the language of love to fulfil the requirements of this courtship ritual; young people commonly used manuals to help them pen love letters.[17] Setalla recommended learning the verses of a poet, such as Becquer,[18] in order to use them along with the missives. If the letter-writer did not know any such poems, she advised against too much improvisation if the hopeful young lover lacked the requisite talent, as was the case of poor "Juanillo," with whom she was uncharacteristically harsh:

> Judging by the sonnet that you sent me as a sample, I can understand why the young lady you love would have chosen to steer clear of you [...] Spend your time more wisely, because I can assure you that the muses are not by your side.[19]

For lost causes such as "Juanillo," there was always the option of heading to Plaza Santo Domingo and paying for the services of the famed scribes or *evangelistas*. Love letters were the most popular request, even though at 18 centavos they were considerably more expensive than normal letters, which cost 5 centavos.[20] Some of the scribes working under the arcade of this square were specialists in romantic missives, and the leading exponents of the genre could charge as much as 2 pesos per letter.[21] Some newspapers also published advertisements for love letters, promising their originality.[22]

Postcards were another option, and these gained popularity at this time as an alternative for those wishing to express their feelings but doubted their ability to do so. These conformed to a template, and used an image to send a love message saved money otherwise spent on manuals. As Margo Glantz mentions, postcards gave a homogenous message within the middle classes, "standardizing the feeling of love,"[23] becoming a sentimental product of mass consumption, whose golden age coincides with the period of our research.[24]

Apart from sending out a standardized message of love, postcards complemented other gifts. Presents were admissible once the period of courtship had developed into a proper relationship. In this case, the differences in gender roles were instrumental in terms of the type of interaction allowed. Men were supposed to make gifts that would become more expensive as the courtship ritual developed over time, whereas women, who still lacked purchasing power and were less free to move around,[25] had to produce homemade gifts, at least in the initial phase of the relationship. The discourse on feminine behavior had crystallized in a series of norms to safeguard public morality, the family, and virtue, confining women to the domestic space. Therefore, the advice for women was to offer home-made gifts, minimizing the need to go out.

Setalla congratulated "MV" for her idea of making a quilt for her boyfriend.[26] She advised "Tosca" (Clumsy) that if it was not possible to offer a gift to her beau that had "the merit of being handmade," such as a sachet for gloves or handkerchiefs, then she could send him a simple trinket on his birthday.[27] The merit of dexterity also worked as evidence of the young lady's skill in regard to forming a home, and in this recognition of a future housewife's abilities, we can see a moralizing discourse that held domesticity in high regard.

The cost of presents was not to be excessive. Members of the middle classes were constantly criticized for boasting a lifestyle beyond their means and imitating the behavior of the upper classes that ended up in poor taste and "vulgar sentimentalism."[28] Hence the recommendation was for modest gifts: "flowers and sweets are appropriate and nice and inexpensive."[29] Setalla recommended them most frequently, at least for the early stages in the relationship, because once the relationship had become more formal, the rules changed. Hence her response to "Huérfana" (Orphan) that she should accept nothing except flowers, or sometimes sweets, but once her suitor had become her boyfriend she could receive other gifts, provided that they were not too expensive.[30]

The gifts that Setalla considered of moderate value confirm that her correspondents generally belonged to the middle classes; for example, she recommended "Perico" (Parrot) to give his girlfriend a gold wedding ring; "Dora" was congratulated for having chosen a fountain pen, with initials engraved in the cap band,[31] while "Manolo" was advised to give his girlfriend a simple gold medallion containing his portrait, adding that she would accept this gift, however delicate she was, because "the portrait is what will make it most valuable, besides which the monetary value of the medallion is nothing."[32] But the cost of such items was still not insignificant, and the lower classes were not in a position to acquire them.[33]

The issue of presents was further complicated when relationships came to an end, and this was also a frequent topic in the letters. This can indicate to us that the reality of personal relationships was not so straightforward, despite attempts for a smooth passage to eventual marriage. For example, Setalla told "Iris Blanco" (White iris) that the code for "breaking up" stipulated that, upon parting company, both the lady and the gentleman should return each other's letters and portraits, "because with the death of the love, those things become valueless." Nevertheless, gifts should be returned or received, hence "young ladies should not accept valuable objects from their suitors during relationships."[34] "Bobo infortunado" (Silly fool) was warned that even though his former girlfriend had indecently accepted valuable jewelry, furniture, and even cash, he could not ask for it all back "without lowering himself to her base level."[35]

For those who had developed successful relationships, the next stage was to ask for the lady's hand in marriage. The idea of an engagement ring became widespread among the middle classes during this period;[36]

this was the man's responsibility and gave rise to some doubts. When young "León" (Lion) was in doubt about a gift for his fiancée, Setalla told him that he should give her a ring that could either be smooth and with some suitable engraving, or even a golden wedding band with two pearls in the "tu y yo" (you and I) setting.[37] "Carlos" was told that he could give a ring with the stone that corresponded to the month of birth, combined with a diamond or two.[38]

A ring's romantic meaning lay in its use. A belief began to spread that the third finger of the left hand connected to a nerve that ran directly to the heart. We can observe, therefore, how consumption linked to love rituals—in this case to the exchange of messages and gifts imbued with a sentimental meaning—helped consolidate the romance. However, as we will see in the following section, consumption did not necessarily go hand in hand with romantic love.

The Market of Despair: From Love Talismans to Marriage Agencies

At the dawn of the twentieth century, Mexico City was undergoing a process of transformation; it was a period marked by the allure of progress and modernity, reflected in the country's rapid industrialization, internal migration, and unprecedented population growth.[39] These factors combined to create an increasingly complex social dynamic. As the domestic market flourished and many small workshops made the leap to industrial manufacturing, businessmen faced the need to adopt advertising strategies to allow them to shift large volumes of merchandise, and love often operated as an effective enticement. If we see love as a product linked to consumption, we can make the connection with strategies and the evolution of publicity itself since the late nineteenth century, understood as a means of spreading a message and a technique of persuasion designed to showcase a product and also stimulate people's desire to acquire it.

Using love as a publicity strategy soon became a common ploy used by advertisers to harness consumers' fantasies and longings. Numerous images of happy couples appeared in advertisements linked to various products, such as Shafer carriages, which included the illustration of a couple in an embrace, with the text reading: "It's far easier to win the heart of a beautiful lady for marriage if you travel in an elegant carriage, in addition to the sheer pleasure of using a Shafer carriage."[40]

However, expectations in these new times also aroused other emotions. Montserrat Cañedo wrote that a "latent anxiety" counteracted the optimism of modernization, threatening chaos and disintegration.[41] This feeling permeated the world of relationships and disturbed the model of romantic love. Alain Corbin wrote that the semantic landscape of this sentiment still consisted of the same elements, but was thrown into disarray:

> The loss of faith in romantic love took place simultaneously with its dissemination and democratization. We could say that it became a consumer object, almost an item of merchandise [...] an uncertain and unstable assemblage of feelings, illusions, memories, and fears replacing the irresistible impulse toward reaching the ideal.[42]

Newspapers reflected this complex mix of emotions. At the same time as ideas spread about the principles of romantic love with its corresponding rules of behavior, practices and products began promising to console those unable to live up to this ideal. One woman, going by the pseudonym "una desesperada" (a desperate lady), asked Setalla whether it was worth following a friend's advice and visiting a fortune-teller. The advice columnist's response was uncompromising: "your friend must be an utterly ignorant, uncouth, and silly woman to suggest such a thing. Emotions are conquered through actions and tenderness, and not by resorting to stupid, deceitful spells that are both useless and dangerous."[43]

Despite vehement opposition to such practices, businesses took advantage of people's yearning for a partner by marketing products as powerful aids in the quest for romantic love. Paradoxically, the same newspapers that published columns criticizing the consumption of such items filled large spreads by advertising products such as the "Seducción" perfume sold by Perfumería Elegante for $5 pesos, with the tag line: "Don't worry, *señorita*, always use 'Seducción,' you will be happy because this perfume is exquisitely concentrated, the best talisman for love."[44] Equivalent objects were also available for men: "There's one gentleman who fears certain disappointments and buys dozens of flasks of 'Talismán del Amor,'"[45] with a case at $2 pesos at the Belga and Zuleta drugstores. Since most workers earned a daily wage of about $1 peso at most, the prices of these products also gave an indication of their target customer.

Apart from talismans, cartomancy was a widespread practice in the market of those "desperate" for love. Since the late nineteenth century, the services of fortune-tellers became well-known as methods to resolve sentimental problems; in the beginning, their advertisements were very brief and found in the "Various Announcements" section of advertising spreads, but by the early twentieth century they began to appear in the "Professional Services" section, alongside advertisements for surgeons and health clinics, and by 1910 an entire section was dedicated to "Cartomancy." This also included international services of the "Oriental Horoscope," which told people to send in their consultations about love to PO box number 5540; "Indian Cartomancy" gave advice on business, love, and marriage;[46] and there was also "Gypsy, Cartomancy" of New York, who charged $5 pesos for love consultations.[47] As competition grew, this advertising became more aggressive, guaranteeing predictions: "what I saw will come true within eight days,"[48] and the services were complemented with the sale of alternative products such as those offered by "Vicente Pasalagua," an Italian astrologer who told fortunes and included "secrets for love and beauty, talismans and amulets."[49]

Cartomancy and other fortune-telling methods were the target of constant criticism as being purely the work of charlatans who exploited the weakness of the credulous, and in August 1913 the government prohibited these services for being fraudulent. According to the newspaper *El País*, the measure was necessary because fortune-telling advertisements had become "very widespread and were out of line with the latest progress of our times."[50] Nevertheless, newspapers continued to publish them and more so than ever, reflecting the strength of the demand for miraculous products.

Marriage agencies and personal advertisements provided other means of directly exploiting some people's desperation to find a partner—practices frowned upon as inappropriate among the middle classes. In one consultation, "Argentino" (Argentine) wondered whether it was a sensible to look for a spouse through an advertisement, and Setalla replied in no uncertain terms:

> Are you going to settle for a woman who shows such a lack of judgement that she might consider marrying a stranger? Try to get out more and let your heart do the choosing. A marriage cannot be happy when simply left to chance.[51]

However, classified advertisements with messages such as "I wish to have a relationship with a young lady or a widow with capital or through a marriage agency,"[52] became increasingly common, with men being the ones who mainly sent in these questions.

One article published in *El Cómico* poked fun at the increasing prevalence of this practice, predicting that marriage would soon no longer be about emotions at all but a veritable business transaction: "What wise financial institutions will be set up! Firms that will improvise marriages!"[53] These agencies would operate as straightforward business establishments that, for a fee, would match a buyer with a partner boasting the desired physical qualities, from a range that appealed to all tastes and budgets.

News stories about marriage agencies—a flourishing business model imported into Mexico—inspired this article. In 1886, *El Siglo XIX* published a long opinion piece about the famous Monsieur de Foy, the founder of the marriage agency in France who had arranged more than 10,000 marriages, charging 3% of the dowry as his fee. Agencies gradually began to multiply, and from 1872 to 1884, Paris already had more than 100 official, first-, second-, and third-class agencies. According to this piece, the most frequent were second-class agencies that provided a service to employees, retired public officials, and the "bourgeoisie" eager to marry.[54] A number of newspaper articles also mentioned agencies in the United States and England.[55]

This vogue began to thrive in Mexico, and, as we saw above, a marriage agency in the country was already planned back in 1880, and by 1906 newspaper sections were already appearing under the title of "marriage agencies" in the small advertisement pages: "for everyone wishing to get married, we will discreetly provide people with whom you can achieve your objective."[56] Although it is not clear how many agencies existed in Mexico, newspapers referred to them with increasing frequency and demand for their services was growing, despite the fact that such agencies were only a fraud. One example was the case of a certain Mrs. Enners, who advertised her services as the owner of a marriage agency. For $2 pesos she promised that she could provide a boyfriend or girlfriend through correspondence. Once she had received said sum by mail, she answered those interested by telling them that they had a wonderful opportunity, "as she had a beautiful and rich *señorita* or wealthy landowner" with whom she could put them in touch immediately for an extra charge; but, as could be expected, once she received the supplementary payment she forgot all about them.[57] As we can see, the mounting pressure to marry caused the expansion of a growing market that departed from the ideals of romantic love. Despite all the criticisms, this business continued to prosper.

Long Live the Bride and Groom! Weddings Great and Small

The journey so far has been toward a single destination: marriage. Whether this came about as a love match or by means of products and services to help those desperately searching for a partner, marriage was the ultimate objective. Weddings could therefore represent the culmination of ideals, the couple's success, and the promise of a lifelong bond. At the turn of the century little guidance was available for men and women about what would happen after the ceremony, something they would discover through experience, often with greater anguish than joy. Therefore, the wedding ceremony would be the crowning moment of the eagerly awaited process, particularly for women, who were the main target of advertising and criticism due to the practice of increasingly lavish weddings.

According to Barbara Penner, in the second half of the nineteenth century US businessmen initiated the custom of staging over-the-top weddings, clearly aiming to connect weddings to the growing market economy. Newspapers lambasted this custom because a ceremony that should display appropriate decorum and respect had become a vehicle for business interests that linked fashion to class aspirations.[58] These reproaches extended to the Mexican media, which attributed the depravity of this commercialization to foreign influence.

By the late nineteenth century, the practice seemed to have already become a tradition. In 1897, *El Imparcial* lamented the exhibitionism that turned an intimate ritual into a form of contest:

> Such were my thoughts the other day, between midday and one o'clock, watching a bride and groom crossing the humped asphalt of the tacky street of Plateros. A rented vehicle with artificial orange blossoms; the

> bride emerging from her white crêpe de Chine dress like a strawberry poking out from an ice-cream sorbet: the husband dressed up in new clothes, three urchins whistling behind the vehicle and at the door to the church a human sandwich of bovine curiosity and plebeian curses [...] $100, $200, $500, $1,000 pesos. What for? For self-exhibition, for a broadcast of the nuptials, for three or five so-called distinguished guests to come along, for a mangling of Mendelssohn's awfully common wedding march, for two lines of people in their Sunday best to disparage the marriage, for wasters hanging out on the street to turn and look; for a chance to wear fancy dress for a portrait. Oh vanity of vanities! Between $100 and $1,000 pesos wasted just to buy phrases like: "How pretty she looked! And the groom, what a catch!" Or else ... "They can't be happy!" "How miserable they looked when exchanging their vows!" "They've already passed San Francisco at least twenty times, showing themselves off!" "The carriage is rented, that poor lad doesn't have two pesos to rub together!"[59]

A clamor of voices complained about ostentatious weddings, especially because they implied an unnecessary expense for middle-class couples. According to estimates by *El Diario del Hogar*, an employee earning a monthly salary of between $80 and $100 pesos had to keep to a tight budget to save up for marriage, but most people preferred not to wait and instead chose to take on a debt that would take years to repay.[60] Along this same line, *El Imparcial* explained that for middle-class individuals love was "an extremely pricey object, a luxury item," that could only be paid through years of sacrifice and indebtedness. Therefore, during the first year of marriage, the new couple would spend their time avoiding their creditors and pawning their wedding gifts.

El Tiempo Ilustrado also published articles on this topic, but with a focus on young ladies of marrying age, who faced all manner of difficulties in their search for a husband. The problem lay in the fact that they themselves scared off potential suitors due to the financial demands of lavish weddings, hence it advised that "young people wishing to make a home should take a step back, if they belong to the middle class, given the onerous, impossible sacrifices that cause so many worries in today's world."[61] The trouble was that marriage implied a series of considerable expenses: the religious ceremony, the bridal dress, the wedding banquet, liquors, music, and much else besides; men who were "despondent about their lack of means to pay for this," simply avoided becoming engaged. Its proposed solution was very simple: cut out unnecessary wedding expenses, "remain oblivious to the rumor-mongering of others by showing character and strength of will, [...] do not buy anything on credit and start out life courageously, showing [...] less vanity and greater thoughtfulness."

In particular, women were blamed for the excesses of these sectors of society: "a growing tendency among women to adopt ostentatious habits must be dissuading many people from wishing to form a family."[62] This finger-pointing is important because it reflects one of the aspects most closely associated with defining the middle classes: *cursilería* (vulgarity) and its connection to women. *Cursilería* is a derogatory term that appeared in newspapers from the late nineteenth and well into the twentieth century, defined as "boasting, but lacking, good taste and elegance. Looking ridiculous or tasteless while trying to appear rich and elegant."[63] According to Noël Valis, *cursilería* arose from a need to keep up appearances but without the requisite financial, cultural, or social means: "the lower-middle class everywhere in the nineteenth century is especially vulnerable to feelings of individual anxiety and collective fear of downward mobility."[64] In the same sense, writes Enrique Tierno Galván, *lo cursi* appears as a femininization of the bourgeois, specifically middle-class bourgeoisie: "it is not unusual to find bourgeois weakness manifested in a notably feminine way, and that *lo cursi* is a particular trait of women";[65] it is not only related to women because of the connotations of weakness, but because *lo cursi* implicitly refers to a naïve imitation,[66] a stereotype attached to women's behavior.

The type of woman with whom a man should walk down the aisle should avoid false luxuries: "A store clerk, young doctor, or lawyer who lives solely off the earnings of his respective work faces an impossible task to marry a decent lady if she feels the need to maintain an image of pomp and luxury."[67] The ideal woman must observe the rules of modesty and moderation, as expressed in the platitudes of the following verse:

> I want a middle-class lady,
> neither ugly nor pretty but true:
> of noble soul and good moral virtue;
> and able to live free of her folks
> Anyway, to live her life beside me
> … let her eat delicacies when there are delicacies
> and bread when there's bread.[68]

But the messages targeted at women could not be more contradictory. On the one hand, society told women to be modest; on the other advertisements relentlessly targeted them with products for marriage. They also had to cope with conventionalisms that commercialized the wedding ceremony. One article in *El Álbum de la Mujer* explained the event's correct—and overwhelming—protocol: the bride's parents were responsible for the trousseau, provided that this was "in keeping with their position, without falling into the regrettably frequent trap of giving the appearance of a duchess and then having to live within the modest means of the middle class." However, if the wedding celebrations followed the protocols espoused by *El Álbum de la Mujer*, it would impose a considerable financial burden. For example, the bride should give a "fairly splendid" camisole and buttons, embroidered handkerchiefs and a pendant for the clock or the tie pin, while the groom should give a dress for the wedding and another one for when they return from church. Finally, on the day of signing the wedding certificate the couple should exchange an item of jewelry.[69]

These conflicting messages produced a profound anxiety. "Afligida" (Heart-broken) confided in *El Imparcial*'s advice columnist that her parents opposed her marriage partly because of the modesty of the proposed event: "No one should criticize, because a wedding should not be ostentatious if the groom is poor. Explain this to your father."[70] For men, the budget for the wedding ceremony and the bride's trousseau was another cause of worry and a frequent topic of consultation. "Modesto Empleado" (Humble employee) inquired about the price of the trousseau: "I cannot give you a detailed budget for the investment of how much you have, but I can assure you that for $300 pesos you can make a simple but pretty trousseau."[71]

Setalla's suggested budget for that hard-up employee was within the range of prices of wedding dresses on sale at El Palacio de Hierro, the city's most famous department store and frequented only by the middle and upper classes of the period. In one of its large advertisements, it promoted a trousseau for newly-weds that consisted of a crêpe de Chine wedding dress with lace frills, a dress for everyday wear with a wool veil, a pair of gloves, a pair of white silk slippers, a box with a book and a rosary, a pair of white silk stockings, a lingerie set consisting of a day shirt, night shirt, a combination of corset cover and trousers, orange blossom tiara and veil, all for $327 pesos.[72]

Another example of the increased commercialization of weddings was the creation of Mexico City's first wedding planning agency that announced in 1908 that from then on, busy people no longer had to worry about the logistics of getting married, because fortunately there was finally an agency in Mexico that provided this service, as found in major European capital cities. Perales Castilla y Cía. promised to handle all wedding arrangements, and although everything suggested that this was designed for the upper classes, they would also cater to celebrations of "any category."[73] We cannot list here the many different wedding-related products and services, but we can observe an exponential growth in the corresponding advertising and demand; an ever-increasing range of nuptial services were available, and department stores included a section in their catalogs for "marriage articles" and honeymoons became a popular custom, with all their associated expenses. As Penner has pointed out, weddings no longer indicated wealth or privilege, despite the constant criticisms and concomitant expense, because middle-class couples increasingly chose this practice.[74]

Final Considerations

As we have tried to illustrate, concern about the declining number of marriages was evident in a series of discourses and practices designed to put people on the right path for married life. By focusing on consumption, we saw the role of romance in creating markets that targeted the swelling middle-class population. The lower social classes were also no strangers to romantic love and its respective rituals of consumption, but during the period in question we can see with greater clarity the construction of a discourse that saw the middle classes as the exponents of sentimental rituals. At the same time, this middle-income sector also needed to navigate and withstand the increasing materialism of love and the contradictions created by the barrage of advertising that steered them toward this flourishing new market-based logic. However, the market and love were not necessarily separate; indeed, the two were complementary and consumption helped elevate sentiments through the meaning attached to the product.

Toward the end of the nineteenth century and in the early twentieth century, the middle classes received a boost—at least in the public discourse—as the sector of society capable of implementing the modernizing drive initiated during the Porfirio Díaz era, and which extended to the revolutionary period. In this sense, we can observe how consumption linked to sentimentalism encouraged practices thought desirable for the middle classes. These practices incorporated the idea of moderation and were linked to a gender code that bolstered the roles of both men and women: men were supposed to occupy the public space as suitors, offering gifts and covering the wedding costs without overdoing it; women, for their part, had to demonstrate their qualities as future wives by showing modesty and making their own presents that would keep them within the domestic space.

After the 1920s, as women began to gain a solid foothold in the job market, ideas and practices related to romance—and love-related consumption—began to spread thanks to the media's greater reach and the emergence of new technologies such as cinema and radio. However, as we have tried to outline here, the origin of this increased commercialization was based on middle-class sensibilities and aspirations.

Notes

1 "Conversación dominical," *La Patria*, May 2, 1880.
2 *El Monitor Republicano*, May 9, 1880.
3 Niklas Luhmann, *El amor como pasión: Hacia una codificación de la intimidad* (Barcelona: Ediciones Península, 1985); Roland Barthes, *Fragmentos de un discurso amoroso* (Mexico City: Siglo XXI, 1982). These texts led the way for subsequent research in recent decades into love-related themes.
4 Peter Gay, *La experiencia burguesa: De Victoria a Freud* (Mexico City: Fondo de Cultura Económica, 1984), 11.
5 Eva Illouz, *El Consumo de la utopía romántica: El amor y las contradicciones culturales del capitalismo* (Buenos Aires: Katz Editores, 2009), 104.
6 Barbosa goes beyond seeking a definition and explores, as he says himself, the meanings of "the middle classes" as a category, analyzing this sector of society's desire to distinguish itself from other social classes. This allows us to

reflect on the complex interconnection of characterizations surrounding them between the Díaz era and the Revolution. Mario Barbosa, "Distinciones y apariencias: La clase media en la Ciudad de México entre el porfiriato y la Revolución," *Oficio: Revista de historia e interdisciplina* 10 (2020): 9–23.

7 By romantic love we also refer to the intense attraction the encompasses an idealization of the other, with the expectation of a future life together. William Jankowiak and Edward F. Fisher, "A Cross-Cultural Perspective on Romantic Love," *Ethnology* 31, no. 2 (1992): 149–155.

8 Rosario Esteinou, "Intimidad y amor romántico entre 1900 y 1950 en México: discursos y normas," *Cuicuilco Revista de Ciencias Antropológicas*, no. 68 (January–April 2017): 36.

9 Martha Eva Rocha, "Los comportamientos amorosos en el noviazgo, 1870–1968: Historia de un proceso secular," *Historias*, no. 35 (1995): 119

10 Sérgio Costa, "¿Amores fáciles? Romanticismo y consumo en la modernidad tardía," *Revista Mexicana de Sociología* 68, no. 4 (2006): 769.

11 "Mexicanismos. Modo de enamorar," *El Popular*, October 14, 1903.

12 According to Martha Eva Rocha, lonely hearts sections only started to appear in newspapers and magazines in 1930. Rocha, "Los comportamientos amorosos," 121. However, during this research we observed that these in fact originated in the early twentieth century.

13 In late-nineteenth-century newspapers there was a proliferation of sections for women, on themes related to the home, fashion, and good manners. In fact, this was not exclusive to sections "for the ladies"; entire newspapers were created by and for women, such as *El álbum de la mujer*, founded in 1884, *El correo de las señoras* (in 1883), and *Violetas del Anáhuac* (in 1888).

14 We cannot be certain that the answers were in response to real questions, but judging by the type of response such as the following: "Azuzena: you are so reticent about your situation that I can barely understand it, let alone give you advice. Please write in again more clearly," we can infer that many of them were based on genuine consultations.

15 "Amor y buenas formas," *El Imparcial*, September 1, 1910.

16 "Amor y buenas formas," *El Imparcial*, July 10, 1910.

17 The manuals were not exclusively the product of the middle classes. Some loose-leaf manuals were sold very cheaply, such as the *Colección de cartas amorosas* published by Vanegas Arroyo. The difference lay more in the content than in the cost, since the instructions in the loose-leaf versions were very short, whereas the manuals included more elaborate verses and texts. Elisa Speckman, "De amor y desamor: ideas, imágenes, recetas y códigos en los impresos de Antonio Vanegas Arroyo," *Revista de Literaturas Populares*, year 1, no. 2 (2001): 72.

18 "Amor y buenas formas" *El Imparcial*, October 3, 1910.

19 "Amor y buenas formas" *El Imparcial*, March 8, 1911.

20 For an idea of the expense, we should recall that laborers earned a daily wage of around 50 to 62 centavos, that a box of cigarettes cost about 4 centavos on average, and that a kilo of rice cost 30 centavos.

21 "Entrevista con el decano de los evangelistas," *El Popular*, March 22, 1903.

22 *El Correo Español*, May 30, 1914.

23 Margo Glantz, *El día de tu boda* (Mexico City: Martín Castilla editores, 1982), 26.

24 Jean Louis Guereña, "Imagen y memoria: La tarjeta postal a finales del siglo XX," *Berceo*, no. 149 (2005): 38.

25 Gabriela Cano, "Ansiedades de género en México frente al ingreso de las mujeres a las profesiones de medicina y jurisprudencia," *Projeto História: Revista do Programa de Estudos Pós-Graduados de História*45 (2012): 24.

26 "Amor y buenas formas," *El Imparcial*, January 4, 1911.
27 "Amor y buenas formas," *El Imparcial*, March 15, 1911.
28 Noël Valis, *The Culture of Cursilería: Bad Taste, Kitsch, and Class in Modern Spain* (Durham: Duke University Press, 2002), 11.
29 "Amor y buenas formas," *El Imparcial*, September 1, 1910.
30 "Amor y buenas formas," *El Imparcial*, November 5, 1911.
31 "Amor y buenas formas," *El Imparcial*, October 3, 1910.
32 "Amor y buenas formas," *El Imparcial*, December 5, 1910.
33 Marie Francois, "Vivir de prestado: El empeño en la Ciudad de México," in *Historia de la vida cotidiana en México, vol. IV, Bienes y vivencias: El siglo XIX*, coord. Anne Staples (Mexico City: El Colegio de México, 2005), 104
34 "Amor y buenas formas," *El Imparcial*, March 17, 1911.
35 "Amor y buenas formas," *El Imparcial*, February 5, 1911.
36 The most common pieces of jewelry in 1873 were gold rings, more than half with diamonds and also popular were rose-cut gems or precious stones. Francois, "Vivir de prestado," 105.
37 "Amor y buenas formas," *El Imparcial*, February 11, 1911.
38 "Sección de respuestas," *El Diario*, March 11, 1910.
39 Mexico City's population increased from 200,000 in 1870, to 250,000 in 1880, to 417,066 in 1910, and 616,367 in 1921. *Estadísticas Históricas*, vol. 1 (Mexico City: INEGI, 1994), 31.
40 *El Imparcial*, January 30, 1906, 5
41 Montserrat Cañedo, *Cuerpos peligrosos en el cuerpo de la ciudad: Medicina y política en el Madrid de finales del siglo XIX* (Spain: Universidad de Zaragoza, 2010), 3.
42 Alain Corbin, *Historia de la vida privada: Sociedad burguesa; Aspectos de la vida privada*, vol. 8 (Madrid: Taurus, 1991), 226.
43 "Amor y buenas formas," *El Imparcial*, October 14, 1910.
44 "Avisos económicos," *El Pueblo*, January 29, 1916.
45 *El Correo Español*, June 3,1899.
46 *El Imparcial*, March 4, 1910.
47 *El Imparcial*, February 5, 1910.
48 *El Pueblo*, February 18, 1917.
49 "Avisos de ocasión," *El Pueblo*, April 23, 1919.
50 *El País*, August 8, 1913.
51 "Amor y buenas formas," *El Imparcial*, November 5, 1910.
52 *El Pueblo*, March 2, 1916.
53 "El matrimonio en el siglo XX," *El Cómico*, May 21, 1899.
54 "El 'Temps' y las agencias," *El Siglo XIX*, April 27, 1886.
55 "Las novias," *Diario del Hogar*, November 3, 1888.
56 "Aviso oportuno," *El Diario*, October 24, 1906.
57 *El Universal*, March 14, 1920.
58 Barbara Penner, "A Vision of Love and Luxury: The Commercialization of Nineteenth-Century American Weddings," *Winterthur Portfolio*, no. 39 (2004): 2.
59 "Mexicanismos," *El Imparcial*, May 10, 1897.
60 "Economía doméstica," *El Diario del Hogar*, February 16, 1897.
61 "Algo sobre el matrimonio," *El Tiempo Ilustrado*, September 5, 1909.
62 "Perfiles de nuestro estado social," *El Imparcial*, August 8, 1899.
63 "Lo cursi," *El Pueblo*, November 12, 1917.
64 The word *cursilería* as defined first appeared in Spain before spreading to Mexico, Cuba, and Argentina. Valis, *The Culture of Cursilería*, 11.
65 Enrique Tierno, "Aparición y desarrollo de nuevas perspectivas de valoración social en el siglo XIX: Lo cursi," *Revista de Estudios Políticos*, no. 42 (1952): 100.

66 Carlos Moreno, "Lo cursi y lo grotesco: Algunos aspectos del romanticismo español," *Revista Hispánica Moderna*, year 48, no. 1 (1995):10.
67 "El lujo," *El Álbum de la Mujer*, March 27, 1887, 102.
68 "Quiero casarme," *El Cómico*, April 30, 1899.
69 "Casamientos," *El Álbum de la Mujer*, November 21, 1886.
70 "Amor y buenas formas," *El Imparcial*, October 6, 1910.
71 "Amor y buenas formas," *El Imparcial*, November 25, 1910.
72 *El Pueblo*, January 25, 1918.
73 *El Imparcial*, September 11, 1908.
74 Penner, "Vision of Love," 22.

9 Tango, Morality, and Nostalgia in the Making of a Middle-Class Subjectivity in Argentina[1]

Enrique Garguin

Tango and the middle class? Is tango not Río de La Plata's quintessentially *popular* music? This has indeed been the view commonly held by scholars and laymen alike. Yet tango possesses a quality that always transcends the popular realm. Perhaps this owes to the musical refinement it acquired in the 1920s with the *Guardia Nueva* movement,[2] or to its poetical sophistication that combined popular, literary, and even avant-garde cultural expressions to an exceptional extent.[3] Or perhaps this is ultimately because "standard" accounts of middle-class Argentina see the world of tango not as something separate to, but instead as an intrinsic part of, that history, with its dances, radio broadcasts, sheet music, and records. In fact, much of the finest literature about tango refers to its middle-class connections.

In her detailed and seminal study on tango poetry, Noemí Ulla suggests that the tango of the 1930s slowly abandoned its humble roots, reflecting "another sector of society—the middle class—that internalized tango and began taking on its traits and passing them on."[4] Eduardo Archetti also writes about a shift in tango's morality at that time, relating it to the expanding middle class: "Guilt and forgiveness are gradually replacing the violence of duels and deaths," he observes, inspired by Georges L. Mosse's studies on the transition from an aristocratic virility to middle-class behaviors.[5] "Who is the narrator?… It seems that the average 'tango man' is single, middle-aged, lower-middle class, or perhaps simply middle class."[6]

Gustavo Varela takes a different view. He emphasizes the specific themes and aesthetics of tango lyrics since "Mi noche triste" (1916), not to make a connection with a hypothetical middle class but to show its close ties with a hegemonic discourse focused on regulating sexuality and moral standards. He also points out that almost every songwriter from that time onward was the product of a state-education system that certainly played a role in conveying moralistic messages.[7] But this sophisticated interpretation glosses over the dissonances in those normative discourses also present in tango. Notable differences exist between perspectives: Archetti refers to multiple masculine personalities rejecting bourgeois morals;[8] Marta E. Savigliano finds in tangos powerful challenges to the concepts of bourgeois gender identity,[9] while Matthew B.

DOI: 10.4324/9781003029311-12

Karush shows a continuing populist classism, with its emphasis on contrasting the honorable poor with the iniquitous rich and their disruptive elements in regard to the (im)possibility of consolidating a homogenous discourse about the nation:[10]

> This classism was combined with consumerist titillation, conformism, the celebration of individual upward mobility, misogyny, and other conservative messages. The result was a deeply contradictory discourse, but one in which class loyalties still resonated powerfully.[11]

As if responding to Ulla's considerations about the changes of the 1930s, he adds: "despite many efforts to modernize, civilize, and improve it, the tango would never lose its popular associations."[12]

We will explore this ambiguity, contradiction, and lack of definition in order to highlight some of the ways that tango's symbolic universe can contribute images and representations to the creation of a middle class in Argentina. Tango lyrics are often said to describe Buenos Aires and its people; over the years, some themes have become crystallized as "themes" identified with tango: the weeping of a forsaken man, the mother as a uniquely pure figure offering refuge, the tough male *guapos* and *compadritos* together with the *milonguita* ladies on the tango scene... and the barrio as the Buenos Aires resident's local stomping ground. Tango's diversity of themes and perspectives is as wide and multifaceted as its relation to the society that produced it. Faced with the various—and in our opinion failed—attempts to come up with a literal interpretation of certain tango representations as reflecting an underlying social reality (whether lower or middle class or related to the bourgeoisie), we consider it impossible to draw a line between a social reality and an artistic creation, or between the messages contained within such a creation and its consumers. Instead, we propose a more elliptical reading. After all, many are the tangos that, far from seeking to describe the surrounding social reality, sought to reflect the feelings of nostalgia, regret and bitterness generated by a rapidly changing world: "sorrow for the barrio that has changed, and bitterness about the dream that died," as Homero Manzi pointed out in "Sur" (1948).[13] And from that wounded subjectivity, the description of the longed-for lost world had no pretensions of objectivity either, as Aníbal Troilo recognized in "Nocturno a mi barrio" (1956)

> That's how my barrio once was, once was, once was...
> What do I know about how it was?
> Yet that's how I remember it was!

In previous studies we have tackled both the (belated) articulation of a middle-class identity in Argentina and the various practices of distinction that made it possible.[14] Here we return to these themes through an analysis of the various ways in which, during the interwar period, tango lyrics invented traditions, idealized the past, created archetypes, and erected moral and social boundaries. We will certainly discover the affinity between these worlds of tango and the more general findings shown by our research into the creation of the middle class in pre-Peronist Argentina; contrary to conventional wisdom, the middle class did not flourish during those years. And if any glimmer of such middle-class identity did emerge, it rapidly become fragmented (for example, in connection to a particular occupation or as a broader identity, such as a popular one). But also, that popular collective already contained many class-ridden tensions pulling in different directions. On the one hand, these tended toward the singularization of a world of work, characterized not only by the solidarity among its members but also by its protest against the oppression and rejection of the privileged and wealthy upper classes. On the other hand, these tensions created new, differentiating boundaries. These marks of distinction were based on the supposedly higher moral values of an element of the popular class, overlooking its more boorish and confrontational aspects. Such elements went on to acquire fresh impetus when the increasing homogenization of the popular collective stalled in the face of political polarization in Peronist Argentina.

From the Fringes

One of tango's recurring themes is that of the underworld of the city outskirts, with its cast of characters including the guapos, compadritos, and milonguitas; an outsider class and possibly the original creators and consumers of tango in the late nineteenth century.[15] However, this milieu was no longer its place of creation when tango gained mass appeal in the second decade of the twentieth century, and particularly following the enormous success of Pascual Contursi's "Mi noche triste" (1916). Recorded on vinyl by Carlos Gardel in 1917, it became a hit when featured in a 1918 play, and it is unanimously seen as the origin of the tango-song.[16] "Mi noche triste" also introduces various classic tango themes, such as the *amurado* (a man abandoned by his lover); the drowning of sorrows in alcohol; the *bulín* (bachelor pad), with its guitar, rickety bed, and other items reminding him of his loved one. In principle, these motifs should not be interpreted as descriptions of a current reality but as continual returns to the topics of Contursi's original tango lyrics.

Another of the great lyricists of the 1920s, Celedonio Flores, also prioritizes the values of the suburbs and several of the female characters are seduced by men known as *bacanes* (local big shots) who lead them astray into the world of the cabaret, a "fictitious world [...] contrasting with the real world of the barrio's tenement buildings, underscoring the positive qualities of such spaces governed by paternal figures and more frequently by the mother."[17]

> Similarly to Pascual Contursi, Celedonio Flores bases his work on popular realism. His work [...] incorporates a wide variety of themes [...] to create enduring character types, using the full range of the local *lunfardo* slang's expressive particularities.[18]

Are we dealing with a "popular realism" or with tango's own poetics, perhaps more attached to an intrinsic logic than to external referents? Its invented traditions, its revived "original" principles, are clear. Did these aspects also reflect *its* reality? Contemporary observers may struggle to see it that way. Writer and journalist Enrique González Tuñón had tango running through his veins, and distanced himself from any literal interpretations when trying to portray its social reality as a journalist. Joining the popular newspaper *Crítica* in 1925, González Tuñón pioneered a new journalistic style, the commentary. Every week, he would use a well-known tango as an intertext to discuss various social issues. In the first of these pieces, González Tuñón defines tango as a "genuine representation of the popular spirit," "our music, the voice of the people," and welcomes "tango that, by distancing itself from fertile mediocrity, introduces an emotional value, thus affirming the prestige gained despite the resentment of the genteel."[19]

González Tuñón's weekly commentaries mainly analyze the barrios and characters furthest from the center. However, they have one fundamental difference to the contemporary tangos that act as an intertext: his *arrabal*—a seedy, marginalized area—is not reduced to somewhere pure and simple, a moral counterpoint to the center of corruption; instead, the writer reconstructs tango's origins among pimps and prostitutes to show "an arrabal that is a den of iniquity, a place of crime and gambling." "Unlike Borges's outskirts, inhabited by compadritos and men armed with knives in the old criollo city, González Tuñón incorporates modern areas of marginalization," concludes Saítta.[20]

In this way, González Tuñón openly challenged the "sanitized" vision of tango of his time that "was introduced into the households of public-sector employees overwhelmed by debts and the whims of their daughters studying French and sol-fa." In his opinion, 1920s tango had hung up its "rags in the closet" and acquired a respectable "family ID card."[21]

González Tuñón therefore substitutes the archetypal, old-school criollo ruffians and compadritos from the arrabal with "modern-day criminals" who "no longer fear the compadrito from another part of town challenging him to a duel, but the snitch who can get them sent to prison."[22] To a large extent, these "modern-day criminals" are also described by Roberto Arlt in his novels through the outsider figures in *El juguete rabioso* (1926) and *Los siete locos* (1929). But what is most interesting here is that González Tuñón explicitly moves away from the symbolic universe of tango to suggest a "real" social world, in the way he understood it. Tango could genuinely express "popular spirit," but it did not say much about its social materiality: it failed to describe the world of contemporary poverty, and overlooked the experiences of exhausted civil servants and their whimsical daughters. We can easily understand why the writer chose to draw that distinction in regard to the texture of tango. But why did tango describe social realities so unlike what Enrique González Tuñón perceived as his contemporary social realities?

We need to revisit other tango themes in order to gain a better understanding of this separation and its possible meanings (both for us and for González Tuñón's contemporaries). The arrabal is not the only ever-present anachronism in tango. There is also a cast of characters considered typical of such surroundings: the guapo, eventually transformed into the compadrito; the modest young lady, who becomes the milonguita. Among these figures, torrid love affairs find both a social and a sentimental setting; hence the theme of the amurado, the figure described by Contursi: the good man forsaken by the girl seduced by the bright lights of the city, the pleasures of the cabaret, the life of luxury offered by a big-shot bacán. According to Ulla, this theme developed essentially in two ways during the 1920s:[23] the resigned fall into disrepute and alcohol consumption (and sometimes searching for the mother's consolation, or the playing down of the event) and the assertion of manhood through revenge, in the form of murder (usually using a knife) either of the unfaithful woman, the love rival, or both. Once these themes became clichéd, other tango songs began to poke fun at them. A naturalist description of contemporary experiences? Nothing could be less certain. Even Ulla, who chose a realist interpretation elsewhere, argues that both responses are

> detached from our social context, and are just empty abstractions... that have persisted for slightly over a decade and that tango uses as a basis, sometimes with a popular aesthetic value or else without any value or originality at all.[24]

This gives us a promising key for an initial reading: this theme, like others we will see below, consist of *topics* more understandable through tango's internal development and aesthetic needs than any possible external social reference points. Ulla proposes this reading for the reactions of the amurado, but it is also dubious whether the compadrito figure was realistic during the 1920s. Everything suggests that he was an idealized, nostalgic figure,[25] similarly to the criollo gaucho. As Borges said in 1945 during a talk in Montevideo, which he concluded with the reading of his *Poema conjetural*:

> Twenty years ago, my country could imagine that undecipherable deities had offered it a benign world [...], separated from all of the rigors of yesteryear. Then, I remember, Ricardo Güiraldes nostalgically recalled [the life of the gaucho].
>
> [And I] pursued with vain perseverance [...] the final traces of the knife-wielding *cuchilleros* from the outskirts. The world seemed to us so tame, so incorrigibly peaceful, that we played around with fearsome

> anecdotes and longed for "the age of wolves, the age of swords" as experienced by other, more fortunate generations. So the gaucho poems were accounts of an irretrievable—and therefore pleasing—past, since no one dreamed that its rigors could return and reach us.[26]

Borges not only tells us that *cuchilleros* were already a thing of the past by the 1920s, but he also gives us a cipher: he sought out these figures playfully from the tediousness of an "incorrigibly peaceful" present. Returning to the theme's development in tango, not all of its new consumers were probably willing to listen—without jeopardizing their moral standing—to tangos as plebeian as those detailing the exploits and crimes of the forsaken guapos. Added to the fact that constant repetition had made the theme clichéd, this can explain why new subject matters came to the fore. However, this topic did not completely disappear from hit records; it made a strong comeback at various junctures. For example, it featured strongly in the repertoires of the 1960s (alongside other tangos in the 1930s and 1940s with fresh poetry and themes). In this sense, Borges's cipher seems of central importance.

Another theme—in parallel to the forsaken lovers in the arrabal (and despite the continued focus on doomed love affairs)—also emerged with a completely different sensibility to the hardscrabble world of the slums, taking tango away from the outskirts to concentrate on lost love among all sectors of Buenos Aires society. Both types of theme coexisted within the work of the same authors, such as García Jiménez or José María Contursi, or on a single Gardel record.[27] This coexistence warns us against succumbing to the temptation of seeking specific social reference points in tango lyrics, or precise social identifications among authors, musicians, and audiences. Instead, this should encourage us to consider plural and heterogeneous subjectivities under development, existing alongside one another under certain tension within the world of tango.

Social Pretensions and Falling from Grace

Along with the lovelorn amurado, we also have the young neighborhood girl who, deceived by a smooth-talking bacán, becomes a milonguita who survives in a downtown cabaret, in the shadow of prostitution—as seen from the moralizing male gaze. With subtle variations, the history repeats itself ad infinitum, and the moral lesson rarely varies: the enticing lights of the city are simply passing illusions; truth lies in the barrio, with the family and the humble boyfriend; but it proves hard for the girl to recover from an earlier misstep.[28] The clear moral and sexual message, together with its transformation into a theme—undergoing significant variations as we will see below—makes this treatment both a mere motif already approved for a tango, and a revealing expression of male concern with certain feminine liberties.

F. García Jiménez's "Zorro Gris" (1921) highlights the contrast between the happiness of a past spent in the humble barrio, and the sentimental and ethical emptiness of the milonguita's life of luxury:

> And while thinking, between a kiss and a tango,
> of your humble and cheerful past
> you hid your sacred tears
> in the folds of your gray fox-fur.

A similar case is found in Cadícamo's "Callejera" (1929), with its contrasts between the barrio and the luxuries of the center, between silk and muslin, youth and old age, which the author repeats in "Cambia de vida" (1938) and "Muñeca Brava" (1929), where the moral recrimination of the milonguita is based on the insult of those assuming false pretenses and hiding their roots:

> Hey madam, you parles in Français
> Spraying perfume all around
> Getting tipsy on nice cool cocktails
> And your gigolo is really proud…
> Fiery baby doll
> So highly prized.
> You're at Trianón…
> Trianón of Villa Crespo…

These lines suggest an unsurmountable, class-based moral divide. Similarly to the tough compadrito, this repeated image of the milonguita seems to refer to an imagined and nostalgic figure (the good girlfriend and humble seamstress) disparaged as a woman who has lost her virtue. Daily life in the barrios was certainly a harder grind and less glamorous. Cadícamo explained this later, still from the confines of a male perspective: "What was the story behind 'Muñeca brava'? Those tangos were caricatures, making fun of someone… They were little digs at the girls you found on the cabaret scene at night in Buenos Aires where we used to hang out."[29]

A.J. Rodríguez's "No salgas de tu barrio" (1927) features an elderly milonguera, now on the scrapheap, who warns others not to repeat the errors of her youth:

> Do not leave your dress-making, little suburban girl […]
> Do not leave your old mother, your street, your tenement,
> Or the simple young lad who begs for your love.[30]

The old lady appears mainly to voice the fears of the "simple young lad."

To heighten the drama to the acts that lead her to perdition, the girl is usually of particularly humble stock, making the advice blatantly ridiculous. Contemporaries were conscious of this: what were the alternatives for the humble seamstress raised in a tenement room, cooped up with her family who barely had enough money for food? To answer this question would also have implied introducing a theme largely absent from tango lyrics: work. This appears in González Tuñón's commentaries where "the world of work is synonymous with exploitation and misery" and "crime and prostitution are presented as valid alternatives."[31] Returning to the theme of the errant seamstress, González Tuñón once again departs from the tango lyrics to deliver a different appraisal; as the love interest of the bacán, she had done well to avoid a life of hardship and penury working in a factory:

> A false step took Regina toward Maipú street. [...] A stuck-up *monsieur* rented her a small flat with a telephone and hot water. She dolled up her slender body with fox-fur and began her first French lessons. She was ready to wash away the humbleness of her soul in a blaze of light. The center was hers. She had conquered it with her proletarian, 18-year-old beauty. She had done the right thing. Choosing between gradually surrendering her youth to the factory of sackcloth bags to end her days with the resignation of a laborer at retirement age, and enjoying it by flirting with the abyss, she opted for the latter. She had done the right thing.[32]

Significantly, the most genuinely feminine version of the female motif of the girl from the barrio also inverts the classic male advice. "Se va la vida"—written in 1929 by María Luisa Carnelli (signed under the pseudonym of Luis Mario)[33]—advises that "if a bacán offers to set you up, don't think twice" because "life goes by... it goes by and doesn't come back" and "It's best to live it and leave your woes behind":

> Tell me, why do you cry over love
> and die, perhaps, of despair?
> Don't think about pain or virtue!
> Live your youth!

Although they certainly risk idealizing the flip side of the coin (the life of the cabaret and prostitution), the ideas of María Luisa Carnelli and Enrique González Tuñon seem to evoke more realistic dilemmas experienced by young, working-class girls. Life in the cabaret certainly led to any number of unhappy endings, but not necessarily more than a life spent locked up in the tenement building or the factory.[34]

Perhaps the situation was different for young girls from higher social and economic strata, but these did not often appear in lyrics themed around the fall from grace. Apart from some exceptions, it is particularly significant to note that the rogue bacán figure escapes censure. Roberto

Goyeneche "De mi barrio" (1923) tells the story of an honest girl who winds up in the cabaret after being cheated by "such a fine, polite man," "of good appearance" and "distinguished manners," and who is introduced like this:

> In my barrio I was the prettiest lass,
> educated in a nun's school
> and though my folks had little cash
> I hung out with the upper-class.
> All the luxuries came fast
> and as I focused on climbing the ladder
> I forgot all about my past,
> and gave my heart to the highest bidder.

This mainly shows how the ideals of upward social mobility (a good Catholic education, connections to "good" families, aspirations of progress) are responsible for the eventual fall from grace. And someone's waywardness is, at least partially, the result of a personal decision and therefore the blame cannot be entirely the fault of the other (the bacán).

In Celedonio Flores's "Por la pinta" (1920)—popularly known as "Margot" since Carlos Gardel's version—we can clearly see the individual guilt of the person who takes a wrong turn in another variation on this same theme that perhaps fits better as a critique of taking on false pretenses, affecting men and women alike:

> It's plain to see, you wretched little thing
> that you come from a shack in a slum...
> Something betrays you, perhaps your gaze,
> how you sit, look, and stand,
> or that body used to rough cotton rags.
> [...]
> Don't give me that. No arrogant layabout guapo
> or immoral pimp drove you to vice...
> You knew the game, you're not naïve...
> your mind's so full of fanciful dreams.
> [...]
> and you even changed your name, just like your fortunes:
> you're no longer my Margarita, now they call you Margot!

Here Margot is solely to blame and any other excuses are bogus. This is not fatherly advice but a stern rebuke of a pretentious lifestyle. An undercurrent of classist essentialism underlies this criticism. Less a critique of prostitution or the choice of a wrong path, this is a direct attack on the attempt to consort with people of a higher social class, the simulation of a social status beyond reach for a girl of a certain background, which therefore becomes an unchanging essence: "that body used to rough cotton rags" constitutes an indelible mark of class. The classic paternalism has become classist elitism. Paradoxically, this also forms part of the "populism" that Karush reveals in Argentina's popular culture in the interwar period, only that here the negative pole of the dichotomy—the enemy of the popular narrative voice—is not the aristocratic bacán but the humble girl who decides to abandon her boyfriend in the barrio and her poor mother to prostitute herself and enjoy otherwise-unobtainable luxuries; as such, it also proposes women's agency not often found in other tangos.[35]

In all these cases, various male fears combine with a plural subjectivity, in turmoil and with themes close to the heart of a national (and middle-class) identity under construction: the longing for upward social mobility, money-related injustices, the strict moral distinction between the legitimate and illegitimate paths of personal development.

This latter topic becomes particularly relevant when male impostors come into the line of fire, as in Cadícamo's "Che Bartolo" (1928) or Agustín Irusta's "Dandy!" (1928), with its moral censure of a man pretending to be "well-bred" and living like a dandy while his "poor sister has surrendered her life to the factory." "Niño bien" (1928) by Victor Soliño and Roberto Fontaina also portrays the figure who turns his back on his own class and fakes an aristocratic background (while his father humbly sells simple pastries). Ridiculing him, he recognizes that he has the right "class" ... to be behind a counter (as a store clerk). In this way, the unbreachable class barrier seems to be raised; it is no longer just those people born "in the misery of a tenement slum" who turn their back on their class, but also presumably those born to be employees, which at that time could signify a higher social class.[36] Already a well-known song since the late 1920s, Tita Merello gave it a major boost when she recorded it at the height of her fame (it was also later recorded by Hugo del Carril, Atilio Stampone, and Mercedes Simone, in that order).

The criticism of those who put on airs and graces, or who "alienate" themselves from their class, also usually comes across as the disappointment at the end of the journey (as self-criticism). And it is frequently linked to having abandoned the barrio—that mythical neighborhood of yesteryear which now seems empty, abandoned, decadent. To be sure, the barrio seems to sum up much of what is being longed for, and imagined as lost. But what has actually been lost and arouses such longing?

The Barrio

Lying at the heart of the Argentina's middle-class origin narrative, every barrio has its own rich social tapestry, frequently channeled through its neighborhood associations, clubs, libraries, street life, stores, cafés, and bars.[37] The barrio therefore occupies a central place, both within tango lyrics and in how the popular classes socialized. The barrio in the tango often connects symbolically with the description of the love affair; at other times, it becomes the sole protagonist. The barrio described is often the arrabal which, with the pretext of representing a longed-for past, idealizes spaces, characters, and traditions. There are exceptions, of course. Homero Expósito dedicates "Farol" (1943) to a working-class barrio; "uncharacteristically," says Noemí Ulla.[38] It was certainly unusual for references to a neighborhood so realistically modern-day and sociologically well-defined. Expósito does not even refrain from referring to the old arrabal with a quote from Carriego. We also saw González Tuñón stepping away from the typical tango barrio to be able to refer to real neighborhoods that he was interested in researching as a writer.

Enthroning tango in the center of the city does not indicate the nonexistence of barrios, but reaffirms their role as a positive hub of activity: "if the center represents loss, [...] the system of positive values is embodied and represented by the maternal figure who holds the barrio within a broad embrace."[39] The barrio and the mother represent the origins, the serenity of lost childhood, the stability of a sheltered world and "all the vital adverse experience is lived by the men (or women) of tango as they move away from their normal place of residence," abandoning their barrio.[40] The longing and the return are produced after distancing that could be the result of the search for individual progress in a competitive and soulless world and/or of a love betrayed. "In all cases [...] the maternal call comes [...] after the break is made with the barrio."[41]

If the barrio represents a nostalgia-filled past, what about the "real" neighborhood that exists and where people actually live? Rather than a simple dichotomy between the barrio and the center, we can glimpse a tripartite situation: between the arrabal (a barrio of yesteryear, mythical symbol of yearning) and the center (a world of modern anonymity, with its uncertainties, opportunities, and dangers), implicitly lies the "real" neighborhood, which acts as a necessary contrast to the other "places" and is the reference point experienced not only by the consumers of tango but also by its composers, lyricists, and musicians).[42] The real barrio is represented to us as the negative of the other two spaces, generally described through indirect imagery—the tranquility and safety of the home, the purity of young love, the maternal residence. On a few occasions, however, the descriptions can also be explicit. In fact, with the passing of time, and especially due to the poetical renewal of the 1940s, the barrio that evokes nostalgia seems to bear a closer resemblance to a (clearly idealized) neighborhood of childhood memory, in counterpoint to the arrabal of the compadritos, that has a far more poetic aspect and one that is doubtfully experienced by the authors themselves.

But during the 1920s, largely because the yearning for the barrio became a recurring theme, what emerges is a feeling of belonging to the slum that sometimes is set in opposition not only to the center, but also to the modern life as experienced in the actual neighborhoods of the time. Therefore,

B. Tagle Lara's asphalt marks the demise of the rough neighborhood of "Puente Alsina" (1926), and Iván Diez smartens up the slum in "Sangre de suburbio" (1938). Here it is not the dissolute center but the employee, the white-collar worker, who replaced, to the author's dismay, the tough guy and gangs who knew a thing or two about knives. There was a yearning for a world of adventures and heroism in contrast to the routine, modern-day life of government, factory or office work, not excluding the barrio.

The guapos and compadritos do not appear to be such archetypal figures of the barrios, at least not in the 1920s—a period when tangos became more widely popular. It is more instructive to see the tango's compadrito as a poetical construct that seems to refer to all that has been lost in the modern and civilized life of the center (contrasting with—and perverting—the guapo from the arrabal), but also of the barrio. The compadrito represents desire, the yearning for all that is instinctive, spontaneous, even almost animalistic, that men must repress in order to participate in civilized life and to enjoy the progress that the vast majority sought in the city, but was not shown so complacently as in the immigrant's dreams. The working-class neighborhood, or the requirement to smarten up, undoubtedly represents the daily life of the barrio in the 1920s more faithfully than the guapo. Yet it is the latter who dominates tango lyrics. So who was this guapo character?

> [...] he was not a thief or a ruffian and not necessarily a fool; he fit Carriego's description: a *cultivator of rage* [...] (always) less unworthy than his current Italian distortion as a *cultivator of infamy*, of a small-time thug or "malevito" smarting from the shame of not being a pimp.[43]

Several tangos criticize this supposed distortion of the guapo in the slums who becomes a compadrito, and several authors seem to follow Borges's ethnic explanation without any other basis.[44] But it is precisely the radical distinction between the guapo criollo of the slums—conveniently no longer on the scene—and the modern Italianized "malevito" that clearly shows the constructed, idealized character of the exalted, much-missed figure. It is easy to imagine, moreover, that most tango-song poets, smartly dressed men, would have taken fright at a face-to-face meeting with one of those guapos whom they enjoyed praising so highly. As much as they may have felt solidarity, the underworld was not their world:

> You will be dismayed/ The author of "Mano a mano,"
> I'm a city kid/ with a good wardrobe
> The one who sings to the girl/ In the tango "Milonga fina,"
> Applies hair oil, seven times per week![45]

What was the reason for this praise of a distant manliness? Among the characteristic traits of the culture of poverty, Oscar Lewis included: "a belief in male superiority which crystallizes in machismo or the cult of masculinity," adding that those who live in the culture of poverty suffer far less repression than the middle classes.[46] The reductionism in these words is hard to accept today. Nevertheless, it is interesting to note how a connection exists to the cult of masculinity in so many tangos.[47] At the same time (even disagreeing with the contrast between a middle class supposedly more likely to repress their feelings and a more violent lower class less prone to suffering and repression), the competitors in the race for upward social mobility during the first half of the twentieth century undoubtedly needed to undergo a significant process of acculturation. They had to jettison certain types of behavior, repress desirable conducts, and the (frequently self-inflicted) disciplining of their own body.[48] Partly this explains why:

> The barrio always looked kindly on the guapo. His well-earned notoriety felt like something that belonged to them. For good or bad, his conduct is a kind of rebelliousness, a romantic non-conformism, not so much for what it is, but for what it has ceased to be: meek submission. He is supposed to have freed himself from all those things that regular folk think make life boring and tedious, irritating, and harsh.[49]

The barrio is in contrast to the guapo. He can belong to it, but he is an individual who stands apart from the other, regular, hard-working neighborhood residents. When the guapo did actually exist, he cut a picturesque figure and was never representative or typical. He stood for freedom from the commitments to family and work, from being a good neighbor and citizen; he represented the spontaneous venting of feelings when faced with the containment required by "modern" and "bourgeois" social norms, molded by school, neighborhood socialization, and the market. The guapo symbolized the embodied conjunction of Eros and Thanatos faced with an existence that in its routine could be experienced as the negation of life itself.[50] In the good times, local barrio residents could feel proud of all that separated them from the plebeian compadrito, but when crises or doubts arose about the chosen life path, this figure emerged as a model of what had been given up in a quest for progress, social status, and a civilized lifestyle that failed to live up to expectations. Similarly to the already-extinct gaucho—a figure extolled in the early-twentieth-century criollismo by those who had also played a part in his downfall—the early-twentieth-century guapo was often the object of yearning for those who had tried to distance themselves from this figure in their life decisions.

I began to think about this interpretation of tango's compadrito elements after David Roediger's interpretation of the minstrel.[51] Later I discovered that Borges had already suggested that tango served a similar "compensatory role."[52] Fiercely critical of the connections between tango and the outskirts,[53] Borges frequently expressed his disdain for the melodramatic and whiney tango since the *Guardia Nueva* period. For Borges, the joy and virility of the milonga and the primitive tango revealed the desire for happiness and valor of the men at the very start of the twentieth century.

> Tango today, by contrast, takes pleasure in misfortune and failure, and only accepts happiness and bravery as nostalgic themes, as assets once owned but now lost. The nineteenth-century dweller of the outskirts sought approval for being fortunate, resolute, and fearless; his contemporary equivalent, for having once had such attributes and, above all, for being mistreated, resentful, a victim. From a classic ideal we have shifted to a romantic ideal, in the most abject sense of the word. [... The milongas of yesteryear] expressed a possible, immediate happiness, and those of today, a paradise lost.[54]

For Borges, the early tangos that spoke of the "guapo," his manliness, bravery, and honor, expressed the rebelliousness "of the man who is alone and expects nothing from others,"[55] and his core mission perhaps was none other than "giving Argentinians the certainty of having been brave, of having met the requirement for bravery and honor."[56] He said it as a corollary to a more general observation made by Oscar Wilde who, according to Borges, had argued that:

> [...] music reveals to us a personal past that up until that point we did not know and that prompts us to regret misfortunes; as for myself, I will confess that I do not usually listen to "El Marne" or "Don Juan" without a precise memory of an apocryphal past, that is both stoical and orgiastic, in which I have fought and laid down challenges before ending up being slain, silently, in a shadowy knife-fight.[57]

Borges saw this "compensatory function" in the early lyrics, and dismissed those of later tangos, from the 1920s, when the partial abandonment of the themes of bravery and virility devalued the tango for him, turning it into a kind of *comédie humaine* of Buenos Aires, with a cynicism presented as a possibly detrimental influence on Argentinians in the 1930s.[58] However, as we have seen above, that "precise recollection of an apocryphal past" was by no means disappearing with tango songs in the middle of the second decade of the twentieth century. On the contrary, it continued undiminished, although not always along a single path, adding to the yearning for the stoical and orgiastic participation in the knife fight of the early-1900s guapo, the multiple meanings of the contrast between the figures of the humble girl and the milonguita, the harmony of the lost barrio and the ever-understanding maternal love. One thing is certain: the vast majority of tangueros and tangueras were neither bad men nor errant women, nor lovelorn men wallowing in alcohol, nor vengeful knife-fighters, nor repentant returnees to their parents' homes. But it is possible that many of them saw many other possible existences in these stories, other ways of living that modern life forbade them. In those often-contradictory mixed meanings (the milonguita could function both as the young lad's fear and the horizon of possibilities for the girl),[59] tango's many other compensatory functions seem to have come into play; in tango, and in its reminiscences about primordial (and shadowy) origins, counterweights and consolations could be found for many of the less-pleasurable consequences created by the disciplining and self-limitations required in exchange for modernity's promises of upward social mobility and progress.

* * *

So let us ask again: Tango and the middle classes? There is no simple answer to this question. But this study helps us rule out a direct and linear answer and indicates a path to follow—one that does not seek *the* middle class in tangos, nor tries to explain them by referring to how its songwriters, performers, or listeners supposedly belonged to that class. But it is a path that can guide us through the constitution of a tumultuous, heterogenous subjectivity—a subjectivity that includes deeply classist melodramatic aspects.[60] These combine with others that point to a non-dichotomous, complex differentiation and include aspects we usually identify with a middle-class subjectivity,[61] without any of this excluding the possibility of other elements which, ultimately, suggest the constitution of a more cohesive subject, a more authentic, homogenous, and trans-classist people of the Rio Plata region, as can be surmised from the study quoted by Varela. All of this exists within the framework of an urban culture that cannot hide its malaise in the form of insistent yearnings for apocryphal—more harmonic, more heroic—pasts. Therefore, tango themes such as decency and moral standards, the barrio and the home, the modern world and the longing for what has been lost, can be re-signified in dialogue with processes of identification and contemporary social differentiation. These processes, in many senses, supported the creation of an inclusive and cohesive people. They also strengthened a simple dichotomy between the general public and the powerful, by rejecting a rich, privileged, and abusive elite. In other ways, however, these same phenomena further engendered internal differentiations and distinctions within this popular collective, creating an "us" and a "them" that would be essential when articulating a middle-class identity during the Peronist years.

Notes

1 I would like to give particular thanks to my friends Gastón "El Colo" Galli and Gabriela Rylands for sharing with me their books and knowledge about tango. I discussed previous versions with various people and I would like to express my appreciation for the comments by Matías Bisso, Ezequiel Adamovsky, Juan Martín Duana, Ayelén Fiebelkorn, Emanuel Correa, Javier Guiamet, Lucía Gandolfi, Paula Román, Sergio Visacovsky, Graciela Queirolo, Claudia Stern, and Jaime Cortés.

2 A consensus exists in the historiography of tango about how the *Guardia Nueva* movement marked a transformation in tango's development. According to José Gobello, the first tango "composer"—as opposed to those who had previously written tangos during moments of leisure and without understanding the techniques of composition—was Juan Carlos Cobián (1896–1937). Gobello remarks how Cobián had studied at the Bahía Blanca conservatoire, a particularly interesting piece of information. Attending a music conservatoire did not necessarily imply a middle-class identity (a sector of society so vaguely defined at that time), but this is worth noting because it shows a significant sign that the make-up of popular sectors of society was becoming increasingly complex. Although the conservatoire did not produce middle-class tango artists, it constitutes a distinguishing and differentiated aspect within the popular sectors. José Gobello, *Letras de tango* III (Buenos Aires: Centro Editor, 1997), 132 of the Appendix, "Mujeres y hombres que hicieron el tango. Biografías".

3 The writing of tango lyrics and/or essays about tango by intellectuals of the stature of Cortázar and Borges is often cited as a distinguishing aspect of this popular music from the Rio Plata region. Eduardo Archetti, *Masculinidades: Fútbol, tango y polo en la Argentina* (Buenos Aires: Antropofagia, 2003); Graciela Montaldo places this cross-over between different cultural spaces at the center of the recent understanding of the place occupied by tango and other cultural activities within the city's mass culture. Graciela Montaldo, *Museo del consumo: Archivos de la cultura de masas en Argentina* (Buenos Aires: FCE, 2016). However, this relation does not only reveal the harmonious way in which Gutiérrez and Romero characterize the popular sectors, but also their conflicts and violence, both internally and between these sectors and the "elites."

4 Noemí Ulla, *Tango, rebelión y nostalgia* (Buenos Aires: CEAL, 1982), 80, 83.

5 Archetti, *Masculinidades*, 212. As we will see, these two reasons (one more virile and violent, the other based on a more romantic form of masculinity) do not necessarily occur chronologically nor respond to different social groups. Instead, they seem to co-exist over time in the universe of tango, perhaps serving different "functions" for both actors.

6 Archetti, *Masculinidades*, 205. Archetti also considers that "the 'milonguita' is young, single, from a lower-middle-class family and born in a barrio [...]. The 'milonguita' escapes the barrio, probably from poverty and a future as a housewife." Archetti, *Masculinidades*, 201. But the typical milonguita fled from the characteristic poverty of the tenement housing or *conventillo*, showing that her background is perhaps more humble than that suggested by the "lower-middle-class" descriptor.

7 Gustavo Varela, *Tango y política: Sexo, moral burguesa y revolución en Argentina* (Buenos Aires: Ariel, 2016).

8 Archetti, *Masculinidades*.

9 Marta E. Savigliano, "Malevos llorones y percantas retobadas: El tango como espectáculo de razas, clases e imperialismo," *Relaciones de la Sociedad Argentina de Antropología, XIX* (1993): 79–104

10 Matthew B. Karush, *Culture of Class: Radio and Cinema in the Making of a Divided Argentina, 1920–1946* (Durham, NC: Duke University Press, 2012).

11 Karush, *Culture of Class*, 16.

12 Karush, *Culture of Class*, 59.

13 All of the original Spanish-language tango lyrics quoted in this article are available at https://www.todotango.com/.

14 Enrique Garguin, "El tardío descubrimiento de la clase media en Argentina," *Nuevo Topo* 4 (2007): 85–108; Enrique Garguin, "'Los argentinos descendemos de los barcos': The Racial Articulation of Middle-Class Identity in Argentina (1920–1960)," *Latin American & Caribbean Ethnic Studies* 2, no. 2 (2007):

161–184; Enrique Garguin, "Diferenciación e identificación de clase media en la esfera pública popular," *IX Congreso Argentino de Antropología Social*, Posadas, Misiones (2008); For a comprehensive study of the middle class in Argentina, see Ezequiel Adamovsky, *Historia de la clase media argentina: Apogeo y decadencia de una ilusión, 1919–2003* (Buenos Aires: Planeta, 2009).

15 Gobello, *Letras de tango*; Horacio Ferrer, *El tango: Su historia y evolución* (Buenos Aires: Peña Lillo, 1968); Blas Matamoros, *Historia del tango* (Buenos Aires: Ceal, 1971; Ernesto Sábato, *Tango: Discusión y clave* (Buenos Aires: Losada, 1965). As we will see below, authors such as Borges and Varela take a slightly different perspective than those named previously by differentiating the popular sectors from the world of pimps and prostitutes, clearly indicating that tango emerged from the latter.

16 Ulla, *Tango, rebelión y nostalgia*; Matamoros, *Historia del tango*; Varela, *Tango y política*.

17 Ulla, *Tango, rebelión y nostalgia*, 91.

18 Ulla, *Tango, rebelión y nostalgia*, 96.

19 Gonzáles Tuñón, quoted in Sylvia Saítta, *Regueros de tinta: El diario Crítica en la década de 1920* (Buenos Aires: Sudamericana, 1998), 105.

20 Saítta, *Regueros de tinta*, 106.

21 Tuñón, quoted in Saítta, *Regueros de tinta*, 106.

22 Saítta, *Regueros de tinta*, 107.

23 From different perspectives, Archetti emphasizes the diversity of relationships between couples and the plural nature of masculinities in play within the world of tango, and Alejandro Ogando deconstructs ten variations in the treatment of women, almost all displaying various kinds and levels of misogyny. Archetti, *Masculinidades*; Alejandro Ogando, *Tango y misoginia: Cultura popular en América Latina* (La Plata: EdULP, 2001).

24 Ulla, *Tango, rebelión y nostalgia*, 76.

25 Sergio Pujol indicates this same retrospective idealization for the dance of tango and from as early as 1903, at a time when "tango had not yet fully emerged and yet people were already talking about its decadence." Sergio Pujol, *Historia del baile: De la longa a la disco* (Buenos Aires: Emecé, 1999), 30.

26 Jorge Luis Borges *Textos recobrados 1931–1955* (Buenos Aires: Emecé, 2001), 225–227.

27 "What I want to emphasize is the co-existence of such uneven love-related perspectives descriptions recorded on vinyl by the same musician in the same period, and also intended for the same audience," says Ulla, *Tango, rebelión y nostalgia*, 79; Despite this heterogenous coexistence and the complexity of the social attribution of the first kind, Ulla contends—as we have seen—a transition from one kind of treatment to the other, socially defined by tango's increasing popularity among a section of the middle class. Ulla, *Tango, rebelión y nostalgia*, 77, 81, 83.

28 The theme already exists in "La costurerita que dio aquel mal paso" (1913), by E. Carriego, but does not seem to be much older, according to Irene López. E. Carriego, *La canción del barrio* (Buenos Aires: CEAL 1967); Irene López, "Morochas, milongueras y percantas: Representaciones de la mujer en las letras de tango," *Espéculo: Revista de Estudios literarios* 45 (2010), http://www.ucm.es/info/especulo/numero45/mutango.html; see also Borges, *Textos recobrados*, 68–69; Varela, *Tango y política*, 103–109; and Pujol *Historia del baile*, 115–135.

29 "Tango needs to stay as it is," conversation between Antonio Rodríguez Villar and Enrique Cadícamo (1986), https://www.todotango.com/historias/cronica/218/Cadicamo-%c2%abAl-tango-hay-que-dejarlo-como-esta%c2%bb-/

30 Celedonio Flores emphasizes paternalistic attitudes toward girls from the barrio in "¡Atenti Pebeta!" (1929), while ironically recommending a

particular kind of empowerment: "Then buy yourself a gun and, catching the first scoundrel, / bid farewell to this love rival."

31 Saítta, *Regueros de tinta*, 107.

32 Tuñón, quoted in Saítta, *Regueros de tinta*, 107.

33 Born into a well-off family of La Plata, Carnelli forged a successful career as a tango songwriter, poet, and journalist. She signed her tangos with a pseudonym to hide from her parents an activity that they considered dishonorable for reasons of class and gender. "I was a girl from a bourgeois family with literary ambitions, and it was deemed rather inappropriate for me to write tangos with all its 'lunfardo' slang. My father never knew I wrote them." María Luisa Carnelli, quoted in Nestor Pinzón, "Biografía de María Luisa Carnelli," Todo Tango, http://www.todotango.com/creadores/biografia/855/Maria-Luisa-Carnelli/. According to Savigliano, less than 2% of tango lyrics were written by women and less than 4% (including, of course, a majority written by men) express thoughts through a woman's voice. Savigliano, "Malevos llorones," 91.

34 See Daniel James, *Doña María: Historia de vida, memoria e identidad política* (Buenos Aires: Manantial, 2014), where the gaze of the woman worker goes one step beyond classism, in this case in relation to a poem by N. Olivari; Savigliano also draws attention to the feminine strategies often implicit in the lyrics and other aspects of the tango world, particularly its dance. Savigliano, "Malevos llorones."

35 Karush, *Culture of Class*; Savigliano, "Malevos llorones."

36 Graciela Queirolo, *Mujeres en las oficinas*. (Buenos Aires: Biblos, 2018).

37 Arturo Jauretche, *El medio pelo en la sociedad argentina* (Buenos Aires: Peña Lillo, 1966); Leandro Gutiérrez and Luis Alberto Rómero, *Sectores populares, cultura y política: Buenos Aires en la entreguerra* (Buenos Aires: Sudamericana, 1995); Garguin, "Diferenciación e identificación."

38 Ulla, *Tango, rebelión y nostalgia*, 57.

39 Ulla, *Tango, rebelión y nostalgia*, 51–52.

40 Ulla, *Tango, rebelión y nostalgia*, 50–52.

41 Ulla, *Tango, rebelión y nostalgia*, 50.

42 For more information about the public life of these "real" barrios, see for example, Gutiérrez and Romero, *Sectores populares*; Archetti considers Buenos Aires was already a modern city with a European population by 1930, displaying a "juxtaposition of three landscapes: the center, a space open to residents, visitors, and tourists; the barrio, a particular 'closed' setting that in some cases was home to various social classes and ethnic groups; and the arrabal, a dangerous and peripheral area, occupied by the marginalized population." Archetti, *Masculinidades*, 26.

43 Borges, *Evaristo Carriego* (Buenos Aires: Emecé Editores, 1965 [1930]), 66–67.

44 For example, Andrés Carretero, quoted approvingly in Ulla, *Tango, rebelión y nostalgia*, 59–60.

45 Quoted in Ulla, *Tango, rebelión y nostalgia*, 98.

46 Oscar Lewis, quoted in Ulla, *Tango, rebelión y nostalgia*, 61

47 Ulla, *Tango, rebelión y nostalgia*, 59–67; Ogando, *Tango y misoginia*.

48 Following the work of Freud, Peter Gay points out the role of repressing feelings in the formation of the Victorian middle class: "The bourgeois character, it proposes, is largely built from prohibitions, from things that middle-class people will not do and words they will not allow themselves to say. But if the bourgeois motto is self-abnegation, that is not because their passions are feeble but harnessed—in Freud's word, 'refined'—[…]. The modern bourgeoisie, on this showing, is the class that sublimates its raw urges more thoroughly than any other class and does so many times […] to its regret." Peter Gay, *Schnitzler's Century: The Making of Middle Class Culture, 1815–1914* (New York: W.W. Norton & Company, 2002), 26.

49 Blas Raúl Gallo, *Historia del sainete nacional*, quoted in Ulla, *Tango, rebelión y nostalgia*, 62.
50 The same break came into play in the passage from the happy and expressive *Morocha* of 1905 to the repressive moralizing of *Milonguera* of 1915. López "Morochas, milongueras y percantas."
51 David R. Roediger, *The Wages of Whiteness: Race and the Making of the American Working Class* (London: Verso, 1991).
52 Borges, *Evaristo Carriego*, 155.
53 Borges, *Textos recobrados*, 217–218; In one of the recently published talks of 1965, Borges insisted that tango was born in the brothels, at the intersection of the lives of compadritos, rich kids, women of ill-repute, and musicians. Jorge Luis Borges, *El Tango: Cuatro conferencias* (Buenos Aires: Sudamericana, 2016, 31–42); Varela offers a similar analysis about tango's multi-class origins. Varela, *Tango y política*, 51–84.
54 Borges, *Textos recobrados*, 230–231.
55 Jorge Luis Borges, quoted in Archetti, *Masculinidades*, 196.
56 Borges, *Evaristo Carriego*, 149.
57 Borges, *Evaristo Carriego*, 149.
58 Borges, *Evaristo Carriego*, 160; Archetti, *Masculinidades*, 196.
59 Savigliano, "Malevos llorones."
60 Karush, *Culture of Class*.
61 Ulla, *Tango, rebelión y nostalgia*; Archetti, *Masculinidades*.

10 Public-Sector Employment, the Middle Classes, and Social Position in Mexico City in the Early 1900s

Mario Barbosa Cruz

Social history has broadened its scope in recent decades to include subjects other than workers, artisans, women, and other laborers organized to varying degrees. Studies now focus on the so-called middle classes, and on a particular subset of this group: public- and private-sector administrative employees. These men and women swelled the size of government and private offices, working in public administration jobs providing services to the public or in businesses. From the late nineteenth century, the nascent discipline of sociology noted the expansion of administrative structures and took an interest in understanding a process related to the growth of a sector of society working in offices and sometimes seeking qualifications to secure such employment. In the early twentieth century, exponents in the emerging field of sociology and in the social sciences (from Max Weber to Siegfried Kracauer) worked to increase awareness of this heterogenous social group at a time of increasing government centralization in Europe.[1]

In my previous work I have highlighted some aspects of men and women working in Mexico City's government bureaucracies. Among other issues, I identified an increase in overall numbers, particularly of women employees, a gradual specialization of jobs reflecting the new need for technical training for certain types of employment, the precarity of some positions, and the job insecurity related to the state not acting as an employer and to the country's political instability.[2]

Analogous studies on Mexico and Argentina, for example, have underlined how these employees worked hard to differentiate themselves from others, despite their living conditions and salaries being comparable to those of other urban workers. Some of the earliest studies on this issue in Mexico focused on how women accessed office jobs and on their working conditions vis-à-vis their male counterparts.[3] Other research has looked at different issues such as tastes, forms of distinction, clientelism, and corruption, as well as the connection between changing methods of administrative organization and the need for labor.

This group's wide range of social and working situations makes it a challenging object of study—a difficulty shared with similar analyses of other workers, particularly sectors of the population considered middle

DOI: 10.4324/9781003029311-13

class. To complicate matters further, answering these broad questions requires research into more than one archive. This chapter seeks to explore the social position of these employees in Mexico City, who are de facto members of the middle classes or intermediate sectors. Instead of analyzing methods of differentiation (the subject of a different article),[4] we explore the working conditions, financial constraints, and social instability of public-sector employees. These employees tend to be pigeonholed in middle-class stereotypes and, unfortunately, our research revealed few specific references or broader characterizations of their lives and working conditions.

We chose the period between 1903 and 1931 as a chronological framework to explore important changes in the lives of Mexico City's public-sector employees. The expansion of Porfirio Díaz's bureaucracy (1883–1911) was combined with significant job insecurity, an undeniable result of the political instability of the Revolution (1911–1917). Other relevant factors were the new conditions imposed by the sectors that held power from 1915 in the city, as well as the unsettled political relationships among the triumphant factions, their clashes in the post-revolutionary years and once they began consolidating the one-party state. At that time, organized social sectors and initial attempts to establish workers' associations played a new role in the regime's structure, and increasing corruption at every level became the subject of complaints.

Within this changing context, this chapter analyzes the social conditions of a sector considered to exist between the popular classes and the elites. It follows up ideas about middle-class ways of life and the potential for upward social mobility among members of this class in early-twentieth-century Mexican society, and perhaps in similar contexts elsewhere in Latin America.

The Relative Social Positions of Employees

Before we can analyze these social subjects, we first need to place them within their socio-economic and cultural context. In my experience of researching the lives of employees, I have tried to pinpoint them within bureaucratic structures and precarious social conditions resulting from political conflicts and social confrontations at the end of the nineteenth and in the early twentieth century. One way of learning more about these sectors' situations is to identify the relative positions of various kinds of employees, not only in the class system but also within the bureaucratic apparatus. We consider that this can provide the first level of analysis based on an assessment of material conditions and salaries of these men and women.

When looking at bureaucratic structures, annual budgets containing employee payrolls, positions, and salaries provide a rich source of information since organization charts frequently changed and are unavailable for many departments. As I have been able to show in other texts, these budgets open a window onto various aspects of a state bureaucracy that emulated European models of administrative reorganization and centralization between 1780 and 1810. They also reveal the separation of government into different ministries (of war, internal and foreign affairs, justice, and finance) and other administrative departments.[5]

During this period in Mexico the structure was constantly shifting and the hierarchies and positions were becoming increasingly complex. Some general references can shed some light on this process. An official decree of November 8, 1821 modified the organization of the colonial government, when the Regency of the Mexican Empire established four ministries (internal and foreign affairs, justice, ecclesiastical affairs, finance, and war). The bureaucratic structure continued to exist largely unchanged until 1917 and with only some name changes and the addition of a new ministry for communications and transport in 1891. Lucio Mendieta asserted in 1942 that the Mexican public administration's basic structure existed since 1821, and some newly created ministries and departments merely carried out these same functions. After the most difficult period of fighting during the Revolution, the Organic Law of Public Administration (April 13, 1917) established a further six ministries and three government departments.[6]

The need for more specific roles was cited as an argument for this expansion of bureaucracy, which also entailed more employees in both federal and city governments. On this subject, Mariano Bárcenas Olalde wrote a bachelor's dissertation in 1939 to graduate as a lawyer, referring to a distinguished French scholar of public law, Léon Duguit:

> the modern state's expanding roles necessitate a radical transformation in its traditional structure if it is to carry out its functions and achieve its objectives of maintaining public order and upholding laws, supporting everything that can be generally said to ensure society's stability and improvement. This transformation is based on the concept of Public Service.[7]

Ariel Rodríguez Kuri has identified how many colonial aspects remained in the Mexican capital's local administrations.[8] He observes the widening range and increasing level of detail in the work of the Federal District's governor and its *ayuntamiento* or city council. This author presents the roles established in the 1840 statutes that defined the relations between the governor and the council, as well as each of their departments' respective functions. He also points to a dispute and an increasing centralization of these functions within the Federal District government, as well as to a gradual stripping away of the council's responsibilities, the central theme of Rodríguez Kuri's work.[9]

For the purposes of this chapter, we look specifically at the increase in government functions. In 1840 the city council was divided into 8 departments; by 1901 this number had increased to 21. This compared to the Federal District's government that had 43 (totaling 64 individual offices).

These included one department called "Markets, promenades, weights and measures, industry, and commerce" included in the 1840 law; 61 years later, this department was split into a number of sub-offices, including "Butchers," "Stables," "Pawnshops," "Weights and Measures," "Markets," "Slaughterhouses," "Promenades," and "Bacon Stores" for the city council; "Lodgings," "Pastries and Biscuits," "Guest Houses," "Cafés," "Purveyors of liquors, wines, and preserves," "Inns," "Ice Cream Parlors," "Cakes," "Hostelries," "Confectioners," and "Tamale Sellers," under the aegis of the Federal District's government.[10] Different trades became much more specific, perhaps in order to boost tax collections or following the appearance of other kinds of businesses and lodgings, as in this case. Areas such as commerce, public infrastructure, communications, and more organized surveillance such as foot and mounted police patrols, the police inspectorate, civil police, and so on, all created the need for specific sub-offices that naturally required employees to perform particular functions.

But over and above the increasing number of employees as noted in other articles, and the fact that men occupied most of these positions,[11] this overall diversity in offices offering such employment in the early twentieth century provides us a context for analyzing aspects of public employees and their social position, factoring in their duties and the working conditions during the period in question.

After Independence and for much of the nineteenth century, some laws changed the profile of employees and civil servants. In the colonial era it was well known that people could buy their way into some positions despite the prohibition of such practices. Some of the earliest regulations drafted in 1814 specifically forbade inherited or temporary positions.[12] Although some authors claim that these rules did not apply to public-sector employees, an analysis of the norms, statutes, and laws reveals that various provisions did regulate working conditions, appointments, elected positions within the three branches of government, and the character of the employees.

The republican legislation gave presidents the authority to designate military leaders and officers, diplomats, and civil servants at the finance ministry and in the federal government. They could also make and approve appointments, and fill vacancies. During the nineteenth century, various regulations defined the executive branch's faculties, becoming increasingly specific over the decades, and particularly toward the end of the 1800s, in regard to appointments, discounts, promotions, leaves of absence, taxation, pensions, and records of newly hired and departing employees.[13] In 1911, when Francisco I. Madero became president, a draft civil service law for federal employees responded to criticism about the job insecurity of bureaucrats, making it harder to dismiss high-level civil servants. But although the Senate debated the bill, it was never ratified.[14] Contemporary accounts refer to this issue only reappearing as the subject of legislation in the 1930s with the passing of the Federal Labor Law (1931), when discussions resumed about the need for a specific law on the subject.

In the first decades of the twentieth century there were broad-ranging discussions about public-sector employees: Could they enjoy full rights as workers? Were they allowed to form associations? Was the state their employer? Legal arguments about these issues referred, inter alia, to the type of contract between the state and its employees, the quality of those participating in this contract, the state as a "non-productive" entity, and the state's role as mediator of social conflicts. These analyses cited France as an example of a country where employees had the same rights as workers when parastatal enterprises had that attribute.[15]

As part of the same debate, Marcelo Bárcenas, for example, signaled the importance of distinguishing between different kinds of employees. He divided state workers into three groups: those in a similar situation to private-sector workers, the ones in managerial positions, and employees with public authority. According to Bárcenas, the first two kinds of state employee should enjoy the same rights as enjoyed other workers, while the third type were more akin to civil servants with closer ties to those in power. These discussions about recognizing rights help us understand the differences between these employees and their relative positions. The increasing personnel and specialization of functions undoubtedly also created correspondingly different social and salary configurations, based on their various duties and areas of work. Continuing to apply Bárcenas' employee classification, we could compare the first group to factory workers and the lower class, and place those in the second group to the middle class.

Public-sector employees had been associated with the middle classes. However, these sources and contemporary analyses reveal social differences due to different incomes and other factors relating to people's positions within bureaucratic hierarchies. Apart from Bárcenas' general classification of three types of state workers, there was a much broader scale in each office. For example, we can refer to the initial structure of the Labor Department established by Congress in December 1911 during Francisco I. Madero's presidency, and whose budget was set in January of the following year (Table 10.1).

Although this office had only recently been created, it already had a similar structure to other federal administrative departments. It must be emphasized that, over and above the different salaries, conditions varied between positions. These budgets reveal differences between the salaries considered for each office, as well as between the type of work, the jobs for men and women or for specific age groups, and the personnel employed for particular activities. It also outlines the nature of managerial positions in public-sector offices.

According to figures reproduced by Diego López Rosado, the minimum wage for public-sector employees was

> $16.20 pesos per month for the years 1877 to 1879; rising to $20.55 in 1880, and to $24.70 in 1881, remaining at that level until 1902; increasing to $27.45 in 1903; reaching $30.00 between 1904 and 1907, and ascending to $36.00 from 1908 to 1910.[16]

Table 10.1 Structure of the Labor Department, Budget, 1911

Item	*Daily amount ($)*	*Annual allocation ($)*
One director	18.00	6,570.00
One deputy director	13.70	5,500.50
One official	12.00	4,380.00
Two inspectors, $3,102.50 each	8.50	6,205.00
One official	7.00	2,555.00
One official	5.80	2,117.00
One registrar	5.80	2,117.00
One primary clerk	2.50	912.50
One secondary clerk	2.00	730.00
Two apprentices, $365.00 each	1.00	730.00
General expenses		15,000.00
Total		46,317.00

Source: *Diario Oficial de la Federación*, vol. CXVII, no. 41, December 18, 1911 (Amounts in Mexican pesos).

In 1941, José C. Valadés wrote that these salaries—together with the poor housing and food shortages affecting these "intermediate strands of society," except for their suits—forced these employees to endure "all the deprivations of the lowest sectors of society."[17]

These sources and accounts are useful for making comparative analyses of structures, working conditions, positions, and salaries. They also expose the precarious conditions of sectors lacking the protection of labor legislation due to the ambiguity of their position and because they appeared to enjoy a stability not borne out by their income. These employees may have been members of the so-called intermediate sectors or middle classes, yet this relative position did not guarantee they could cover basic needs for themselves and their families.

The Importance of Social Distinctions, Beyond Salaries

Records in personnel files, service records, and archive documents can also contribute to this research into public-sector employees' social position and conditions. This material is naturally incomplete, since record-keepers selected information to provide samples according to specific criteria, or for much more strategic reasons to cover up or emphasize certain actions or decisions made by the administration itself at a given moment.[18]

In the case of employees' career development, hundreds of fragmentary references to employees exist, in the form of small files containing some notification about an appointment, or perhaps as a document providing a very concise notice of dismissal. This information shows that, on the whole, these employees held onto their jobs only briefly, and perhaps also reveals some of the specific causes of dismissal: budgetary shortfall, performance-related issues, or the decision to eliminate a certain position from the organizational structure. It also brings to light the social consequences of losing a job for these sectors considered middle class both by themselves and by public opinion; it also points to the risk of a possible loss of social status.[19] These sectors walked on a "tightrope": they lived amid personal constraints, and with a constant fear of slipping down the social ladder if they lost their job, if a political or economic crisis hit, or if their circle lost political power to give them jobs or support.

This precariousness is evident in documentation on housing, the composition of their families, their personal vicissitudes, as well as career developments recorded in more comprehensive files. In some cases, my research revealed where these employees lived and worked so that I could identify their physical whereabouts in the city and make some observations about their social position.[20] These documents also detail the requirements (education, training, experience, physical appearance) and the importance of recommendations and the membership of (or proximity to) circles of power in order to access public-sector jobs. Social positions were intertwined with maintaining personal relationships with family and friends who formed the basis of clientelist networks—networks that provided the foundation of personal and political positions, and *compadrazgo* relationships.[21]

References also exist to public-sector employees who held onto their jobs for years, sometimes even decades, and who formed part of the privileged group who could request and sometimes even secure a pension. The very few employees in this situation matches information found in other sources about the dearth of state pensioners, a subject as yet unexplored by historiographical studies in Mexico. Further details on this issue appear in the budget headings on pensions, confirming the meager amounts spent on paying pensions to lifelong employees.

In a handful of cases, the files include descriptions of employees' longer-term career developments, letters of recommendation, and transfers between different departments. They even allow us to follow up the various positions occupied by these civil servants. These data enable deeper analysis of job insecurity and differences between the clientelist practices of the Porfirio Díaz era and those found in the competing political factions during the Revolution. Some of these differences appear in the supporting arguments of those recommending others for jobs or requesting employment themselves. In the case of the former, we find family networks, *compadrazgos*, friendships, or memberships of groups attached to a local *caudillo* or strong man, military leader, or a politician within the circle of power.

The following analysis uses as an example some files from the Ministry of Labor held in the General Archive of the Nation (Archivo General de la Nación), which provide information about the conditions for securing a public-sector job. These files about men seeking to hold onto their jobs, for example, include correspondence in which they offer their services and tell personal accounts[22]—as in this letter addressed to the Director of the Labor Department, dated January 17, 1916:

> I am writing to kindly request an employment application form, since I am currently unemployed and have a family to provide for, hence my need to secure the most reliable means of support. Therefore I am hopeful that after due deliberation of this Department under your distinguished directorship I may be successful in my application. However, if by misfortune there is no vacancy or it proves impossible to find the job that I seek, I have no objection to working in any other capacity in agriculture or mining, either as an office clerk or a manual laborer...[23]

Such documents make it possible to follow up these requests and to see how government departments and successive governors tried to dodge the many applications made by the unemployed desperately seeking work during the crisis facing the Mexican capital due to the armed conflict and the nationwide political instability. In this case, the signatory even referred to his willingness to take other jobs, as an extreme alternative that would involve a loss of social status entailed by requesting the favor from the recipient of his missive. These job applications, or the creation of departments specifically to handle them, reveal the severity of the unemployment problem for people who had previously held government jobs and found themselves walking on the tightrope mentioned above. These mechanisms (specially created forms or departments) constitute some of the means of containing the difficult problem of social instability caused by the Revolution in the second decade of the twentieth century. Rodríguez Kuri points out that the newly installed political groups in this period took time to settle into their new national role and this affected people's living conditions: "It caused an impact on every monetary and financial variable for factory workers, artisans, day laborers, storekeepers, employees, teachers, and business owners." For example, the exchange rate fell drastically and the prices of basic goods rose by between 200% and 900% during 1914 and 1915, according to the American Red Cross. This same author uses three words to sum up the effects of the crisis on the general populace: shortages, inflation, and hunger.[24]

In times of crisis, unemployment and a lack of opportunities motivated some people to seek work using the means at their disposal. By analyzing a particular office, as in the case of this Labor Department toward the end of the 1910s and in the early 1920s, we see personnel movements and continuous changes, in all likelihood the result of budget cuts. Documents also show people using various strategies to secure, maintain, or recover jobs. Some of these refer to the type of work, the career path, and personal aptitudes:

> Should the proposal be accepted [...] for the promotion of Víctor Álvarez Sáenz, if you have no objection I respectfully request that he be replaced by Rodolfo Medina, the young *Oficial Cuarto* working in this Ministry who has demonstrated competence and performed well in his duties.
>
> Please note that I am not putting forward the names of other employees from this same Office, since they are less senior or have only recently been promoted.[25]

In this instance the recommendations are strictly work-related and offer a glimpse of the practice of internal promotions. Other files show the weight of political recommendations and the importance of personal connections for people to maintain their social and employment status. Given the constant dismissals and changes in the bureaucracy at that time, clientelist strategies become clearly visible in this world of favors and exchanges. A letter signed in February 1924 makes specific references to political affiliations in a request for re-employment:

> I am pleased to submit for your consideration Javier Fernández, a friend and fellow party member, who informed me that he was dismissed from his job as Labor Inspector in the Ministry under your authority, without any reason provided.
>
> This recommendation is made only for those people such as Señor Fernández who are truly deserving of special consideration.
>
> Señor Fernández has been an Obregón supporter since the outset, from the times when loyalty was tested.
>
> Rest assured that you would be acting most fairly in reinstating him in his job, and I trust in this possibility because I am aware of your just actions in public life, and particularly in regard to serious, competent, and worthy fellow party members.[26]

At this time of clashes between factions and the consolidation of political leaderships, such requests speak of labor insecurity and strategies adopted to maintain a job and, by the same token, a social position. The first example shows the extreme measures taken to maintain jobs and the privilege associated with being a member of the bureaucracy.

At this juncture it is worth detailing some reasons for the social and labor insecurity evident in the federal ministry archives (such as the Ministry of Labor) and in those of the government offices of the Federal District, an administrative entity with its own governor directly appointed by the president. Tensions provoked by the functions of these newly created government departments continued to grow throughout the nineteenth century and became more pronounced under the increasingly centralized government of Porfirio Díaz. These government offices took over duties formerly within the remit of city government offices, leading to their aforesaid marginalization. Mexico City's Historical Archive (Archivo Histórico de la Ciudad de México) contains information about several aspects of the work of Mexico City's municipality and the other 13 municipalities in this administrative entity, whose members were elected by popular vote since the start of the republican period. The division by function and the increasing number of offices (considered part and parcel of modernization) clashed with this council structure and stirred up tensions at a time when these new administrative units were considered more efficient than their counterparts in the city council. Political instability increased these frictions in the early 1900s, making it more difficult to hold down a job in government when obtained thanks to personal relationships with the government in turn.

In Mexican historiography, it is a commonplace observation that the Revolution only partially affected the capital's population. According to such documentary evidence, the population of a city that mainly provided services suffered the crisis differently to the rest of the country: job instability or losses, as well as shortages, public health problems caused by epidemics, and restrictions on movement caused by the activities of revolutionary forces.[27]

Analyzing the history of social instability caused by the Revolution requires understanding the context of how political shifts affected society during a process of constant change and gradual consolidation of a new public administration since the late 1800s. At this level, investigation reveals employment conditions and the role of the state and its institutions as an employer. It also outlines the practices of recruitment and clientelism, the increasing respect for workers' rights, and even the political persecution that also affected the precarious working conditions of public-sector employees, as we will see in the following section.

Secret Surveillance of Public-Sector Employees

Since the start of the republican era historians can find reports by secret agents with important information for the ruling political elites. Laura Muñoz has written about the work of these undercover agents sent by the recently formed government of independent Mexico to neighboring countries, to the land borders, but above all to countries in the Caribbean that posed a risk due to the constant rumors of a possible Spanish reconquest that would spread out from the Caribbean islands. These agents "reported on all events or rumors, especially during the third decade of the nineteenth century, not only about plans for a reconquest, but also about the movements of ships or the trafficking of slaves and other merchandise."[28]

Some decades later, when Porfirio Díaz's government was under threat, reports began to circulate about the activities of the *acordada* or secret police. John Kenneth Turner, author of *Barbarous Mexico* (1908), wrote one of the fiercest criticisms of the Porfirio Díaz regime, reporting twice as many secret police as there were regular ones on his visit to Mexico City:

> You see a uniformed policeman standing in the middle of the street. That is all you see, or at least all you notice. But leaning against the wall of that alley entrance is a man whom you take to be a loafer; over on the other side lounges a man whom you think is a peon. Just start something and then try to get away. Both of those men will be after you. There is no getting away in Mexico City; every alley is guarded as well as every street!
>
> [...] they know your business as well as you do yourself. They talk with you and you never suspect. When you cross the border they take your name and business and address, and before you've reached the capital they know whether you've told the truth or not. They know what you're here for and have decided what they're going to do about it."[29]

Why did Turner refer to the secret police's activities at such length? Here we will not cite examples of political espionage or discuss the many civil servants engaged in this activity; instead, for the purposes of this chapter, we show the surveillance and information-gathering related to Federal District employees, in particular with reference to their loyalty and commitment to the "government's stability." At a time when a new regime was still consolidating its rule and people feared changes of political leadership, some public-sector employees became targets of these secret investigations ordered by high-ranking civil servants in the Interior Ministry during the period covered in this chapter. Therefore, the Confidential Department's files held in the Interior Ministry's General Archive of the Nation provide examples of records that reveal the surveillance of public-sector employees. They also give an insight into how civil servants experienced clashes between rival political factions, providing yet more evidence of their precarious employment and their difficulties is maintaining a stable social position.

Unfortunately, these archives are not comprehensively indexed, making it difficult to locate the files needed for a more in-depth analysis of public-sector employee surveillance. For our purposes, these files contain two particularly relevant elements: the nature of civil servants' work, and their surveillance duties. What were their main aims? What relevant information could this surveillance provide about the issues mentioned previously in this article—in other words, about public-sector employees' social structures, as well as their individual possibilities and conditions?

We were fortunate to find the text of a talk given by a secret agent to his fellow agents on February 4, 1925. It is relevant to note that Plutarco Elías Calles—a post-revolutionary *caudillo* with a reputation for persecuting his political rivals and radical Catholic groups—was the country's president at this time. Many files held by the Confidential Department from this period are accessible to researchers. In his talk, Carlos I. Flores, identified as an agent attached to "la primera delegación número 4," defined himself as self-taught, an orphan, and someone who took on "menial jobs" in order to earn a living. He added that he was commissioned to give a talk and "to explain the many cases this Department handles on a daily basis." He focused on a number of main themes: What are secret agents, what do they need to know, and what are their duties and obligations?

What this talk reveals about the type of work carried out by these police agents is more relevant than a detailed description of its actual contents. Flores said it was untrue that agents only spent their time "constantly harassing people who opposed the government." On the contrary, agents should be utterly discrete, have a broad social network, be unquestioningly loyal to the government, well versed in political science, history, geography, electoral law, the Constitution, government bulletins, and the state of the country: "[The agent] must be knowledgeable about revolutionary trends in order to know which states or areas of the nation have implemented reforms, where they are in jeopardy, who is obstructing them, and how." One of his pieces of advice was "to encourage discussions about issues other than the one of interest and then carefully steer the conversation toward the relevant topic in order to gather observations, opinions, views, and information from your interlocutor."[30] It is possible to compare this role with the surveillance files containing reports of the actual implementation of this work.

This department's investigations offer clues about the relationships between public-sector employees and the population at large, and therefore about the qualities required by these civil servants and how their work triggered debates among their contemporaries—an important discussion since it related both to the values and loyalty to the political leader's project, as well to public-sector employees being considered as workers with rights. In the case in question, we can supplement Flores' self-awareness with pronouncements by politicians or administrative departments on the issue. As already indicated, some Law dissertations also addressed this role of civil servants that differentiated public-sector employees from workers elsewhere in society. This idea is comparable to early sociological studies on bureaucracy that emphasized this particular characteristic of government employees[31] and a particular quality that precluded them from enjoying labor rights. This situation gradually began to change from the 1930s, as said above, with the entry into force of the Federal Labor Law.

These reports by secret agents also give insights into the mechanisms of Plutarco Elías Calles government's surveillance of state-employees' activities. This was not merely political persecution but a response to accusations of official corruption or favoritism. Perhaps both reasons enter the picture in some cases, but at least the documents highlight accusations of corruption among employees with a degree of power on the hierarchy in each department. These accusations are repeated in some of the complaints lodged by citizens of the capital held on file. The interesting aspect of this case is the research into the background of those involved and the campaign to find enemies of the Revolution within the bureaucracy itself. On the one hand, there was an interest in ensuring the loyalty of the bureaucratic apparatus to the political *caudillos* in power and, on the other, the sources expose acts of corruption. Records from the time of Venustiano Carranza's presidency include forms detailing the backgrounds of public-sector employees, particularly their connections to previous administrations—either with governments seen as friends (Madero's, in particular), or as enemies (Victoriano Huerta, Emiliano Zapata, and of course Porfirio Díaz). The various sources provide examples of the various types of research into the past of public officials, the weight of recommendations in securing employment, the increasing clientelism of political factions, as well as suspicions raised by employees' membership of the early worker associations.

Accusations of corruption focus on those groups benefitting most—particularly inspectors and commissioners. Records often refer to bribes, favors in exchange for money, nepotism, and family networks in public employment. This issue not only indicates this world of interrelations and favors—it also shows the instability and strategies of certain social sectors to maintain their grip on power. But in the case of employees, these reports reveal their capability of agency, their strategies for holding onto jobs, the political relations they established, and the clientelist structures whereby everyone sought to profit. The bureaucracy gave politicians and military officers free rein to help maintain and reinforce their circles of power. State employees used various methods to sustain or increase their income: some supplemented their salaries with bribes or their low level of prestige through the exchange of favors. Others boosted their income by offering protection to those engaged in illegal or prohibited commercial activities. Complaints can shed some light when researching this murky world of corruption, and so too can the evidence revealed by these investigations about government malpractice.

Gabriel Vommaro and Hélène Combes consider clientelism as an analytical category to understand these mutually beneficial relationships and exchanges, as well as an ethical label to certify these practices as an expression of a malfunctioning democracy.[32] Staying at the first level of analysis and understanding these material and symbolic clientelist relations between asymmetrical actors can help us understand their relative positions, as well as the tension inherent in trying to maintain these positions based on this complex network of unequal exchanges. In the case of the social subjects analyzed in this chapter, this improves our knowledge of their attitudes and practices, over and above disparagement or labels of unethical behavior attached to bureaucrats.

Conclusion

An article on the work of Natalie Davis unearths some of the implicit aspects of social history in recent years:

> The focus on social issues implicitly brings up the debate over the liberty of individuals, their ability to face their world with creative and resolute strategies that are, in Davis' work as a historian, the ones that give men and women their sociocultural form, beyond the limitations of material and intellectual structures.[33]

This quote about Davis's work brings up again these two levels of analysis chosen for this chapter and that enable us to explore, based on documentary sources, the social positions of public-sector employees in the midst of shifting sands of bureaucracy and the relationships established between the various social subjects interacting in this sector of society. It also enables us to consider the need to delve further into clientelist relationships based on the differential positions of those involved in the network of favors and exchanges.

The issues explored in this chapter provide an opportunity to consider that these so-called middle-class sectors are varied and disconnected from the stereotype of social groups with a privileged social standing. Although they do not suffer the ordeals of extreme poverty, they still struggle to meet basic needs: they walked a tightrope every day on meager salaries and with little job security. However, in their efforts to differentiate themselves from other sectors (especially those whom they considered to be socially inferior) they worked hard to maintain their social positions in the face of the vicissitudes caused by political crises and the financial constraints of the period under study.

The modernization and expansion of the bureaucracy continued a trend that had begun in the nineteenth century, despite the political upheaval caused by the Mexican Revolution. In this process, public-sector employees continued to be considered—by themselves and by public opinion—as members of the middle class. Political instabilities had social repercussions, and for some of these subjects "being in the middle" entailed the risk of slipping down the social ladder. By strengthening the clientelist networks explored in this chapter, these employees were able to maintain the social and labor position of these sectors. Apart from recognizing themselves from a social perspective, and engaging in activities that set them apart from others, public-sector employees also increasingly strengthened their political connections and loyalties and sought other means to maintain and increase their income. Some years later, those loyalties would form the basis of grassroots organizations that supported the one-party state and the post-revolutionary project already in place. In the meantime, those tumultuous years show how, for this social group of public-sector employees, maintaining a social position implied making personal efforts to strengthen ties with political groups in the ascendency, and thus defending the project of a newly established ruling class put in place by the forces that triumphed after the Revolution.

By incorporating new historiographical sources, we have been able to analyze the social characteristics as well as the possibilities and restrictions in the agency of the social groups included in broad categories such as the elites and middle-class or popular sectors (that should be the subject of more specific studies). History faces the challenge of rethinking these categories, historicizing them, and fleshing them out on the basis of a dialogue between theory and the particular realities visible through a permanent confrontation with evidence and observations from various sources. For this chapter, we researched the possibilities and different ways public-sector employees related to other social sectors in order to maintain their social position, and, in the process, we saw the limitations experienced by those who identified themselves as members of the middle class.

This chapter is an invitation to historicize and ascribe meaning to categories in which we positioned social groups. This is obviously not a simple task. However, exploring their living and working conditions takes a new approach to received opinion that fails to take into account the considerable differences to other contexts, even when compared to other Latin American countries.

For the case examined in this chapter, we cannot use the experience of public-sector employees to generalize the situation of sectors considered as middle class. However, studying these specific actors reveals some of their characteristics. Such a wide range of men and women fit into the middle-class category that further studies need to locate them within their specific spatial and temporal contexts, and to explore their living conditions in the midst of the crises triggered by Mexico's political transformations in the early twentieth century.

Notes

1 Lutz Raphael, *Ley y orden: Dominación mediante la administración el siglo XIX* (Madrid: Siglo XXI Ed., 2008).
2 Mario Barbosa, "Empleados públicos en la ciudad de México: Condiciones laborales y construcción de la administración pública (1903–1931)," in *Cuestión social, políticas sociales y construcción del Estado social en América Latina, siglo XX*, eds. Fernando Remedi and Mario Barbosa (Mexico City: Centro de Estudios Carlos E. Segreti; UAM-Cuajimalpa, 2014), 137–158.
3 Graciela Queirolo, *Mujeres en las oficinas: Trabajo, género y clase en el sector administrativo (Buenos Aires, 1910–1950)* (Buenos Aires: Biblos, 2018); Susie Porter, *From Angel to Office Worker: Middle-Class Identity and Female Consciousness in Mexico, 1890–1950* (Lincoln: University of Nebraska Press, 2018).
4 Mario Barbosa, "Distinciones y apariencias: La clase media en la Ciudad de México entre el Porfiriato y la Revolución," *Oficio: Revista de Historia e Interdisciplina*, no. 10 (2020): 9–23.

5 Raphael, *Ley y orden*, 65ff.
6 Lucio Mendieta y Núñez, *La administración pública en México* (Mexico City: UNAM, 1942), 68–73.
7 Mariano Bárcenas Olalde, "El Estado patrón: Crítica al estatuto jurídico de los trabajadores al servicio de los poderes de la Unión" (Bachelor's diss., Mexico City: UNAM, 1939), 26. Underlining in the original.
8 Rodríguez Kuri writes: "for much of the nineteenth century, and even after the enactment of the 1840 ordinances, municipal authorities had to resort, discretionally and opportunistically, to a traditional interpretation of colonial law and "derecho gaditano" (the legal framework for municipal administrations based on the Constitution of Cádiz)." Ariel Rodríguez Kuri, *La experiencia olvidada: El Ayuntamiento de México; Política y gobierno, 1876–1912* (Mexico City: El Colegio de México; UAM-Azcapotzalco, 1996), 23.
9 Rodríguez Kuri, *La experiencia olvidada*, 29ff.
10 Rodríguez Kuri, *La experiencia olvidada*, 29–30.
11 According to population surveys, in 1900 there were 11,534 male employees and 423 women employees. By 1930, that number had grown considerably, to 143,134 men and 10,209 women. In percentage terms, during this period the proportion of women rose from 3.6% to 7%. Barbosa, "Empleados públicos," 144.
12 See Articles 25 and 26 of the Constitutional Decree for the Freedom of Mexican America, Apatzingan, 22 October 1814, quoted in Carolina Pérez Rodríguez Lara, "La relación de servicio entre el Estado y sus trabajadores," (PhD diss., Mexico City: UNAM, 1968), 20.
13 For example, in 1885 decrees and bulletins defined these areas and even specified the travel expenses of federal employees. Similarly, in 1896, the regulatory laws of Articles 104 and 105 of the 1857 Constitution established penalties for dismissal, payments for labor immobility, and the granting of promotions. Rodríguez Lara, "La relación de servicio," 26, 27.
14 Adelaido Ezquerra Hernández, "El Estado patrón" (PhD diss., Mexico City: UNAM, 1939), 19.
15 Mariano Bárcenas Olalde, "El Estado patrón: Crítica al estatuto jurídico de los trabajadores al servicio de los poderes de la Unión" (PhD diss., Mexico City: UNAM, 1939), 56.
16 Diego López Rosado, *La burocracia en México: México independiente* (Mexico City: Secretaría de Comercio, 1980), 348.
17 José C. Valadés, quoted in López Rosado, *La burocracia en México*, 349.
18 The composition of these administrative archives and the reasons for keeping them remain a mystery for researchers analyzing the volumes without any clues about how they were put together. The archives' organization—with their repetitive information, undoubted omissions, and more complete records for specific periods—also clearly reveals the temporary limitations and the specific characteristics of the various government departments.
19 This text will not refer to the social identity of these sectors. Their social activities and efforts to distinguish themselves from others undoubtedly show that they saw themselves as part of the middle class. This issue was the subject of detailed analysis in Barbosa, "Distinciones y apariencias."
20 Mario Barbosa, "Los empleados públicos, 1903–1931," in *Los trabajadores de la ciudad de México, 1860–1950: Textos en homenaje a Clara E. Lida*, eds. Carlos Illades and Mario Barbosa (Mexico City: El Colegio de México, 2013), 117–154.
21 A term that describes a relationship that is either formal (between parents and godparents) or a very close, informal friendship of mutual support.

22 Unfortunately, we did not find women's files with this kind of details in the information to help our understanding of measures taken to apply for or hold down a job as a public-sector employee. A possible explanation is the fact that, as mentioned above, most employees were men (95% in the second decade of the twentieth century).

23 "Solicitudes de trabajo. Miguel Aguilar." Archivo General de la Nación, Departamento del Trabajo. Sección: auxilios, caja 109, exp. 2.

24 Ariel Rodríguez Kuri's book is one of the few studies on the impact of the crisis and the war on Mexico City from 1914 to the end of this decade. Ariel Rodríguez Kuri, *Historias de desasosiego: La revolución en la ciudad de México, 1911–1922* (Mexico City: El Colegio de México, 2010), 143–162. Research into the impact on the job market remains pending.

25 From the Chief of the Labor Department to the Chief Administrative Officer, May 21, 1920. Archivo General de la Nación, Ramo del Trabajo, caja 139, exp. 1.

26 Letter addressed to General Manuel Pérez Treviño, Minister of Industy, Commerce and Transport, February 14, 1924. File of Inspector Javier Fernández. Archivo General de la Nación, Ramo del Trabajo, caja 514, exp. 4.

27 Ariel Rodríguez Kuri's aforementioned work provides illuminating detail on the problems of supplies and the movements of the revolutionary forces in and around the Mexican capital. Rodrígez Kuri, *Historias de desasosiego*, 99ff.

28 Laura Muñoz, "Agentes confidenciales y funcionarios consulares en el Golfo-Caribe: La labor de Feliciano Montenegro," *Secuencia*, no. 48 (2000): 73.

29 John Kenneth Turner, *México bárbaro* (Mexico City: Ediciones Leyenda, 2008), 102.

30 "Carlos I. Flores. Su expediente," Archivo General de la Nación. Fondo: Secretaría de Gobernación. Departamento de Investigaciones Políticas y Sociales. Confidencial, caja 50, exp. 1.

31 Mario Barbosa, "Los empleados públicos," 117–154.

32 Gabriel Vommaro and Hélène Combes, *El clientelismo político desde 1950 hasta nuestros días* (Buenos Aires: Siglo XXI Editores, 2016).

33 María José de la Pascua Sánchez, "Natalie Z. Davis o la historia de las mujeres desde una historia social renovada," *Historia Social* 75 (2013): 97.

11 "Cheerful, Attentive, and Polite"

Store Clerks and the Middle Class in Early-Twentieth-Century Mexico City[1]

Cristina Sánchez Parra

On August 23, 1924, the communist newspaper *El Machete* published an article criticizing the appalling living conditions of clerks, identifying them as representatives of Mexico's middle class and suggesting that their only goal in life was to avoid losing their job, "by defending it, if not quite by any means, at least by hunching their backs at the expense of their pride, sometimes their dignity, shuddering at the mere mention of the word 'dismissal.'"[2] This same article also referred directly to the economic hardships facing these workers on account of their meager salaries:

> The financial situation facing the middle class is unimaginably grim. For store and office clerks [...] society's demands are a ball-and-chain worn by this hapless member of the middle class. Clothing, housing, and everything else required to keep up appearances forces them to skimp on food and lose sleep over the domestic shortages that they can never remedy.[3]

This statement categorizes store clerks as members of the middle class and perceives their working conditions to be unjust. Based on these two premises, this chapter analyzes the workplace environment of store clerks employed in medium- and large-sized clothes shops in Mexico City at the dawn of the twentieth century.[4] The particular aspects of their job reveal not only where these employees worked, but also the skills required to obtain and hold onto their positions.

This study will therefore refer to places and skills as components of store clerks' life experience.[5] Therefore, we must clearly define the workplace and identify aspects of the store clerks' job that both connected these workers to, and distinguished them from, other employees. In short, an examination of locations and skills uncovers what it meant to belong to this sector of society.

Knowledge in Class Practices: An Analytical Proposal

Considering the middle class as a category is not straightforward. Given this concept's long history, any attempt to analyze it requires various

DOI: 10.4324/9781003029311-14

initial clarifications. If we seek to understand the social universe of a particular group of workers (who do not exactly represent the center of a class struggle), then there is only limited usefulness in using the traditional references to the middle class as society's "happy medium," acting as a kind of catalyst between the antagonistic positions occupied by the upper classes and, at the other end of the spectrum, the lower or popular classes.[6] Similarly, a structuralist focus on the relationship between class and the means of production falls short when attempting to understand a group of employees' aspirations in addition to their places of work.

Mario Barbosa's studies on the aspirational element of the lifestyle and everyday habits as fundamental aspects of white-collar workers in the Mexican bureaucratic apparatus in the early 1900s. Apart from focusing on living spaces and education as a factor in social mobility, Barbosa also explores how these sectors of society sought to differentiate themselves, particularly from popular sectors. This raises the issue of appearances and consumption[7]—another layer of analysis included in this chapter that enriches the study of the middle classes.

Without overlooking these theories' significant contributions to defining the middle class, we should also indicate the concept's history, in other words its particular characteristics in the time and space in question. Hence the usefulness of considering the idea of class as a *practice*, or as a "constantly developing category and reality."[8] Along these same lines, we can also understand class as a community's particular experience, considering a social group's capacity to perform, form relationships, and generate its own discourses.

For E.P. Thompson, the notion of experience requires an understanding of class as: "a relationship, and not a thing [...] if we watch men over an adequate period of social change, we observe patterns in their relationships, their ideas, and their institutions."[9] In this sense, experience calls upon some practices which, according to Ricardo López-Pedreros, represent a useful category to move beyond the idea of class linked to the economic structure, and to rescue it as a real and discursive notion.[10] But thinking about class as a set of practices also enables us to rescue the historicity of a social group, in this case store clerks in early-twentieth-century Mexico City.

To discuss these clerks on the basis of their practices, this study has two main analytical focuses: firstly, the subjects, their inter-relationships and places of sociability; and secondly, the knowledge generated through their daily experience as a social group performing comparable functions and with similar aspirational horizons.[11] This division into two themes does not imply two separate categories; knowledge cannot exist without identifying those who generate it, nor can there be labor relations without spatial conditions.

Class practices—the relationship between subjects and the knowledge they generate—will therefore provide this chapter's common thread. We can learn about a social group's practices through its discourses, hence the importance of understanding that:

> "Knowledge" is defined as a space that is fairly open to learning; it is a space where we can find discourses on many different levels, ranging from those that are only beginning to have discursive objects and practices to differentiate them from other discourses and to become specified, to those that achieve a systematicity that does not yet conform to formal criteria.[12]

The breadth of the notion of *knowledge* opens up a wide range of possible analyses. From this perspective, we can understand as a discourse everything from a store clerk's job skills to the political thought expressed in the demands for their profession to have a higher status. This accumulation of knowledge comprised in the discourse of store clerks reveals the construction of class identities, as we will see below.

These discourses arise from a particular set of working conditions, in terms of their space. The store is the place where the clerks carry out their work, but it is also the locale for power relations, individualization, and corporal discipline, which, according to Michel Foucault, open the door to social stratification in efforts to control labor practices. Hence "the place, the condition, the field of emergence, the authority to differentiate between individuals [...] defines the possibilities of appearance and delimitation of that which gives meaning to the sentence."[13] In this sense, both discourses and their contexts of emergence define subjects' experiences. Therefore, characterizing the workplaces where store clerks sold clothes in Mexico City is a necessary step toward understanding their practices.

Clothing Store Spaces

The Porfirio Díaz government's distinctive idea of progress expressed itself, among other ways, in the consolidation of specific districts for clothing stores—notably along the main streets around Mexico City's central square, the Plaza de la Constitución. The capital's infrastructure was rapidly modernizing in the final decade of the nineteenth century; the government wanted to put Mexico on the same level as other capitals around the world such as New York, Paris, and London by widening streets, expanding the tram network, building new drainage systems, increasing electrification, constructing new buildings, and demolishing or renovating older ones.

As part of this modernization drive, discussions also focused on the city's cleanliness and beautification as an essential part of the civilizing project of the era. The local authorities supported all kinds of initiative to improve the aesthetical appearance the capital's inhabitants and to lend them distinction—hence the proliferation of specialist, sophisticated, and tasteful clothes stores met with the approval of the socially ambitious Porfirian society.

French-owned stores[14] specialized in clothes retailing were within the spheres that shaped such ideals. Department stores were the prime example of the "spirit of the times"; they boasted imposing architecture and also demarcated luxury shopping districts. The streets of Plateros and San Francisco (today's Madero) became an established shopping precinct due to the wide range of clothing offered to an equally diverse clientele.

During the first decade of the twentieth century, the streets in the capital's center became lined with shops. The most prestigious boutiques, department stores, and hat shops were mainly on the streets of Monterilla (now 5 de Febrero) and San Bernardo (now Venustiano Carranza). Fashion houses and sewing workshops were located a few blocks further out from the city's first block. Tailors were scattered across this central area, alongside pawnbrokers and other more modest businesses.

The development of an increasingly well-defined precinct of stores selling textiles, clothing, and accessories was accompanied by improvements in these establishments' health and hygiene standards, particularly in the case of medium- and large-sized stores with open interior spaces that were well-lit and ventilated. The department stores were at the vanguard of modernity in their upmarket approach;[15] they aimed higher than providing basic standards of cleanliness, and in the finest Parisian style their magnificent interiors became showcases of beauty and elegance. New consumer patterns and behaviors developed as customers could move freely along wide corridors, clearly demarcated departments stocked different kinds of merchandise,[16] and visitors had direct access to products. These stores generally had more than three floors: they used the lower levels for retail sales and the upper ones for wholesale, nationwide transactions. Employees sometimes even had accommodation at the top of some of the largest stores.[17]

Our analysis focuses on the employees behind the counters in these stores. Ensconced in glamorous surroundings, they embody the store's philosophy, giving them a twofold social role: they represented European cosmopolitanism and aspired to climb the social ladder by becoming partners within the stores where they worked or, at least, to save up enough money to return to their places of origin. Apart from identifying the particular spatial characteristics of these store clerks' workplaces, we also need to examine their working conditions as a way of putting together the puzzle of this sector of society's *practices*.

Life As a Store Clerk in Mexico City

In 1911, the marketing of a well-known brand of "blood-purifying" sarsaparilla syrup targeted store clerks, referring to how "their duties prevent them from going for walks or doing other forms of exercise to stay healthy. They generally gain weight or become bloated as a result of their sedentary lifestyle."[18] The message conveyed in the frequent advertisements for this syrup reveals how society viewed these store clerks as physically inactive. However, this bears little relation to reality because, apart from having to stand up throughout the working day behind the counter,[19] these store employees had be agile enough to climb up and bring down the different fabrics upon request, among their other duties.

The physical demands of their work was a matter discussed among the employees themselves, and it also differentiated them from other types of employee. The issue of physical aptitude also cropped up in public debates about gender at the time. For example, in relation to the changes brought about by the Revolution, a recurring theme was that women's "lack of physical strength" made them suitable for certain professions and jobs. This situation prompted a message targeted at men who were "usurping" these positions:

> Currently men are taking jobs that are the preserve of women; men have no right to such employment. For example, should not young ladies replace those men who stand behind counters, polishing little watches, measuring fabrics, selling lace and ribbons?[20]

These discussions about women in the workplace were not new; at the turn of the twentieth century, various columns in Mexican newspapers dwelled on the issue, and gender demarcated the boundaries of the jobs suitable for men and women. This debate continued for decades. For example, Susie Porter's study on public-sector female employees in the 1930s identifies how these workers were not only the first to escape the (traditionally female) teaching profession, but that they also played leading roles in the struggle to carve out a space in offices predominantly occupied by men.[21]

Returning to the period in question, employees accepted their allegedly "physical disadvantage," but argued in their defense that although the job may not have been physically demanding, the working hours were exhausting long. In their own words, "laborers are, as we all know, strong men who are used to heavy and tiring work, but they work shorter hours than us, [and we] are generally weaker due to our upbringing."[22] In addition to these reflections on feminine capabilities and their corresponding suitability for certain jobs, paradoxically women formed part of a modern context yet one in which they continued to be seen as the "fairer sex," steering them toward more domestic, peaceful, and parsimonious occupations. The idea of the lack of women working behind the store counter[23] stands out in the Mexican case; generally speaking, contemporary sources reveal that men mainly occupied these positions.

In discussions about class, some people criticized the apathy of middle-class men, including store clerks, in relation to the Revolution. An editorial of *El Pueblo* demanded the participation of members of this social sector: "what are you indolent members of the middle class—public-sector employees, office workers waiting idly for business, store clerks, and small business owners—all waiting for?[24]

This begs the question: Who are those store clerks, accused of being feeble and sitting on the political sidelines? As mentioned above, the clothes business was mainly in foreign hands, controlled particularly by French and Spanish merchants, who consequently developed links of solidarity with their fellow countrymen, hiring young employees aged between 18 and 30 who had recently arrived in Mexico. According to the 1921 census, records for the Federal District showed a total of 8,182 people who stated their employment as being a store clerk, a figure that may vary if we take into account occupations that are similar yet considered separately, such as window dressers. If the Mexican capital's entire population was 901,121, as stated in this survey, 1% reported that they worked in sales. Since this information does not distinguish between the types of employer, we cannot know the precise number of store clerks exclusively selling clothing and accessories. The records' lack of clarity not only makes it difficult to identify these workers but also to gain an idea of their daily lives. However, we do have some clues about the vicissitudes of their line of work thanks to press articles that refer directly to these employees, and some letters sent by foreign store clerks to their families.

Store clerks were naturally a common feature in Mexico City given the concentration of many types of business in the capital. Yet the sheer ubiquity of these clerks around the city obscures our view of them. Some people considered store clerks as puerile, and that this kind of work stunted their mental faculties. These detractors included representatives of the working class, one of whom described these employees in a newspaper by stating that a "[the] store clerk has a job anyone could get, one that can be learned in a few weeks; store clerks don't muddy their clothes or get blisters on their hands, but because their job is easy, it's badly paid."[25]

Moreover, in the social imaginary of the period, the French and Spanish store clerks had a reputation for being effective (though pushy) salespersons. Courteousness was a weapon to make a sale. In a story published in *El Imparcial*, the author recounts his experience of shopping at one of these stores, joking that,

> if the store clerk had been French or Spanish, you can be sure that I'd have been sold the cheap lamps at the price of the expensive ones. You can also be sure that I would have left the store thrilled by my purchase. And you can count on the fact that the lamp would never even have worked.[26]

This teasing reference confirms society's value judgment on store clerks in general: a savvy salesperson can persuade a client to make a purchase and earn a commission. At least in the larger stores, the commission-based system encouraged competition among store clerks, as their priority was to earn enough money to start up their own businesses or put aside some decent savings. Therefore, it was important to maintain good relationships with more senior employees, as reflected in the account of an employee of

Las Fábricas Universales, Léon Martin, who referred to similar situations in the large Parisian department store, Au Bon Marché, where the counters were veritable battlefields for store clerks to curry favor with their bosses.[27]

Mistrust was also a relevant factor in relation to store clerks; stories about swindling the bosses, stealing cash or goods, and even attempted homicides put this sector of society in the spotlight of public opinion. Some cartoons and jokes referred to how these youngsters managed to appear that they were busy, but without actually working. Take these two examples:

> "Young man, I began as a store clerk earning 50 centavos a week, and now I run my own business."
> "Yes, sir. But nowadays stores all have cash registers."
>
> "That store clerk of yours looks like a hard-working young man."
> "Yes, that's his forte."
> "What? Working hard?
> "No! Making it look like he's working."[28]

Given such contrasting opinions, we must focus on an idea that was undisputed (yet still paradoxical): these store clerks belonged to the Mexican middle class, yet they did not earn enough money, nor did they have the same access to cultural spaces as enjoyed by other groups classified as middle class. Nor were they all Mexican, because as mentioned above the majority were European. Porfirio Díaz himself alluded to the complexity of this part of society when characterizing the Mexican population:

> ... and so we are left with the middle class, [a sector of society] almost entirely dependent on public funds: artists, store clerks, workshop bosses who have not become rich and who have not yet moved up into the ranks of the aristocracy, hairdressers, *pulque* vendors, bar owners, and sacristans; the others are employees which is where you genuinely find the intellectuals, and in that category I include everyone from ministers to deputies and school teachers.[29]

The Store Clerk's Knowledge: An Experience of Class

Classified advertisements and personal recommendations provided access to this kind of employment. Advertisements were usually very short, and sought to attract "clerks with good recommendations," and generally targeted Mexican clerks for smaller stores. This shows that a network of French immigrants predominantly hired salespeople at higher-end clothes stores. On the whole, newly arrived youngsters in Mexico already came with the recommendation of a family member normally already involved in some kind of business.[30]

Once hired, the division of labor depended on two factors: seniority and the young employee's aptitude for learning. Store clerks carried out various duties in the workplace: sweeping, cleaning showcases, organizing and classifying fabrics, window dressing, managing cash registers, serving customers, among other jobs depending on the store's size. Over the years, the modernization of the establishments introduced new jobs. We can take the example of El Nuevo París. The accountant, window dresser, wholesale manager, traveling sales agent, and retail managers were at the top of the hierarchy. Next in seniority came the billing supervisor, retail store clerk, collection agent, cashier. At the bottom of the pile were the (least-experienced) sales clerk, typist, assistant cashier, office clerks, wholesale clerks, warehouse assistants, and porter.[31]

In the specific case of the store clerks, some characteristics pertain to their required *knowledge* as employees, including literacy, writing skills, basic mathematics, and sometimes other languages (particularly English and French), knowing the different types of fabric for sale, and the dexterity required to measure, cut, and fold cloth.[32] There were also other types of know-how to maximize success, such as judging where the boundary lay between friendliness and pushiness in order to make the sale. The art of selling was a socially recognized skill; one press report appealed to lady shoppers not to waste store clerks' time, showing respect for their work, "[...] since store clerks make a certain commission from sales, and this constitutes most of their income. All your chit-chat stops them serving genuine customers and deprives them of their earnings, because their time is literally money."[33]

Technology also played an important role in the specialization of the store clerks' job: calculators helped them do their sums and improved cash registers facilitated their work (some new machines even kept a separate tally of each employee's sales during their shifts). These provide examples of objects that employees used and required particular knowledge. One cash register advertisement also encouraged business owners to acquire it to "avoid losses, avoid mistakes, avoid temptation, increase sales, and increase profits."[34] The employees' ability to earn extra income through their sales skills is another important factor in this analysis. Making sales was essential for these clerks to make enough money, as shown both in the aforesaid advice given to women shoppers and in the technical improvements made to cash registers.[35]

Politeness and a good personal appearance were two other elements to consider alongside store clerks' *experience*. Polished manners, friendliness, and elegance were the qualities of "good" clerks. The *Correo Español* refers to the transformation of an immigrant who arrived in Mexico as an uncouth young man, yet who, after some training, acquired "very refined and distinguished manners, and a polished, clear, flexible, trustworthy speech, attainments of which he was rightly proud."[36] Smart attire was similarly important. When discussing the sale of clothing, the clerk needed to promote values related to elegance, good taste, and beauty (Figure 11.1).

Figure 11.1 Store Clerks of "Fábricas de Francia", Guadalajara.
Source: Courtesy of L'Unité Patrimoniale de Photographie du Musée de la Vallée à Barcelonnette.

Period photographs show these young men neatly lined up behind the counter, with serious expressions, waiting for customers. Their appearance denotes a cleanliness and courtesy that set them apart from those engaged in hard, physical labor. Male store clerks always wore suits and ties, hats (though only when outdoors), and highly polished shoes. An advertisement from this time gives an idea of a department selling clothes for this sector of society:

> We understand that you are busy and it is hard to find the time to go out shopping, so we are pleased to offer you our Premises as well as our telephone service. This makes it easy for you to place your orders at your convenience. We stock the most comprehensive selection of top-quality fabrics for suits, overcoats, formal trousers, silk waistcoats, hats, shoes, ties, shirts, jerseys, waterproof coats, umbrellas, and in general, every kind of article for gentlemen.[37]

The consumer needs of the store clerks themselves became the subject of fierce debates between 1910 and 1913 as part of calls for stores to close on Sundays. One of the many arguments put forward referred to the time needed by store clerks to obtain the necessary items—food and clothes—to lead a dignified life. Without any days off during the week, store employees were deprived of the right enjoyed by everyone else to make purchases in stores around the city: "How do these unfortunate employees do their shopping in the same way as you [the store owners] who protest? When will they be able to buy a modest pair of shoes or a democratic shirt if stores are closed on Sundays?"[38]

As we can see, the knowledge that formed part of store clerks' class experience ranged from physical requirements, intellectual abilities, and the appearances of "good" employees. Stores were a stage for social appraisals, places where workers competed among themselves to gain their boss's favor and developed their ambitions. Many planned to save up with a view to returning to their places of origin with enough money to establish themselves and raise a family. Although consular correspondence shows that male store clerks did marry Mexican women, remaining celibate was certainly an objective for these young men, as we can ascertain in letters sent to their families. Some of the most radical of such accounts referred to two basic guiding principles for Mexico City clerks: to save up and remain single.[39]

Of course, these aspirations were subject to all manner of external factors: the type of store and its status, the social connections made both in and outside the store, and the realistic saving prospects all contributed to their class experiences. Therefore, showing some situations perceived as unfair by store clerks can help build up a picture of their class identity.

Store Clerks' Working Conditions As a Praxis of Class Identity

Store clerks developed relationships—not only working ones—by virtue of coexisting in the same space. Although *knowledge* partly shaped their class experience, these employees' daily working lives, regulated by codes of conduct, contributed toward the identification of shared values that created a group cohesiveness. One display of this kinship was how they rallied to defend their profession, despite the unsatisfactory working conditions. Store owners gave these young workers an insight into the latest market trends, and this led to their increasing social refinement, combined with their everyday contact with customers who reflected the store clerks' *aspirations*.

This value system, rooted in their pride as foreigners, converted these employees into the embodiment of cosmopolitanism. This quality—combined with the knowledge they acquired to do their job—created a set of subjectivities particular to store clerks, blended with the experience of working alongside other young men with similar aspirations. The types of relationship appear here as a factor when analyzing this social group's class experience, because "the workplace is the setting for social practices and ways of experiencing, thinking about, and perceiving gender relations."[40]

Society at the time did not ignore the construction of masculinity among these store clerks, as we saw above with the criticism made by the working class about men taking jobs that should be the preserve of women. These young store clerks represented a particular masculine aesthetic: they were elegant, well mannered, impeccably dressed, and, of course, ambitious, because they constantly strived for social advancement through savings, sales commissions, and good relationships with their bosses. Although this opens up another analytical dimension that lies beyond the scope of this chapter, it is still important to mention that "masculinity refers to a social and historical process through which men commit themselves to a gender position inextricably linked to the evolution of the class experience."[41]

Alongside the element of masculinity, discipline also shaped their experience: these young men needed to abide by a set of rules they accepted as part of their contracts. Job regulations are an ideal source for analyzing this issue. For instance, El Palacio de Hierro—one of the most iconic department stores—still has its first set of employee regulations, dated 1891, that remained in force until the 1920s. This concise document consists of eight points, briefly describing the store clerks' duties, emphasizing their relationship to clients who "must provide services as required by anyone entering the store for any reason, whether they have come to make a purchase or simply visit the establishment."[42]

This same document stipulates that "store clerks must work diligently during their shifts, without attending to personal matters or those not connected to selling."[43] An account from the time detailed the working hours:

> I'm writing to you today on Sunday and I'm in a rush because during the week we have little time. We return in the morning at half past seven and stay until half past one and from half past two to half past eight. At half past one we go to eat, and again at half past eight. We have to be back at night, by ten o'clock. We also work on Sunday mornings and we only have the afternoon free; we get a whole Sunday off once every three weeks. So you see how much time I have to see Mexico City—I haven't got to see it at all.[44]

The issue of working hours takes on particular importance if we think about time as a factor of the praxis of the class experience. The long working hours left store clerks no option but to remain in the workplace from early in the morning until nightfall, drastically reducing their leisure activities, rest time, and social life in general, all of which are factors of class identity. This poses a paradox: studies often cite recreation and the pursuit of certain cultural activities as examples of middle-class aspirations. However, store clerks—considered in literature as being separate from manual laborers and connected to the middle class—were not at liberty to enjoy such activities.

These employees' housing situations add further complexity to the analysis. As we saw above, large stores had employee accommodation until the mid-twentieth century. In fact, the regulations quoted above specifies the existence of house rules. Number seven on its list stated that "employees who have their lodgings in the store must return before midnight; this requirement will be enforced by a store employee or supervisor working every day in shifts who will ensure compliance."[45]

These working conditions fed into a sense of injustice, prompting store clerks to stage protests to demand their right to rest, training, and recreation. Although under discussion for many years, the issue of working hours (though not wages) became the subject of public debate between 1911 and 1913, with the demand for days off on Sundays:

> We want to have a rest. We only ask for one day a week when we're not forced to wake up at dawn like farmers at first light to carry out our duties, and then, enduring conditions worse than those endured by peons, we have to wait until eleven o'clock at night before resting in our beds, tormented by the idea of having to return the following day to our miserable jobs.[46]

These protests by store clerks were not isolated events.[47] On the contrary, they occurred within the context of broader transformations within Mexican society. On 22 September 1912, the establishment of the Casa del Obrero Mundial, a syndicalist organization representing workers from different industries, in parallel with the creation of the Labor Ministry during Francisco Madero's administration, revealed that previously invisible sectors of society were beginning to stand up for their rights. During the period in question, the Mexican capital saw protests by various groups, including store clerks.

In defending their right to a rest on Sundays, store clerks were keen to differentiate themselves from manual laborers. According to these clerks, they needed time to train, so that they could serve customers better and do their jobs more effectively. In other words, the day off would make them more competent employees, because

> there is no question that the honest and reliable store clerk always strives to better himself and keep up with the latest developments of modern commerce. Culture is the one guiding star that can lead him to this goal, and this is only attainable by reading instructive books and illustrated newspapers.[48]

These store clerks also emphasized their difference to manual laborers, claiming that they, unlike manual workers who flocked to cantinas on Sunday, would use their free time to associate with their friends. They referred to their wish to go for walks in the countryside, see plays, or go to cafés. Another gripe was that other workers' organizations had beaten them to it and prevailed in their protests:

> ... it is regrettable that factory workers are setting the example to us on a daily basis. Their solidarity has earned them many privileges, such

> as shorter working hours and equal pay. We cannot believe that these laborers can achieve more than we can [...] it is high time that we awake from such a long slumber and show the world that we are not inferior to the humble day laborer; we must show we can do what they have done, and achieve even more than they have managed.[49]

Various organizations of store clerks proliferated at this time,[50] with memberships based on the criteria of nationality or—more frequently—the type of the employer's business. These organizations often moved quickly to find premises for their meetings. These same spaces doubled up as venues for recreational activities, dances, dinners, literary gatherings, and music concerts.

In this way, the store clerks used the demand for days off on Sunday as an opportunity to open up spaces of sociability—something previously denied to them. The behavioral patterns and tastes, which varied according to their different activities, reveal the differentiating practices that incorporated the idea of elegance, training, and good manners, establishing their class experience and widening the gulf separating them from manual laborers.

Conclusions

Studying the middle class as a practice gave me an understanding of clerks working in clothes stores as a vehicle for gaining a sense of their working conditions based on *knowledge*. In other words, the study considered every discourse—from the simplest to the most elaborate—about their identity as a social group. These different areas of knowledge were the common thread that enabled me to historicize these subjects and to ascribe them the particular characteristics of the middle class.

Their practices also enabled me to distinguish between some elements of time and space that added nuances to the lifestyles of these employees, who perceived themselves as different to laborers and aspired to hold onto their jobs, put aside money, become partners in business, return to their places of origin with a nest egg, participate in contemporary culture, enjoy days off, and so on. This perspective ultimately opened up the possibility to address a complex, diverse, and contradictory class experience.

In this study approach, spaces and skill sets played an important role in the characterization of store clerks as part of the varied Mexican middle class. Furthermore, the focus on daily life as glimpsed in the sources opens a window onto two defining aspects of the middle class: consumption and gender relations. Although barely touched upon, these two elements add an extra dimension to the study of class experience and introduce new analytical paths that could contribute to historiography on this subject. Finally, the Mexican Revolution and World War I set the stage for social transformations during the first decade of the twentieth century. These changes transformed commerce in Mexico City, enabling women to begin taking their place behind the counters and allowing workers to set up new labor organizations, thus undoubtedly redefining Mexico's middle class.

Notes

1 The phrase is taken from the headline "A Social Occurrence in the Annals of Mexican Commerce," *El Diario*, October 3, 1911, 4.
2 *El Machete*, August 23, 1924, 3.
3 *El Machete*, August 23, 1924, 3.
4 Newspapers at the time used the following various terms in Spanish for store clerks interchangeably: "vendedores de mostrador," "dependientes de comercio," vendedores de comercio," and "empleados de comercio."
5 Clerks working in stores selling all kinds of products were referred to generically as "dependientes" in Mexico. It is interesting to note, by comparing different sources, that this word is not widely used in South America, where they are called "vendedoras" or "vendedores." In Spain and Mexico, however, "dependiente de comercio" is the most commonly used term. In French, sources refer literally to "employés de commerce."
6 For a detailed analysis of the concept of the middle classes, see Geoffrey Crossick, "Clases medias ¿Formación o invención de las "clases medias?," in *Clases medias: Nuevos enfoques desde la sociología, la historia y la antropología*, eds. Ezequiel Adamovsky, Sergio Visacovsky, and Patricia Vargas (Buenos Aires: Ariel, 2014).
7 For a study of public-sector employees in Mexico City, see Mario Barbosa, "La capacitación y posición social de los empleados públicos en la Ciudad de México a comienzos del siglo XX," *Historia* Mexicana 68, no. 2 (2018): 747–781. The same author also wrote an analysis of middle-class aspirations, Mario Barbosa, "Distinciones y apariencias: La clase media en la ciudad de México entre el porfiriato y la revolución." *Oficio: Revista de historia e interdisciplina*, no. 10 (January–June 2020): 9–23.
8 Ricardo López, "Nosotros también somos parte del pueblo": Gaitanismo, empleados y la formación histórica de la clase media en Bogotá, 1936–1948," *Revista de Estudios Sociales* 41 (December 2011): 88.
9 E.P. Thompson, *The Making of the English Working Class* (New York: Vintage, 1966), 11.
10 López, "Nosotros también," 88.
11 Reinhart Koselleck proposed the "horizon of expectations" to insist on the historicity of social groups, because, according to this author, the horizon of expectations will be formed by a social group's present level and future aspirations. This juxtaposition of time frames indicates the importance of experiencing the present in the construction of a project by a characteristic social group. Reinhart Koselleck, *Futuro pasado: Para una semántica de los tiempos históricos* (Spain: Paidos, 1993 [1979]).
12 Olga Lucía Zuluaga, *Pedagogía e historia: La historicidad de la pedagogía, la enseñanza, un objeto de saber* (Bogotá: Siglo del Hombre Editores, 1999), 26.
13 Michel Foucault, *La arqueología del saber* (Buenos Aires: Siglo XXI, 2003).
14 By way of qualification, I should mention that, together with the French community, Spaniards were also dominant in this sector of the economy. According to Vilar Guerra, in 1930 the Spaniards "had a total of 137 establishments that comprised specialties including tailors and shops that sold shirts, hats, umbrellas, and women's fashion." Vilar Guerra, *Directorio de la Colonia Española* (n.p., 1937), 470–473.

15 For the period in question there were more than a dozen large stores: El Palacio de Hierro, El Surtidor, La Francia Marítima, La Reforma del Comercio, Las Fábricas Universales, Al Progreso Mercantil, El Puerto de Veracruz, Al Puerto de Liverpool, La Ciudad de Londres, La Bella Jardinera, El Centro Mercantil, Sorpresa y Primavera Unidas, La Nueva Bella Jardinera, and Las Fábricas de Francia. These names appear in press articles and a document called *Principales maisons du commerce Françoise au Mexique* (1900) in "Raíces Francesas en México, Racines," Unclassified archive.

16 On this subject, Steven Bunker points out that "certain departments were undoubtedly bigger than others, but the point is that the stores were organizing, categorizing, and separating goods that displayed both the abundance of modern society and the modern penchant for quantification and categorization." Steven Bunker, *Creating Mexican Consumer Culture in the Age of Porfirio Díaz* (Albuquerque: University of New Mexico Press, 2012), 145.

17 The stores are described in: *El Mundo Ilustrado*, Sept. 18, 1914, 52–67; François Arnaud, *Les Barcelonnettes au Mexique* (Barcelonnette: Musée de la Vallée, 2014), 14–15. Moreover, a plan of Las Fábricas Universales demonstrates this layout by showing that the ground and first floors were used for retail sales; wholesale operations were carried out on the next two levels up; the workshops were located above them; and the lodgings were on the top floor, in Hélene Homps-Brousse, *L'aventure architecturale des Émigrants Barcelonnettes: France-Mexique* (Barcelonnette: Musée de la Vallée, 2013), 34.

18 *El Mundo Ilustrado*, December 17, 1911, 28. The advertisement began with "The office and store clerks [...]"

19 The so-called "chair law"—permitting employees to sit down when there were no customers to serve—was the victory of these social sectors after much debate and protest. In Spain, this law was passed in 1912. In the case of Argentina and Chile, the law came into effect in 1914. There are no records referring to such a law in Mexico, although from press articles we can infer that the law was passed in around 1918.

20 *El Abogado Cristiano*, January 18, 1912, 10.

21 Susie Porter, "Empleadas públicas: Normas de feminidad, espacios burocráticos e identidad de la clase media en México durante la década de 1930," *Revista Signos Históricos* 11 (January–July, 2014): 42.

22 *El Pueblo*, March 16, 1915, 5.

23 Note the contrast with other countries where, during this same period, store clerks were predominantly women. See Graciela Queirolo, "Vendedoras: Género y trabajo en el sector comercial (Buenos Aires, 1910–1950)," *Estudios Feministas, Florianápolis* 22, no. 1 (January–April 2014); Jacqueline Dussaillant, *Las reinas de Estado: Consumo, grandes tiendas y mujeres en la modernización del comercio de Santiago, (1880–1930)* (Santiago: Ediciones Universidad Católica de Chile, 2011).

24 It is interesting to note the different sectors named in this article and that they seem to belong to the middle class of the time. *El País*, November 15, 1912, 7.

25 *El Machete*, August 23, 1923, 3.

26 *El Imparcial*, March 13, 1912, 12.

27 Arnaud, *Les Barcelonnettes au Mexique*, 82.

28 *El Imparcial*, September 29, 1900, 4.

29 *La Patria*, May 3, 1912, 3.

30 A detailed account of these circumstances is included in Jean-Luis D'Ànglade, *Un gran patrón barcelonnette en México: Joseph Ollivier y su familia, 1850–1932* (Puebla: Benemérita Universidad de Puebla, 2012).

31 Sergio Valerio Ulloa, *Los barcelonnettes en Guadalajara, siglos XIX y XX* (Mexico City: Universidad de Guadalajara; Instituto Mora, 2015), 227.

32 In 1920, the "Miguel Lerdo de Tejada" School of Commerce proposed its "study program for store clerks for the academic year 1920." This source not only reveals the arrival of women behind the sales counters, but also shows the professionalization of working in sales on the shopfloor. The subjects over the three years of the course give an insight into the knowledge required for the job: "Spanish Language, Commercial Arithmetic, Commercial Writing, Commercial Geography, Shorthand, Typing, English, French, Bookkeeping. The course also included choral singing, gymnastics, and sports," in Archivo Histórico de la Ciudad de México, AHCDMX, Sección: Secretaría del Gobierno del Distrito Federal, Serie: Instrucción Pública, 5: 356, 1f. 1920.
33 *El País*, April 21, 1911, 4.
34 *El Imparcial*, December 29, 1912, 12.
35 On the issue of wages, in some press articles young workers state that they earn $3 per week, and others mention that they had a monthly wage of $50, or just over $1 per week. In one case, an employee of Las Fábricas Universales wrote a letter to his family in which he stated that he received $75 in the month. This would mean daily earnings of more than $2, an amount that is certainly higher than the average wage received by Mexican laborers, which was 45 cents per day, cf. Arnaud, *Les Barcelonnettes au Mexique*, 85.
36 *El Correo Español*, August 5, 1912, 1.
37 *El Correo Español*, August 20, 1914, 8. The advertisement has the suggestive tagline: "¡Interesante a los señores dependientes!" (Store clerks take note!) and it also specifies the store's location, on 3ra calle de Tacuba No. 12, a few blocks away from the stores where its potential customers worked.
38 *La Patria*, January 23, 1913, 1.
39 These success stories are frequently mentioned in the Barcelonnettes' own historiographical production. This account is of an ambitious young man who left his hometown, worked in Mexico City as a store clerk for many years and then, by dint of hard work and discipline, became a shareholder in a respectable business, making him a fortune with which he returned triumphantly to his place of origin, covered in glory.
40 Hernán M. Palermo, *La producción de la masculinidad en el trabajo petrolero* (Buenos Aires: Editorial Biblos, 2017), 29–30.
41 Palermo, *La producción de la masculinidad*, 30.
42 Archivo Histórico del Palacio de Hierro, AHPH, "Reglamento," unclassified, 28 June 1891, n.p.
43 Archivo Histórico del Palacio de Hierro, AHPH, "Reglamento," unclassified, 28 June 1891, n.p.
44 Arnaud, *Les Barcelonnettes au Mexique*, 81.
45 Archivo Histórico del Palacio de Hierro, AHPH, "Reglamento," unclassified, 28 June 1891, n.p.
46 *La Patria*, December 13, 1913, 2.
47 For more information about sites of employee protests, see J. Cristina Sánchez Parra, "'Detrás del mostrador': Espacios de trabajo y lugares de sociabilidad de los empleados de comercio en la ciudad de México a inicios del siglo XX," *Estudios del ISHIR* 26 (2020): 1–19
48 *El Faro*, May 24, 1912, 12–13.
49 *El País*, November 15, 1912, 7.
50 The following organizations of sales clerks participated in the demand for days off on Sundays: La Sociedad Mutualista de Empleados Libres, El Centro Cosmopolita de Dependientes, and La Unión de Dependientes Católicos.

Part III

The State, Social Movements, and the Cold War

Introduction to Part III

Mario Barbosa Cruz

Figure III.1 Ñuñoa, Santiago de Chile, late 1960s. Private Collection.

DOI: 10.4324/9781003029311-15

Tensions between the left and the right took various forms in Latin America during the twentieth century. Multiple social sectors aligned themselves with political groups and with leaders who represented different parties and transnational political tendencies. Such affiliations were defined by the kind of inter-relationships established between the political parties and their potential voters, by the role of intermediaries seeking political bases among the electorate, and by the dynamics related to the broadening of participative democracy and to a larger electorate. They were also related to transnational discussions and the spread of political ideas, forms of organization, and identification with political platforms. The political left became increasingly organized in Latin America from the late nineteenth century, causing concern among the ruling elites. As a result, public debates raged about this merging of sectors of society into groups amid mutual accusations and sometimes even political persecution.

As they became established, nation-states experimented with various new ways of doing politics and the creation of opposition groups that confronted the establishment. International social and political identities related to liberalism, anarchism, and communism among other political trends expanded, bolstered by new knowledge and the communication of ideas. Political loyalties ceased to be solely a matter of private arrangements or pressures; the expansion of publishing and journalism helped to stimulate debates and gave visibility to ways of challenging political adversaries. Meanwhile, transnational political networks gained strength and expanded their reach with the organization of society. Social movements were inspired by experiences of other contexts with their own specific aspects, and some of them were related to groups from other countries whose influence spread beyond their borders. Tensions between global powers in times of war caused governments to take sides, and also led to domestic polarization among social groups that supported or opposed left- or right-wing political groups.

Several works of social historiography have shown the contribution of various sectors of society to social organization in Latin America. Intellectuals, political leaders, unionized laborers, campesinos, the indigenous, and other workers were among those who joined and actively participated in political groupings of various stripes. Under these circumstances, middle-class groups were also active depending on the particular context and juncture.

In this third part, we can see how middle-class sectors aligned with left- or right-wing political movements in Colombia, Chile, Ecuador, and Mexico. The five chapters reveal the political conflicts related to the organization and creation of group identities constituted or self-identified as belonging to the middle classes. Each context obviously entails particular historical problems, means of organization, and the intervention of national and international agents and groupings. During the first half of the twentieth century, groups appeared that supported the international left, fascism, and the western powers. Following the Second World War, the frictions of the Cold War spread beyond the borders of the United States and the Soviet Union, and had an impact on Latin American countries. The following contributions not only show the creation of political subjectivities related to the middle classes, but also explore specific examples of social practices, as well as the creation of collective representations and identities. International tensions continually arise that frame these political positions.

In Ecuador, some middle-class army officers joined with popular sectors in the late nineteenth century to support alternative governments representing the radical party and the incipient socialist movement that contrasted to the traditional, oligarchical government's programs and actions. During the first half of the twentieth century in Mexico, sections of the middle classes joined anti-Communist organizations such as the Confederation of the Middle Classes (Confederación de la Clase Media, CCM), while simultaneously keeping an open line of communication with President Lázaro Cárdenas. These fluid relations reveal the region's social and political complexities, as well as the possibilities and the functioning of political and clientelist networks of charismatic leaders in Latin America. Meanwhile, in Colombia and Chile during the 1970s and 1980s—in the middle of the Cold War—sectors of the middle class considered petit bourgeois (in Colombia's case), or Integral Chileans, actively participated in left-wing movements. In Colombia, they were a generation of young people who benefitted from their parents' greater opportunities for education. In Chile, the agency of these groups was constructed from the intersection between masculinities, State education and Chileanness. These students, white-collar workers, and professionals championed social and political processes, as well as transnational values of equality and fairness. As for another moment in Ecuador's history, when the middle classes joined in the protests of the Rebelión de los Forajidos in 2005—a leftist movement rebelling against the establishment—and promoted new means of collective representation. In the early twenty-first century, there were similarities and crossovers between academic discourses, overarching narratives, and daily life about the middle classes.

Over and above the discourses, this part's analyses show the experiences and the processes of forming identities, as well as values defended at any time. The chapters have various common threads: strong political and class-based affinities stand out in the type of action taken and in the groups of men and women who formed part of the groups considered in these five texts. These identities gained strength in the midst of political struggles, the strengthening of political opposition movements, and the consolidation of nation-states.

The cases share the analysis of tensions between various polarized and conflicting groups framed by specific contexts and particular transnational influences: the consolidation of hegemonic oligarchies in the late nineteenth century, the political polarization during the interwar period, the fear of Communism as an international specter, and the anxieties of the Cold War. The case of Ecuador in the early twenty-first century reveals how these sectors have settled into place after the conclusion of confrontations between the West and the Eastern bloc countries. This bears witness to middle-class aspirations at both a personal and a political level. It also sheds light on the role of these social sectors during the rise of so-called progressive governments in countries such as Argentina, Bolivia, Brazil, Ecuador, and Uruguay. These contributions show that the tensions between East and West extended over a longer period since the late 19th century. Therefore, we can speak of a broader concept of Cold War politics.

The essays in this part reveal specific subjectivities of the groups that played a leading role in these five cases. Within these subjectivities, we can glimpse values that these groups represent and that form the basis for radicalization, to the extent of taking up arms or resorting to violence as a means of expressing opposition to the hegemonic ruling class or local governments.

12 The Middle Classes and Anti-Communism During the Cárdenas Presidency in Mexico

Nationalist Dynamics in a Transnational Framework

Sebastián Rivera Mir

Following his tour of Yucatán in 1935, Lázaro Cárdenas sent a letter to the writer Luciano Kubli, referring to the importance of continuing the momentum of his visit through other channels:

> You must write a short booklet, mentioning the benefits of the collective *ejidos*; a short, five-or six-page booklet to be printed in a large-sized font, explaining concepts understandable for campesinos and with a paragraph for the middle class [...] and another paragraph on socialist education.[1]

At the end of this handwritten letter, Cárdenas suggests a title: *El ejido en Yucatán*. In this publication, containing almost an entire page of text, Kubli wrote:

> The state of Yucatán's middle class, another victim of the injustices of the capitalist production regime, crushed by its cogs, must rally to the cause of the campesinos in Yucatán's ejidos in the knowledge that this will sow the seeds for its own financial reward.[2]

Lázaro Cárdenas, despite his attention being diverted toward other problems, did not forget to include the middle class as part of his propaganda plans.

This chapter seeks to analyze the disputes over "the middle class" that broke out between unions and government entities and some organizations or individuals that were the self-styled representatives of this social sector. These groups shared a common belief that they supported the national cause, accusing Lázaro Cárdenas of being a puppet of foreign interests. Nevertheless, they needed to articulate their own brand of nationalism with transnational dynamics imposed by the global context, something that ultimately affected their daily practices.[3] For example, this required forming a relationship with Ibero-American or US organizations with the common goal of opposing social reforms, social education,

DOI: 10.4324/9781003029311-16

and Cardenista diplomacy. Hence the paradoxical situation of a strongly nationalist sector needing to insert itself coherently within a transnational setting without betraying the central tenet of its discourse.

For this research, I chose to focus on the Confederation of the Middle Class (Confederación de la Clase Media, CCM), which appointed itself representative and true mouthpiece of the middle class. This proved useful for this case study, though by no means do I intend to conflate this organization with the actually-existing middle classes. At best, the CCM disputed the meaning of the political implication of the "middle class" as a category. In this regard, the historian Javier Garciadiego classified it as one of the main anti-Cardenista groups, and drew attention to how the Cárdenas government disparaged the middle class. Garciadiego considered the CCM as Cárdenas's principal opponent in civil society:

> It aimed to mount a Social Defense of the Middle Class—a class that, despite being "the driving force behind civilized nations," in Mexico found itself 'as a pariah of society,' deprived of 'all rights' and without an institution "to defend it."[4]

According to Garciadiego, the goal of its founders (a group that included the brothers Gustavo and Enrique Sáenz de Sicilia) was to bring together professionals, students, industrialists, farm owners, landholders, business owners, employees, and artisans—a proposal of the Mexican president himself, as stated in one of his speeches. This was something that, according to Ricardo Pérez Monfort, the CCM never achieved; instead, it represented only the "most reactionary" sectors.[5] Therefore, at no point in this chapter do we intend to consider the middle classes in Mexico as synonymous with the CCM.

Although the CCM was set up for very specific political ends, in our analysis we can clearly view its organizational processes, as well as consult the abundant and mostly unexamined printed texts and propaganda produced by this organization and its like. As we will see, their efforts could result in a text produced in Spain or Chile, for example, turning up on the streets of Mexico City to "expose the foreign threat." In particular, they made notable efforts to set up an Ibero-American publishing house to specialize in producing books, booklets, and pamphlets, along with other initiatives.

We have chosen two of the aforesaid areas—largely overlooked by Mexican historiography—to develop a fuller understanding of the ideas about the middle classes during the Cárdenas presidency.[6] Firstly, we examine the constant references to "outside" processes to justify the need to strengthen these sectors in Mexico. This appears to be a standard political practice, a series of specific mechanisms that incorporated actions by the subjects involved in order to secure certain political returns.[7]

The second area I intend to discuss relates to the apparent molding of the CCM's objectives to those proposed by Lázaro Cárdenas in the same vein. This was clearly Enrique Sáenz de Sicilia's strategy in his letters to the president that sought to create a link with him. The CCM leader's proposals indicate to us that "civil society" actors took part in the disputes over the middle class at the time, while facing a government offensive. The conflict between the dynamics of the government and its opponents drew the boundaries of the discourses, hence the political proposals centered on the hegemonic intentions of both sectors. In contrast to the aversion as observed by Garciadiego, the government clearly intended to support middle-class groups whose aims were compatible with its own.[8] Political practices focusing on the "middle class" informed my decision to explore a history that is often elusive.[9] We shall begin by analyzing the development of the clashes between the Mexican government and the CCM.

The Disputes

In 1938, the Autonomous Department of Press and Publicity (Departamento Autónomo de Prensa y Publicidad, DAPP) published a short booklet entitled *Fuerza y flaqueza de la clase media* (Strengths and weaknesses of the middle class). This text set out the principal official view of this sector of society, starting with a description of its diversity and importance within political processes. Consisting of professionals, artisans, owners of small businesses, small rural landholders, "[...] it's a group forever being pulled in two opposite directions. The elite are on top, with the proletariat down below."[10] Following this description, the booklet underlines the importance of education in explaining the rise [of the middle class] in society, elevating it directly to the propertied class. "It can be said," it explains, "that all middle-class education shares the same aim: to develop the student's mentality for an upward social trajectory."[11] The issue was more complex because those who failed to join the ruling classes were equally excluded from the proletariat, hence they could turn into a point of entry for capitalism. And in one of its sentences that aimed to recover certain existing representations, the booklet stated: "Some people substitute their own names and surnames by aping foreign equivalents. And so Juan Rivera becomes John Brink, and José Cabañas turns into Joe Cabines."[12] The arguments also centered on certain situations such as strikes in which the middle class was called upon to support one group or another, but as it found itself caught up in the middle of the fight, "they're ignorant and incapable," In this no man's land they no longer formed part of the story and disappeared from view.[13]

According to the DAPP booklet, however, this was not necessarily the only destiny for the middle class. The processes initiated by the authorities offered them potential acceptance, either by supporting the oil industry expropriation, taking part in the struggle against business monopolies, or, in particular, by not believing the "deranged" rumors that undermined the government.[14] The list of possible actions was long and could be taken "[...] in the classroom, lecture theater, and union offices."[15] Any such measures could also be taken from the planned popular sector of the Party of the Mexican Revolution (Partido de la Revolución Mexicana, PRM): "[...] the middle classes could certainly aspire to achieving the objectives of organizing the distribution of goods, tackling monopolies, eliminating intermediaries, securing small landholdings and coordinating work with ejidos, and imbuing professions with a sense of social service."[16]

The unearthing of this text is important because it allows us to deepen our research into some elements proposed by historiography. Firstly, it is necessary to establish whom the official booklet considers a member of the middle classes. Nowhere does it mention those usually considered the sole objectives of such a state policy: public-sector employees or those working within the state's bureaucracy.[17] This absence was not unintentional. There was an effort to completely disassociate these sectors from the middle classes, whether specifically or in terms of symbolic representations. Erasing such a connection helped the government reinforce the link it wanted to have with other kinds of workers and manual laborers. The issue of who did or did not qualify as middle class was therefore the subject of fierce disputes. Again, this contrasts sharply with the prevailing historiographical idea that emphasizes Cárdenas's disinterest in this sector of society. It certainly lacked the same importance as manual laborers or campesinos, but the middle class remained present in government policies and discourses. A member of the Confederation of Mexican Workers (Confederación de Trabajadores de México, CTM), Rodrigo García Treviño, gave one plausible explanation for this situation in 1937 when describing Lázaro Cárdenas taking over the presidency:

> The force that brought down Callismo lacked a homogeneous class identity. Its leader, General Cárdenas, had a rather strange mix of supporters invented by history, a makeshift combination of highly dissimilar groups and classes. This appears legitimate but is becoming more dangerous by the day.[18]

This unstable situation—a particular focus of revisionist historiography—forced the government to maintain a constant lookout to prevent its support base from disintegrating.[19]

Since the CCM was set up during the context of the break between Cárdenas and Elías Calles, public-sector employees and the bureaucracy was the main aim of their propaganda. One of the Sáenz de Sicilia brothers had worked at the Palacio de Hierro department store as a collection agent, and the other, Gustavo, in various public-sector jobs. However, for some reason they claimed to have no links at all with the Cardenista bureaucracy.[20] This might explain what Ricardo Pérez Monfort considered to be CCM's decision to concentrate on three areas: "university schools and polytechnics, employees and workers, and military personnel."[21]

The CCM's supporters therefore sought to characterize some of the problems facing these sectors. They considered that employees were exploited and that military personnel led nomadic lives; after ten years of service a captain could only expect to earn $5 pesos per day.[22] In its declaration of principles, the CCM declared that

> employees of retail stores and firms have pitiful salaries. It takes so long for the labor tribunals to resolve their cases that they are forced to make painful choices, rendering it very difficult for them to find new jobs and they are always extemporaneous.[23]

Other sectors complemented these three areas as part of the CCM platform, especially if we consider their type of work, and could include manual laborers, campesinos, and artisans. In fact, their proposal to come up with a financial system to organize the middle class was almost exclusively mediated by the creation of cooperatives of distribution, of consumption, credit unions, and social security programs that strengthened the work of the "national industries."[24] To some extent this overlapped with the government proposals for certain groups of urban artisans or the working classes, and in a broad sense it sought to make the most of the cooperativist drive toward the hegemonic construction of Cardenismo.[25]

However, if we broaden our scope to include the CCM's anti-Communist stance, we can discern an even larger audience for its discourse. Its declaration of principles was explicit in pointing out that Communism was "[...] a chaotic and unworkable utopia that disorganizes and divides Mexicans and only became fashionable thanks to champagne socialists and false prophets, as a perverse machination to influence and divide the country's factory workers and campesinos."[26] Since the CCM mainly focused on anti-Communism, we can consider that apart from employees, bureaucrats, and military personnel, factory workers and campesinos were bundled together at the heart of its political messages. This was particularly the case at a local level. For example, the Iztacalco campesino sector, attached to the Acción Nacionalista (a part of the CCM), bluntly stated that: "Conscious of the harmful Communist machinations that have set up a major obstacle in the path of progress in Mexico, we address the proletariat to agree on a common position on the conquests of the Revolution."[27] Along with its anti-Communist obsession, the CCM even came to the defense of the ejido, which potentially contradicts its ideas about private property associated with small farm owners, according to the Confederation's own general principles.

The CCM's leaders acknowledged a significant difference when setting up its political practices. While its anti-Communist drive encompassed all these sectors, the rights of public-sector employees, members of the bureaucracy, and military personnel also needed consolidating.[28] This perspective was crucial to understand how the limits of their idea about the middle class connected to the needs for political action they deemed essential. This dialogue concluded with a reconstruction both of its practices and its ideological definitions: unlike discourses about the middle class in other countries that emphasized an anti-working-class position, the CCM placed particular emphasis on aspects that linked both sectors within the same political objectives.[29] This variable is important in order to grasp the particular aspects of the Mexican situation and very probably we must associate it with the creation of forces that opposed the post-revolutionary project. In the words of Diane Davis: "With Cárdenas as president, Mexico City's middle classes and many sectors of the urban poor not only lacked national institutional mechanisms for political participation on a par with labor and the peasantry, they also lost out in urban service amenities."[30] Therefore, the platform that tried to establish this organization was subjected to the accumulation of problems affecting the relationship between government and some social sectors that appeared adversely affected by its proposals.

But to what extent did groupings such as the CCM oppose the Cardenista project? Once again, their stance was defined more by political selectiveness rather than by essentialist ideas: the CCM's leader wrote to Mexico's president in November 1937, congratulating him for his efforts to resolve the agrarian problem and boost the nation's economy: "The CCM welcomes the well-judged decree issued by the executive branch."[31] And this was not a one-off message. One CCM press release praised the government's initiative to regulate the country's civil service as follows: "it cannot be better," "our most sincere and complete congratulations," "this project will uphold the rights of employees." It only identified one problem: the possibility for political parties to charge fees, something that could exclusively benefit the nascent official entity.[32] Otherwise the text expresses complete agreement with the government's proposals. Of course, these eulogies were not unconditional, as the CCM strongly criticized government figures such as the education minister, Gonzalo Vázquez Vela; interior minister, Ignacio García Téllez; and the CTM's leader, Vicente Lombardo Toledano.

Perhaps as a result of this kind of ambiguity, the CTM was one of the most vocal opponents of the CCM's work.[33] It considered that "[...] it was not a confederation and does not even have a middle-class membership. Instead it's a fascist organization funded by the ruling class, particularly by German industrialists and merchants."[34] Vicente Lombardo Toledano based his comments on some documents that appear to have fallen into the hands of government authorities and that provided details of the CCM's financial structure. The union boss claimed that every month the CCM received several thousand pesos from its German, Italian, and Japanese patrons.[35]

However, these accusations were an opening shot, prompted by General Cedillo's revolt in May 1938. Up until that point, the main criticism levelled at the CCM was that the *useful middle classes* were already in the ranks of the CTM, "[...] in other words, the middle class that is the physical and intellectual force, such as the institutions of professionals, school teachers and even professors, chemists, etc., proving that the workers' movement in Mexico is not simply a financial struggle."[36] The CCM made no reference to teachers belonging to the middle classes, probably due to the education sector's close links to government and the Communist influence within the teaching profession.[37]

The dispute over middle-class diversity, although without referring to this class in the plural, was another variable in the period's discourses and practices. Middle-class unity was maintained among different sectors, highlighting its internal diversity, and there were mutual accusations of organizations only representing a small section of it in detriment to the majority.[38] Xavier Icaza, who held several government positions during the period in question, wrote a long text called the "Decálogo de la clase media mexicana" (Decalogue of the Mexican middle classes), accusing Luis Cabrera of seeking to create his own intellectual middle class. "Perhaps it would be useful for Señor Cabrera to know that there is a union of salaried intellectual workers registered with the Federal District's council and that they form one of the country's most important central committees."[39] Icaza was defending the idea of a middle class committed to political change. Interestingly, he did not query whether Cabrera belonged to this social sector or not, but instead focused on his intellectual failure to conceive the political membership and role of Mexico's middle classes.

The debate also raged in universities, called upon to participate in discussions about what was meant by the middle class. Different groups adopted different positions in publications, magazines, and even in conferences. The League of Socialist Agronomists (Liga de Agrónomos Socialistas) suggested various alternatives, especially linked to the relationship between the middle classes and agrarian reform. Meanwhile, a new journal called *Revista Mexicana de Sociología* contributed by publishing various articles on this subject in its early issues, including a text by Maurice Halbwachs.[40] In this article the eminent French researcher asked whether the heterogeneous mass that formed the ranks of the middle class really deserved to be referred to as a "class." In his view, one possible way of analyzing them as a whole was their connection to a "technical" form of knowledge as a principal work tool. Halbwachs concluded by saying that the middle classes needed to join forces with other social classes and no longer be "dominated," chiming with the position of some government officials. The resumption of certain intellectual stances was not accidental, either. Lucio Mendieta y Núñez—the driving force behind the *Revista Mexicana de Sociología*, and the institutionalization of sociology more generally—had initiated Cardenismo when at the helm of the political, economic, and social research institute of the National Revolutionary Party (Partido Nacional Revolucionario, PNR), which sought principally to combine academic and political efforts to support government programs.[41]

However, if we return to the DAPP booklet, we can see that one of its main bones of contention was about education as a means of consolidating social and economic disparities. This was not a controversy about theory but formed part of the disputes between different sectors about the so-called socialist education. In this regard, Cárdenas perceived the National University as one of the main obstacles facing his project. This partly explains the creation of a series of institutions and mechanisms to reduce its importance in the field of education and politics. Of course, the National University viewed this with concern and took various countermeasures, from creating the Departamento de Acción Social in 1936 to mounting fierce opposition to institutions such as the Instituto Hispano-Mexicano Ruiz de Alarcón.[42]

The CCM—and particularly some of its affiliate organizations seeking to increase their membership figures—took advantage of this conflict between the government and the National University. A confidential report on students at the National Preparatory School (Escuela Nacional Preparatoria, ENP) associated with the CCM contained an analysis on how to reach out to the students and how to win the local elections. In this process, the candidate of the groups connected to the Confederation, José Luis Noriega, reported that he had given more than ten speeches a day and even organized a rally attended by more than 700 students (out of a total of the 2,000 enrolled at the ENP). In fact, he claimed that armed Communist militants were present in order to intimidate their opponents, making it "necessary" for them to arm their own gunslingers. On the day of the elections, a number of scuffles broke out and ultimately the university's authorities had to adjudicate, and they awarded victory to the group linked to the CCM. Over and above this particular triumph, the important issue was the intensity of political clashes within centers of higher education.

The CCM also disseminated its views through the debate over public-sector employees' legal status. These discussions lasted between June 1937, when Cárdenas submitted a draft workers' statute to the executive branch, almost until the day the decree passed into law, on December 5, 1938. The Senate extended its applicability to the judicial and legislative branches. In this instance, the legislative branch became the principal public opposition to the CCM. In fact, according to Pérez Monfort, the lower chamber of congress proposed a motion to dissolve it for its pernicious campaign defending the rights of public-sector employees. "Since September 1937, there has clearly been a threat to some government ministries in which the CCM is recruiting large numbers of government workers."[43]

From the organization's perspective, the new statute failed to improve working conditions for public-sector employees but instead reinforced their unfair treatment:

> Public-sector employees are still exploited and harassed at all levels of government; they are unfairly dismissed; ridiculed on the most trivial pretext; forced to accept deductions from their already-meager salaries; and obliged to adopt certain political and social positions or else risk dismissal; and the financial needs of female public-sector employees lead to the abuse of Mexican women who should be the mainstay of our country's moral virtue and traditions.[44]

The CCM referred to the absurdity of comparing public-sector employees to blue-collar workers, implementing the right to strike or even turning the state into an employer. In its view, Congress's amendments sought to sabotage the process and divert attention from the genuinely important issue, namely prohibiting the dismissal of public-sector employees on account of reorganizations or due to their political beliefs.[45]

Although some deputies perceived that the CCM was a threat due to its expanding influence among public-sector employees, the outlook was less promising within the organization's own ranks. Despite its steadily growing university student membership, it had less success among public-sector employees and had been a little impetuous (in contrast with the ENP's aforesaid electoral campaign). According to the CCM, the problem lay in the training of its members, which required greater thoroughness. Another weakness was employees' apathy when dealing with organizational processes. Albeit somewhat ambiguously, its statements emphasized that "public-sector employees have organized themselves thanks to their own efforts and the government's understanding of the need to define their situation and regulate its relationship with them."[46]

Congresses and Publications

As one of its main activities, the CCM made continual accusations that international Communism had taken over the Mexican government, and by doing so hoped to attract a membership of more than half a million people around the country. According to its own statements, the CCM comprised some 40 organizations with a total of 162,000 members engaged in all kinds of activities, not excluding armed militancy targeting the Cardenista government and the Mexican Communist Party.[47] "This febrile middle-class activity reflects the unprecedented political agitation dominating Mexico over the past two years,"[48] wrote George Stern, a journalist from the United States in the introduction to his interview with Enrique Sáenz de Sicilia. The fact that this interview was given to a US journalist was no coincidence.[49] Although the CCM made no reference to belonging to an international network either in its statement of principles or in its programs, its supporters made a special effort to use potentially beneficial transnational webs. The interview was just one link in this chain of activities.

Perhaps the best way to analyze the CCM's political maneuvers in this regard is by focusing on the organization of the First Ibero-American Anti-Communist Congress, scheduled to take place in Havana from September 1 to 15, 1937. Cuban military officers Jaime Mariné y Montes and Manuel S. Pérez Alfonso intervened to ensure the local government's backing for the CCM.[50] In Mexico, the Argentinean ambassador, Roberto Leviller, had pledged to support the event and the country's legations in Chile, El Salvador, Costa Rica, Guatemala, and Honduras had welcomed the organizers with open arms. The Bolivian ambassador, Alfredo Sanjinés, had conveyed the invitation to the president of his country's military junta, David Toro. In March of that same year, a group of graphic artists produced the "allegories" for the propaganda effort across the continent, while some intellectuals were allegedly writing keynote speeches.[51] In August 1937, the organizers even sent a letter to the Mexican president, informing him about the event.

In the end, the CCM canceled the Congress, exculpating itself and explaining that the pledge of support from the Cuban authorities had failed to materialize:

> Our delegate had grounds to conclude that it was not advisable to hold the Congress on the Island due to the vacillation of the man who was supposed to have the last word, who seeks to accommodate all the different political parties on the Island in order to hold onto power, the leftism of the island's large Spanish population, and the characteristics of Havana's population itself, something that we are more than familiar with, in addition to the radical background to the Cuban Revolution.[52]

This was not the only problem facing the organizers. The first setback came when Mexico's foreign affairs ministry made concerted efforts to prevent the event from going ahead. The diplomatic corps in Mexico generally supported the Mexican government, hence they rejected the CCM's proposals, as these could sour its relationship with the country's authorities. However, this situation did not prevent the media of various countries across the continent from publishing the invitation to the event, hence the battles between the CCM and the government began to be waged in Latin American newspapers and magazines.

Venezuela's *La Esfera* newspaper published the following: "If countries in the Americas are anti-Communist; if, as has been said, they have all enacted anti-Communist legislation to challenge Soviet doctrine, then it is to be inferred that our governments—without exception—will rush to be represented."[53] This was designed to pressure the Venezuelan government, which had already expelled a number of Communist militants and union bosses. Mexico was the country that had given them asylum, and the CCM's campaign, replicated systematically across various Latin American countries, also criticized its policy of providing shelter to those suffering political persecution. The Mexican government became the target of continual attacks with each publication about the Congress. Mexico's foreign affairs ministry, despite playing down the event's importance, still sought to minimize its potential impact.[54] As a first step, it sent out to all Latin American governments a press release indicating that an unofficial organization had issued the invitation and that Mexico would not participate. This needed clarification, since the CCM's printed invitation read: "The statements on this issue by the President of the Republic, General Lázaro Cárdenas, make it relevant for Mexico."[55] Moreover, Sáenz de Sicilia told the media that José Vasconcelos, Federico Gamboa, and Antonio Díaz Soto y Gama would be attending as Mexico's representatives.

The strengthening of the organization's publishing structure was a core objective of the CCM's political work, though its 1936 declaration of principles did not make any direct reference to it. The organization's founders' idea was that

> there is no modern scientific, literary, or political body that can disseminate its doctrine by word of mouth alone; it must have a newspaper for it to endure, so that it can be surrounded by converts and withstand attacks or hostility from opponents.[56]

The CCM had failed to achieve this, but its presence in various national and international media represented an important step forward in this direction. This also implied the possibility of promoting its middle-class "values."

At the time of the CCM was planning the Ibero-American Anti-Communist Congress, publishing was important for two reasons. On the one hand, the organizers openly declared the initial aim: an advertising bureau to print anti-Communist propaganda across the continent. They considered this an essential step toward creating a continent-wide organization equipped to lead the anti-Communist struggle and to *clarify* its underlying principles.[57] The idea was to counteract "[...] the pro-Communist radicals who slander national governments with all their fallacious demagoguery."[58]

The second reason was less explicit, and its themes were copied from the titles of an anti-Communist series of booklets that began to circulate around Latin America, entitled *El Socialismo y el Comunismo ante el Sentido Común* (*Socialism and Communism versus Common Sense*).[59] These booklets were published in Mexico after mid-1936 by Acción Cívica Nacional, one of the CCM's member organizations.[60] The texts addressed important issues for Mexico's right-wing elements: socialist education, agrarian reform, and the relationship between Church and

State,[61] but focusing on the debate on theoretical principles of Communism and the experiences of Spain and Russia (during this period the propaganda of these organizations did not generally refer to the Soviet Union). Its conclusion and basic principle was that "in Mexico we live under a Socialist regime. A tendency exists to implement the dictatorship of the proletariat. If we do not prevent it, this will cause the same misfortune that has befallen Spain and Russia."[62] Wearing these ideological blinkers, Acción Cívica Nacional and CCM launched perhaps one of the most vigorous and long-lasting publishing ventures of all the small anti-Communist groups of the time (Table 12.1).

Table 12.1 El Socialismo y el Comunismo ante el Sentido Común (Socialism and Communism versus Common Sense), a series published by Acción Cívica Nacional

No. 1	*Qué cosa es el socialismo y qué el comunismo; La verdadera finalidad del socialismo; El materialismo histórico* (What is Socialism and Communism; the true purpose of Socialism; a history of materialism)	*1936*
No. 2	*El socialismo y la propiedad* (Socialism and property)	1936
No. 3	*El socialismo y la familia* (Socialism and family)	1936
No. 4	*El socialismo y el gobierno* (Socialism and government)	1936
No. 5	*El socialismo y Dios* (Socialism and God)	1937
No. 6	*Los horrores del antiteísmo socialista en España* (The horrors of Socialist atheism in Spain)	1937
No. 7	*Los horrores del antiteísmo socialista en Rusia* (The horrors of Socialist atheism in Russia)	1937
No. 8	*Los horrores del antiteísmo socialista en México* (The horrors of Socialist atheism in Mexico)	1937
No. 9	*Cómo desarrolla su acción el socialismo* (How does Socialism work in practice)	1937
No. 10	*La dictadura del proletariado; ésta y el campesino* (The dictatorship of the proletariat; dictatorship and the campesino)	1937
No. 11	*La dictadura del proletariado y el obrero* (The dictatorship of the proletariat and the laborer)	
No. 12	*Malos resultados del socialismo y el comunismo* (The harmful effects of Socialism and Communism)	1937
No. 13	*El O. G. P. U. o Cheka* (The OGPU or Cheka)	1937
No. 14	*Solución católica a la Cuestión Social* (The Catholic solution to social issues)	1938
No. 15	*Refutación de las falsedades que contra la Religión, la autoridad y la pureza, enseña la Escuela Socialista* (Refuting the falsehoods of the socialist school's education that attacks religion, authority, and purity)	1938
No. 16	*Frutos del comunismo* (The results of Communism)	1938
No. 17	*Resumen de todos los folletos anteriores* (Summary of previous booklets)	1938

Although published in Mexico, the texts were most probably written in Spain in the context of the Civil War, since most of the issues were not related specifically to the Cardenista government, and instead took a more general approach. Only issue number 15, published two years after the launch of the series, dealt with Mexican subjects, although since the third issue some Mexican case studies were discussed, evidently tacked on to a pre-existing text.[63] The same collection also appeared in Chile during the same period.

Although the Congress did not go ahead, CCM's assessment remained positive. The anti-Communist movement had strengthened across the continent. Also, the confederation claimed progress in establishing an anti-Communist doctrine adapted to the reality of the Americas. It definitely proved that the projection of local problems onto a Latin American context could benefit anti-Communist organizations, and especially in the CCM's positioning thanks to its propaganda efforts.

> But to demonstrate the effectiveness of our work, we simply need to refer to our adversary's reaction: speakers and writers attached to the CTM, the Communist Party, the Chamber of Deputies' Committee for the Proletariat's Defense, all mention CCM at every opportunity.[64]

This process, although cut short at that time, also undoubtedly produced one of the important variables that defined middle-class disputes at the time. Cosmopolitanism, or what we now call the global middle class, would appear implicitly in CCM's every action. Combined with nationalist views, this conflictive atmosphere created a specific discourse, with the need to make an impact in the mass media. Therefore, analyzing this particular position reveals how those who appointed themselves representatives of the middle classes could articulate several levels of discourse, taking advantage of specific political situations.

By way of a Conclusion

A number of issues are completely absent from the CCM's proposals, such as discussions about their differentiation and consumption patterns. In fact, when referring to consumption, the texts discuss beans, chilies, and corn—in other words, the basic diet of the Mexican population. This is relevant because the CCM did not seek to frame discussions by emphasizing social differences but by combining its efforts with those of the broader Mexican public. As we have seen, the key to understanding this situation was its founder's deep-seated anti-Communist views.

This anti-Communism was essential for increasing the organization's number of active members and to generate processes of identification through its ideological stance. However, we can ask ourselves: To what extent did focusing on this variable prompt the CCM to abandon or minimize the importance of the particular demands of the Mexican middle class? Or, from a different perspective: How did this organization relate to the sector of society it claimed to represent? There is scant evidence that its activism had much effect on private-sector employees or on members of the armed forces. However, it seems to have enjoyed fleeting success with public-sector employees. In this regard, different processes could have been important, including the staunch anti-Communism of groups belonging to the public administration, the dominant role assumed by Communist activists and their monopolization of certain positions within the state bureaucracy, among other processes.

Another important line of inquiry is the extent of a convergence between "middle classes" and "anti-Communism" during this period. The CCM—as perhaps one of Communism's most virulent opponents—offers a possible response. But we must not forget that the strategies behind this organization's political activities, including the planning of an international congress, were based on one possible reading of Mexican reality. But this was not the only possible one, hence the inevitable disputes. However, the fact that it provided an alternative calls for a deeper research into the proposals of such organizations.

This text shows a series of elements defining the ambiguities and conflicting discourses about the middle classes in Mexico during Cardenismo. To conclude, we should recall E.P. Thompson's words on this issue: "By class I understand a historical phenomenon, unifying a number of disparate and seemingly unconnected events, both in the raw material of experience and in consciousness."[65] To what extent these discourses were capable of entering into dialogue with the construction of the middle class, is a topic that requires further research.

Notes

1 "Carta de Lázaro Cárdenas a Luciano Kubli," February 27, 1935, in Archivo General de la Nación de México (AGN), Fondo Lázaro Cárdenas (LC), caja 1301, exp. 704.1/73, n.p.

2 No author [Luciano Kubli], *El ejido en Yucatán* (Mexico City: Talleres Gráficos de la Nación, 1935), 14.

3 Alan Knight, "Cardenismo: Juggernaut or Jalopy?" *Journal of Latin American Studies* 26, no. 1 (1994): 73–107.

4 Javier Garciadiego, "La oposición conservadora y de las clases medias al cardenismo," *Istor*, no. 25 (2006): 44. The author quotes excerpts from AGN, LC, exp. 565.4/1391, which includes a letter from the CCM to the president.

5 Ricardo Pérez Monfort, *"Por la patria y por la raza": La derecha secular en el sexenio de Lázaro Cárdenas* (Mexico City: Facultad de Filosofía y Letras-Universidad Nacional Autónoma de México, 1993).

6 In this sense, the idea is to take a similar approach as proposed by Mario Barbosa in relation to the "middle-class category," although in his case he discusses public-sector employees. The author's ultimate objective is to analyze the exterior perspective on these sectors. See Mario Barbosa Cruz,

"Distinciones y apariencias: La clase media en la Ciudad de México entre el Porfiriato y la revolución," *Oficio: Revista de Historia e Interdisciplina*, no. 10 (July–December 2020): 9–23.

7 This could also be connected to the embryonic construction of a certain global middle-class identity.

8 See Soledad Loaeza, *Clases medias y política en México* (Mexico City: El Colegio de México, 1988), 78–98.

9 Here I have come back to Ricardo López's proposal in "Nosotros también somos parte del pueblo: gaitanismo, empleados y la formación histórica de la clase media en Bogotá, 1936–1948," *Revista de Estudios Sociales*, no. 41 (2011): 84–105.

10 Departamento Autónomo de Prensa y Publicidad, *Fuerza y flaqueza de la clase media* (Mexico City: DAPP, 1938), 2.

11 Departamento Autónomo de Prensa y Publicidad, *Fuerza*, 2.

12 Departamento Autónomo de Prensa y Publicidad, *Fuerza*, 3.

13 The CCM's discourses almost invariably began with a rejection of strike action. See George Stern, "Habla la Confederación de la Clase Media," *Futuro*, no. 12 (February 1937): 13.

14 This was a key exercise in the construction of the political project at the time. Rumors became an important means of action for various sectors. This can be seen in various spheres, including the proliferation of apocryphal texts. On this subject, see Alan Knight, "México y Estados Unidos, 1938–1940: Rumor y realidad," *Secuencia*, no. 34 (1996): 129–154.

15 Departamento Autónomo de Prensa y Publicidad, *Fuerza*, 4.

16 Departamento Autónomo de Prensa y Publicidad, *Fuerza*, 4. This process crystallized in 1943 with the emergence of the National Confederation of Popular Organizations (Confederación Nacional de Organizaciones Populares, CNOP). See Tiziana Bertaccini, *El régimen priista frente a las clases medias, 1943–1964* (Mexico City: CONACULTA, 2009).

17 To understand the importance of these sectors, for example, according to Susie Porter, 5% of the Mexican population depended on the salaries of public-sector employees. Susie Porter, "Empleadas públicas: Normas de feminidad, espacios burocráticos e identidad de la clase media en México durante la década de 1930," *Signos Históricos*, no. 11 (January–July 2004): 41–63.

18 Rodrigo García Treviño, "Ejidos, 'mordidas,' hombres y clases," *Futuro*, no. 13 (March 1937): 25. See an analysis on this topic by Víctor Bravo Ahúja and Marco Antonio Michel, "Alianza de clases y dominación: México, 1930–1946," in *La democratización fundamental: El populismo en América Latina*, coord. Carlos M. Vilas (Mexico City: CONACULTA, 1995), 309–338. The CCM was considered part of the historic block that had defeated Callismo.

19 As discussed in Knight's "Cardenismo," 73–107.

20 Stern, "Habla la Confederación de la Clase Media," 14.

21 Ricardo Pérez Monfort and Lina Odena Güemes, "*Por la Patria y por la Raza*": *Tres movimientos nacionalistas 1936–1940; Documentos* (Mexico City: Cuadernos de la Casa Chata; CIESAS, 1982), 44.

22 Although the minimum wage in 1936 was $2 pesos, in many sectors of the population people earned less than $1 peso a day. Therefore, a daily income of $5 pesos per day was far above the average.

23 *Declaración de principios, programa de acción y estatutos de la Confederación de la Clase Media* (n.p: Mexico City: 1936), 4. This declaration of principles was published in the national and local press. See, for example, "La clase media en la vida política y social de México," *El Porvenir* (Monterrey), June 14, 1936, 4. In this case, the editors added some references to the social conditions in Nuevo León. Two weeks later, excerpts were published that had not

been selected in this issue. "La Confederación de la Clase Media da a conocer su programa," *El Porvenir* (Monterrey), June 29, 1936, 4, 8.

24 *Declaración de principios*, 6.

25 Further studies on this topic appear necessary. See a brief reconstruction of this process in Eduardo Nava Hernández and Beny Oliver Barajas Pérez, "Cooperativismo, autonomía y poder: el movimiento cooperativista en México durante el cardenismo," *Revista Cooperativismo y desarrollo* 23, no. 106 (2015): 25–34.

26 *Declaración de principios*, 3.

27 "Manifiesto a los obreros y campesinos del país," July 1937, in Archivo de la Confederación de la Clase Media (ACCM), CIESAS, 158.

28 "Informe de la Confederación de la Clase Media," November 30, 1937, in ACCM, CIESAS, 193.

29 See, for example, some of the chapters in the book by Ezequiel Adamovsky, Sergio E. Visacovsky, and Patricia Vargas, comps., *Clases medias: Nuevos enfoques desde la sociología, la historia y la antropología* (Buenos Aires: Ariel, 2014). I also suggest the compilation by David S. Parker and Louise E. Walker, *Latin America's Middle Class: Unsettled Debates and New Histories* (Lanham, MD: Lexington Books, 2012).

30 Diane E. Davis, *El Leviatán urbano: La ciudad de México en el siglo XX* (Mexico City: Fondo de Cultura Económica, 1999), 126–127.

31 "Carta de la CCM al Gral. de División Lázaro Cárdenas, Presidente Constitucional de los Estados Unidos Mexicanos," November 6, 1937, in ACCM, CIESAS, 170.

32 Quotes from "Boletín de prensa," July 7, 1937, in ACCM, CIESAS, 174–175.

33 This was one of the CCM's objectives from its outset: "We need considerable mental strength to confront the unchecked hostility of the union bosses who do not and will not accept the creation of a powerful social group—one that is undoubtedly the most influential in Mexican history, by joining together the country's entire middle class—and has to fight it using the exotic means in vogue, whose most popular slogan is that the end justifies the means," stated Querido Moheno Jr., one of the signatories of the CCM's articles of incorporation. Querido Moheno Jr., "La clase media en México," *El Porvenir*, June 1, 1936, 3.

34 "Absoluto orden tuvo el desfile," *El Nacional*, August 4, 1938, 7.

35 This retrieved the assessment of Manuel Fernández Boyoli and Eustaquio Marrón de Angelis, *Lo que no se sabe de la rebelión cedillista* (Mexico City: Grafi-Art, 1938). Although it is more likely that it received resources directly from the group of businessmen from Nuevo León who saw Cárdenas as the reincarnation of Bolshevism.

36 "En la CTM está ya la clase media," *El Nacional*, March 20, 1937, 1.

37 In some parts of Latin America, teachers were instrumental in forming the middle class. Enrique Garguin, "Intersecciones entre clase y género en la construcción social magisterio: La Asociación de Maestros de la Provincia de Buenos Aires durante las primeras décadas del siglo XX," in *Clases medias*, comps. Adamovsky, Visacovsky and Vargas.

38 It is interesting that the CCM's texts often accuse officials of one class of intervening in the organizations of other classes. In its view, class purity ensured a well-functioning society.

39 Xavier Icaza, "Decálogo de la clase media mexicana," *Futuro*, no. 14 (April 1937): 26.

40 Maurice Halbwachs, "Las características de las clases medias," *Revista Mexicana de Sociología* 1, no. 3 (1939): 95–109. See also Valentín Feldman and René Barragán, "El Problema de las Clases Medias en la U. R. S. S.," *Revista Mexicana de Sociología* 2, no. 2 (1940): 15–40 and Raymond Aron,

"El Concepto de Clase," *Revista Mexicana de Sociología* 1, no. 1 (1939): 97–108. On the debates in question, see Klaus-Peter Sick, "El concepto de clases medias: ¿Noción sociológica o eslogan político?," in *Clases medias*, comps. Adamovsky, Visacovsky and Vargas.

41 Margarita Olvera Serrano, *Lucio Mendieta y Núñez y la institucionalización de la sociología en México, 1939–1965* (Mexico City: UAM-Azcapotzalco; Miguel Ángel Porrúa, 2004).

42 In particular, see Sandra García de Fez, "Una escuela desconocida del exilio: La polémica en torno al Instituto Hispano Mexicano Ruiz de Alarcón," *Educació i Història: Revista d'Història de l'Educació*, no. 17 (2011): 213–235. Although she only mentions its conflict with the UNAM in passing.

43 Pérez Monfort and Odena Güemes, "*Por la Patria y por la Raza*," 45.

44 *Declaración de principios*, 3. The ideas about gender are essential to understand some aspects of how the middle class formed in Latin America. On this issue, see Susie Porter, *From Angel to Office Worker: Middle-Class Identity and Female Consciousness in Mexico, 1890–1950* (Lincoln: University of Nebraska Press, 2018); López, "Nosotros también," 84–105.

45 "Carta de la CCM a la Cámara de Diputados," February 19, 1938, in ACCM, CIESAS, 182–183.

46 "La Conf. de la Clase Media propugnará la expedición de la Ley de Servicio Civil," *El Porvenir*, July 11, 1936, 4.

47 For a list with the names of notable activists, see AGN, Fondo Dirección General de Investigaciones Políticas y Social (DGIPS), vol. 205, exp. 1.

48 Stern, "Habla la Confederación de la Clase Media," 13.

49 The CCM presented its program and action plan of the Republican Party in search of aid. See "Conexión de los elementos del fascismo," *El Nacional*, August 7, 1938, 1 and 6.

50 "Carta de la CCM al Comandante Jaime Mariné y Montes," March 17, 1937, in ACCM, CIESAS, 199–200.

51 "Memorándum de los trabajos desarrollados hasta la fecha para el Primer Congreso Iberoamericano Anticomunista," March 17, 1937, in ACCM, CIESAS, 197–198.

52 "Informe de la Confederación de la Clase Media," November 30, 1937, in ACCM, CIESAS, 188. The close relationship between Batista and Cárdenas very probably impeded any attempt to hold this congress in Cuba. The organizers later attempted to move it to Colombia, but the local government also refused to provide any support.

53 "¿No han invitado a Venezuela?," *La Esfera* (Caracas), June 15, 1937. Transcription in "Informes Primer Congreso Iberoamericano Anticomunista," 1937, in Archivo Histórico Genaro Estrada de la Secretaría de Relaciones Exteriores (AHGE), Fondo Diplomático (FD), exp. III-353-4, n.p.

54 According to the files, the person who initially seemed least informed was the Mexican ambassador in Cuba, Alfonso Craviotto. While memorandums were flying back and forth around almost the entire continent, the ambassador in Cuba said that he had received no information about the event. "Informes Primer Congreso Iberoamericano Anticomunista," 1937, in AHGE, FD, exp. III-353-4.

55 "Informes Primer Congreso Iberoamericano Anticomunista," 1937, in AHGE, FD, exp. III-353-4, n.p.

56 Moheno Jr., "La clase media en México," 3.

57 Invitation available in "Informes Primer Congreso Iberoamericano Anticomunista," 1937, in AHGE, FD, exp. III-353-4.

58 "Informes Primer Congreso Iberoamericano Anticomunista," 1937, in AHGE, FD, exp. III-353-4, n.p.

59 In specific, see the set of themes about the doctrine.
60 Pérez Monfort, "*Por la patria y por la raza*," 163–169.
61 On this subject, see John W. Sherman, "Reassessing Cardenismo: The Mexican Right and the Failure of a Revolutionary Regime, 1934–1940," *The Americas* 54, no. 3 (1998): 357–378.
62 Acción Cívica Nacional, *Malos resultados del socialismo y el comunismo* (Mexico City: Acción Cívica Nacional, 1937), back cover.
63 It is interesting to note that the 15th issue deals with religious issues. This theme is practically absent from the CCM's statements. However, its organizational effort is readily comparable to certain excesses of Catholic syndicalism, which had aimed to create a League of Middle Classes since the 1920s. See Manuel Ceballos Ramírez, "El sindicalismo católico en México, 1919–1931," *Historia Mexicana* 35, no. 4 (April–June 1986): 621–673.
64 "Informe de la Confederación de la Clase Media," November 30, 1937, ACCM, CIESAS, 191.
65 E. P. Thompson, *La formación de la clase obrera en Inglaterra* (Barcelona: Crítica, 1989), XIII.

13 “Tigers, Cholo-Jacobins, and Red Government Officials”

Roles and Discourses of the Radical Middle Class in Ecuador between 1895 and 1938

Valeria Coronel

This chapter analyzes the discourses and political interventions of the Radical Party’s middle-class activists who were instrumental in the revolutionary war of 1895 and in the subsequent institutionalization of the national state up until the mid-1920s. By researching the formation of the National Army and the Ministry of Public Education—two pillars of social integration and citizenship—we can observe how this sector of the middle-class responded to calls for integration from the popular classes.

We contend that the shift in Ecuadorian politics in 1925 ushered in by the Juliana Revolution confirmed and expanded the sphere of influence of middle-class activists who helped build the nation-state; it also broadened the organization of the lower-income sectors that called for the upholding rights connected to the nation-state’s democratic construction. This sector of the middle class became most visible during this time of change due to its sustained interest in public education and in the social programs of the newly formed state agencies. These state organs provided a locus for a dialogue between the middle classes and the popular classes demanding rights; they were also at the center of (often-conflictive) encounters with a ruling elite that had a firm grip on property ownership and class privileges, and that fiercely opposed regulations that both the secular and reformist state sought to impose on it during a period of global upheaval. While the revolutionary forces and political antagonisms saw the middle-class leaders and lower-class militia joining forces during the republican wars, the state organs provided a place where the lower classes, public officials, and where those pushing for the country’s democratization throughout the first half of the twentieth century could enter into dialogue. Members of the ruling elite bristled when these middle-class actors spoke as figures of public authority; the former considered the latter’s close relationship to the lower classes to be politically motivated, both in terms of collective political action and in the use of law and litigation. The middle class was in fact pivotal as a political connection with the expanding, organized popular processes to help promote the creation of an inclusive state that also embraced the popular

DOI: 10.4324/9781003029311-17

classes, and to foster a public environment that was supportive of this process—a factor still largely overlooked by current historiography.

We must analyze the militant discourse of the middle classes connected to the public administration and the creation of the nation-state in light of the experiences of its dialogue, antagonisms, and political connections with actors of other social classes. It gained its own identity and voice in a "relational" space—in other words, within the context of conflicts and power relations in which these middle-class members often acted with various degrees of decisiveness as agents representing a nation under construction.

To interpret this process requires us to consider a number of elements: war, political rivalries, public debate in the Parliament, the national teaching profession, land disputes, ministerial reports, and in the public sphere (including newspaper articles and literary works). There we can find records left by the actors closely involved in social events and learn about their discourses from the perspective of public officialdom. Moreover, literature from this period offers us a key to understanding some actors who faced certain risks and who showed sensitivity in situations of social conflict. They emerge as agents who activate and strengthen the meanings of republican democratic language, and their self-reflection, among other things, leads to a shift in aesthetic and political language. In this sense, rather than considering them as technical tools of the state, these people were reflexive subjects within certain fields who opened up a democratic path through the political struggles of two historical cycles, and formed their own identity during this process.

Although there are clearly many different ways of defining the middle class, here we focus on public officials who supported the aims of the democratic transition as proposed by the national-popular discourse of the democratic revolution. We have chosen not to examine those aspects of the middle class relating to the social mobility coordinated by ethnic communities, mainly connected to strategies of creating social rifts within the popular sectors and among campesinos who managed to raise some of their members into higher-status positions through market-oriented, identity-based, and cultural strategies.[1] Nor do we intend to reveal the different processes of social differentiation and middle-class formation based on employment or income in Ecuador during the decades in question, a specific subject area in Ecuadorian historical studies.[2]

In the following section we refer to various historiographical studies on the role of these middle-class actors with links to the state. We refer to a paradoxical coincidence, a negative image of the radicalized middle class contained in conservative early-twentieth-century historiographical, revisionist, Latin American neo-Marxist, and post-modern accounts. Countering these academic approaches, our aim is to reconstruct the significant contribution made by this sector of the radical, socialist middle class toward supporting the integration and rights of the popular class as part of two democratic programs: the state reforms following the 1895 democratic revolution and during the decades of global crisis until the late 1930s. We reappraise this sector's role in building democratic institutions, supporting the suffrage of the popular classes, developing social rights, and fighting to include the popular sectors in Ecuador's national culture. We analyze the discourse that seeks to delegitimize the middle class, while also reconstructing the perspectives of radical public officials and leaders about their role in giving visibility to the lower classes as full members of Ecuadorian society and participants in the construction of its democracy.

Reassessing the Signs of Inter-Class Political Connections

Ecuadorian historiography frequently returns to the image of subjects belonging neither to the ruling elite nor to the popular classes, but who nevertheless played a leading political role in establishing state institutions between the late nineteenth century and the end of World War II. Liberal historical accounts often use the trope of a leadership based on military fraternity rather than status. This image suggests that republican clashes gave birth to the modern political nation and the democratic process.[3] In contrast, conservative historiographical studies have insisted on defining the revolutionary military leaders' rise to power as part of dictatorial processes due to these figures' middle-class backgrounds and the context of popular classes clamoring for their rights; these studies have defended a vision of social order being linked to the concept of authority, and viewed the distinguished members of the educated elites as the sole legitimate leaders of the Catholic Nation. At the same time, conservative Hispanism delegitimized the heroism of the radicalized middle class and of the Indigenous communities who aspired to be part of an Indo-American political nation. For Hispanist historiography, the communities mentioned so frequently by the radicalized middle class were not heirs to any remarkable ancient civilization and their struggle was merely a result of their leaders' manipulation; only colonial Catholic institutions and Hispanism could be identified with the origin of Ecuador as a nation.[4] An academic and party-political debate over the nation's cultural origins and classes between the liberal, radical, and conservative forces was overshadowed by the pessimism of the new Marxist's view on Latin American republicanism.

Alongside the narrative of the predestined failure of the democratic dispute in Latin America came a pessimistic reading—rooted in dependency theory—about middle-class aspirations for agency in the democracy, with an ability to mitigate the violence between the elites and the general public in a racist society. From this perspective, the middle-class militants who had challenged Hispanism, *gamonalism*,[5] and imperialism during the first half of the twentieth century had been a naïve group that had diverted the popular revolution into the treacherous terrain of bourgeois democracy.

Cultural studies connected to Latin America's school of sociological and scientific thought of the 1970s tended to take a pessimistic view, sometimes ridiculing middle-class intellectuals and figures in their attempt to supplant the culture of power handed down through the generations of the ruling elites by calling upon the national-popular discourse, introducing concepts such as ventriloquy and manipulation.[6] Others referred to a hidden agenda behind this middle-class democratic discourse, namely the aim to build a mestizo nation. This prompted literary critic Abdón Ubidia to refer to the impossibility for the liberal mestizo to play a role in Ecuador's history: "[...] the full-length mirror that he needs to recognize his own identity does not actually exist: his mestizo existence is merely a series of fragments that are impossible to connect..."[7]

The postmodern discourse has keenly adopted this gloomy perspective in global cultural studies as the basis for disparaging regional political processes and key moments in Latin American plebiscitary democracies, writing them off as authoritarian, populist movements, while simultaneously searching for a cultural otherness as the continent's offer in the midst of the crisis in late-stage capitalism.[8]

Taking a different tack, this chapter examines some lessons learned from new Latin American political history, showing how lower-class republicanisms and popular national processes in Latin America constituted experiences in political connectedness; in these instances, heterogeneous political subjects applied creativity and complexity in using political languages in disputes for power, proving effective to counteract the de facto power of oligarchic pacts. As such, they provided a field of comparative analysis on the formation of the modern world and the nation-state.

This chapter argues that in the dynamics of power negotiations that underlie the more abstract political rhetoric, the Ecuadorian state contains—among its legacies and sediments—aspects that translate into formative processes of democratic political mediations, including social agency and negotiations between inter-class movements that incorporated a section of the middle classes, particularly in the first decade of the liberal state and during the 1930s. Ecuador is the case of a country in which radicalism shaped the state's development during the first two decades of the twentieth century and where the global crisis was the backdrop for a state reform driven forward by a cross-party block that combined democratic and socialist elements.[9] In relational theories applied to the state, research reveals the creation of a relatively autonomous public power that inspired initiatives that tended toward establishing control over the forms of imperialist and oligarchical domination and accumulation, constituting processes based on plebiscitary legitimacy.[10] This type of question arises specifically in early-twenty-first-century Latin America when disputes over alternatives to neoliberal governments consider the formation of states with contrasting outlooks.

This chapter seeks to indicate areas in which the middle class operated after they made the transition from revolutionary activities to building up public power and the national imaginary as a platform for a cultural discourse. Its own identity is questioned by the different class extremes; its knowledge encompasses scientific rules and technical procedures, but it only takes effect to challenge the power of the ruling elites.

The Divisive Social Status of Radical Leaders and of "Cholo-Jacobins" in the Democratic Process

In 1894, Ecuador had four officially recognized political parties. A portrait of their respective leaders was taken for a photographic composition in a catalog sent by Ecuador to the Universal Expo of Chicago in that same year.[11] Those appearing were Camilo Ponce (Conservative Party); Pedro Carbo (a patrician member of the Liberal Party); José María Plácido Caamaño (an aristocrat and leader of the ruling Progresista Party); and Eloy Alfaro (the son of storeowners from the Manabí province and a military commander with strong support among the popular classes, included as the leader of the Radical Party).

Eloy Alfaro's inclusion reflects President Luis Cordero's aim to ensure peace during a time of global economic expansion, lifting the censorship of the Radical Party and inviting its leader to sit at the same table as the parties of the ruling elite. In contrast to other countries, attempts to stamp out radicalism in Ecuador had failed. If the idea of including radical leaders alongside the predominant oligarchical parties had been successful, it would have changed the course of history. In this chapter, we propose that two factors prevented the forces of ultramontanism from modeling the nation-state in the late-nineteenth-century transition: (a) radicalism was formed as a political tendency that articulated sectors of the regional elite and the smaller, more local elites on the peripheries, as well as a heterogeneous mix of popular collectives and classes in Ecuador's different regions; (b) the ruling class was not a homogenous entity, partly due to the influence of the transnational clergy, which limited its capacity to drive forward a process of efficient political integration and imposed the superiority of the Church's interests and its state agents.

Even at the dawn of the twentieth century, this situation continued to prevent the success of conservative republicanism. Conservatives and progressives adhered to the ultramontane creed. In 1894, the clergy objected to the participation of senator Felicísimo López, elected by popular vote to represent Esmeraldas in the Senate, because of his past as a liberal, excommunicated for criticizing the clergy's financial accounts. The clergy weakened the state, threatened its finances, stirred up conflicts among regional elites, and usurped their control over the most important areas of social interventions, preventing institutionalization itself.

Bishop Schumacher, the head of the clergy, warned against the political use of patriotic symbols, accusing the "Reds" of entering into an "impious competition" for patriotic and sacred symbols; he criticized the erection of the statue of Sucre on Plaza de Santo Domingo in Quito (on April 24, 1894); he lodged complaints against the *Diario de Avisos* (Guayaquil) and *Democracia* (Portoviejo) newspapers for entering into the debate over the hierarchy of laws. Along with Massiá—the Carlist bishop of Loja—Schumacher attempted to prevent the veneration of patriotic symbols among the lower classes for being the proselytizing work of "committees" and the "Red" and liberal literary circles. In 1895, Schumacher sent urgent letters to protest against the small regional elites and radical leaders' "rabble-rousing" among the popular classes to lower the level of politics "with false democratic rhetoric." He said that they had been impious in raising up the lowest strata of society—"the radical hordes in the Chone jungles."

The radical leaders had indeed stirred up conflict through the radical press, and using a tried-and-tested republican language they succeeded in alerting public opinion by protesting against "the sale of the flag"—namely, President Cordero's lending of Ecuador's national flag to Chile, enabling the latter to sell a ship to Japan, triggering a public outcry across the country. The lower-class elements among the democratic republican supporters took over the lead from the elite parties in the political sphere. Alfaro did not represent a regional oligarchical faction, but led a party that had sealed a pact between the bourgeoisie and the campesino population around the country, inviting them to join in a national ideal, which, according to the Gramscian definition, constituted a Jacobin route. This was a historic movement that had survived throughout the nineteenth century and had built up significant power on successive occasions, as well as experience in government.

By launching a campaign to protect patriotic symbols from the power of the transnational clergy and the oligarchy's secret deals, they managed to organize various sectors of society into something that Alfaro called a new revolutionary cycle. In this process, they articulated the most deeply rooted class disputes, involving Indigenous campesinos who had long opposed the expansion of the hacienda system and the payment of the *diezmo* or tithe to the Church, while also fanning the flames of the struggle for democracy—a cause supported by the middle classes and peripheral elites in various parts of the country. The connection made by leaders and radicalized middle classes with patriotic symbols was not merely part of a doctrinaire rhetoric; it lay at the heart of a strategy of making political linkages between different social groups for collective action.

This situation explains how, at the cusp of the twentieth century, this body that had accumulated power over the years, holding up the flag of the national discourse, triumphed over the conservative armies, and pronounced itself in charge as the national revolutionary government in 1895. After Alfaro had secured his definitive rule with transitional governments led by political-military leaders, the revolutionary government decided to give institutional democratic shape to the military triumph and announced a constitutional assembly in 1896. Deputies from existing parties attended this assembly and, although the presence was required of members of the ultramontane progressive and conservative opposition, the liberal and radical parties formed the largest contingent. The political elites viewed the rise of radical leaders to the position of deputies, and the presence of the popular classes around Parliament, as illegitimate—an affront to the nation they considered the property of the patriotic aristocracy of the *cabildos* or councils, in other words, of the educated elites rather than the masses.[12]

The elites feared encounters with assemblymen of lower-class origin, as opposed to the patrician members of the cabildo of Guayaquil, whom they recognized as the Liberal Party elites. After the war they found themselves sitting next to radicals who had acquired their status as leaders during the military campaign and who demanded a nation that included the lower-class militia, Blacks, and Indigenous people. They consistently sought to delegitimize their representation in Congress, despite controlling the executive branch. This rejection was always connected to their mocking of "tropical men" not of the educated elite but instead surrounded by "manipulated" campesinos who tried to act as though they had equal political rights or who were supported by international Freemasonry. From exile, the transnational clergy incited anger about the "debasement" of politics that invigorated these radicalized, middle-income sectors:

> [...] that mass of arrogant, impious, and ill-mannered men taken by the Freemasons into the galleries of the National Congress, that group of Cholo-Jacobins were brought and paid to drown the voices of all the Catholic speakers and intimidate them with their howls and threats, whereas upon a signal they applauded any impious proposition made by the Masonic lodge.[13]

Nevertheless, records show that there were as many educated men as military leaders among the Radical Party's representatives, and even among the radical deputies of the congresses from 1896 to 1898.[14]

The liberal elites found common cause with their conservative counterparts on this issue. Luis Felipe Borja, for example, agreed with the conservatives in describing the phobia displayed toward the military leaders acting as senators and the ranks of soldiers supporting their arguments. He called them "uncouth soldiery" who disguised themselves as civilians to attend Congress and to intimidate the genuine public following the orders of their leaders, the upper level among the plebeians who manipulated them. This connected the anti-plebeian and anti-military discourses: the revolutionaries—due to their humble origins and despite their efforts to pacify political forces and settle differences by democratic means—became associated with dictators who protected themselves by manipulating the lower classes.

Manuel María Arízaga and Juan de Dios Corral, representing ultramontane forces, along with the liberal aristocrats Luis Felipe Borja and Juan Benigno Vela, launched a defamation campaign against the revolutionary leader, Manuel Antonio Franco, whom they considered one of the most influential members of this imagined lower-class "tyranny." Franco had forged his leadership as a commander of guerrilla forces in the Esmeraldas province among young patriots and militia of African descent. He had been appointed the political and military leader in the Pichincha province, setting up a revolutionary government in Quito known for redistributing lands and empowering the organized Indigenous workers on the haciendas of Conservative leaders. Strongly supported by the militia, Franco was elected representative for the Assembly, and touted as Alfaro's potential successor to be presidential candidate imagined by the radical majorities.

The Conservative newspaper *Fray Gerundio* referred to him as "humble" on account of his origins, insulting him as "riff-raff" and a "tiger" for his military career and campaigns in the countryside, an "innkeeper" for his style of communicating with different classes, and a "tyrant" for imposing power of the people. The ultramontane figures called for the "tigers" to be removed from Parliament and prevented from submitting their candidacy for the executive branch:

> Outlaws, showing off some talent or other, somehow recruit fellow soldiers for their criminal enterprises, like Abelardo Moncayo, for example [...] seducing gangs of hardened upstarts. But what kind of riff-raff, unbearable men, a cross between gorilla and tiger, lacking any higher quality, can find support among the sons of a nation that so often has proclaimed itself KING, hardworking and educated, kind and just; this is the most abject disaster. What answer will we receive from these humble men, to describe them politely, who conjured up what has now become a dreadful reality, supposing that traces of patriotism still exist in the leader of the hordes of 1895? Let us all perish before consenting to a former innkeeper from the coast of Ecuador laying his blood-stained hands on the presidential staff.[15]

The radicals responded by saying that the Revolution had regenerated the nation and restored its sovereignty, and that they could legitimately form its government. They also argued that the way forward was to show their majority support, both in the National Assembly and in the ballots, referring to a majority that included even the most reluctant liberals, who remained prepared to ratify their power in the ruling party. Meanwhile, the ultramontane conservatives oscillated between war and attempting to regain their positions of power within the state. Therefore, the constitutional agenda of the radical liberal block imposed the idea of separating Church and State and broadening suffrage to go beyond the strictures of religion. It achieved this objective through a number of means: by launching a campaign to redefine electoral registers, removing the clerical and gamonal control on voting, and including sectors of the population mobilized during the years of conflict. These sectors established a presence in strategic towns, and included all those who had learned how to sign, such as the troops and those who had become literate thanks to the priority given to the state's public, secular, and compulsory education system. This agenda led to the "threat" of an expanding democracy, in a move whereby the top echelons of radicalism used electoral means to attract the support of the armed forces and a hitherto-invisible general public.

The reactionary discourse, meanwhile, focused on leveling accusations of widespread electoral fraud, connected to the idea of plebeian leaders as manipulators of "garroteros"—a term used in Ecuador by conservative forces to disparage the lowest strata of the militia, national guards, and volunteers, described as paupers, wretched mercenaries of the tyrannical designs of the plebeian "innkeeper" leaders and "tigers" who had risen to power. Even after the assassination of the radical leadership in 1912, the defamation campaign continued to discredit the electoral processes that gave predominance to the Liberal Party until 1923.

As I discussed in another article on the elections in the first decade after the revolution,[16] the rapid conversion of voluntary militia forces into public officials—in addition to the literacy campaign—constituted a genuine political force capable of reflecting the democratically elected power achieved through mobilization. In 1896, there were 1,646 public officials with military backgrounds, including second lieutenants, captains, sergeants, colonels, as well as eight generals who were war veterans. Between 1896 and 1902, the year of the first presidential elections, organized under electoral laws that benefitted the secular voting rights for the public, these numbers swelled with the army's formal establishment, with 6,000 troops and the recognition of 50,000 volunteers enlisted as national guards, causing a veritable political tsunami.[17]

Soldiers from the lower classes entertaining electoral ambitions, and the mushrooming of the National Guard, struck fear into the heart of the political elite. Thanks to their presence on the 1902 electoral register, the military and others now included in a broader electoral register could submit their candidate: Manuel Antonio Franco. This threatened to mark a radical path that could play into the hands of the lower classes in the future. In his 1896 report as Minister of War, Juan Francisco Morales emphasized how the revolutionary militia formed a completely new core of the national army, and how the army's identity and social base was instrumental in defining the nation:

> Almost the entire Army is new; and even though its ranks include some older veteran soldiers who understand strategies, ordinances, and more military laws, we should remember how it formed. The vast

> majority of Ecuadorians rushed to improvise battalions on the battlefields to wash away the stain that the party of terror stamped on the glorious flag left to us by our forefathers, clean and pure, by giving us our Nation, Independence, and Liberty.[18]

Responding to the elite's discourse, the minister argued that that section of the population had virtues,

> [...] that making up for the (continued) lack of education and discipline that distinguishes the true soldier with studies and a professional career, their love of country inspired them to enter the fray. Their intelligence and bravery have counted for more than previous education, and served them best in battle...

he also proposed reforming the laws of 1876, 1885, and 1886, which contained a series of exceptions through privilege so that the national guards could be formed through a universal, compulsory draft, to include men from all social classes and political stripes:[19]

> We must do our best to minimize the many exceptions in the law [...] note the homogeneity in the troops of the National Guard, of its individual members, in order to remove any excuse for avoiding enlistment, which must be compulsory for everyone [...] to militarize the population.[20]

The radical leaders were not delicate, novice members of the middle class who had reached political power simply to simulate fake alternatives to gamonal and oligarchical power, as suggested in revisionist historiography. On the contrary, they owed their leadership and most probably governance of the nation-state to dialog, representation, and political management; the radicalized middle class achieved this among a much broader and more mobilized section of the population under the slogan of the people and therefore followed the path of forming that nation-state and an electoral democracy. The elites' reluctance to follow an alternative path of integration, complete with a discourse with a wider appeal, paved the way for an alternative, bottom-up democracy in which the radicalized middle class in public positions played a critical role in connecting different classes and, at the same time, creating a nation-state's political intelligence.

Building the Nation-State and Establishing a Militant Bureaucracy

The party's internal negotiations prevented Franco from becoming the first president elected by popular vote in 1902. Alfaro's preference for pacification—instead of allowing the popular forces to define the path of the revolutionary and democratic process through electoral means—led to a peace agreement with the rebel faction of the ultra-conservative forces. They laid down their arms in exchange for a middle-class candidate less radical than Franco: Leonidas Plaza. The party was the predominant political force at the ballot box for two decades, during which the reactionary forces made constant accusations of fraud as they failed to acknowledge the Revolution and the people at the heart of the democracy.

Between 1900 and 1925, the institutionalization of the National Army and the Ministry of Public Education created employment for a middle class instilled in republican values and knowledge and who by then were on a mission to make an impact on society from a position of power.

The bureaucratic apparatus linked to the National Army went through phases of professionalization. Of particular note were those who entered the bureaucratic apparatus through collective action during the revolution and those who followed the route offered by the Colegio Militar, the Escuela de Oficiales, and the Escuela de Clases entering as students. These institutions connected military strategy, civilian authority, and other areas of knowledge to the state's program of territorial integration through the fields of engineering and national infrastructure. Even before this, the army was an institution that assembled revolutionary militia, troops, and leaders from the country's peripheral areas into a force that defended the democratic constitutions. It is no coincidence that one of the fundamental debates about the growth of democracy and people's suffrage focused on the issue of the votes of soldiers from campesino backgrounds, and their radical leaders who undertook training and consolidated their power of constitutional supervision in the institution of the nation-state.

The field of public education was also instrumental for the plans of the popular classes' national integration and an area of work of the republican middle class. They accepted the constitutional mandate for children's compulsory education across urban and rural parts of a country that had reached a higher level than religious education had ever aspired, or been able, to achieve. Education initiatives were handled by planning departments and with local follow-up; participants included interdisciplinary educators, inspectors, infrastructure works, curricula, assessments, and the state also produced unprecedentedly accurate statistics. These show the evolution in the number of schools, enrollments, and the teaching profession's structure. The size, composition, and other characteristics of the profession reveal how the constant efforts to support an expanding middle class linked public commitments to the general public. Compulsory secular education laid the foundations for technical and professional education, and promoted a critical perspective on national reality that formed a part of the civic education for the majorities and permeated the approach of teachers, journalists, and intellectuals. Our contention is that this formed part of the democratic strategy and that it made a lasting impact on the creation of a citizenry that demanded its rights between

1925 and 1945. The civilian and military junta that took over control of the state in 1925, in opposition to the banking elite, and in the midst of the crisis, grouped together representatives of the middle class with professional military experience and imbued with civic values thanks to the liberal radical school, socialism, and the Italian school. This junta supported education as the basis for social integration and the "consolidation of nationality." The horizon of Alfaro's revolution was broadened by socialist public officials of the reformed state.[21]

In this sense, the socialist educationalist Emilio Uzcátegui, a participant in the liberal government and then in reformist politics in the field of public education, formulated a key argument in understanding how education had been fundamental for the progress of the militant middle class and society in its broadest sense, defined as the "pueblo" during four decades. He argued that the state reforms between the 1920s and 1940s had deepened the cardinal principles established by Alfaro's revolution of 1895. He emphasized the importance of integrating populations to the nation "freeing them from gamonalism," by providing an education in law, moral virtues, and national identity. That had been the work of the radicals, continued by the liberal regime, and later resumed in the 1930s during the left's most intense effort to produce politicized citizens: lawyers, teachers, and socialist technocrats who not only thought about matters of state but also contributed to them. To deepen and consolidate the progress of the reformed state, educators called for functional representation at the highest level of government—in parliament and other areas—demanding the commitment of an increasing state budget, converting this duty of political representation into a new chapter in the state's role as an upholder of legal protection. After referring to the ministry's core principles of free primary and secular public education, Uzcátegui argues that the reformist constitutions between the 1920s and 1940s, under the banner of democratic socialism, bolstered these values already established in the strengthening of liberal radical governance since 1905. Uzcátegui also emphasized the progress of the 1929 Constitution which, alongside radical issues such as the social role of property, created the functional representation of teachers in the National Congress and ordered the annual increase in the national budget, demanding 20% of the total national income. The 1944–1945 Constitution confirmed education's position at the core of the state's organic function—the foundations of Ecuador's education—starting by declaring it to lie within the state's remit. The broadening horizons are shown by the articulation between the central state and municipal districts campaigning against illiteracy, expanding technical education, and guarantees of teachers' and students' freedom to organize in national unions, and the stability of those working at every level of the teaching profession.[22]

An analysis of public education statistics reveals the trend for budgetary increases in education between 1938 and 1942, rising from 13.69%

of the total budget for 1938 to 18.5% in 1941.[23] This increase led to more schools and teachers: the number of teachers rose from 5,253 in 1938 to 6,404 in 1942. The majority of these educators belonged directly to the fiscal regime, including the trainee teachers or *normalistas* whose number increased from 852 to 1,279. The information about primary school teachers broken down by length of service for the years 1942–1943[24] reveals that 795 teachers—equivalent to 12.37% of all teachers—had joined the primary school system in the later stages of the liberal period (1918–1923), whereas 1,655 (25.74%) had done so during the "Juliano" period (1924–1933) and 3,979, corresponding to 61.89% of all teachers, had signed up between 1934 and 1943.[25]

In 1929, after the enactment of a constitution that promised to uphold citizens social and legal rights, the education sector's growth was consolidated with a complementary focus on organizations focusing on social problems. The state facilitated means of integral planning, oriented toward creating holders of rights.[26] The Ministry of Work and Social Welfare (Ministerio de Previsión Social y Trabajo, MPST) became the center of legal and political knowledge, with its technocrats studying and guiding state justice to address issues about rural landownership, and intervening to regulate the relationship between labor and capital. Public officials, who were members of the politically informed middle class, referred to "repairing" sections of the population through exercises in distributive justice to guarantee the economic autonomy of the lower classes, as a means of expanding their political rights.

The 1928 Constitution promoted by Julianos and socialists gave priority to the role of property in society, requiring social organization as a right, as well as its democratic representation as social citizenry within the framework of the legislative branch and state control. The joint labors of the education and social welfare ministries formed part of a political program that sought relative autonomy of public power, based on an expansion and appraisal of the lower class as an active political subject in processes of plebiscitary legitimation. The push for public officials' functional representation in the legislative branch accompanied the equivalent representation of workers and Indigenous people, among other subjects of social citizenship.

The militant middle class working in the public sector not only engaged in rhetoric, and its organization was not simply about union demands; it also developed a program of democratic expansion and the construction of social rights. In shaping the national union, one of the main objectives was to defend the state's expansion of the citizenry. The "social citizenry" was a new category of legal and political citizenry with recourse to justice and state institutions. Therefore the teaching union—recognized as the result of the agreement between the leaders of liberal socialism, Alberto Enríquez Gallo, and the assemblies of teachers from every province in April 1938—established objectives that were not solely related to union activities. For example, it sought to set up assemblies to consider and form elected representatives, ranging from the level of communities up to a national scale, and including every category of teaching professional being treated as equal.

Egalitarianism was not limited to the different hierarchical levels; women could participate as citizens who could vote and stand for elections for government positions, and, notably, middle-class women could also run for Senate positions, and Indigenous communities, workers, along with other collective actors, were able to enjoy upward social mobility between 1929 and 1946.[27]

Whereas the judiciary traditionally curbed the transformative zeal of constitutions and legislations to uphold citizens' rights inspired by radical and socialist ideas,[28] the MPST tribunal—a key locus for legal and sociological issues relating to the middle class—was able to resolve social conflicts to mitigate inequalities with a view to boosting national economic integration and increasing guarantees of political rights. Public officials and technocrats were connected to the Socialist Party, while left-wing militants were the union lawyers for the communities involved in conflicts. The middle-class elements of the popular fronts and in public-sector employment found an important space in the MPST. Together with the Education Ministry, it formed a part of the functional representation before the Parliament.

Legal experts and intellectuals working closely with communist Indigenous movements added dynamism to this state department, supporting claims and constructing a public sphere supportive of ministry officials' controversial decisions on property and the business sector's compliance with the progressive social rights promoted by these two political forces in the legislative branch. The landowning elites initially reacted with incredulity to this institution represented by the middle class—which examined land issues and encouraged isolated sectors of society to join in national affairs. Then they turned violent and embarked on a political reorganization of the political right.

In *El maestro Mariano Guamán, según la versión de su colega Aurelio Benítez*, the socialist narrator Ángel Felicísimo Rojas evokes a middle-class subject who puts himself at risk while working as a public official for the Ministry of Education, representing the government in rural Ecuador. The story describes Guamán from the public perspective, and as a mediator in the field of social conflict.[29] This public official moves between apparently disconnected settings and his subjective voice emerges from how he is affected by the destabilization of his role within the framework of the varied fields or territories of social relations and discursive authority. This instability is his strength, as it produces a critical gaze, a modern sentimental education—a modernity that enables him to think about the national republican and democratic project in a colonial society.

Various reports from the MPST technocrats in the territories of conflict between landowners and communities translate the tension they experienced as militants in the construction of citizenry and holders of rights; they bear witness to the fragility of its middle-class condition, the result of social mobility rejected on two levels by the elite: for its inferior status, and for aspiring to represent power at a national level. As such, they relate the impact of losing the status gained through education, appearance, and employment due to the humiliation that placed them on the side of the nation marked by racial prejudices and by the complex mission of representing the country from a position of public power.

Rojas's account describes a character attached to the Education Department whose emotional distress prevents him from rising up the ranks of the liberal profession. Forced into becoming a rural school inspector, he has to apply the positivist techniques to evaluate rural schools. In a critique about the shortcomings of a functionalist perspective on society, Benítez distances himself from the director of studies, "an enthusiastic supporter of endocrinology" and its influence on emotions, and his journey takes him to the "famous school of the *cacique* Curimillma" and to the bright professor Mariano Guamán, in whose hands the community had deposited "with some solemnity, old documents" that triggered numerous lawsuits filed by citizens from rural parts of the country, who travelled to the capital to lodge their complaints with the MPST and the National Congress.

When describing the indigenous teacher, the writing transcends the ministerial style and Benítez's identity; Guamán's identity refuses to be "essentialized" in indigenous stereotypes. Guamán knew how to read the opportunities to accumulate wealth, and was adept at moving between the campesino and business worlds, connecting the official documents and languages of the country's central government to its heterogeneous territories and communities. Guamán moved between the interior rural world, the business world, and the leadership that activated the memory of long-running conflicts. Benítez read in Guamán's reflection his own condition as a subject transiting between various settings and having to construct his feeling about this experience. The technical layout of the form sought to tie the bureaucratic report to technocratic and positivist questions. However, Benítez—a middle-class radical and reflective public-sector employee—adds a twist to the narrative by voicing deep, political thoughts and connections to the indigenous teacher Guamán. This subjective connection is expressed in the narrative, highlighting to the reader that the formation of that nation-state is produced in the relationships between subjects in the territory, political relations, narratives, and encounters of historical records in the formation of modern Ecuador.

Several studies have described the social hygiene movement in the strategy of the liberal and reformed states' governance,[30] a discourse developed around the thesis of the Ecuadorian state's authoritarian path. In contrast, this chapter proposes that governability was based on complex political calculations and on the development of democratic instruments, including the offers of integration and gradual democratization that ran through the formation of the state's different branches; in this regard, the creation of a middle class closely connected to labor and the production of the public discourse was essential. An integral assessment of this problem of democratic mechanisms in play calls for an in-depth study. Those enrolled and the civil servants, as well as the population involved in the society–state arrangements that provide a public service, are relevant, similarly to the middle-class categorization linked to the civil service and the type of the political language that it produces.

In the civil service we can observe languages used in political disputes. These do not correspond to the image of a depoliticized society or to a sector of society seeking to climb the social ladder under the guise of representing the popular classes: the middle class participates strategically in public discourses, builds up expert knowledge and critical perspectives, and creates literary accounts. Together this suggests the creation of a voice that emerges in the interpretation of the social conflict, the existence of subjects who collaborate in the political and cultural debate to ensure the reproduction of the state and nation against other alternative power configurations tied to the construction of the people. Both cycles of disputes over the consolidation of public power in Ecuador between 1895 and 1945 created conditions that, despite boosting economic growth and leading to new forms of inequality, can also be considered cycles of democratic experimentation going against the tide of oligarchical power. The discourse around this issue, and the public gaze constructed by the militant middle class, takes shape through social conflict, threatened by those opposing the involvement of the lower classes in politics, thus restoring the status and power of the "Republic" and the "People."

Notes

1 See Christiana Borchart de Moreno's "Las tierras de comunidad de Licto, Punín y Macaxi: Factores para su disminución e intentos de restauración," *Revista Andina*, no. 2 (December 1988) and Karen Powers, "Señores dinámicos e indios vagabundos: Riqueza migración y transformación reproductiva de los cacicazgos de Quito, 1600–1700," *Memoria*, II (November 1992).

2 Cecilia Durán, *Irrupción del sector burócrata en el estado ecuatoriano, 1925–1944: Perspectiva a partir del análisis de la vida cotidiana de Quito* (Quito: Abya-Yala, 2000) and Eduardo Kingman, *La ciudad y los otros: Quito 1860–1940; Higienismo, ornato y policía* (Quito: Flacso; Universitat Rovira i Virgili, 2006).

3 Modern radical historiography reveals the influence of Roman authors, such as Tacitus, in books on the Revolution. For the Ecuadorian case, see Pedro Moncayo, *El Ecuador de 1825 a 1875, sus hombres, sus instituciones y sus leyes* (Quito: Imprenta Nacional, 1906 [1886]), or for the Colombian case, included in Sergio Mejía, *La Revolución en Letras: La Historia de la Revolución de Colombia de José Manuel Restrepo (1781–1863)* (Bogotá: Ceso; Ediciones Uniandes; Universidad EAFIT, 2007). This narrative is also present in autobiographical accounts, for example in Eloy Alfaro's *Narraciones*

históricas (Quito: Corporación Editora Nacional, 1983 [1884]), in Jorge Isaacs' Liberal novel, *María* (Caracas: Biblioteca Ayacucho, 1974 [1867]) or Luis A. Martínez's *A la costa* (Madrid: Instituto de Cooperación Iberoamericana; Ediciones de Cultura Hispánica, 1992 [1906]).

4 Guillermo Bustos, *El culto a la nación: Escritura de la historia y rituales de la memoria en Ecuador, 1870–1950* (Quito: FCE; UASB, 2017).

5 Gamonalism is the term given by Andean socialist thinkers to a power structure related to land ownership blending religious, political, and private-sector interests, benefitting local elites.

6 Andrés Guerrero, *Administración de poblaciones, ventriloquía y transescritura* (Quito: Flacso, 2010).

7 Abdón Ubidia, prologue to *El Cojo Navarrete* by Enrique Terán (Quito: Campaña de Lectura Eugenio Espejo, 2009), 9–11.

8 Guerrero argues that the indigenous only expressed themselves directly in 1991, without the mediation of democratic language.

9 Valeria Coronel, *A Revolution in Stages: Subaltern Politics, Nation-State Formation, and the Origins of Social Rights in Ecuador, 1834–1943* (New York: ProQuest, 2011).

10 This idea also forms a part of historical sociology's relational theories of the state. See Viviane Brachet-Márquez and Mónica Uribe Gómez, coords., *Estado y sociedad en América Latina: Acercamientos relacionales* (Mexico City: El Colegio de México, 2016).

11 Gobierno Nacional, *El Ecuador en Chicago* (New York: A. E. Chasmar & Cía, 1894), 30.

12 Federica Morelli, "Entre el Antiguo y el Nuevo Régimen: El triunfo de los cuerpos intermedios; El caso de la Audiencia de Quito, 1765–1830," Procesos, *Revista Ecuatoriana de Historia 21* (II semester 2004): 89–113.

13 Pedro Schumacher, *¿Teocracia ó Demonocracia? ¿Cristo ó Lucifer? ¿Quién ha de vencer? ¡Quién como Dios!* (Lima: Imprenta y Librería de San Pedro, 1897), 16.

14 On the origins of radicalism's military leaders, see Tatiana Hidrovo Quiñónez, *Estado, sociedad e insurgencia en Manabí 1860–1895* (Quito: UASB; Corporación Editora Nacional, 2018).

15 *Fray Gerundio* (Lima), Nov. 4, 1900.

16 Valeria Coronel, *Revolución, republicanismo democrático e intransigencia: Contienda en torno al sufragio popular en el Ecuador de 1895 a 1902* (forthcoming).

17 Juan Francisco Morales, *Informe del Ministro de Guerra y Marina a la Convención Nacional de 1896* (Guayaquil: Imprenta del Comercio de J. B. Amat y Luna, 1896).

18 Morales, *Informe del Ministro.*

19 Morales, *Informe del Ministro.*

20 Morales, *Informe del Ministro.*

21 Durán, *Irrupción del sector burócrata.*

22 Emilio Uzcátegui, "Visión panorámica de la Educación en el Ecuador," *Revista Ecuatoriana de Educación*, year VII (September–October 1954).

23 In collaboration with Fernando Muñoz-Miño in *Sociología Histórica y Política del Estado ecuatoriano* (Quito: Flacso; Fondo de Desarrollo Académico 2019–2020).

24 Dirección Nacional de Estadística, *Ecuador en Cifras 1938–1942* (Quito: Imprenta del Ministerio de Hacienda, 1943), 101.

25 According to Fernando Muñoz-Miño, an analysis of statistical sources about the budget's development reveals that primary education was the main budgetary item during the liberal period, showing a marked rise during the

welfare state, although this was in addition to secondary and higher education. See Dirección Nacional de Estadística, *Ecuador en Cifras 1938–1942* and Ana María Goestchel, *Educación de las mujeres, maestras y esferas públicas: Quito en la primera mitad del siglo XX* (Quito: Flacso; Abya-Yala, 2007).

26 For information about the states of integral planning and populism, see Hugo Dalbosco and Graciela Falvine, *El Estado peronista: Los planes quinquenales del peronismo; La primera experiencia argentina de planificación integral* (José C. Paz: Edunpaz, 2018) and María Teresa Gómez, *Manuel Gómez Morin, 1915–1939* (Mexico City: Fondo de Cultura Económica, 2008).

27 Rafael María Avilés, "Sindicalización magisterial," in *Educación*, Órgano oficial del Ministerio de Educación, no. 2 (1938): 76–79.

28 See Roberto Gargarella, *La sala de máquinas de la Constitución* (Buenos Aires: Katz Editores, 2014).

29 Ángel Felicísimo Rojas, "El maestro Mariano Guamán, según la versión de su colega Aurelio Benítez," in *Un idilio bobo: Libro de relatos* (Quito: Casa de la Cultura Ecuatoriana, 1946).

30 Eduardo Kingman, *La ciudad y los otros*, and Sonia Fernández Rueda, *La construcción moderna de los maestros y de la infancia en el Ecuador (1925–1948)* (Ph.D. diss., Universidad Andina Simón Bolívar, 2013).

14 Towards a New Cultural Sociology of the Latin American Middle Class

Ecuador's Middle-Class Revolution as a Collective Representation

Celso M. Villegas

Introduction

The beginning of the twenty-first century looked like a century of middle-class revolutions. Massive, largely peaceful protests against illegitimate dictators and democratically-elected presidents and prime ministers took place around the world: from the Philippines and Thailand, Argentina to Venezuela, to Ukraine, Tunisia, and Egypt. In Ecuador, elected as a left-leaning populist with the support of Ecuador's Indigenous movement, Lucio Gutiérrez had embraced neoliberalism and allied with right-wing elements to reorganize the Supreme Court, ostensibly to drop the charges against former ousted populist president Abdalá Bucaram. Protests began in late 2004, but by April of 2005, the heavily-choreographed return of Bucaram from exile sparked a tremendous popular response from the middle-class residents of Quito, Ecuador's capital city. In a dramatic "defense" of Quito, protesters blocked Gutiérrez supporters from the city and attempted to thwart Gutiérrez from leaving the country by gathering on the airport tarmac. On April 20, 2005, opposition lawmakers voted 60 to 2 to declare Gutiérrez had vacated the presidency. In the following presidential election, Ecuadorians elected another populist: US-trained economist Rafael Correa. Correa has attacked the foundations of electoral democracy through plebiscitary rule, claiming support from *la clase media forajida* (the outlaw middle class). Subsequently, *los forajidos* and their middle classness would be central to the populist project of Rafael Correa. As much as Correa and his plan for a *Revolución Ciudadana* (Citizen's Revolution) conform to previous models of populist rule in Ecuador and Latin America as a whole—top-down, co-optive, and anti-liberal—Rafael Correa was more than simply just an incarnation of the Ecuadorian *pueblo*—he was *los forajidos* incarnate.[1] This is most evident in the public support for the 2008 Constituent Assembly which observers agreed was impelled by the middle class.

In this sense, the on-the-ground political question is the same as the analytical one. Is this middle class *for real*? It is here that despite the advances that historians have made on middle-class formation from the

DOI: 10.4324/9781003029311-18

linguistic turn to the transnational turn that comparative-historical sociology has been unwilling to follow.[2] This chapter argues instead that through the neo-Durkheimian branch of cultural sociology we can synthesize the innovations of the linguistic and transnational turns to sociology in a new way. Using a close reading of print media, academic writing, and political discourse about "the middle class" and its relationship to the economy and democracy in Ecuador, this chapter describes the concept's changing collective representation. Those representations are built on a binary language of sacred decency and profane indecency which then links symbolically to the civil-democratic and uncivil-anti-democratic qualities of middle classes.

While representations of the middle class through the 1970s marked it as a profane, indifferent political actor amidst regional and economic tensions, the 1980s and 1990s saw a reimagining of the middle class as a tragic representation of Ecuador's economic and political instability. The 2005 Rebelión de los Forajidos crystalized a representation of a sacred and revolutionary middle class. In the "defense of Quito" against the presumably uncivil, darker-skinned supporters of Lucio Gutiérrez, a new *forajido* (outlaw) middle class reinforced divisions in Ecuador's civil sphere. At the same time, this affirmed the rise of a largely Quiteño middle class that formed the indisputable base for Rafael Correa's early government.

The Limits of a Materialism and the Promise of Cultural Sociology

That "primitive desire" to define the occupation and income of the middle-class subject is perhaps less an issue of deriving an exact definition as it is a hope that defining the relations of production and consumption will unlock the mysterious relationship between the middle class and political change.[3] To be sure, left-Weberian analyses of middle-class politics have emphasized this fickle quality to the middle class' attitudes towards democratic politics. In this view, their contradictory structural location between dominant and subaltern classes allows them to be allies for both reactionary and progressive democratic politics, if they are capable of looking past their own preferences toward consumption and comfort.[4]

Moving the question to the developing world and the variegated capitalisms that emerged there does not resolve the middleness issue. Whether state-driven, consumption-based, or the "new petty bourgeoisie" of a new and insecure global economy, middle strata have political potential but need (and are often taken by) other classes whose interests are more fully expressed as democratic or dictatorial. Either way, a search for material interests for the middle class leads back to an analytical pessimism.[5]

If the solution to "the problem of the inter-temporal, inter-societal, and inter-linguistic translatability of the middle-class concept" cannot be found in political-economic structures, then we should turn to innovations in cultural sociology instead. Cultural sociology's neo-Durkheimian branch insists on the relative autonomy of culture from economic and political structures.[6] It focuses on the internal architecture of meaning-making structures—especially narratives and semiotic codes—in historically-situated contexts. This allows us to rethink the Durkheim's notion of *collective representation* as containing contested and multivalent parts, but ultimately structured as a shared discursive object.[7]

Binary Oppositions and Sacred Decency

If it is Aristotle who contributes the virtuous middle to political and economic discourse, then the polluted characteristics of the middle perhaps come even earlier from Plato's Callicles in *The Gorgias*.[8] It is the "mediocre" middle that is duped by power and distracted by daily life, its blind adherence to law and justice evidence of its own cowardice. Nietzsche, Marx, Weber, C. Wright Mills, and Bourdieu insinuate this link between mediocrity and middle-classness in their work. In the theoretical debates within and against Modernization theory, the middle class with "no horizons of its own" à la Fredrick Pike and José Nun emerge from the then-surprising observation that both frustrated upward mobility and elite manipulation were to blame for the failure of the heroic Aristotelean Latin American middle class.[9] In the Durkheimian tradition, the sacred qualities of the middle class—moderation, balance, asceticism, self-expression, self-reliance—are counterposed and given power by their profane opposites—immoderation, fickleness, indulgence, narcissism, and dependence.[10]

Middle-class discourse is therefore a Janus-faced symbolic structure—for every claim for comfort is an implicit binary opposite: decency against indecency, stability against instability, asceticism and hard work against indulgence, enlightened action against indifference (see Table 14.1). Again, this is not to say that material interests and conditions have no effect, but rather to rethink the kinds of tools and meanings available to social actors as they narrate the middle class. And again, to be sure, these binary oppositions are not values, but rather a set of stable signifiers with which social actors can apply to variable signifieds.

Table 14.1 Binary Oppositions in Middle-Class Discourse

Sacred Symbols	*Profane Symbols*
Decent/Respectable	Indecent
Stability	Instability
Mobility/Rising	Decline/Falling
Moderate	Polarizing
Ascetic/Hard-Working	Indulgent
Enlightened/Educated	Indifferent
Confident/Comfortable	Insecure
Modern/Progress	Backwards

Narrating the Middle Class

Recent historical work has posited that the middle class is an ontological indivisible entity: the idea of the middle class, its quantifiable and measured forms, and the stories told about it are one in the same. For cultural sociology, this dovetails with work on working-class formation and narratives.[11] Metanarratives, public and institutional narratives, and personal narratives do not simply recount historical memory, but can also be subjunctive and prospective. In a similar vein to symbolic oppositions, narratives help provide and situate action as meaningful.

For studying the middle class in Latin America a cultural-sociological way, this sensitizes us to the varying ways that the middle class has been *reified* in narrative form. The facticity of statistical measures of middle-classness can really only make sense when they are understood in the context they are evoked in a story. In this sense, "facts" become "fact-totems" as governments, businesses, cities, movements and others attempt to call on "objective" measures to describe middle-class subjects.[12] Aggregate talk about the middle class in public and institutional narratives may describe it with varying degrees of self-coherence and organization. In other words, what we would attribute to being evidence of class formation in the classic sense may be story-specific characterizations. Personal narratives may narrate the mundane and quotidian lifeworld, or, as Brian Owensby puts it, they may bout with the maelstrom of modernity itself.[13]

Of course, in any one empirical case, stories are a bricolage. They will draw from disparate discourses—family, politics, nationalism, development—and objects, actors, and their actions are given meaning and meaningfully-understood when narrated in creative ways. Quotidian objects are given unique powers in protests (e.g. *cacerolazo* noise barrages, cell phones). Dry statistics provide a scientific facticity, but that facticity can anchor different kinds of political and economic stories. Indeed, metanarratives about revolution and capitalist development draw from such "objective" data; they, in turn, inform governmental and personal decisions. Politically, the potentials for class alliances require in some sense a coherent story about a worthwhile (or unnecessary) middle-class coalition partner. A cultural sociology of the middle class in this vein would see a collective representation flecked with *both* verisimilitude and myth, available to social actors as they create new meanings and try to understand events around them.

The Moral Uses of the Middle Class in Ecuador, 1918–1978

To see how this cultural and interpretive approach can be used, let us look at how public discourse connected the middle class to political and economic changes in Ecuador. In the first few decades of the 20th century, talk about the middle class in Ecuador had similar discursive patterns to its neighbors. Public discussion about "la clase media" first began to emerge surrounding the lifestyles and social roles of the growing number of Quiteño bureaucrats. Liberal governments had started the process of bureaucratization to better manage their expanding use of the state. Eduardo Kingman notes that "the growth of the middle sectors is notorious in the case of Quito, so much so that it started to be seen as a 'ciudad burocrática'."[14] These rapid changes pitted the rising social aspirations of these bureaucrats with the staid conservatism of the sierra landholding elite. The first avowedly sociological analysis of Ecuadorian society, Alfredo Espinosa Tamayo's *Psicología y Sociología del Pueblo Ecuatoriano* (1918), described the middle class as an unruly element in what should be a harmonious society:

> [House parties amongst] the middle and inferior classes and amongst the people, under the influence of alcohol, become disgusting orgies, of which many times the events do not come out well-reported, thusly producing scandals and quarrels in which clubs and punches play a principal role.[15]

Cecilia Durán notes a particular lack of self-esteem on the part of these new bureaucrats that developed out of this realization of their low status.[16] For their part, these bureaucrats did employ class language to describe their situation; paid like the proletariat, their status as representatives of the state required a certain level of consumption which their salaries could not match. A pair of commentaries written by self-described middle-class bureaucrats in 1920 offers a window into this attitude. The first, written by an anonymous author, titled "El Proletario de Clase Media" (The Middle-Class Proletarian) makes a case that their "hard-pressed situation for the need to maintain a standard of *decency* ["la presentacion *decente*," emphasis in the original], he is touching the boundaries of the proletariat".[17] The second, written in a mocking, sarcastic tone by "Un Futre" (a dandy) and simply titled "La Clase Media," describes the conditions for a status-seeking bureaucrat so occupied by outward appearances that he has neglected to purchase "underwear! Oh Underwear! Let's not dwell on this point, because tears would pour like water from our own faucets; that is spontaneously and abundantly".[18] In this sense, Quito's new bureaucratic middle class in the 1920s shares much in common with the white-collar workers around the same time in Peru who sought to distinguish themselves as *empleados* against what they saw as the low status of *obreros* (workers) by equating "la clase media" with being *gente decente* or "decent people," i.e. the upper class.[19] The major difference here is that Ecuador's fight over the *empleado/obrero* distinction through class language originates from state bureaucrats whereas white-collar workers in Lima's private businesses led the charge in Peru.

The Middle Class and the Political Economy of the Oil Boom

Ecuador prior to 1972 was squarely in the global economic periphery, living and dying on the export prices of first cacao from the 1920 onwards, then bananas at mid-century.[20] As such, the coastal origin of both crops served to intensify regional political and economic distinctions, mainly between the export city of Guayaquil and bureaucratic Quito. Lower-class demands for political participation and incorporation into the body politic would increase, especially among *empleados* and university students in Quito.[21] To avert a hegemonic crisis from the emergence of subordinate classes, both coastal and sierra elites begrudgingly accepted a populist solution—specifically, they backed recurring bouts of populism under five-time president José Maria Velasco Ibarra (1934–1935, 1944–1947, 1952–1956, 1960–1961, 1968–1972). Ibarra would cast a long shadow on Ecuadorian politics, identifying himself with *mi chusma* (my rabble), declaring himself dictator four times, and only completing the full mandate of his presidencies once (1952–1956). Still, Velasco Ibarra's populism served as a means by which lower classes could participate in politics.[22]

On February 15, 1972, a military junta headed by General Guillermo Rodriguez Lara deposed—for the last time—President Velasco Ibarra, in anticipation of the election of another populist to the presidency, Assad Bucaram. Inspired in part by the Peruvian military junta under Juan Velasco Alvarado, Rodriguez sought to bring "social justice" to the excluded classes saluting them "as an armed citizen and as a citizen of your middle class…"[23] In establishing himself as a "citizen" and "armed," Rodriguez sought to make a solidarity claim between the military and civilians. In establishing himself as a "citizen of your middle class," Rodriguez pushed past the people vs. elite populism of the Velasco Ibarra era. He rooted his political power in the idea of an ideal citizen, a middle-class one. The point being that here for the exercise and performance of political power, Rodriguez thought the idea of the middle class was key.

While growth during the 1970s allowed the state to make inroads against regional economic powers, the drastic drop in oil prices in the 1980s weakened the power of all presidents to enact centralizing projects, further state expansion, and redistributive policies. As for the role of the middle class during these political economic changes, few found it to be the protagonist. Former national deputy Juan Tama Márquez concluded in 1980,

> The army of the decade of the 60s and later of the 70s will be in the service of the social sectors that hold real power. The middle class, suffering from the evil of bureaucracy and its own monotonous, delicious abulia, will be with both. Today the debate is between the oil enclave and the inflationary spiral: we shall see where the balance tilts.[24]

For Tama, the middle class' indifference heightens the stakes for the new democratic Ecuador, but as it chooses between oil and decadence, so would go the fortunes of the country.

The choice, however, turned out to be emigration. The economic downturns of the '80s and '90s evinced a major out-migration of middle-class Ecuadorians. Brad Jokisch and Jason Pribilsky note that "in just two years (1999 and 2000) more than 267,000 Ecuadorians emigrated (net) and remittances increased to more than $1.41 billion in 2001 from an estimated $643 million in 1997."[25] While they argue that this new explosion of emigration finds people of all socio-economic statuses traveling to the United States and Europe (Spain especially), authors like Franklin Ramírez and Jacques Paul Ramírez argue that the vast bulk of the new emigration from Ecuador came from middle-income and middle-sector groups from Sierra provinces.[26] The patterns of remittances and emigration also changed significantly. While in previous decades, business networks offered Guayaquilenos the opportunity to emigrate, push factors in Ecuador have overwhelmingly sent emigrants from highland provinces like Azuay, Canar, and Loja.

To sum up, dependent development amplified the size of the urban middle sectors associated with the state and Quito. Neoliberal reforms and their subsequent social effects—emigration, heightened social conflict. This led observers to narrate the middle class as regionally-isolated victims of elite political pacts and economic policies. In the larger scheme of things, however, these political and economic dynamics made the state vulnerable from below—as evidenced by the ousting of Abdalá Bucaram in 1997, the 2000 Indigenous uprising against Jamil Mahuad, and *los Forajidos* in 2005. In the crucible of the protests against President Lucio Gutiérrez in 2005, and combined with the regionalized concept of class, protesters would generate an explicitly *Quiteño* rejection of the entire political class. Unlike Tama's pessimistic reading in the early 1970s, however, *la clase media* as victim was the first step to it becoming a justified political agent; protesters and observers alike constructed a history of a social class that came of age during the crises of the previous two decades.

New Discourses of Ecuadorian Democracy and the New Discourses of the Middle Class

The new middle-class collective representation is a bricolage of new narratives that emerged from the late 1970s. As Pablo Andrade points out, there have been two discursive understandings of Ecuadorian democracy "from above." The first is the "original democratic discourse" prominent in the 1979 constitution. Conceived of as a "national project" which would help to consolidate the youthful democracy, this discourse was based on an understanding of the socio-economic changes of the last decade as creating the social basis of the new democracy.[27] Assuming a more rational and more educated public, the "original democratic discourse" assumed a "contractual" relationship between the state and society wherein said educated citizens would form a new social contract with the state—"in reaction to the political project of [populist politics] and the meanings of the old regime".[28] The problem was that a "reform from above" did not square with the liberal vision of the citizenry as free-thinking. This contradictory discourse was not simply the purview of explicitly self-described statists. The neoliberal project "broke the identity between the reformist model, the state, and the Nation" wherein "the State stopped being the 'natural' representative of the nation…" while at the same time reproducing the same "state-centric matrix" of the past.[29] These discursive disjunctures gave way to two opposed discourses: one, the return of populism in the form of neopopulism; and two, the discourse of *gobernabilidad* (governability) which took root among liberal academics and politicians. Governability suggested that the political system suffered from a "crisis of representation"—that it was not that citizens were irrational, but that the political elite had failed to reflect their interests.[30]

On the other hand, the absence of a strong working-class left and the high political organization of the Indigenous movement thrust into view attempts to reconstitute vision of citizenship in a populist way.[31] The Indigenous movement allied with elements of the military to force President Jamil Mahuad from power in 2000. Ironically, Ecuadorian populism took on neoliberal form in the 1990s, joining the region's neopopulist trend. Presidents Abdalá Bucaram (1997–1998) and Lucio Gutiérrez (2004–2005) campaigned with promises to the poor, but once in power, either maintained or intensified austerity measures. Bucaram was sent into exile in Panama and his return in 2004 would help precipitate *la Rebelión de los Forajidos*.

"Hay Clase Media!" Los Forajidos and Revolution from the Middle

The middle class that emerged from the April protests formulated a "renegade republican" image of itself, tired of the libertine allowances of the liberal vision of Ecuadorian democracy and also against neopopulism. The several occurrences between April 14 and April 16, 2005 in Quito were crystalized into a narrative with the middle class as the central actor. First is the immediate cause of the April protests: Gutiérrez's stacking of the Supreme Court with loyal judges in December of 2004. Second was the return of deposed populist president Abadalá Bucaram on April 2, 2005, with the support of Gutiérrez. Then, the "-azo" ("cacerolazo," "mochilazo") appended protest events throughout Quito, the "defense of the city" from Gutiérrez´s supporters, and Gutiérrez´s removal by a hastily-gathered Congress, egged on by crowds who chanted a borrowed slogan from the Argentine protests of 2001—"¡Que Se Vayan Todos!" The name *forajidos* is a reappropriated one, given to the protesters by

Gutiérrez. Each of those moments was interpreted as middle-class-driven, and when taken collectively, they make up a larger narrative of the *rebelión forajida* that gave the middle class an agential role—really for the first time—in Ecuador's long and uneven history of democracy.

How did Ecuadorian scholars, pundits, and participants identify the protest's class origins and their moral significance? The process of class formation required an assessment of recent history to square the events of April with the political, economic and discursive context. That is, these occurrences needed to be understood as *events*, and this required a new narrative. With this historical hindsight, the vision of the middle class that emerged from the *Rebelión* would be dramatically different from previous protests and a distinct form of Ecuadorian left-radicalism formed from this middle class.

Multiple authors and observers remarked on the creativity of these protests, partly driven by the fact that among the ranks of *los forajidos* were the materially-comfortable and educated middle class. Juan Francisco Morales, a member of the civil society group Ciudadanos por la Democracia in Ecuador, recalls his experience during the 2005 protests against populist Lucio Gutiérrez:

> Then, since February, I could see many of my relatives, first cousins, second cousins, third cousins, morally and socially-organized families; writers, musicians; university graduates, that is to say, the thinking class of Ecuador. Naturally, I carried out an analysis of the social composition of the marchers, of the immortal *forajidos* [outlaws], and upon seeing so many of my relatives as much as my school and university comrades, I could appreciate, in effect, that it was the upper middle class that mobilized, not for economic pretenses, but rather to rescue human dignity; people absolutely honest, hard-working, honorable, clamoring for a rule of law in which liberty is not conceived of as a demand, but rather that the dignity of a person as a condition to exercise liberty limited[,] from my point of view[,] in these past 25 years by economic elites and politicians, without any exceptions[32]

In this statement, we can see several features already discussed above in regards to a rebellious republicanism. Romantically, Morales tells a hero's journey of finding one's path toward identity and political action alongside friends and family. In his point of view, he writes, the opposition to the upper middle class are the elites "without any exception." The author speaks of human dignity, and the limits placed on that dignity by politicians and elites. However, Morales is careful to note that it was not for "economic pretenses" that the middle class mobilized, that "honest, hard-working, honorable" people were making claims for liberty. These positive valuations of the middle class allow for a creative, moral linkage between class identity and political change.

Another picture of this heroism locates the Ecuadorian middle class in comparative perspective. Franklin Ramírez Gallegos' *La Insurreción de Abril no Fue Sólo una Fiesta* (April's Insurrection Wasn't Just a Party) (2005) recounts the events La Rebelión against this type of analysis. As a participant and observer to the protests, he counters the criticism that they were an exhibition of middle-class narcissism with no deeper motives. He describes the anti-neoliberal mood of the protests, precipitated by neopopulist "postmodern dictatorships" like Alberto Fujimori's in Peru, and embodied in Ecuador's populist president Lucio Gutiérrez.[33] He writes: "April's insurrection starred middle sectors without organizational or party ties, which were progressively added to by popular sectors and militants of social and political organizations that were more or less radical."[34] Ramírez goes on to describe how the protests were different from labor strikes as they occurred mainly at night and represented by symbols like backpacks and pots—markers of education and the family life of middle-class people.[35] For Ramírez, the heroism of the middle class is found in high mimetic moments, it links to the transformation of the quotidian into the morally and symbolically meaningful, and draws from a counter-discourse towards neoliberalism and regional trends.

Ironies of Race, Region, and the Self-Indulgence of Politics

At the same time, other observers expressed surprise that the Ecuadorian middle class even existed at all. In a piece originally printed in *Hoy* titled, "¡Hay Clase Media!" (There is a Middle Class!), Omar Ospina García notes:

> What remains clear is that, despite their pauperization, there is a middle class whose view of the government [with each uprising] has become more demanding. For if in the manifestations against [Abdalá] Bucaram [in 1998] featured aristocratic and illustrious last names, [during the *Rebelión de los Forajidos*], the representatives of the middle class thought to be non-existent went into the streets.[36]

To imagine a middle class in that instant as becoming a political actor—literally seeing class formation happen before his eyes—suggest that the representations of the middle class in Ecuador's anti-populist protests contained an implicitly apolitical, if not possibly antagonistic quality. Again, the theme of a democracy captured and limited by economic and political elites provides the experiential origins of middle-class protest:

> What remains clear is that, despite their pauperization, there is a middle class whose view of the government [with each uprising] has become more demaqtding. For if in the manifestations against Bucaram featured aristocratic and illustrious last names, [during the *Rebelión de los Forajidos*], the representatives of the middle class thought to be

> non-existent went into the streets. A middle class that went to take out the trashcan that carried to power the opportunism of the supposedly vanguardist sectors and the lack of education of a people whose level of instruction does not permit them to choose their leaders well...[37]

Ospina continues in a more ironic mode, offering that inasmuch as *los forajidos* aimed for a moralization of politics, their actions were strongly self-indulgent and narcissistic and would thus leave the work of politics post-Gutiérrez unfinished:

> Only when the State and its directing classes understand that a well-educated public does not vote for vulgar rogues and commits to educational reform that the country has demanded for decades will antiseptic social movements like these become unnecessary. For the two most-mentioned motives [of the *forajidos*] were for more ethics, more aesthetics, and for hygiene than for more politics.[38]

Ospina's ironic distance here allows him to retain and reproduce the popular understanding of a purifying middle class, but now he disempowers the middle class by turning its supposed strengths against itself. Would that this middle class establish the basis for a stable (that is, governable) country—instead, it only sets the stage for more moral but anti-institutional politics.

In addition to the limits of the middle class' moral revolution, some interpretations noted the racial characteristics of pro-Gutiérrez forces reconfirmed the racism of Quito's middle class—a simple repackaging of previous social distinctions within new discursive frameworks. "The confrontation [between pro-Gutiérrez forces and *los forajidos*]," writes Carlos de la Torre,

> ... had, in some cases, marked regionalist and classist tones. Quiteños defended their city from the supposed Gutierrist hordes that were coming in buses from the Amazon and the coast. To be Quiteño meant not being black, nor Amazonian, nor from the coast, nor 'a monkey', as if those weren't characteristics of citizens of the capital.[39]

And as Omar Ospina writes above, the tripartite combination of ethics, aesthetics, and hygiene links a particular habitus to who should make up the citizenry and who should lead. In other words, the image of the middle class that emerged from these protests projected a "new" political project built around a common morality; that morality, however, was also linked an exclusionary politics.

In this form, the negative edge of middle-class discourse was more "republican" than "liberal" in the sense that it emphasized how good citizens should comport themselves. However, both the romantic and sacred middle class of Morales and Ramírez and the ironically-narrated and tragic middle class of Ospina and De La Torre form a shared discourse of positive and negative framing. Welded together, they are both in direct contrast to the "original" liberal model of democracy Andrade highlighted—a democracy that encouraged libertinism more than liberty and focused on deal-making and acclamatory politics rather than consensus. This "republican" middle class sought to renew Ecuadorian democracy from a moral core, in part developed over years of living under political failures as well as built on the street. But this new moral character of this middle class was contrasted to their opponents and their forebears, portending both romantic transformation and the tragic reproduction of inequality at the same time.

The Social Fact of Correa's Middle-Class Support

Now with the concept of the middle class narrated and analyzed in Ecuadorian public discourse, political action *La Rebelión de los Forajidos* and *los forajidos* were seen to have powered the rise of Rafael Correa. In Durkheimian terms, the *forajido* middle class was now a collective representation. But also in Durkheimian terms, the middle class was now a *social fact*, its narrated actions condensed into an analytical concept to explain the particular qualities of Ecuadorian populism in the form of Rafael Correa. Together representation and fact combined to provide a distinguishing feature for the political and economic changes implied by Correa's presidency—changes which in 2007 indicated more promise than fact.

Inasmuch as Ecuador was exhibiting a left-turn as many of its regional neighbors, the middle-classness of *los forajidos* allows for academics to establish how distinct Ecuador's left turn would be. For example, in an article situating Correa's 2006 election in the larger leftist wave in Latin America, Hernán Ibarra identifies the new *forjadismo* of the middle class as a motive force for Correa's victory:

> ...Chávez and Evo Morales. The first has a plebiscitary and caudillistic tendency and supports a growing popular revindicated mass and opposed to the middle classes, and the second is supported by a social and political coalition based on ethnicity. Within this framework, the Correa government, whose strongest support is in the urban middle sectors will be outlined around political-economic and social policy decisions that depend on the ability to return legitimacy and authority to the state[40]

Indeed, Ibarra says, "The recent novelty in Ecuadorian politics consists in the activation of the middle class, a social group that is barely made feasible and even less studied, excepting impressionistic opinions..."[41] To add scholarly heft to the concept, Ibarra executes an short historical analysis the development of the middle class, tracing developments in the economy and civil society that set the stage for a middle class that "now enters the scene[,] that looks for representation outside the [existing] parties.".[42] But it is its structural heterogeneity that maps well with "[Correa's] Alianza País... precisely... [because it is a] heterogenous front in which dominates the middle sectors.".[43] Here, Ibarra narrates in a low mimetic mode, turning impressionistic middle class into a middle class as a social fact. He deflates the romantic intentions behind the "protagonist" middle class, but retains the newness of its intervention in politics to explain the potential uniqueness of Ecuador's position in the left turn.

On the other hand, as much as the middle class could differentiate Ecuador from other countries, it could also mark Ecuador's similarity too—and, as such, the familiar plotlines of the failures of political change in Latin America. In an analysis of Correa's new Constituent Assembly to rewrite the Ecuadorian Constitution, Pablo Dávalos Aguilar argues that "a political system cannot be replaced if there do not exist groups in power who can assume the political tasks of the renovation of the discourses, the practices, and the institutions that would replace the previous one."[44] For him, "this subject exists,"

> ... and it is the Ecuadorian middle class. An emerging middle class, that does not differ much from the middle classes of other countries, except for the fact that in Ecuador it has become a real political subject and believes in the status of the citizen, with which he identifies himself in the meanders of politics, it is almost ontological.[45]

He says later, "[the middle class'] critique is always and in every moment permeated by the moralization of politics and for demands for stability," echoing the symbolic associations emergent from the 2005 protests.[46] Like Ibarra, Dávalos marries the idea of an emerging middle class with political change. But Dávalos treats the relationship between the middle class and change in a more law-like way, affording the middle class a subjectivity that elevates it above being an indicator of change to being an "almost ontological" truth. Later though, Dávalos notes that the middle class' demands are uncritically "liberal" and create a "fetish" for stability over a critical analysis of foreign bank power in Ecuador and capitalism in general.[47] As such, Dávalos does not narrate a romantic high mimesis, but rather a tragedy common to "other countries"—a fatal flaw hidden among the arguments of this new middle class potentially undermining the change it wishes to bring about.

In both these scholarly articles, the middle classness of the next stage in Ecuador's politics was a reason for deeper analysis. Insofar as both authors attributed different powers of action for the middle class as they defined it, the middle class acted as a narrative trope, capturing the tensions in a political moment in the early Correa presidency, lived in the subjunctive. For Ibarra, an analytic narrative connects a heterogeneous middle class to a heterogeneous political movement, deflating romantic notions of the middle class' protagonism while turning on its head arguments about the class' solidarity. For Dávalos, the consistency of the middle class' claims on democracy, morality, and stability limited its vision for thoroughgoing change.

But similarly, the social and historical fact of a middle-class protest could be used for political claim-making. In a book opposing the new Constituent Assembly, failed assembly candidate and former Secretary of Education and Culture under Jaime Roldós, Ney Barrionueva Silva provides a list of the reasons why the middle class during the protests was so important:

> Because they [the middle class] awoke, created awareness, and rose up against such indignity as a president looking to found his own personal satrap
> Because this middle class was educated, university-trained, and professional, read newspapers, magazines, books, and a good number of them used the internet and cell phones, which made it difficult to fool them
> Because it was an unemployed middle class, the majority of it
> Because it was in solidarity with its absent relatives who had to leave the country for the lack of jobs in a genocidal migration
> A middle class, that sensed the country was being robbed from them, that the Republic was being robbed from them, that democracy was being robbed from them, that their families were being robbed from them, that joy and hope were being robbed from them
> Because the middle class bridged the gap, linking to the people from below and on the other side, to the progressive and nationalist bourgeoisie...
> The middle class achieved a synthesis of what the people demanded: to be done with the dictator Gutiérrez, to be done with the Supreme Court, to be finished with the National Congress, to be done with everything and everyone!
> Because the middle class took the initiative for the *Rebelión de los Forajidos*
> Because the middle class was not opposed by other class sectors
> Because the middle class catalyzed the process [la Rebelión] without declaring itself "leader" nor "director", but rather it disseminated and penetrated through all the pores of the people how to think and act like a unified people[48]

Barrionueva's vision of the middle class parallels much of the discourse that described the protest back in 2005: public indignation by a group which was far from political power, and yet rational enough to somehow organize itself without organization and generate a legitimate vision of anti-politics, its dignified suffering enabling it to make a claim on removing Gutiérrez, the Supreme Court, and the National Congress. In the context of his book, these social and historical facts contrast to the undemocratic quality of the Constituent Assembly. And in the context of a post-*Forajidos* Ecuador, the middle class—for worse or better—was now a fundamental touchstone for explaining Ecuador's political futures.

Conclusion

Instead of assuming a simple teleology from economic conditions to class consciousness, this chapter has approached middle-class formation as an active process of interpretation. Looking at the process by which *La Rebelión de los Forajidos* was explained as a middle-class phenomenon, this chapter argued that such a construction of middle-class consciousness required reinterpreting the economic, cultural, political, and discursive history of the last 30 years of Ecuadorian history. Using the tools of the neo-Durkheimian tradition, binary codes and narrative illuminate how the public debate about the middle class retains consistent basic qualities, with social actors using binary codes and narrative bricolage. The result was a specifically-Ecuadorian construction of a middle class whose supposed origins were born of the recent transformation of the Ecuadorian economy, but explicitly more so from the failure of democracy in the past 30 years and contrasted against non-middle class populisms in Venezuela and elsewhere. Thus, taking a neo-Durkheimian approach, we have cause to infirm or reverse the causal arrow that relates the middle class to democracy in Ecuador—the cultural discourses around Ecuadorian democracy strongly inform the ways in which public talk defined the middle class.

Notes

1 On the illiberal character of Ecuadorian populism, see Carlos de La Torre, *La Seducción Velasquista* (Quito: Ediciones Libri Mundi, 1993); and Carlos De La Torre, "The Resurgence of Radical Populism in Latin America," *Constellations* 14, no. 1 (2007): 384–397.

2 Dror Wahrman, *Imagining the Middle Class: The Political Representation of Class in Britain, c. 1780–1840* (Cambridge: Cambridge University Press, 1997); Sarah Maza, "Luxury, Morality, and Social Change: Why There Was No Middle-Class Consciousness in Prerevolutionary France," *Journal of Modern History* 69 (June 1997): 199–229; A. Ricardo López and Barbara Weinstein, eds., *The Making of the Middle Class: Toward a Transnational History* (Durham, NC: Duke University Press, 2012).

3 Robin Muncy, "Commentary on Part IV" in *The Making of the Middle Class*, eds. López and Weinstein, (Durham, NC: Duke University Press, 2012), 383.

4 Dietrich Rueschemeyer, Evelyn Huber Stephens, and John Stephens, *Capitalist Development and Democracy* (Chicago, IL: University of Chicago Press, 1992); Cihan Tuğal, "Elusive Revolt: The Contradictory Rise of Middle-Class Politics," *Thesis Eleven* 130, no. 1 (2015): 74–95.

5 David S. Parker. "The All-Meaning Middle and the Alchemy of Class," *Estudios Interdisciplinarios de América Latina y el Caribe* 25, no. 2 (2014): 13–29.
6 Ezequiel Adamovsky, Review of *The Making of the Middle Class: Toward a Transnational History*, eds. A. Ricardo López and Barbara Weinstein, *Social History* 38, no. 3 (2013): 411.
7 Jeffrey C. Alexander and Phillip Smith, "The Discourse of American Civil Society: A New Proposal for Cultural Studies," *Theory and Society* 22, no. 2 (1993): 151–207.
8 Ezequiel Adamovsky, "Aristotle, Diderot, Liberalism and the Idea of 'Middle Class': A Comparison of Two Contexts of Emergence of a Metaphorical Formation," *History of Political Thought* 26, no. 2 (2005): 303–33.
9 José Nun, "The Middle-Class Military Coup," in *The Politics of Conformity in Latin America*, ed. Claudio Véliz (London: Oxford University Press, 1967), 68–118; Frederick B. Pike, "Aspects of Class Relations in Chile, 1850–1960," *Hispanic American Historical Review* 43, no. 1 (1963): 14–33.
10 Alexander and Smith, "The Discourse of American Civil Society," 157.
11 Brian P. Owensby, "Commentary on Part III," in *The Making of the Middle Class*, eds. López and Weinstein (Durham, NC: Duke University Press, 2012), 288–295; Margaret Somers, "The Narrative Constitution of Identity: A Relational and Network Approach," *Theory and Society* 23, no. 5 (1994): 605–694.
12 Martin de Santos, "Fact-totems and the Statistical Imagination: The Public Life of a Statistic in Argentina 2001," *Sociological Theory* 27, no. 4 (2009): 466–489.
13 Brian P. Owensby, *Intimate Ironies: Modernity and the Making of Middle-Class Lives in Brazil* (Stanford, CA: Stanford University Press, 1999).
14 Eduardo Kingman, *La Ciudad y Los Otros: Quito 1860–1940: Higenismo, Ornato, y Policía* (Quito: FLACSO Ecuador, 2006), 89fn37.
15 Alfredo Espinoza Tamayo, *Psicologia y Sociologia del Pueblo Ecuatoriano* (Guayaquil: Biblioteca Ecuatoriana, Imprenta Municipal, 1918), 93.
16 Cecilia C. Durán, *Irrupción del Sector Burócrata en el Estado Ecuatoriano: 1925–1944;* Perspectiva a Partir del Análisis de la Vida Cotidiana de Quito (Quito: Ediciones ABYA-YALA, 2000), 30–31.
17 Un Futre "La Clase Media," *El Dia*, July 20, 1920, quoted in Durán, *Irrupción*, 78; and J. Hernan Ibarra, "Notas Sobre Las Clases Medias Ecuatorianas," *Ecuador Debate* 74 (August 2008): 40–42.
18 Durán, *Irrupción*, 77; Ibarra, "Notas," 40.
19 David S. Parker, *The Idea of the Middle Class: White-Collar Workers and Peruvian Society, 1900–1950* (University Park, MD: Pennsylvania State University Press, 1998).
20 David W. Schodt, *Ecuador: An Andean Enigma* (Boulder, CO: Westview Press, 1987).
21 Agustín Cueva, *The Process of Political Domination in Ecuador* (New Brunswick, NJ: Transaction Books, 1982).
22 See De La Torre, *La Seducción*.
23 *El Comercio*, "No Habrán Privilegios; Todos Los Ciudadanos Cumplirán Obligaciones," February 17, 1972, 1.
24 Juan Tama Marquéz, "La Clase Media en la Política Ecuatoriana, 1830–1980," in *Política y Sociedad en Ecuador: 1830–1980*, ed. Enrique Ayala Mora (Quito: Corporación Editora Nacional, 1980), 372.
25 Brad Jokisch and Jason Prebilsky, "The Panic to Leave: Economic Crisis and the 'New Emigration' from Ecuador," *International Migration* 40, no. 4 (2002): 76.

26 Franklin Ramírez Gallegos and Jacques Paul Ramírez, *La Estampida Migratoria Ecuatoriana: Crisis, Redes Transnacionales y Repertorios de Acción Migratoria* (Quito: CIUDAD; ABYA YALA; UNESCO, 2005).
27 Pablo Andrade, "El Imaginario Democrático en el Ecuador," in *Antología. Democracia, Gobernabilidad, y Cultura Política*, ed. Felipe Burbano de Lara (Quito: FLACSO; Sede Ecuador 1999), 387–388.
28 Andrade, "El Imaginario Democrático," 390.
29 Andrade, "El Imaginario Democrático," 393.
30 Andrade, "El Imaginario Democrático," 394–395.
31 Andrade, "El Imaginario Democrático," 400–403.
32 Juan Francisco Morales, "Reflexiones Iniciales," in *Ciudadanos por la Democracia: Democracia Sí, Dictadura No* (Quito: Imprenta La Union, 2005), 14–15.
33 Franklin Ramírez Gallegos, *La Insurreción de Abríl No Fue Sólo una Fiesta* (Quito: Taller El Colectivo, 2005), 30.
34 Ramírez Gallegos, *La Insurreción de Abríl*, 70.
35 Ramírez Gallegos, *La Insurreción de Abríl*, 78.
36 Omar Ospina, "¡Hay Clase Media!," in *El Abril de los Forajidos*, ed. S.D. Araujo (Quito: EDIMPRES, 2005): 128.
37 Ospina, "¡Hay Clase Media!," 128.
38 Ospina, "¡Hay Clase Media!," 128.
39 Carlos De La Torre, "El Gobierno Cayó en las Calles," in *El Abril de los Forajidos*, ed. S.D. Araujo (Quito: EDIMPRES, 2005), 51.
40 Hernán Ibarra 2006, "La Victoria de Rafael Correa y la Ola Progresista en América del Sur," *Ecuador Debate* 69 (2006).
41 Ibarra, "La Victoria de Rafael Correa," 12.
42 Ibarra, "La Victoria de Rafael Correa," 13.
43 Ibarra, "La Victoria de Rafael Correa," 13.
44 Pablo Dávalos Aguilar, "Economia Política de la Asemblea Constituyente" in *Asemblea Constituyente y Economía: Constituciones en Ecuador*, ed. Juan J. Paz y Miño Cepeda (Quito: Ediciones ABYA-YALA, 2007): 67.
45 Dávalos Aguilar, "Economia Política," 67.
46 Dávalos Aguilar, "Economia Política," 85.
47 Dávalos Aguilar, "Economia Política," 88.
48 Ney Barrionueva Silva, *Rebelión Forajida Traicionada y El Proceso Constituyente Trunco: Poder Cidudadano; Poder Constituyente* (Quito: Ney Barrionuevo Silva and Sur Editores, 2007), 132–133.

15 Silences, Confessions, and Taboos

The Petite Bourgeoisie's Dissident Memories of Political Radicalization in Bogotá

A. Ricardo López-Pedreros

As part of a transnational radicalization of everyday life during the 1960s and 1970s in Bogotá, many professionals and white-collar employees experienced a profound political change in their lives. Although intimately connected with developmental programs such as the Alliance for Progress as well as the expansion of the service sector, they began to question their political and social identifications as middle class in an effort to redefine what they thought their role should be in a changing society. Such new subjective experiences shaped—and were shaped by—a transnational Left which led these historical actors to claim, consciously and unconsciously, a classed and gendered position as petit bourgeois working for a revolutionary cause. Elsewhere I have argued how this political radicalization—understood as moving toward the left of the political spectrum, joining revolutionary parties, participating in street protests, politically committing to the masses, proletarianizing oneself, embracing (in some cases) feminist positions and participating in armed rebellions—translated into a massive petit bourgeois activism as a social movements of class politics.[1]

In so doing, I have invited scholars to historicize Cold War politics as a struggle between and among heterogenous classed and gendered mobilizations, happening simultaneously within revolutionary and counterrevolutionary movements, and through which competing visions of class rule as well as opposing forms of domination were contested and legitimized. To be sure, scholars have identified the important role played by the middle classes during the 1960s and 1970s in Latin America. There are historical studies that offer descriptions of the participation of certain historical actors who are usually labeled as coming from a "middle class background."[2] Other authors concur that, in the context of revolutionary politics, "most New Left activists were indeed middle class."[3] Yet others tend to historicize any political radicalization of the middle classes as fundamentally alien to its very formation, as the middle class were, the argument goes, forced by a social polarization to at times ally with working classes' political project to participate in revolutionary politics and on other occasions to reproduce oligarchical interests and thus become a reactionary force.[4]

DOI: 10.4324/9781003029311-19

Although I have relied on these recent studies of the Cold War in Latin America, they often leave two fundamental questions unasked: if, as most studies concur, middle classes participated in larger process of radicalization and social awakening during the 1960s and 1970s, what was middle class or petit bourgeois about those experiences? And what did it mean to be petit bourgeois during revolutionary times? In what follows, I revisit these questions as a matter of memory-making. I discuss how professionals and white-collar workers—in particular, those who first participated in developmental projects such as the Alliance for Progress in the early 1960s and then joined the Left, broadly understood, in the second half of the 1960s and 1970s—remembered multiple experiences of political radicalization and social awakening. I argue that memory became not only a highly contested field but also the vehicle through which certain historical actors—former left-wing activists—made a claim to a hierarchized past according to class stratifications and gendered divisions. As part of "memory struggles," I submit, professionals and white-collar workers sought—consciously and unconsciously—to remember the past as a way to position themselves as belonging to a gendered petite bourgeoisie in the present.[5] I then trace a political genealogy for those gendered and classed dissident memories—their silences, confessions, and taboos—within the Left in order to show how such genealogy played a pivotal yet forgotten role in the political execution of José Raquel Mercado, a working-class Black leader, by the guerrilla *Movimiento 19 de Abril* (M-19) in 1976.

Contested Pasts—Neoliberal Memories

In Colombia, amid a political polarization first produced by Alvaro Uribe Vélez's democratic security regime and then intensified by peace negotiations between the *Fuerzas Armadas Revolucionarias de Colombia* (Revolutionary Armed Forces of Colombia; FARC) and Juan Manuel Santos's government, the Left's revolutionary projects in the 1960s and 1970s have been explained, with few important exceptions, through one-dimensional, nostalgic narratives of romance, failure, and defeat.[6] Often evoking objectivity and impartiality, some scholars, journalists, and politicians have reduced the complexity of Left political ideas, experiences, and projects to an undifferentiated, transcendental evil, usually referred to as "terrorism," that has historically sentenced Colombia to years of unending violence.[7] A crucial aspect of Uribe Vélez's regime, for instance, was to legitimize his so-called democratic security by criticizing a national past of perpetual violence in which he as democratic messiah—often described as the most "virile" of all rulers, the great Colombian, the second Simón Bolivar—had finally arrived to overcome a past of violence.[8] In this dominant narrative, petit bourgeois who participated in Left activism were often depicted as villains who became foolishly enamored with armed rebellion thereby perpetuated illegitimate and unnecessary violence against the National

Front's "reasonable" liberal democracy, a political coalition between the Liberal and Conservative parties that proposed an experiment for national peace and reconciliation. In comparison to dictatorships elsewhere in Latin America, the argument goes, the National Front provided multiple spaces for democratic dissent.[9] Such reality, some scholars and politicians alike insist, was accompanied by the development of an important degree of political stability, a relative expansion of economic prosperity, and significant moments of sustained peace, conditions that presumably consolidated a middle class.[10] In the aftermath of peace negotiations of 2016, this narrative gained further traction with state-sponsored endeavors to rescue visions of a harmonious past, a middle class past, through which Colombia emerges as a neoliberal peaceful society, a nation "free of conflict," and thus available for economic extractivism and tourism consumption.

In this context, scholarly and popular discourses have tended to trivialize certain political experiences by arguing that, given the revolutionary temporality of the 1960s and 1970s, middle-class sectors suffered a "revolutionary voluntarism"—indeed a "belligerent enthusiasm"—that led them to join the Left in general and armed rebellion in particular. Unlike laboring groups, they contend, middle classes had neither material need nor an ideological legitimation for their own radicalization. Middle classes moved toward far-left politics via a "youthful idealism" during a historical moment when becoming radical was merely "fashionable."[11] It is at the core of these arguments that the Left, broadly understood, gets essentialized as a "mismatch" with the rules, the institutions, and practices of democracy, precisely because such argument works on the assumption that the role of the middle classes must function as the normative foundation for politically "peaceful" liberal democracy.[12]

Simultaneously, another narrative—one that has become dominant as dissident voice—explains the revolutionary temporality of these decades as a product of an exclusionary and anti-communist policies implemented by the National Front that sought to repress political resistance, oppositional parties, and confrontational styles of politics, the combination producing the conditions for an inevitable radicalization of some members of the middle class who, now together with popular groups, were excluded from a "two-party constitutionalism."[13] Indeed, the radicalization of society in general and some members of the middle class in particular sprung, these narratives propose, from the fact that the National Front's social policies just disguised its realpolitik, the consolidation of an exclusionary, cynical, antidemocratic oligarchical rule based on expanding counterinsurgent policies.[14]

Dissident Memories—Creating Silences

These are the narratives, memories, and explanations that multiple professionals and white-collar workers evoked, contested, expanded, and reproduced, as they remembered their political radicalization and their critical participation in revolutionary times.[15] Interviewed first in 2009–2010 and then in 2015–2016, these members of a petite bourgeoisie recalled the experiences of the late 1960s and 1970s as the critical moment when they drastically changed what they thought, felt, and perceived themselves to be. It was a decade, they recalled, of important social awakening, passionate debates, new political horizons, new class consciousness and gendered emotions. Nowhere was this clearer than in the need to discuss what they at first remembered as one of the most important, if unavoidable, questions that their generation had to face: How could they be part of a petite bourgeoisie and yet, in seeming contradiction, want to participate in revolutionary movements?

For some professionals and white-collar workers, a political radicalization and social awakening were intimately connected with the transition away from a middle-class identity, often remembered as social climber (*arribista*), into a petit bourgeois position, evoked as the encounter with radical discourses from the Left. It was indeed important to qualify such a petit bourgeois radical past as the manifestation of their participation in making Colombia democratic. They narrated their participation in revolutionary movements because, in a present from which they were speaking from, nobody wanted to see how they had desired "to make society more democratic." They recalled participating in different sites of left activism as formative because they became "politically consequential individuals." They were part of a larger collective struggling for the "most important political ideals than any decent society should achieve equality, solidarity, equal distribution of wealth, in a word true democracy."[16]

Yet as these petit bourgeois men and women attached many political hopes to these decades, they simultaneously remembered those years as a moment of classed frustration and gendered disillusionment. When I asked Hernando Rincón, a professional who worked for over thirty-five years as part of the Colombian developmental state and a former militant of a Maoist group, about his radicalization, he recounted how different his present and past were. He expressed disillusionment at the current stage of politics:

> We have grown to be a very individualistic society... Politics is not fashionable anymore... and those who participate in politics they do that just to be cool... to check a box... the middle classes just want to be able to travel around the country, go to their *fincas*, and enjoy their cars... they do not care about anybody else but themselves.[17]

With nostalgia, he recalled his participation in a recent rally in which a bystander had yelled at him "this is not the 1960s anymore... get over it... get a family... be productive for society," which highlighted how, unlike the late 1960s and 1970s, for so many Colombians, "politics [had] become boring." A manifestation that translated into what the Uribe

Vélez regime sought to achieve: to criminalize social protest, silence dissent, and implement "a neoliberal society." In contrast, in the late 1960s and 1970s "politics were boiling… everything was political… everyone wanted change… everyone wanted to be together and worked for the same cause—a democratic revolution."[18]

But it is at the core of these three dissident memories—as a transition from middle class to a radical petite bourgeoisie, as disillusioned activists of a radical past, and as makers of democracy—that these historical actors tended to disavow their class position and gender identity because, in a context of massive criminalization of the Left, they wanted to legitimized an authentic, if pure, revolutionary past, in stark opposition to those narratives that figured their experiences as a manifestation of "terrorism." It was crucial for members of this petit bourgeoisie to *reivindicar*—to reclaim and recuperate—how change was possible and necessary. Their radicalization was now remembered as a product of a "revolutionary decade"—usually the second half of the 1960s and 1970s—that affected everyone in society except the oligarchies. These memories posited political radicalization as a product of radicalization itself. In a tautological and circular explanation, they understood a revolutionary moment as generating successive radicalizing events. And yet they simultaneously assumed that such radicalizing events ignited the radicalization and polarization of society. As a result, radicalization was explicated away as a historical inevitability: "nobody could avoid radicalization… you would breathe it, you would feel it… it was there… you could see it."[19]

Thus, a "revolutionary moment" became the telos to recall their experiences of radicalization. Along the way, their memories silenced specific classed and gendered experiences as rather inconsequential elements to understand a radicalized past. My conversations with some of these professionals and white-collar workers became tense because they now found my questions "unfruitful." My queries seemed to interpellate them, as they reacted in a defensive manner. These professionals and white-collar workers wanted to end our conversations by telling me what they thought I had to know. As César López, a former white-collar worker, for instance, vehemently concluded,

> … [e]veryone was creating social consciousness… To radicalize oneself was to become aware that you were part of the popular sectors… if we were middle class that did not matter… To become a revolutionary was to be part of the people… it must be difficult for you to understand because you are from another generation. Revolution was all around us… You knew when you saw a revolutionary… a revolutionary was a man who was politically committed to social change and committed to the popular sectors… Your unfruitful questions are part of a familiar story that was seeking to divide the people who participated in revolutionary movements…[20]

In this context, furthermore, some professionals and white-collar workers began to remember awakening and radicalization as a process of social proletarianization—a class amalgamation—into an undifferentiated and homogenous group they recalled as "popular sectors, working classes... the people, the proletariat, the masses." Although there were professionals and white-collar workers who reclaimed their role as middle class as part of a revolutionary movements, proletarianization became the emblematic—if dominant—memory of radicalization that simultaneously posed a transcendental binary understanding of society as the proper measure of such radicalization. Along the way, their previously celebrated revolutionary role as petit bourgeoisie had to be silenced precisely because political radicalization was now remembered as becoming socially aware that the only class struggle for social change was between two united and homogenous groups: a radicalized society—the product of the amalgamation between a working classes and middling sectors—and an all-powerful oligarchical elite.

Gendered narratives figured in very important ways to legitimize such emblematic memory, since radicalization as proletarianization was remembered as a process of masculinization, of becoming a "true revolutionary man."[21] Professionals and white-collar workers began to tell epic stories of how they sought to extirpate any manifestation of a petit bourgeois status, one that they imagined as a feminine reality, an infantilized past, a sporadic situation, and a regretful moment of false consciousness: "at first I was scared... I did not have the balls to face my reality... I acted like a little woman... a petit bourgeois child."[22] But then, as product of a revolutionary environment, they embraced the popular groups' practices, imagined as masculinizing force, which allowed them to proletarianize themselves. A classed and gendered descending transition from a superior petite bourgeoisie into the presumably inferior popular group now characterized as masculine, a pure form of class consciousness, and the final source a revolutionary experience.

In other cases, "gender demands" were remembered as an obstacle to a proper radicalization as proletarianization. These historical actors recalled gender demands sought to create divisions within "the popular sectors." Hernando Rincón, for instance, recounted that, although there were some "irrelevant" discussions about the role of the petite bourgeoisie, such discussions were, for the most part, a "feminine tendency." For him, the "fatal mistake" was precisely "an ideological confusion [and] fragmentation" produced presumably by the emergence of "cultural questions... postmodern approaches"—feminist's concerns understood as petit bourgeois vices—which destroyed the "ideological precisions needed for what the revolution was supposed to do: create more spaces for the proletariat, who wanted to have access to the fruit of their labor... their land... to the wealth they produced."[23]

Confessions

I am not interested in demonstrating whether these professionals and white-collar workers were right—or wrong—about how they remembered a past. Rather, what I want us to discuss is how this willingness to extirpate class belonging became a foundational condition to a classed and gendered memory of petit bourgeois radicalization and social awakening. Indeed, because of the need to question a dominant memory that posed their radicalization as politically naïve or as "terrorism," some professionals and white-collar employees imagined their past as a fantasy of *classless experience of proletarianization*. A productive fantasy of authentic radicalization in which the question of class politics could be silenced, denied, and, above all, disregarded as irrelevant because a political radicalization and social awakening had to be about a pure binary polarization of society.

It was indeed a contradictory process in which memories were often delivered as reluctant confessions. On the one hand, they wanted to purposefully disavow any manifestation of "petite bourgeoisie privilege," and thus made a claim to have experienced a proper proletarianization experience to become part of the popular groups. They confessed they had been purified away from any petite bourgeoisie classed privilege because "[o] ur ideas became proletariat, our behavior became proletariat… our lives became proletariat… We had to smell and breathe as proletariat [and] we did…"[24] Unsurprisingly, they evoked Marx—from the *Eighteenth Brumaire* to *Capital* to the *Communist Manifesto*—in order to substantiate their memories. In capitalism, they said, there were three classes in society: the bourgeoisie, the petite bourgeoisie, and the proletariat. The petite bourgeoisie was destined to sink into the proletariat because, given the structural conditions of capitalism in Colombia, "real social classes" were groups of individuals who could appropriate somebody else's labor as a result of one's location in the economic structure. Thus, the petite bourgeoisie, always oscillating between the other two classes, had a diminutive capital, forcing it to undergo proletarianization or politically to join the elites in a process of "social climbing." As a social class, the petite bourgeoisie, they concluded, could not exist at all.

On the other hand, they simultaneously claimed they were indeed part of a petite bourgeoisie in order to demonstrate how, in a process of proletarianization, they overcame such particular "class background" so that a remembered process of political radicalization and social awakening could be properly authenticated in the present. Thus, their memories of this revolutionary decade were replete with stories searching for purified working-class origins, of anecdotes tracing social origins to "proletarian cribs," of perceived downward social mobility to embrace proletarian lives. These memories became, furthermore, a plethora of endlessly heroic stories of "natural born rebels," heroes from infancy who, as seemingly classless subjects, had challenged social rules, familial authorities, educational institutions, and political orders. These commemorations told stories of individuals who were radical party militants of the Left since their mothers' womb, fed since childhood with radical ideas and commitment to "the social question... and radicalism... troublemakers, rebellious people [who] did not follow the rules."[25]

In these epics of masculine class belonging, petit bourgeois men also recalled this radicalization in which their class privilege was eradicated in public rites of passage as a way of overcoming former classed and gendered selves. Evoking Mao or Che, they told plenty of stories on how they, as true men, "burned bourgeoisie books... personal libraries... LP records, put petit bourgeois music on the bonfire" to set a public example of how any manifestation of petit bourgeois "vices" had to become ashes.[26] Yet these rites of passages—and the memories about them—unconsciously revealed a petit bourgeois gendered position in at least two ways. First, in their memories there was an exclusion through hierarchical homage of the proletarian, as they glorified this supposedly socially inferior other as the source of simplicity and manual labor whereas assigning some of the petit bourgeoisie as the representation of intellectual sophistication, abstraction, and culture.[27] And precisely because the task was to leave intellectual labor behind—presumably a petit bourgeois "vice"—, a task in which a certain "dosage of manhood" was required. Second, in order to show the authenticity of the proletarianization process, they *first* had to demonstrate they were part of a petite bourgeoisie, that is, other than the proletariat, in order to legitimize the perceived process of class purification.

Some petit bourgeois women challenged this association between proletarianization as masculinization by remembering it as the product of feminine predispositions—care, perception, feelings—that allowed them to develop a sensibility for social questions. Unlike men, who were rational and insensitive, they embraced those female predispositions to "feel the pain of the poor."[28] And they radicalized themselves as they became aware of how they could "work with the popular classes to better a society." Women and their natural feeling could "lead the most important rebellion in history."[29] Yet again, the silences in women's memories were quite telling. They, as did petit bourgeois men, remembered the experience of getting closer to popular sectors as provoking an inescapable and inevitable form of radicalization. Simultaneously, they imagined themselves having a class superiority, given their female and classed predispositions, that allowed them to "go down" to the reality of popular groups and legitimized their radical preoccupation with those conceived as being in an inferior position and thus in need of being uplifted. The imperative task, they remembered, was twofold. On the one hand, they wanted to avoid being called petit bourgeois because that was an insult. On the other, they had "to behave like a proletariat, change [their] ways... and to live *as if* we were poor and marginal."[30] It is in this context that some women remember their radicalization in a specific way. Yolanda Villar, a white-collar female employee who would eventually join the *Alianza Nacional Popular* (National Popular Alliance; ANAPO) in the late 1960s and then strongly sympathized with the M-19, recalled:

> ... since I can remember, we had different maids throughout the years... all of them were my friends... I felt their problems... I just wanted to be like them but of course my family did not let me. I had to be professional about it... I wanted to get on my knees, get to their level and see how they felt. I wanted to get on my knees and wash the floors. I wanted them to be with me at all times... I loved them.[31]

As we turned to discussions about intimacy, these contradictions at the core of the memory of radicalization as proletarianization further revealed gender and class hierarchies. These memories were delivered as voluntary confessions. Some men told stories of failed love relationships in which they wanted to get closer to popular sectors, stories demonstrating what they perceived an unquestionable proletarianization. Indeed, men began, or so they remembered, to date "working-class women" in a gendered public competition with their masculine "peers on the left... over who" could abandon their petit bourgeois ways.[32] The class and gender politics of proletarianization shaped whom they loved and had sex with. Yet, in our conversations, they remined themselves that "the task was to uplift working classes" into a more conscious class position for revolutionary change, one that could follow the lead of a radical petite bourgeoisie. "[I]t was an experiment of proletarianization... of love... I confess that it was through love we wanted them to be part of a larger cause... via love I proletarianized myself..."[33]

In contrast, for others this question was indeed remembered as the *limit* of proletarianization. After eagerly making the case for radicalization and a social awakening as proletarianization, some of these professional and white-collar workers men made yet again another confession:

> ... my political militancy, my proletarianization did not go that far. I liked... a type of a petit bourgeois woman for the pleasures and intellectual preparation and in some cases for the political militancy she could offer. I swear to god, I could not have engaged into a relationship with a woman worker [*obrera*] or a woman peasant [*campesina*].[34]

And women, too, remembered what now one might call classed and gendered impossibility: "proletariat men, no way, they were too *machos* to my liking. Would I have something to discuss with them? Sure, but to develop a love relationship... not sure about this... In this sense, petit bourgeois men were better."[35]

The silences and confessions at the core these memories sought to legitimize, consciously and unconsciously, a gendered and classed petit bourgeois past. Consciously, they remembered the very experience of getting closer to the popular sectors as provoking an inescapable and inevitable political radicalization as proletarianization. Yet unconsciously, they wanted to make evident that they had been the product of a classed position from which they had been able to purify themselves and thus proved their proletarianization. In their memories, these petit bourgeois men and women defined themselves as Others to the popular classes—the poor, the working class, the peasants, the people, the proletariat—as those who were able to "go down" to a perceived socially inferior group to join, to listen, to celebrate, to glorify, to provide the ontological measure through which political radicalization and social awakening could be legitimately remembered. Against an emblematic memory of the Left as in opposition to democracy, these memories allowed these petite bourgeoisie to legitimize their radicalized past, one that was not radical at all without this gendered and classed Other.

Taboos

But where do these memories—their silences and confessions—come from? What is the political genealogy for their historical production? These petit bourgeois women and men mobilized perhaps one of the most important transnational discussions during the 1960s and 1970s throughout the Old and New Left in Latin America: *the question of proletarianization* as a classed and gendered condition for becoming militant for social change.[36] In the Colombian case, from the Communist Party to Maoist groups, from guerrilla movements to liberation theology, from ANAPO to Trotskyist positions and countercultural politics, one finds countless references to this specific question. The *Partido Comunista Colombiano–Marxista Leninista* (Colombian Communist Party—Marxist-Leninism; PCC-ML,) a Maoist political party, founded in 1965, that perhaps most decisively promoted the practice of proletarianization, "recognized"—or confessed—from the very beginning that most of their members, at least in its urban cells, were of a "petit bourgeois background," thus giving the political party an "imperfect and faulty social makeup."[37] The Communist Party complained that they were becoming a party supporting "workerism without workers." Other political organizations complained that the "petit bourgeois origins" of their revolutionary members had produced some "deficiencies... *deviations*, abnormalities" in the consolidation of a "proletariat leadership" for the revolution."[38] Trotskyist groups discussed whether the petit bourgeoisie should compose, along with a worker leadership, the "cuadros del movimiento." Some urban guerrilla organizations, like M-19, also worried that the presence of "too many petit bourgeois members" would put the military preparation for revolution at risk.[39]

These confessions raise important questions once we try to trace those historical actors who participated first in the Alliance for Progress. In their search for partial answers to their class frustrations and gendered anxieties, these actors found themselves in a new discursive conjuncture, in which the political imperatives of the New Left—from Che Guevara to Mao Tse-tung and from Althusser to God—dictated that it was the proletariat, rather than the middle class, as most developmental projects would advocate, who would be the sine qua non revolutionary subject. This paradox of initially considering oneself middle class, and thus imagining oneself in a democratic role, while yearning dearly to hold onto the idea of the proletariat as the source of political radicalization and revolutionary horizon provoked among these professionals and white-collar employees a classed unconscious *desire*—a repressed obsession—to become and represent what they thought the proletarian class should do.

Precisely because most members of these Left parties first saw themselves as part of the petit bourgeoisie, this task of transforming their classed selves was defined as the most revolutionary of all. If a revolution were to succeed, they would need to normalize their putative class deviation and legitimize their revolutionary potential. The ample teaching material produced in different Left political parties, university work-study groups, plays, and movies suggests it was mandatory to eradicate "*the original sin* of every revolutionary… to overcome any trace, mark, or print of a petit bourgeois custom, habit, or pattern," because those "vices" prevented them from becoming proper revolutionaries.[40] As some of these manuals of the New Left envisioned this proletarianization in the late 1960s,

> The internal struggles are often the most difficult ones… We have to start locating the enemy within ourselves, inside our own petit bourgeois lives… This is not an easy enterprise, to eradicate the petit bourgeois vices from our minds and our bodies that have been imposed upon us in the family, the school, in religion… but we need to implant a proletarian life in ourselves…[41]

Marx, Lenin, Camilo Torres, Che Guevara, Paulo Freire and, above all, Mao Tse-tung became the sources of political education for this disciplinary project of adopting what this petite bourgeoisie considered the genuine virtues, thoughts, practices, and experiences of the so-called proletariat. In so doing, the proletariat became a desire of classed and gendered exclusionary otherness through which petit bourgeois subjects would be able to claim hierarchical political recognition and social distinction as proper revolutionaries. In order to do so, these professionals and white-collar workers imagined themselves as fleeing what in the second half of the 1960s was referred to, following the German poet and theater director Bertolt Brecht, as the "seven capital sins of the petit bourgeoisie."[42] These sins, part of a shared economy of desires among those participating in this disciplinary project, as these petit bourgeois women and men's memories make clear, were usually performed in public spaces, constantly examined in teaching materials, endlessly discussed in everyday conversations, and continuously practiced in the bedroom.

Those capital sins, intimately associated with notions of femininity, were the source of classed inspiration on how to behave as an authentic proletariat, that is to say, to define oneself as masculine petit bourgeois revolutionary. The first and perhaps most important sin was the putatively feminine petit bourgeois "preoccupation with… thinking [and the tendency to follow] the subjectivity of abstraction." By implication, the masculine petit bourgeois—the imagined proletariat-to-be—had to distinguish himself from other classes by his "practicality, thingness, concreteness, and objectivity of experience."[43] In a twist on the common gendered distinction between thinking and doing, now a feminized petit bourgeois would prefer to abstract—rather than experience, as the properly masculine revolutionary subject would—the conditions of revolutionary change. In order to avoid such a capital sin, it was mandatory, as Mao dictated, to navigate the masses "as a fish swims in the sea,"[44] to experience the putative concreteness of proletarian life. All the following capital sins of the improper and thus feminized petit bourgeois emanated from this foundational distinction between abstraction and concrete experience: *laziness* (the preference to stay behind a bureaucrat's desk instead of finding the practical truth with the proletariat), *pride* (to think of oneself as different from others and thus not being able to "go down" to work with the masses), *silence* (to think, rather than experience, social injustices and thus not to do anything practical about it), *luxury* (embracing excess rather than the "material scarcity" so central in the life of the masses and hence to the coming revolution), *greed* (losing one's "brain… what [one] think[s]… for the benefit of money"), and *envy* (to "resent the life of others" and not be content with one's own life).[45]

Instead of these cardinal sins, proper masculine petit bourgeois subjects would embrace the purported objective virtues of the proletarian revolutionary class—"simplicity, plainness, bareness, austerity, scarcity, material-driven decision-making, and objectivity."[46] Hence, at the core of this disciplinary process of proletarianization, the petit bourgeoisie, as a class seeking self-praise as radical revolutionaries, imagined the proletariat as an excluded Other, relentlessly represented in its hierarchical alterity. In so doing, the very political desire to proletarianize oneself meant to legitimize—unconsciously, no doubt—a masculinized, petit bourgeois hierarchical fulfillment of a process of radicalization. Such hierarchy was protected by the fact that—like a taboo, one that often was characterized as a political insult—this petit bourgeois identity had to be treated as *the* repressed secret.

"What happened to José Raquel Mercado was a Mistake"[47]

During the late 1960s and 1970s, the discourses and practices I have detailed here soon became foundational, if not common sense, within the

Left. This gendered and classed radicalization at the level of subjectivity played a fundamental role in expanding the political mobilization of professionals and white-collar workers.[48] Indeed, it is in this context that the political decision to join rural guerrilla groups became the practical manifestation of such fulfillment. And yet again, as they tried to demonstrate their proletarianization, the imagined proletariat told them they were in fact very much part of a petite bourgeoisie:

> I went there and I found only hostility. For them [*campesinos*; peasants] we were just *niños pequeños burgueses* with some ideas but no practice in the revolution. When we complained about physical labor, they told us we were lady *burguesitas*. They treated us like we were women with no strength. We treated us with suspicion... because we were from the middle classes.

They found themselves demasculinized and delegitimized through the very values that made their petit bourgeois revolutionary identity possible. Peasants called them "little dolls... little ladies... playing to be revolutionaries." And precisely because these decisions were seen as a manifestation of masculinity, those women who joined rural guerrilla groups had the hardest time. Peasants told them that they were "little... small... petit bourgeois women" who had to "behave like real men" to keep up with the revolution. Otherwise, some of these women wrote in their diaries, they better return to their "privileged city life." After all, these women reported, they were told that they were "pretending to be men and revolutionaries."[49]

Those experiences soon invited or forced these revolutionaries, both women and men, to think of what else they could do in a context in which, they insisted, the combination of all forms of struggle had become inevitable:

> I returned to Bogotá very disillusioned and with no prospects for what to do. I had left my job, I had left my family, I had left everything. I had to work the land and we walked a lot and we had very little intellectual discussion. I thought that all the things I would contribute to the revolution were a waste there... I began wondering if the revolution had to take place in the countryside or in the cities. Perhaps I was a petit bourgeois after all.[50]

Those ambivalent about joining rural guerrillas learned through friends' stories, some important books, and stories about executions carried out for anti-revolutionary behavior that a proper petit bourgeoisie needed to develop via a means besides proletarianization.[51] Others would insist that, along with political projects of education and awareness, armed rebellion remained critical, given the oligarchies' intransigency and the exclusionary democracy of the National Front, but they now emphasized that it was urban, rather than rural, guerrillas who would play a leading role in creating the conditions for a revolutionary change.

This was the case of the M-19, a guerrilla movement that emerged as splinter group of the ANAPO and as a product of presidential fraudulent election of Misael Pastrana in 1970. In close conversation with the Tupamaros in Uruguay and the Montoneros in Argentina, the M-19's early efforts sought to secure a degree of legitimacy by implementing, among other efforts, educational projects to "conquer the masses for a revolution" and to "put capitalism on trial." In so doing, the M-19 wanted to represent "the people" while making evident the bourgeoise's "intransigency to democratize the nation." In particular, the M-19 questioned the bourgeoisie justice system and instead proposed a "popular or revolutionary justice" predicated on the expansion of "people's prisons."

These popular trials are often explained as a product of larger "urban romance, a myth propounded by middle-class radicals" about armed rebellion in particular and political radicalization in general. Indeed, as John Beverly has argued, in recent years scholars have tended to dismiss these projects of the Left as politically naive or as a result of an adolescent irrationality—an exertion to play to be a revolutionary with no real political agenda—which propelled state violence and right-wing reaction and thereby prevented the consolidation of a "viable democracy."[52] These explanations seek to legitimize state terror while silencing the radical petite bourgeoisie's more inclusive and challenging democratic demands.[53] In more critical accounts, scholars concur to describe the middle class or petit bourgeois background of some members of the M-19, to then say they dedicated themselves, in a process of proletarianization, to represent the interests of the working classes. Concurrently, those who directly participated in these popular trials, and from a present recall a petit bourgeois past, remembered them as a fatal political mistake, as they simultaneously performed the role of "judges, jury, and executioners."[54]

Although these are highly competing narratives, they are grounded on a silence that, as described in the second section of this chapter, is also foundational to the memories of radicalization and social awakening. This silence is often translated into unasked question: What is specifically middle class or petit bourgeois about these popular trials as part of a societal political radicalization? During the 1970s, the M-19, in its effort to materialize political legitimacy across society, located itself hierarchically above both the oligarchies and the working classes, as the former were seen an anti-democratic force while the latter had revolutionary potential but needed political representation to finally arrive at a real democracy. It is not accident that this guerrilla group detained what one might call the two class and hierarchical others of a radicalized petit bourgeois revolutionary.[55] On the one hand, the M-19 captured what they thought were the representation of the undemocratic oligarchies or failed bourgeoisie: Hugo Ferreira, an agro-industrial African Palm Company (INDUPALMA) manager, to put pressure on the resolution of a strike of its workers; and Camila Michelsen, daughter of a powerful banker. On the other, the M-19 imprisoned José Raquel Mercado, the president of the *Confederación de Trabajadores de Colombia* (Confederation of Workers of Colombia; CTC), to face a popular justice trial given Mercado's role as a working-class union leader.

As a way of conclusion, I want to focus on the latter, as it shows how a petite bourgeoisie radicalized identity—their memories and silences—has a longer genealogy that often goes unaddressed. Questions of proletarianization intimately shaped the claims about justice, forms of legitimate violence, and visions of self-determination that M-19 reclaimed at the core of this popular trial. The M-19 put into practice the professional skills of some of its members and offered research about the rapid—and presumably questionable—upward mobility Mercado had experienced from the 1950s to the mid-1970s: from a bracero, working-class Black man in Cartagena to a union leader of one of most important labor unions in the country.

They also provided ethnographic accounts on the work Mercado had done as a union leader. Such research discovered that, as a working-class Black man, women were the union leader's "major weakness." Thus, the M-19 set up surveillance measures and coordinated undercover work executed by a woman who, most accounts concur to say, exploited Mercado petite bourgeoisie's desires for women whose class background was sharply different from his.[56] Indeed, mobilizing a larger racialized discourse, these guerrilla members assigned a hypersexuality to Mercado as a Black man, one that presumably privileged (masculine) bodily pleasures/energies with elite women over a political commitment to the interests of the working classes. It was both his "weakness" for women of a higher status and his hypersexuality, the ethnographic research reported, that allowed the M-19 to abduct Mercado, as he was supposed to meet his "mistress"—a guerrilla female member who, as undercover, presented herself as a middle class—in an apartment in downtown Bogotá but instead found two-armed M-19 men militants.

By presenting copious research before the public, the M-19 sought to demonstrate how Mercado embodied some of the seven sins of the petite bourgeoisie. He was brought to "popular justice" because he was an *improper proletariat* and thus, as the M-19's first accusation made clear, "the enemy of the people." Indeed, for some male members of the M-19 "he was weak," a feminized and politically lethargic working-class leader, a less than fully man, a Black man, who could not stand up before the oligarchies and imperial powers, as he often preferred to promote a harmonious relationship, rather than conflict, between capital and labor. Indeed, Mercado, as a partially feminized body, represented an absolute victim of capitalist exploitation. For others, mostly women, Mercado was a "macho… a womanizer" politically unprepared subject and the embodiment of a false consciousness.[57] And it was these anti-political attitudes that did not allow him to embrace proper masculine role of confronting the struggle against the oligarchies (Figure 15.1).

Following his presumably questionable manifestations of masculinity, Mercado endorsed a union bureaucracy that disallowed the development of working-class democracy since he dedicated himself to please—and collude with—the oligarchies with a *sindicalismo patronal*. In some cases, as a feminized subject, in others as hypersexualized body, he was not a politically autonomous agent and thus was a "servant often kneeing before imperialistic forces."[58] As a result, he was accused of being a "traitor to the fatherland," as the second charged by the M-19 made evident in the popular trial. Mercado, the M-19 contended, also embodied the sin of pride, that eagerness to do whatever possible to differentiate oneself from the working class, its origins, values, and interests. This was manifested, again, in Mercado's longed-for sexual gratification and love relationships with women from a higher status. Indeed, in M-19 explanation of the charges, women often appeared as a sexualized source of classed corruption/improperness and gender weakness of an otherwise pure, mestizo, and proletarianized working-class masculinity. It was through these gender relations that Mercado became an improper proletariat, as he was now behaving like a feminized petite bourgeoisie in his effort to climb the social ladder and thus forget his true class origins. As a result, the M-19 issued the third accusation: Mercado was a "traitor to his class." And if this was not enough, the M-19 also offered evidence to the press, in particular *El Bogotano*, that Mercado also embodied that sin of luxury, often perceived as feminized trait, which led him to glorify material excess and consumption instead of embracing material scarcity, as a proper proletariat should

Figure 15.1 "Mercado is Guilty", *El Bogotano*, April 6, 1976, 4.

Source: Courtesy of *El Bogotano*.

do. In practicing these petite bourgeoisie's sins and vices, which simultaneously prevented him to embrace proletarianization, he halted "the historical [revolutionary] mission of the proletariat" (Figure 15.2).[59]

The M-19 offered this evidence for "the people" of the nation to decide whether Mercado was guilty or not. Although it remains unclear how such process played out, the guerrilla group contended that "the people" had spoken loud and clear on streets of Colombia and had written the verdict on walls across different urban centers: José Raquel Mercado was guilty as charged. By claiming democratic representation, the M-19 assigned itself, as presumably a proper proletariat, that is to say, as a revolutionary petit bourgeoisie, the right to inflict legitimate violence on a body defined as improper proletariat. After 64 days in captivity, M-19 informed the public Mercado would face a death penalty.[60] The inaction of the government contributed to the situation. And although the M-19 proposed to vacate this verdict if Alfonso López Michelsen's administration met certain demands in favor of working-class leaders, public employees, and teachers, such a proposal fell on deaf ears. The state exercised violence by omission because it shared the gendered, racialized and classed connotations that underwrote this manifestation of violence. On April 19, 1976, the M-19 executed—*ajusticiar*—Mercado and his body was found nearby a popular park in Bogotá. And the pictures were sent to *El Bogotano* as a spectacle of the violence inflicted on a Black body (Figure 15.3).

Figure 15.2 "Petite Bourgeoisie Consumption," Photos by Jorge Bermúdez, *El Bogotano*, April 21, 1976, cover page.

Source: Courtesy of *El Bogotano*.

Figure 15.3 "Petite Bourgeoisie Consumption," Photos by Jorge Bermúdez, *El Bogotano*, April 21, 1976, 7.

Source: Courtesy of *El Bogotano*.

Conclusion

This popular trial proved that the question of proletarianization was much more than an abstraction or a rhetoric device. It was part and parcel of a larger project of class politics for legitimizing a masculinized petit bourgeois revolutionary as proper rulers in a real democracy in which they could govern over oligarchies and improper proletariat. Indeed, a real democracy—what was often mobilized as revolutionary change—was unimaginable without the rehabilitation of a class, racialized, and gender project. In the 1970s, the M-19 sanctified the execution of Mercado by claiming ownership over the sovereign representation of "the people" as a radicalized petite bourgeoisie. And the state exercised violence by silence. The improper proletariat was imagined as the political inferior other—relentlessly discussed in its hierarchical otherness, a transcendental embodiment of class lack, gender defect, and racialized indiscipline—that allowed petit bourgeois revolutionary women and men to imagine themselves as proper proletariat, as those who could experience proletarianization and thus make a legitimate claim to radicalization and class rule. In this popular trial, these political claims became quite evident: For Mercado to be a proper proletariat—and overcome all the charges elaborated by M-19—he had to become a radicalized petit bourgeois revolutionary as the representation of "the people." But as this was not possible, Mercado, and the gendered, racialized and classed otherness he was assigned, had to be eradicated—discursively, figuratively, and literally—in order for the proletarianized-petit bourgeois revolutionary to exist at all as the hierarchical proper ruler in a "real democracy."

Notes

1 A. Ricardo López-Pedreros, *Makers of Democracy: A Transnational History of the Middle Classes in Colombia* (Durham, NC: Duke University Press, 2019); when requested I have used pseudonyms.

2 Eric Zolov, "Expanding our Current Horizons," *Contracorriente* 5, 2 (2008): 47–73; Hal Brand, *Latin American Cold War* (Cambridge, MA: Harvard University Press, 2010); Mauricio Archila, *Idas y venidas: vueltas y revueltas; Protestas Sociales en Colombia, 1958–1990* (Bogotá: CINEP, 2003); James Green, *We Cannot Remain Silent: Opposition to the Brazilian Military Dictatorship in the United States* (Durham, NC: Duke University Press, 2010); Jaime M. Pensado, *Rebel Mexico: Student Unrest and Authoritarian Political Culture During the Long Sixties* (Stanford, CA: Stanford University Press, 2013); Lilian Guerra, *Visions of Power in Cuba: Revolution, Redemption, and Resistance, 1959-1971* (Chapel Hill: The University of North Carolina Press, 2012), 14, 17: Marco Palacios, *Between Legitimacy and Violence: A History of Colombia, 1875–2002* (Durham, NC: Duke University Press, 2006), 180.

3 Jeffrey Gould, "Solidarity Under Siege: The Latin American Left, 1968," *The American Historical Review* 114.2 (2009): 349.

4 Greg Grandin, "Living in Revolutionary Time," in *A Century of Revolution: Insurgent and Counterinsurgent Violence during Latin America's Cold War*, ed. Greg Grandin and Gilbert Joseph (Durham, NC: Duke University Press, 2010).

5 Steve Stern, *Remembering Pinochet's Chile: On the Eve of London 1998* (Durham, NC: Duke University Press, 2004), xviii; Gonzalo Sánchez, *Memorias, subjetividades y política* (Bogotá: Crítica, 2020).

6 For an exception see Mauricio Archila et al., *Una Historia Inconclusa: Izquierdas políticas y sociales en Colombia* (Bogotá: Cinep, 2009).

7 See the countless editorials in *El Tiempo*, by José Obdulio Gavira, the so-called ideologue of Uribismo; Dario Acevedo, "Terrorismo y comunismo," July 20, 2015 in http://ventanaabierta.blogspirit.com/about.html. See also Álvaro Uribe Vélez "testimony" before the Truth Commission https://comisiondelaverdad.co/

8 These daily glorifications happen in *La hora de la verdad*, a radio program hosted by Fernando Londoño Hoyos, Minister of Interior under the first regime of Uribe Vélez.

9 Posada Carbo, *La nación soñada: Violencia, liberalismo y democracia en Colombia* (Bogotá: Grupo Editorial Norma, 2004); Isidro Vanegas, "Las Guerrillas, la democracia y el Frente Nacional," in *Ciencuenta años del regreso de la democracia*, eds. Carlos Caballero Argáez, Mónica Pachón Buitrago and Eduardo Posada Carbó (Bogotá: Ediciones Uniandes, 2012).

10 Michael J. LaRosa and Germán R. Mejía, *Colombia: A Concise Contemporary History* (Lanham, MD: Rowman & Littlefield, 2012). LaRosa and Mejía work on the assumption that a history of a cohesive Colombia and a history of violence/division can be easily compartmentalized. For a different history of peace see Rob Karl, *Forgotten Peace: Reform, Violence, and the Making of Contemporary Colombia* (Berkeley: University of California Press, 2017).

11 Gustavo Duncan, "Exclusión, insurrección y crimen," in *Contribución al entendimiento del conflicto armado en Colombia*, Comisión Histórica del Conflicto y sus Víctimas (Bogotá: Ediciones desde Abajo, 2015), 7–8; Jorge Giraldo Ramirez, "Política y Guerra sin Compasion," in *Contribución al entendimiento*. For a different reading, see Maria Emma Wills, "Los tres nudos de la Guerra colombiana," in *Contribución al entendimiento*.

12 Isidro Vanegas, *Todas son iguales: Estudios sobre la Democracia en Colombia* (Bogotá: Universidad Externado de Colombia, 2011), 384–437.

13 Some examples are Frank Safford and Marco Palacios, *Colombia: Fragmented Land, Divided Society* (Oxford: Oxford University Press, 2002), 324–334; Fernán González, *Poder y violencia en Colombia* (Bogotá: CINEP, 2014), 320–325. Elsewhere I argue that, contrary to what most studies contend, in the second half of the 1960s, a middle-class radicalization materialized within, rather than without, the National Front and its development programs; López-Pedreros *Makers of Democracy*.

14 Archila, *Idas y venidas*, 346–347; Palacios, *Between Legitimacy*, 170–213. For an alternative understanding of the National Front, see Fernando Gutiérrez Sanin, *¿Lo que el viento se llevo? Partidos políticos y la democracia en Colombia, 1958-2002* (Bogotá: Grupo Editorial Norma, 2007).

15 Elsewhere I contrast these memories with those that sought to legitimize a neoliberal society. See López Pedreros, *Makers of Democracy*.

16 Alberto Otalora, interview with the author, June 2010.

17 Hernando Rincón, interview with the author, June 2010.

18 Rincón, interview.

19 Rincón, interview.

20 César López, interview with the author, June 2010

21 López, interview.

22 López, interview.

23 López, interview.

24 Samuel Cifuentes, interview with the author, June 2010.

25 Mauricio Florez, interview with the author, June, 2010.

26 Florez, Interview

27 Jacques Rancière, *The Philosopher and His Poor* (Durham, NC: Duke University Press, 2003), xxvi.

28 Amanda Torres, interview with the author, June 2010.

29 Torres, interview.

30 Amanda Gonzalez, interview with the author, June, 2010. My emphasis.

31 Yolanda Villar, interview with the author, June 2010.

32 Ignacio Sanchez, interview with the author, June 2010.

33 Sanchez, interview.

34 Mauricio Leal, interview with the author, June 2010.

35 Villar, interview.

36 As a point of comparison see Claudia Stern in this volume. See also Aldo Marchesi, "Revolutionaries without Revolution: Regional Experiences in the Forging of a Radical Political Culture in the Southern Cone of South America (1966–1976)" In K. Young (Ed.), *Making the Revolution: Histories of the Latin American Left*. Cambridge: Cambridge University Press, 2019, 185–211.
37 Partido Comunista de Colombia, ML, *Combatiendo unidos venceremos* (Medellín Editorial 8 de junio, 1975), 45.
38 Partido Comunista, *Combatiendo unidos venceremos*, 91.
39 Encuesta interna de la organización político militar. c1975. Movimiento 19 de Abril Archive.
40 Partido Comunista de Colombia, ML, *Proletarización*, 1969 (CRPA).
41 Partido Comunista, *Combatiendo unidos venceremos*, 69, 253,
42 Carlos Duplat, *Siete pecados capitales del pequeño burgués*, theater work (Bogotá: Biblioteca Nacional de Colombia, 1984).
43 Duplat, *Siete pecados capitales*, my emphasis.
44 Mao Tse-tung, *Las Tres Permanentes* (CRPA).
45 Duplat, *Siete pecados capitales*, 3.
46 Partido Comunista, *Combatiendo unidos venceremos*.
47 Otty Patiño, interview with the author, July 2010; See also Vera Grave, *Razones de Vida* (Bogotá: Planeta, 2000), 77.
48 López-Pedreros, *Makers of Democracy*
49 Clara Barrero, interview with the author, June 2010.
50 Marta Espinosa, interview with the author, June 2010.
51 Jaime Arenas, *La guerrilla por dentro* (Bogotá: ICONO), 2009.
52 David Stoll, *Rigoberta Menchú and the Story of All Poor Guatemalans* (Boulder, CO: Westview Press, 1999), 282; John Beverley, "Beyond the paradigm of disillusion," in *Latin Americanism after 9/11* (Durham, NC: Duke University Press, 2011), 95–109.
53 Elsewhere I show how these petit bourgeois men and women experienced state terror, as they attempted to redefine democracy. López-Pedreros, *Makers of Democracy*, 247–254.
54 Grave, *Razones de Vida*, 77.
55 For a description of these trials, see Mario Aguilera Peña, *Contrapoder y justicia guerrillera: Fragmentación política y orden insurgente en Colombia, 1952–2003* (Bogotá: IEPRI, 2014).
56 This description is based on *El Bogotano* and Efraín Motatto, *Los testigos M-19* (Bogotá: Presencia, 1977). For a fictionalized account see Ramón Molinares Sarmiento, *El saxofón del cautivo* (Bogotá: College Editores, 2018).
57 Grave, *Razones de Vida*, 77.
58 "Mercado sí es culpable," *El Bogotano*, April 6, 1976, 6.
59 M-19 Con el pueblo con las armas al poder. Organo del Movimiento Anapista, 19 de abril, No. 13, February 15, 1976, M-19 Archive.
60 Ibid.

16 "Young People Committed to the Motherland"

Middle-Class Masculinity, Radicalization, and the Fragmentation of the "Integral Chileans" in the 1970s*

Claudia Stern

Introduction

The 1972 *Unidad Popular* (Popular Unity, UP) government poster, which bore the message "*La juventud se compromete con la Patria*" (Young people committed to the motherland, Figure 16.1),[1] invited young people to engage in a day of reflection. It is an appropriate image with which to introduce the climate of the period, to express the ways in which young Chilean UP sympathizers, followers, and left-wing activists in general were invited to become actively involved in the Chilean road to socialism, and to emphasize the role played by the youth during the period. Vicente Larrea, designer of the graphics used by Allende's government, generously shared with me the rationality behind his team's creations and stressed that they were given creative free rein. Accordingly, the graphics included neither political ideologies nor the hammer and sickle, as the intention of Larrea, his brother, Antonio, and Luis Albornoz was to communicate in a simple and colorful manner the Chilean philosophy and values system; instead, posters always included the Chilean flag. In reference to the design presented in Figure 16.1, Vicente indicates that

> the aim of this poster can be seen in the 'speech bubble'; strong colors, simple but well-defined forms, with attractive and optimistic graphics, direct language and basic concepts. Everything was conceived with a view to reaching out as effectively as possible to all Chileans and motivating them to take part in this social activity.[2]

Within the figure's head, a multiplicity of activities are depicted, representing the diverse rights and duties of the Chilean youth which would be discussed at the meeting called in the speech bubble. Vicente, himself a freethinking member of the middle classes, a progressive left-wing sympathizer with no party affiliation either then or now, represents the spirit of the "Integral Chilean," a social archetype that is central to understanding the proletarianization of the left-wing youth of the 1970s. The impact of local young people under the UP government was

DOI: 10.4324/9781003029311-20

Figure 16.1 "Young people committed to the motherland". Graphic used by Salvador Allende's Popular Unity government. Concept and illustration by Vicente Larrea, Santiago de Chile, 1972.

Source: Courtesy of Vicente Larrea.

a result of an historical evolution of the notion of the youth and of their social role from decades past. The group came to the fore within modern culture and its diverse members were people whose specific task was to study and to prepare themselves for the challenges posed by society in an era of national modernization.[3] From the 1930s onward, young people gave shape to both new political parties and a new political order,[4] and the development of the Chilean middle classes can therefore be said to have gone hand-in-hand with the social evolution of the youth.

The image of the committed youth first emerged at the beginning of the twentieth century.[5] Later on, notions of Chile's democratic tradition and alleged stability gained prominence during the golden age of national capitalism, when democratic values and Chilean middle-class cultural and social capital became instrumental in shaping social and class identities. These distinctions led to the emergence of the profile of the Integral Chileans, to which the middle classes began to aspire from the 1930s onward. Their political radicalization decades later exposes their evolution as an expression of democratic normativity. The Integral Chileans embodied the ideal of modern middle-class masculinity—a new elite destined to lead both society and the state[6]—of whose proliferation the state was a defining agent. By the 1970s, the increasingly polarized Chilean society was not indifferent to these idealistic middle-class profiles as the nation passed in rapid succession by three historical milestones that would have a profound impact on the history of the country and its citizens: Salvador Allende's Popular Unity government (UP), Augusto Pinochet's 1973 coup d'état, and the 17-year military dictatorship that followed. These milestones caused a rupture in the foundations of the middle-class ethos, which not only highlighted gendered and intergenerational differences but transformed pre-dictatorship expressions of civic agency.

Following the 1970 election, Chile influenced a new era of the United States' Cold War agenda in Latin America.[7] The Chilean road to socialism brought together "the best of the Cold War's two worlds," and the UP government symbolized a new step along the continent's path to liberation.[8] However, the Chilean road to socialism was complex and, in many senses, utopian. Among the measures implemented by the UP, two were particularly critical. Firstly, the unanimous decision by Congress to nationalize the copper industry (Law 17,450, July 11, 1971) presented a threat to US interests, while at the same time exposing Chile's complete awareness of its own value as a country. Secondly, the *Escuela Nacional Unificada* (Unified National School, ENU) project, under discussion since 1971, was viewed by the majority of Chileans as a socialist ideological educational program and therefore unacceptable. For the middle classes in particular, education was a central aspiration,[9] and the project presented a threat to their status, as I will detail in the next section. Ultimately, the impact of the ENU was indeed ideological, and the UP period brought profound social transformation that ended in the breakdown of democracy.

Across Chilean society, exaggerated importance began to be given to possession of a university degree. The middle classes in particular fell victim to this discourse, as they were also the primary beneficiaries of public education, which enjoyed a golden age between 1932 and 1973.[10] The very experience of education lent added weight to the university degree and opened the door to civic agency. As centers of political activity in the runup to 1973, schools and universities were not immune to change. I will discuss this point in order to contextualize the radicalization of the middle-class youth, whose class consciousness was key to their practice as agents of change, in keeping with the image of the Integral Chilean.

As an introduction to social identity in this chapter, I argue that throughout the decades of mid-twentieth century and up until the coup, the Chilean middle classes moved on multiple planes in terms of what they produced, what they consumed, and how they viewed themselves. Although the middle classes presented many differences and contradictions, they also shared certain values and beliefs. Additionally, the myriad identities that made up the Chilean middle classes were influenced by legal regulations and state policies. These identities were contextualized at the national level as the common people, the cosmopolitans, and the immigrants, and the masses, the "bourgeoisie," and the elite.

There were contradictions between different versions of the middle classes, and particularly between different archetypes of Integral Chileans, with some pursuing pleasure and easy riches, and others seeking *eudaimonia* through spiritual refinement and the appreciation of nature.[11] The two attitudes highlight the underlying problem of the Chilean public education system, present from its earliest conception: that of segmentation.[12] From the very inception in the early 1930s of the concept that I have defined as the Integral Chilean, there was an apparent gap between this middle-class ideal and reality. This aspirational Chilean identity was marked by a strong sense of moral and social duty. As soon as they entered the humanities-based public secondary schools, students were exposed to the image of the Integral Chilean, which placed a high value on the human being and on democracy. Key elements of this social profile included a civic spirit, patriotism, and social commitment to the country in general, and to the disadvantaged in particular, all from a paternalistic perspective suited to the notion of middle-classness. The Integral Chilean was also characterized by individualism, as befits the success-oriented project with which the image was associated. Thus, the contradictions inherent to the Integral Chilean ideal gradually gave rise to different versions of Integral Chilean men and women.

The political component evolved gradually and was instrumental in the split between Integral Chilean men and women on the right and left of the political spectrum from the late 1950s until the early 1970s, i.e., the Chilean "age of youth."[13] Within the scope of this chapter, I will focus on the experience of men within the left-wing middle classes.[14] While this decision accentuates the dominant masculine hegemonic perceptions of political radicalization, it is worth noting that Integral Chilean women on the radicalized left questioned this heteronormative model and participated just as actively in the revolutionary struggle, but without having to refer to a manual for the "new man," such as that provided by Ché Guevara.[15] Nevertheless, the figure of the Integral Chilean woman on the radicalized left found herself challenged by conventions related to gender.[16]

Historically, the figure of the Integral Chilean man embodied the intersection between the middle classes, the country's youth, and nationalism. This ideal of manhood is inextricably linked to the performance of modern men in the public sphere. Consequently, the Chilean state was a central agent in strengthening the hegemonic forms of masculinity[17] that legitimized and perpetuated the patriarchal models that went hand-in-hand with the country's modernization[18] and, as such, with the institutionalization of modern masculinity.[19] Furthermore, their proletarianization during the 1970s embraced a class elitism that perpetuated middle-class paternalism over the working classes.

Due to the length of this chapter, I will not elaborate on the disputes between the various middle-class hegemonic masculinities of the period or their connection with the imaginary of caste that I have introduced elsewhere.[20] The latter, inherited from the Colonial period,[21] overlaps with the notion of modern masculinity performed by the middle classes, and perpetuates it even though the ideal of class does not encompass lineage.[22] I suggest that caste is clearly distinguishable vis-à-vis modern masculinity within monolithic nationalism, and the other as anti-national was very much the norm at the time.[23]

The radicalization of left-leaning Integral Chileans was powered by three factors directly related to the dynamics of the all-encompassing Cold War, which went beyond economics and politics. First, from a cultural perspective, intellectuals called attention to the role played by knowledge production in political processes, as military, political, economic, and cultural funding from the United States began to be questioned throughout the region.[24] Second, the same continental context had already led to the fragmentation and radicalization of Integral Chileans. The 1960s brought greater potential for mobilization in Chile. The political discourse was dominated by exclusionary projects, motivating some but terrifying others.[25] Additionally, when Brazil and Argentina, until then leaders in intellectual production, fell victim to military dictatorships in 1964 and 1966, respectively, the primary role of hosting and producing knowledge in the Southern Cone fell to Chile. Third, the Chilean capital, Santiago, was home to important middle-class centers for knowledge production, such as the *Facultad Latinoamericana de Ciencias Sociales* (Latin American School of Social Sciences, FLACSO), the headquarters of the *Comisión Especial para América Latina* (Special Commission for Latin America, CEPAL), and other research centers with ties to the Catholic Church and to the reforms taking place at the University of Chile and the Pontifical Catholic University of Chile, such as the *Centro de Estudios Socioeconómicos* (Center for Socioeconomic Studies, CESO) and the *Centro de Estudios de la Realidad Nacional* (Center for the Study of the National Reality, CEREN).[26] These centers boosted political radicalization and counteracted the policy recommendations of the early Chicago Boys, the right-wing Integral Chileans who were instrumental in the economic policies implemented during the dictatorship. The writing produced by both political positions was heavily laden with nationalistic ideology.[27] One key factor connected directly with the Chilean youth was the University Student Reform Movement (*Movimiento de Reforma Estudiantil*), which began in 1967. The events of May 1968 in France further reinforced the movement as ideas of profound worldwide change led by students and workers gained strength.[28] This environment contributed to regional academic exchange, as many exiled thinkers found Chile to be an intellectual hotbed of the new left,[29] a sentiment that was enhanced when Salvador Allende came to power in 1970 and Chile came to be seen as a "laboratory country."[30]

Additionally, as seen in the poster (Figure 16.1), there was particular sensitivity toward young people under the UP government. The *Secretaría General de la Juventud* (General Secretariat for Youth) was created in December 1970 at the beginning of Allende's term, and the president argued that the youth—i.e., those aged 30 years or younger—constituted more than 60% of the Chilean population, maintaining that Chile was a "young country."[31] However, the secretariat was institutionally weak, depended exclusively on the presidency, did not have paid officials, and was allocated an insignificant budget.[32] In contrast, the dictatorship raised the youth to an institutional position never before achieved, and the regime's *Secretaría Nacional de la Juventud* (National Youth Secretariat) became the first state agency to be linked to a specific ministerial organization.[33] Needless to say, besides age itself, the youth embodied the desire for transformation.[34] This examination will help to reveal how, through the intersection between volunteering, knowledge production, and proletarianization, the leftist middle-class youth became an inherent part of the Chilean road to socialism.

The present study is part of broader research into the transformation of the Chilean middle classes and their gender identities, which are examined from a transnational perspective, through the lens of cultural trauma between 1970 and 1990. The testimonies recounted in this chapter were obtained by the author and are part of a broader corpus of oral histories collected for this research. They reflect two main branches of the middle classes of the period, and these can be distinguished by their emphasis on either cultural or economic capital. To complement these testimonies, I will also examine some of the graphics used by the UP government and the Santa Marta Cultural Association. This combination of sources will serve to elucidate the experience of those Integral Chileans on the left of the political spectrum who played a leading role as agents of change. From the viewpoint of memory, their testimonies are a lively development of meaning-making[35] that enable me to address their subjectivities.

By viewing the experiences of left-wing Integral Chileans as an ongoing attempt to live a life of *eudaimonia*, both before and after the coup, the present study calls for a reexamination of both the general assumptions of the middle classes as a mirror of the upper classes, and of the class distinction of these idealistic youths and their methods of driving forward the revolution. At the same time, it seeks to recover the human dimension of the radicalization of Integral Chileans as the expression by individuals of their own civic agency, as well as the subsequent ways they found to cope with cultural trauma under dictatorship.[36] This is directly related to middle-class values and the way in which their identification with these values led young people from the middle classes to engage in both social and class transformations. Likewise, by focusing on the experiences of middle-class human agency and their proletarian performances, the present examination proposes the variable of class as a novel factor in the study of memory.[37]

This chapter focuses on the experience of Ramón, a representative of the Integral Chilean social taxonomy. He participated in and indeed dedicated his life to the political radicalization of the left-wing middle classes through his membership of the *Movimiento de Acción Popular Unitaria* (Popular Unitary Action Movement, MAPU). Ramón began his affiliation with the MAPU while at school, moving on to study pedagogy at university where his involvement continued. He then took part in the reorganization of the party in 1976 following the harshest period of political repression in Chile's history.[38] His experience, along with those of Axel, Agustín and Raúl, whose testimonies will be quoted later in the chapter, exposes the true significance of the UP government's "Young people committed to the motherland" poster (Figure 16.1) during a period in which engagement in a proletarian role could have horrific consequences.

The Incubator of Integral Chileans: National Spirit, Ideology and Knowledge

Ramón's experience as a secondary pupil in San Antonio—a coastal city located in the Valparaíso Region—and subsequently as a university student in the Chilean capital, Santiago, clearly exposes both the degree of politization taking place in schools during the late 1960s, and the roots of the evolution of Integral Chileans as radicalized practitioners of civic agency. The Integral Chileans aspired to this image partly as a consequence of the education they had received, and partly thanks to the example set by their teachers, who had themselves been inspired by a missionary calling. Teachers in general were agents of change, and students, rather than being mere passive subjects, aspired to make their own contribution to society, thus, unconsciously, becoming agents of change themselves.[39] By the 1960s, this image fit with endorsement by intellectuals in the Southern Cone of the link between "political commitment and knowledge."[40]

The state secondary school model turned out to be highly elitist, as was the case with universities, and until 1960, the Chilean education system continued to exacerbate the social gulf between classes rather than reduce it.[41] Drop-outs during the later years of state-provided secondary education were high, reducing higher education enrollments, with many students opting to pursue vocational qualifications instead. This was a widely available and more accessible option that promised better income prospects, often even than the university degree, which nevertheless maintained its supremacy. However, between the censuses of 1960 and 1970, the percentage of higher education students between the ages of 20 and 24 more than doubled, rising from 6.0% to 12.4%. Despite the constant increase in the overall level of education, by 1970 the difference in primary and secondary student numbers was stark. Attendance figures of 68.5% for ages 5 to 9 and 91% for ages 10 to 14 dropped sharply to 48.9% for ages 15 to 19 and yet more abruptly to 12.4% for ages 20 to 24.[42] Under the UP government, democratization of study became more profound and many students gained access to higher education through the program entitled "The First 40 Measures of the Popular Government." Measure 28 offered grants to students at all educational levels—primary, secondary, and university—based on academic performance and family circumstances.[43]

The model installed by the secondary state education system prior to 1970, was value-based and vocational, and led to an intergenerational rift in the family nucleus as the system began to mold the idealistic youth into Integral Chileans. Parental aspirations for their children and the prospect of bringing those aspirations to fruition were challenged by the teachers who, in general, embodied an erudite, missionary, and above all vocational spirit.[44] This model had significant repercussions over the course of the 1960s, when everyday nationalism became polarized in Chile and the culture of rebellion became more tangible, no longer simply a youthful impulse, but a way of viewing the world. Meanwhile in Argentina, radicalization was evident within an increasingly fractured Peronism, where students in the city of Mar del Plata and the Peronism of left-wing university students contrasted with the Peronist nationalism of the right.[45]

As a second-year student, Ramón ran for president of the *Centro de Alumnos* (Student Council, CAA) at his secondary school, the *Liceo Fiscal de San Antonio*, a post he held throughout his third year. Ramón recounts that "it wasn't a small school; it was the largest in the area with 1,500 to 1,800 students. At that time, secondary schools offered a different quality of education."[46] Ramón's experience, which highlights the quality of Chilean state education at the time, can be viewed as a middle-class memory; as highlighting the definitive nature of the state secondary school for the education of the middle-class youth up to the breakdown of democracy, as well as for its "relationship with the conditions of modernity."[47] In this context, modernity is seen in terms of the change brought about by the dictatorship, during which the state educational model was lost as a result of intervention in centers of education by the military regime, followed by its commercialization.

For some Integral Chileans, the exercise of democracy motivated a more decisive form of action, and ideals were put into practice. In this sense, the reformist government of Eduardo Frei Montalva and its *Revolución en libertad* (Revolution in Freedom, 1964–1970) paved the way to the UP government and the Chilean road to socialism, especially considering the growing frustration with which its promises were met by increasingly exigent revolutionary rhetoric.[48] The political radicalization of Catholic left-wing progressive sectors belonging to the center-left *Democracia Cristiana* (Christian Democratic Party, DC) prompted the creation of the MAPU in 1969. The DC's young intelligentsia was limited in terms of electoral weight, but very significant in terms of cultural and social capital, also playing a role in recruiting the "technocrats" who led the progressive reforms of Frei Montalva's DC government, including the Agrarian Reform and the Popular Reform.[49] Although this chapter does not offer a study of the history of the MAPU, the middle-classness of its members—different sectors of Integral Chileans—was a key factor in the communication of their message and recruitment of young people who would become radicalized under the UP. Although the MAPU did not have electoral weight with regard to the UP government either,[50] their "intellectual weight" was crucial then and during the dictatorship, as well as under the governments of the post-dictatorship *Concertación*.[51] The MAPU's members were a paradigm of the intersection between the middle classes, knowledge production, and masculine radicalization.

The political message permeated every area. The missionary profile of teachers was not exempt from the effects of radicalization: "They were engaging and very likeable teachers; through resolute political action they began to influence their students with their ideas. Thus, their enthusiasm spread." [52] The enthusiasm mentioned by Ramón included the creation of after-hours political education courses held at schools. In the case of the *Liceo de San Antonio*, MAPU members would go from Santiago to give classes:

> They displayed an extraordinary intellectual quality. And the first manual appeared: the "Nature of the Chilean Revolution"—a catechism that discussed the class structure. This is when the term *lumpen proletariat* was first used in Chile [...] They're guys who, through a highly ideological approach, breathed new life and introduced new elements into Chilean politics [...] The movement came towards the end of the 1960s and the *Unidad Popular* triumphed. This was the period when I got involved in politics, in the MAPU.[53]

This is Ramón's account of his motivations to join the movement, which played a central role when it came to applying to university. However, idealism and the secondary school reality also impacted in the private sphere. Parents of these politicized young people were far from indifferent to the positions adopted by their children:

> My rebellion against the family tradition was taken very badly, especially by my father. Partly because I went to the left; my posters of Ché

> Guevara, of Vietnam [...] He stopped speaking to me: 'take all of that down' [...] Once you start studying, you find yourself in Marxism, in Marx or Engels. Fundamentally, the most ideological thing in terms of ideas [...] As a result, I became an atheist.[54]

Just like Ramón, many young people saw themselves at a crossroads between religion and Marxism-Leninism. Not all moved from one extreme to the other, but they did begin to question their identities and ideologies, contributing to and perpetuating their sense of *eudaimonia*, which explains their attempts to shed their middle-class identity, a basic tenet at that time. Their middle-class ethos caused them to question both ideology and knowledge, and to search for what gave their lives meaning.[55] The fact that the Integral Chileans applied their intellectual advantage to the benefit of others makes it clear that the democratization of knowledge cannot be viewed exclusively under the lens of political radicalization. Ramón's decision to study at the Pontifical Catholic University of Chile (UC) was purely ideological. The opportunity to participate in the democratic education project, as proposed by the ENU, represented a chance to take more decisive action as part of his university experience, in accordance with the evolving approach of the left-leaning Integral Chileans and the civic agency of the 1970s. Ramón sums up his decision as follows:

> For a very practical reason. Two of the teachers who visited San Antonio from Santiago and who were members of the MAPU were assistants at UC [...]. They were creating this new collaborative experience with ENU. They told me: 'study at UC, you'll get the grades you need', so I applied and I got in.[56]

Ramón also applied to a university in Valparaíso, but he ended up studying pedagogy at UC in Santiago in order to participate actively in the ENU project. Ramón's testimony, as well as revealing that the MAPU "attracted middle-class Catholic segments; reformist university students," reveals the influence of the party on the "UC decision-making bodies."[57]

Axel, who identified himself as middle-class, was a young administrative officer in the armed forces, and his memories help to contextualize the social climate in regard to ENU. He worked for the undersecretary of aviation before and after the coup and recalled the ENU as a major factor of social dissatisfaction:

> I remember that when the ENU tried to intervene in education, this generated discontent within the population. When the state is telling you what you should do with your kids from a social point of view, that was what really sparked unhappiness. And then came all the rest.[58]

By 1973, the threat posed by ENU to the right-wing cultural hegemony through education accelerated the military intervention.[59] Ramón's recollections of the ENU reflect those of Axel, as well as the segmentation of Chilean education:

> A strong ideological position was developed: the UP's position against the classical one that was becoming radicalized and defended the history of education in Chile; the ENU was unthinkable. It was a distraction that put the right, the Church and everyone on high alert, because it meant that education would become entirely ideological. If this were not the case, the class struggle element was very decisive.[60]

The political education classes illustrate the association between radicalization and knowledge, permeating all areas. Education of the Integral Chileans in the late 1960s included an unprecedented component. The secondary school was the incubator in which the middle-class youth were radicalized through debate, study, camaraderie, and human interaction in all its splendor, and these activities were reinforced at university, the ultimate center for debate. The mingling of knowledge production with political activism on the ground nourished a renewed sense of class and belonging that included various forms of working-class practice (*obrerización*) and which sustained the shared middle-class roots of the Integral Chileans, as will be analyzed in the next section.

University: Between Democratic Ideals and Practices of Radicalization

On the edges of the disputes over the political options and affiliations of those Integral Chileans from the more conservative households, middle-class roots relating to access to higher education maintained their position of importance. Ramón, who still expresses a firm sentiment of class struggle and the subjectivities thereof, recalls that, although his parents were aware of his political activities:

> The fact that I was at university was important to them. Especially at UC. To be honest, I didn't go there just because it was the UC [...] I never would have adopted that social climber attitude. But the fact that it was the Catholic University—Pontifical—may have been far more important than anything else for my mother. My father... he was just happy that I was at university, that I was studying. He was glad I was there.[61]

Politicization within universities meant that faculties and programs became associated with certain political positions. The University of Chile in Santiago was divided into the "North," corresponding to the left and the UP, and the "West," associated the right and the DC. Prior to the coup, the institution's students had been on strike. Agustín, a young employee at the Faculty of Economics, recalls that he was not a member of any political party, but supported the coup despite genuine concern for his colleagues who disappeared. Even in the tense UP environment, there was mutual respect: "Although our opinions were divided, we were still colleagues and there was no rivalry between us. Before the coup we got on very well."[62]

Historically, the left and right had opposing views as to how the country should be built, and Allende's government, the coup, and the Pinochet dictatorship accentuated these differences, permeating social foundations and producing a profound rupture in perceptions of social and national identity. The notion of Chileanness was a rhetorical resource to which both sides would strategically appeal, and its meanings were reshaped as a result of the rupture. Such appeals to competing definitions of Chileanness were "a symptom of divisions rather than of unity."[63]

The construction of Chileanness became a political project towards the end of 1930s. Numerous parties incorporated the rhetoric into their programs, and other social organizations took advantage of their relevance in society.[64] From a transnational viewpoint, it also exposes a local expression of the parallel evolution of nationalism, modern masculinity, and the middle classes;[65] the proper Chilean middle-class man was disputed in the press by both political sides under the UP, while under the dictatorship the notion of proper Chilean saviors men was out of the question.

Ramón moved to Santiago to begin his university education in 1972. He explains, "naturally, I kept up my political activism at university—everything from street demonstrations to voluntary work."[66] Some deeply committed priests led youth voluntary work in the city's peripheral shantytowns, and Ramón, as a MAPU and then MAPU/OC militant, joined in, beginning his volunteering in the Lo Hermida shantytown in eastern Santiago. Following the coup, he continued to volunteer under the umbrella of the *Pastoral Universitaria Católica* (University Catholic Chaplaincy) and despite his atheism, Ramón maintained ties with the priesthood. The connection between the Catholic Church and political action was not exclusive to Chile and can also be observed on the other side of the Andes. In Argentina, the progressive working priests (*curas obreros*) of *Acción Católica* (Catholic Action) worked with young political activists.[67]

Under the UP, left-wing Integral Chileans already studying at university found a place where they could shed their middle-class identity and put into practice what they preached. The Chilean social and political context of the time not only permitted but actively promoted this process. Consequently, the UP government promoted a number of ways to volunteer and, according to Allende, the General Secretariat for Youth gathered together some 70,000 people.[68] The poster "*A trabajar por Chile*" (Let's work for Chile, Figure 16.2) exposes the protagonism of Chileanness under the UP government, with the young volunteer wearing a t-shirt emblazoned with the national flag.[69] As Vicente Larrea explains:

> The poster "Let's work for Chile" was designed to encourage young people to engage in voluntary work. We based it on the Titan Atlas who here bears the working world on his shoulders. We were always sure to include the Chilean flag, but deliberately omitted the political emblems of the UP.[70]

Figure 16.2 "Let's work for Chile". Graphic used by Salvador Allende's Popular Unity government. Concept: Vicente Larrea, illustration: Luis Albornoz, Santiago de Chile, 1971.

Sources: Courtesy of Vicente Larrea.

The image harks back to Greek mythology and the young Atlas, condemned by Zeus to hold up the sky for eternity, and reflects the task Allende bestowed upon the Chilean youth of committing to the motherland and engaging in voluntary work the length of the country. The image also reinforces the idea of the performance of modern masculinity: as a prominent political and social force, it symbolized the hopes and ideals of society.[71]

Raúl, another Integral Chilean and radicalized DC member who went on to join the MAPU, enrolled in 1967 at one of the most prominent intellectual centers of the time, the *Instituto Pedagógico* (Pedagogical Institute, University of Chile). He points to the distinctions that were beginning to emerge between the different types of Integral Chileans as the key to his radicalization: "We were more *intellectuals* at that time. We adopted the title to distinguish ourselves from the theorists who just sat around the university campus debating, while the country moved forward at a hundred miles per hour."[72] This sentiment is illustrative of a period when Integral Chileans on the left—those who were keen for their actions to match their words—began to view campus debates as insufficient. Integral Chileans wanted to radicalize and take action, a purpose related directly to abandoning one's class position and the subjective well-being associated with it.

Raul's social commitment reflected his educational background at the National Institute (a prestigious secondary school) and subsequently at the University of Chile's Pedagogical Institute, which inspired him to follow his inclination toward political activism. Although not a Marxist-Leninist, he identified with the radical church, becoming involved with the *Movimiento de Iglesia Joven* from 1968 to 1969. During the same period, he also become a member of MAPU and then the MAPU/OC (*MAPU Obrero Campesino*). For Raúl, laying aside his class position meant leaving the university and participating in a program created by two MAPU members from Allende's Ministry of Education, which provided supplementary education to workers.[73] As he recalls: "I proletarianized myself (*me obrericé*)." However, for Raúl, this was part of his middle-class performance as a radicalized left-wing Integral Chilean: at the end of each day spent at the factory teaching workers, he went back to his parents' house in Ñuñoa, a middle-class quarter in eastern Santiago. The particularity of their human agency shaped the ways in which Integral Chileans reconfigured the *eudaimonia* that had led their counterparts in previous decades to experiences of social sharing, exchange, and knowledge. Through a more contemplative spirit that sought the common good and was defined by the act of giving as a "specific human capacity,"[74] Integral Chileans endorsed this agenda, and with time even came to appreciate the mistakes made during that period, as Raúl recalls.[75] From the transnational perspective, parallels can be identified between the *eudaimonia* of the Integral Chileans men and the German self-cultivation of the individual—or *Bildung*—in which achievement of true manhood was the objective.[76]

From Revolution to Repression: The Reinventions of the Left-Wing Integral Chileans

The dictatorship, through its interventions in secondary schools and universities, caused a profound rupture in social relations, human interaction, knowledge, and action. Under the dictatorship, those left-wing Integral Chileans able to reinvent themselves and continue as agents of change did so, either covertly or through grassroots organizations, some supporting the cause within Chile and others from exile. Raúl was sought out again in 1976 to help resurrect the MAPU: "So we started all over again, forming a popular front, with us working in the cultural arena; but various actions were taking place in other areas, always with links to the parish churches." Because of the harsh repression dealt out at that time, groups needed some form of protection: "The cover provided by the Church afforded us a certain degree of safety."[77] Six of the 40 bishops openly supported the coup, and it took six months for the *Comité Permanente de la Conferencia Episcopal* (Permanent Committee of the Chilean Episcopal Conference, CECH) to officially criticize Pinochet's regime.[78] Nevertheless, immediately following the coup, Raúl Silva Henríquez, Archbishop of Santiago, together with Lutheran bishop, Helmut Frenz, began to work committedly in defense of human rights,[79] initially through the ecumenical organization *Comité Pro Paz* (Committee of Cooperation for Peace in Chile)—prior to its dissolution by the regime in 1975—and then Silva Henríquez continued through the *Vicaría de la Solidaridad* (Vicariate of Solidarity).[80] In the long run, the military junta was conflicted by the lack of support from the Church,[81] and by 1980 the Church was considered an opponent of the regime.[82]

The *Agrupación Cultural Santa Marta* (Santa Marta Cultural Association) was created towards the end of 1976 with a view to reorganizing social spaces, a move which reflected the magnitude of social division in the country. It was affiliated with Santa Marta church in Ñuñoa, run by progressive Dutch priests who supported the Association economically. Raúl led the creation of the group in the hope of eventually realizing the vision and the ideology held so dear by the leftist middle-class youth. Integral Chileans such as himself who were now able to re-establish values that had been sidelined by the coup through its disruption of social life, dismantling of meeting places, and police suppression of dissenting voices. The Santa Marta Cultural Association pamphlet (Figure 16.3) invited people to a cultural meeting at the *Cariola* Theater and shows a gentle representation of Chileanness in the form of flag-bearing man and woman, along with the call *"La cultura al servicio del hombre"* (Culture at the service of man), all in green as a sign of hope. The call to action—in which the word "man" refers to both mankind and men—and the superimposition of the dark green figure of a man over the paler shadow of his female counterpart reinforced the prominent role of men in the public

Figure 16.3 The Santa Marta Cultural Association pamphlet.

Source: Courtesy of Santa Marta Cultural Association Archive.

sphere, revealing that although the gendered narrative was progressing at the time, masculinity remained unconsciously dominant. This message was aligned with the middle-class nature of the Integral Chileans and the ways these groups found to maintain morale. Music, poetry, folkloric ballet, modern dance, and theater were all included in the schedule.

The schedule brought together well-known artists from the left-wing scene, incluiding the band Congreso, folk musicians Catalina Rojas and Pedro Yañez, a founding member of celebrated folk group Inti-Illimani, and artists from the *Canto nuevo* musical movement, which was a continuation of the *Nueva Canción Chilena*. With its "folkloric style," the latter soon became emblematic of young people at the time.[83] For many, the *Llanto nuevo* (a variation on the name *Canto nuevo*, substituting the word 'song' for 'cry') arose as a musical response to the reality of the time,[84] and groups such as Wampara and Cantierra played an important role at such events, not only raising the morale of the audience, but slipping in a political message, recalls Raúl.[85] Roberto Parra Sandoval (1921-1995), widely known as *el Tío Roberto* (Uncle Roberto), was an iconic folklorist who regularly participated in the *peñas*, *fondas* and other cultural gatherings at Santa Marta, and composed the *cueca* "Ña Martuca," a familiar contraction of the name Doña Marta, for the Santa Marta Cultural Association. The discovery was made among Parra's unpublished *cueca* notebooks by his widow, Catalina Rojas, and Raúl and other ex-alumni of the Santa Marta school went on to record it more than 40 years later.[86] The song bears immeasurable value and helps to illustrate both the cultural scene and the scope of cultural production during the period; el Tío Roberto and Catalina Rojas both were active, committed Santa Marta artists and very much a part of its bohemian scene. The *cueca* now stands as material memory of a time in which voices were stifled and, as such, reflects bravery and hope through folklore. The organization of these activities formed part of his "double life"—as Raúl called it—and were made possible by the platform provided by Santa Marta. These cultural events can be viewed in terms of middle-class memory: the majority of artists that participated in such programs were members of the middle classes, and the meetings themselves recreated middle-class cultural leisure prior to the coup.[87]

As mentioned previously, Ramón was also part of the group responsible for reviving the MAPU in 1976. His experience reveals the extreme demands of revolutionary activity, in particular an incident that occurred at the iconic Gran Palace theater which forced him into a clandestine existence. At the end of May 1976, coinciding with the anniversary of the founding of MAPU, a major event was organized in downtown Santiago downtown Santiago theater—famous for its beautiful architecture and decoration, and with a seating capacity of 1,200 people—an ideal venue for a day of cultural events. Ramón was asked to read a speech, which he describes:

> It was definitely inappropriate for that venue; very political, very confrontational. Suddenly, they began to close the curtains behind me, those giant theater curtains, and said 'Finish up, the DINA [secret police] are here.' So, I spoke hurriedly: 'Comrades, we'll have to continue this conversation later.' They closed the curtain and got me out of there and put me in a change of clothes. I wasn't aware that this elaborate security protocol existed; they got me up and out of there and I disappeared.[88]

Ramón was unfamiliar with the security protocols for mass events. The Gran Palace event was one of the first large-scale gatherings to be held in the wake of the coup, and it symbolized a repairing of the social fabric. Ramón recalls that "in the days that followed, I began to realize that people were avoiding me around university because everyone had been at the Gran Palace—all the political leaders of the time were there; I was in the spotlight." The presence of the *Dirección de Inteligencia Nacional* (National Intelligence Directorate DINA, Pinochet's secret police) at the theater raised the threat of serious consequences for such a high-profile appearance. The theater had been full and Ramón had no choice: "I had to put my studies on hold again. Nobody knew which side anyone was on."[89]

Ramón's experience illustrates the magnitude of what was happening at the time. Aside from the danger involved in the organization and execution of such activities, Raúl points out that: "culture is what makes it possible, to a certain degree, to repair the social fabric."[90] Radicalization was accompanied by new expressions of class subjectivity, which by that time were inherent to the political activism in which Integral Chileans on the radicalized left were already engaged. The gatherings became commonplace and were seen as legitimate spaces for socialization and cultural engagement beyond political purposes.

In order to be a consistent Integral Chilean, one had to sacrifice comfort while demonstrating that education is an agent for change. Radicalization can therefore be seen as a "total liberation;" as "radical (or revolutionary) humanism."[91] Ramón, who was forced into a clandestine existence on more than one occasion and had a more radical profile, was involved with different parties at different times during the dictatorship. This can be understood in terms of his own class subjectivity; as a consequence of his shedding of his class identity when the MAPU/OC moved away from classical Marxism and its worker politics:

> In the MAPU/OC, at the youth level, a good number of those of us who were working in poorer districts, working with that struggle, identified more closely with the popular movement. At that point we made a decision to move to the Communist Party.[92]

His involvement with the Communist Party (*Partido Comunista*, PC) began with the collapse of the underground production of print publications, and Ramón was made responsible for reviving the distribution mechanism for PC press material.

During the 1980s, disappointed by the rigidity of the PC, he moved further to the left and began his *foquista* affiliation with the newly formed *Frente Patriótico Manuel Rodríguez* (Manuel Rodríguez Patriotic Front, FPMR), which led him to take up residence in the La Legua shantytown. There he worked on assembling militias of local young people, and he continued to live there even after his short period at the FPMR. Among the many activities in which he was involved, he created an NGO, studied Waldorf education, visited Germany, and launched a Waldorf teaching project which grew and endured in the shantytown. His activities are an illustration of how the Integral Chileans persevered in their varied commitment to the dispossessed. The Waldorf school that he set up engaged with the parents of pupils through carpentry and masonry workshops, Mapuche textiles, jam making, and the production of children's clothing. These were the same parents who, in their youth, had problems with drugs and delinquency, and who Ramón had recruited into the political militias. The scope of this shedding of class was immense.

As the project grew, its management became a full-time responsibility for Ramón. Teaching was extended to the fifth grade and there were two kindergarten groups. When democracy returned, members of the *Concertación*, the mayor, and deputies made committed contributions to the cause, and Ramón's entire network of acquaintances joined in, connecting contacts in order to find, for example, music teachers and musical instruments, as music education began in fourth grade. By that point, Ramón was no longer receiving support from Germany—in a democracy, needs had to be met through other channels—and he recalls: "Socially, the experience was an extraordinary success. We resisted; we managed to keep it going for ten years,"[93] and the initiative even received attention from UNESCO (the United Nations Educational, Scientific and Cultural Organization). There were winter parties, voluntary contributions from parents, and guardians "based on their income. If you can't pay, come and do some cleaning at the school."[94] In this way, the project was kept alive until the year 2000, when it succumbed to financial problems. Ramón's experience of living in the shantytown exposes how the middle-class roots of these idealistic students led to diverse, extreme, but meaningful expressions of what it meant to perform a masculine proletarian role. From the formation of the militia to his creation of the Waldorf school, the performance of modern masculinity on the part of this Integral Chilean was clearly ingrained in his nature.

Integral Chileans were able to lay aside their class positions and put their social commitment into practice under the UP government. This shaking off of their class—or proletarianization—was the mantra of left-leaning Integral Chileans at that time, a trend that endured in various forms during the dictatorship and even after the return of democracy, as seen with Ramón. In their encounters with the working classes, these young people believed that their various contributions were making a real difference to the people and to the country. The Chile of the 1970s was a prominent example of the shift in the Latin American struggle from the elites to the working classes during the late twentieth century.[95] From a transnational viewpoint, the Chilean middle classes played a central role in the local class struggle, and their expressions of human agency included diverse instances of Integral Chileans leading the shift. Thus, the masculine tone of the proletarian performances of left-leaning Integral Chileans men perpetuated a twofold elitism of gender and class that reproduced democratic normativity.

Final Comments: The Integral Chilean and the Resignification of How "Young People Committed to the Motherland"

The notion of youth and the role played by this group cannot be explained simply as an attempt by the Allende government to co-opt young people in support of their cause; rather, it must be understood as an expression of the state of Chile's political and social development during the twentieth century, embodied in the public sphere by modern middle-class men. This maturity is also associated with the elitism of the educated youth, personified by the Integral Chileans and associated with the meaning attributed to democracy, civics, and civic agency in Chile. Together, these aspects deepened political divisions and reinforced the turn to the left, making it possible for Salvador Allende to succeed democratically upon its fourth electoral attempt. To this can be added knowledge production on the part of the middle classes as a cornerstone of both the evolution of the twentieth-century Chilean youth and the political radicalization at either end of the political spectrum. From a transnational perspective, the Chilean road to socialism was a local reflection of the Cold War, depicted in the colorful posters that first called out to the Chilean youth and then placed an Atlassian burden on their shoulders.

An examination of the testimonies of the activists recounted here—whether in terms of the notion of the Integral Chilean or of the elitism of political organizations such as the MAPU—reveals the segmentation of Chilean state education and the different forms of expression of social commitment to the dispossessed which, in reality, served ultimately to perpetuate this distance. For their part, the radicalized left-wing youth of the middle classes was divided among the democrats and revolutionaries (aligned to *foquismo*). The shedding of class is evident both in the case of the workers' school set up in the factory by Raúl under the UP government, and in that of the dictatorship-era Waldorf school established by Ramón. As such, these actions—as masculine performances in the public sphere—can be also seen as both class subjectivities and middle-class memories.

Under the dictatorship, the reinventions of the young left-wing Integral Chileans continued to express their sensibility and commitment to the country. Consequently, in this new version of the national, the cultural, and the social, the Integral Chileans found the courage to express a renewed sense of *eudaimonia* in terms of how "Young people committed to the motherland."

Notes

* The archival research for this study was conducted during my postdoctoral fellowship with the Minerva Foundation

1 For further details: vlarrea@larrea.cl

2 Vicente Larrea, interview with the author by telephone, April 13, 2020.

3 Fabio Moraga, "'Ser joven y no ser revolucionario': La juventud y el movimiento estudiantil durante la Unidad Popular," in *Frágiles suturas: Chile a treinta años del gobierno de Salvador Allende*, comp. Francisco Zapata (México: El Colegio de México, 2006), 383.

4 Alfredo Riquelme S. and Joaquín Fernández, "La vida política," in *Chile: Mirando hacia adentro*, vol. 4 (1960–1930), dir. Joaquín Fermandois and coord. Olga Ulianova (Madrid: Fundación Mapfre; Taurus, 2015), 22.

5 Moraga, "Ser joven," 376.

6 George L. Mosse, *The Image of Man: The Creation of Modern Masculinity* (New York, Oxford: Oxford University Press, 1996), 134.

7 Tanya Harmer, *Allende's Chile and the Inter-American Cold War* (Chapel Hill, University of North Carolina Press 2011), 9.

8 Aldo Marchesi, "Southern Cone Cities as Political Laboratories of the Global Sixties: Montevideo (1962–1968); Santiago de Chile (1969–1973); Buenos Aires (1973–1976)," *E.I.A.L* 28, no. 2 (2017): 65.

9 Claudia Stern, "La sobredimensión de la educación estatal en Chile: El Liceo experimental Manuel de Salas y el 'chileno integral' (1932–1962)," *Historia 396*, no. 1 (June 2017): 265.

10 Stern, "La sobredimensión," 265.

11 Aristóteles, *Ética a Nicómaco* (Gredos, Madrid, 2014), 39–40.

12 Stern, "La sobredimensión," 286.

13 For details about the post-war baby boom vis-à-vis the Chilean long sixties, see: Tanya Harmer, *Beatriz Allende: A Revolutionary Life in Cold War Latin America* (Chapel Hill: The University of North Carolina Press, 2020), 10; For the political entanglements of the Chilean long sixties, see: Isabel Torres Dujisin, "La década de los sesenta en Chile: la utopía como proyecto," *HAOL* No. 19 (Primavera, 2009), 141–144.

14 The *Gremialismo* (guildism) was the liberal-conservative movement of the rightist youth that opposed leftist youth and university reform and then has a renewed attention under dictatorship, for details: Yanko González, *Los más ordenaditos: Fascismo y juventud en la dictadura de Pinochet* (Santiago: Hueders, 2020); Guillermo Campero, *Los gremios empresariales en el período 1970–1983: Comportamiento sociopolítico y orientaciones ideológicas* (Santiago: Series ILET 1984); Marcelo Casals, "Estado, contrarrevolucion y autoritarismo en la trayectoría política de la clase media profesional chilena: De la oposición a la Unidad Popular al fin de los Colegios Profesionales (1970–1981)," in *1988–1968: De la transición al largo '68 en Chile*, ed. Andrés Estefane (Santiago: Ariadna, 2019); Gonzalo Rojas, Andrea Botto, Jorge Soto and Confederación de la Producción y del Comercio, *Historia del gremialismo empresarial* (Chile: Confederación de la Producción y del Comercio, 2000).

15 Hillary Hiner, "Memory Speaks from Today': Analyzing Oral Histories of Female Members of the MIR in Chile through the Work of Luisa Passerini," *Women's History Review* 25, no. 3 (2016): 386.

16 Harmer, *Beatriz Allende*, 3.

17 R. W. Connell and James W. Messerschmidt, "Hegemonic Masculinity: Rethinking the Concept" *Gender and Society*, Vol. 19, No. 6 (December 2005), 832, 836.

18 In 1941 the existing state education program included a Chileanness Program, that reinforced social heteronormative mandates by teaching home economics. *Programa de chilenidad: Resumen de las actividades en pro de la chilenidad en las distintas asignaturas* (Santiago: Liceo Experimental Manuel de Salas, 1941), 35.

19 Mosse, *The Image of Man*, 133.

20 For an overview of gender, caste and class, see Claudia Stern *Entre el cielo y el suelo: las identidades elásticas de las clases medias (Santiago de Chile, 1932–1962)* (Santiago: RiL editores 2021), 37, 97, 118, 336; Regarding connections between caste and the idea of race, see Stern, *Entre el cielo y el suelo*, 29–30, Claudia Stern, "La paz neutra y el 'chileno abnegado'. Inmigrantes y sectores medios en Chile 1930–1960," *Revista de Paz y Conflictos* Vol. 9 (2) (2016), 129, and Claudia Stern "Otherness in Convergence: Arabs, Jews, and the Formation of the Chilean Middle Classes, 1930–1960" in Raanan Rein, Stefan Rinke, and Nadia Zysman, Eds., *The New Ethnic Studies: Jewish Latin Americans in a Comparative Perspective* (Brill, Leiden and Boston, 2017), 104; For an examination of caste imaginary, decency and middle classes, see David Parker's study of Peruvian employees: David Parker, *The idea of the Middle Class, White-collar Workers*

and Peruvian Society, 1900–1950 (University Park, PA: Pennsylvania State University Press, 1998), 24–40, 208–211, 224–238; For a wider dialogue with other Latin American realities and the idea of race and pigmentocracy, see Barbara Weinstein's and Mara Vivero-Vigoya's chapters in this volume, along with Susie Porter's and Miriam Shakow's chapters concerning the idea of race and women.

21 For the entanglements of the caste imaginary, the idea of race, and the social structure during the Chilean War of Independence, see Hugo Contreras "Las tropas afroamericanas y mulatas durante la Guerra de Independencia de Chile. Casta, segregación y pretensions sociales, 1810–1820," *Cuaderno de Historia Militar No.15*, (2019): 90–91, 99-100; For a description of the Chilean colonial period, see Azun Candina's chapter in this volume.

22 Stern, *Entre el cielo y el suelo*, 35–36.

23 Stefan Rinke, *Encuentros con el yanqui: norteamericanización y cambio sociocultural en Chile 1898–1990* (Santiago de Chile: DIBAM, Centro de Investigaciones Diego Barros Arana 2013), 468 ; Claudia Stern "'To live with honor, or die': The metamorphosis of place, national symbols, masculinities, and practices under state terrorism (1973-1990)," *Journal of Urban History*. doi:10.1177/00961442221083043 (2022): 1-20.

24 Aldo Marchesi, "Imaginación Política del antiimplerialismo: Intelectuales y política en el Cono Sur a fines de los sesenta," *E.I.A.L* 17, no. 1 (2006): 138.

25 Torres Dujisin, "La década de los sesenta en Chile," 144, 145.

26 Marchesi, "Southern," 66.

27 Julio Pinto and Gabriel Salazar, *Historia Contemporánea de Chile I: Estado, legitimidad, ciudadanía* (Santiago: Ediciones LOM, 1999), 171.

28 Torres Dujisin, "La década de los sesenta en Chile," 146.

29 Gonzalo Cáceres, "Santiago de Chile: La capital de la izquierda," in *Ciudades Sudamericanas como arenas culturales: Artes, medios, barrios de élite y villas miserias, intelectuales y urbanistas; Como ciudad y cultura se activan mutuamente*, comps. Adrián Gorelik and Fernanda Aréas Peixoto (Buenos Aires: Siglo Veintiuno, 2016), 386.

30 Claudio Rolle, "La 'NO historia' de un año crucial," in *1973: La vida cotidiana de un año crucial*, coord. Claudio Rolle (Santiago: Planeta, 2003), 30.

31 For details, see the Allende Archive at the Marxist Internet Archive: Marxist Internet Archive, "Misiones y tareas de juventud y Nacionalización del cobre, discurso en la Plaza de la Constitución pronunciado ante el pueblo de Santiago," last modified February 2, 2016, https://www.marxists.org/espanol/allende/1970/diciembre21.htm.

32 González, *Los más ordenaditos*, 63.

33 González, *Los más ordenaditos*, 47.

34 Harmer, *Beatriz Allende*, 10.

35 Alessandro Portelli, *The death of Luigi Trastulli and other histories: Form and meaning in oral history* (Albany: State University of New York Press, 1991), 52.

36 Claudia, Stern, "Cuando Chile dejó de ser una 'copia feliz del Edén': Redefiniendo clases medias en trauma en la década del 70," *Journal of Iberian and Latin American Research* 25, no. 2 (2019), 170, 172–3.

37 Stern, "Cuando Chile dejó," 159.

38 Steve J. Stern, *Luchando por mentes y corazones: Las batallas de la memoria en el Chile de Pinochet* (Santiago de Chile: Ediciones Universidad Diego Portales, 2013), 138.

39 Stern, "La sobredimensión," 283.

40 Marchesi, "Imaginación," 138.

41 Felícitas Klimpel, *La mujer chilena: El aporte femenino al progreso de Chile, 1910–1960* (Santiago: Editorial Andrés Bello, 1962), 226.

42 Hector Gutiérrez, *La población de Chile*, CICRED Series World Population Year 1974 (Paris: CICRED, 1975), 63.
43 "Las primeras 40 medidas del gobierno popular." Document available at: http://www.archivochile.cl/S_Allende_UP/doc_de_UP/SAdocup0003.pdf (accessed August 01, 2018).
44 Stern, "La sobredimensión," 267.
45 Mónica Bartolucci, *La juventud maravillosa: La peronización y los orígenes de la violencia política, 1958–1972* (Argentina: EDUNTREF, 2018), 180.
46 Ramón, interview with the author, November 5, 2017.
47 Maria Rosaria Stabili, "Introducción: Los desafíos de la memoria al quehacer historiográfico," in *Entre historias y memorias: Los desafíos metodológicos del legado reciente de América Latina*, coord. Maria Rosaria Stabili (Madrid: AHILA; Iberoamericana, 2007), 8.
48 Harmer, *Beatriz Allende*, 9.
49 Presentation of Eugenio Tironi in Cristina Moyano, *MAPU o la seducción del poder y la juventud: Los años fundacionales del partido-mito de nuestra transición (1969-1973)* (Santiago: Universidad Alberto Hurtado, 2009), 25.
50 As a reference, in the parliamentary election of March 1973, the party achieved only 2.6% of the vote. Details: Esteban Valenzuela, "El MAPU y el rol transformador de las élites iluministas: Revolución, pragmatismo y disidencia," *Revista de Ciencia Política* 31, no. 2 (2011): 198, 202.
51 Valenzuela, "El MAPU," 197.
52 Ramón, interview.
53 Ramón, interview.
54 Ramón, interview.
55 Erich Fromm, *Del tener al ser: Caminos y extravíos de la conciencia* (Barcelona: Paidós, 2016 [1991]), 16.
56 Ramón, interview.
57 Valenzuela, "El MAPU," 202.
58 Axel, interview with the author, December 4, 2017.
59 For the role of ENU as precursor of the coup, see Jorge Olguín, "La derecha chilena y los principios legimitadores del pre y post golpe de Estado de 1973," *Izquierdas*, 38, febrero (2018), 144.
60 Ramón, interview.
61 Ramón, interview.
62 Agustín, interview with the author, December 4, 2017.
63 Jorge E. Iturriaga, "Proletas, limpios, cobardes y burgueses: El fútbol en 1973," in *1973*, coord. Rolle, 320.
64 Stefan Rinke, *Cultura de masas: Reforma y nacionalismo en Chile 1910–1931* (Santiago de Chile: DIBAM; Centro de Investigaciones Diego Barros Arana 2002), 137.
65 Mosse, *The Image of Man*, 7.
66 Ramón, interview.
67 Bartolucci, *La juventud maravillosa*, 24.
68 Moraga, "Ser joven," 400.
69 For a visual art study of the UP graphics see: Camilo D. Trumper, *Ephemeral Histories: Public Art, Politics and the Struggle for the Streets in Chile* (Oakland: University of California Press 2016), 113–127.
70 Ilustration: Luis Albornoz. Concept: Vicente Larrea, interview with the author by telephone, April 13, 2020. For further details: vlarrea@larrea.cl
71 Mosse, *The Image of Man*, 16.
72 Raúl, interview with the author, March 5, 2017.
73 For details on Raúl experience at the factory, see: Stern, "Cuando Chile dejó," 168–169.

74 Erich Fromm, *El arte de amar* (México: Paidós, 1983 [1959]), 33.
75 Raúl, interview.
76 Mosse, *The Image of Man*, 8.
77 Raúl, interview.
78 Veit Strassner, "La Iglesia chilena desde 1973 a 1993: De buenos samaritanos, antiguos contrahentes y nuevos aliados; Un análisis politológico," *Teología y Vida*, XL VII (2006): 81.
79 Stefan Ruderer and Veit Strassner, "Recordando tiempos difíciles: La Vicaría de la Solidaridad como lugar de memoria de la Iglesia y la sociedad chilena," *Archives de sciences sociales des religions* 170 (April–June 2015), 45.
80 Valeria Navarro-Rosenblatt, "The Untold History: Voices of Non-affiliated Jews in Chile, 1940–1990," in *The New Ethnic Studies: Jewish Latin Americans in a Comparative Perspective*, eds. Raanan Rein, Stefan Rinke, and Nadia Zysman (Brill, Leiden and Boston, 2017), 142.
81 William Sater and Simon Collier, *Historia de Chile, 1808–2017* (Madrid: Ediciones Akal, 2018), 452; Needless to say, there were bishops and Church factions that supported the regime, such as the priest Raúl Hasbún or the *Capellanía Militar* (Military Chaplaincy), the Archbishop of Valparaíso Emilio Tagle and its congregants, to name a few.
82 For a chronology of the CECH's relationship with the regime, see: María Angélica Cruz and Camilo Ramírez, "Memorias subalternas sobre la dictadura militar en Chile," *Archives de sciences sociales des religions* 170 (April–June 2015): 20–22; For the role of the Church during the 1980s, see: Strassner, "La Iglesia chilena," 85–86.
83 Brenda Elsey, *Citizens and Sportsmen in Chile: futbol and politics in twentieth-century Chile* (Austin: University of Texas Press, 2011), 222.
84 Details at the *Enciclopedia de la musica chilena*: "Canto Nuevo," Musica Popular.cl: la enciclopedia de la música chilena, accessed May 23, 2020, http://www.musicapopular.cl/generos/canto-nuevo/
85 Raúl, interview.
86 Recording of the *cueca* as a tribute to Roberto Parra available at: https://www.facebook.com/groups/22165065545/permalink/10158555229930546/?sfnsn=mo.
87 Stern, "Cuando Chile dejó," 171.
88 Ramón, interview.
89 Ramón, interview.
90 Raúl, interview.
91 Fromm, *Del tener*, 25.
92 Ramón, interview.
93 Ramón, interview.
94 Ramón, interview.
95 Marchesi, "Imaginación," 148.

Part IV

Social Mobility, Neoliberal Discourses, and the "Pink Tide"

Introduction to Part IV

A. Ricardo López-Pedreros

Figure IV.1 Marcha de los Indignados, Bogotá, 2012.

Source: Photo by Gabriela Díaz Montealegre.

DOI: 10.4324/9781003029311-21

James Ferguson has provocatively argued that scholars have become accustomed "to a debate pitting triumphalist accounts of the global spread of 'free-market' capitalism (decreeing the end of history, or telling us the world is flat) against critical accounts of that same ascendancy that tell a formally similar story but with the moral polarity inverted."[1] With some remarkable exceptions, this narrative continues to be dominant particularly for Latin America, as scholars often see neoliberalism's triumph as the almost inevitable product of "shock therapies" implemented by military regimes and crafted by US-trained economists.[2] Neoliberalism is mostly depicted as an imperial imposition (or, at least, a calculated strategy disseminated globally from Europe and the United States) with which Latin American societies had to either comply or reject. Indeed, most scholars have criticized neoliberalism as an anti-democratic capitalist ideology and political economy advancing only the interests of transnational financial elites. We thus have studies demonstrating the consolidation of what widely celebrated economist Thomas Piketty calls "patrimonial capitalism" or famous philosopher Alan Badiou refers to as an "oligarchical capitalism," in which a social order, often seen as unified and homogenous, has emerged only to concentrate income for the upper brackets of society.[3] Such narratives have often translated into a transhistorical metanarrative of neoliberalism in which elites have been scripted as in favor of neoclassical economics while subaltern groups have unanimously been against those political economies.

As important as these historical explanations have been to dismantle triumphalist accounts of neoliberalism as democratization, such analyses readily sidestep the role of the middle classes. These scholars criticize neoliberalism as an anti-democratic by highlighting the historical process through which neoliberal policies have vanished the middle classes and have simultaneously produced a two-class society, thereby widening economic inequality, political polarization, and class conflict. In this specific context, scholars are inclined to locate a two-class society as the struggle of our times and thus in imperative need of critical appraisal.

Yet again, as the region experienced the consolidation of left-leaning political projects since the beginning of the century, scholars further assigned no important role to the study of the middle classes. For some, this "pink tide" consolidated the struggle between the people and the oligarchies in which the middle classes were forced to join the popular against the oligarchies or unite forces with the elites against popular groups. As a result, scholars have created powerful explanatory narratives in which the middle classes appear at best vestigial—that is, as a class that does not matter—in what is considered a "proper" analysis of power relationships either in the consolidation of neoliberal societies or in the formation of alternative political economies across the region.[4]

This part puts these narratives to rest in four specific ways. First, they show how the idea of the middle class has been discussed since the late 1940s and has recently been mobilized in neoliberal rationalities to legitimize multiple forms of exploitation and vast material inequalities at the core of those rationalities. In so doing, they show how neoliberal policies and practices emerged partially as a response to—and an attempt to address—middle-class radical mobilization during the 1970s and 1980s. Second, these contributions also offer a detailed ethnographic work to demonstrate how the competing discourses and practices of social mobility simultaneously foreground both neoliberal societies and left-leaning political projects. Although there were competing meanings of upward mobility, the very notions of middle-classness were indeed shared in both neoliberal and progressive definitions of democracy since those notions served as the source of legitimization for class hierarchizations and multiple forms of inequalities. But they also parted ways on what the very model of social mobility entailed. Some, as in the case of Brazil and Bolivia with left-leaning political projects in place, legitimized upward mobility through which solidarity became a crucial feature whereas others promoted competition and exclusion as different historical actors tried to move up in the social latter. The former imagined upward mobility as a potential common good whereas the latter naturalized hierarchized social mobility as a quintessential individual endeavor.

Third, by paying attention to ethnographic approaches and discourse analysis, this part also offers specific answers as to how vast material disparities have become a foundational characteristic of a neoliberal order. As in the case of Mexico during the twentieth century or Brazil since the beginning of the twenty-first, these essays explain how diverse social groups within the middle classes challenged but also reproduced multiple forms of inequalities and their intrinsic forms of gendered exploitation. Fourth, by critically approaching the notion of myth, these chapters also discuss how the middle class, as a discourse, has shaped overarching moral narratives that seek to legitimize political order in moments of social mobilization. Indeed, as in the case of Chile and Argentina, these chapters demonstrate how the idea of the middle classes is not just empty rhetoric but rather a potent political discourse through which material inequalities at the core of neoliberalism have historically been naturalized.

As a whole, by studying the interlocking process of economic policies, political rationalities, gendered discourses, classed interests, racialized desires, and social struggles, these essays question a narrative that presuppose a teleological, clear-cut transition from free-market absolutism to left-leaning, state-driven economic policies and it demonstrates the crucial role of the middle classes in the consolidation of different, but intimately related political economies. What this part proposes is a less assured and more historically grounded approach to understand the social foundations of neoliberalism. In so doing, it invites readers to think that, far from being only an imposition by an elite and thus merely a process benefiting such group, a neoliberal rule occurred through an ample, if fragmented, common sense across different social groups.

Notes

1 James Ferguson, *Give a Man a Fish: Reflections on the New Politics of Distribution* (Durham, NC: Duke University Press, 2015), 1.

2 See, among several others, Naomi Klein, *The Shock Doctrine: The Rise of Disaster Capitalism* (New York: Henry Holt and Company, 2010); Renán Vega Cantor, *Capitalismo y despojo: Perspectiva histórica sobre la expropiación universal de bienes y saberes* (Bogotá: Impresol Ediciones, 2013); Renán Vega Cantor, *Los economistas neoliberales: nuevos criminales de guerra; el genocidio económico y social del capitalismo contemporáneo* (Colombia: CEPA, 2010); Luis Rojas Villagra, coord., *Neoliberalismo en América Latina: Crisis, tendencias y alternativas* (Buenos Aires: CLACSO, 2015); Greg Grandin, *Empire's Workshop: Latin America, the United States, and the Rise of the New Imperialism* (New York: Metropolitan Books, 2006). For remarkable exceptions see Carla Freeman, *Entrepreneurial Selves: Neoliberal Respectability and the Making of a Caribbean Middle Class* (Durham, NC: Duke University Press, 2014); Verónica Gago, *Neoliberalism from Below: Popular Pragmatics and Baroque Economies* (Durham, NC: Duke University Press, 2017); and Heidi Tinsman, *Buying into the Regime: Grapes and Consumption in Cold War Chile and the United States* (Durham, NC: Duke University Press, 2014).

3 Thomas Piketty, *Capital in the Twenty-First Century* (London: Belknap Press, 2017); Alain Badiou, "Twenty-Four Notes in the Use of the Word 'People,'" in *What is a People?*, Alain Badiou et al. (New York: Columbia University Press, 2016), 29.

4 For some remarkable exceptions, see Miriam Shakow, *Along the Bolivian Highway: Social Mobility and Political Culture in a New Middle Class* (Philadelphia: University of Pennsylvania Press, 2014); Mara Viveros, Mara Viveros Vigoya. *El Oximoron de las clases medias negras: Movilidad social e interseccionalidad en Colombia*. (Guadalajara: Universidad de Guadalajara. Collección CALAS, 2021) Carla Freeman, *Entrepreneurial Selves: Neoliberal Respectability and the Making of a Caribbean Middle Class* (Durham, NC: Duke University Press, 2014); Verónica Gago, *Neoliberalism from Below: Popular Pragmatics and Baroque Economies* (Durham, NC: Duke University Press, 2017); A. S. Dillingham, *Oaxaca Resurgent: Indigeneity, Development, and Inequality in Twentieth-Century Mexico* (Stanford University Press, 2021).

17 A "Middle-Class Country"

Social Mobility, Progress, and Genealogical Origins in the Public Discourse in Argentina (2002–2015)

Sergio E. Visacovsky

The headline of an editorial published in *La Prensa* in October 2018 read: "La Argentina será de clase media o no será" (Argentina must be a middle-class country or else it's nothing). In this piece, the author wrote:

> For several decades, the emergence, upward mobility and prosperity of the middle class has undoubtedly made this country civilized and dignified—desirable to this day for millions of foreigners—and this is almost always synonymous with modernity because its material symbols come from the present and cosmopolitanism on account of its mainly European origin. "Argentina must be a middle-class country or else it's nothing." This slogan is a good starting point to rebuild this battered country we all call home.

These ideas—of a country "synonymous with modernity," "civilized," and "dignified"—referred to the "European origin" of a modern Argentina that was not born at the start of the nineteenth century but toward its end, and in the early twentieth century:

> Thanks to the deluge of foreigners arriving in the late nineteenth century and during the first decades of the twentieth, our country has been fortunate to develop a much broader, middle-class base than the Latin American average (with good salaries, due to labor shortages). Modern Argentina, in fact, is the result of mass immigration from Europe and not from the May Revolution...

The history and nature of the middle class included the possibility of restoring the Argentinians' "battered" country in which they had to cope with high rates of inflation, cyclical adjustments to the economy, high unemployment, widespread poverty, and a significant drop in consumer spending among much of the population. As such, the call for Argentina to "be a middle-class country" represented a hope for a brighter future after decades of decline.

DOI: 10.4324/9781003029311-22

The newspaper piece equated the influx of European immigrants with the origin of Argentina's middle class, a sector of society associated with prosperity, modernization, and civilization. This large-scale immigration had been state policy, a means of populating vast swathes of uninhabited areas, increasing land productivity, and, in particular, altering the population composition by incorporating new arrivals from Western Europe.[1] A total of 5.9 million immigrants arrived on Argentina's shores between 1871 and 1914, and nearly 3.1 million became permanent residents.[2] Although we must be careful about overstating a generalized upward social mobility among immigrants,[3] the editorial still painted a rosy picture of the good old days of "progress"; therefore, a reconstructed Argentina needed to return to that middle-class country of yesteryear. In the same vein and shortly before, neurologist and neuroscientist Facundo Manes (a bestselling author with a high media profile) wrote: "We must be a middle-class country once again, I think that's what society is asking for."[4]

Since the beginning of this century, during a bout of severe economic and political crises in Argentina, politicians and other public figures have frequently called for it "to become a middle-class country again." They clung on to the belief—one that took hold in the mid-twentieth century—that Argentina was "a typical middle-class country," an "island in a polarized Latin America,"[5] and more akin to Anglo-America and Western Europe.[6] The core argument for such statements was the country's many descendants of European immigrations who had improved their quality of life through hard work and education.

Nevertheless, the idea of a middle-class country where hard work led to upward social mobility seemed an anachronism, something only possible in the past. During the ethnographic fieldwork that I began in 2003, many interviewees who had slipped down the social ladder after the 2001 crisis spoke of the disappearance of the middle class, giving up hope of future progress. They also saw themselves as hard workers who had got ahead through tenacity, determination, effort, and sacrifices, emulating their forbears who had emigrated from Europe to Argentina. However, unlike these ancestors, their hard work and sacrifices went unrewarded: many faced the harsh reality of losing everything for which they had worked so hard. Yet they had no regrets, and saw their personal lack of success as the failure of the national project: they argued that at some point Argentina lost its way, and that it needed to get back onto the right path in order to improve the country's present-day problems. In other words, the route toward upward social mobility taken by their descendants remained a central tenet—immune to the effects to the country's continual financial crises in recent decades.

The nostalgia for being "a middle-class country again" became a recurring theme following the crisis in early-twenty-first-century Argentina, as it suffered a dramatic economic and financial meltdown, mass unemployment and poverty, riots, and a loss of confidence in government institutions and the country's political leaders. A particular facet of the crisis was that the situation was already being discussed in the press, academic articles, and books, during the first weeks of December 2001, and even beforehand.[7] Writers argued that the origins of the existing problems lay in the country's more distant past. From this perspective, the "crisis" was solely the latest episode in a long history of failures and that the country's woes began many years earlier. Clamoring for Argentina "to become a middle-class country again" presupposes the idea that Argentina had been such a country in the first place, and that once upon a time the nation had reached a level of progress and general wellbeing.

By analyzing newspaper articles and editorials in newspapers, together with other texts published mainly between the early 2000s and 2015, I have focused on various discourses of political candidates, presidents, and leaders representing various parties and ideological perspectives, as well as the views expressed by journalists and other writers. I argue that these calls to "be a middle-class country [again]" renewed an overarching moral narrative in order to appraise the past and consider a possible future for the country. Although this narrative assumed the existence of a reality it was referring back to (often drawing from sociological, historical, and economic data and concepts), here I am particularly interested in its *narrative aspects*. I am not suggesting that the notions of "class" and the "middle class" can be reduced to a "linguistic" or "rhetorical" problem,[8] nor that the middle class is an objective situation from which the origin narrative developed (though this does not mean that these narratives are unrelated to specific social conditions). Instead I consider ways of thinking expressed narratively as events organized in a temporal sequence, with a particular subject (in this case, the middle class) that is a protagonist in a plot that narrators and audiences can identify with, or differentiate themselves from.[9]

By examining the period between the end of Argentina's crisis in the early years of the twenty-first century and the 2015 national elections, I will show how this middle-class origin narrative (communicated orally and in writing as an exemplary or paradigmatic case,[10] which could take the shape of a personal story or one relating to a company or a nation), was widely and actively used in public narratives as a way of framing the nation's problems and, at the same time, of finding solutions to them.

Times of Crisis, the Middle Class, and "Nouveau Pauvres"

The "December 2001 Crisis" was objectively one of the worst and deepest calamities in Argentina's history from its outset: in September 2001, 14 million out of a total of 37 million people lived below the poverty line—in other words, 38% of the population.[11] As a corollary of the region's neoliberal policies implemented during the 1990s, unemployment figures rose sharply between 1991 and 2000, largely due to the privatizations of state-owned companies. In Gran Buenos Aires, Argentina's most populous conurbation, unemployment rose from 6% to 17.9%.[12] In May 2002, Argentina's unemployment reached the unprecedented level of 21.5%, increasing the number of people out of work to 2.8 million. In parallel, 53% of Argentinians were living below the poverty line and almost a quarter were destitute. Extrapolated to a national scale, this percentage represented a total of 19 million Argentinians living below the poverty line.[13]

Upward social mobility was therefore largely out of the question during the 1990s and at the dawn of the twenty-first century. During the period of this study, the diminishing size of the formerly numerous middle-class population was an important issue, and several studies claim this caused a deep socio-economic shift in Argentina, making it more similar to other Latin American nations. "Argentina, we now realize, is no longer Latin America's middle-class kingdom," according to an article entitled "Adiós al país de la clase media" (Farewell to the middle-class country), based on a 2004 report by the Economic Commission for Latin America and the Caribbean (ECLAC).[14] According to income statistics, from the mid-1970s to the late 1980s (a period during which there were various hyper-inflationary crises), the middle class accounted for 45% of the population, compared to a lower-class population of 44.6%. In 1994, the middle classes represented 63.8%, as opposed to 26.1% in the lower classes. In 2002, in the midst of the crisis, only 26% of the population could be classified as middle class, whereas the number of poor doubled.[15] The aforesaid rise in unemployment and underemployment, falling incomes, and more widespread informal and precarious jobs without welfare benefits led to people sliding down the social ladder; in the view of many specialists, this created a new stratum of "nouveau pauvres" who were different from the "structurally poor."[16]

After the economic recovery that began in 2003, statistics estimated that by 2006 the middle-class accounted for 58% of the population, compared to 32% in the lower-income sectors.[17] A World Bank report published in November 2012 showed that Argentina's middle-class population had doubled since it emerged from its crisis at the start of the twenty-first century and during the following ten years, making it Latin America's fastest-growing economy in proportion to the region's total population. The report indicated that Argentina's middle class had grown from 9.3 to 18.6 million, equivalent to 45% of the total population, defining as middle class those earning between US$10 and US$50 per day, per capita.[18]

I do not cite these reports as an "objective" confirmation of the existence of a middle class; apart from revealing income distribution and its fluctuations over a specific period, this information often supported people's claims that a country that had ceased to exist should be revived, or that a country had re-emerged and everything should be done to maintain it. Since the start of the twenty-first century political leaders constantly invoked the middle class as a force for building a new country, whereas in fact they were trying to recreate a country from the past that was more prosperous but had already disappeared. From those years up until the 2015 national elections, the middle class was a conduit for a public controversy about progress in relation to a desired or an undesired national image.

From Restoring Upward Social Mobility to Returning to Core Values

During the 2015 presidential campaign, candidates Daniel Scioli and Mauricio Macri set out their potential government's positions on the middle class. Almost two months before the first round of elections, Scioli referred to the aforementioned World Bank report as proof of the success of the economic stimulation policies rolled out by the governments of Néstor Kirchner (2003–2007) and Cristina Fernández de Kirchner (2007–2015). Macri, meanwhile, cast doubt on this middle-class revival, predicting that a Scioli presidency would be disastrous. During an event in early September, he claimed that Argentina needed to return to being a middle-class country—an objective that required everyone to make progress, choose where to live, work, and study. Whereas Scioli alluded to a recovery of the middle class based on higher incomes (stimulating consumer spending on goods and services), Macri took a liberal stance by emphasizing individual aspirations for progress through free choice. Macri's message reflected the misgivings of a section of the population that chafed against the restrictions imposed on the purchase of dollars imposed in 2011 to prevent capital flight. During his presidential investiture speech on 10 December 2015, he made no specific references to the middle class; however, during a meeting with entrepreneurs in 2017, he mentioned that "… Argentina needs to strengthen its entrepreneurial spirit, just as our parents and grandparents decided to travel here when there was no internet or WhatsApp and they boarded ships without any idea what to expect when they disembarked." He added: "With that same spirit and those values that run in our blood, we're going to make progress…"[19] Macri was invoking an "entrepreneurial spirit" and "values" that ancestors had passed down biologically through the generations ("in our blood")—ancestors who had emigrated to Argentina from Europe in the early twentieth century. Macri counted himself among these immigrants of European descent: his father, Francesco Raúl Macri, was born in Rome in 1930. He arrived in Argentina when he was still only 18 years old and went on to become one of the nation's most powerful businessmen. Macri was referring to the middle-class origin narrative and as such considered himself to be carrying the virtues inherited from his father that guaranteed progress. As we will see, Macri's idea of progress stemmed from values inherited from immigrant forebears—an element missing from Scioli's version.

The aspiration to (re)build a middle-class country was nothing new. As president, Néstor Kirchner said during a radio interview in 2005 that "we need our middle class to be society's driving force again."[20] As a starting point, Kirchner could refer to the words of his predecessor, Eduardo Duhalde, whose inaugural address in the Legislative Assembly on January 1, 2002 referred to the demise of the middle class. In 2003, during a public event, Kirchner said:

> We must also give new impetus to the driving force behind Argentine society, re-enabling upward social mobility for the country's middle class. Remember when our parents and grandparents told us "my son's going to university, my son and grandchildren will have better opportunities than I had." I've seen how grandparents and parents have cried because their children are worse off than they were. We're turning things around, and I know that soon we'll be seeing our parents and grandparents smile again because their children are going to be doing better than them, we're going to recover our hope—that's what Argentinians want most.[21]

This speech was along the same lines as his inaugural address at the Legislative Assembly on May 25, 2003 when he stated the need for a middle class with better income distribution, as part of an overarching strategy to lift many Argentinians out of poverty by rebuilding "a national capitalism that creates alternatives for renewed upward social mobility." In the midst of a severe socio-economic crisis the recovery of the middle class implied better living conditions for large sectors of the population suffering poverty and unemployment, an aim based on images of Argentina's level of material comfort in the past that are so powerful that they transcend party lines.[22]

The "Mediocre" Genealogy of a "Selfish" Class

On becoming president on December 10, 2007, Néstor Kirchner's successor, his wife Cristina Fernández, also made it a priority "to improve the upward social mobility that has been the defining quality of this country, giving us a powerful middle class." Referring to her own life story as an example, she stated: "that gives the children of manual laborers the chance to become president. That is the country Argentinians have to rebuild…" She repeated this line some years later: "Look at this daughter of a bus driver who has been elected president twice."[23] The former president saw herself as a member of the middle class whose main characteristic was its constant progress. During her eight years in power, Cristina Fernández consistently identified with belonging to the "middle class," championing its importance for the country and the need to rekindle upward social mobility. She continued to give this same message in 2012, just over a year after beginning her second term in office and one week after a major opposition protest on November 8, described by the media as a "middle-class" movement; in a speech broadcast on national television, she repeated once again: "... I've always felt proud to be part of that formidably ambitious and entrepreneurial Argentinian middle class..." and that "I've understood that it's the result of the country's political project."[24] This latter comment introduced a new and distinctive message: politics versus individual aspirations.

Sometime before, she had questioned a middle class that "believes its achievements are purely the result of their own work, without realizing that in fact they're made possible by an economic model."[25] Cristina had framed the issue in this way after the unfavorable outcome of the so-called "farm crisis" when many sectors—described in the media as the "urban middle class"—supported the farmers. This conflict between March 11 and July 18, 2008 consisted of a lockout and roadblocks, and was coordinated by the country's four farming associations (Sociedad Rural Argentina, Confederaciones Rurales Argentinas, Confederación Intercooperativa Agropecuaria Limitada, and Federación Agraria Argentina), in response to Resolution 125, which proposed a return to a sliding-scale taxation system for soybean, wheat, and corn exports.

In this conflict—defined by many media outlets as a dispute between the government and the middle class[26]—Cristina Fernández shifted from the first to the third person when referring to the middle class. For example, she challenged the supposed middle-class support to the farming businesses during the 2008 conflict, suggesting that it was due to "cultural reasons," that meant it "sometimes ends up acting against its own best interests."[27] Sometime later, at a political rally in 2010, she said that the middle class "often fails to understand," since "it believes that it's better off standing apart from the dark-skinned *morochos*."[28] A few years on, when she announced on national television that she had submitted to Congress a bill for a moratorium on pensions, she said that the middle class "benefits the most, yet complains the most too."[29] In these three public statements, Cristina Fernández distanced herself from that middle-class country (in other words, one that promised upward social mobility) that had to be rebuilt: The middle class had assumed a specific role in the present, differentiating itself from the *morochos* (that is, people with dark complexions). Cristina Kirchner used this last category evoking another, typically derogatory: "cabecita negra", but she did so with the pretense of showing the implicit racism of the middle class. According to the then president, the middle class wanted to differentiate itself from the *morochos* for cultural reasons; that is why it was not aware of its interests. Nor did the middle class show empathy with the poorest sectors of society.

However, few of Cristina Fernández's statements were as bizarre as the one given in September 2012 at an event where she unveiled plans for a new social housing project on state-owned land—a development that had sparked protests from local residents. Defending the program, the president interpreted the situation as a struggle between the poor and the middle class who saw themselves as being different and rejected any contact with the former. Cristina Fernández thus invoked the stereotypical image of the immigrants who disembarked "dying of hunger from the ships," but instead of taking the same line as Macri, for example, by considering the values passed down by these immigrants to their descendants, she associated the "poor" with immigrants "dying of hunger." As such, she compared the future beneficiaries of the housing program to the ancestors of those who opposed their arrival in their neighborhood. And those origins gave the idea that their descendants were mediocre, contrary to their self-image:

> To hear some of them talk it's as though they were descendants of the Romanovs [a Russian dynastic family established in Moscow since the seventeenth century]. Here they wrinkle their nose, and I wonder, why are they being so snooty because, to be honest, they don't have much to be snooty about [...] Members of the middle or upper-middle classes need to understand that other people also have the right to become middle class and, why not, upper class too.

And they could even have ignominious family backgrounds: "Many patrician families come from smuggling backgrounds. I'm not here to judge anyone, but they started making their fortunes 200 years ago as smugglers."[30]

As we have seen, Cristina Fernández embraced her middle-class status yet also distanced herself from it, as if it was the Other to which she did not belong—the Other that was attributed certain qualities that it actually lacked, hence invalidating its insistent pretense at differentiation and superiority, both on account of their financial situation and their skin color. This challenge met with a swift response, as people rallied to defend their ancestors' honor.

Defending the Honor of Ancestors

In June 2012, as the conflicts between Cristina Fernández's government and some members of the opposition was escalating, writer Marcos Aguinis published an article in *La Nación* called "Elogio de la clase media" (In praise of the middle class),[31] that would later be included in a book.[32] Rising to the defense of the middle class, he pointed out:

> Stale prejudices continue to disparage the middle class. It is mentioned with a certain shame, because it lacks clearly defined limits and is linked to mean, cruel, and insensitive bourgeois and petit-bourgeois traits that fill the major works of universal literature [...] the time has come to extol [middle-class] virtues, especially those of the Argentinian

> middle class, who became the most important and productive in Latin America. In our country it developed exceptionally. Nowhere else was did it become as successful or acquire such importance so quickly, and over such a vast and largely barren territory.

This defense could be seen as a response to Cristina Fernández herself who, as we saw, drew attention to some of these undesirable traits associated with the middle class. Nevertheless, these negative qualities were connected to a stereotyped version that continued to resurface frequently; for example, sociologist Agustín Salvia, director of the Universidad Católica Argentina's social development research unit (Observatorio de la Deuda Social, ODS), whose reports on poverty had a strong impact on public opinion, declared in September 2017 (during Macri's government): "the prosperous middle class is very selfish. Its members are navel-gazers without any ideology beyond choosing how to vote in each election. They'll buy a pig in a poke."[33]

Let us now return to Aguinis. This writer divided his argument into what we could identify as sections. The first examined the role of European immigration in the origins and progress of the middle class:

> The Organización Nacional, a period that began in in 1853, sparked an influx of immigration that gathered strength until it became a veritable flood, to the extent of causing some people to fear it posed a threat to the foundations of the country's identity. The risk was not to national identity but the backwardness associated with reactionary colonial traditions. In the space of a few decades, most of the immigrants who arrived penniless had learned the language and become familiar with the customs to become fully and definitively integrated. They were the main protagonists of the phenomenon that swelled the ranks of this new, hard-to-define class that had once been far smaller. The new arrivals came with their pockets empty, exhausted by hunger and persecutions. They wanted to work hard to improve their lives. They came to a country that had a new, inclusive Constitution that gave people hope. The rural and urban populations grew, with a better demographic structure. The country's positive developments shook the foundations of the old structures. Argentina was growing at a dizzying speed and was becoming a global success story.

Aguinis centered his argument around the idea of a fundamental opposition between the "new," represented by immigration that ushered in a period of modernization, against the "old" (unspecified, but implicitly referring to representatives of the sectors of the Argentinian population that existed before mass immigration), that denoted backwardness. The stereotype of poverty-stricken immigrants arriving in Argentina is at variance with wealth (as progress). This is a dynamic contrast, because it is in fact a shift from one state to the other, and this transition requires work—which serves a dual function: as a type of activity and as a value that makes this activity possible.

At this juncture, Aguinis introduces what we might call his second section: the intrinsic values of immigration that enabled the emergence of the middle class:

> Values were sown like seeds both in the countryside and in the cities. These values supported three cultures: the culture of work, the culture of striving, and the culture of honesty. There was a consensus that nothing came for free, and that rights came with obligations. It was possible to prosper, but only by dint of hard and honest work. Such was the disapproval of dishonest behavior that families would be appalled if one of their members committed a crime. Their new country was not a land of milk and honey, because exceptions were everywhere. But the three aforesaid cultures predominated. Thanks to the mood of optimism, both in the home and on the street, progress was within grasp [...] It was common for people to aspire to lead dignified lives, form solid families, educate children, enjoy culture, and get ahead. People did not seek enormous wealth but to achieve the undeniable (and wonderful) objectives of a respectable life, a solid family, a good education for children, and reasonable progress. I repeat these aspirations because they are the ones we need to recover.

This leads to the third section, the issue of individual competence as a value, which rewarded hard work and punished laziness:

> During that predominantly middle-class period, merit and tenacity were virtues. It was inconceivable to drag down those who had climbed up as a means of consoling those at the bottom, because that implied pulling everyone down to the lowest level and removing incentives (the terrible policy of later times). Competitiveness was not something to be feared or mistrusted, but a motivation for people to make an effort and improve the end result for everyone. This was the opposite approach to what came later.

In this section Aguinis updated the narrative, wading into public debates about meritocracy and, in particular, about the criticisms launched by liberal sectors against what they identified as populism, which they saw as the top of the slippery slope toward the nation's decline. For example, he argued that small and medium-sized companies do not

> ... live off hand-outs or subsidies [but] groan under the burden of extortionate taxation. The money extracted from them is not invested in infrastructure projects or a more efficient state, but maintains an

> elephantine bureaucratic apparatus that is voracious, myopic, irrational, and whimsical, frittering away money on red tape, friends, gnocchi, and political opinion leaders.

In this way, the three cultures that had paved the way for progress "began to be dismantled during the first half of the twentieth century" and were replaced by mendacity, expediency, and corruption, respectively, in the name of "utopian egalitarianism." The poor became "victims of a perverse system that promised to defend them while actually alienating and using them," through social welfare programs. This encapsulated the "...awful populism that is poisoning us [...] as you need hordes of poor people to bribe them and rob them of their vote." In the case of "those vast numbers of Argentinians who cannot see the horizon [have been] convinced that 'they have the right' to subsidies without there being any reciprocal obligations [...] of work, effort, and honesty." As a corollary, Aguinis proposed that instead of disparaging the middle class, "projects should be rolled out to help convert those suffering from poverty and misery into the middle class, in the place they strive to integrate." Therefore, it was "time to revive the pride of belonging to the middle class that made Argentina great."

Aguinis supported Macri and was staunchly anti-Peronist. He defined himself as a liberal and a republican, and fiercely criticized the governments of Néstor Kirchner and Cristina Fernández. He also referred to a middle-class origin narrative, decrying this as a period of decline in Argentinian history,[34] sharing the neoliberal view of the paternalistic state oppressing the individual.

Over the following years, it was common to find reactions to Cristina Fernández. For example we have the case of the reader of *Clarín*, Juan José Quinteros, who wrote in a letter introducing himself as "a middle-class citizen who took a break from his work to defend the honor of my grandparents, those who disembarked from their ship 'dying of hunger,' in order to build the nation that we are now losing." According to Quinteros, the president had sullied the memory of the country's European immigrant ancestors, denigrating "our grandparents," offending "those honest men" by describing them as "dying of hunger," instead of paying them tribute. Similarly to Aguinis, Quinteros contrasted the European ancestors and their descendants with the thousands of poor whom (he considered) received state benefits in exchange for their votes. This was how he narrated the origins:

> One day, while still a very young man over in Europe, the grandfather looked toward the horizon and thought that perhaps there was another way. His hands, soft and strong, were empty. And then one day the grandfather left Spain on a ship. Or perhaps, on a different day, like so many others, he left Italy, filled with hope. He carried the image of his old village and surrounding mountains close to his heart, when the old

> ship took him away from Spain, or from Italy. Those who were "dying of hunger" [...] were the ones who gave our country its prosperity, turning it into the world's sixth-largest economy [...] they created a prosperous Argentina, a country of peaceful hard work. Through their commitment to hard work, these same people who were "dying of hunger", *Señora* [Fernández], were the first ones ever to plough the land in most of the Argentinian territory to make it "the breadbasket of the world". They were the ones who went to work carrying a piece of bread, two onions, a half-liter of wine, in order to save up enough to bring over their wife and children to share this blessed land. They loved this land in a way that you cannot even begin to imagine; they not only sowed wheat but produced many children and grandchildren, those of us who *today are the Argentinian middle class*: those children and grandchildren learned that men's dignity begins with work, because it means obeying the Bible's message that "by the sweat of your brow you will have food to eat.[35]

Some years later, during the fourth year of Macri's presidency, Alejandro Poli Gonzalvo, an accountant and member of the Club Político Argentino—a space for intellectual meetings and discussions, founded in 2008 in the midst of the farm crisis as a group critical of Kirchnerism and closely allied to the Cambiemos government—published another article in *La Nación* (February 5, 2019) describing most of the narratives given by Aguinis and Quinteros. Firstly, the immigrants' origins:

> Our parents and grandparents came from the backwaters of the world. They only had the scantest information about this far-off land at the southern tip of the Americas, or else some relative forced to emigrate due to poverty or to pursue the dream of a different future encouraged them to make the journey.

As in the previous iterations, this kind of immigration brought hard work and sacrifice, on the one hand, as well as an acknowledgement of the importance of education, to transform the old Argentina (represented as a barren desert) into the modern-day version, described in the well-worn terms: "All of them, with sweat on their brows and through hard work, created the modern Argentina, where the desert became breadbasket of the world and education reigned supreme." Those immigrants

> [were] often cheated ... [but] always worked and continued inculcating in their children the values of their parents and grandparents. It did not matter whether their families were in the fourth or fifth generation of Argentinians or recently arrived from abroad. The values of personal effort and the love of a shared *patria* united them.

But now they must

> suffer the consequences of decades of populist governments. Therefore, we are paying tribute [to the descendants of those immigrants, the middle class] at this time when they are again under attack, a serious test as they carry the weight on their emaciated shoulders of an economy derailed by decades of populism.

The difference in Gonzalvo's version is how he identified the middle class with the values of freedom and democracy: "it stood up to dictatorships and populist governments and paved the way for Alfonsín's victory (in 1983) and the return of democracy." On the aim to continue Kirchnerism in 2015, he wrote: "the same middle class is and will continue to be a thorn in the side of any hegemonic plot to threaten liberty and democracy."[36]

As we can see, the praise of European immigrant origins was coupled with intimately associated values genealogically passed down from one generation to the next. The idea of being a middle-class country "again" went beyond the simple recovery of upward social mobility: such a return was primarily a moral issue. This country's restoration was no more and no less than the complete reinstatement of those values that made Argentina great (hard work, honesty, and a desire for progress), values brought over from Europe by ancestors and passed down through the subsequent generations. In connection to the idea of the present as a period of national decline, this exemplary narrative questioned the political and moral stance of the Kirchner governments characterized as populist. The only way to revert the decline was therefore to return to that middle-class country of yesteryear, a nation created by ancestors.

Epilogue: A Genealogy for the Moral Rebirth of the Nation

Above I described the perception of Argentina's period of "crisis" as a series of continual failures in the country. A common view was that Argentina suffered from a type of malign, age-old influence, and that unless this idea is quashed once and for all, it will always be lurking in the background. One of these arguments was the narrative of decline, which painted the picture of a prosperous past interrupted at some point, never to be revived. Whether the times were seen as bountiful or decadent clearly depended on individual perspectives of national history. This narrative opened up exciting potential, which could be imagined morally as the restoration of a past that promised a brighter future: it enabled the formulation of genealogical relationships between events, figures, and ideas of the past and present, distinguishing between "virtuous" and "malignant" relations, between those that were morally acceptable and unacceptable.[37] The middle-class origin narrative carried out this role perfectly: it was a perfect fit for the public discourse and widely shared as a means of making sense of progress and it helped crystallize an image of the country's future horizons. However, contradictory versions of this same, widely shared narrative postulated a country in which upward social mobility was plausible, and these expressed contrasting perspectives on the nation's woes and, therefore, very different political projects.

The governments that faced the crisis in the early twenty-first century referred to the poverty afflicting more than half of the Argentinian population as something immoral. Restoring upward social mobility through a proactive state was seen as the means of improving life for these citizens, giving them access to what the public discourse defined as the "middle class." At that time, the broad consensus held the previous decade's neoliberal policies responsible for the crisis, hence the need to close the circle and start again.[38] But after the conflict with the farming sector in 2008, a mounting opposition found in the middle-class origin narrative a means of interpreting the present as part of a long period of decline. The response to the increases in customs tariffs in 2008[39] and, subsequently, restrictions imposed on the purchase of foreign currencies,[40] was an over-estimation of the genealogical virtues brought over by European ancestors and passed down through the generations. Any progress achieved without individual hard work aroused suspicion. But with a virtuous genealogy, this version excluded those unable to invoke or demonstrate such ethno-national origins.[41] Aguinis wrote that a perverse exchange of welfare programs for votes manipulated sectors that depended on state aid for their survival.[42] From this perspective, the moral imperative was not to drag down those higher up, but to lift up those lower down on the social ladder. The repeated description of poverty-stricken ancestors appears analogous to the current hardships faced by sectors dependent on state support: it would imply that today's poor could make progress—as these ancestors once did—if instead of waiting for the state to help them they had the desire or ambition to seek a better life. However, in this narrative the values enabling such progress possible are passed down genealogically, hence the difficulty in applying this approach more universally.

Former president Cristina Fernández also waded into the moral argument (how else could you describe her referral to "middle-class selfishness"?). This led to people's moral response to the offence caused to their forebears. Defending ancestors' honor was akin to defending their values that people believed were under threat or disappearing. This worship or devotion of essentialized, transcendental ancestors[43] who influence the present continued to underpin an idea of community based on a European origin and, therefore, a shared kinship.[44] This is what prompted Cristina Fernández to challenge this ancestor worship by stripping these people of their transcendental qualities and, consequently, their virtues. There was nothing special about their genealogy: if progress was not about the individual, if membership of the middle class did not depend on kinship, then anyone could be middle class if national policies made it possible.

Invoking the middle class updated an overarching moral narrative about the future of the Argentine population. In its various versions we can see how a society like Argentina's has a dramatic and conflicting view of its past, its future, and the pathways to upward social mobility. Many of the events and political disputes described in this article could certainly be subject to a more conventional political analysis. The public debate that began about the version that defines the origin of the middle class as deriving from immigration had plenty of overlap with neoliberal criticism of what its proponents described as "populism." This was not a debate exclusive to Argentina; since the second decade of the twenty-first century, several Latin American countries have seen major shifts in political direction compared to the previous decade. Neoliberal governments aligned with the United States were coming into power after free elections, as in the case of Sebastián Piñera in Chile (2010) or Macri (2015). Another instance was the election of Jair Messias Bolsonaro as Brazil's president (2019), after serious institutional crises triggered by the ousting of former president Dilma Rousseff from office in 2016 (who had succeed Luiz Inácio Lula da Silva, arrested at the start of that same year). Other changes came after coup d'états with the active involvement of the military, as in the case of Juan Evo Morales Ayma's resignation as president of Bolivia in November 2019.

The staunch defense of the middle class since 2008 in Argentina, centered mainly around the importance of individual freedom, is explainable by a situation that went beyond Argentina's borders. However, as I have tried to show, even when the circulation and presence of these ideas is clear to see, they evolved from versions of a pre-existing standard narrative. These versions constituted entrenched views of the nation that gave a historical dimension to political debates, framing them in a specifically localized manner. This does not necessarily mean addressing these issues in isolation from their broader context, but it does shed light on the particular experience of these processes.[45]

Notes

1 Fernando J. Devoto, *Historia de la inmigración en Argentina* (Buenos Aires: Sudamericana, 2003).
2 David Rock, *Argentina 1516–1987: From Spanish Colonization to Alfonsín* (Berkeley: University of California Press, 1987).
3 Ezequiel Adamovsky, *Historia de la clase media argentina: Apogeo y decadencia de una ilusión* (Buenos Aires: Planeta, 2009), 45.
4 Micaela Pérez, "Tenemos que volver a ser un país de clase media: Creo que la sociedad está pidiendo eso," *El Cronista*, May 20, 2016.
5 Ezequiel Adamovsky, "El color de la nación argentina: Conflictos y negociaciones por la definición de un ethnos nacional, de la crisis al Bicentenario," *Jahrbuch für Geschichte Lateinamerikas* 49, no. 1 (2012): 184.
6 Joseph Galen, "Taking Race Seriously: Whiteness in Argentina's National and Transnational Imaginary," *Identities* 7, no. 3 (2000): 333–371; Emanuela

Guano, "A Color for the Modern Nation: The Discourse on Class, Race and Education in the Porteño Middle Class," *The Journal of Latin American Anthropology* 8, no. 1 (2003): 148–171.

7 Flavia Fiorucci, "Fascinated by Failure: The 'Bestseller' Explanations of the Crisis," in *The Argentine Crisis at the Turn of the Millennium: Causes, Consequences, and Explanations*, eds. Flavia Fiorucci and Marcus Kein (Amsterdam: CEDLA, 2004).

8 Philip Nicholas Furbank, *Unholy Pleasure: The Idea of Social Class* (Oxford: Oxford University Press, 1985).

9 Jerome Bruner, "Life as Narrative," *Social Research* 71, no. 3 (2004): 691–710; Jerome Bruner, "The Narrative Construction of Reality," *Critical Inquiry* 18, no. 1 (1991): 1–21.

10 Dan Sperber, *El simbolismo en general* (Barcelona: Anthropos, 1988).

11 Claudio Lozano, "Contexto económico y político en la protesta social de la Argentina contemporánea," *OSAL-Observatorio Social de América Latina*, no. 5 (2001): 5–10.

12 Gabriel Kessler and María Mercedes Di Virgilio, "La nueva pobreza urbana: Dinámica global, regional y argentina en las últimas dos décadas," *Revista de la CEPAL*, no. 95 (2008): 31–50.

13 Instituto Nacional de Estadísticas y Censos (INDEC), "Encuesta Permanente de Hogares, mayo," 2002.

14 *Página 12*, October 26, 2004.

15 Walter Sosa-Escudero and Sergio Petralia, "'I Can Hear the Grass Grow': The Anatomy of Distributive Changes in Argentina," *CEDLAS, Working Papers* (2010).

16 Kessler and Di Virgilio, "La nueva pobreza urbana"; Daniel Lvovich, "Colgados de la soga: La experiencia del tránsito desde la clase media a la nueva pobreza en la ciudad de Buenos Aires," in *Desde abajo: La transformación de las identidades sociales*, ed. Maristella Svampa (Buenos Aires: Biblos, 2000); Alberto Minujin, "Estrujados: La clase media en América Latina," in *Pobreza: Un tema impostergable*, ed. Bernardo Kliksberg (Mexico City: Fondo de Cultura Económica, 1997); Alberto Minujin and Gabriel Kessler, *La nueva pobreza en la Argentina* (Buenos Aires: Planeta, 1995); Alberto Minujin and Eduardo Anguita, *La clase media: Seducida y abandonada* (Buenos Aires: Edhasa, 2004).

17 Sosa-Escudero and Petralia, "I Can Hear."

18 Banco Mundial, "Argentina duplicó su clase media en la última década, dice informe del Banco Mundial," press release November 13, 2012; Francisco H. G. Ferreira et al., *La movilidad económica y el crecimiento de la clase media en América Latina* (Washington: Banco Internacional de Reconstrucción y Fomento; Banco Mundial, 2013).

19 "Macri, con emprendedores: 'No renuncien a sus sueños y sigan apostando por el país,'" Casa Rosada: Presidencia, November 30, 2017, https://www.casarosada.gob.ar/slider-principal/41371-macri-con-emprendedores-no-renuncien-a-sus-suenos-y-sigan-apostando-por-el-pais.

20 Infobae.com, May 24, 2005; *La Nación*, May 25, 2005.

21 "Palabras del Presidente de la Nación, Néstor Kirchner, en el Club Platense, en Vicente López," Casa Rosada: Presidencia, October 4, 2005, https://www.casarosada.gob.ar/informacion/archivo/24827-blank-21158391.

22 On December 12, 2010, when Macri's future ally, Elisa Carrió, announced her candidacy for the October 2011 presidential elections representing the Coalición Cívica-Afirmación para una República Igualitaria (CC-ARI) in the city of Buenos Aires, she pledged to build a nation in which the children and grandchildren of the poor could aspire to become part of the middle class; she

repeated this line at every campaign event, during various media interviews, and in her book, *El futuro es hoy*, launched at the end of April 2011. Her version here is similar to that of Kirchner and Scioli, candidate in 2015 and, therefore, contrasts to Macri's one.

23 *Ámbito Financiero*, September 20, 2012.

24 *La Nación*, November 15, 2012.

25 *Ámbito Financiero*, July 25, 2008.

26 *Clarín*, August 31, 2014; José Natanson, "Una política para la nueva clase media," *Le Monde Diplomatique*, 2012.

27 *La Política Online*, June 18, 2008.

28 *Diario Popular*, September 15, 2010. Cristina Kirchner's use of the word *morocho* implied racism among the middle classes.

29 *Infonews*, June 5, 2014.

30 *La Nación*, September 21, 2012.

31 *La Nación*, June 22, 2012.

32 Marcos Aguinis, *Incendio de ideas: Lo que el siglo XXI tiene para aprender del siglo XX* (Buenos Aires: Sudamericana, 2017).

33 Catalina de Elía, "Agustín Salvia: 'La clase media argentina es egoísta, no tiene ideología y compra espejitos de colores,'" *Infobae*, September 14, 2017.

34 Sergio E. Visacovsky, "Intérpretes públicos, teodiceas de la nación y la creación del futuro en la crisis de inicios del siglo XXI en Argentina," in *La ilusión de la justicia transicional: Perspectivas críticas desde el Sur global*, ed. Alejandro Castillejo-Cuéllar, (Bogotá: Universidad de los Andes, 2017); Sergio E. Visacovsky, "The Days Argentina Stood Still: History, Nation and Imaginable Futures in the Public Interpretations of the Argentine Crisis at the Beginning of the Twenty-First Century," *Horizontes Antropológicos* 24, no. 52 (2018): 311–341.

35 *Clarín*, "Ellos hicieron rica nuestra patria," September 29, 2013.

36 Gonzalvo also stated that a part of the middle class had become Peronists in the mid-1940s; he acknowledged the existence of the criollo descendants of the Spaniards who had come to the Americas in the sixteenth century, who lived in an "empty land" that they called "the desert," connected with "native peoples," who fought for independence and produced the 1853 National Constitution. This recognition of a period prior to the massive influx of immigrants led him to conclude that the combination of this earlier phase in the country's history with the more recent immigration is what created "Argentina's unique demographic profile," evocative of the idea of the melting pot.

37 Visacovsky, "The Days Argentina Stood Still," 316.

38 Edward Epstein and David Pion-Berlin, ed. *Broken Promises? The Argentine Crisis and Argentine Democracy* (Lanham: Lexington Books, 2006); Aldo Ferrer, "Los mitos neoliberales versus la capacidad económica estatal," *Clarín*, December 11, 2001; Pedro Pírez, "¿Qué pasó en la Argentina? Algunas piezas de un rompecabezas para intentar entender." *Estudios sociológicos* 20, no. 2 (2002): 455–467; Mario Rapoport, ed., *Crónicas de la Argentina sobreviviente: el presente en el espejo de la historia* (Buenos Aires: Norma, 2004); Miguel Teubal, "Rise and Collapse of Neoliberalism in Argentina: The Role of Economic Groups," *Journal of Developing Societies* 20, no. 3–4 (2004): 173–188.

39 Osvaldo Barsky, Osvaldo and Mabel Dávila, *La rebelión del campo: Historia del conflicto agrario argentino* (Buenos Aires: Sudamericana, 2012).

40 Mariana Luzzi and Ariel Wilkis, "Soybean, Bricks, Dollars, and the Reality of Money: Multiple Monies During Currency Exchange Restrictions in Argentina (2011–2015)," *HAU: Journal of Ethnographic Theory* 8, no. 1–2 (2018): 252–264.

41 Enrique Garguin, "'Los argentinos descendemos de los barcos': The Racial Articulation of Middle Class Identity in Argentina (1920–1960)," *Latin American and Caribbean Ethnic Studies* 2, no. 2 (2007): 161–184.
42 Julieta Quirós, *El porqué de los que van: Peronistas y piqueteros en el Gran Buenos Aires; Una antropología de la política vivida* (Buenos Aires: Antropofagia, 2011).
43 Maurice Bloch, "Why Religion Is Nothing Special but Is Central," *Philosophical Transactions of the Royal Society B: Biological Sciences* 363, no. 1499 (2008): 2055–2061.
44 Katherine Verdery, *The Political Lives of Dead Bodies* (New York: Columbia University, 1999), 41–42.
45 Marshall Sahlins, *Islands of History* (Chicago and London: The University of Chicago Press, 1985); Michel-Rolph Trouillot, *Silencing the Past: Power and Production of History* (Boston: Beacon Press, 1995).

18 Middle-Class Sensorial

Conceptualizing the Experience of Inhabiting "the Middle" in Brazil's Post-Neoliberal Public Housing

Moisés Kopper

> Here we are all *Classe* C! Where I lived before there was no class. People were expendable. Now they are proud users of cards and buy in stores. Even their skin looks better; they are smiling more often. All this affects your mind: you start to *develop* a class.[1]

Introduction

It always baffled me that a country so widely known for its endemic inequality is also a country mostly averse to the idea of overt class conflict. For over a century, Brazil's national identity was celebrated as one of cultural miscegenation[2] and "racial democracy,"[3] a utopia of conciliation in which the poor try to become more like the rich while navigating informal (and asymmetrical) networks of reciprocity[4]. Having worked among first-time homeowners for years, I had never heard any of my interlocutors speak of their socio-economic predicaments in a prospective class language. While—at times deprecative—references to "we, the poor," and "the people" were regularly invoked to describe experiences of institutional exclusion and subjective stagnation, the notion that by overcoming socio-material obstacles one would become upwardly mobile remained largely unarticulated for the bottom half of Brazil's society throughout the twentieth century.

Seu Juliano's words in the epigraph of this chapter seem to defy this reality. He voiced them more or less spontaneously over an informal conversation that took place in the living room of his new apartment. In September 2014, Seu Juliano, along with other 160 families, moved to a model housing project constructed in the outskirts of Porto Alegre, the capital of Brazil's southernmost state of Rio Grande do Sul. Before that, Seu Juliano had been a member of a grassroots organization, mobilizing for years to earn the right to become a beneficiary of public housing under *Minha Casa Minha Vida*, Brazil's nationwide program launched in 2009.[5]

Seu Juliano's commentary about the ubiquity of "Classe C" is evocative of a time in Brazil's recent political-economic history when the country figured among the fastest-growing economies in the developing world.

DOI: 10.4324/9781003029311-23

Between 2003 and 2014, a range of successfully implemented social and economic policies—including monetary stability, controlled inflation, low unemployment, credit expansion, minimum wage increases, and conditional cash transfers—redistributed wealth and reduced the Gini coefficient—the world's most accepted measure for inequality—to levels only seen during the "Economic Miracle" of the 1970s, when Brazil also grew significantly, albeit without generating income redistribution. The socioeconomic transformations of this period were ferociously debated, in Brazil and the world,[6,7,8] among public intellectuals, policymakers, journalists, politicians, and marketers.

Far-flung theories to explain and label this heterogeneous populace rapidly surfaced in public debates. In 2008, for example, world-class economist Marcelo Neri[9] performed a series of statistical and income-based calculations that would lead to his famous intervention that Brazil had finally become a "middle-class country"—a shimmering catchphrase embraced by Dilma Rousseff's cabinet to proclaim the end of endemic poverty as swiftly as Neri himself was made a leading intellectual figure within the federal government.[10] Dozens of millions of individuals like Seu Juliano—previously warded off from markets and government programs—found a way to not only profit from the consumer-targeting policies from the Workers' Party's era (2003–2016), but they also benefitted from public debates that hailed the emergence of a "new middle class," Neri's renowned "Classe C."

In this chapter, I reflect on what it means for first-time homeowners and housing activists to subscribe to ideas of the middle class in the context of a growing and "post-neoliberal" economy.[11] I draw on ethnographic and survey research conducted between 2012 and 2017 among community leaders, beneficiaries, policymakers, public planners, architects, and representatives of the state and the market. Throughout this period, I followed the practices and exchanges that made possible the local implementation of a large-scale housing program, and the moral and subjective travails set forth by people like Seu Juliano to actualize a model community and set themselves apart from the failed housing initiatives of the past. Although this project was not initially framed as an ethnography of the middle class, I increasingly came to perceive and piece together a larger social map of the trajectories of social and economic mobility of Brazil's once-rising poor. What is more, the lived experiences of upward mobility seemed to foreground structures of belonging fundamentally distinct from the conventional understandings of class as fixed positionalities based exclusively on income or occupation.

In what follows, I first discuss the insufficiency of Marxian and Weberian theories of class alone to grasp processes of stratification and transformation in Latin America and recent Brazil in particular. Together with the social and material aspects that shape class belonging, we must also consider the affective, sensorial, and infrastructural dimensions whereby class positionalities are apprehended and projected onto time and space. I refer to the social maps that result from the active experimentation with tropes of past and future being, and the socio-material ensembles that ensue, by the term "middle-class sensorial." The second part explores three brief empirical cases that highlight different dimensions of the middle-class sensorial in practice: the capacity to spatialize social difference; the ability to temporalize personal transformation; and the role of infrastructure in drawing the contours of the middle-class sensorial. In conclusion, I summarize the main arguments and propose a research agenda, offering methodological insights on the implications of considering the middle class a dynamic collection of affects and materialities for the study of Latin America's recent sociopolitical transformations.

From Classic Sociology to the Sensorial and Affective Dimensions of Class

The concept of social class is foundational of classic sociology. Both Karl Marx and Max Weber devised theories about the emergence and workings of capitalism that deeply hinged on ideas about the theoretical status, social composition, and structural position of different social strata in so-called advanced societies. The question and location of the middle class, in particular, is one of the "more persistent and more strongly colored by both ideological commitments and political context"[12] problems of twenty-century social theory. In Latin America, middle classes were long thought to be an impossibility given the region's political instability and economic cycles of boom and bust, not to mention the epistemological discrepancies between class theories developed in the Global North and the diverse realities of Developing Societies. This section presents a brief overview of such debates, arguing that recent ethnographies of class are a welcome, if yet timid, effort at bridging the theoretical and empirical impasses left open by classic sociological theory.

In Marx's binary analytics of class structure, based on the opposition between owners of the means of production (the bourgeoisie) and sellers of labor power (the proletariat), all intermediate groups are expected to morph into a growing, and increasingly homogeneous, working class.[13,14] However, at the turn of the nineteenth century the exponential growth of white-collar occupations in the Weimar regime gave way to the "revisionist debate." Sociologists like Gustav Schmoller[15] and Eduard Bernstein[16] emphasized the distinctive social status and political ideology of white collars, which substantiated the claim of a "new middle class"[17]. Similarly, Erik Olin Wright's theory[18] of contradictory class locations, which emphasized secondary forms of exploitation—including control over organizational assets and upon ownership of monopolized skills—introduced less antagonistic Marxist approaches to class structure.

The Weberian treatment of class presumed the interaction of a variety of positional and multidimensional variables, such as property, occupation, authority, education, and prestige. This led to more nuanced pictures of the middle class that move beyond considerations of production, income, and ownership. White-collar educational and technical qualifications were understood to yield effects of authority and status that can reinforce or subvert cleavages between the middle and working classes.[19] Weberian theories thus saw intermediate groups—defined by the interaction of both economic and noneconomic structures—as heterogeneous and fragmented, requiring more nuanced sociological descriptions of their boundaries.

While Marxist and Weberian theories of class have been synthesized in a number of ways, the French school of thought has been particularly influential in the critical reading of the sociological classics. In the 1970s, Pierre Bourdieu and Luc Boltanski led research agendas that dislodged concerns with social structure as an already given and preconstituted entity. Instead, Bourdieu's theory of practice introduced a symbiotic mediation between structure and action. The "social space" resulting from this dialectics is at once a structured constellation of positions and a dynamic field of struggles over the legitimacy of determining the very criteria for group formation, what Bourdieu calls "classification struggles"—"indeed a forgotten dimension of the class struggle."[20]

As Wacquant[21] aptly notes, this requires a theory of the middle class that is attentive to "both responses to preexisting sociopolitical perceptions of these groups and attempts to influence these perceptions." Conversely, in his study of the social formation of a French group between 1934 and 1945, Boltanski[22] argues that the appearance and public recognition of the cadres reflected the social conflicts and identity contradictions of a society that was projecting a new social order. Overall, these empirically situated studies underscore the fact that "the middle class, like any other social group, does not exist ready-made in reality. It must be constituted through material and symbolic struggles waged simultaneously over class and between classes; it is a historically variable and reversible effect of these struggles."[23]

Class formation and boundary-drawing have stood at the center of ethnographic accounts of the middle class. Anthropologists interested in socio-economic dynamics followed Karl Polanyi's vision[24] of the embeddedness of all economic activity and the substantivist argument that the principles of economics cannot be applied to understanding economic integration in noncapitalist societies.[25] Anthropologists exploring class dynamics and globally connected patterns of capitalist transformation in economies of the Global South have taken seriously the challenge of capturing "class (...) as, in fact, it eventuates."[26] Recent ethnographies portray these ambivalent sectors in all their contradictions as producers and consumers of goods and services, attending to the structural forces and subjective perceptions of what it means to occupy the intermediate strata.[27,28,29]

In the introduction to the volume *Global Middle Classes*, Heiman, Freeman, and Liechty[30] inscribe the anthropology of the middle classes into a broader tradition of globalization studies and, within that framework, of the appearance and expansion of neoliberal political regimes. They consider middle-class groups the driving forces, the target populations, and the empirical outcomes of globally interlocked practices, programs, and identities that seek to produce, capture, or reinforce middle-classness. In this view, middle classes are also tools of neoliberal governance: technologies of governing that travel and reshape localities, spatialize difference, and remake political consciousness. While acknowledging class as a lived and situated experience, a "social process over time," the authors also pay attention to the broader historical and socio-economic conditions of possibility that allow for the conceptualization of the middle class as a coherent category of social analysis without falling into a historical teleology that takes Europe as the epicenter. In this sense, Mark Liechty[31,32] thinks of socio-spatial interrelatedness and scalar (rather than categorical or epochal) differences to locate the interjacency of middle classes in the social structure. The challenge, he suggests, consists in finding empirical connectors that bring local, regional, and global dynamics into productive theoretical conversations—without giving up the empirical diversity and singularity of emic discourses, sentiments, and practices through which actors themselves define the "experience of being in the middle."

Extolled as signals of modern, democratic, and less unequal societies, middle classes were only seldom conceptualized in Latin American scholarship.[33] Too long, the region's cultural distinctiveness and chronic political instability were said to have thwarted "middle-class hopes for stability and improvement."[34] However, in countries such as Argentina and Chile, middle classes have been constitutive of identity politics and technologies of nation-making.[35,36,37] Conversely, Brazil forwent broader debates about stratification—particularly the middle class—throughout much of the twentieth century,[38] until recently, when the prospects of envisioning middle-class futures drove experts, politicians, and marketers to hail the dream of a middle-class country. In short, recent empirical research has painted a much more intricate, layered, and diverse picture, showing that the promises and protractions of the middle class have long been structural to Latin America's politics.[39]

In what follows, I will outline an alternative mode of thinking about the ever-elusive social experience of "being in the middle." I draw on sociological and anthropological insights to conceptualize the specificity of this space at once as the reflection of particular conditions of possibility, forms of biopolitical and market intervention, and intersubjective categories of apprehension. Middle-class quarrels often stem from exclusionary concepts that see it either as an intrinsic, objective reality; or as an external, conceptual apparatus; or as a lived experience. To adequately apprehend the uses, practices, and experiences associated with Brazil's "Classe C" over the last decade, we must consider these three intersecting dimensions of class—as reality, language, and experience—through the workings of a *middle-class sensorial*. By middle-class sensorial, I refer to the assemblages of images, words, and material affects through which class mobility is experienced and located in time and space. While sensorial qualities and affective modes of belonging have recently entered experimental definitions of the middle class,[40] ethnographic theories about the multi-scalar articulations of infrastructure and political economy, and of socio-historical forces and situated dynamics of inclusion and distinction, are still lacking in conceptual definition.

"Developing a Class"

This section presents three brief ethnographic cases that foreground different dimensions of the middle-class sensorial: its interactions with space-making; its ability to work as a time machine; and its intrinsic articulation to socio-material affects.

Spatial Sensorial

Seu Juliano is a retired electrician in his sixties and one of the leaders of the housing association I accompanied during fieldwork between 2012 and 2017. He became famous after moving to the construction site in 2013 and residing in a container for months before the condominium was ready for habitation. Living amid debris, he put together a makeshift office and attended to the association's members as they called or visited for updates on the construction.

In January 2015, I visited Seu Juliano in his new apartment. Anyone familiar with his crumbling living conditions in the container would have been hard-pressed to recognize the elegantly dressed man standing before me. A comfortable environment, crowded with technological objects, emerged in place of sand and debris. Seu Juliano even brought along the stray dog that kept him company while he lived by himself at the construction site. The animal was now groomed, leashed, and elevated to the condition of a "pet" by his owner.

Throughout our encounters, Seu Juliano reported on the new composition of forces within the condominium. Circulating between common areas, giving people advice on how to become a "*proprietário*," and on how to adhere to condominium bylaws, Seu Juliano envisaged new everyday responsibilities for himself as the respectable owner of a condo. In January 2015, Seu Juliano confided that "where I lived before, there was no class. Here, we are all 'Classe C.' People came from the bare bottom. There was no house; there was nothing. This is a game-changer."

Over time, Seu Juliano developed a critical stance of the condominium's problems and expressed them in a language of informed consumerism. Such as when he overheard gatekeepers call the project "Carandiru"—the name of Latin America's once-largest prison.

Dissatisfied with their job, Seu Juliano confronted the security company's manager, who undermined the episode as a misunderstanding. "No!"—Seu Juliano bellowed—"it was not. It got to everybody's ears. We are *consumers* of your services. We are paying you, and you give us defamation in return. Did you know we have the right to go to Procon?!"[41]

It was reflecting about such a context that Seu Juliano told me, almost a year and a half later, that

> before, people were expendable. Now we have a voice as informed consumers of services. They are proud to use their cards and buy in stores. Even their skin looks better; they are smiling more often. All this affects your mind: you start to develop a class.

Up to that point, the question of class belonging had not yet surfaced in informal conversations with research interlocutors. By directly talking about it, Seu Juliano was dovetailing on prevalent narratives of the emergence of a "new middle class," whose circulation in mainstream media crested around 2014.[42,43,44] The idea that economic stability, systematic wage increases, easier access to credit and consumer markets, and conditional cash transfer programs had pulled some 40 million out of poverty became the flagship argument in the Workers' Party's campaign to reelect Dilma Rousseff. Market research institutes and corporate media also helped disseminate identity narratives that engaged middle-class tastes, expectations, and consumers through commercial campaigns, soap operas, and live audience shows targeting women, youngsters, and black populations—who were pinpointed as key beneficiaries of the middle-class expansion.[45,46]

Crucially, then, Seu Juliano was mobilizing a multi-scalar set of discourses and practices of intervention that helped him recast his class identity to meet the subjective experience of belonging to the middle of Brazil's shifting social stratification. The sensorial and affective dimensions of this process eventuated as Seu Juliano moved across urban space—"from the hills to the asphalt"—and developed new ways of navigating and experiencing the city. The urban map, anthropologist Gilberto Velho[47] notes, is best understood as a "social map in which people are defined by their place of residence," to the point that they "change social class when moving from one neighborhood to another."

Survey data collected both in 2015 and in 2017 among 160 households of a public housing project in Porto Alegre helps situate Seu Juliano's everyday experiences of stratification, distinction, and inclusion within a broader locational and affective middle-class language. After covering questions to gauge life and financial improvements over the last ten years, respondents were asked to position themselves within a wide array of preestablished class nomenclature. The point of this exercise was to probe the public circulation of different classification systems ingrained in Brazilian public debates. Juxtaposing them with inductive categories collected

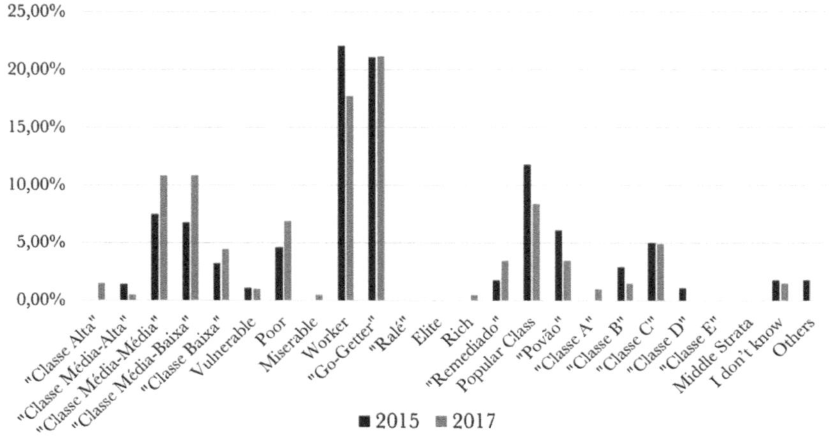

Figure 18.1 How would you define your current situation?

throughout fieldwork, I aimed to track the interplay between scientific and emic systems of thought in the production of new moral vocabularies to conceptualize the experience of inhabiting the "middle" (Figure 18.1).

Both in 2015 and 2017, I found that "worker" [trabalhador] and "go-getter" [batalhador] were the most cited categories, closely followed by "popular class," "middle-class," "poor," and "Classe C." However, while go-getter remains at the top in both time series, the categories "worker" and "popular class"—typically associated with left-leaning and insurgent movements—gave way to "middle-class" and its offshoots. This suggests that, two years into the housing project, perceived upward mobility gravitated toward languages emphasizing the midpoint in different scales of stratification. Moreover, this shift toward the middle despite a nationwide economic recession indicates that the taxonomy used to describe upward mobility is only loosely linked to broader political and economic changes. Instead, it seems to foreground the affective and moral attunement of a middle-class sensorial, reflected in the dynamic ways people conceptualize personal and familial development over time.

Thus, when Seu Juliano spoke of a "before" and an "after," he was alluding to the spatial dimensions of his middle-class sensorial: a past spent in the hills—a space of stagnation that hampered his chances of progressing in life—and a hopeful future envisioned as a citizen who, for the first time, saw himself as part of the urban infrastructure. In doing so, he was defying decades-long debates in Brazilian urban sociology, which decried the impossibility of upward mobility for those inhabiting the fringes of Brazil's big ailing cities despite hopes to "'move upwards' (…) to the legitimacy that exists by the asphalt."[48] Through spatial flux, Seu Juliano activated words, imageries, and socio-political practices of *becoming* middle class.

Temporal Sensorium

"There was a time... When I arrived, I used to spoil the environment. I am no longer that person. These days, I strive to improve my surroundings." I heard these words from Guilherme, a young man designated to become the first building manager of the housing project in Porto Alegre. Living for decades in an impoverished and informal settlement with his wife and kid, Guilherme had learned from an early age how to navigate the shifting terrains of precarious infrastructures, lack of opportunities, and scarce resources of Brazilian peripheries. Soon, he became the spokesperson for the new kind of life envisioned by politicians, marketers, and community leaders by the asphalt. In June 2013—one year before moving—he told me:

> This project unleashed the best in me. It's like cleaning the dust off a person. For too long, because of so much sorrow in a person's life, you get stuck, fagged, stagnated in time. It locks you in; it becomes a burden you no longer can carry.

As a building manager, Guilherme oversaw the unfolding of life in the projects, anticipating problems, monitoring the usage of collective equipment, and proposing new infrastructure projects—such as fences and surveillance designs—to keep the collective dream of upward social mobility underway. Two years into his role as a building manager, he told me: "Outsiders sometimes compliment me and say, 'there are many middle-class high-rises that don't have all this infrastructure.' This makes my day. We are not lagging behind that much, after all."

Engaging new materialities and re-organizing everyday sociability in the condominium, Guilherme carried on with his plan of self-transformation. "The idea is to move up the social ladder, but people are not yet aware of this goal," he told me in September 2016.

> I am here today. I don't know if I'm going to be here tomorrow. If it were up to me, I would be in an even better place. Each of us has a 10-year mortgage; 10 years that we have to stay before moving up again. Like a clock, ticking... towards the future.

What stands out in Guilherme's rendition of the middle-class sensorial are the plays of scale with time, which he sees as moving parts in a larger project of continuous personal improvement. Time, here, conjures images of past, unrealized desires, and their re-morphing into future-oriented configurations of wellbeing. Much like Seu Juliano, the fear of stagnation accompanies Guilherme's dynamic ideation of life in the condominium—it provides the grounds upon which new aspirations are inscribed.

Conversely, just as Seu Juliano's experience of inhabiting the middle is informed by broader debates in Brazilian society, there are political-economic elements and larger socio-historical forces at play in Guilherme's narrative of class. To the extent that he gauges his accomplishments as building manager against the backdrop of external benchmarks—the residents of middle-class high-rises—he is also invoking novel distinction patterns between Brazil's traditional intermediate segments and the emerging "new middle class."[49]

Guilherme's narrations are evocative of broader patterns of subjective belonging in the aftermath of Brazil's public housing program. Throughout fieldwork, I encountered many other activists and residents with a similar profile—young couples, singles, or nuclear families driven by ambitious and prospective visions of their future, a keen understanding of their rights as citizens and consumers, and a passionate will to thrive by building on the opportunities enabled by public policies. For these people, moving to a model housing project became an important, if transitory, stepping-stone towards upward mobility, a journey toward "an even better place," as Guilherme put it.

Another example of how the middle-class sensorial reveals itself in the very process of aspiring for homeownership is found in a second survey question. Both in 2015 and 2017, I asked residents to pick up to five words in a pool of dozens of expressions inductively compiled from ethnographic fieldwork that best defined what it meant for them to live in the housing project (Figure 18.2).[50]

In 2017, interviewees conceptualized the experience of owning their apartments with expressions such as access to citizenship, access to dignity; personal effort; struggle [luta]; worthiness [merecimento]; and unique opportunity. Compared to 2015, the 2017 survey reveals a sharp

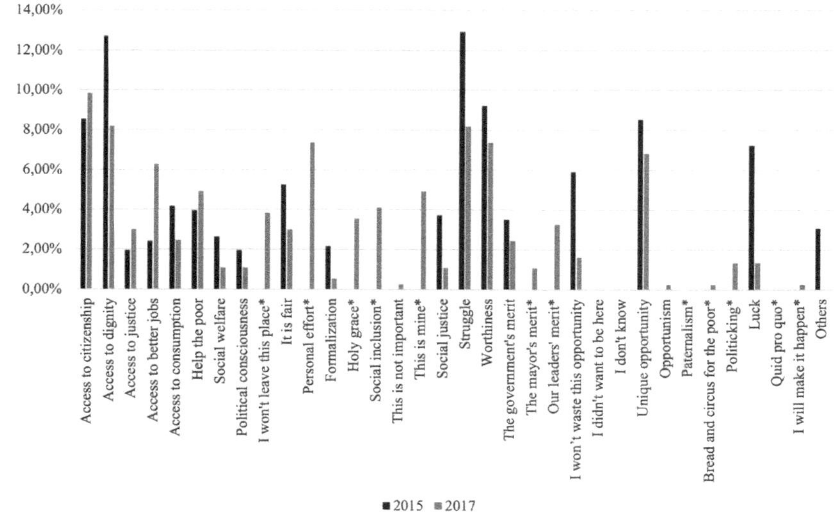

Figure 18.2 What does it mean to live in a housing project in Porto Alegre?

decline in expressions commonly identified with the experience of being part of collective mobilization, including access to dignity; "I won't waste this opportunity;" social welfare [assistencialismo]; and struggle [luta]. On the other hand, values such as personal effort; "this is mine;" "I won't leave this;" holy grace [graça divina]; and social inclusion were on the rise—especially among young families like Guilherme's—pointing to new spheres of belonging and social action that foreground personal development and privacy. Moreover, apartments were associated with access to justice and better jobs, validating data on employment, which suggest a gradual formalization of job posts among working-age residents.

Resorting to values and spheres of circulation that foreground individual improvement over collective mobilization, people like Guilherme are weaving together middle-class temporalities that reveal orientations toward the future.[51] While such temporalities contain references to desirable endpoints, they cannot be apprehended in terms of fixed positionalities alone. Instead, an ethnographic account of the sensorial and affective realities must center on how the constellations of these positions move in time and space; the moral, practical, and material efforts people put forward attempting to muster such goals; and the fragments of identity and history that surface as people move closer to accomplishing these goals.

Socio-material Sensorium

Jussara is 34 years old and lives in a new apartment unit of the housing project in Porto Alegre with her husband and an 8-year-old daughter. In our first conversation after she moved in, she spoke of past housing experiences in the hilltops, shifting familial configurations, and the process of becoming the beneficiary of public housing. Jussara has access to a range of other social programs, including *Bolsa Familia*, Brazil's eye-catching conditional cash transfer program pioneered in 2003. Throughout her college years, attending a prestigious federal university and majoring in the field of public health—a traditional white and upper-middle-class environment—Jussara qualified as a "low-income citizen," thus receiving financial subsidies to cover the material and logistic costs of studying, on top of free tuition and *Bolsa Familia* benefits.

When Jussara lost her job, her household was maintained exclusively with her husband's minimum wage earnings. The supplemental money received from *Bolsa Familia* proved decisive in keeping the couple's finances afloat. "It was the cash for kitchen gas, groceries, clothes for our daughter to go to school, sneakers for me to go look for a job." Jussara's point was that provisional cash allowed her family to set aside time to think of long-term projects while adjourning difficult decisions. By covering immediate expenses and stabilizing her household economy, *Bolsa Familia* opened up new sociomaterial spaces for autonomy and for the future to materialize.

Still, Jussara does not believe that social policies such as *Bolsa Familia* or *Minha Casa Minha Vida* should be made readily available to the poorest among the poor. Not everyone is equally prepared to take advantage of the opportunities made possible by governmental intervention: some will need additional support before being able to commit to a house mortgage, however heavily subsidized. In contrast, others will first need to be persuaded about the life improvements that come with paying for a home. Amidst the rapidly changing financial and material conditions of the poor, the key was to detect each own's tempo and will to thrive.

In her reasoning, also shared by many others, state-distributed benefits should not be ends in themselves; instead, they were meant to operate as springboards through which inner aspirations meet (otherwise improbable) chances for a better life. In so thinking, Jussara actualized a middle-class sensorial rooted in active aspiration[52] and opportunity structures,[53] and concretely experienced through the transformed architecture of the built environment and its material objects—a kind of life ideal at which she directed her present-day efforts.

Jussara had a clear vision of the interactions between state interventionism and citizen's personal will to thrive. Housing movements, like the one in which she partook to earn an apartment, have it as their goal to steer governments into allocating public services—such as health, education, or daycare—and accompany the beneficiaries of such services in their personal development. Trying to square demands for an accountable and operative state with residents' quest for a middle-class spatial aesthetics would ensure enfranchising pro-poor politics. Moreover, the combination of social protection and individual freedom would create sustainable emancipatory channels the poor to free themselves from the addictive entrapments of welfare. This movement, she suggested, would be the ultimate transition toward the middle class.

In response, I asked her whether she believed she had succeeded in this endeavor:

> I now own a house; I am attending college; we have food on our plates, washing and drying machines, all that is needed. With such tools, I can manage to better develop my life. I think I improved on my class condition, not because I am already where I want to be, but because now I have the conditions to go beyond. Class is not a state of being; it is like investing in the stock market. You will earn money, but does that make you rich? No. I invested; I have money, I have things, but they are not yet mine. *I simply have the conditions to invest in my future for the first time*. To be able to harvest in the future what I am seeding now.

Jussara's stance on the middle class as a subjunctive technology, a socio-material ensemble of becoming, was also illustrated by another paradigmatic example she distilled from her everyday experiences as a condo owner. The day before, during the week's grocery shopping, she asked herself whether she should buy chicken breast, priced at R$10.90 per kilo, or chicken thighs, going for R$5.49 per kilo.

> I was going for the breast to make lunch for my college girlfriends, because it doesn't come with skin or bones. But I also grabbed a package of thighs which will be dinner and lunch for my family. These calculations sound obvious for the upper classes who already learn how to ask certain kinds of questions from an early age,

Jussara continued her reasoning,

> but if you have to make ends meet you can't just spend all your monthly earnings on a weekend barbecue only to look cool in front of your friends. You have to make decisions responsibly. Unfortunately, among the poor, such wisdom is in short supply.

In these examples, Jussara spoke of everyday moral calculations whereby abstract aspirations for upward mobility met socio-material opportunity structures. It was the capacity to enact such forward-looking reasoning concerning the infrastructures of her new life in a condominium that ultimately distinguished the "deserving" from the "undeserving" poor. Decisions about the type of meat to buy were also seen as opportunities to project specific images of oneself to networks of acquaintances—the middle-class friends deserve chicken breast, whereas the immediate family is fine with thighs—and exercise voice as informed middle-class consumers.

> These things make all the difference. Your life has changed, you now live by a major avenue, next to a big supermarket chain, you don't want to leave that place feeling frustrated, just like any other poor. You want to be prepared for this new lifestyle.

Conclusion

This chapter laid the grounds for an ethnographic theory of the middle class, one capable of providing an alternative framework to the classic sociological synthesis between agency and structure. Discrepancies between how people conceive the experience of inhabiting a determinate social position and how intellectuals classify the social structure in which they live have always been a central impasse in the literature of social class. What takes precedence in the analytical treatment of the middle class: agency or positionality? Experience or discourse? Production or consumption? History or political economy? Past or future? Aspiration or distinction? While these questions certainly matter, in this chapter I returned to the problem of how class, in fact, eventuates,[54] which is a historical as much as a discursive and an experiential one. Looking at the joint workings of these dimensions and moving beyond the emic versus ethic debate allows to see the imbrications of time, space, consumption, infrastructure, and becoming that make up middle-class positionalities.

The empirical materials this chapter drew from were collected in the context of the implementation of Brazil's emerging networks of social and economic protection of the 2000s. This included beneficiaries of the country's largest public housing program, the *Minha Casa Minha Vida*, but also of conditional cash transfer initiatives like *Bolsa Familia* and university entrance programs based on racial quotas. The stories of class belonging and class becoming I unearthed in previous pages illuminate tangled worlds of aspiration, desire, and experimentation through which existing structures of stratification and mobility are experienced, contested, and woven into openings for hope against enduring inequality. But they also reveal broader discursive alignments with nationwide projects of development, such as the one that coalesced around the widespread circulation of the catchphrase "new middle class." Overall, then, these vignettes gave human form to the changing political, economic, and subjective realities of middle-class makings in post-neoliberal Latin-America—a period marked by redistributive shifts, economic growth, and diffused poverty governance mechanisms in much of the region's pink-tide governments.

Against this backdrop, the concept of the middle-class sensorial advances our understanding of class in at least four ways. First, it departures from context-specific variables and takes seriously the challenge of letting actors intuitively place themselves within broader constellations of social, political, and economic forces affecting their experience of "being in the middle." Methodologically, this requires keen attention to the vocabularies, affects, and practices that surface in casual settings and interactions, rather than attempting to extract commentaries on class from interlocutors by asking them direct questions on class positionality. If it stands that middle classes are not real because they exist in theory, but because people exist in "classed ways" that can be theorized,[55] it is no less true that people's classed existence is the dynamic outcome of myriad scales, rationalities, practices of intervention, and everyday affects.

Secondly, a middle-class sensorial approach avoids isolating historical, political, economic, conjunctural, or even subjective dimensions. Instead, it seeks to draw a social map of these moving constellations of forces as they come to matter in the experiences of particular individuals and groups in time and space. To grapple at once with the dynamics of inclusion and exclusion, past and future, distinction and aspiration that make up the middle-class sensorial, we need new cartographic approaches to class mobility. Cartography is here envisioned as a collection of tropes of place and time through which individuals conceptualize the experience of moving toward as the middle. Rather than hierarchical positions linked through well-defined class positions, cartographies are horizontal and dynamic portraits of the mental and experiential maps people draw as they navigate challenging realities to pursue their dreams of upward mobility. Cartographies of the middle-class sensorial are best equipped to capture the intermediate scales of historical/political/economic/spatial transformation and human becoming through which a politics of class mobility gains traction in the aftermath of governmental and market interventions.

Thirdly, the middle-class sensorial beseeches a nuanced social and material grasp of the senses, languages, and affects that pervade the experience of being in the middle. In the aftermath of Brazil's public housing program, infrastructures and materialities became key mediators of class.

They enabled a politics of wellbeing that was rooted both in conditions of political and economic possibility, and in everyday experiences of hope, experimentation, and subject-making that destabilize entrenched imaginaries of class and hierarchy. Consider, for example, Guilherme's intriguing contrasts to high-rises and Seu Juliano's narrations of a past where "there was no class." Here, the imagined "Others" are not located "above" and "below" the speakers—as in an abstract and hierarchical stratification system. Instead, they emerge as moving cartographies within an affective, material, and urban geography of horizontal forces: the rich neighborhoods and the impoverished hills; spaces of a "before" and an "after." The emerging patchwork of imagined places and temporalities lend infrastructures a sense of belonging, both to the city and to one's own becoming. The middle-class sensorial surfacing from these aspirational experiments with past and future tropes of infrastructure thus reveals ideals of the good life that are both linked to a broader constellation of inter-class imaginaries and seek to transcend them.

Finally, this means that ethnographies of the middle class must move beyond reductionist discourses of distinction to capture more nuanced and symbiotic dynamics of distinction *and* belonging. People's efforts to actualize ideals of comfort, security, and inclusion speak of the looming desire to be included in networks of consumption and the temporalities of the credit economy. At the same time, such efforts redraw the built environment of the city, engendering new forms of social distinction and urban seclusion. Yet as the ethnographic vignettes showed, these forms of everyday distinction are not lived as the enactment of inter-class boundaries, but as moral, aspirational, and material discontinuities by which new senses of dignity and respectability come to stabilize.

As we gloss the middle class as a processual, horizontal, cartographic, and encompassing sensorial—one that restitutes immanence and unfinishedness to life worlds and desire[56]—we also seek to capture broader constellations of historical and spatial change under way. The consequences of this radical shift in class conceptualization will be even the more dramatic in the post-pandemic world ahead. With the progressive dismantling of social, economic, and racial rights that has characterized Brazil's turn to far-right politics since the election of Jair Bolsonaro, what politics and experiences of class are in the horizon? To what extent have the disruptive social and economic effects of the coronavirus pandemic impacted the projects, affects, and already frail expectations of Brazil's "new middle class," bringing back tropes of the hills that many thought belonged to a bygone era? Amid fears of downward mobility and return to poverty, the middle-class sensorial is uniquely equipped to explore the interjacent dynamics of distinction and belonging, hierarchy and aspiration, past and future that define everyday human journeys toward territories of dignity, belonging, and respectability.

Notes

1 All names of individuals, groups, and places have been anonymized to respect the privacy of my research interlocutors.
2 Renato Ortiz, *Cultura Brasileira e Identidade Nacional* (São Paulo: Brasiliense, 1994).
3 Gilberto Freyre, *Casa Grande e Senzala: Formação Da Família Brasileira Sob Regime Da Economia Patriarcal* (Rio de Janeiro: José Olympio, 1978).
4 Sean Mitchell, *Constellations of Inequality: Space, Race and Utopia in Brazil. Constellations of Inequality* (Chicago: University of Chicago Press, 2017).
5 Introduced by the Workers' Party (Partido dos Trabalhadores, PT) as part of the government's Growth Acceleration Program (PAC), the multi-billion-dollar initiative was intended to fix almost half of Brazil's entire housing deficit through the construction of nearly four million two-bedroom apartment units across the country's peripheries. In its entry-level bracket, families with monthly incomes of up to three minimum wages—some US$650—were eligible to apply for government-subsidized mortgages that could, in some cases, amount up to 81% of the property cost.
6 Francisco Ferreira, Julian Messina, Jamele Rigolini, Luis-Felipe López-Calva, Maria Ana Lugo, and Renos Vakis. "Economic Mobility and the Rise of the Latin American Middle Class" (Washington, DC: The World Bank, 2013).
7 Homi Kharas, "The Emerging Middle Class in Developing Countries" (Paris: Development Centre Working Papers, 2010).
8 Martin Ravallion. "The Developing World's Bulging (but Vulnerable) Middle Class," *World Development*, 38:4 (2009), 1–31.
9 Marcelo Neri. *A Nova Classe Média: O Lado Brilhante Dos Pobres* (Rio de Janeiro: CPS/FGV, 2008).
10 Moisés Kopper. "Measuring the Middle: Technopolitics and the Making of Brazil's New Middle-Class," *History of Political Economy*, 52:3 (2020), 561–88.
11 Arne Ruckert, Laura Macdonald, and Kristina R Proulx, "Post-Neoliberalism in Latin America: A Conceptual Review," *Third World Quarterly*, 38:7 (2017), 1583–1602.
12 Löic Wacquant. "Making Class: The Middle-Class(es) in Social Theory and Social Structure," in *Bringing Class Back In: Contemporary and Historical Perspectives*, edited by Scott McNall, Rhonda Levine, and Rick Fantasia (Boulder: Westview Press, 1991), 39.
13 Karl Marx and Friedrich Engels, *The Communist Manifesto* (New York: International Publishers, 1948).
14 Wacquant, *Making Class.*
15 Val Burris, "The Discovery of the New Middle Classes," in *The New Middle Classes: Life-Styles, Status Claims, and Political Orientations* (London: Macmillan, 1995), 15–54.

16 Eduard Bernstein, *Evolutionary Socialism: A Criticism and Affirmation* (New York: Schocken Books, 1961).
17 Arthur J. Vidich, ed., *The New Middle Classes: Life-Styles, Status Claims, and Political Orientations* (London: Macmillan, 1995).
18 Erik Olin Wright. *Class, Crisis, and the State* (New York: Verso, 1978).
19 Anthony Giddens, *The Class Structure of the Advanced Societies* (New York: Harper & Row, 1975).
20 Pierre Bourdieu, *Distinction: A Social Critique of the Judgment of Taste* (Cambridge: Harvard University Press, 1984), 483.
21 Wacquant, *Making Class*, 50.
22 Luc Boltanski, *The Making of a Class: Cadres in French Society* (Cambridge; New York: Cambridge University Press, 1987).
23 Wacquant, *Making Class*, 57.
24 Karl Polanyi. *The Great Transformation: The Political and Economic Origins of Our Time* (Boston: Beacon Press, 2001).
25 Chris Hann and Keith Hart, *Economic Anthropology* (Cambridge: Polity Press, 2011).
26 E. P. Thompson, *The Making of the English Working Class* (London: Vintage, 1964), 150.
27 Carla Freeman, *Entrepreneurial Selves: Neoliberal Respectability and the Making of a Caribbean Middle Class* (Durham; London: Duke University Press, 2014).
28 Joska Samuli Schielke, *Egypt in the Future Tense: Hope, Frustration, and Ambivalence before and after 2011* (Bloomington: Indiana University Press, 2015).
29 Li Zhang, *In Search of Paradise: Middle-Class Living in a Chinese Metropolis* (Ithaca: Cornell University Press, 2010).
30 Rachel Heiman, Carla Freeman, and Mark Liechty, "Introduction: Charting an Anthropology of the Middle Classes," in *The Global Middle Classes: Theorizing through Ethnography*, edited by Rachel Heiman, Mark Liechty, and Carla Freeman (Santa Fe: School for Advanced Research Press, 2012).
31 Mark Liechty, *Suitably Modern: Making Middle-Class Culture in a New Consumer Society* (Princeton: Princeton University Press, 2002).
32 Mark Liechty, "Middle-Class Déjà Vu: Conditions of Possibility, from Victorian England to Contemporary Kathmandu," In *The Global Middle Classes: Theorizing through Ethnography*, edited by Rachel Heiman, Mark Liechty, and Carla Freeman (Santa Fe: School for Advanced Research Press, 2012), 271–300.
33 Davida S. Parker, *The Idea of the Middle Class: White-Collar Workers and Peruvian Society, 1900–1950* (Pennsylvania: Pennsylvania State University Press, 1998).
34 Michael Jiménez, "The Elision of the Middle Classes and Beyond: History Politics, and Development Studies in Latin America's Short Twentieth Century," in *Colonial Legacies: The Problem of Persistence in Latin American History*, edited by Jeremy Adelman (London: Routledge, 1999), 209.
35 Ezequiel Adamovsky, *Historia de La Clase Media Argentina: Apogeo y Decadencia de Una Ilusión, 1919–2003* (Buenos Aires: Editorial Planeta, 2009).
36 Sergio E. Visacovsky, "Estudios Sobre Clase Media En La Antropología Social: Una Agenda Para La Argentina," *Avá: Revista de Antropología*, 13 (2008), 9–37.
37 Ezequiel Adamovsky, Sergio E. Visacovsky, and Patricia Vargas, eds, *Clases Medias: Nuevos Enfoques Desde La Sociología, La Historia y La Antropología* (Buenos Aires: Ariel, 2014).

38 Brian P. Owensby, *Intimate Ironies: Modernity and the Making of Middle-Class Lives in Brazil* (Stanford: Stanford University Press, 1999).
39 David S. Parker and Louise E Walker, *Latin America's Middle Class: Unsettled Debates and New Histories* (Lanham: Lexington Books, 2013).
40 Samuli Schielke, "Living in the Future Tense: Aspiring for World and Class in Provincial Egypt," in *The Global Middle Classes: Theorizing through Ethnography*, edited by Rachel Heiman, Mark Liechty, and Carla Freeman (Santa Fe: School for Advanced Research Press, 2012).
41 Procon is an entity that protects consumers' rights in Brazil. It was established in 1970 and is responsible for providing information and guiding consumers through their complaints.
42 Kopper, *Measuring the Middle*, 581–588.
43 Moisés Kopper and Arlei S. Damo, "A Emergência e Evanescência Da Nova Classe Média Brasileira," *Horizontes Antropológicos*, 24:50 (2018), 335–376.
44 Charles H. Klein, Sean T. Mitchell, and Benjamin Junge, "Naming Brazil's Previously Poor: 'New Middle Class' as an Economic, Political, and Experiential Category," *Economic Anthropology*, 5 (2018), 83–95.
45 Moisés Kopper, "La Invención de La Nueva Clase Media Brasileña: De La Antropología de Los Números a Las Políticas de Movilidad Social," in *Clases Medias: Novos Enfoques Desde La Sociología, La Historia y La Antropología*, edited by Ezequiel Adamovsky, Sergio Visacovsky, and Patricia Vargas (Buenos Aires: Ariel, 2014).
46 Guilherme Xavier Sobrinho, "A 'Classe C' e Sua Alardeada Ascensão: Nova? Classe? Média?," *Indicadores Econômicos FEE*, 38:4 (2011), 67–80.
47 Gilberto Velho, *A Utopia Urbana: Um Estudo de Antropologia Social* (Rio de Janeiro: Jorge Zahar, 1973), 80.
48 Claudia Fonseca. *Família, Fofoca e Honra* (Porto Alegre: Editora UFRGS, 2000).
49 In previous decades, before the "new middle class" became a discursive reality, this binary distinction took on different cloaks. (See Moisés Kopper and Matthew Richmond. "Subjetividades Periféricas: Uma Conversa Interdisciplinar," *Novos Estudos Cebrap*, 39:1 (2020): 9–17. See also Matthew Richmond, Moisés Kopper, Valéria Oliveira, and Jacqueline Garza, "Introdução: Espaços Periféricos, Ontem e Hoje," in *Espaços Periféricos: Política, Violência e Território Nas Bordas Da Cidade*, edited by Matthew Richmond, Moisés Kopper, Valéria Oliveira, and Jacqueline Garza (São Paulo: UFSCAR/CEM, 2020).) The formation of traditional middle and upper middle classes in the country dates back to mid-twentieth-century when industrialization policies and the economic programs of the military governments fostered the expansion of these sectors against a peripheral, ultra-exploited, and unqualified working class (See Waldir José de Quadros, *O 'Milagre Brasileiro' e a Expansão Da Nova Classe Média*. PhD Dissertation (Campinas: Unicamp, 1991). See also Maureen O'Dougherty, *Consumption Intensified: The Politics of Middle-Class Daily Life in Brazil* (Durham: Duke University Press, 2002).) The "new middle class" of the 2000s is commonly criticized for being a political-economic construct associated with the expansion of neoliberal consumerism and governance in the region, ensnaring the poor into depoliticization by having them believe that their vulnerable status in society has finally changed. (See Marcio Pochmann, *Nova Classe Média? O Trabalho Na Base Da Pirâmide Social Brasileira* (São Paulo: Boitempo, 2012). See also Marilena Chauí, "Uma Nova Classe Trabalhadora," in *Lula e Dilma: Dez Anos de Governos Pós-Neoliberais No Brasil* (São Paulo: Boitempo, 2013), 123–34.)
50 Expressions marked with a star (*) were only available for respondents in 2017 to choose.

51 Rebecca Bryant and Daniel M. Knight, *The Anthropology of the Future* (Cambridge: Cambridge University Press, 2019).
52 Samuli Schielke, "Living in the Future Tense: Aspiring for World and Class in Provincial Egypt," in *The Global Middle Classes: Theorizing through Ethnography*, edited by Rachel Heiman, Mark Liechty, and Carla Freeman (Santa Fe: School for Advanced Research Press, 2012).
53 Edward F. Fischer, *The Good Fife: Aspiration, Dignity, and the Anthropology of Wellbeing* (Palo Alto: Stanford University Press, 2014).
54 Thompson, *The Making of the English Working Class.*
55 Wacquant, *Making Class.*
56 João G. Biehl and Peter Locke, eds, *Unfinished: The Anthropology of Becoming* (Durham; London: Duke University Press, 2017).

19 Residential Practices of Three Generations of a Middle-Class Family

Mortgages, Honor, and Inequalities in Mexico City

Claudia Zamorano

Introduction

> We thought we'd copy our parents who bought their first house to get onto an easy-to-climb property ladder. Since the crisis we've been stuck in this tiny two-bedroom apartment with its tiny living room. Can you imagine the children having to share the same bedroom?[1]

This is how Facundo—a young architect employed by one of Mexico's main real-estate firms—explained to me how the 1994 Mexican peso crisis dented his aspirations for social mobility, keeping him trapped in an apartment he considered too small for his family, and with a crippling debt. Nine years had elapsed since the fateful "December Mistake" when Mexicans saw the peso lose its parity with the US dollar, the doubling or tripling of interest rates, the progressive bankruptcy of banks and businesses, and increasing unemployment.

Facundo's story highlights one aspect I would like to explore in this article: how several generations passed down a strategy, or even a "know-how," for climbing the property ladder by using mortgages. This transmission was rooted in a practice that originated in the early 1900s and became established by the 1960s, but fell apart during the extensive structural reforms linked to neoliberalism, and after a series of crises triggered by speculative investments.

This same context exists in different forms all around the world, and is a cause for concern in various political and academic circles. The social sciences have tried to gauge its impacts through longitudinal studies, such as my approach in this chapter. These analyses reveal profound differences between the generations that enjoyed the period of financial stability and the more recent ones that have mainly experienced cyclical crises and stagnation. I have included education, income, identity, and consumption as some of the principal variables in order to understand these effects.[2]

This chapter focuses on how the physical characteristics, accessibility, and location of housing reflects and informs a set of three main, closely related

DOI: 10.4324/9781003029311-24

elements: intergenerational transmission of assets and knowledge; socio-economic and political contexts; and, finally, strategies and practices that are not only residential but also related to professions, marriages, migrations, and social mobility. My aim is to examine these elements through the prism of three generations of a family with a working-class background that settled in Mexico City in 1926 and profited from one of the very few post-revolutionary social housing projects. After benefitting from the socio-economic boom or "Mexican Miracle," structural crises caused a divergence in their respective experiences, between the "winners" in the new economic situation[3] and those who took out mortgages and generally lost, as in the case of Facundo. The chapter has three main parts that describe the family members' professional and residential history, as well as the social and urban context of each generation. I will begin by providing some notes on my methodology.

Remarks on the Methodology

This chapter is the result of a broader study entitled *Vivienda y familia en una colonia central de la ciudad de México* (Housing and family in a Mexico City neighborhood).[4] For that research, I compiled the stories of 35 kinship groups who founded the Colonia Michoacana, one of the first areas of social housing to be built in Mexico following the Revolution. I interviewed most members of these groups, attempting to encompass three different generations. I carried out 71 semi-guided interviews, including with people no longer living in the neighborhood itself.

For the purposes of this chapter, I have followed up with the Zepeda family, as it provides one of the most complete case studies.[5] I interviewed four members of the second generation (aged between 60 and 70 at that time), and two members of the third generation (in their late 30s).

I combined two tools for the study. I examined the family genealogies, emphasizing the development of the three generations' professional and housing situations. Secondly, I used the "marketing maps" drawn up by the Buró de Investigación de Mercado, S.A. (Market Research Bureau, BIMSA), a market research tool used by marketing agencies and planners from retail chains to define the geographical location for their investments. Narrowing down to the neighborhood scale, they classify homes by socio-economic levels, with definitions based on four types of variables: (a) sociocultural factors (education, children's education level and their enrolment at public or private schools, use of banking services, sports club membership, life and car insurance policies); (b) profession; (c); type of housing and durable goods; and (d) monthly household income.

In summary, BIMSA describes the profiles of six socio-economic levels (Table 19.1).[6]

According to BIMSA, the different tiers of the middle class are between the C+ and D+ levels. This practical and operational principle has its limitations (as referred to in my article "Los hijos de la modernidad").[7] In this

Table 19.1 BIMSA's socio-economic levels by education level, profession, housing characteristics, and monthly family income in Mexican pesos (1998)

Level	*Education*	*Profession*	*Housing**	*Income in 1998 / smmw*** (Mexican pesos)*
A/B	University degree (minimum)	Businessmen in large or medium-sized firms, directors of major companies	> 6 rooms	> $50,000 (52 smmw)
C+	University degree (generally)	Independent professionals, managers, or second-tier executives in important companies	> 5 rooms	$21,000–$49,000 (22–51 smmw)
C	High school (or higher)	Traders, public-sector employees, salespersons, teachers, technicians, and skilled workers	4 rooms (sometimes in social housing developments)	$6,000–$20,000 (6–21 smmw)
D+	Primary or secondary school (completed)	Taxi drivers, vendors (in premises or door-to-door), couriers, laborers	3 rooms (sometimes in social housing developments)	$4,000–$5,000 (4–5 smmw)
D	Primary school (complete)	Laborers, maintenance workers, vendors	2 rooms (often in social housing developments)	$1,500–$3,000 (1.5–3 smmw)
E	Primary school (incomplete)	Under-employed or temporary workers	1 or 2 rooms (often coinhabiting with different generations)	< $1,500 (< 1.5 smmw)

* Housing characteristics have little influence on the classification, especially the home's ownership status, which appears normal in a country where more than 70% of the population claims to own their own home.

** Statutory minimum monthly wage (1998 = $957 pesos, figure subject to rounding up/down). BIMSA's ranges leave a gap between $20,000 and $21,000 pesos, $5,000 and $6,000, and $3,000 and $4,000.

BIMSA indicates that some people in the D+ level might have a higher level of education, but they lost their jobs after the 1995 crisis.

Source: compiled by author, based on BIMSA's data.

study, they offer a frame of reference for the Zepeda family's social class at the time of the interviews.

The Pampered Children of the Revolution: The First Generation

The family's founding couple formed a relationship in around 1920, after the armed phase of the 1910 revolutionary struggle had abated. They settled in the city of Tampico, in northern Mexico, where Roberto Zepeda was a skilled worker at an oil company and Diana worked in the home after leaving her job as a rural schoolteacher. In 1926, already with one daughter and one son, the family moved to Mexico City.

Despite its endemic poverty, the country's capital was a magnet for internal migration as the seat of federal government and due to increasing industrialization in post-revolutionary Mexico. The city had therefore attracted many migrants fleeing the poverty and violence left in the wake of the armed struggle in the countryside and provincial towns and cities. Between 1900 and 1930, Mexico City's population swelled from 541,516 to 1,229,576 inhabitants, representing 3.9% and 7.4%, respectively, of the country's population.[8]

In 1926, upon the arrival of the Zepeda family, Mexico City was already a socio-spatially segregated city. The former elites of the Porfirio Díaz era who had survived the tumult of the Revolution lived in a handful of neighborhoods south-west of the center (Roma, Juárez, Condesa), along with a new post-revolutionary bourgeoisie. In the center, north, and north-east, neighborhoods such as Peralvillo, Tepito, Merced, and Tlatelolco were slums and *vecindades*, a particular form of subdivision of old mansions into smaller dwellings. People in those places lived in extremely overcrowded conditions: families with as many as six to eight members shared communal patios, clothes-washing areas, and toilets, with other families.

On arrival, the Zepedas moved into a room in a vecindad in the Tepito neighborhood, the birthplace of another one of their children and where they had the unconditional support of Roberto's mother and sisters. This family network helped Roberto to find employment quickly; he secured a job as a skilled worker in a factory that produced plastic products, a job he kept for the rest of his life.

They remained in this same residential situation until 1936, when Diana became aware of the social housing programs offered by the state-owned development bank (Banco Nacional Hipotecario Urbano y de Obras Públicas, National Urban Mortgage and Public Works Bank BNHOUOPSA), the first of their kind in post-revolutionary Mexico. A group of left-wing architects who styled themselves as the "Arquitectos Radicales" led this ambitious project, with the support of government and some pioneers of modern urbanism in Mexico. This was the first time that the state had ever joined forces with private firms, architects, and artists to produce workers' housing.[9]

Roberto met the requirements to submit his paperwork to the bank, which specified that applicants needed to be "Mexican citizens, heads of household, between 18 and 45 years old, and earning a minimum of $75 pesos a month,"[10] equivalent to the recently established minimum wage. The houses were obtainable through another innovation in housing policy: mortgages with monthly repayments of $22.5 pesos, a third of the minimum wage.[11] Unionized employees such as Roberto had priority access to this new mortgage system.

Diana handled the paperwork on behalf of her husband, who spent his days at the factory. That same year, the Zepedas were one of the 750 families who benefitted from the social housing with a government loan in the Michoacana neighborhood. Built on a 150-square-meter lot, the Zepeda's house had two bedrooms, a living room, bathroom, kitchen, and a 75-square-meter backyard where, over time, the family built three extra rooms. The houses had electricity, running water, and drainage—exceptional services for a working-class family at the time. The neighborhood also had a remarkable range of services for Mexico City: parks, recreational areas, sports facilities, as well as a 5,000-square-meter plot set aside for a primary school for up to 2,000 pupils. This school became one of the centers of an ambitious project spearheaded by President Lázaro Cárdenas (1935–1938): Socialist Education, the route to social equality. "The active proletarian school should form an integral part of the workers' neighborhoods, in order to make a clean break from chronic exploitation by bringing about social equality, at least in opportunities for education [...]."[12]

The Zepedas were undoubtedly privileged to gain access to these homes and facilities in a city where more than 80% of people lived in poverty,[13] with most migrants ending up under-employed and living in rented rooms in vecindades in more central parts of the city, or in shacks on the outskirts. How did this factor affect the careers and housing strategies of the subsequent generation? It certainly gave them access to formal education, laying the foundations for upward social mobility, thus allowing them to benefit from the "Mexican miracle," a bonanza that only worked miracles for a privileged few.[14]

The Pampered Children of the Revolution: Second Generation

The government abandoned its socialist education project in the 1950s. However, it had a lasting effect on the Zepeda brothers, who finished their primary education at their local school that formed part of this initiative. In common with many families from the emerging middle classes in Mexico, they sought upward social mobility through diplomas.[15] In 1940, the eldest daughter, Sonia, finished her training course as a secretary at the age of 16, and began to work in a law firm. In the 1950s, her two brothers, Horacio and Esteban, aged 33 and 26 respectively, graduated as accountants from the Instituto Politécnico Nacional, another institute of higher education created by Lázaro Cárdenas that expanded the offer of education for young people from the popular classes.

Diplomas gave the Zepeda family's second generation a chance to make a break from their father's professional background, leaving manual labor behind to join the growing numbers of white-collar employees. This training, combined with their mother's residential practices, defined the residential future for the Zepeda family's younger members after their marriages.

In 1945, at the age of 19, Sonia married a Mexican air force officer and, in 1951, she moved to the United States where her husband found a job in a commercial airline. Sonia soon found a job as a secretary, helping her to swiftly integrate into US society. She even told me during an interview that her three children speak more English than Spanish.[16]

Sonia's two brothers married later, after completing their degrees. In 1957, Horacio married Raquel, a secretary from a northern border city. Esteban wed Mago, a young girl without any educational qualifications who lived in a nearby neighborhood. While Horacio set up home in his parent's house, Esteban (who earned more) rented an apartment in the middle-class Narvarte neighborhood in the west of the city, one of the areas considered bastions for the capital's "decent families" (see Sara Luna's chapter in this book).

Toward the end of the 1950s, their mother—Diana—found out about a new social housing program in the Balbuena neighborhood, very near to the Colonia Michoacana, and persuaded her children to apply for a housing loan there. Afterwards, Esteban left his apartment in the Narvarte neighborhood and moved into his parents' home. Both brothers began to save up for the down payment required by the new loan system.

The choice of a government housing loan as a way of getting onto the property ladder shows that the residential strategy for the first and second generations was remarkably similar, and this is by no means coincidental. Once again, Diana played a pivotal role in passing on the information, an essential part of any strategy. Nevertheless, the social housing system's conditions had changed since the parents' time. Firstly, the Mortgage Bank of Public Works S.A. (Banco Hipotecario de Obras Publicas S.A. BAHUOPSA) had morphed into National Bank of Public Works and Services (Banco Nacional de Obras y Servicios Públicos BANOBRAS), establishing its presence in producing social housing and loans available for the middle classes, especially public-sector employees (as discussed by Sara Luna in her chapter).

By 1970, there were already 17,250 homes in housing complexes in Mexico City and other states across the country.[17] Qualifying for a loan had new rules attached: young families now had to make a sizeable down-payment and the monthly installments were almost at the same level as the minimum wage. This required the Zepeda brothers to work harder than the preceding generation. A factory worker in the same mold as Roberto would have been unlikely to qualify for a loan under such conditions. But Horacio and Esteban could bring to bear other resources that their parents lacked. They earned far more than the minimum wage, thanks to their qualification as accountants; and their family owned a property large enough to accommodate them all for as long as it took them to save enough for the down-payment.

In 1961, the two young couples each took ownership of their apartment in the Balbuena neighborhood. From then on, Horacio and Esteban entered a kind of competition in the family and professional spheres. Each brother had six children. However, in terms of their work and housing, a gulf began to open between them. Esteban became a senior manager in the private sector and also a university professor; Horacio maintained his senior role in the public sector, but without much stability. In terms of their housing situation, in 2001 (at the time of the interview), the younger brother had a large house in an upscale area (A/B), as well as a second home in Mexico and another in the United States, a situation that positioned him as a member of the upper class. Horacio, meanwhile, only had one house able to accommodate his large family, located in a gated condominium classified as C+ by BIMSA, in other words, a middle-upper class area. What accounted for these divides? What repercussions would they have on the following generation? What other sociocultural changes affected their residential practices?

Ruptures, Continuities, and Inequalities

The career of the younger brother (Esteban) soon affected his housing situation. In 1962 he purchased a lot in Ciudad Satélite. This suburb located in the north of the city was designed in 1954 for the upper-middle class—a sector of society rapidly growing at the time.[18] Esteban planned to build his house there, but in 1964 he had the opportunity to buy a house in San Jerónimo, an area in the south of the capital which the Mexican elite had chosen for their weekend residences since the early 1900s. Esteban was impressed by this house that had a built area of more than 800 square meters, complete with garden and swimming pool. In order to make the purchase, he sold his apartment in Balbuena and his plot of land in Ciudad Satélite, raising a total of $50,000 pesos. He received a loan to cover the remaining $200,000 pesos. On this occasion he deviated from the family tradition: the money did not come from the government but from a private bank—such loans were the preserve of the well-off given their stringent repayment conditions. When I asked him whether he was anxious about taking out such a large loan, he replied in the negative:

> At that time I already had my degree and was earning good money, so of course I wasn't afraid. In fact, I think I took the decision too quickly. As soon as I saw the opportunity, I told myself: "let's sell the apartment

> and the land, and let's go for it." I was earning between $12,000 and $15,000 pesos a month.[19] So the house represented a year and a half's salary. Perhaps that's why I wasn't worried.[20]

As mentioned above, Horacio was less upwardly mobile. His different jobs in the senior public-sector positions prevented him from severing ties from government housing loans, requiring him to continue living in state-built houses until the late 1970s. In 1968, seven years after buying his apartment in Balbuena, he was able to access a single-family property in Villa Coapa,[21] a housing complex with more than 6,000 units built by BANOBRAS to house the staff working at the Olympic Games, to be sold subsequently with affordable loans targeted at middle- and lower-middle-class families.[22] As in the case of the Balbuena neighborhood, these properties required an initial down-payment and monthly installments near to the minimum salary.

Another difference between the brothers is that Esteban was the family's sole breadwinner and the only one paying off the mortgage. Horacio's wife had begun contributing to the family income after taking a job as a secretary in a government office after the birth of her youngest child in 1965. This employment even allowed her to maintain the family for one year while Horacio was unemployed and, at the same time, maintain the Balbuena apartment and pay the monthly installments for the new house in Villa Coapa.

In 1976, the family bought a larger house in the outskirts of Villa Coapa,[23] where various property developers had built horizontal condominiums. Horacio and Raquel sold two properties in order to make the down-payment on the new house, and took out a mortgage for the remaining amount. On this occasion, Raquel was the one who managed to obtain a private bank loan thanks to her job. Raquel's active intervention in the family's residential strategies invites an analysis of the main intergenerational shifts revealed by the Zepeda case study: the role of middle-class woman in the family's economy and in its residential strategies.

Honor, Gender, and Mortgages

In rural Mexico, there appears to be a rule whereby the men and those on their side of the family make the main economic and material effort to assist the younger generations in their residential strategies. In working-class urban environments—particularly where people build their own houses—the idea has continued more as an aspiration. In practice, women are instrumental in negotiating the purchase of lots, participating in neighborhood committees and assemblies, and even in the actual building of the house.[24] Hence it is paradoxical to hear a woman say: "There I was, building as if I were a man."[25] What can be said about the urban middle classes?

The ability to maintain a home and provide a house is also at the core of the idea of male honor among members of the middle class whom I have interviewed. Although in their residential practices I have found traces of a complex system of financial, practical, and business factors, male honor also enters the picture[26]—yet this is not the only reason why the Zepeda brothers lived in their parents' home at the start of their married life; their family home was large enough for them to share with a certain degree of comfort. Raquel's parents were not in a position to offer accommodation because they lived in a different city; Mago's mother and family could not do so either, since their family rented a small room in a vecindad.

However, this approach is neither strictly utilitarian nor does it constitute a clean break from the predominantly patrilineal logic of rural Mexico, as shown by the episode recounted by Raquel: in 1961, when they were going to buy in the Balbuena neighborhood, Raquel's father offered the couple some money to help them buy a house, instead of an apartment. Horacio turned down the offer, arguing that—as head of the household—he was responsible for providing a house for his family. Therefore, by symbolically rejecting his father-in-law's donation, Horacio prioritized his idea of social and family respect or, as Raquel put it, "saving his honor."

Nevertheless, such a posture can be flexible. Horacio eventually ended up accepting his wife's intervention, by allowing her to contribute both to the family income and to the purchase of the house. Raquel took out the mortgage in her own name—an unimaginable situation for her mother-in-law, Diana, in whose days women were expressly excluded from applying for housing loans.[27] These changes became more deeply entrenched in the following generation: Raquel's three sons bought apartments thanks to the generous support of their parents-in-law. Their wives and sisters also worked as salaried employees from the outset of their married lives, then a common practice among most middle-class women in Mexico, and one that continues to this day.[28]

As Ricardo López-Pedreros observes in the case of Colombia,[29] this new order did not appear to pose any radical threat to the masculinity of these middle-class subjects. Some women find a way around with comments such as: "Well, he pays for house expenses and we use my salary for vacations and our little luxuries" (Lilia, wife of Facundo).[30] This undoubtedly helps give the impression that the woman's income is an ad hoc support and not, as we have seen since Raquel's experience, a new family division of paid labor.

We must consider these changes in the light of the experiences of this family's third generation, who lived at a time of financial and political crises, the winding-down of the import-substitution model, and the advent of neoliberal policies.

Those Condemned to Live in the Present: Third Generation

The residential odysseys of Esteban and Horacio, sons of a factory worker, clearly show upward social mobility, essentially reflecting their rise into white-collar employment. Their rise would certainly have been impossible without Mexico's economic boom from the 1950s to the 1970s. The parallel development of the oil industry and the welfare state enabled some children from families of modest financial means to secure more comfortable lives, mainly thanks to their employment in liberal professions. The "Mexican miracle" enabled this generation not only to make a break from their parents' type of employment but also from their residential aspirations and lifestyles.

Despite their differences, the Zepeda brothers were both privileged in comparison to Mexico City's average inhabitants, who suffered increasing socio-spatial inequalities. The capital's population was also swelling—it grew from 3,050,442 to 6,874,653 between 1950 and 1970—with high rates of immigration among poor campesinos.[31] Poverty and socio-spatial fragmentation persisted over that period, and different socio-economic sectors had notably unequal access to housing. Private property developers began to rapidly expand the number of housing projects for the middle and upper-middle classes, social sectors that qualified for mortgages from private banks. Government housing loans also became more widespread, generally targeting the middle and lower-middle classes. Finally, the proliferation of lots for self-build projects (the principal means for the working classes to access housing) meant that toward the end of the twentieth century such housing accounted for 60% of total residential construction in the city.

The capital was becoming a fast-growing metropolis mainly due to poor migrants who faced under-employment and lived in makeshift housing in neighborhoods without public services and infrastructure. The middle class was struggling to maintain or improve their situation, assisted to a large extent by a credit culture that had become firmly established within the space of 60 years. We can now turn our gaze toward the third generation of the Zepeda family and their particular socio-economic context. Their generation faced a creaking mortgage system and, to paraphrase Wallerstein, was condemned to living in the present.[32]

Crises and Currency Devaluations

Horacio and Raquel seem to have anticipated the future by signing for their last property purchase just months before the Mexican peso devaluation of 1976. A series of agreements signed in 1954 between Mexico, the United States, and the International Monetary Fund had kept the Mexican currency stable at $12.50 pesos to the dollar. In 1971, this agreement came to an end and in mid-1976 the dollar climbed to almost $20 pesos. This was the first indication of a succession of financial crises that continue to this day, and which have worsened since 1979 due to the oil crisis, the mainstay of the Mexican economy.

Margarita Estrada refers to three defining moments in this period of financial trouble.[33] Firstly, in 1982, when the international banking systems' interest rates increased while oil prices plummeted. Then in 1987, when the Mexican government launched a neoliberal program to adapt the country's economy to the new international dynamic. In this period, salaries remained stagnant and Mexican firms were going bankrupt, disappearing, or merging, while the government privatized formerly state-owned enterprises and encouraged foreign investment. The inflow of foreign capital helped mitigate the crisis somewhat, and created jobs. However, in late 1994, during the crisis that came to be known internationally as the "Tequila effect," the peso underwent another devaluation, this time by nearly 100%. This crisis affected each region and sector of society differently, and hit members of the middle class the hardest. After having grown accustomed to a culture of taking out loans, they suddenly saw a doubling of interest rates, and those who had taken out dollar-based loans found themselves sinking into exponentially worsening debt.

The population of Mexico City and the surrounding metropolitan area—which had already exceeded 16 million people in the 1990s—also faced the cancelation of certain state subsidies available to them since the 1930s, as well as with the challenge posed by the reconstruction after the 1985 earthquake. This string of crises and challenges was the inheritance received by Diana and Roberto's grandchildren as they embarked on their independent lives. What resources could they muster in order to get onto the property ladder under these new circumstances?

For this generation, the parents' situation played a significant role, deepening the inequalities between the cousins. Their varied careers and residential situations show some aspects of the different population profiles that we tend to include within the middle-class category. Below I will focus on two profiles in particular: "the winners" and "the mortgagors."[34]

The Winners

Three of Esteban's five daughters emigrated to the United States. As in the case of their aunt Sonia, their experience was a world away from that of undocumented Mexicans who cross the Rio Grande to find work in the agricultural or service sectors. They travelled with their residence papers in order, following their young Mexican husbands, already senior managers who had graduated from private universities. Only one of these girls had a university education (in Medicine); the other two had completed their high-school education at private schools that gave them enough English to integrate rapidly into US society.

Studies on the geographical mobility of Mexicans heading to the United States have not addressed the emigration of certain sectors of Mexico's elite. However, Guadalupe Loaeza's novel described the intensity of this phenomenon as a reaction of the middle and upper classes to the various problems (including urban violence, the bankruptcy of companies, professional uncertainty) affecting the Mexican capital since 1982.[35]

Meanwhile, Esteban and Mago's two daughters who remained in Mexico, as well as their eldest son, now form part of the upper-middle class. Only the son completed a degree (in Legal Studies), and he worked in his father's firm, while the two daughters attended private high schools and became housewives. They lived in upper-middle-class neighborhoods (C+). The expansion of the capital's elites certainly explained their ability to "marry well." However, they were still nowhere near reaching their father's socioeconomic status.

Raquel and Horacio's children had more varied financial situations. They all obtained degrees, which, despite being from universities that had lost some of their prestige for certain liberal professions, still enabled them to have fixed employment and one or two cars per family. In terms of their housing, four of the six children own their own home outright or else are paying a mortgage, one of them rents a property, and the other one (a single mother) lives with her parents. The siblings' housing experiences varied considerably.

As indicated above, the eldest daughter, a single mother, lived with her parents. Her brother who came next was on his second marriage when he obtained a home in a social housing project for low-income residents in the northern outskirts (D+). The next eldest, Facundo, bought an apartment in the south of the city (C). The other sister, Amelia, managed to set up a medium-sized company and lives in an exclusive gated community. The other two brothers also live in the south of the city in a (C) zone. The interviews provided a more in-depth understanding of the careers and residential situations of Amelia and Facundo—siblings who represent two aspects I wish to analyze: the "winners" and the "mortgagors."

Amelia finished her degree in Computer Engineering in 1988 and married Raúl, who had graduated as an architect. Some months later they migrated to the United States. However, they did not have their papers in order (unlike Amelia's cousins). They only had a tourist visa and they never succeeded in swapping it out for a residence permit. However, while living in the United States they built up their professional qualifications: Amelia took English lessons while Raúl learned about local construction techniques thanks to his work as a master builder and after taking various technical courses.

In 1993, the young couple returned to Mexico with the goal of setting up their own business. They thought that their return to Raúl's parents' house would only be temporary, but over time the two generations became so closely bonded that they continued the arrangement, even after the young couple had bought their own separate apartment. In 2004, having saved up a substantial amount and making the most of the construction techniques Raúl had learned while in the United States, they bought a lot measuring more than 1,000 square meters in one of the new, luxury gated communities in the north of Mexico City. There they built two enormous adjacent houses that enabled them to maintain mutual intergenerational cooperation, while gaining some independence at the same time.

A practical logic lay hidden behind this patrilocal relationship: Amelia managed the family business with Raúl as the architect and his father the manager of the team of workers. The three of them formed the pillars of this company that sometimes gave employment to more than 30 workers. After the North American Free Trade Agreement (NAFTA) entered into force in 1994, the family even worked for one of the large US companies that had set up an office in Mexico. This implied frequent journeys and a considerable investment of capital, time, and effort. Amelia and Raúl would never have been able to dedicate themselves so fully to their work had Raúl's mother not taken care of the young couple's two children and the housework. The family had strong intergenerational connections both domestically and professionally. It could weather the various crises and devaluations—in the words of Amelia's mother, whom I interviewed—by working hard, buying and selling properties, and thanks to a healthy savings account in US dollars. Amelia's brother Facundo also worked in the construction industry but had a very different experience.

The Mortgagors

Facundo began his career in 1987 working for one of the country's largest property developers. He was an on-site architect and received various minor promotions. In 1989 he married Lilia, a primary school teacher, whose parents (storekeepers) gave them an apartment in a working-class area in the north of the city. Due to transport complications, Facundo decided to return to the south, the area where he worked. During his parents' day, commuting to work did not pose a problem if you owned a car. But increasing distances and the sheer volume of traffic has changed the situation; Facundo spent around four hours every day driving to and from his workplace.

To avoid the difficulties of finding a new job at a time of increasing job cuts, he persuaded his wife to move to the south of the city. The young couple sold their apartment and applied for a mortgage from a private bank to buy somewhere new and slightly larger in a socio-economically more desirable part of the city. Lilia requested a job transfer so that she could work in the south and their life remained stable until December 1994, when the peso devalued by more than half against the dollar, the country's GDP fell by 6.2%, banks collapsed, and hundreds of thousands of people became unemployed.

In fact, during Mexico's brief economic recovery between 1989 and 1994, banks granted loans for housing, cars, and luxury goods in a flexible and even rather cavalier fashion. This breathed new life into certain sectors such as the real-estate market, and almost a million Mexicans entered into debt.[36] The 1994 Mexican peso crisis then triggered a doubling of interest rates, and, by extension, levels of debt.

Debtors had four options: (1) lose their properties through foreclosures; (2) pay the new amount of the debt according to the terms of the original contract, tripling or quadrupling the monthly installments compared to the original amounts; (3) join El Barzón,[37] a new movement of debtors who refused to negotiate their debts or to abandon their homes; or (4) negotiate a reimbursement in a unit of account or UDIs (Unidades de Inversión para Préstamos Hipotecarios; Investment Units for Mortgage Loans), whereby they could double or triple the amortization period. Facundo and Lilia chose this last option. However, the UDIs operated as a kind of stock market instrument, whose value fluctuated depending on inflation, obliging debtors to pay compound interest.

When I interviewed Facundo in 2004, the banking situation had stabilized and mortgages had high interest rates (around 12% per annum) and incorporated numerous safeguards. In common with many others in the same position, Facundo avoided taking out another loan. He had to work within the resources available. However, it was too late to make a break from the mortgage culture inherited from his grandparents, his parents, and his contemporaries, because he will have to pay his debt for at least another 15 years. But the "UDI deal" not only undermined Facundo's faith in bank loans. It also confined him—as we read in the quote at the beginning of the introduction—to a residential situation that he considered unsuitable for his family at the time. His children (an adolescent girl and a younger boy) already needed more space and independence. His ambitions of rising up the social and property ladder had come to nothing.

Within this framework, it is surprising how many of my middle-class interviewees were adamant about avoiding any involvement in El Barzón, a movement that rescued past-due portfolios, paid off debts, and even amended the Mexican Civil Code.[38] When I asked Facundo why he had opted against joining El Barzón, he dismissed the idea out of hand: "Who's got the time to get mixed up in all that stuff? To be honest, I think they're just a bunch of troublemakers, and they'll just end up losing their homes."

Conclusion

This chapter has focused on the emergence, continued presence, and differentiation of the middle classes in Mexico City through residential practices and situations across three generations of a kindred group. The period in question, which spans more than 80 years, reveals the transformations of a city whose population grew from 1.2 million inhabitants in 1930 to 16 million in 2000. We have seen how the government housing loan system developed into a specialist source of mortgages for the lower and lower-middle classes. In parallel, private property developers expanded the housing stock, accessible for the upper and middle classes through mortgages subject to the performance of national and international economies.

The couple who founded this kindred group was one of the 750 families who obtained a highly subsidized mortgage from the post-revolutionary state that was beginning to explore means of addressing the growing shortfall in urban housing. However, the state's response fell short of solving the problem and the program only benefitted a handful of "pampered children of the Revolution." During the "Mexican miracle"—a miracle that only benefitted a select few—the subsequent generation enjoyed more favorable circumstances in terms of their professional training and ability to climb the property ladder. They initially accessed a property through government loans, after Esteban and Horacio's mother played a pivotal role in passing on information and her experience. However, the increasing availability of such loans was also instrumental in a country whose governments sought to assimilate the model of the welfare state.

Gradually, each of the children began to go their different ways, closely following slightly disparate career paths. Esteban found himself in a privileged position that brought him within reach of an upper-class status, while Horacio joined the ranks of the upper-middle class. Their residential situations mirrored these developments, and the involvement of Raquel—Horacio's wife—made another important difference to the family's financial situation by obtaining their last mortgage.

This undoubtedly reveals one of the most fundamental changes in Mexican families during the twentieth century, as reflected in the third generation, though also unevenly. While Horacio's daughters and daughters-in-law have jobs outside the home, Esteban's daughters (members of the upper class) are housewives. The interviews do not provide detailed information about Esteban's sons' living arrangements. However, they did open a window onto how inequalities began to form within the kindred group, and particularly in the third generation—one that had to cope with cyclical crises and neoliberal policies and to learn to live in the present.

In those years, government housing loans targeted the lower and lower-middle classes, whereas the middle classes gravitated toward private bank loans—between the 1980s and the early 1990s, a well-established and flourishing credit culture swept people along in a tide of indiscriminate bank loans of all kinds.

The 1994 Mexican peso crisis undoubtedly exacerbated inequality between members of the middle classes, some of whom almost fell into poverty (Horacio's eldest son, for example, lived in a social housing development classified as D+ in the BIMSA map of 1998). As Minujin and Kessler wrote,[39] these were the newly poor who were significantly different to the structural poor, due to their education and consumer habits. This perhaps explains why, despite their precarious financial situations, this son and his brothers rejected the idea of building their own home by acquiring a lot through a grassroots movement which now accounts for 60% of the Mexican capital's housing constructions.

This study took two examples to explore in greater depth the heterogeneity of, and the inequality between, members of the middle class. On the one hand, there were the "winners," with a particular focus on Amalia's family and how it benefitted from the new trade relationship between Mexico and the United States strengthened by NAFTA (January 1994). On the other, there were the "mortgagors" who lost, as in the case of Facundo, who kept his job in the stagnant local construction sector under the constant threat of redundancy.

The residential situations of these two brothers also affected not only their professional situations but also their place within the national economy and politics. While Aurora and her extended family had two large homes in a luxury country club, Facundo remained (to use his own expression) "chained" to a small apartment and a large debt. In the same way that his elder brother refused to contemplate joining a local neighborhood association to build their own house, Facundo rejected the idea of signing up to El Barzón to salvage his property without having to mortgage everything. This reveals political stances in residential and class situations. But that will be the subject of another study.

Notes

1 Facundo, interview with the author, April 2004.

2 See (inter alia), Ezequiel Adamovsky, *Historia de la clase media argentina: Apogeo y decadencia de una ilusión, 1919–2003* (Buenos Aires: Planeta, 2009), 538; Sergio Visacovsky, *'Hasta la próxima crisis': Historia cíclica, virtudes genealógicas y la identidad de clase media entre los afectados por la debacle financiera en la Argentina (2001–2002)* (Mexico City: CIDE, Cuadernos de trabajo, 2010); Genaro Aguilar, "¿Está desapareciendo la clase media en México? Análisis de la polarización del ingreso," *Revista de Ciencias Sociales*, XIX, no. 1 (2013): 57–69; Camille Peugny and Cecile Van de Velde "Repenser les inégalités entre générations," *Revue française de sociologie* 54, no. 4 (2013): 641–662; Luis López-Calva et al., "Clases medias y vulnerabilidad a la pobreza: Reflexiones desde América Latina," in *El Trimestre Económico* 81, no. 322 (April–June 2014): 281–307.

3 Maristella Svampa, *Los que ganaron: La vida en los countries y barrios privados* (Buenos Aires: Biblos, 2001), 282.

4 Main findings in Claudia Zamorano, "Los hijos de la modernidad: Movilidad social, vivienda y producción de ciudad en el México posrevolucionario," in *Revista Alteridades* 34 (2007): 75–91 and Claudia Zamorano, *Vivienda mínima obrera en el México Posrevolucionario. Apropiaciones de una utopía urbana, 1936–2004* (Mexico City: Casa Chata, 2013), 266.

5 These interviews were conducted between 2000 and 2004. By 2021, all members of the second generation have already passed away. To preserve the anonymity of my interviewees, all the names and surnames were changed.

6 BIMSA, *Mapa mercadológico de la megaciudad de México* (Mexico City: Buró de Investigaciones de Mercado, S.A., 1998). I found four editions of

BIMSA maps: 1978, 1993, 1998, and 2004. I chose to work with the 1998 edition, because it uses a neighborhood scale and provides significant detail. This represents a problem of anachronism which I will indicate where necessary.

7 Zamorano, "Los hijos de la modernidad."

8 INEGI, "Fifth Population Survey (1930)," Basic tabulations, accessed February 2, 2011, http://www.inegi.org.mx/sistemas/TabuladosBasicos/default.aspx?c=16767&s=est

9 Zamorano, *Vivienda Mínima Obrera*.

10 DDF, *Departamento del Distrito Federal y la vivienda para obreros y empleados* (Mexico City: Imprenta Mundial, 1934), 73.

11 This loan system was the result of various discussions within the post-revolutionary government since the drafting of the 1917 Constitution and began to take shape with the establishment of the state pensions in 1925. See Zamorano, *Vivienda Mínima Obrera*.

12 Francisco Reyes-Palma, *Pablo O'Higgins: De estética y soberanía* (Mexico City: Gobierno del Distrito Federal, Fundación Cultural María y Pablo O'Higgins, 1999), 71.

13 Estimate by Pablo González Casanova, *La democracia en México* (Mexico City: Era, 2006), 114.

14 Louise E. Walker, *Waking from the Dream: Mexico's Middle Classes after 1968* (Stanford, CA: Stanford University Press, 2013), 321.

15 Soledad Loaeza, *Clases medias y política en México* (Mexico City: El Colegio de México, 1988), 437.

16 Migration introduces variables into the equation that lay outside the scope of this study. In fact, it is one of the pending contributions that the social sciences need to make to aid in the understanding of the middle class. It is interesting to see that one part of the Zepeda family's third generation emigrated to the United States.

17 Concepción Vargas, "Conjunto habitacional Narciso Mendoza: Villa Coapa," in *El espacio habitacional en la arquitectura moderna*, eds. Enrique Ayala and Gerardo Álvarez (Mexico City: UAM; CONACYT, 2013), 220.

18 Martha de Alba et al., eds., *Satélite: El libro: historias suburbanas en la ciudad de México* (Mexico City: UAM; Iztapalapa, 2011), 278.

19 In other words, between 95 and 120 minimum monthly wages—an amount that seems distorted by a trick of the memory. However, it is not completely out of the question, given the levels of inequality that still plague Mexico.

20 Esteban, interview with the author, July 2001

21 In 1998, located in the D+ category, according to BIMSA.

22 Vargas, "Conjunto habitacional Narciso Mendoza."

23 In 1998, located in the C+ category, according to BIMSA.

24 Alejandra Massolo, *Mujeres y ciudades: Participación social, vivienda y vida cotidiana* (Mexico City: El Colegio de México, 1982), 297.

25 Claudia Zamorano, *Navegando en el desierto: Estrategias residenciales en un contexto de incertidumbres; Ciudad Juárez* (Mexico City: Casa Chata, 2008), 326.

26 Zamorano, *Vivienda Mínima Obrera*.

27 Among the 35 kinship groups interviewed, I only found one woman who took out the bank mortgage for the Michoacana neighborhood in 1936; she was an exceptional case on account of being one of the teachers in the education center that formed part of the project.

28 Rosario Esteinou, *Familias de sectores medios: Perfiles organizativos y socioculturales* (Mexico City: CIESAS, 1996), 183.

29 A. Ricardo López-Pedreros, "'It Is Not Something You Can Be or Come to Be Overnight': Empleados, Office Angels, and Gendered Middle Class Identifications in Bogotá, Colombia, 1930–1955," in *Latin America's Middle Class: Unsettled Debates and New Histories, David S. Parker and Louise E. Walker* (Lanham, MD: Lexington Books, 2012), 151–170.
30 Lilia, interview with the author, 2001.
31 Jorge Montaño, *Los pobres de la ciudad en los asentamientos espontáneos: Poder y Política* (Mexico City: Siglo XXI Editores, 1976), 224.
32 Immanuel Wallerstein, "The Bourgeois(ie) as Concept and Reality," *New Left Review* I/167 (January–February 1988): 91–106.
33 Margarita Estrada, *1995: Familias en la crisis* (Mexico City: CIESAS, 1996), 102.
34 Svampa, *Los que ganaron*.
35 Guadalupe Loaeza, *Debo, luego sufro* (Mexico City: Océano; PFC, 2000), 342.
36 "El espejismo de los UDI's," *La Jornada* (Mexico City), October 9, 1996, 2.
37 El Barzón originated in agricultural parts of Mexico following the 1995 Mexican peso crisis that forced many farmers and livestock owners into bankruptcy. The name derives from a folk song about campesinos' debts to the company stores. Members of the middle class facing excessive mortgage debt repayments joined the movement when it spread to cities.
38 Silvia Bolos, "Los movimientos sociales, actores de la democratización en la ciudad," *Democracia y exclusión: Caminos encontrados en la Ciudad de México*, coords. Lucía Álvarez, Carlos San Juan, and Cristina Sánchez Mejorada (Mexico City: UNAM; Plaza y Valdés; UACM; INAH, 2006), 73–90.
39 Alberto Minujin and Gabriel Kessler, *La nueva pobreza en la Argentina* (Buenos Aires: Editorial Planeta, 1995), 278.

20 Class Transvestism in Chile

When the Poor Became Middle Class

Azun Candina Polomer

Transvestite Identities

The right-wing coalition Chile *Vamos* has been in power in Chile since March 2018. In May 2019, the authorities announced the creation of the "Clase Media Protegida" welfare system. The government website reveals that this is not a new social program but a collection of links and online information about pre-existing public policies and social welfare programs, such as unemployment insurance, financial and medical assistance for senior citizens, and applications for housing subsidies. In terms of its target audience, this government site explains that it is intended:

> For all the people who are the driving force behind our country and faithfully embody the importance of work, merit, and effort. With the conviction and sole objective of giving a better quality of life to their families and loved ones.
>
> Yet despite all their effort, work, and determination, these people still live in precarious conditions and accept that, without the right safeguards, they face situations that can potentially jeopardize their progress and wellbeing.[1]

Researchers into the middle classes will recognize in this brief text various words commonly associated with this sector of society: "work," "merit," and "effort." However, we can also read the second paragraph as an acknowledgement that some people, despite all of these virtues, continue to be poor—if we take poverty to mean financial precariousness that prevents people from leading dignified and stable lives. So why did the government present this project to protect the middle classes? On the one hand, the answer is simple. Since between 70% and 80% of the Chilean population defines itself as middle class, it is unsurprising that professional politicians single it out: they need votes and must appeal to the majority. This is not a local phenomenon; politicians of all stripes—Barack Obama, Donald Trump, Luiz Inácio da Silva and Mauricio Macri, to name but a few—have cast themselves in the role as knights in shining

DOI: 10.4324/9781003029311-25

armor riding to the defense of the middle class. However, the question in itself is complex: How and why do predominantly poor societies such as Chile's end up considering themselves middle-class countries? Why have so many people chosen to identify themselves with this social category instead of the alternatives? What does this apparent contradiction between people's financial status and self-identity tell us, or hide from view?

This text proposes the (working) concept of "class transvestism" as a way of answering those questions. A transvestite is defined as someone who dresses up in clothes appropriate to the opposite sex, either out of personal preference or as part of a performance. Without wishing to enter into a debate over the concept's dissident heteronormal connotation, this proposal borrows one of its elements or meanings: the appropriation and public use of something socially and historically assigned to others. We propose it because it seems more suitable than the classic concept of alienation, or the more colloquial and derogatory descriptions of snobbism (*cursilería, siutiquería, esnobismo*) used in Chile to refer to individuals or groups imitating others' behaviors or pretending to be something they are not; we contend that members of this mainly poor population do not define themselves as middle class through any kind of blindness to their precarious living conditions, nor because they consider these conditions natural or legitimate, nor because they are seeking to deceive other people, consciously or otherwise. Class transvestism falls into the category of a performance, where the actors are aware of appropriation and of wearing clothes normally assigned to others, for "staging a public performance" that they consider desirable or necessary. This "cross-dressing," therefore, refers to a performance or interpretation that we consider important as a means of understanding—at least partly—the contradictions, tensions, and feelings of frustration and loneliness that often accompany people who define themselves as belonging to the middle class in our recent history.

This text is developed from my previous research into primary and secondary teachers working in Chile during the twentieth century, public-sector employees in the mid-twentieth century, and the dramatic shift in direction of the Colegio Médico during the Chilean dictatorship (1973–1990).[2] In the first of these studies mentioned above, for example, one of the conclusions was that teachers had a turbulent relationship with other political and social actors in society, and amongst themselves. Tensions throughout the twentieth century existed between those educators who identified themselves with the proletariat, and therefore should rightly belong to a union, and others who claimed a middle-class status and should therefore form professional teacher associations or colleges. Furthermore, the collection of accounts revealed an unresolved contradiction between teachers who claimed that they worked purely out of love for their job and their pupils, and not for money (calling this the teaching profession's "mística"), while also complaining bitterly about their unfairly low salaries as university-educated professionals. A number of them even justified some teachers' poor performance as a consequence of their meager salaries: What more could they be asked to do for such a paltry wage? For their part, public-sector employees and doctors, despite the differences in their jobs, had a shared grievance that society expected them to dress, spend, and consume in a way that was not commensurate with their income that was always falling in real terms due to inflation. Doctors were also irked by the public perception that they belonged to the upper classes. This did not correspond to their reality: many had problems maintaining their status as middle-class professionals, and some doctors even suffered poverty. These examples prompted the idea of defining the middle class as a performance, one that is considered either an obligation (although it is unclear what or who is behind such a requirement), or a right, thanks to certain level of formal education, social or ethnic origin, or expectations. Again, this begs the question: Why did people feel "obliged" to adopt this middle-class guise despite the difficulties involved? What can explain such a high percentage of the population unwilling to self-identify as wage earners or as "proud members of the working class," or at least why they gradually stopped doing so over the course of the twentieth century?

In the following two sections, this text approaches this issue from two angles: firstly, by taking a cultural and long-term perspective, and proposing that the middle-class performance has deep roots in the definition of what is respectable and decent in postcolonial societies such as Chile's; and secondly, by examining top-down social categorizations and affiliations, as well as economic transformations, since the 1980s.

Middle-Class "Decency"

Performing in public, cross-dressing, wanting to be a body wearing clothes normally assigned to another type of body, is not a new reality for the middle and lower classes. In early-twentieth-century Chile, Tancredo Pinochet Le Brun poked fun at people who—being poor and in need of work—avoided manual labor despite the better pay, because they were not blue-collar workers but "decent people." He recounted this in one of his testimonial works:

> I've always seen that all young Chileans prefer a decent job that pays between $60 and $80 pesos. In other words, they'll choose to work as an office clerk in a dark, unpleasant room, or selling fabrics in a suburban store, instead of taking a job that pays twice as much but is called "indecent" because instead of working with a pen in hand, they have to handle a hammer or chisel. A lady once came to the school to apply for a vacant position. She hoped to earn $60 or $80 pesos. The vacancy was for a job managing a laundry workshop and the salary would be from $150 to $200 pesos. I'll never forget her look of indignation and arrogant protests when I told her what the job entailed.

"But *señor*, I thought that you knew that I'm a decent person!" she replied.[3]

Clotario Blest, Chile's most prominent and well-respected trade unionist, also refers to his failure to set up an association of fiscal employees in the 1930s, because the public-sector employees—most of whom earned pitiful salaries—opposed that definition of workers, whom they identified with manual labor, in other words people of a lower social status than they had as white-collar employees:

> Clotario was excited to observe the growth of the working class from a distance, as a middle-class government employee. At that time, public-sector employees (apart from teachers) were not represented by any kind of organization. They did not feel the need. As they were mostly members of the middle class, the idea of trade unionism struck them as "uncouth." In his concern for such matters, he appeared like a shipwreck survivor marooned on an island, misunderstood and surrounded by social climbers.[4]

In a well-established cultural matrix dating back to the colonial era's caste system, Latin American societies were built upon the perception of two social groups: "decent" people (whose decency was associated with a European and Christian lifestyle and background, with non-manual employment such as the management of properties and businesses, political affairs or intellectual pursuits) and the lower classes or "plebs" who worked in manufacturing or domestic jobs and were assumed to lead messier lives: campesinos, farmhands, day laborers, servants, and general vagrants. Some "White" people down on their luck fitted into this second category, but it generally consisted of mestizos, indigenous, and those of African ancestry, which was used to explain the "barbarity" of their uneducated and disorderly ways of life and their dubious morality and cleanliness.

That social construction was clearly based on "Derecho indiano"—a set of laws applicable to Spain's Latin American dominions—that gave a legal footing to a social hierarchy defined by ethnic background. According to Araya, the word "castas" was

> used in every colonial territory by different authorities (clergy, governors, viceroys, intellectuals, etc.) in various contexts: for example, it cropped up principally in geographical reports, civil and ecclesiastical population surveys, marriage files, legal dossiers, travelogues, from the sixteenth to the eighteenth centuries.[5]

Broadly speaking, this constituted a form of classification rooted in ancestry and bloodlines, and was designed to regulate what Viceroy Amat referred to in 1770 as the "unusual products" of the American territories;[6] in other words, new people and new bodies created by the joining of different races that had not previously encountered one another in human history.

At the top of the ladder were the Spaniards and their criollo descendants, considered "White," followed by the indigenous peoples, and finally Blacks or those with African ancestry, who were mainly slaves or, in the best-case scenario, freed slaves. Very soon, and during centuries of colonial rule, the inter-racial unions that began in the sixteenth century made it very difficult to define "pure" categories and the caste system had to include intermediate groupings classified as "mulattos," "zambos," and "pardos," including some names that now appear bizarrely whimsical, such as "albarazados," "tente en el aire," and "tornatrás."

Although from a contemporary perspective this mélange of different terms designating various racial combinations might appear laughable, their very existence and enduring use reveals a fundamental issue when defining social classes and groups in Latin America: the variable of ethnic origin or race. This was established not merely to distinguish between people's different physical appearances, but as criteria to define social superiority or inferiority, and, to an even greater extent, the opportunities for individuals' and families' social mobility. Scholars of the colonial period often insist that in practice the caste system could be overcome, and this did indeed happen in practice. Some people managed to become classified as "Spanish" despite being technically "mestizos" or "castizos"; or they assumed a "mulato" identity whereas they were in fact "moros." But the effort in itself and these acts of deception reveal their importance for citizens and the society to which they belonged. In colonial times, if someone had indigenous, African, or Oriental "blood" (ancestry), this did not constitute a simple fact about their background, as we have already mentioned; it also had negative connotations about their characters and trustworthiness. This was seen as sullying the Spanish ("White") heritage, in the sense of producing less reliable, physically and morally feeble, or lazier individuals. The Black population in particular, and especially the men, were deemed to be more violent and lewd than other people, with a natural inclination for committing rape and crime, and they therefore needed closer supervision and to receive harsher punishments.[7] In July 1551, for example, Santiago's council decreed that no one of any kind or caste should be on the city streets after curfew. If the person caught disobeying this order was a Spaniard, he could be asked to hand over his weapons and detained. If the offender was Black or indigenous, then they would be sent to jail or tied up and given 100 lashes in public.[8] Hence the interest in being a "Spaniard"—in other words, fair-skinned—or in being defined or perceived as white as possible, became an important need and one that added complexity to the understanding of the origin and the development of Chile's social classes.

Perhaps, therefore, our first social "transvestism" existed in the caste system, before becoming applicable to classes, or a hybrid of both. Latin

American class relations and structures cannot be properly comprehended without considering that past which, as we have touched upon here, rested on two basic elements of those social relationships: the pre-eminent social and financial position of families and groups of European origin and who lived as elites, and at the opposite end of the spectrum, the disparagement of indigenous cultures and African descendants, and of the individuals and communities who belonged to these groups, or whose skin color, hair, body shapes and features, speech, attire, or lifestyles identified them as belonging to such categories. When analyzing our current reality, we should recall that the concept of social classes, which emerged in Europe in the eighteenth century, is classified on the basis of differences in property ownership, political power, and social status, that are attached to people's varying levels of wealth. When studying these differences in Latin America, we cannot overlook the ethnic influences on these factors. A Spaniard from Spain who arrived with only the clothes on his back and an ambition to seek his fortune in the New World would be inserted into a society where he would be afforded greater opportunities than those available to a "mulato," an "albarazado" or a "tente en el aire." Latin American class structures—and therefore studies on them—must include this inseparability of class and caste, despite being virtually invisible and sometimes very subtle and well-concealed.

This chapter is not the place for a detailed description of the drive to "civilize"—understood as Europeanizing and Whitening the local populace—that began with the European conquests of the Americas and continued with the republican projects of the nineteenth century. Suffice it to say that, over the long term, Latin American societies were not only built upon status and economic power, but also upon identities in which virtues such as reliability, honesty, and refinement were attributed to Europeans and their descendants, while the wide variety of non-Europeans and non-Whites were treated with suspicion and subject to discrimination. The efforts by the poor in Latin America to escape from poverty and ascend to join the ranks of the middle class was certainly a financial issue, but it has also often been a process of becoming less indigenous and fairer-skinned than one's ancestors, and thus attain more easily a Western lifestyle and its canons of virtue, beauty, and elegance.

This is no small matter. The majority of those who, during the twentieth century and to this today, have been defined in Chile as middle class did not come from the impoverished White elites or upper classes, but from popular sectors of society that consisted of large numbers of mixed-race people of the Americas. Therefore, they lacked a guarantee of upward social mobility due to their ethnic background and physical appearance, and were obliged to use other symbolic and material methods such as formal education, material wealth, and cultural consumption. They needed to equip themselves in order to climb the socio-economic ladder, as well as to go through a process of physical and cultural "Whitening." They were obliged—to return to this chapter's guiding concept—to cross-dress as Europeans and Whites despite not actually belonging to these groups. This is what converted them, at least partially, into "decent people."

As Ezequiel Adamovsky pointed out in the case of Argentina—and we believe that the Chilean case was not dissimilar—in societies with fewer people, smaller cities and a not-too-distant colonial past, most people were well aware who was decent and who was not, both generally and in daily life:

> Differences in wealth during this period were still not as notable as they became some decades later; the distance between the richest and poorest members of society was less extreme. The houses of "patrician" families in that era were humble dwellings compared to the palaces and mansions that sprung up in the second half of the nineteenth century. The owner of a textile import business could easily belong to the "decent" classes, and it was not unusual for the children of even the most prominent families to work as store clerks. In any case, in those years it was abundantly clear who was who: in towns and cities that were still small, decent people knew each other, so that there were few opportunities for anyone to be misplaced in the social hierarchy.[9]

This quote reveals various phenomena. Firstly, since the late nineteenth century, the Chilean elites became increasingly wealthy and developed more refined tastes, thus setting themselves apart from common folk. At the same time, public administration, trade, education, service sector, and industry were growing, and this required more public officials, teachers, professionals, and technically qualified workers. The relatively clear-cut distinction between the patrician classes and the lower orders of society became more blurred. For example, many people could also style themselves as "decent" due to their level of education, style of speech and dress, and their white-collar jobs—despite lacking old criollo roots. However, we propose that this identity-based duality between the patricians (or "decent" people) and the masses may have changed but did not disappear. Whoever managed to become a schoolteacher or a clerk at a new and modern store, a bank employee, or an accountant at a factory, attained a higher cultural status than domestic workers, laborers, or those in informal employment. Sometimes those "decent" jobs also promised higher salaries and less-arduous duties, as in the case of independent professionals or senior managers in the public and private sectors; but in other cases, skilled laborers or informal workers earned salaries that were not much lower than those earned by junior public officials or primary school teachers. Perhaps for these groups, and from a modern perspective, defining oneself and performing publicly as a member of the middle class was a way of resolving that tension: it was a broadly defined area but one that marked the difference between the rich and the poor, allowing them to show that they were decent people, even without belonging to the traditional class of "decent" people.

The important thing to note here is that some people managed to carry off this requirement to dress, consume, and live like "decent people" with certain ease, whereas for others it was a grueling process that caused them permanent stress given their genuine financial means. Amanda Labarca, who addressed this issue in the 1940s, calculated that Chile had a middle-class population of 800,000, out of a total of 5.5 million (in 1946), based on their income levels, income tax declarations, and an approximate calculation of four people per family.[10] Labarca highlights two phenomena about the middle classes, a minority group within Chilean society: firstly, that the "families of the urban and rural lower classes are aware that their children will have greater opportunities than their own limited ones"[11]—in other words they could join the ranks of the middle classes; and secondly, that it was a tough and competitive struggle, and victory did not necessarily ensure glittering success. For example, although a public-sector employee's salary was on average higher than what a laborer earned, their lives were complicated by the "conspicuous consumption" that they considered necessary to maintain their status as white-collar (non-manual) workers and as "decent people," and this took its toll on their confidence and their nerves:

> Chile's middle class is *poor*. The strong competition to achieve well-being and that "conspicuous consumption" which forms a part of their social needs makes its members unhappy, bitter, envious, and severely critical. In addition to poverty, we should now add the insecurity generated by inflation, and how it is partially mitigated by the benefits of social welfare programs.[12]

We are talking about a society undergoing a transformation. New social identities (viz. the working class and proletariat) were growing and becoming more entrenched, and traditional identities remained (such as the landowning aristocracy and the campesinos). Some blue-collar, salaried employees were also making progress and by dint of their labors were considered "decent." Therefore, as Labarca says, these employees felt the "social need" to perform in this decent way in their daily working and family lives, despite the material costs and with the added complication of living in countries plagued by inflation and political and economic crises.

Ever since the "middle-class" concept came into use, it was related to a performance. Being or becoming "middle class" entailed Westernized and modern styles of dress and speech which, up until that point, had been the preserve of a social minority identified as "patricians," "decent people," or, to use more contemporary terms, elites or oligarchs. For some, this "performance" was relatively straightforward since they had the requisite income and stability. For others, however, it was a constant struggle: the reality of being lower class in a strictly financial sense, and the awareness of being "middle class/decent," in terms of their employment, was a driving force behind the performance that we have defined here as class transvestism.

Top-Down Innovation

This chapter contends that if class transvestism or the middle-class performance was a tendency with roots in long-standing social identities and developed over the course of the twentieth century, then the neoliberal transformations related to employment and labor caused this tendency to increase in Chile, from the 1980s until the present day.

From this perspective, we should recall that the graphic representation of social classes tends to resemble a social pyramid, generally in the form of an equilateral triangle. This figure suggests the existence of social and economic inequality, with a minority of the rich, a robust and growing intermediate sector, and just a bottom layer made up of the poor. In the mid-twentieth century and possibly even today, the received wisdom was that this held true in the case of Chile's social structure: a country of both rich and poor, to be sure, but also one with a solid and promising middle class. However, the financial data fail to back this up, and for Chile the equilateral triangle does not apply. According to a survey by the Fundación Sol in 2017, in Chile 54.3% of workers earn a net income of less than $350,000 pesos, 74.3% of workers earn less than $500,000 pesos (net) and only 16.1% earn more than $700,000 pesos (net). A very small segment of workers (1%) earn salaries of over $3 million pesos, with the highest earners making $40 million pesos per month.[13] Chile also has one of the highest concentrations of wealth in the world. According to ECLAC's *Social Panorama of Latin America*, wealth distribution in Chilean homes is highly unequal: "50% of the poorest homes had an average net wealth of $5,000 dollars, the wealthiest 10% had an average of $760,000 dollars, and the richest 1%, around $3 million dollars."[14] Furthermore, the wealthiest 1% also accounts for 26.5% of GDP. If we add that *within* that 1% we must consider a much smaller percentage of the "ultra-rich," the graphical representation would not look remotely like an elegant, equilateral triangle; Chile's social pyramid would instead appear like a strange skyscraper: a fat lower level representing various levels of poor, below a small minaret and then tapering to a stratospherically high pinnacle.

Why, therefore, if that dream of a "middle-class country" failed to materialize, does it continue to exist as a social category, and one that has even grown? What makes people prefer to identify themselves as "impoverished," "threatened," or "struggling" members of the middle class, rather than admit their actual poverty? We propose that this cannot be solely attributed to a pre-existing identity matrix in society, but relates to discourses about social classes and identities constructed in universities and global organizations and centers of learning.

Figures released by ECLAC show a reduction in poverty in Latin America from 40.5% to 33% of the total population between 1980 and 2008.[15] Most of those considered to have escaped poverty, according to this study, were deemed members of the "vulnerable," "emerging," or "new" middle class. These adjectives refer to those who—at least statistically—have recently risen out of poverty but who could easily relapse. Nevertheless, we should exercise great caution when analyzing this information: those classified as being formerly poor, in other words the "new" middle class, are persons with a yearly income of between $5,000 and $15,000 dollars. In Chile, for example, this means including within that "middle-class" range people with an average monthly salary of $417 dollars, an amount that is only slightly above the current minimum wage, which is approximately $400 dollars. In other words, and at least at the lower end of the spectrum, among those people considered to have escaped poverty and joined the middle class are individuals and families that remain impoverished.

Table 20.1, taken from the same ECLAC survey of 2010, points to another important phenomenon. It provides information about the percentage variation in household incomes, and distinguishes between the middle- and lower-income strata of society. An optimistic interpretation of this data would conclude that the variations have been upward; in other words, that a higher variation in the average income is a sign of improvement of people's financial situation and quality of life. However, when examining these variations we must factor in some major financial crises, as in 1994 and 2001, which give reason to believe that these variations show frequent decreases more often than governments and people themselves like to admit.

The editors of this research project sum up the situation clearly in the following extract, which is worth citing in full:

Table 20.1 Percentage variation in average household income, by employment strata

Country	*Years*	*Middle-income stratum*	*Lower-income stratum*
Brazil	1990–2007	23	35
Chile	1990–2006	47	49
Costa	1990–2007	41	20
Rica	1990–2007	12	24
Honduras	1989–2006	15	11
Mexico	1991–2007	10	41

Source: ECLAC, based on special tabulations of the countries' household surveys.

> New areas of social theory focus on other objects—or subjects—where currents such as "stratificationism" and Marxism lost relative importance. Precarious employment and the impact of financial volatility, combined with the crises that shook the region over the final two decades of the twentieth century, turned people's gaze toward the most vulnerable groups. These included a section of the middle class that fell onto hard times and lost their jobs. In this sense, the remaining middle class faced the threat of relapsing into poverty rather than enjoying continued stability. Far from being autonomous subjects, masters of their own fate, and protagonists in political alliances and in relation to the state, the focused social policies during the 1980s and 1990s simply revealed the scattered remains of the dismembered and impoverished middle-class who need assistance.[16]

We should emphasize the importance of the first part of that quote. During the first half of the twentieth century some academics and politicians were already aware that a sizeable proportion of the supposedly growing middle-class population were in fact a "transvestite" lower class, but the crisis of welfare states and labor market flexibilization that ravaged the region since the late 1970s made their performance even harder. People seemed to doubt that, despite their public performance and a lifetime of work and profound faith in education as a key for upward social mobility, they would ever reach that much-coveted horizon. Another important phenomenon also exists: privatizing reforms have gradually reduced the number of manufacturing jobs, thus downsizing an established unionized working class. The group of employees that grew strongest since the 1970s was a new proletariat clustered in sectors such as business and services, with low salaries and highly precarious employment conditions—although the nature of their work still categorized them as white-collar employees. In other words, they could continue to define themselves as middle class due to their type of activity but not thanks to employment stability or financial security.

Table 20.2 shows that the "managers and administrators of medium- and large-sized companies" and "salaried employees with university-level education in public administration and in medium- and large-sized companies in the private sector," only correspond to 4.2% of the total workforce; in contrast, "independent professionals and technical workers, and owners of microbusinesses with directly supervised staff" and "salaried technical workers with vocational qualifications and office clerks" (significantly, with the latter being referred to as "non-manual proletariat") represent 20.9% of jobs, plus 23% of workers defined as "specialized and non-specialized members of the salaried proletariat with employment contracts." These numbers can give us clues to understand the performance aspect of defining the middle class: although this classification in particular does not use the term "middle class," we know that,

Table 20.2 Class structure in Latin America (A. Portes and K. Hoffman)

Class	*Subtypes*	*Percentage of workforce*
I. Capitalists	Business owners and managing partners of medium- or large-sized businesses	1.8
II. Executives	Managers and administrators of medium- or large-sized businesses	1.6
III. Elite workers	Salaried professionals with university-level education working in public administration and in medium- or large-sized businesses in the private sector	2.8
IV. petite bourgeoisie	Independent professionals and technical workers and owners of microbusiness with directly supervised staff	8.5
Va. Non-manual workers in the formal proletariat	Salaried technical workers with vocational qualifications and office clerks	12.4
Vb. Manual workers in the formal proletariat	Specialized and non-specialized salaried proletariat with employment contracts	23.4
VI. Informal proletariat	Salaried laborers without work contracts, street vendors and unpaid domestic workers	45.9

Source: Camilo Sémbler, "Estratificación social y clases sociales. Una revisión analítica de los sectores medios" (Santiago de Chile: CEPAL, División de Estudios, 2006), 44.

culturally speaking, this heterogeneous mix that encompasses managers, owners of a neighborhood store, IT technicians, and store clerks working in a shopping mall, perform in public as white-collar employees in the proud tradition of "decent" work. As such, they occupy a superior position to waste collectors, gardeners, domestic employees, or street vendors who form part of the daily urban landscape.

Conclusion

We began this chapter by referring to a program of the right-wing coalition government, Chile Vamos, and it would seem appropriate to conclude with a reference to a poster that circulated on social networks and on the streets, in Chile's "social rebellion" that began in October 2019 (Figure 20.1).

Posters such as this have been part of a social protest movement with collective leadership structures. One of this movement's principal aims has been to "awaken" consciousness and rebel against the country's drastic social and economic inequality, the abuses of large-sized companies and the corruption and ineptitude of the political class. For those studying the

Figure 20.1 "Remember: You're not middle class. You're working class… with a salary and debt." Plaza de la Dignidad (formerly Plaza Baquedano) Santiago de Chile, December 2019.

Source: Photo by the author

middle classes, this definition has also undeniably applied to the many grievances and public discussions triggered by this protest movement. Significantly, the first word of the poster is "Remember," making it a call for people to recognize themselves and take a fresh look at pre-existing definitions. This message is reinforced by the image accompanying the text, a drawing or engraving of three people wearing clothes identified with the poor and the working class, characteristically left-wing imagery of the low-income, popular sectors of society: a possible campesino, a woman wearing a *chamanto* or poncho with a babe-in-arms, and a young, dark-skinned youth. The importance of the poster is that its message is not that the middle class has become impoverished and run up debts, but that many people were never even middle class in the first place, and that underneath the Westernized, urban, and modern dress, the world of mestizaje, *chamantos*, campesinos and laborers continued to exist. The poster—affixed to a wall in an area dubbed by the media as the "ground zero" of the protest movement (in Plaza de la Dignidad, in the heart of the city of Santiago)— can be read, within the context of this analysis, as a kind of stripping-off of this middle-class attire, an angry critique of what was always seen as a performance. To some extent it responds to the definition made by the Chilean government, just five months previously, indicated above, and which seems much closer to the concept of the "good people" or the "good poor" of paternalist capitalism: poor *but* (?!) honest, hard-working, domesticated, and "Whitened" folk, who pose no threat to the status quo, accepting financial hardship as an individual problem and therefore deserving state aid. The poster can hypothetically be read as a public wake-up call as if to emphasize: "yes, there are people poorer than you, but you're still poor." In the eyes of its critics, this transvestism has turned these people into a depoliticized and individualistic "trashy middle class" who, according to Barozet, "[…] only eat fast-food, live in apartments that have destroyed the typical neighborhood houses, and supposedly act aggressively and impolitely." She describes a phantom social class that supposedly exists but that no one can properly identify.[17] We do not believe it coincidental that this poster is allegedly the work of the Bloque Vegan Straight Edge—a group identified with radical activism that seeks to reject the established daily routines and policies of late-stage capitalism.

This class transvestism possibly exposes and exonerates itself most powerfully during political and economic crises, when performing as a member of the middle class while remaining poor becomes even more arduous. It is no coincidence that the crises of Argentina (2011) or in the United States (2008) led researchers to reappraise definitions about the middle classes, thus creating a renewed interest in them. The self-defined middle-income sectors' claim of being "unprotected"—rich people do not need help from anyone, and the poor receive "everything free" from the state—is a kind of basso continuo of its voice and self-definition. In times of crisis, that perception of fragility and lack of protection becomes even more pronounced. In this chapter we propose that during turbulent times, the issue goes beyond the fear of losing a job or a certain social status; it casts doubt on the same strategies that have been used to meet these expectations. We can refer to Enrique Garguin's description of the situation in Argentina:

> In the public sphere, the idea of the "middle class" is instrumental in the struggle to establish a specific vision and division of the world; struggles of classification and identification that, as we will see, become particularly critical at times of uncertainty, either because a crisis shakes the very foundations of the status quo, or because public

> protests for democratization broaden people's expectations with disruptive effects on what is accepted as "normal."[18]

We could therefore say that this performance that we have called class transvestism is de-normalized more frequently in times of instability and crisis, and moreover is revealed as the performance that it is. Optimistic ideas about social change lead us to believe that the progress of neoliberalism, combined with societies and economies with advanced technologies, have created a new "global middle class" that communicates, works, and moves both physically and virtually around the world. More pessimistic observers point out that these groups are in the minority, and that while economic growth can be global, economic crises, precarious employment conditions, and frustrated ambitions can be equally widespread.[19]

It is difficult to know how the crises of the neoliberal project around the world, which appear to be increasingly frequent and profound, will affect the definitions of class and identity in specific societies. It seems clear that, after the 1970s and 1980s, the concepts of "the people" and the "working class" lost their power as rallying cries, and the "middle class" became more prevalent and suitable within systems that praised individual effort and merit, and where there was predominantly white-collar, salaried employment. It remains to be seen whether those white-collar, salaried employees who consider themselves middle class by default, by expectation, or by type of work, and who seem to have lost their faith in the benefit of credit and conspicuous consumption, will rediscover the concept of the working class, imbue new connotations and meanings to the definition of the middle class, or create new terms with which to describe themselves.

For the time being, we can conclude by quoting another (anonymous) text on the Chilean protests, written on a blackboard in October 2019. With a deft use of street slang and art, it effectively sums up a Latin American oasis questioning itself and the clothing it has worn:

> We're doing worse
> yet still we're better off,
> because before we had it good
> but that was false.
> Not like now that things are bad
> though it's the truth.

Notes

1 "Clase Media Protegida," accessed June 2019, https://clasemediaprotegida.gob.cl.
2 Azun Candina, *Clase media, Estado y sacrificio: La Agrupación Nacional de Empleados Fiscales (1943–1983)* (Santiago de Chile: LOM Ediciones, 2013); Azun Candina, "Vivir una dictadura: Historia y memoria de los profesores en Chile (1973–1990)," *Historia 396* 4, no. 2 (2014): 187–216; and Azun Candina, "Studying Other Memories: The Colegio Médico de Chile under Socialism,

Dictatorship, and Democracy, 1970–1990," *Latin American Perspectives* 43, no. 6 (2016).

3 Tancredo Pinochet Le-Brun, *Un año de empleado público en Chile* (Santiago de Chile: Casa Editora Tancredo Pinochet, 1915), 56.

4 *Collipulli* (pseudonym), "Clotario Blest: Cristiano, sindicalista, revolucionario," *Revista Aportes para la Renovación*, no. 2 (1979): 15.

5 Alejandra Araya Espinoza, "¿Castas o razas?: Imaginario sociopolítico y cuerpos mezclados en la América colonial; Una propuesta desde los cuadros de castas," in *Al otro lado del cuerpo: Estudios biopolíticos en América Latina*, comps. Hilderman Cardona and Zandra Pedraza (Colombia: Universidad de los Andes; Universidad de Medellín, 2014).

6 Carlos López Beltrán, "Sangre y temperamento: Pureza y mestizajes en las sociedades de castas americanas" (Mexico City: Directorio UNAM, electronic publication, 2008).

7 Eduardo Cavieres and René Salinas, *Amor, sexo y matrimonio en Chile tradicional* (Valparaíso: Universidad Católica de Valparaíso, Serie Monografías Históricas no. 5, 1991), 33.

8 Cavieres and Salinas, *Amor, sexo y matrimonio*, 33.

9 Ezequiel Adamovsky, *Historia de la clase media argentina: Apogeo y decadencia de una ilusión, 1919–2003* (Buenos Aires: Planeta, 2009), 20.

10 Amanda Labarca, "Apuntes para estudiar la clase media en Chile," *Revista Atenea*, no. 500 (November–December 1950), 8.

11 Labarca, "Apuntes para estudiar," 8.

12 Labarca, "Apuntes para estudiar," 8. Italics in the original.

13 Gonzalo Durán and Marco Kremerman, "Los bajos salarios de Chile: Análisis de la Encuesta CASEN 2017," *Fundación Sol* (2019), http://www.fundacionsol.cl/wp-content/uploads/2019/04/Salarios-al-L%C3%ADmite-2017-NV2-1.pdf.

14 CEPAL, *Panorama Social de América Latina 2019* (Santiago de Chile: CEPAL, 2019), 63.

15 Alicia Bárcena and Narcís Serra, eds., *Clases medias y desarrollo en América Latina* (Santiago de Chile: CEPAL, Santiago de Chile, 2010), 27.

16 Bárcena and Serra, *Clases medias y desarrollo*, 15.

17 Emmanuelle Barozet, "Serie sobre la clase media chilena (2): Ese gran miedo a resbalar," *Ciper*, Apr. 4, 2017, https://ciperchile.cl/2017/04/13/66957/.

18 Enrique Garguín, "La clase media en el discurso público," *Revista Cuestiones de Sociología*, no. 9 (2013).

19 A. Ricardo López-Pedreros with Barbara Weinstein, "Introduction: We Shall Be All; Toward a Transnational History of the Middle Class," in *The Making of the Middle Class: Toward a Transnational History*, eds. A. Ricardo López-Pedreros and Barbara Weinstein (Durham, NC: Duke University Press, 2012).

21 Taxonomy, Identity, Mode of Being, or Political Project?

Epistemologies of "Middle Class" in Latin America Since 1948

David S. Parker[1]

In August of 1948, the newly established Social Science Section of the Pan American Union's Department of Social Affairs chose as its inaugural research project an ambitious, comprehensive multi-nation study of Latin America's middle class.[2] Theo Crevenna, the Social Science Section's first director, believed that understanding the evolution of the middle class offered essential insights into Latin America's broader economic, social, and political trajectory, and to that end he set out to organize a genuinely continental group of experts that included such notable figures as Argentina's Gino Germani and Chile's Amanda Labarca. Twenty Latin American and seven U.S.-based scholars, sociologists and anthropologists in the majority, researched and wrote monographs published in six volumes over the course of 1950 and 1951, covering eighteen countries with only Guatemala and Peru omitted. Though published in a rough, almost typewritten format in a mix of Spanish, English and Portuguese, the volumes made a considerable impact: they were reviewed in several academic journals at the time and continue to accumulate citations today.

In this chapter I return to the 1948 Pan American Union project, a unique international collaboration that marked, I would argue, a noteworthy moment in the early history of social science writing on Latin America's class structure, as a jumping-off point for an interpretive essay that seeks to highlight questions that have cropped up repeatedly in subsequent scholarship. On what empirical basis do we assert that a middle class in fact exists? What kinds of sources do we utilize and what methodology do we apply in order to prove or deny its existence, to delineate its boundaries, to measure its size or to chart its growth or decline? I identify four distinct approaches that experts tend to adopt—taxonomical, identitarian, focused on *habitus*, or centered on politics—and discuss why they so often lead to wildly divergent conclusions. This chapter does not present a comprehensive account of the historiography of the Latin American middle class nor does it endorse any one methodology over another; rather, it hopes to employ examples from both academic and policy-oriented writing to show how profound the disconnects between

DOI: 10.4324/9781003029311-26

these four approaches are. Contributors to the Crevenna project wrestled with precisely these same challenges, which is why I consider it so appropriate to begin there.

Prologue: Why Focus on the Middle Class? And How?

In 1940, Chilean author Francisco Pinto described the middle class as "the thermometer that marks the vigor and strength of a nation, the class to which present-day civilization owes its formidable material progress."[3] Although this idea of the middle class could be traced through the Western canon all the way back to Aristotle,[4] it would become a particularly compelling vision in the aftermath of fascism's defeat in Europe and the dawn of the Cold War.[5] Crevenna embraced it fully, and in his preliminary communication to the scholars who enlisted in the Pan American Union project he articulated what he considered at stake:

> Why study the middle class separately? Why insist on studying this social group that is so unstable and difficult to define? It has been said that a powerful middle class contributes to social and economic stability. It has been said that the new middle class that has emerged—slowly in some countries, more rapidly in others—holds decisive importance for the stabilization of the world's problems.[6]

Writing without irony or intentional hyperbole about the "stabilization of the world's problems," Crevenna betrayed one of the unique characteristics of the middle class as a research topic: its intimate link to a normative vision of economic progress, social stability, and democracy.[7] Brian Owensby describes the optimistic hope of many post-World War II-era scholars, that "by rejecting patronage and hierarchy, by embracing individualism and merit," the middle class "would deliver Latin American nations from 'backwardness'."[8] Not to mention from Communism as well. Nowhere is the *durability* of that normative ideal better illustrated than in a 2011 OECD Development Centre working paper:

> [F]ocus on the middle class in developing countries is justified by its potential contribution to economic and social welfare. Several channels through which the middle class might promote economic growth have been identified: fostering entrepreneurship, shifting the composition of consumer demand, as well as encouraging policy reforms and institutional changes conducive to growth. Empirical studies have shown its relevance to economic growth and prosperity in several respects. It contributes to mediation between rich and poorer classes—in Marx's words, "it limits class conflicts"—an essential element of a sound democracy. Furthermore, democratic regimes are more likely to occur in countries with middle classes.[9]

Latin America, however, had also long been home to the counternarrative that it was a region without a genuine middle class, or whose middle class had failed to fulfill its role as a transformational bourgeoisie.[10] So it was no trivial matter for contributors to the Pan American Union project to seek to determine through empirical investigation whether the objects of their research did, in fact, constitute a true middle class, of the kind that might hold "decisive importance for the stabilization of the world's problems."

This inevitably raised the question of how to define the middle class. At first Crevenna's team in the Social Science Section contemplated setting out a definition a priori in order to impose some unity on the country studies, but they quickly discarded that option as unworkable, choosing instead to provide six different definitions to consider, and instructions to the authors to make their own conceptualizations explicit.[11] One of the six options came from project contributor Germani, already recognized as one of the giants of Argentine sociology; the other five were translated excerpts from works by European and U.S. academics first published between 1897 and 1942.[12] Several of the definitions focused on occupation, with Germani's stressing the distinction between an "old" middle class of independent proprietors defined by their autonomy and a "new" middle class of salaried employees defined by the nonmanual or high-tech character of their work.[13] But there were also key differences between approaches. Johannes Wernicke privileged education, while also bringing in supervision of other workers and "a moderately elevated income and even some degree of capital."[14] Jean Lhomme made central to his definition *the consciousness of not belonging* to either the upper or lower class, and the absence of hope of reaching the former or fear of falling into the latter.[15]

Crevenna's inter-American team of contributors crafted their monographs in response to 34 questions that ranged in their phrasing from narrowly empirical to highly interpretive. Some representative examples of both:

- Is there a middle class in the geographic area you are dealing with? What is its size? What percentage of the total population? What groups of people comprise it?
- Does a middle class exist outside urban centers? Has industrialization caused the middle class to grow? To what extent?
- Has the increase in technicians and professionals in service to government and private enterprises favored the tendency to foster a middle class?
- Do you consider unionized workers to belong to the middle class? If so, to what degree?
- Have the recent world wars had an influence on the growth and development of the middle class? What specifically has their influence been?

- Is there a minimum living standard that characterizes the middle class?
- Is there a typically middle-class cultural pattern (*patrón*)?
- Are there, or are there not, difficulties in moving from one class to another, be it downward mobility from the upper class as a result of economic ruin or matrimonial union, or ascent from the lower class to the middle class?
- At present, does the middle class enjoy a living standard that members of lower classes cannot easily attain?
- Is there a typical mentality ("*actitud mental*") that is peculiar to the middle class? Does there exist a certain psychological pattern? Is this mentality recognized by other social groups?
- Do people who belong to the middle class readily admit that they belong to this group?
- Do you believe that belonging to the middle class owes more to a "state of spirit" than to economic, social, or religious factors?
- What, in your opinion, is the influence of the middle class on the political, economic, social, and religious life of the country? To what degree does that influence affect the stability of the country?
- Do you believe that the growth of the middle class will have a beneficial effect on political stability and democratic forms of government?
- Do you believe that a considerable growth of the middle class is desirable?[16]

As leading as some of these questions were, revealing both the conceptual blinders of what would come to be known as modernization theory and the preoccupations of Cold War diplomacy, the 27 country monographs were nevertheless surprisingly nuanced in their observations, reflecting serious independent work by some of the region's most influential social scientists. The modern-day divorce between purely academic and policy-centered research was, one could argue, yet to emerge.

I would contend, however, that the challenges inherent in defining a middle class (and in defining it, affirming its existence) were nonetheless evident from the very first page of the Crevenna collection's very first monograph. Above and beyond the middle class's indefinite boundaries, above and beyond the challenge of importing theories of class developed in wealthier countries to analyze poorer ones, there was the deeper question of which facts to examine and what rules of evidence to apply to what kinds of sources. At issue, in other words, was epistemology: finding an appropriate methodology for the study of social class, rooted in a defensible theory of knowledge. In her critical review of Sara Maza's *The Myth of the French Bourgeoisie*, Jan Goldstein described three fundamentally different ways of conceptualizing class:

> Like every key word with a long history and wide resonance, its meaning is hard to pin down... It can be a taxonomic concept, used from an

> external vantage point to describe the make-up of society and to analyze social processes. It can be an identity or identity-element, self-consciously and linguistically appropriated by a speaker to refer to a group to which he or she belongs and whose membership shaped the speaker's sense of purpose. Or it can be a *habitus*, in Pierre Bourdieu's term, in which case it is inhabited without linguistic self-consciousness but in a manner that shapes its possessor's mode of physical and mental being in the world and is recognizable to the observer.[17]

These three conceptualizations of class are not simply alternatives to one another; they rely on radically different sorts of evidence and involve incompatible modes of inquiry. Looking back over seven decades of research on Latin America's middle class, what stands out above all else is the dispute over the kind of evidentiary test we need to apply to determine whether such a thing as a middle class exists in the first place. Taxonomy, identity, or habitus: let us consider the implications of each.

Taxonomy Versus Identity: Observer's Gaze or Agent's Self-Expression?

There are countless possible taxonomical approaches to the middle class, "used from an external vantage point," of which the most common is the statistical focus on living standards. In its crudest form, locate those whose incomes lie closest to the mean and we have found our middle class, but obviously there are millions of possible nuances and refinements. Is it better to define the middle according to a global standard, or to speak in national or local terms? Should we set the middle at the third quintile or the middle two or four deciles, or do we instead define an absolute income threshold far enough above the poverty line that people have access to status goods and leisure opportunities surpassing basic needs?[18] Alternatively, do we define middle-classness as a function of possession of some emblematic consumption good such as an automobile?[19] The choice affects what can be discerned. Setting an absolute standard for middle-class membership enables arguments about the class's growth over time, something that relative measurements based on income percentile cannot. But absolute measures of middle-class membership do not, of course, capture differences in what societies value.

Alternative taxonomies reject economic criteria as the sole or even the principal factor defining a middle class. Some identify middle classes structurally-functionally, based on the place of occupations in the division of labor. Works on the "professional-managerial class" or Erik Olin Wright's idea of "contradictory locations" in the division between capital and labor are examples.[20] Others have focused on education, or on occupational prestige rather than function. The diversity of approaches is limitless, but all qualify as taxonomies because they share two assumptions:

first, that class originates in the unequal distribution of resources, power, and status that exists in a society, and second, more importantly, that scholars are capable of discerning those structures of inequality, and in so doing, *they* are the ones who define the middle class and delineate its boundaries. No matter the complexity, this is unproblematic epistemological territory. Finding a middle class is a matter of the external observer examining data and making sense of society's hierarchies as they are, out in the "real world" as the analyst interprets that real world to be.

Over recent decades, however, methodological critiques within the social sciences have called into some question the propriety of experts in richer countries creating a priori models to characterize social structure in the poorer countries that are the object of their gaze.[21] If our imperative is to de-privilege "-etic" analyses in favor of more "-emic" ones, we need at least to question the idea that a meaningful middle class can be found simply by analyzing a society's unequal distribution of resources, power, and status, without taking into account how members of that society conceptualize their identities within the social order of which they form a part. For historians, embrace of the cultural and linguistic turn has tended toward a consensus that identifying a middle class requires that we find subjective acts of self-recognition *as* middle-class, a language of middle-class identity expressed in the public sphere. A middle class cannot exist, in other words, in the absence of a self-aware middle-class agent.

We need not retrace the well-worn path from Marx's distinction between a "class-in-itself" (*klasse an sich*) and a "class-for-itself" (*klasse für sich*), through E.P. Thompson's contention that only through the experience of acting as a class-for-itself does a collectivity come to constitute a class-in-itself, to Gareth Stedman Jones's and Dror Wahrman's insistence that there *are* no classes-in-themselves, only discursive constructions of imagined classes.[22] For our purposes the important thing is that the middle-class-as-identity approach sends us not to the census or tax rolls or other measurable socio-economic data to find a middle class, but to the kinds of sources where evidence of class-identified agency might be found. It leads us to the public pronouncements of small business associations or white-collar worker unions, to newspapers and pamphlets, to strikes and rallies and conferences, to opinion surveys and letters to the editor, in short, to individual and collective acts of self-definition and self-expression. These are very different kinds of sources, and can lead to very different kinds of conclusions.

People have long been aware of the tension between class as externally observed and class as a subjective identity claim. Gino Germani's opening contribution to the Crevenna collection began by noting the distinction between what he called "structural" and "psycho-social" criteria for defining the middle class. Germani defined as "structural" a diverse and thoughtful list of functional, economic, and status attributes. These included occupation, individual or family wealth, education, whether one's standard of living matched culturally-assumed expectations for members of a particular class, and society's general collective judgment of a person's value. The criteria he defined as "psycho-social" included the attitudes, expectations, beliefs, norms, and values that "govern the subjective life" of middle-class individuals and shape their conduct.[23] Germani believed that in normal times, structural and psycho-social attributes of class tended to coincide, but that in crises the correspondence could be lost, potentially producing "social conflicts of profound repercussion."[24] In times of hyperinflation, for example, it would not be unusual for people to lose the income and living standards that had defined them as middle class, yet still cling tightly to middle-class habits, attitudes, expectations, and self-identifications. Germani was especially interested in these recurrent moments of instability, which he considered characteristic of, and in their frequency and intensity unique to, Latin America in general and Argentina in particular.[25]

Writing about Cuba, Lowry Nelson made an almost identical distinction between structural and "socio-psychological" criteria for class definition, but in his view the absence of any collective middle-class subjectivity in Cuba called into question the class's very existence, notwithstanding that there certainly were, in Havana especially, large numbers of professionals, government employees, teachers, commercial and bank clerks, and others who would fit an external observer's definition.[26] One of the Argentine contributors to the Pan American Union project, Sergio Bagú, similarly questioned the existence of a middle class, making a case that was philosophically identical to Nelson's, even though socially fluid Argentina was arguably the antithesis of the static two-class order that Nelson perceived in pre-revolutionary Cuba with its slaveocratic plantation legacy, divided between "those who hire servants and those who do not, or those who work with their hands and those who work with their heads, or do not work at all."[27] Bagú asserted that in Argentina "the middle class is an unknowable entity when one hopes to illuminate it with figures," because historically elevated industrial wages and high levels of social mobility rendered it "impossible to tell if a person earning a salary of, say, 8000 pesos a month was a white-collar or skilled blue-collar worker."[28]

Reviewers of the Pan American Union collection at the time highlighted these unresolved doubts about the definition and even the existence of a middle class. Harold E. Davis wrote that the collection "still seems to leave unanswered one of the basic questions which disturbs our age—that of the extent to which the middle class is a social reality or a social myth."[29] B.R. Wilson concurred that "more problems are raised than are solved by these studies—if, indeed, any are solved." Among them: "Must a class be aware of its own existence to be considered a class at all?"[30]

The distance between externally defined middle classes and people's self-identification *as* middle class, which the Davis and Wilson reviews highlighted, remains an intractible problem for contemporary scholars and policy experts from multiple disciplines. The authors of a 2011 Inter-American Development Bank Working Paper entitled "Latin American Middle Classes: the Distance Between Perception and Reality" tested seven income-based definitions of the middle class typically used by economists against how Latin Americans identified themselves by class in a 2007 World Gallup Poll. Their goal was to choose out of those seven definitions the one that was least out of step with people's identitarian perceptions, an exercise rooted in the hope that it might yet be possible to find a meaningful "objective" definition of the middle class that reasonably tracked with self-affirmed identities.[31] An argument can be made, however, that the global diffusion of ideas associating the middle class with entrepreneurship, progress, democracy, and meritocracy has increased the likelihood that people of highly diverse socio-economic circumstances will all identify as middle-class, to the point that the term loses meaning, or at least loses correspondence with any conceivable taxonomy of classes as observed "from an external vantage point." In a 2010 article entitled "Middle Class: Sociological Category or Proper Noun?" Raka Ray noted that Indians most likely to describe themselves as middle-class, particularly the so-called "new middle class" who derive their income from market activity rather than state employment, tend to be upper-caste individuals with incomes in the top 15%, nowhere remotely near the middle.[32] Ray concluded that self-identification as middle-class has little to do with one's true position in a hierarchy of wealth, power, or status. It is, instead, an ideological construct. In the mid-twentieth century the term invoked a set of attitudes toward modernity: "setting aside the primordial loyalties of caste and citizenship, and opening oneself to new affinities and associations based on merit."[33] In more recent years, the idea of a middle class has served to "conjure up a universal, unifying identity that summons legitimacy for projects that favor elites in the nation."[34] According to Rachel Heiman, Mark Liechty, and Carla Freeman, the term achieves that legitimating function by "shifting the desires of marginalized groups away from liberatory politics (which would threaten the state's capitalist and, in some instances, repressive underpinnings) and toward relatively depoliticized aspirations for middle-class goods and lifestyles."[35]

We should not be surprised that identitarian invocations of the middle class seem designed to perform ideological work: legitimation, claims-making, or support for one political cause or another. But for the historian in particular, the distance between—and fundamental incompatibility of—analyses based on outsider taxonomies versus those predicated on evidence of conscious class agency poses a clear challenge. Countries and time periods that an external observer might describe as having large middle classes can yield scant evidence of middle-class subjectivities, and vice versa. The classic example is again Argentina, long thought to be the Latin American nation with the earliest and largest middle class. By the turn of the twentieth century, Argentina had a dynamic economy, excellent public education by regional standards, near-universal literacy, and high social mobility, all supposed attributes of a middle-class society. But when historians Ezequiel Adamovsky and Enrique Garguin examined the kinds of sources best suited to reconstructing middle-class identity claims, what they found came as a surprise. There was little evidence of a self-aware middle-class agent, of "political or labor or gremial organizations" or indeed anyone in Argentina using the term "middle class" as a discursive flagpost on which to hang their collective grievances or demands.[36] To the extent that the phrase entered into public discourse at all prior to about 1950, its function was political rather than social, invoking conceptions of the *juste milieu* rather than the interests of a defined socio-economic or occupational group.[37] In contrast, Peru's middle class was objectively far smaller than Argentina's, no matter what defining criteria observers might bring to their taxonomies. Poorer than Argentina, Peru was more deeply stratified by race, with an entrenched elite and significantly less social mobility. Yet in Peru a self-consciously middle-class agent appeared surprisingly early: in the aftermath of World War I white-collar employees couched their labor demands in an explicit discourse of middle-class needs and justly deserved rights.[38]

The paradox begins to make more sense once we understand that in Argentina, the middle class for the longest time did not speak its own name because middle-income professionals, white-collar employees, businessmen, and small property owners were so numerous that they thought of themselves simply as people, or, in Adamovsky's words, as representatives of "the entire Argentine nation."[39] Only with the rise of Juan Perón, who championed industrial workers as the heart and soul of the Argentine nation, did those professionals and property owners and clerks abandon their former universalizing discourse and gravitate toward promoting their interests using a language of "middle class." In so doing they implicitly recognized that Perón spoke for other Argentines, against whom they now defined themselves for the first time in class terms.[40]

Extending Adamovsky's interpretation back to Peru, white-collar employees in Lima were never numerous enough to pretend to speak for all Peruvians, so it makes perverse sense that they might embrace a middle-class identity from a much earlier date. Indeed we could argue that it was *because* Peru was a more hierarchical, less socially fluid, less middle-class society, where movement into the elite was rarer and the social and racial distance between manual and nonmanual workers was great, that it was logical for commercial and bank employees to portray themselves as a "middle class." Not only did it reflect people's common sense, but it also made tactical sense, legitimating those nonmanual workers' clamor for labor rules and benefits that elites might agree a middle class deserved, but which they would never concede to all workers.[41]

The contrast between Argentina and Peru reminds us that identities are not just expressions of an inner sense of collective belonging and solidarity rooted in some degree of shared experience. They are also—indeed they are primarily—strategic speech acts, with intended audiences and desired effects, and which operate in an epistemological space that could not be more distant from the world of social science taxonomies. Again, the point is nothing new—Crevenna's contributors realized the tension—but we do need to remind ourselves how radical the implications of this fact truly are. Not only is there no positive correlation between the externally observed size of a country's middle class and the presence or absence of public expressions of middle-class subjectivities; indeed, the correlation is every bit as likely to be negative.

Mode of Being in the World or Project for Transforming the World

Goldstein's third sense of class was a "mode of physical and mental being in the world" that does not require "linguistic self-consciousness" or expression in the public sphere but is either recognizable to the outside observer, understood in real time by members of a society, or both.[42] Using Bourdieu's concept of habitus, this conception is predicated on the idea that there are values and behaviors that are deeply internalized even when unarticulated, in how people form families and organize their households, in attitudes toward education and consumption, in aesthetic tastes and preferences, in ways of self-presentation including but not limited to dress and grooming and speech and etiquette, and in millions of other unconscious everyday practical and moral choices.[43]

Bourdieu's originality was in expanding our imagination of the universe of human activity that should be viewed as manifestations of class, and in showing the different ways that these class characteristics are reproduced for some and denied to others, generation over generation, in ways that mystify and naturalize the whole process. Considered epistemologically, in terms of the distinction between class residing in taxonomies of the social scientist's invention or class defined by the subject's self-awareness, habitus inhabits an ill-defined space between the two. Bourdieu was not averse to taxonomizing—in *Distinction*, he was the one who told the reader which tastes in art and music were highbrow or middlebrow, for example. But Bourdieu also relied on surveys and interviews to better understand how members of society perceived—and in perceiving, constructed—differences that they saw and acted upon but might not think of explicitly as "class."[44] This middle position between a taxonomical and an identitarian conception of class opened up new avenues for research, allowing the historian or sociologist to look for middle classes in places and time periods where the phrase "middle class" went unvoiced, while still employing an inductive methodology focused on what people said, did, and thought, rather than first formulating analytical models.

Several contributors to the Crevenna collection outlined elements that Bourdieu would later define as habitus. Regarding Chile, Julio Vega wrote that members of each class—upper, middle, and lower—shared what he described as an almost caste-like "unity of activity, unity of interests, and unity of formation":

> The members of a class graduate from the same schools; they possess similar knowledge; they share the same beliefs and have the same sentiments. This is visible to the observer in their similar ways of behaving; by a particular vocabulary; by specific forms of entertainment; specific expenses that we might call ritual expenses; the luxuries that certain classes must spend on and which some of its members do, at times, at the cost of huge sacrifices in order to adhere to established norms.
>
> Lastly, classes like castes are more or less endogamous. It is true that this is not always so rigorous in the upper class, and marriage is precisely one of the pathways to enter the higher class, but the fact that each time this occurs it calls attention to itself and is motive for scandal is the best demonstration of this de facto endogamy.[45]

One of the first-order questions that divided contributors to the 1948 Pan American Union project was whether a distinctly middle-class habitus existed in their countries, or whether what separated Latin America from more developed societies was precisely the absence of a set of embodied values, habits, and practices, a "mode of physical and mental being in the world" that was unique and exclusive to the men and women that the contributors identified as middle-class. For Lowry Nelson, otherwise middling Cubans had no real culture or lifestyle of their own, looking always to the upper class as their model.[46] Writing about Colombia, T. Lynn Smith expanded on the theme of a middle class comprised of the "sons, grandsons, and great-grandsons of persons who once occupied positions at the apex of the social pyramid:"[47]

> Among these descendants of the upper classes who can no longer keep up appearances, the class consciousness remains with the elite. They do not identify themselves with any middle class group. Instead they consider themselves as persons whom the force of circumstances has been against; "the breaks" have reduced them to a level below that to which they are legitimately entitled. They have been wronged in that they are no longer able to live in the style to which they were once accustomed and which they feel is their birthright.[48]

For Amanda Labarca, a fundamental and unique characteristic of Chile's middle class was that their economic means did not support the mode of being that their social milieu demanded of them, a lament long echoed throughout the region. "The Chilean middle class is *poor*," she argued. "The intense competition to find well-being and the 'conspicuous consumption' that comprises one of their social necessities, makes them discontented, bitter, suspicious and sharply critical."[49] All three of these authors shared the presumption that an essential characteristic of a properly developed class system was the existence of a stable middle-class mode of being, but they believed that distinctly middle-class lifeways did not currently exist in the countries they were studying.

This presence or absence of a middle-class habitus distinguishable from that of other classes above and below is a fundamental question to which anthropologists, sociologists, and historians have returned repeatedly over the subsequent seventy years. Although Brian Owensby's *Intimate Ironies* did not use Bourdieu's term, his argument about "the making of middle-class lives" endorsed the case that a clear middle-class habitus—with unique behavioral, psychological, and political characteristics—coalesced in Brazil between the early and mid-twentieth century.[50] More recently, the authors of *Mexico: A Middle Class Society* argued that the middle class may be heterogeneous in occupation and income, but is homogeneous in ways "that are essentially cultural, sharing attitudes and consumption patterns:"

> [T]he middle classes of practically all modern societies, and all developed ones, share a common characteristic: those who are part of the middle class earn enough income to live in an urban environment and want to systematically improve their social and economic standing... The definition of the middle class also includes a positive worldview, an interest in enjoying life beyond the day-to-day, an expectation of systematic economic advancement, and a belief that education is essential to the development of one's children.[51]

The authors present a portrait of a Mexico in 2012 whose economic growth, decline in fertility rates, and educational development succeeded in fostering consolidation of a distinctly middle-class way of being, despite ongoing challenges.[52]

Scholars continue to debate the implications and consequences of a uniquely middle-class habitus. Numerous books and articles written in the aftermath of Argentina's 2001–2002 economic collapse emphasized the objective impoverishment of a middle class "seduced and abandoned," fighting to preserve appearances and hopes.[53] Rodolfo Barros's portrait of the Buenos Aires middle class in these years highlighted the stubborn persistence of belief in upward mobility via education and hard work, an optimism, his informants believed, that distinguished the formerly-and-perhaps-still-middle-class "new poor" from other impoverished Argentines who were more resigned to their lot in life and allegedly eschewed self-improvement for themselves and their children.[54] Much as Germani had written in 1950 of hyperinflation creating a gap between failing economic fortunes and middle-class identities, Barros and his informants believed that despite financial hardship, something essential endured to be passed on from generation to generation. A distinctly middle-class habitus, in other words, might not correspond to any definable measures of wealth or status but was ingrained as a set of embodied habits, attitudes, and aspirations.

But how, practically, does the researcher operationalize this idea of habitus to find a middle class or verify its presence or absence, if on the one hand—returning to Jan Goldstein—taxonomies "from an external vantage point" are ill equipped to capture such an inchoate sense of a "mode of physical and mental being in the world," and on the other hand habitus is "inhabited without linguistic self-consciousness" and may not register in the kinds of sources where discursive expressions of class identity would be given voice? One historian who rose to this methodological challenge was Patrick Barr-Melej, whose 2001 *Reforming Chile: Cultural Politics, Nationalism, and the Rise of the Middle Class* made the following argument:

> [W]hen considering the Chilean case, defining who composed the middle class is a complicated endeavor because "class"… is not merely a socioeconomic category but a cultural one as well. In early twentieth-century Santiago, for example, it was not entirely uncommon to see the progeny of the upper class take jobs as journalists, teachers, or bureaucrats, join the Radical Party, and, in general, immerse themselves in, and contribute to, a characteristically mesocratic cultural milieu. In this changeful urban setting, genealogy did not necessarily correlate with a distinct lifestyle, ideology, or identity; many mesocrats-by-choice shared with mesocrats-by-station certain cultural tastes and ideological sympathies that, in many ways, differed significantly from those of aristocrats. A mesocrat's being in the world, then, was not solely the function of economic activity and a comparable social standing; it was also tied to cultural norms and a cultural outlook… In short, it may be argued that locating or identifying a mesocracy during this period, by, say, examining employment data or breakdowns of occupations or census reports would not take into full account the pliability of "class" and, for that matter, the significance of culture and cultural practices in the elaboration of classes and identity.[55]

Identifying the limitations of both taxonomic and identitarian constructions of the middle class, Barr-Melej chose to take membership in Chile's Radical Party and participation in Radical-aligned intellectual circles as one key indicator of a middle-class habitus that transcended taxonomies of income or occupation. He viewed participation in the Radical political-intellectual milieu as more than just politics, more than a voting preference: it was a "cultural practice," a "being in the world" that expressed a middle-class habitus.[56]

As a description of the meaning of Radical Party membership in early twentieth-century Chile, Barr-Melej's argument brings enormous insight.

In less capable hands, however, correlating class with political party affiliation creates a potential for epistemic slippage that should set off alarm bells. A good deal of writing on the Latin American middle class since the Crevenna volumes, including some of the most influential, has been driven by an idea that there is a distinctly middle-class project of social change, discernable in the political arena. This idea constitutes a fourth conceptualization of class that Jan Goldstein did not contemplate, which intuits the existence of a middle class whenever and wherever governments have pursued, or political parties have advocated, policies that seem to embody what the scholar views as "middle-class" goals. Such approaches look for empirical evidence not in the distribution of resources, power, and status as gauged from the outside, nor in the identitarian pronouncements of agents who call themselves middle-class, nor even in an unarticulated but arguably middle-class "mode of physical and mental being in the world," but in the presence of demands for economic, social, and political change along purportedly middle-class lines.

The alleged attributes of that political project run the gamut: promoting democracy; curbing the power of "feudal" landed interests; exalting entrepreneurship in general and industrialization in particular; advocating for juridical equality and secure property rights under the rule of law; embracing meritocracy and public education; championing cosmopolitanism and modernity or, alternatively, nationalism and nostalgia; "civilizing" society through the repression of baser instincts and the diffusion of "bourgeois" norms; approaches to gender that include separate spheres, the cult of domesticity and moral puritanism; the specific list goes on, but its general contours should be quite familiar. Some of these elements appear in Marx's concept of the bourgeois revolution, while others are later-arriving elaborations or variations on Marx. Some writers subject these "bourgeois" moral and political objectives to intense critique or outright derision, but others view them as precisely the kinds of reforms that define development, progress, and the transition to modernity.

Research that focuses on the programs and actions of political leaders, and from there perceives middle-class agency behind the scenes, comprises a significant percentage of scholarship on Latin America's middle class. Several contributors to the Crevenna Pan American Union project included in their analyses extended discussions of the political history of the countries they were writing about.[57] When one plumbs the footnotes of other books, articles, and dissertations with "middle class" in their titles, one often finds that much of the source material comes from political leaders, parties or movements that seek to win the votes of literate urbanites by employing an insurgent discourse critical of the traditional elite, a status quo-affirming discourse critical of working-class radicals, or both at the same time.[58]

The best example of this kind of approach to middle-class politics in Latin America also happens to be the most-cited book ever written on the subject, John J. Johnson's *Political Change in Latin America: The Emergence of the Middle Sectors*, published in 1958. Johnson's influence is best measured by the fact that the phrase "middle *sectors*" still remains in common use.[59] Johnson explained that he chose the word "sectors" rather than "class" to "convey a sense of 'middleness'" without confusing Anglo-American readers accustomed to equating class with income cohort, and without imputing to the middle sectors "the central condition of a class: [a] common background of experience."[60] His middle sectors lacked objective sociological unity or any publicly articulated sense of class belonging. They were defined, in other words, not by an external observer's taxonomy, nor by a subjective affirmation of identity, nor by an observable habitus. Johnson's reason for treating them as a meaningful collectivity resided instead in their alleged political unity of interests, favoring pro-urban government policies, the expansion of public education, industrialization, nationalism, and statist interventionism.[61]

This intentionally vague and undefined conception of middle sectors freed Johnson from having to do anything other than focus on how those hypothesized middle-sector interests found expression in government policies and party platforms. Once Johnson moved into his five case studies the book turned into little more than insightfully-rendered political history, or, in the words of one reviewer, "an account of what happened in Buenos Aires under Perón, in Rio de Janeiro under Vargas, in Mexico City during the administration of President Ruiz Cortines, and so on."[62] While he made an effort to show that reformist politicians were more likely than the men they opposed to hail from taxonomically middle-sector origins, there was scant empirical data to demonstrate that these politicians uniquely or even preferentially attracted middle-sector votes. Neither finding nor really looking for evidence of a self-aware middle-class agent, Johnson inferred middle-sector influence from the content of the reforms adopted or proposed.

The issues raised by this use of political action as a proxy for class agency are twofold: first, there is the question of whether political leaders can ever really be thought of as organic intellectuals giving voice to the collective will of a social class, or whether they should instead be viewed as mercenary "interest entrepreneurs," who strategically build a power base by articulating the demands of target groups in exchange for those groups' votes.[63] While the two characterizations are not mutually exclusive, *which* image one chooses shines a particular light on the acts of political parties and leaders, with cynical observers tending toward the transactional paradigm. A second concern is the potential for self-confirming circular reasoning. Who decides what values, goals, discourses, and policy demands are to be identified as typically middle-class? What was it that led Johnson, for example, to zero in on public education, state-led industrialization, nationalism, and social welfare policies as the principal indicators of a middle-sector agenda? What was it that has led other scholars to focus instead on the rhetoric of democracy, or entrepreneurship, or domesticity and moral reform? Is there not at least some danger that scholars in search of a middle-class project of political transformation will inevitably find politicians and parties that espouse whatever they have decided in advance that they are searching for?

At one level studies of government policies or party programs may make a credible case for behind-the-scenes machinations by a middle class, insofar as professional politicians and partisan propagandists may carry out tasks that look a lot like those performed by individuals who fit our taxonomic models of a middle class, insofar as a government or opposition party may invoke identitarian shout-outs to the middle class in pursuit of legitimacy and supporters, or insofar as politicians may embody and/or project an unarticulated "mode of being in the world" that outside observers would identify as middle-class. But first defining a middle class via taxonomy, identity or habitus, and then looking at what that group advocates politically, is a different mental exercise than starting with an a priori understanding of what a middle class should want, and then searching for empirical evidence of a political force promoting that agenda.

Self-Awareness and Triangulation: By Way of Conclusion

It may seem as if my goal in this chapter has been to project a defeatist vision of an inevitably inconclusive debate between incompatible epistemologies, all talking past one another. By starting in 1948 with the questions raised by the Pan American Union's novel and ambitious contribution to Latin American social science, I might appear to be making a case that nothing new has been learned in seven decades. But I hope in this brief conclusion to convince the reader otherwise. On the one hand, there *is* an argument to be made that no easy way exists for scholars to avoid the disconnects between approaching the middle class as the creation of an external observer's analytic taxonomy, as a publicly expressed subjective identity, as a recognizable but unarticulated habitus, or as an agenda for political change. These competing approaches embody radically distinct logics, each rooted in its own conception of where class is found, each asking different questions, and each relying upon entirely different types of evidence. While scholars can and do study the middle class on more than one track simultaneously, the tracks themselves inhabit profoundly distinct spaces.

On the other hand, otherwise incompatible methodologies can talk to one another so long as two conditions are present. First, scholars must be careful never to lose sight of what their chosen approach can and cannot illuminate, its potential for unique discoveries but also its inevitable blind spots. Taxonomical approaches from an external perspective will always have the power and clarity that comes with the dispassionate analysis of hard data on the structure of occupations, the distribution of income, and potentially thousands of other measurements of power and status. But they will not crack the mysteries of human consciousness. Methods and sources that capture public expressions of class identity will always be dogged by humans' infinite ability to lie to one another and to themselves as they perform strategic, instrumental, ideological speech acts. Efforts to understand the vagaries of middle-class culture, lifeways, and psychology raise almost as many questions as they resolve: where exactly does one look to find a middle-class habitus, and is that evidence coming from an outsider's "-etic" perspective or an insider's "-emic" one? And studies of middle-class politics will—or at least should—always be challenged by questions of cause and effect: do politicians, parties, and movements that speak in the name of the middle class reflect and give voice to a social collectivity that actually exists, or are they the ones who conjure that alleged collectivity into being, as Dror Wahrman and so many others have long contended? Sensitivity to how we know what we are able to know is paramount.

Requirement two is triangulation. There have always been researchers who pursued their understanding of the middle class on several methodological fronts. Perhaps, like Dennis Gilbert, they went door-to-door with a questionnaire that asked informants how *they* defined the middle class, in order to confirm and flesh out their taxonomical model.[64] Perhaps they looked for those who first voiced in the public sphere an identitarian discourse that used the actual words "middle class," then subjected those individuals to sociological scrutiny based on income, occupation, consumption, and other measurable criteria.[65] Perhaps, like Ricardo López-Pedreros, they studied how people of radically varying habitus, but all self-identifying as middle-class, differed in how they interpreted and acted upon the ubiquitous political idea that the middle class was the backbone of democracy.[66] These are just a few of the ways that scholars have combined approaches, and by triangulating between them have arrived at conclusions that leverage the insights and partly overcome the limitations of each. We should, therefore, perhaps not be overly concerned that epistemological questions identified seventy years ago continue to crop up today, so long as we always remember to use the methodological tools at our disposal carefully, deliberately, precisely, and without illusions.

Notes

1 Earlier formulations of ideas presented in this chapter went through their test paces at the 17th Annual Workshop of the Department of Middle East Studies, Ben-Gurion University, Israel, June 2015, and at the Facultad de Humanidades y Ciencias de la Educación, Universidad Nacional de La Plata, Argentina, November 2015. The current text has benefited from the questions asked and comments received. Special thanks to Relli Shechter and Enrique Garguin.

2 Theo Crevenna, "The Social Sciences in the Organization of American States," *UNESCO International Social* Science *Bulletin* IV, no. 3 (1952): 483–89. The Pan American Union was the institutional precursor to the O.A.S.

3 Francisco Pinto S., *Clase media y socialismo* (Valparaíso: Imprenta Victoria, 1940), 19–20.

4 Ezequiel Adamovsky, "Aristotle, Diderot, Liberalism and the Idea of 'Middle Class': A Comparison of Two Contexts of Emergence of a Metaphorical Formation," *History of Political Thought* 26, no. 2 (Summer 2005): 301–333.

5 A. Ricardo López-Pedreros, *Makers of Democracy: A Transnational History of the Middle Classes in Colombia* (Durham, NC: Duke University Press, 2019), 28–37.

6 "Suplemento II: Sugerencias para el estudio de la clase media en América Latina," in *Materiales para el estudio de la clase media en América Latina*, Vol. 1, *La clase media en Argentina y Uruguay: Cuatro colaboraciones*, ed. Theo Crevenna (Washington, DC: Pan American Union, 1950), 94. Original in Spanish except where indicated; all translations mine.

7 López-Pedreros, *Makers of Democracy*.

8 Brian P. Owensby, *Intimate Ironies: Modernity and the Making of Middle-Class Lives in Brazil* (Stanford, CA: Stanford University Press, 1999), 5.

9 Francesca Castellani and Gwenn Parent, "Being Middle-Class in Latin America," OECD Development Centre Working Paper No. 305 (October 2011): 8. Quote is edited to remove two parenthetical citations.

10 That counter-narrative would later become a central tenet in most versions of Latin American dependency theory, but it had a well-established pre-1948 pedigree. David S. Parker, "Asymmetric Globality and South American Narratives of Bourgeois Failure," in *The Global Bourgeoisie: The Rise of the Middle Classes in the Age of Empire*, eds. Christof Dejung, David Motadel and Jürgen Osterhammel (Princeton, NJ: Princeton University Press, 2019), 275–294.

11 "Suplemento I: Procedimientos en la organización de estas monografías," in *Materiales para el estudio de la clase media en América Latina*, Vol. 6, *La clase media en Colombia, Ecuador y la República Dominicana: Cuatro colaboraciones*, ed. Theo Crevenna (Washington, DC: Pan American Union, 1951), 91.

12 The scholars translated were Alfred Meusel, Johannes Wernicke, Jean Lhomme, Leo Miffelman, and Gustav Schmoller. Crevenna, *Materiales* vol. 6, 93–95.

13 Gino Germani, "La clase media en la cuidad de Buenos Aires," *Boletín del Instituto de Sociología*, no. 1 (1932): 105, cited in Crevenna, *Materiales* vol. 6, 94.

14 Crevenna, *Materiales* vol. 6, 94.

15 Crevenna, *Materiales* vol. 6, 94.

16 Crevenna, *Materiales* vol. 6, 95–98.

17 Jan Goldstein, "Of Marksmanship and Marx: Reflections on the Linguistic Construction of Class in Some Recent Historical Scholarship," *Modern Intellectual History* 2, no. 1 (2005): 89.

18 Homi Kharas, "The Emerging Middle Class in Developing Countries," OECD Development Centre Working Paper No. 285 (January 2010).

19 Uri Dadush and Shimelse Ali, *In Search of the Global Middle Class: A New Index* (Washington, DC: The Carnegie Endowment for International Peace, 2012), 1.

20 Barbara Ehrenreich and John Ehrenreich, "The Professional-Managerial Class," in *Between Labor and Capital*, ed. Pat Walker (Boston, MA: South End Press, 1979), 5–45; Erik Olin Wright, *Classes* (London: Verso, 1985). For a historian's overview of earlier similar literature: Peter Stearns, "The Middle Class: Towards a Precise Definition," *Comparative Studies in Society and History* 21, no. 3 (July 1979): 377–96.

21 Renato Rosaldo, *Culture and Truth: The Remaking of Social Analysis* (Boston, MA: Beacon Press, 1989).

22 E. P. Thompson, *The Making of the English Working Class* (London: Victor Gollancz, 1963); Gareth Stedman Jones, *Languages of Class: Studies in English Working Class History, 1832–1982* (Cambridge: Cambridge University Press, 1983); Dror Wahrman, *Imagining the Middle Class: The Political Representation of Class in Britain, c. 1780–1840* (Cambridge: Cambridge University Press, 1995); Sara Maza, *The Myth of the French Bourgeoisie: An Essay on the Social Imaginary* (Cambridge, MA: Harvard University Press, 2003).
23 Gino Germani in Crevenna, *Materiales* vol. 1, 4–5.
24 Gino Germani in Crevenna, *Materiales* vol. 1, 5.
25 Gino Germani in Crevenna, *Materiales* vol. 1, 28.
26 Lowry Nelson, "The Social Class Structure in Cuba," in *Materiales para el estudio de la clase media en la América Latina*, Vol. 2, *La clase media en México y Cuba: Cuatro colaboraciones*, ed. Theo Crevenna (Washington, DC: Pan American Union, 1950), 69–70. Original in English.
27 Nelson in Crevenna, *Materiales*, vol. 2, 70.
28 Sergio Bagú, "La clase media en la Argentina," in Crevenna, *Materiales* vol. 1, 49–50.
29 Harold E. Davis, Review of "Materiales para el estudio de la clase media en la América Latina," *BBAA: Boletín Bibliográfico de Antropología Americana* 14, no. 2 (1951): 144.
30 B.R. Wilson, "Review of Crevenna, Materiales para el estudio de la clase media en la América Latina,'" *British Journal of Sociology* 2, no. 4 (December 1951): 375–76.
31 Eduardo Lora and Johanna Fajardo, "Latin American Middle Classes: The Distance Between Perception and Reality," Inter-American Development Bank Working Paper Series No. IDB-WP-275 (December 2011).
32 Raka Ray, "'The Middle Class': Sociological Category or Proper Noun?," *Political Power and Social Theory* 21 (January 2010): 315–16.
33 Ray, "Middle Class," 316.
34 Ray, "Middle Class," 319.
35 Rachel Heiman, Mark Liechty, and Carla Freeman, "Introduction: Charting an Anthropology of the Middle Classes," in *The Global Middle Classes: Theorizing Through Ethnography*, eds. Rachel Heiman, Carla Freeman, and Mark Liechty (Santa Fe: School for Advanced Research Press, 2012), 18–19.
36 Ezequiel Adamovsky, *Historia de la clase media argentina: Apogeo y decadencia de una ilusión* (Buenos Aires: Planeta, 2009), 479–80; Enrique Garguin, "'Los Argentinos Descendemos de los Barcos': The Racial Articulation of Middle-Class Identity in Argentina, 1920–1960," in *The Making of the Middle Class: Toward a Transnational History*, eds. A. Ricardo Lopez-Pedreros and Barbara Weinstein (Durham, NC: Duke University Press, 2012): 355–57, 367.
37 Ezequiel Adamovsky, "Acerca de la relación entre el radicalismo argentino y la 'clase media' (una vez más)," *Hispanic American Historical Review* 89, no. 2 (2009): 248–251.
38 D. S. Parker, *The Idea of the Middle Class: White-Collar Workers and Peruvian Society, 1900–1950* (University Park: Pennsylvania State University Press, 1998).
39 Adamovsky, *Historia de la clase media*, 281–2.
40 Adamovsky, *Historia de la clase media*, 281–2.
41 David S. Parker, "Middle-Class Mobilization and the Language of Orders in Urban Latin America: From Caste to Category in Early Twentieth-Century Lima," *Journal of Urban History* 31, no. 3 (March 2005): 367–381.

42 Goldstein, "Of Marksmanship and Marx," 89.
43 Pierre Bourdieu, "The Social Space and the Genesis of Groups," *Theory and Society* 14, no. 6 (November 1985): 723–744; Pierre Bourdieu, *Distinction: A Social Critique of the Judgement of Taste*, trans. Richard Nice (Cambridge, MA: Harvard University Press, 1984), especially Part II, "The Economy of Practices."
44 Bourdieu, *Distinction*, Part III, "Class Tastes and Life-Styles."
45 Julio Vega, "La clase media en Chile," in *Materiales para el estudio de la clase media en la América Latina*, Vol. 3, *La clase media en Bolivia, Brasil, Chile y Paraguay: Cuatro colaboraciones*, ed. Theo Crevenna (Washington, DC: Pan American Union, 1950), 65–66.
46 Nelson in Crevenna, *Materiales*, vol. 2.
47 T. Lynn Smith, "Observations on the Middle Classes in Colombia," in Crevenna, *Materiales* v. 6, 10. Original in English.
48 Smith in Crevenna, *Materiales*, vol. 6, 13. One caveat: Smith cited Antioquia and Caldas as exceptions to this rule.
49 Amanda Labarca, "Apuntes para estudiar la clase media en Chile," in Crevenna, *Materiales* v. 6, 88. Italics in the original.
50 Owensby, *Intimate Ironies*, for example 68–71.
51 Luis De la Calle and Luis Rubio, *Mexico: A Middle Class Society: Poor No More, Developed Not Yet* (Washington, DC: Mexico Institute, Woodrow Wilson International Center for Scholars, 2012), 6–9.
52 De la Calle and Rubio, *Mexico: A Middle Class Society*, 90–92.
53 Alberto Minujin and Eduardo Anguita, *La clase media: Seducida y abandonada* (Buenos Aires: Edhasa, 2004).
54 Rodolfo Barros, "We Were the Middle Class," in *Latin America's Middle Class: Unsettled Debates and New Histories*, eds. David S. Parker and Louise E. Walker (Lanham, MD: Lexington Books, 2013), 320–345.
55 Patrick Barr-Melej, *Reforming Chile: Cultural Politics, Nationalism, and the Rise of the Middle Class* (Chapel Hill: University of North Carolina Press, 2001), 6
56 Barr-Melej, *Reforming Chile*, 6.
57 Julio Vega, for example, connected a middle-class political presence all the way back to Chile's early-nineteenth-century conflicts between reformist "*pipiolos*" and aristocratic "*pelucones*." Vega, "La clase media en Chile," in Crevenna, *Materiales*, vol. 3, 69–71. See also Sergio Bagú, "La clase media en la Argentina," in Crevenna, *Materiales*, vol. 1, 45; Antonio Miguel Grompone, "La clase media en el Uruguay" in Crevenna, *Materiales*, vol. 1, 84ff.
58 Adamovsky, "Acerca de la relación," 209–251, discusses the Argentine literature in this genre. For other examples: Jaime García Covarrubias, *El Partido Radical y la clase media en Chile: La relación de intereses entre 1888–1938* (Santiago: Editorial Andrés Bello, 1990); Iñigo García-Bryce, "A Middle-Class Revolution: the APRA Party and Middle-Class Identity in Peru," in *The Making of the Middle Class*, eds. Lopez-Pedreros and Weinstein, 235–252; Bryan McCann, "Carlos Lacerda: The Rise and Fall of a Middle-Class Populist in 1950s Brazil," *Hispanic American Historical Review* 81, no. 4 (2003): 661–696.
59 OECD, *Latin American Outlook 2011: How Middle-Class is Latin America?* (Paris: OECD Publishing, 2010).
60 John J. Johnson, *Political Change in Latin America: The Emergence of the Middle Sectors* (Stanford, CA: Stanford Univerity Press, 1958), viii–ix, 3.
61 Johnson, *Political Change*, 5–11.
62 George I. Blanksten, "In Quest of the Middle Sectors," *World Politics* 12, no. 2 (January 1960): 323–7.

63 Philippe C. Schmitter, *Interest Politics and Political Change in Brazil* (Stanford, CA: Stanford University Press, 1971), 208.
64 Dennis Gilbert, *Mexico's Middle Class in the Neoliberal Era* (Tucson: University of Arizona Press, 2007), 105–117.
65 As for example Parker, *Idea of the Middle Class.*
66 López-Pedreros, *Makers of Democracy.*

22 From White-Collar Employment to Managerial Influence Among the Middle Class in Early-Twenty-First-Century Mexico City

Terioska Gámez

Introduction

This text forms part of my wider research that analyzes how inequality between individuals evolves progressively and cumulatively through subtle differences that become increasingly entrenched until constituting unbridgeable chasms. By using anthropological tools, this chapter seeks to shed light on the origins of this process, its development, legitimation, and reinforcement.

In this chapter, I aim to show that economic inequality is not necessarily at the root of differentiation in capitalist societies and that such disparity stems from cumulative efforts made elsewhere. Social differentiation begins this process that subsequently becomes consolidated in financial advantages, because capital ownership is not synonymous with prestige.

I have therefore chosen to analyze a process of differentiation within a specific, privileged segment of society: university-educated professionals with cultural, economic, and social capital sanctioned by the society in which they live and work—in this case, Mexico City in the early twenty-first century. This differentiation takes place for these individuals to secure access to positions offering greater material benefits (earning higher incomes than the vast majority of the population) and symbolic ones (legitimizing their positions as being the result of a meritocratic system). Specifically, I emphasize how, in a highly stratified society in which neoliberalism operates as a system of governance, performance is an extremely effective way to create the small but crucial differences that legitimize a sub-group's access to upper management.

The pendulum swing of performance between the material and symbolic spheres shows the strategies of these individuals: although good execution is an important factor for promotions within businesses, it does not necessarily explain the requisite differentiation given the overwhelming number of individuals with university degrees. Hence the particular importance of using symbolic codes, relevant to the specific knowledge base, within cognitive capitalism.

DOI: 10.4324/9781003029311-27

The fieldwork for this research consisted of interviews with 32 professionals whose upbringing, education, and early careers were in Mexico City, and who held managerial positions in corporations that were preferably transnational at the time of the interview (2016–2019). The interviews sought to discover, challenge, and find answers that reveal more than the standard and predictable meritocratic and perfectly well-structured discourse permeating the classic narratives of these figures presented as the embodiment of success within the cultural dimension of neoliberalism: senior managers, entrepreneurs, sportspersons, artists, opinion leaders, and, more recently, influencers, and so on.

The anonymization of the narratives serves an important methodological purpose. Due to the consistency in the accounts, I chose the ones that most effectively summed up the central themes—differentiation for upward career trajectories and the construction of Class in that sense. Ethical issues and people's right to privacy also informed this decision. I provide the most relevant (but least-possible) information about the individuals in question: the position held at the time of the interview and the kind of employer. For their job titles to be comparable and useful, sometimes they do not match the positions specified on the business cards. Nevertheless, in each case the individuals were fully representative of Mexico's managerial class based on their incomes, decision-making powers within their companies, and their employers' reputations as major international and local corporate players.

During the interviews, the interviewees used semiotic-discursive elements to differentiate themselves both in their narratives and in their non-verbal exercises, and to find a meaning for their access to, and profit from, prestigious corporate positions. The interviewees mentioned categories such as gender, sexual preference, ethnic-racial background, body type, among other factors, to explain these processes. All of these factors intertwine in Mexico City's highly stratified society. However, in this text I will make an artificial cut-off and focus solely on Class—understood as a native category of the interviewees—in terms of its communication, its underlying meanings, as well as its consequences and results for individuals in managerial positions in Mexico City.

Membership of Mexico City's Managerial Class in the Early Twenty-First Century

Mexico City is the capital of a strongly centralized country with an unequal economic and cultural integration and in a subordinate position within the North American regional block; furthermore, Mexico—in common with the rest of Latin America—has severe inequalities. Therefore, although individuals in managerial positions within transnational companies may be deemed members of a middle class as a sociological category, matters become more complex if we consider this sector of society as a cultural project and if we place individuals specifically within the Mexican context, in other words as an elite, as detailed below.

A university education is a basic requirement for anyone aspiring to a senior position within a transnational company and to its corresponding financial benefits. OECD figures for Mexico reveal only 17% of the population aged between 25 and 64 have access to higher education, and just 7% of this group earns more than $800 dollars per month. Furthermore, specialized business media define managerial positions as those with a minimum monthly salary of $1,600 dollars,[1] in other words double the figure mentioned above. Holders of these jobs therefore belong to a privileged group whose members have a clearly different financial situation compared to the vast majority of the country's population. This differentiation also derives from this group's access to higher education and its members' ability to develop tight-knit social connections at their alma maters, in their corporate environments, and even in the circles of consumption affordable to them thanks to their income.

These managerial positions represent the professionalization of the leadership of companies that have grown to a certain size and developed an entire internal command network, prompting the owners to choose someone else to take over their management. Such positions are linked to the holders of capital with the resulting exposure to their spheres of meaning (and a certain desirable communion with this exposure); a power exercised through market-based and organizational decisions that affect the lives of consumers and collaborators. There is also a prestige associated with the desirability of occupying such positions as they constitute an image of social progress legitimated by a meritocratic discourse. Thanks to their advantageous situation in terms of cultural capital (having a university education as a minimum), financial capital (earning more than most people), and social capital (accessing actionable networks at certain levels), these groups enjoy highly differentiated and privileged positions compared to the rest of the population in these three areas.

Another way to highlight the privilege of these positions is to approach them as important nodes within the Network Society[2] in counterpoint to the Service Proletariat,[3] since the latter positions are easily replaceable in the Information Age. If we consider that the individuals in both groups have university-level qualifications (and somehow comparable types of capital), their roles in the job market lead to highly differentiated positions, showing the aggressive segmentation of the middle class into (at least) two very dissimilar clusters, this produces a change from interclass antagonism to an ethos of intraclass status competition.[4]

To explore this competition in the corporate job market, it is important to establish that the late-twentieth and early-twenty-first centuries' mode of production is cognitive capitalism[5]—an economy that mainly produces new kinds of value through the creation of knowledge. If the role of cultural capital is important in the formation of classes (especially for the middle class), a full understanding of what kind of knowledge is relevant in the prevailing economy provides means of differentiation and access to desirable roles.

Specific knowledge bases are associated with innovation in each sector—analytical for the science-based sector, synthetical for industrial settings, and symbolic for cultural industries[6]—and each sector has held a particular importance at different historical junctures. This has a connection to class-based labor or professional reconversion, which is particularly notable in generational studies of social mobility. Once neoliberal policies have been implanted, certain professions have blossomed: those that rely on aesthetic inputs, which depend on the tacit knowledge of certain actors, have a particular connection to the management of symbolic elements, and therefore depend on that specific knowledge base for innovation.[7]

It is interesting to explore the connection between the growing relevance of some professions in a society with a neoliberal governmentality and such subjectivities associated with individuals in said professions. In the specific case of this research, the profession is related to mediation and authority in companies where individuals work, rather than in the field in which they obtained their university degree, or in the type of industry in which the company operates. By analyzing the subjectivities of a specific group of individuals who skillfully use a set of symbolic codes to differentiate themselves and obtain rewards for doing so, we can discover the desired moralities and values in the spheres of meaning associated with corporate power and prestige. This makes it necessary to identify the communicating vessels with society at large.

Individuals place several bets on a symbolic level, placing them in different corporate roles and as such are part of an iterative process of cause and effect around the creation, operation, and legitimization of differences that are not strictly material within the large conglomeration referred to as the middle class. Therefore, this (already-diverse) segment becomes even more fragmented and generates severe internal inequalities that are not exclusively based on differing financial means, but that lead to such differences. However, the job market does not exist in isolation and individuals make various efforts to differentiate themselves in other areas, such as consumption, within the corporate sphere. These accumulated effects reconfigure society and alter class structures.

Creating Differences: Class as a Native Category

In this research I explore social class not as a pre-existing category consisting of individuals, but as a specifically situated cultural process that they are continuously constructing themselves. Various anthropological approaches help us understand the creation of differences between individuals. For example, we can include Class as a native category, in other words one used to describe and understand everyday events.

The use of the word Class in various daily settings and situations reveals a human desire to classify, to separate elements of perceived reality, and to place them in different groups in order to be able to give this reality meaning, building tools that make it possible to navigate this world. The natural and social sciences have co-opted the term.[8] Classifying people means placing them in categories based on arbitrary characteristics (given the absence of an intrinsic cause, however much we think we can see one).[9] But such classifications are significant as a way of explaining differences between individuals. This was a tacit message in the following narrative by a marketing manager, who refers to the meaning of Class in a daily context and its use as a container of shared meanings in society, with the consequent extra layering of complexity afforded to him by his profession when contrasted with another category with which he is familiar:

> Social class? I'd rather use the term Socioeconomic Level,[10] which is how everyone likes to call it in today's "inclusive language" [air quotes used by the interviewee], [...] in theory you don't use social class, but in practice it's obvious that everyone knows that's what we're talking about... that basically means your level of... you know... your income level, lifestyle, and kind of surroundings.
> (marketing manager, global market research conglomerate)

The manager refers to Class as a native category, a well-understood system of classification that is used and even problematized. He establishes a difference between two discourses: (a) one that establishes (social) Class as something in full effect in the society to which he belongs, but that forms a part of a classificatory system that is off-limits in daily conversations. In other words, Class is understood as something experienced, a system of differentiation full of meanings constituting levels, but which represents a certain taboo when spoken about with an other according to the comment that there is another term used for it within "inclusive language;" and (b) another discourse that, in fact, aligns itself better with the terminology used within his profession (as the Socioeconomic Level) and that for the interviewee this is a euphemism, though not entirely an equivalent, of this classification. Taboos are well-known to have a cultural basis and they are inherently important to the societies that create them.

Later on, this same manager explicitly states that Class does not solely refer to income, but to a certain lifestyle, to markers in experiences such as consumption or in places where daily life unfolds:

> [So] it isn't always [about] income, [but] how you live your life. Say if you earn $200,000 or $300,000 pesos per month but if you don't travel to Europe, you don't go on holidays, but just go around *puebleando*,[11] [then] that aspect of your life defines your socioeconomic level

> or social class. For example, someone from the Central de Abastos[12] and someone from Las Lomas[13] may have the same level of income, but they're not going to be from the same social class!

This empirically resolves a constant problem in discourses that consider social class to be a purely financial phenomenon and therefore something experts consider is only a part of people's identities,[14] neglecting to see Class as a native category that helps problematize and enrich the concept. In this narrative we can see how despite a similar income there can be profound differences in activities, routines, and experiences of reality, and therefore how one is perceived, all thanks to divergent symbolic markers attached to each specific role: in other words, in people's performance.

The interviewee's comment appears commonsensical, tallying with a popular saying in Mexico: "la Clase no se compra" (Money can't buy Class). Given this disconnect from financial considerations, which is not absolute, it is helpful to consider Pierre Bourdieu's idea as it brings up the roles of cultural, social, and symbolic capital in addition to economic capital.[15] However, I am interested in showing that, by analyzing access to the managerial class in Mexico City in the first decades of the twenty-first century, the emphasis is not solely on the ownership of these kinds of capital but on the art of this performance in order to access that sphere of prestige and power even without truly possessing these forms of capital. Another popular saying in those circles expresses this idea succinctly: "*fake it till you make it*."[16]

The aim of this strategy implies individuals differentiating themselves from one group in order to identify with another, according to the respective groups' implicit hierarchical positions. That established order justifies unequal access to valuable but scarce positions and resources. Studying the differentiation that the individuals themselves produce and strive toward requires focusing on a process of forming groups, not on specific markers. This shift is essential because markers lose their relevance in different times and spaces; however, the process of legitimizing small but cumulative differences makes it possible to understand the accumulation and consolidation of advantages.

In this text, climbing up the corporate ladder—as a personal experience—is about observing a set of values and meanings associated with a sphere of privilege and prestige[17] intended to include or exclude. This process begins by creating a perceived difference to others that subsequently translates into material inequalities. These disparities then act as symbolic differentiators as established in the following narrative that effectively serves the dual purpose of marking a separation from one group and an affiliation with another, as well as translating this into financial reward:

> I have indeed succeeded in outshining [...] the rest of my generation, [...] my school group, my peer group. I don't have much contact with that group... the truth is that [I've only had contact] with very few of them,

the few that I have seen... it's like they got stuck, repeating that same story, I mean, like it's a cycle on that same level, you know? You study... but it's like you study and climb, right? And then you fall back down. I mean you never really move up from there because it's a cycle. When you manage to climb to the next rung it's like a challenge... and I think it's important to believe in yourself, to show why you're different from the others, that's why you climb, because then those in upper management see you and say "hey, this guy's like us" and you're not scared... you lose some of the fear at facing those situations, then... I don't mean you become arrogant and don't look... I mean, it's more like you look down on [people] [he gestures], right? [...] the truth is that it does open the door to better career opportunities, to a better financial reward.

Marketing Manager, Transnational Consultancy Firm

This second marketing manager clearly expresses his feeling of differentiation from his classmates at school, and the lack of contact with them indicates a social distancing due to the rift that has opened up. Clearly, he perceives that they have remained stuck at the "same level," underneath him, and it is obvious when he describes identifying himself with the "upper management," the group to which he now feels that he belongs. He explains that this is the result of a display of specific and sanctioned attitudes and behaviors that have brought rewards. The material result of this approach has been a higher income, which, at the same time and in a virtuous circle, consolidated his perception of being different and enabled him to feel like that and to act correspondingly, with attributes and attitudes that he associates with the managerial class.

The Middle Class: A Background

Before continuing, we should consider that individuals in managerial positions in companies, including upper management positions, occupy a particular space in which they connect financial capital and labor. They work as intermediaries, as the hinge between the individuals who possess the means of production and those with only their labor to sell. Furthermore, this intermediate position is not exclusive to those in managerial positions; owners of small businesses, liberal professions, the self-employed, civil servants, etc., also find themselves in that in-between space. To understand how people working in such a variety of activities can all occupy this intermediate space, I have chosen two criteria, both addressing the concept of class from beyond the strictly economic dimension.

The first criterion is based on how Bourdieu considers different types of capital in his problematization of class. For this purpose, it is useful to visualize the ownership of these forms of capital as if they could be counted numerically, and by using values that grow gradually and infinitesimally.[18] If we imagine that we could express each kind of capital (economic, social, and cultural) as axes on a chart, they would determine a specific position for each individual in a three-dimensional space with specific coordinates. This creates an infinite number of possible positions, with each individual represented in a single point on this matrix, looking at it closely. However, if we pull back we begin to see clusters, leaving it up to our criteria how to draw arbitrary lines between the number of them that we consider optimal and significant, as well as where we mark the boundaries. In this text, without falling into the trap of relativization, we seek to establish the fact that the middle class is inherently the result of an arbitrary decision of classification, yet one that is also useful and significant.

The second criterion is to consider the middle class as part of a cultural project not born of a neutral process, and not far removed from its vision as a political buffer. For our purposes, behind the middle class is an idea that associates it with modernity, with citizenship based on consumption, and on a country's development or progress, and which is also responsible for its progress through customs and values, creating a specific imaginary of individuals who act as reliable repositories of the nation's future. However, in common with any cultural project, it is important to understand it as a process and therefore we should explore its historical background.

The Mexican Revolution was a foundational moment of the country's middle class as we understand it today. Among the revolutionary movement's various results, a number of government programs began to stimulate upward social mobility through a vision of formal education that led to a shift from manual to non-manual labor from one generation to the next.

However, creating the modern citizen was not solely linked to labor. Many other similar initiatives existed. For example, Mexico made efforts to modernize and show its citizens to live correspondingly, among other programs designed to give access to and promote patterns of consumption associated with a modern lifestyle.

In Mexico, this led to the idea that the middle class had four main markers, according to Claudio Stern's seminal work,[19] which is worth problematizing:

1) Urban residence. Urban living has greater prestige, due to the association of cities with modernity, and rural areas with tradition.
2) At least nine years of formal education. Educational qualifications are seen as the sole and unquestionable certificates of competence and preparation for jobs deemed to confer higher status.
3) Non-manual employment, implicitly meaning a higher income than earnings from manual labor. This draws a line between white- and blue-collar workers, with the former being desirable and valuable.
4) Consumption over and above basic needs. Classifying what constitutes "basic" is difficult given human beings' inherently social nature.

This makes it clear that any social category—in this case the middle class—does not exist in an ideological vacuum. The categories are created within a specific cultural space, the boundaries are blurred between groups, and, most importantly, they reveal values specifically relevant to their originating societies. Furthermore, assigning specific categories to subjects is based on how those who create them are situated and what they wish to explain. The cultural space also has a specific place and time, as proved in a brief analysis of markers, which are no longer relevant, shifting the differentiation elsewhere.

Urban life in the 1930s (during the period of the post-revolutionary regime's consolidation) was a highly differentiated experience: only 34% of the entire population was considered urban. By 2020, this percentage grew to 79%.[20] Moreover, if we consider that in 2012 the Mexican government made high-school education obligatory (in other words, 12 years of formal education), the nine years became obsolete. Similarly, the differentiation between manual and non-manual employment assumed a constantly growing demand for skilled jobs, a typical aspect of early-stage industrialization programs. Additionally, subsequent processes were not taken into account, such as the massification of higher education that led to the supply of university-educated workers outstripping demand, devaluing the qualifications obtained. This created an education market in which differentiation not only existed between public and private education centers, but also within the private sector, in terms of their cost. In this way, education replicated processes in other spheres of consumption, where various bets and tools (such as loans, intermittent consumption, and a combination of public and private offers) give access to goods and services and in this way show them to be a performance as part of a shared code of signifiers.

From White-Collar Worker to Manager in Mexico City during the Neoliberal Era

The expansion of market rationalities into other fields, as described above in relation to education, is one of the effects of neoliberal governmentality that also entails specific subjectivities. With markets that are both massified and hyper-segmented, performance constitutes a means for individuals to explicitly establish their membership of groups formed through the access and display of each option on offer. In the analysis of narratives, the creation of the discourse specifies affiliations and differentiations that also help explore how historical and social processes translate into individuals' experiences—as reflected in the following narrative:

> [My father] studied business administration at the UNAM[21] and then worked in HR [...] with all the labor market contacts, for him the TEC was ideal,[22] since it's the best university, right? Because he saw

> that the TEC alumni got good jobs [...] I think that it's also an inherited perception, right? Over many generations where perhaps some time ago it made a difference, and the perception sticks: a private name [university] has greater value than a public one.
>
> (Director, transnational finance company)

Here we can read how access to a public university education gave this woman director's father access to a white-collar position within a company, which also allows him to notice the shifts in the desirability of symbolic elements in the job market: educational qualifications from a private "name" (university) enjoyed a level of prestige previously afforded by public ones. Despite structural factors limiting the agency of the father's position, his gatekeeping role within the company allows him to invest in private education for his daughter as an investment for a better future. It is also clear that, for this director, upward social mobility is at least a result, not only of her efforts, but also of those made by her father, and of the possibility to take advantage of changing markers. We can summarize by saying that social progress is a cumulative and contingent process, and by highlighting both the shift in symbolic elements and their increasing effectiveness in the value system of said family and of those gatekeepers who paved the way to a successful professional career.[23]

Symbolic elements are by no means the sole criteria for gaining access to the managerial class in Mexico City. The contention here is that their role has assumed particular importance in differentiating between individuals. We can refer to the narrative once again: she always brings us back to the sphere of perception as there is no discussion about knowledge, capabilities, or execution of alumni from private or public universities. She also discusses a long-standing process that would validate such a perception—even when we see that it is not precisely the case in accordance to her father's access to a public education and subsequently to a white-collar job within a private-sector firm.[24] Additionally, the differentiation between public and private universities makes us think about the university as a commercial brand that remains attached to its graduates, offering a quantifiable and specific value on the job market. This becomes a tangible difference once they reach specific positions, with commensurate salaries. It is worth pausing here to note how inequality—resulting from different levels of access to material and symbolic benefits—is created through these shifting and infinitesimal discrepancies between individuals of the same group, or, more specifically, between members of the same class. If she had followed in her father's footsteps and attended a public university, without earning a more desirable qualification for the job market, that might have been enough to have prevented her from reaching the same level of corporate seniority, with all its associated benefits. To paint a clearer picture of the contingency and flexibility of the gambles made, as well as the effectiveness of symbolic codes of differentiation in other fields, we can analyze the same director's narrative below:

> Because my mother worked in a [government office] she received discounts at hotels in Acapulco and that kind of thing... sometimes things didn't go [so great], [...] but when times were good, [...] we went to Disneyland, [...] and then we went to Orlando... and then we went... Yes! From there we went to Las Vegas... Yes! On the same trip, that was the *top* vacation.[25]

The advantages stemmed from not only having a father employed by a private firm, but also a mother working in a government department. This arrangement gave the household the necessary flexibility in times that were not "so great," a euphemism for Mexico's different economic crises following the collapse of the industrialization model. In its place, a service-based and free market economy began to drive economic growth, with neoliberal administrations actively disregarding the traditional roles of government. At the same time it is not only goods that move around the world but also those products and symbols that are part of the cultural hegemony, thanks to the growth of technological and cultural industries. However, only some individuals have a similar range of movement. In this sense, and corroborating the marketing manager's narrative above, going on vacation—apart from being a classic example of conspicuous or non-basic consumption—is centered on the experience as its material roots quickly vanish. It also points to the important difference between going on vacation abroad or to domestic destinations, in order to have access to places imbued with a greater prestige and desirability as they belong to touristic circuits full of meanings, which translates into a globally recognized lifestyle. Simply being present in such places turns the body into a symbol of distinction on account of its mobility and for announcing its affiliation with a specific group through a shared symbolic code.

These two examples about education and vacationing (consumption) show that the analysis, in absolute terms, of access as markers of differentiation between classes must shift toward considering symbolic aspects, too. This leads us to conceiving them as part of a code that operates in the deeply fragmented groups within the middle class, and in which individuals' skillful communication in these aspects takes place through perception-based processes.

Classifying Through Perception and Exercising Power Through Influence

> People can't judge you by your intrinsic value, so they have to find some kind of proxy, whatever's easiest, most superficial... this *wey*

> [dude] dresses well, he's well-structured. Do you give him the role? What's your value? What's your worth?
>
> (Senior Managing Consultant, international consultancy firm)

This narrative shows how categorical thinking[26] or the halo effect[27] become useful but dangerous tools as shortcuts to classify individuals, processing our perceptions in a world saturated by data that need processing for it to become information and help us navigate our social surroundings (in addition to the sense of urgency required by our culture of immediacy). Such mechanisms lead us to infer mistakenly that if the individuals we perceive have specific characteristics, then they will have others because "they fit together." If someone displays a character trait considered desirable, we expect this quality naturally to go hand-in-hand with other, similarly positive characteristics, as well as vice versa.

This managing consultant admits that it is impossible to rely on an exhaustive assessment, hence he acknowledges that simple and superficial tricks will suffice: dressing well and having a properly structured speech will ensure the person can access a certain position, and this will be used as a proxy for his or her value and legitimacy in it. The codes referred to are important in a company's sphere of managerial positions, but this does not mean that they are the only valuable attributes or simply replace others such as diligence, intelligence, etc. The point is that they are used to swiftly infer an individual's category. However, homophily is an influential factor in the desirability of the traits associated with corporate elites.[28] People in such positions of power consider that their characteristics to be of most value, and conceive merit on that basis. Therefore, as gatekeepers they often let in the people with whom they identify. The very concept of meritocracy was conceived as an exercise to show how a meritocracy would lead to an intensification and reinforcement of social filters, at the same time as legitimizing those individuals with accumulated advantages that would be read as merit;[29] furthermore, access to highly selective positions in itself acts as a Rite of Institution,[30] establishing it as legitimate and unarguable.

Since these processes represent a pendular movement between the symbolic and material realms, the concept of performance is extremely useful when exploring access to the corporate elite with its semantic double helix, in accordance with Anne Johnson:[31]

- The material component of corporate performance is definable as the achievement of quantifiable results: sales targets, financial goals, inventory targets, share value, etc. However, obtaining these tangible results is associated with personal characteristics and attitudes such as rapport with clients, "vision," ingenuity, "proactivity/assertiveness," etc., which are socially sanctioned and fall into a non-material category.
- This leads to the symbolic aspect of performance by talking about the "presentation of Self in Everyday Life"[32] (or image, in native

> terms), as well as the "restoration of behavior"[33] (or attitude, in native terms). Both elements are related to a class-based aesthetic and knowledge, read as an adequate repertoire for use in these areas, to create affiliations, to communicate membership, and to prove sufficiency in the legitimate codes in the same way as performing a role effectively (causing an effect) in front of an audience.

When the first helix relates to the kind of knowledge acquired in higher education, the second helix becomes a tool to make the difference with regard to others with the same qualifications and to assert the privilege of accessing a more senior position. This claim can be either conscious or unconscious, successful or unsuccessful, but the idea is to present it as legitimate through the use of codes seen as requirements for said positions:

> Because when you see yourself there, you want to see yourself like that. Once you're there you say, right, now I've got to wear the right clothes, buy myself a suit, you begin to see what kind of ties they wear, you have to buy yourself a watch, to look the part, right? [standing up straight and drawing attention to the watch he is actually wearing by raising his arm slightly as if to tell the time]. You've got to put on some kind of disguise, because that's what it really is: you've got to go out there and put on your mask that includes everything from how you look to how you dress, so it has been a little like… […] "When in Rome…" right? So it is like blending in once you've reached the next level, and you've got to present yourself like that.
>
> (Manager, transnational consultancy firm)

Performance works by building bridges and erecting barriers between individuals, creating representations of how legitimate managers should see themselves and act through specific objects and behaviors. These visions are not solely based on subjective levels, as they help to express reality by making it intelligible through a proposed classificatory system of individuals that provide meanings to relations between them through identities and alterities.

A classificatory system validating acceptance or exclusion in certain spheres is based on hierarchies; this is an expression of power in interpersonal relations, hence a political process. Therefore, in climbing the corporate ladder, clusters that create a larger group conceived as being middle class show dynamics of conflict due to the access to material markers through specific symbolic codes. Two particularly relevant studies that specifically explore the middle class, and that reflect the same concepts that arose in interviews, are:

- Mark Liechty's analysis of the emerging middle class in Nepal[34] which uses the word "suitability," which contains various possible meanings in this context: being adequate and not being out of place in certain spaces, standing out appropriately among colleagues to aspire for a more senior position, showing yourself to be compatible with certain values, being appropriate in line with certain characteristics (even in the physical sense), being considered right for a role, etc.

- Beverley Skeggs's work about respectability as a desired value dividing working-class and middle-class women in the United Kingdom.[35] This concept turned up in interviews, but with a twist: not as something one desires to have, but as respect, something that one hopes to inspire in others, so that they behave that way towards you. It was also presented as being closely connected to the value that needed to be inferred by others and that would lead to the treatment you received.

However, the interviewees constantly and expressly stated the desire to have an influence on others as the embodiment of power, as this manager tells us:

> I have the power to decide, [...] to determine the kind of environment for lots of people, to make visible changes, a stroke of my pen decides the fate of x-number of people, how big is my sphere of influence? [...] I think it's a recent trend too, that people want to be influential, because I do something then everyone follows me, right? Today it's far easier to have influence over people and then we have the human ego, I think that's always the case, right? [laughter] that's an ego boost for me, isn't it? To see that now I've got that power [...] (Key Account Manager, technology firm)

The creation of differences between individuals on the corporate ladder relies heavily on symbolic elements; therefore, the motivation to climb the ladder is not only about financial incentives. Monetary satisfiers are a consequence of greater obligations and responsibilities, but the interviewees reveal that money by itself does not explain their efforts. As the above narrative suggests, for this group of individuals in managerial positions, the capacity of influencing others becomes the true measure of their position. In this sense, some of them directly mentioned the role of social-network influencers, as if this represented the ethos of this era. As such, for managers and directors, influence is today's symbolic and material embodiment of power, in the same way as "leadership" used to be. This power behind their positions is represented in how their decisions affect other people. The number and level of their decisions therefore defines the power they have accumulated over the course of their careers.

Conclusions

Creating differences between individuals is an exercise derived from the effort to categorize and navigate reality; however, hierarchies form at the same time to justify access to scarce positions and assets, and this represents a political process.

One example of such processes is the creation of Class as a native category which has symbolic origins used to legitimate access to material benefits through the perception of the order established as irrefutable. In turn, these material advantages create and reaffirm symbolic elements that form a feedback loop.

This path of analysis shows the fragmentation of the heterogeneous middle class: a cultural project that represents social and financial progress both at an individual level and as a social role within modernity. However, with the implementation of neoliberal governmentality policies, obsolete markers become explicitly inoperative after structural processes in Mexico City during the first decades of the twenty-first century.

By using the idea of performance as an analytical tool, it is possible to explain the predominance of the symbolic sphere of this term for creating differences in cognitive capitalism, and its skillful use by a cluster within the aforesaid group. In this case, such a cluster—through the projection of an image and specific attitudes—creates not only a representation but an elite: the managerial class.

Being a member of said managerial class becomes a path for its members not only to gain access to specific advantages compared to the rest of the country's population, but also to attain what they describe as influence, which in turn represents their power over other individuals.

Notes

1 Forbes Staff, "¿Qué sueldo puedes tener en las empresas que mejor pagan en México?," *Forbes Mexico*, Mar. 26, 2018, https://www.forbes.com.mx/cuanto-puedes-ganar-como-gerente-en-las-empresas-mas-grandes-de-mexico/.
2 Manuel Castells, *La sociedad red V1* (Madrid: Alianza, 2000).
3 Gøsta Esping-Andersen, *Changing Classes: Stratification and Mobility in Post-Industrial Societies* (London: Sage Publications, 1993).
4 Mark Liechty, *Suitably Modern: Making Middle-Class Culture in a New Consumer Society* (Princeton, NJ: Princeton University Press, 2003).
5 Yann Moulier-Boutang, *Cognitive Capitalism* (Cambridge: Polity Press, 2003).
6 Bjorn Asheim, "Differentiated Knowledge Bases and Varieties of Regional Innovation Systems," *Innovation* 20, no. 3 (2007): 223–241.
7 Ezequiel Adamovsky, *Historia de la clase media Argentina: Apogeo y decadencia de una ilusión, 1919–2003* (Buenos Aires: Planeta, 2009), 427.
8 Giampietro Gobo, "Class: Stories of Concepts. From Ordinary Language to Scientific Language," *Social Science Information* 32, no. 3 (1993): 467–489.
9 Claude Lévi-Strauss, *El pensamiento salvaje* (Mexico City: FCE, 1970).
10 In particular, the interviewee refers to Socioeconomic Level in accordance with the association of market research agencies, the Asociación Mexicana de Agencias de Investigación de Mercados.
11 Puebleando means traveling by road to visit different towns and villages. This marks a contrast between something local and backward (traditional) and the international and cosmopolitan (modern).

12 The Central de Abastos is a wholesale market located in an area of Mexico City perceived to be highly marginalized.
13 Las Lomas is a residential district for Mexico City's highest-income sectors.
14 The article "No, no eres clase media" reduces the middle class simply to its income level and in a sermonizing tone determines who can and who cannot be considered a member. Viri Ríos, "No, no eres clase media," *The New York Times*, July 6, 2020, https://www.nytimes.com/es/2020/07/06/espanol/opinion/clase-media-mexico.html.
15 Pierre Bourdieu, "Capital simbólico y clases sociales," in *Estrategias de reproducción social*, eds. P. Bourdieu and L. Wacquant. (Buenos Aires: Siglo XXI, 2011).
16 Individuals in these circles use this saying in English as another social marker.
17 Iuri Lotman, *La semiosfera I: Semiótica de la cultura y el texto* (Madrid: Ediciones Cátedra 1996) talks of spheres of defined meanings specific to certain groups, where whatever lies beyond its boundaries requires translation, whereas Alice Krozer, *Inequality in Perspective: Rethinking Inequality Measurement, Minimum Wages and Elites in Mexico* (PhD diss., Cambridge: Centre of Development Studies, University of Cambridge, 2018) refers to a bubble in which the Mexican economic elite live in isolation thanks to their privileged status. Both figures are combined for the symbolic analysis of the country's corporate managerial positions.
18 Even economic issues are difficult to fully quantify since they are not completely comprised by income.
19 Claudio Stern, "Notas para la delimitación de las clases medias en México," *in Las clases medias en la coyuntura actual: Seminario llevado a cabo en el Centro Tepoztlán, A.C. Tepoztlán, Mor., 26 de septiembre de 1987*, eds. Soledad Loaeza, and Claudio Stern (Mexico City: Cuadernos del CES 33, 1990).
20 According to information obtained from: https://www.inegi.org.mx/programas/ccpv/2020/#Datos_abiertos, the website of the Instituto Nacional de Estadística y Geografía (consulted on April 4, 2021).
21 The National Autonomous University of Mexico (UNAM) is the largest and most important public university in Mexico.
22 Business sectors consider the Tecnológico de Monterrey, or TEC, to be one of the country's leading universities, though the country's elite do not necessarily share this view.
23 Charles Tilly, *La desigualdad persistente* (Buenos Aires: Manantial 2000). The author emphasizes the fact that individuals do not promote themselves, but it is the gatekeepers who promote them.
24 It is not about seeking the truth, as absolute facts, but the meaning, as plausible facts.
25 See also note 17. This native Spanish speaker uses an English word here to indicate a higher social standing.
26 Tilly, *La desigualdad persistente.*
27 Edward L. Thorndike, "A Constant Error in Psychological Ratings," *Journal of Applied Psychology* (1920): 25–29.
28 Sam Friedman and Daniel Laurison, *The Class Ceiling: Why it Pays to be Privileged* (Bristol: Policy Press, 2019).
29 Michael Young, *The Rise of the Meritocracy, 1870–2033: An Essay on Education and Equality* (Baltimore, MD: Penguin Books, 1961).
30 Pierre Bourdieu, "Los ritos de institución," in *Honor y gracia*, eds. J. Pitt-Rivers and J.G. Peristiany (Madrid: Alianza, 1993).
31 Anne Johnson, "¿Qué hay en un nombre?: Una apología del performance," *Alteridades* 24, no. 48 (2014): 9–21.

32 Erving Goffman, *The Presentation of Self in Everyday Life* (Edinburgh: University of Edinburgh Social Sciences Research Center, 1956).
33 Richard Schechner, "Restauración de la conducta," in Estudios avanzados de performance, eds. D. Taylor, and M. Fuentes (Mexico City: FCE, 2011).
34 Mark Liechty, *Suitably Modern: Making Middle-Class Culture in a New Consumer Society* (Princeton, NJ: Princeton University Press, 2003).
35 Beverly Skeggs. *Formations of Class & Gender: Becoming Respectable* (London: Goldsmiths; University of London, 1997).

23 Equality or Hierarchy? Solidarity with Those Above or Below?

Dilemmas of Gendered Self-Identification in a New Bolivian Middle Class

Miriam Shakow

Introduction

In January, 2018, I watched a Bolivian-made movie, *Sueños Cumplidos*, with Aide, a forty-year-old nurse, in her rural home community in central Bolivia, alongside her family. They had purchased the film, a recent production by students in a rural, highland Bolivian teachers' college, from amongst Bollywood, Japanese anime, and Hollywood horror offerings in a local bootleg-DVD shop. This multigenerational audience included Aide's elderly mother, two of her middle-aged sisters, a teenaged nephew, and her four-year-old son. We watched on Aide's large, flat-screen TV, laughing at the low production values and amateur acting, even as we were all riveted. It quickly became clear that this film encapsulated Aide's own family history, complete with word-for-word statements that they uttered in their own daily lives to refer to their hopes for middle-class upward mobility and pride in their achievement of it.

The movie begins with Don Faustino, an impoverished construction worker who lives in Bolivia's rural highlands, supporting his family lovingly on his meager income. He declares frequently to his teenaged children that they must help their parents, such as by taking the sheep to pasture, but also study hard to become professionals (*profesionales*) so they won't "suffer as I have suffered." Aide's father, a former bus-driver's assistant and peasant farmer, had repeated this phrase, a truism among rural, peasant-Indigenous parents in Bolivia, since I met him in 1995. Aide and her siblings frequently quoted him saying those words to explain their dogged efforts to graduate college with professional degrees. Several of them, including her, had accomplished that goal.

An early scene depicts Don Faustino's family in their adobe house. His wife wears a worn *pollera*, the Indigenous- and peasant-identified gathered skirt; on her head is a ragged bowler hat and her hair is in two braids. Her clothing and hairstyle mark her clearly as a rural *chola*, a peasant-Indigenous Bolivian woman. She blows through a metal pipe to stoke the fire in her wood-burning adobe stove as she serves the family dinner. Suddenly, Aide's twentysomething brother exclaimed to me, in a tone that combined

DOI: 10.4324/9781003029311-28

his dry humor with disgust: "That's how we used to live, Miriam! Like animals! Everyone in one room: the guinea pigs, the wood-burning adobe stove (*q'oncha*), everyone all mixed together." Where their small corner store stood now, he continued, there had been a sheep corral. Now, finally, by contrast "We live like people!" (*vivimos como gente*). He thus marked the existential stakes of upward mobility, in which each material goal (e.g., to build a multi-roomed house with separate bedrooms) were laden with moral symbolism and aspirations for social mobility.

By the end of *Sueños Cumplidos*, the protagonists have moved to El Alto, twin city of the Bolivian capital, La Paz. The children are depicted on the campus of the large public university wearing urban- and middle-class-identified clothing—the sister has swapped her *pollera* for a pair of pants—speaking confidently to classmates and professors. The eldest son has gained prosperity by founding a construction company while studying for an architecture degree. He hands his mother stacks of cash, supporting her social elevation within the *chola* category: she now dresses in a new, more stylish *pollera* and Borsalino hat (known to cost hundreds of US dollars). He also pays for his sister's expenses as she completes her own *profesional* degree. In the final scene, he proclaims triumphantly at his father's graveside: "Your dream is accomplished, Papá!" Bright-yellow Spanish subtitles appear: "One additional effort and what would have been a failure has become a glorious success," ending the film. The individualist ideal of upward mobility through hard work has triumphed. Aide's family exclaimed frequently that they loved *Sueños Cumplidos* and watched it nightly for quite some time.

This film depicts a longstanding individualist model of upward mobility and progress via professional education, made possible through the hard labor of older, Indigenous peasant-laborer parents and studious, hard-working children. This dominant model for people of impoverished backgrounds hoping to join the middle class is so utterly familiar as to be unremarkable in Bolivia, as well as in much of Latin America and the Third World. It also expresses the common Latin American notion that "money whitens": racial categorization is deeply intertwined with class determinants such as wealth and education. The Andean particularity of this model holds that working-class, rural parents are also racialized as Indigenous and they can rise to the mestizo middling racial category as they gain income and professional status. The marked, gendered category of the *chola* as the encapsulation of working-class Indigenous Bolivian identity is symbolized in the film by the mother's and sister's *polleras* and braids. A major sign that the family has achieved upward mobility via assimilation is the sister's switch from wearing a pollera to pants as she embarks on university education.

Yet the film was also notable for leaving out a significant challenges that upward mobility in Bolivia entailed. First, it ignores social and economic demands of friends, family, and neighbors who may feel left behind or rejected. Furthermore, new models of upward mobility that had gained increasing purchase in Bolivia during the previous two decades presented a competing path for would-be new middle classes. These new models emphasized social solidarity between middle and lower socio-economic classes, anti-racism, support for nationwide redistribution of wealth from the rich to the poor, and indigenous pride (rather than the imperative to become mestizo or mestiza), expressed through watchwords like "interculturality" (*interculturalidad*) and "development with identity." This alternative definition of middle-class mobility developed from the social agitation of indigenous and leftist social movements that made possible the 2005 election of Evo Morales as Bolivia's first self-identified Indigenous president, on the MAS (*Movimiento al socialismo*, Movement Toward Socialism) party ticket.[1] In response to the "free marketization" of the Bolivian economy and neoliberal multiculturalism in the 1980s and 1990s, social movements protesting neoliberal economic policies and demanding economic redistribution were accompanied by some groups promoting Indigenous cultural pride and the dissolution of Bolivia's entrenched racial hierarchies. They derided as "pluri-multi," shorthand for "pluricultural and multilingual," reforms such as bilingual education that had presented a watered-down notion of culture that celebrated Indigenous folklore but denied the inextricability of indigenous cultural claims from demands for economic redistribution, an end to racism and to free market reforms.[2] The MAS party built on these diverse movements, from coca growers in the tropics to militant indigenist Aymara-speaking highland groups. The MAS party even, temporarily, won over well-established, urban upper-middle classes.[3]

This model of "intercultural" upward mobility expanded after Morales took power and his MAS party gained electoral dominance in both houses of Congress and many municipal and regional governments. Highly visible cabinet ministers wearing homespun ponchos and *polleras* and speaking Quechua and Aymara in the halls of power portrayed themselves as new exemplars of upward mobility, who could gain prosperity and political power while retaining their social identification as working-class, peasant, and indigenous. Subaltern Indigenous and *campesino* categories became increasingly associated with increasing political and social power in many realms of life, from Congress to universities to mass media. Young people who would earlier have been urged only to leave behind an Indigenous and *campesino* identity as they pursued educational and economic opportunities were now told that they could both acknowledge their "roots" and enjoy a prosperous life, while helping to dismantle the colonial hierarchies of Bolivian society.[4] It is important to note, however, that even many fervent social movement activists did not identify themselves explicitly as "Indigenous" (*indígena*, *originario*, or *nativo*). As Andrew Canessa has shown, many Bolivians whom foreigners or even upper and middle classes would term "Indigenous" instead identified themselves through more local and national categories of identity.[5]

Expanded political opportunities for women formed an important element of social movement demands and political leaders' promises for societal transformation. The Bartolina Sisa women's agrarian union federation had played a key role in social movements since the 1970s and gained numbers and power through members' leadership in national protests between 2000 and 2005. President Morales appointed a woman who identified as a *cholita* to his Cabinet for the first time in Bolivian history: Casimira Rodriguez as Minister of Justice. Other women, some but not all *cholitas de pollera*, served in subsequent cabinets, including Nemecia Achacollo, a Bartolinas Federation leader, who served as Minister of Rural Development and Lands from 2010 to 2015. With these appointments, MAS leaders rhetorically signaled a shift away from what anthropologist Rob Albro had termed the calculated use of "the populist *chola*" as a symbol in Bolivian politics during prior decades.[6] During the 1980s' and 1990s' "pluri multi neoliberalism," male political leaders frequently surrounded themselves with *cholas* in public events to signal to voters that they would act in solidarity with peasant and working-class Bolivians. The women, as mostly-silent companions onstage at political speeches and inaugurations of local public works, had become both "relatively powerless" but "politically crucial for men" who frequently failed to address their economic hardship.[7] By 2018, by contrast, women of all socio-economic classes comprised nearly 50% of elected leaders, owing both to 1990s-era laws requiring that women comprise one-third of political candidates and to the social movement and MAS party initiatives outlined above.[8]

Middling people in the central Bolivian region of Cochabamba, in which I carried out my research, in fact have a longer history of attaining upward mobility and of asserting multiple and shifting identities than do Indigenous-identified peasant farmers in other regions of the country. Brooke Larson and Laura Gotkowitz, for example, have shown that in the early twentieth century, many people in the Cochabamba region were considered "Indian" while working as serfs or small-scale peasant freeholders, but, with a quick change of clothing, could present themselves as upwardly mobile mestizos.[9] The social category of the "*chola*" was multifaceted then, as well. While men's ponchos and sandals signaled their peasant and indigenous status, the *chola*'s *pollera*, petticoats, jewelry, and braids carried a more complex assortment of meanings because women who occupied this category served as economic and social mediators between rural and urban populations, peasant and middle class, indigenous and mestizo. Women frequently owned and operated taverns (*chicherías*) and brokered the sale of agricultural products in cities.[10] As Albro notes aptly, "The chola has shown a considerable capacity to put up particular resistance to imposed social classifications, while demonstrating deft skill in navigating among them."[11] Yet this ability to shape their own identities and assert upward mobility had limits. On the one hand, *cholas* were able to assert a higher status as mestizas relative to poorer and more rurally-identified "Indians" from whom they bought corn, wheat, or vegetables to sell in urban markets. On the other hand, they faced frequent social demotion to the "Indian" category when interacting with the "decent people" of middle and upper classes in Cochabamba City.[12]

The 1952 Bolivian revolution's state-building model of ethnic assimilation intensified, as well as transformed, this relational social hierarchy in which individual people could potentially shift races and classes depending on the context, but only sometimes in ways that they controlled. The Revolutionary government, as part of its support for peasant demands for Agrarian Reform, taught through centralized school curricula and public proclamation that all Bolivians were mestizos, erasing the public use of category of "Indian" by fiat, even as the connotation of racial inferiority persisted in the class term "peasant" and the frequent racial slur "Indian."[13] Rural peasants were encouraged to speak Spanish instead of Quechua and women to drop their *pollera*-wearing in favor of straight skirts. For instance, young women were prohibited from wearing *polleras* in high schools until the MAS government overturned the rule in 2006, as were young women who were visibly pregnant.

My primary field site of Sacaba, where I have carried out ethnographic field research since 1995, reflects these historical and contemporary trends. It is a diverse municipality of 180,000 people, bisected by a major highway, that spans rural, provincial town, and wealthy housing developments that blend imperceptibly into Cochabamba City. This peri-urban setting has long been the launching pad for many families' attempts to *salir adelante*, even as it also has been home to many movement activists and MAS party loyalists.

If these models of middle-class self-identification entailed competing cultural, racial, and gendered ideals during the past three decades, it is important to note that the economic possibilities for families and individuals attempting to "get ahead" were shaped by repeated economic booms and busts. Dramatic economic expansions and contractions followed the coca and cocaine boom of the 1980s and its 1990s bust owing the US-led War on Drugs; neoliberal structural adjustment and austerity; political decentralization that distributed modest funding for infrastructure; recurrent droughts and other extreme weather; a significant redistribution of wealth, anti-racist legislation, and quota programs for Indigenous and peasant-identified workers in the public sector under President Evo Morales' three terms (2006–2019); economic prosperity generated by high world prices for natural gas, Bolivia's chief export. Most recently, additional economic pressures have resulted from a drop in world prices for gas, a right-wing coup in late 2019 that shrank many government redistribution mechanisms, and a severe economic crisis brought on in 2020 by the global coronavirus pandemic. Bolivia's upwardly mobile groups have thus been alternately buffeted by myriad economic challenges and buoyed by economic opportunities. The new middle classes upon which I focus in this chapter are even less insulated from the economic shocks than are the traditional middle classes (*clase media*), long identified with a relatively small cohort of professional families based in Bolivia's largest cities.

The gendered dimensions of class status have also changed over time. In the colonial and Republican periods, Bolivian women frequently gained in status as sexual partners of European and elite men, and as social and economic intermediaries between elite and subaltern groups. The rising social status of *cholas* in early-twentieth-century central Bolivia reflects this role.[14] Yet during the course of the twentieth century, echoing what Marisol de la Cadena has found in Peru, Bolivian rural *cholas* became "more Indian" than men.[15] As education became more available for rural folk in the mid-twentieth century, rural families frequently prioritized their sons' education over that of daughters. In more recent decades, however, in response to initiatives such as the Millennium Development Goals, girls and young women had achieved near-parity with boys and young men in education. Since 2010, as the MAS party funneled increased funding to education on a national level, approximately 90% of teenagers of both sexes attended high school.[16] Similarly, official estimates of gaps in literacy between young men and women dropped to zero, though gaps persist for elderly Bolivians.[17]

The most extreme shocks of the past twenty years have occurred since November, 2019, when upper- and middle-class protests against apparent fraud in the presidential elections degenerated into a right-wing military coup. The Organization of American States reported that Evo Morales had won the election (his fourth) through fraud. Though this claim was challenged months later by several independent investigations, a little-known right-wing Senator, Jeanine Áñez, took power as interim president.[18] She and her hastily-assembled cabinet immediately began supporting military control as well as symbolic, cultural, and political attempts to root out the more progressive of the MAS platform and policies. The military and newly-formed paramilitary forces carried out massacres of MAS supporters, including the murder of 10 coca-growers in Sacaba.[19] She and her allies infamously tried to stamp out Indigenous and MAS symbols, such as the *wiphala* flag.[20] The coronavirus pandemic began shortly afterward, leaving Bolivian society and economy in a deeply uncertain state.

Latin American Middle Classes: A Minority in the Global South

Aspirations for middle-class upward mobility in Bolivia bore some similarities to self-identified middle classes elsewhere. As scholars examining middle-class experiences from the Global North and Global South have noted, middle-class social and economic existence is frequently fraught with anxiety, from "fear of falling" economically to enormous energy spent displaying one's distinction through consumption, education, and fine taste to convey their own superior morality, hard-workingness, individual entrepreneurial agency, and respectability.[21] Scholars find that class is formed relationally, rather than via the occupation of static categories, and that experiences of upward mobility have simultaneous economic, social and cultural meanings.

Furthermore, the older Bolivian model of individual upward mobility through ethnic assimilation and climbing of Bolivia's hierarchies (rather than dismantling them) resonates strongly with those in many post-colonial countries, within and beyond Latin America. Anthropologists examining middle classes, usually focusing upon more established urban middle classes in the Global South, contrast First World countries, where majorities consider themselves middle class (regardless of income) and who generally feel confident in their geopolitical and economic power, with Third World middle classes who must contend with their small numbers amidst a majority of desperately poor and the overwhelming power of the economic and racial super-elite. Furthermore, the legacies of extractive colonialism mean that, in contrast to the Global North, middle classes in the Global South have more to prove to assert distinction and respectability as superior to that of the majority impoverished and indigent fellow countrymen and their worth relative to both the super-rich of their own country and the middle and upper classes of the Global North.[22]

Yet, as I show below, Bolivia is unusual in several ways. First, egalitarianism as a popular value among its models of middle-class upward mobility is unusually prominent in Bolivia. Furthermore, unlike other countries in which the middle class serves as normative, in Bolivia political discourse has long assumed the existence of "Two Bolivias," comprised of a popular, Indigenous, *campesino* majority and a super-rich, white minority. Despite relatively new public discourse identifying an "emergent middle class" in Bolivia, few Bolivians I knew used those terms to describe themselves or others.[23] The recent nature of upward mobility means that Bolivians who were one generation away from peasant farming face a perplexing array of shifting options and restrictions: competing models of class status introduced by Bolivia's left-indigenist movements; social and economic commitments to poorer and lower-status families, friends, and neighbors; and volatile economic conditions that rapidly expanded and shrank opportunities for accumulating capital and securing professional jobs. That the *chola* served as a gendered symbol that engaged these competing imperatives made the dilemmas confronting young Bolivian women particularly vexing.

Struggles Over Competing Models of Upward Mobility

I witnessed a public, charged debate over these gendered models of upward mobility in October 2005, during Evo Morales' first successful presidential campaign, when the prospect of deep social and economic transformation in Bolivia was palpably new. This debate took place during a workshop on "Social Communication," part of leadership certificate course, sponsored by foreign development agencies, to train women leaders of the Bartolina Sisa women's agrarian federation (see above) and members of other historically marginalized groups to become municipal leaders. Topics ranged from fiscal management to the UN Millennium Development Goals. A rotating series of professional sociologists, agronomists, and accountants taught the classes, held at Cochabamba's large public university, over two long days every other weekend for six months. Many instructors were then enthusiastic supporters of leftist and indigenist social movements and the MAS party.

Some of the students in this workshop were members of social movements that had formed the MAS party, such as the Bartolinas, and infused the discussion with their visions for societal transformation. Others, such as the young women I accompanied from my field site of Sacaba, were quite apolitical and attended primarily to gain an educational credential; this less politically engaged group also included shopkeepers and university students.

Sociologist Elsa Andrade taught this particular workshop. After several hours discussing the concept of "citizenship," she announced that we would discuss the theme of "interculturality," the favored term at that time among MAS-affiliated social movements, mentioned above, that conveyed the need to push beyond multiculturalist state reforms that accompanied neoliberal economic reforms, to decolonize Bolivia, dismantle racist structures of society, redistribute wealth, and valorize indigenous culture.

If interculturality was intended to convey the ideal of Indigenous pride and economic redistribution for equality in contrast to liberal multiculturalism, however, the ways in which this concept might apply to individual people's subjectivity was still up for debate. Andrade launched a tumultuous discussion by asking students to relate their own identities to that of the *chola*. In what seemed to me a deliberately challenging tone, Andrade asked a young woman sitting directly in front of her, "you no longer dress like a *cholita*, right?" This young woman wore pants and her hair was gathered in a ponytail. She replied earnestly in Spanish that her mother had always urged her not to wear a *pollera:* "[My mother] said to me, 'You need to learn to read and write' and to not be like her, who didn't study. That's why I don't wear a pollera." This statement, echoed innumerable times in my fieldwork in Sacaba, as well as in the film *Sueños Cumplidos*, described above, represented a straightforward explication of Bolivia's dominant model of upward mobility via education and cultural assimilation; that *polleras* had been forbidden dress for young women entering high school for the prior century made this decision symbolic as well as material. In a national context in which high school graduates constituted a minority, the act of completing high school was a sign of distinction, an important first step for many Bolivians striving to reach the middle class.

But another young woman, who wore a *pollera*, responded angrily. She declared emphatically in Quechua that the first young woman's acceptance of her mother's exhortations to not wear a *pollera* conveyed both cultural disrespect and racist and classist belittling of those who did. "We have become devalued! (*desvalorasqas*)," she exclaimed. She then described her own somewhat unusual circumstances. "I used to be *de vestido*": like the prior speaker, she had worn a pencil skirt or pants, rather than a *pollera*, throughout most of high school, adopting the same assimilationist norms of upward mobility. But indigenist NGO workers had come to her rural town when she was a high school senior and urged her to wear a *pollera* in order to practice "interculturality." Their admonishment made her realize, she told us, that "our culture needs to be recognized (*Noqancheqta culturancheqta reqsina tiyan*)" and she began wearing a *pollera*. She repeated scathingly that the first young woman was denigrating everyone who wore *polleras*.

The first woman began to cry. She protested that she was not putting anyone down (*criticar*). She said, resorting to a model of individual choice with which most residents in Sacaba explained how women decided whether or not to wear *polleras*, "I believe that anyone should wear what they want." What she was trying to explain, she continued, was simply that her mother had cared deeply about furthering her daughter's upward mobility. In warning her away from wearing a *pollera*, her mother wanted her children to "*salir adelante*" (get ahead in life), she concluded tearfully.

The teacher, clearly trying to defuse some of the anger she had provoked, changed the topic by asking someone else if they would wear a homespun, hand-embroidered *pollera* from Tapacarí, a Bolivian region heavily marked as Indigenous. Yet the political and symbolic stakes of the conversation in fact became more explicit as her question sparked continued argument over what form of women's clothing could be considered acceptable. A man responded in Quechua, explaining that the reason why he and other classmates (that is, their womenfolk) would not wear a homespun *pollera* was because it would counteract the "civilization" that they had already attained. He then bolstered his argument by stating that national progress demanded that individuals choose racial assimilation: "No one can prevent you from wearing a *pollera*, because we have rights. But we also need to enter into civilization." His apparent need to admonish women regarding their clothing choices, and his statement that dressing as a *chola* could facilitate or block the national spread of "civilization" highlighted the deep and tangled symbolism of *cholas* within Bolivia. To this, a woman who had spoken earlier to condemn disrespect aimed at women wearing homespun *polleras* retorted heatedly in Spanish, "We are all *Indios*. I don't understand why some people claim that they aren't. We should demand respect!" (*Debemos darnos nuestro lugar*).

Another young woman, whose poverty was reflected in her ragged *pollera* and tousled hair from the long truck-ride to the university campus, appeared to agree this debate over what women should wear and who should choose had important implications for Bolivia's deeply entrenched racism and classism. She said that people who came to Cochabamba dressed in those very homespun *polleras*, whom we all knew were from desperately poor, drought-stricken, highland regions, and came seasonally to beg on city streets in the agricultural off-season, were often the target of racist insults. "They get called, '*campesino*, *Indio*, *Lari* [hick], *sonso* [stupid],'" she spat in outrage. She echoed the woman who had declared earlier that she had donned a *pollera* after graduating from high school by declaring: "We need to make ourselves respected! (*respetachikuna*). We need to be proud (*orgullosos*)!"

The rhetoric of different students showed clearly which were activists in social movements such the Bartolinas women's agrarian union federation. The high school graduate who had donned a *pollera* and the woman who urged classmates "to be proud!" were enunciating social movement principles of both "interculturality" and anti-racism, at that time also promoted by Evo Morales' MAS party and models of collective indigenous uplift. These classmates were arguing that most Bolivians should identify as Indigenous, and implied that this cultural and racial reframing of upward mobility should be part of a national process of economic, social, and cultural "decolonization" accompanied by redistribution of wealth. By contrast, the man who argued that homespun *polleras* betrayed a lack of "civilization" clearly was not immersed in social movements, despite speaking in Quechua as his native language; nor was the young woman who justified in Spanish her mother's choice not to dress her in a *pollera* to help her to "get ahead." While both may have supported the policies of Evo and MAS for economic redistribution, they did not at that moment express the need to dismantle Bolivia's racial and cultural hierarchies or rethink their own place in them.

Ximena, a young communications professional who worked for an indigenist NGO, spoke up. She added that not only could individual upward mobility be compatible with Indigenous identity and solidarity with working-class roots, but that this change was already underway. Ximena declared excitedly to the workshop attendees, "A *pollera*-wearer (*uj pollerayoq*) is graduating from the Law School [right now]! All of our moms wear *polleras*." Bolivians should acknowledge that they sprang from "two cultures" and that both were equally worthy of respect, she urged. We needed to speak "both" languages: Indigenous Quechua *and* Spanish.

This argument between workshop classmates outlined the competing models of upward mobility among Bolivians, as well as the intense struggles—introspective and social, private and public—provoked by these competing models. Newly-powerful national movements defined societal progress and individual upward mobility away from individual striving and racial assimilation and toward a model of collective political action, Indigenous identification, and economic redistribution. The emergence of these competing paths compounded the dilemmas upwardly mobile Bolivians already faced in moving up the social ladder themselves.

Newly-Middle Class Women Wrestle with Competing Models of Upward Mobility: Celia and Aide

Far from a straightforward, linear, process of an individual person's economic and social improvement, as depicted in *Sueños Cumplidos* and in the ubiquitous Bolivian ideals of *salir adelante*, then, the experience of upward mobility was emotionally fraught, gendered, and subject to accusations of racism, disrespect, and snobbishness by others. In this final section, I trace the ways in which two women, Celia and Aide (mentioned above watching *Sueños Cumplidos* with her family), articulated their own newly middle-class subjectivity during the past twenty-five years. I focus on women's narratives because as a female researcher, I developed more intimate relationships with women during my fieldwork. Both exceptionally strong and independent, they each experienced different degrees of economic vulnerability and gendered burdens as women. They drew upon different specific bases for their own middle-class distinction.[24] They also expressed contrasting political commitments. Yet they both struggled with their social and economic choices, which offered a confusing mix of opportunities and constraints. From disappointing marriages to accusations of snobbery while confronting racism themselves, they rode the ups and downs of the Bolivian economy and expressed frustration at the pull of the dueling models of upward mobility. In their conversations with friends and family members, as well as with me, they conveyed that their aspirations for upward mobility involved a complex web of political allegiances, economic hopes, and connection to and distinctions from loved ones.

Celia

In January 2017, Celia told me that she had achieved many of her long-held dreams of upward mobility. As a teenager in 2006 when she worked with me as a research assistant, she had frequently expressed deep frustration at her poverty and what she saw as her mother's cultural backwardness. Celia was the only child of a destitute, chronically-ill widow. They lived in a small, ancient, dirt-floored house with a leaky tiled roof—visibly among the poorest families in her rural community. Celia complained to me that her mother's worldview was anti-scientific and old-fashioned: she visited folk healers (*yatiris*) rather than doctors and believed in animist powers of lightning and thunder. Celia worked in a dead-end job for several months following her high school graduation, as an assistant at a *chicha* (home-brewed corn beer) tavern owned by prosperous cousins. These cousins were also longtime supporters of the MAS party and President Morales; one of them was reputed to have been Evo's former girlfriend. In late 2006, another cousin, a wealthy *cholita*, hired Celia to work in her business importing Chinese-manufactured home-appliances. Brimming with excitement, Celia moved to the eastern Bolivian boom city of Santa Cruz to pursue this opportunity.

Celia's fortunes rose steadily, she recounted to me when I visited her in 2017 after we had not seen each other for over ten years. With her cousin's economic support and encouragement, Celia completed a technical certificate in marketing, though she dropped out before completing the final two years of her professional (*licenciatura*) degree after becoming pregnant. Yet she expressed a great deal of satisfaction with her life's upwardly mobile trajectory. "I wish my mother could see me now!," she exclaimed proudly, with a tinge of sadness. Her mother couldn't witness how Celia had built three businesses from scratch: two home appliance stores and a snack bar on a bustling commercial avenue in downtown Santa Cruz. Using her experience and contacts from her wealthy cousins, she had begun importing appliances from China to sell in her own shops.

Celia also conveyed pride in her upward mobility when describing her life, and she showed me photos of her social and family life, marked by racialized colorism, new amusements and forms of consumption, and new class horizons for her children. Celia explained that she never would have expected to fall in love with a man from the north of Potosí, a region known throughout Bolivia as a center of both poverty and highland Indigenous culture, whose inhabitants were frequently considered the archetypical "Indians" and "hicks" (*indios, laris*), as described above in the 2005 "interculturality" workshop. Celia told me in a tone of amazement that her husband's family was *vecinos* (small-town elites) from a beautiful North Potosi town whose residents were all light-skinned people. To her surprise, they had "white, white!" skin she exclaimed. Her own husband had pale skin and green eyes, she said proudly. Also, he was kind (*bueno*) and creative and energetic in working with her to make their businesses succeed.

Celia and her husband also clearly shared similar aspirations for consumption and middle-class distinction. She was a sharp dresser and wore her hair short and tinted, attesting to frequent trips to the salon. In one recent photo, she wore a gold lamé dress at a wedding, accompanied by her husband in a suit. Celia also showed me a video her husband had taken, in which she rode down a roller-coaster in a Santa Cruz amusement park with two women friends, their screams of excitement turning to laughter as they hugged each other after landing in a pool of water. Her daughter attended a private kindergarten, out of the economic reach of most Bolivians, where she was developing public speaking skills, Celia told me proudly. She and her daughter wore matching Tinkerbell pajamas to bed (wearing pajamas is a distinctly middle-class, urban style in

Bolivia). The family's home sported many home appliances and electronics from their shops: several enormous flat-screen TVs, large smartphones, air conditioners, microwaves—all items far out of economic reach of even more highly educated first-generation middle-class people I knew, such as Aide, the nurse.

Though Celia's rented rooms were small and dingy, and she expressed some concern about having become deeply indebted to launch her business ventures, she clearly saw herself as economically and socially ascendant in 2017. She told me excitedly that, though they had not yet accumulated enough savings, she and her husband hoped to buy their own home within the next few years and also planned to visit Disneyworld in Florida with their children. Her husband was so enraptured by the idea of visiting "Disney," she said, that he sometimes exclaimed "I'm going to work as hard as a burro" to pay for the trip.

Celia supported the MAS platform of economic redistribution, though at this moment in which her economic and social status seemed to be rising, she expressed mixed feelings about the MAS government. "Look, I was in favor of Evo—I'm in favor of [his policies]. He has done much good." Like many MAS supporters, however, Celia was also concerned about the MAS leaders' "corruption": "So much money going into their pockets!" Yet despite deep concerns about some MAS leaders' stealing of public funds (*corrupción*), she never completely gave up on the party because she agreed with its core platform.

Yet Celia's economic situation as a self-employed businesswoman turned out to be quite precarious. By 2020, she had divorced her husband after he began drinking heavily and only returned home every few days. This is a familiar pattern in Bolivia, where alcohol consumption quite high among both sexes but male drinking, as well as intimate partner violence, is reported to be the highest in Latin America.[25] He had left her to pay back their huge debts alone. She regretfully closed the snack bar and one appliance shop and was struggling to staff the one remaining shop without hiring employees. With the school closures owing to the coronavirus in 2020, Celia had to leave her nine-year-old daughter to take care of her four-year-old brother while she worked. She scrambled to sell what she could from her shop illicitly despite the lockdown, like so many market sellers and businesses whose owners did not have an economic safety net.

Celia was deeply opposed to Áñez's right-wing interim government on multiple counts, which she framed as an expression of solidarity with "poor people" (*los pobres*)—among whom she did not seem to count herself—as well as outrage at the news reports that many government leaders were pocketing public funds. Celia said she had known from the outset that the charges of electoral fraud against Evo were themselves fraudulent; the US government had obviously plotted the coup in order to claim Bolivia's large lithium deposits (Elon Musk's tweets of support for Evo's ouster certainly support Celia's analysis). She asserted that evidence that the Áñez government favored only "rich people" could be seen in the government's response to the coronavirus. Áñez had forced the closure of open-air markets, in which "the poor" shopped and made their living, purportedly to combat the spread of the coronavirus. Yet the president allowed indoor supermarkets, patronized by the rich and owned by the super-rich, to remain open, despite being vectors of contagion. Meanwhile, the government's malign neglect had sparked runaway case-counts and deaths from the virus, Celia declared.

Celia's analysis of her life history echoed many common elements of the two models of upward mobility in Bolivia and their gendered variants. She portrayed a trajectory of economic triumph through individual hard work and determination, with a will to leadership as an entrepreneur. Celia marked her middle-class distinction through her acumen as a businesswoman as well as her consumption practices—expensive ball gowns, trips to water parks, home appliances—and aspirations—plans to buy a home and travel to Disneyworld. At the same time, she expressed solidarity with impoverished Bolivians through her condemnation of Bolivia's widespread poverty and support for the MAS party's promises of economic redistribution. As a woman, she experienced the intense personal pain of betrayal by her alcoholic, absent husband and the unequal, gendered burden, all too common, of supporting their two children on her own. Meanwhile, her most recent economic suffering echoed those of most Bolivians in the wake of the recent political crisis and coronavirus pandemic.

Aide

Aide, the nurse introduced above watching *Sueños Cumplidos* with her family, had much in common with Celia: similar wealth, income, and origins in similarly classed and raced campesina, and Quechua-speaking families from the same rural home community in Sacaba municipality. They also shared similar aspirations for upward mobility. On the other hand, however, Aide's political commitments and explicit articulation of her own distinction from impoverished and indigenous Bolivians diverged strikingly from Celia's.

During the twenty-five years that we have known each other, since shortly before she graduated with her nursing degree, Aide proudly affirmed both her satisfaction at become a *profesional* and with her family's elevated status in their rural hometown. Her *campesino* parents were widely admired locally because Aide's elder sister was "the first" professional to graduate from their rural community, and Aide and her younger brother and sister had followed in her footsteps. As described above, her parents each perpetually exhorted their children to *salir profesional* to avoid "suffering as I have suffered." Aide's mother wore a *pollera* and spoke very broken Spanish, but she told me frequently that, as one of the first children to complete elementary school in their community in the early 1950s, she had tried her best when their teacher exhorted the students to speak Spanish, rather than Quechua, in order to acquire "civilization." By 2020, Aide's siblings included an architect, doctor, lawyer, and communications professional.

Aide's *profesional* status was at the core of her sense of self. Unlike Celia, however, Aide's family paid for her education before the MAS party took power and thus did not attribute any of their upward mobility to social movement power or the MAS's policies, such as increased support for public education. Aide's family's upward mobility via professional education had been largely funded by their production and sale of coca, as well as her grandfather's veteran's pension (though several nieces have benefitted as current university students in Cochabamba's public university).

Like Celia, Aide's analysis of her middling economic prospects fluctuated between current satisfaction, hopeful aspirations, and anxiety. As a nurse with secure tenure in a government clinic, she had a steady paycheck. She owned a flat-screen TV, purchased home internet access in 2020, and was building herself a house. Yet Aide's mother's home, where Aide frequently stayed with her daughter while her husband traveled for work, lacked a bathroom with flush toilet and kitchen sink—found in every urban middle-class home I have ever seen. In 2018, with much trepidation, she took on a large loan to finance her husband's trucking business.

Over the years, it became clear to me that Aide and her siblings and parents, more overtly than Celia, accepted the racist and classist hierarchies of Bolivian society. While I heard racial slurs and colorist comments that darker skin was ugly from middling people on all sides of the political spectrum—such as Celia's deep attraction to her husband and his family's "white, white" skin—among Aide's family, racist commentary was constant. From Aide's younger sister complaining in 2018 for the hundredth time that she couldn't find clothing that looked good on her because of her "too dark" skin, to Aide's insistence that my son was the most handsome of all of their mother's many godchildren "because of his blue eyes," to their frequent barbed "jokes" about each other being "ugly, black, Indians."

This deep and vocal racism shaped their political subjectivity and self-identification. Aide and her siblings, in direct contrast to Celia, had been deeply opposed to Evo and the MAS from the start on all grounds, including the characterization of him and his non-*profesional* political allies and cabinet members in those same racialized terms. For example, they complained about Evo's ugly "Indian face." Like Celia's longtime support of MAS policies, if not leaders' actual practices (such as nepotism and fraud), Aide's opposition to MAS was based upon multiple personal experiences: the views of her particular social networks (including long-time right-wing family friends), the historical moments she lived through, and analysis of her own precarious place in Bolivia's social and economic hierarchies. Aide had come of age in the 1980s, before the rise of Indigenous pride and working-class solidarity movements that had apparently shaped Celia's consciousness more deeply. As early as the late 1990s, soon after I met them, Aide's family expressed frustration with Evo's disruptive political role as the coca growers (*cocalero*) union president, when coca grower unions were marching and blockading roads, eliciting violent state repression.[26] In 2005, when Evo Morales was campaigning for president, they expressed disgust and shock at the idea that a non-*profesional* "Indian" could become president. Aide complained frequently that Evo and his government were "discriminating" against *profesionales* like her.[27] In contrast to their firm expression of support for coca growing in 1995 while they were still growing coca themselves or earning ample income from coca grower clients, as lawyers for example, by the early 2000s they expressed the view that all coca growers were "narcotraffickers" and Evo was aiding and abetting narco-traffic, representing a gradual right turn in their political subjectivity.

As the MAS government settled into governing following Evo's first presidential election in 2005, Aide and her siblings repeatedly declared their staunch opposition to the MAS and its platform. They shared Celia disgust at MAS leader's "corruption", but also expressed consistent opposition to the politics of "redistribution," claiming with prominent right-wing Bolivian pundits that "socialism" was a Cuban-inspired ideology that would limit individual freedom of choice by repressive measures to make "everyone the same." In addition to outrage at the MAS party's elevation of campesinos and other non-university-educated people to scarce leadership positions (and job opportunities), Aide and her siblings, in contrast to Celia, evinced little empathy for or solidarity with "poor" people. They also, throughout the years, spoke scornfully of people who did not have professional degrees as less "cultured" (*cultos*). Aide's opposition to the MAS and Evo was so staunch that, even after having been diagnosed with life-threatening leukemia in 2017, she supported a nationwide doctor's strike that year that they held in protest of a government revision of Bolivia's Penal Code (later withdrawn) that would charge doctors with criminal negligence if their patients died without cause. The strike delayed her treatment by several critical months, yet she never wavered in her support. In 2020, Aide and her family are part of a small minority of Bolivians who continued to support the right-wing Áñez interim government despite the government's support for a massacre of coca growers just down the road, the implosion of the Bolivian economy, and an uncontrolled coronavirus epidemic.[28]

Yet Aide, like Celia, experienced contradictory class, gendered, and racialized experiences in her personal life. She also conveyed frustration and pain at the competing imperatives to rise within Bolivia's traditional social hierarchies and to find solidarity with people whom she viewed as lower in the hierarchies. In her romantic relationships Aide had always appeared to be torn between her affinity for men from rural hometowns like hers while also aspiring to find a husband who was a *profesional*, not to mention the challenge of finding a partner who would value her strength and independence in a country with rampant overt misogyny and domestic violence.[29] Where Celia had been attracted as a young woman to a racially superior "white"-skinned man with green eyes who turned out to be an alcoholic and abandoned her, Aide remained wary of this very situation. She told me several times over the years that she had a "fear of getting married" precisely because a husband might become an alcoholic or try to limit her autonomy.

In her late thirties, Aide wound up marrying a kindly truck driver, Tomas, with whom she found a relationship of love and deep mutual respect. Yet several of her *profesional* siblings caused her great pain because they refused to accept Tomas. When her brother Pedro, a lawyer, glimpsed Aide's husband on the street in January 2018, Pedro stiffened and exclaimed to me "I don't want to see that *Indio* of my brother-in-law." When I asked why, Pedro said that he didn't know why, "but I hate him." Their sister, a doctor, frequently made similar disgusted comments to me. A family friend concluded that Aide's siblings rejected Aide's husband "because he's not a *profesional*."

Aide offered the same analysis, that her siblings rejected Tomas out of classist snobbery. In 2018, after Aide had finally secured leukemia treatment (currently in remission) through personal connections, she told me tearfully about her brother and sister's rejection of her husband. "I like Tomas," I said. Why didn't her brother and sister like him? Aide replied "They don't have any justification. If you ask them, they won't be able to give you a good answer. It's [really] because he is not a *profesional*." Starting to cry, she told me that when she was hospitalized for an entire month the prior year for leukemia treatment, Tomas had stayed "by my side, day and night." Yet her siblings refused to see that he was a good person.

Aide had thus managed to find a devoted partner who respected her autonomy and intellect as a woman, but, ironically, faced rejection from her siblings with whom she had long shared her striving for middle-class upward mobility and scorn for people of their generation who had not become *profesionales*.

Conclusion

These conflicts reveal how upwardly mobile Bolivians have struggled with their self-identification, their intimate relationships, and political allegiances amidst a precarious economy. Throughout the twentieth century, young Bolivians were overwhelmingly urged to leave the category of Indigenous "campesino" to become a successful mestizo "professional" or entrepreneur. The *chola*, in particular, was a heavily politicized, gendered, social category in this mobility narrative. As a highly individualist model of mobility, the ideal of *salir adelante* did not acknowledge the interpersonal and internal conflicts that this could generate. And since the late

1990s, a new model of upward mobility emerged that focused on solidarity and upon dismantling racism and classism instead of rising within those hierarchical systems; in some quarters, this includes Indigenous cultural pride. I have also shown how both of these models are deeply gendered, but have both affirmed, at least in theory, the rights of women to pursue professional and entrepreneurial aspirations. The existence of competing models of upward mobility have further complicated the decisions Bolivians make about how to navigate their aspirations.

The economic basis for upward mobility is exceedingly volatile: a commodities boom that lifted the value of natural gas, Bolivia's chief export, from the mid-2000s to the mid-2010s, was followed by declining commodities prices, and, more recently, an economic and health crisis precipitated by the coronavirus pandemic. This was compounded by the political whiplash experienced by many Bolivians as, under the right-wing government of interim president Jeanine Añez, civil liberties have been stifled, Indigenous pride rejected, economic redistribution frozen, and several massacres of protesters by the military with the government's support have spread fear of political repression.[30] I show that, despite significant movement toward social, economic, and gender-based equity in Bolivian society, the middling social categories remain conflicted and ridden with considerable social and economic insecurity, though in diverse ways.

Notes

1 Nancy Postero, *The Indigenous State: Race, Politics, and Performance in Plurinational Bolivia* (Berkeley: University of California Press, 2017); Radoslaw Poweska, *Indigenous Movements and Building the Plurinational State in Bolivia: Organization and Identity in the Trajectory of the CSUTCB and CONAMAQ* (Warsaw: University of Warsaw Center for Latin American Studies, 2013); Raquel Gutiérrez Salazar, *Rhythms of the Pachakuti: Indigenous Uprising and State Power in Bolivia*, trans. Stacey Alba D. Skar (Durham, NC: Duke University Press, 2014).

2 Charles Hale, "Neoliberal Multiculturalism: The Remaking of Cultural Rights and Racial Dominance in Central America," *Political and Legal Anthropology Review* 28, no. 1 (2005): 10–28.

3 Miriam Shakow, *Along the Bolivian Highway: Social Mobility and Political Culture in a New Middle Class* (Philadelphia: University of Pennsylvania Press, 2014).

4 Miriam Shakow, "Digital Alteration and the Law Against Racism: Conflicting Models of Citizenship Among New Bolivian Middle Classes," in *Citizenship in the Latin American Upper and Middle Classes: Ethnographic Perspectives on Culture, Politics, and Consumption*, ed. Fiorella Diaz Montero and Franka Winter (Abingdon: Routledge, 2019); Emily Achtenberg, "Economic Growth with More Equality: Learning from Bolivia," *NACLA Report on the Americas: Rebel Currents Blog*, February 2, 2013, https://nacla.org/blog/2013/2/15/economic-growth-more-equality-learning-bolivia; Jake Johnston and Stephan Lefebvre, "Bolivia's Economy Under Evo in 10 Graphs," Center for Economic and Policy Research, *The Americas Blog*, October 8, 2014, https://cepr.net/bolivias-economy-under-evo-in-10-graphs/.

5 Andrew Canessa, "Who is Indigenous? Self-Identification, Indigeneity, and Claims to Justice in Contemporary Bolivia," *Urban Anthropology* 36, no. 3 (2007): 195–237.
6 Robert Albro, "The Populist Chola: Cultural Mediation and the Political Imagination in Quillacollo, Bolivia," *Journal of Latin American Anthropology* 5, no. 2 (1997): 30–88.
7 Albro "Populist Chola," 33.
8 ONU-Mujeres [United Nations-Women], *Annual Report: Bolivia.* (La Paz, Bolivia: UNESCO, 2019), http://uis.unesco.org/country/BO.
9 Brooke Larson, *Cochabamba 1550–1900: Colonialism and Agrarian Transformation in Bolivia* (Durham, NC: Duke University Press, 1998); Laura Gotkowitz, *A Revolution for Our Rights: Indigenous Struggles for Land and Justice in Bolivia, 1880–1952* (Durham, NC: Duke University Press, 2007); see also Susan Paulson, "Familias que no 'conyugan' e identidades que no conjugan: la vida en Mizque desafía nuestras categorías," in *Ser mujer indígena, chola o birlocha en la Bolivia postcolonial de los 90*, ed. Silvia Rivera (La Paz, Bolivia: Ministerio de Desarrollo Humano, 1996), 85–154; Maria Lagos, *Autonomy and Power: The Dynamics of Class and Culture in Rural Bolivia* (Philadelphia: University of Pennsylvania Press, 1994).
10 Laura Gotkowitz, "Trading Insults: Honor, Violence, and the Gendered Culture of Commerce in Cochabamba, Bolivia, 1870s–1950s," *Hispanic American Historical Review* 83, no. 1 (2003): 83–118.
11 Gotkowitz, "Trading Insults," 83–118.
12 Albro, "Populist Chola," 32.
13 Gotkowitz, "Trading Insults"; Larson "Cochabamba 1550–1900." See also Marisol de la Cadena, "Women are More Indian: Ethnicity and Gender in a Community Near Cuzco," in *Ethnicity, Markets and Migration in the Andes: At the Crossroads of History and Anthropology*, eds. Brooke Larson, Olivia Harris (Durham, NC: Duke University Press, 1995); Marisol de la Cadena, *Indigenous Mestizos: The Politics of Race and Culture in Cuzco, Peru, 1919–1991* (Durham, NC: Duke University Press, 2000); Linda Seligmann, "To Be in Between: The Cholas as Market Women," *Comparative Studies in Society and History* 31 no. 4 (1989): 694–721; Mary Weismantel, *Cholas and Pishtacos: Stories of Race and Sex in The Andes* (Chicago, IL: University of Chicago Press, 2001).
14 Gotkowitz, "Trading Insults."
15 de la Cadena, "Women are More Indian."
16 ONU-Mujeres, "Bolivia: Annual Report."
17 ONU-Mujeres, "Bolivia: Annual Report."
18 Glen Greenwald, "The U.S.-Supported Coup in Bolivia Continues to Produce Repression and Tyranny, While Revealing How U.S. Media Propaganda Works," *The Intercept*, July 23, 2020, https://theintercept.com/2020/07/23/the-u-s-supported-coup-in-bolivia-continues-to-produce-repression-and-tyranny-while-revealing-how-u-s-media-propaganda-works/.
19 Linda Farthing, "In Bolivia, the Right Returns with a Vengeance," *NACLA Report on the Americas* 52, no. 1 (2020): 5–12.
20 Farthing, "In Bolivia," 5–12.
21 Barbara Ehrenreich, *Fear of Falling: The Inner Life of the Middle Class* (New York: Pantheon, 1989); Pierre Bourdieu, *Distinction: A Social Critique of the Judgment of Taste* (New York: Routledge, 1984).
22 Sara Dickey, "Permeable Homes: Domestic Service, Household Space, and the Vulnerability of Class Boundaries in Urban India," *American Ethnologist* 27, no. 2 (2000): 462–489; Sung won Kim, Kari-Elle Brown, and Vanessa L.

Fong, "Chinese Individualisms: Childrearing Aspirations for the Next Generation of Middle-Class Chinese Citizens," *Ethos* 45, no. 3 (2017): 342–366; Mark Liechty, *Suitably Modern: Making Middle-Class Culture in a New Consumer Society (*Princeton, NJ: Princeton University Press, 2002); Maureen O'Dougherty, *Consumption Intensified: The Politics of Middle-Class Daily Life in Brazil* (Durham, NC: Duke University Press, 2002).

23 "Editorial: La Clase Media Emergente," *El Diario*, Jan. 18, 2018, https://www.eldiario.net/noticias/2018/2018_01/nt180118/editorial.php?n=28&-la-clase-media-emergente; "Arce Catacora: Yo soy un representante de la clase media emergente," *Página Siete*, Jan. 1, 2020, https://www.paginasiete.bo/nacional/2020/1/24/arce-catacora-yo-soy-un-representante-de-la-clase-media-emergente-244455.html#.

24 Bourdieu, *Distinction*.

25 ONU-Mujeres, "Bolivia: Annual Report."

26 See also Thomas Grisaffi, *Coca Yes, Cocaine No: How Bolivia's Coca Growers Reshaped Democracy* (Durham, NC: Duke University Press, 2019).

27 See Shakow, *Along the Bolivian Highway*, 2014.

28 CELAG Opinión Publica, "Encuesta Panorama Politico y Social," July 8, 2020, https://www.celag.org/encuesta-bolivia-julio-2020/.

29 ONU-Mujeres, "Bolivia: Annual Report."

30 Farthing, "In Bolivia"; Greenwald, "The U.S.-Supported Coup in Bolivia."

Epilogue: "Was It Worth Coming?"

The Global Drama of Middle-Class Lives in Latin America

Brian P. Owensby

It has been the best of times, it has been the worst of times—for the world's middle classes.

In 2010, an OECD researcher breathlessly announced that the global middle class was poised to surge. Seven years later, he confirmed his prediction, heralding an "unprecedented expansion of the global middle class." By 2018, he stated, more than half the world's population had crossed the "tipping point" to being "middle class or wealthier," "for the first time ever" (where the definition of "middle class" included people earning between $11 and $110 per day in purchasing power parity adjusted dollars; for some, anyone earning more than $2 a day qualified).[1] Such people, it was said, could now buy cellphones, washing machines, televisions, and eat out, see movies, and take vacations. It was proof, crowed neoliberals, of the miracle of preceding decades—not only had the U.N. Millennium Development goal of halving global poverty been met but a majority of the world's population was now middle class.

Not everyone was so quick to celebrate. Cautious observers noted that most of this expansion involved those previously among "the vulnerable" (earning between $2–10 a day) who had just barely crossed the trip-wire to $11 a day, mostly unaware of their accomplishment and often no better off than before. The phenomenon, others pointed out, was a statistical artifact and could be accounted for almost entirely by rising household incomes in Asia, chiefly in China. At best, it indicated a reduction in the number of people living in abject poverty and precarity. Yet even this outcome, said critics, involved statistics artfully cherry-picked to yield the desired result—proof of the emergence of stable middle classes across the globe.[2] Much depended on how, and who, was doing the measuring. Moreover, the movement appeared to owe as much to government policy in Beijing as to "free" global markets. To many the claim of a massive increase in the "global middle class" seemed overblown, "deterministic," and insufficiently contextualized.[3] Even boosters of a growing global middle class noted that most of these freshly turned-out middling folk did not live in "middle class societies."[4] For instance, Latin America's middle classes, defined as those unlikely to fall back into poverty, were said to be

DOI: 10.4324/9781003029311-29

"surging" in 2012, though it remained unclear whether they were "really a force for change." Researchers noted that most of the "former poor" in Latin America remained "vulnerable, not yet middle class."[5] This may have been widely the case elsewhere as well, leading to "fear and loathing" that the global middle class might take up anti-democratic sentiments.[6]

Not surprisingly, academic interest in the middle class exploded through this period. Two volumes on the global middle classes were published in 2012 (one ethnographic, one historical). In 2016, a team of historians put out another major collection of essays on the global bourgeoisie, with studies spanning nations and regions.[7] Sociologists discussed the need to refine a definition for "the global middle class," while more or less taking its expansion for granted.[8] Contemporary middle-class lives and becoming were explored in Angola, China, India, and South Africa, to name a few places where a middle class might once have been thought not to exist, or in circumstances where a middle-class story might previously have been considered irrelevant.[9]

At the same time, some have begun to clang a discordant bell. Anxiety about the U.S. middle class has seemed to grow, as the "American Dream" vanishes and as "meritocracy" serves only to "feed inequality" and "dismantle the middle class."[10] Worry extends to the world at large. One observer has warned the "global middle class," and everyone else, of the "coming neo-feudalism." Scholars remind us that global middle classes may as likely be autocratic as democratic. Alarms have been raised that "the rise of the new global super-rich" will lead to "the fall of everyone else." It might even be that the "end of the middle class" is nigh.[11] Latin American authors recall, with an ironic nostalgia, that "there was a beautiful time" when Latin America dreamt of becoming a region of middle classes, a future, many now admit, that may never have been more than an "illusion" in the face of inequality and precarity.[12]

We are, in other words, amid another period of *Sturm und Drang* regarding the global middle classes. Of course, there has been talk of the middle class since at least the dawn of modern market-industrial regimes in nineteenth-century Europe and, as some of the essays here note, in Latin America as well. That discourse has ebbed and flowed, with greater or lesser intensity, depending on historical conjunctures. Crisis periods in capitalism's economic model have tended to raise the volume of contention—think the Great Depression. So too have periods of ideological struggle, as during the Cold War and the debate over "modernization." More recently, efforts to justify market fundamentalism at global scale have called forth encomiums for a planetary middle class, only to be followed by cautionary, even panicked assessments following the Great Recession in 2008. Through this long and uneven process, the middle class has become an unavoidable trope of avowedly "modern" societies across the globe, and of those aspiring to be. Its staying power is due to its conceptual range and to the fact that it is entangled with the very idea of what is for a society to be considered "modern." As Sankaran Krishna has noted, the middle class as an idea "works to produce political affects, hierarchize peoples, prioritize projects, create and unmake nations, and embody complex and varying relationships with other equally 'dramatic' concepts, such as nation, democracy, economic growth, and the future."[13] Given simultaneous celebration and hand-wringing over the middle class's fate, the current moment is a propitious one for rethinking fundamental questions.

~

Rather than rehearse what the introduction and essays in this volume have so brilliantly accomplished, my goal in what remains of this epilogue is to make explicit the framework I think this book lays out for future historical study of the world's middle classes. The editors and authors here operate within a global frame, but do so in relation to the heterogeneous histories of Latin America from the nineteenth century to the present day. In the aggregate, the essays' central claim is that middle classes as transnational and global phenomena must be anchored in the particular historical milieux of region, nation, and locality. The point is to bypass sterile arguments over whether Latin America, or this or that country, has a middle class, or is more or less middle-class than other places in the world. The idea instead is to propose a global picture formed by a mosaic of regional specificities, thus allowing the insights of area studies to inform and shape a wider panorama of commonalities. Relying on abundant evidence over wide areas and long periods, the volume begins from the premise that middle classes have long formed part of Latin American social, political, and discursive realities. And while to speak of the middle class is necessarily to invoke *class* as a category—and cognate concerns of income, occupation, status, material inequalities, and the state—the essays here look beyond such criteria to make sense of middle-class lives in terms of their complex articulations to gender, sexuality, race, and ethnicity, and to the ways consumption, art, morality, emotions, and subjectivities express middle-class identities. Above all, I take the book to be advocating a perspectival view of people who cannot avoid a label that means many different things at once—status, identity, a kind of freedom, a basis for larger commitments—and therefore cannot be contained by any one conceptual apparatus.

This approach allows for greater categorical autonomy in thinking about the middle classes in Latin America, especially in relation to "normative" middle classes in supposedly more "advanced" places. The volume thus pushes back against the false universalism of seeing the middle class always from the perspective of the U.S. or certain European countries. But the essays also insist that the middle class be understood as a focus of diverse societal influences, some rarely considered when discussing the falsely normative notions of the middle class. Building on scholarship of the last couple of decades, these essays slip the straitjacket of "modernization," with its taken-for-granted teleology, and loosen the tethers to class, with its irreducible antinomies. In this way, and as several of the essays in the collection demonstrate, the middle class becomes a position from which to rethink society as a whole, not because the middle class is more central to some autonomous force or project than other social groups, but because middle-class people, perhaps more self-consciously than others, have lived the contrarieties of modern economic, social, and political regimes. Thus, sub-national identities sit uneasily alongside national and even transnational ones. Gender and race intersect with notions of decency and status anxiety. The comforts of taxonomy fade into class transvestism. Frustration over unrealized past promises slide into nostalgia for a future seen as already lost. The sectarianism of politics comes hard against desires for greater unity. Nothing in the life of modernity is alien to middle-class people, who feel and think, act and react in ways that reveal the agita of being on the knife's edge between a hope for stability and the reality of social unsteadiness.

~

To think about the middle class, therefore, is to inquire into the ontology of modern market regimes as variously expressed in global context. *Middle-classness* may be understood as revolving around an axis connecting two competing axioms—a principle of order and a principle of movement. Ezequiel Adamovsky has observed that the concept of class emerged during the eighteenth and nineteenth centuries, as an incipient market regime destabilized notions of rank, order, and estate that had long structured social relations. Market competition, and the individual pursuit of gain that propelled it, posed the question of what could ensure social cohesion in circumstances of universal economic competition. The idea of a *middle class* took form to answer this riddle. Through a reading of European writers, Adamovsky argues that the middle class represented an updated version of Aristotle's doctrine of the mean—virtue as the balance point between extremities of excess and deficiency—expressed socially. Thus, Diderot held that an intermediate social group would avoid harmful "collisions" among men and spread enlightenment "down to the people and up to the great," thus ensuring society's equilibrium.[14]

This stood as the dominant understanding through the early nineteenth century—the middle class as a principle of hierarchy and order for newly turbulent societies, a countervailing force against challenges from below and stratagems from above. Originally, the idea of the middle class was limited to those, neither aristocrats nor commoners, who had learned that economic competition offered a means to gain and status. But as Adamovsky notes, the middle class ultimately could not remain a static postulate of order in the spirit of ranks and estates. Because the new monied classes understood themselves as having *come to* their position, rather than having inherited it from an unbroken past, the *middle class* implied a certain openness to movement, a principle of mobility allowing for people to arrive at a new station and status. Although there was no determinate principle as to who such new arrivals might be, they were drawn especially from the ranks of small property owners and even "respectable" wage-earners who made their fates in new lines of work broadly tied to money, commodities, and their circulation. The middle class thus came to embody the idea that those who successfully deployed their talents, energies, and luck in accord with the novel rules of an emerging new market regime could imagine themselves apart from the lower orders, who had no basis for Icarian hopes.

By the twentieth century, this principle of movement came to be broadly understood in terms of an expectation of mobility within and among social levels. As an ideological expression, the middle class stood for the proposition that those who disciplined their talents to the demands of market competition might reasonably hope for a measure of freedom from raw economic necessity. In the aggregate, this would guarantee a dynamic mean between rich and poor. The middle class became, in other words, the effort to square the Enlightenment's aspirational egalitarianism with the market regime's pronounced tendency to inequality of economic outcomes, which Adam Smith himself (or at least the Adam Smith of *The Theory of Moral Sentiments* (1759)) had declared socially destructive. It did so by overvaluing certain kinds of "non-manual" work, by promising levels of consumption beyond mere social reproduction, and by celebrating the role of "middling" folk as industrial civilization's balance wheel. As a matter of experience, the middle class represented not so much a particular fragment of society, as it came to stand for the outcome of a generalized struggle to move up—and, for those who did, the no less enervating struggle not to fall. Middle-class people came to be seen as those who had achieved an unstable combination of income, prestige, status, education, and networking potential sufficient to stand apart from those below them who could only be counted among the (manual) "working" classes or the poor. The middle class thus represented an internally generated answer to the corrosions of income and wealth disparities that appear to be an ontological condition of competitive market orders.

But the supposed moderating influence of the middle class was not an automatic outcome or a structural effect of its mere presence. Decades ago, Karl Polanyi argued that nineteenth-century liberals had pursued a self-defeating "utopian endeavor" to create a self-regulating market that would keep the individual pursuit of gain at the expense of others—the anti-social economic war-of-all-against-all upon which day-to-day life was premised—from spinning out of control. No government action was necessary for this to happen, insisted liberals. To the contrary. The system itself would obviate all need for political meddling and government intervention could only interfere with the market's invisible hand.[15] The hubris of this ambition, and its social consequences, called forth a reaction among society's most vulnerable, and others, to balance the equation, lest society itself collapse. Polanyi called this reaction a "countermovement" to the idea of a homeostatic market. Only political struggle calling for pro-social government action could meet the "social catastrophe" of market-economy, liberals' "stark" and unrealizable utopia. It was this "double movement"—the "free" market sparking political countermovements from below to restrain the market's socially ruinous tendencies—that powered the political dynamics of capitalist regimes.[16] Against liberals' own prescriptions, government responded to the countermovement by creating new institutions that sought to soften the blows of market life. This, argued Polanyi, was the origin of late nineteenth- and twentieth-century welfare systems that aimed to check the worst excesses of markets and furnish protections and public goods capitalists seemed uninterested in supporting—workplace regulations, limits on the workday, health care, education, social services.

As this role for government came to be widely, if unevenly accepted in modernizing social orders, a new group of white-collar employees—social workers, teachers, state functionaries, inspectors—joined the ranks of bank clerks, commercial employees, professionals, and small property owners who kept money and commodities flowing. These new workers, as essays in this collection show shared worries and hopes with other middling folk regarding respect and recognition, if from a perspective that allowed for the possibility of a distinct outlook on issues of broad social concern. From the vantage of such workers, the middle class might be thought of as expressing an organic principle of equilibrium not unlike the one Diderot had envisioned in the late eighteenth century. The market regime as it developed in the nineteenth century had no moderating principle or mechanism of its own, beyond the supposed automaticity of the market. It would seem no accident, as Adamovsky suggests, that the idea of the middle class emerged just as this new regime was taking root in Europe. By allowing some to rise above the scrum of everyday existence, even by just a little, the middle-class idea became the closest thing to an in-built mechanism of social regulation and equilibration the market regime was ever to have. Polanyi was not entirely oblivious to this fact, though in his account the middle class remained a shadowy figure, the "bearer[ ] of the nascent market economy" but also the focus of modest aspiration for humble craftsmen and tradesmen (what has sometimes been called the *lower middle class*). Apart from such casual mentions, however, the middle class played only a bit part in Polanyi's broader analytical scheme. Arguably, this absence is one of the central weaknesses of his argument, for it underplayed the middle class's role in the "double movement" that defines market economies.

Sitting at the uncomfortable pivot between order and movement, Latin America's middle classes have been organized around this central tension. Mobility as separation from those below, or even the hope for it, has been crucial to middling people's self-conception. At a time when middle-class status was still new, those who became middle class thought of themselves as arriving from somewhere else. Having ridden the momentum of newly dynamic economies and expanding states, they could understand their rise as an achievement and experience their situation as one of relative freedom—freedom from abject want, freedom to make certain choices regarding their lives—compared to those below who had no margin. Spared the indignity of utter necessity, they could think of themselves as central to market society's fundamental order, the group whose way of being, as decent, moral, hard-working, understanding people, could heal a social order premised on producing winners, who could suppose they had made their own way, and losers, whose lot it was to accept their fate uncomplainingly. In this context, however, middle-class folk could imagine cultivating, even promoting aspects of their selves that might otherwise have gone unexpressed, itself a privilege of their position but one not strictly limited to it. This allowed some of them to take radical stances on points of political principle. Of course, most knew they were but a job loss or financial crisis away from falling into the lower realms. And so, they could not avoid the anxiety that the middle-class house of cards might one day collapse in on them through no fault of their own.

It is crucial to have such close regional treatments of middling peoples' lives, because through them we can sharpen our understanding of the middle class in global context. By reversing the direction of the gaze that always proceeds from some mythical center (the West) to an equally mythical periphery (the Rest), this volume speaks forcefully to the sociological reality of modernity at global scale. The middle class is central to that reality. Indeed, the middle class is, or has been understood to be, a marker of what it is to be socially modern. What these essays show, taken together, is just how rich and dense study of the middle class can be once it is freed from the center–periphery gaze and made part of a recomposed global phenomenon, and once the middle class is no longer the poor cousin of class discourse, that is, always secondary to "real" classes, be they rich and poor, or working class and bourgeoisie. Put another way, the Latin American middle classes in their own right can be the basis for historicizing and theorizing relations of global market regimes, rather than stand merely as exemplars of a placeless (but ultimately Western) notion of the middle class, serving only to fill in gaps of what might be termed the standard account (rooted in the falsely universalized experience of U.S. and Western European middle classes).

~

"Are we rich or poor?," a six-year-old girl asks her father, who is tying his tie while looking into a mirror. "Neither rich nor poor," says the distracted man, "we came to be middle class." Face framed by ear-length black hair, with a bow on top, the girl grimaces in apparent bafflement.

"We came?" she asks, eyes wide, "We came to be middle class?" "Uh-huh," says her father, still futzing with his tie. "And tell me," she says, "in order to be middle class, was it worth coming?" Her father, deadpan while turning down his collar and finally breaking the mirror's gaze, raises his eyebrows, as though considering the question for the first time.[17]

The girl in this small exchange, of course, is Mafalda, the famously precocious, curious, idealistic, and penetrating six-year-old of Quino's comic strip that ran from 1964 to 1973 in Argentina, in syndication across Latin America for many years after, and in books translated into twenty languages. Mafalda was, in many ways, the diminutive embodiment of middle-class life at a crucial moment in Argentine, Latin American, and even global history. Her milieu coded the economic growth, increasing prevalence of higher education, growing "respectable" employment, and rising consumerism of the 1940s through the 1970s, phenomena widely if unevenly experienced as "modernization"—with all its antinomies.[18]

I take Mafalda's colloquy with her father as a fair summary of what this volume of essays accomplishes, and where it might point us. With a few words and images, the strip hints at middle-class lives defined not only by a desire for upward mobility, or a fear of falling, but also by questioning what it means to be middle class, asking whether there is something beyond the doubts and ironies of classed lives in the middle. This is deep probing from what Claudia Stern has called the "incisive wit" of cartoon humor depicting middle-class lives.[19] The father is absorbed in the routine ordeal of tying a tie, that sartorial emblem of distinction from the lower orders. He gazes upon his own reflection, though chiefly to prepare for the social judgment of life beyond the home. His daughter poses the sort of question children might ask in a world that seemed made of stark opposites. Calmly, with no break in his practiced dexterity, he rejects the premise of Mafalda's query, asserting their position as the culmination of a journey, a kind of passive arrival—*we came to be*—from an unnamed somewhere else. Almost a teleology, but not quite. As her father may have expected, Mafalda follows up with another question, one that by its tone and inflection seems to demand an answer—"we came to be middle class?" And so, pulling the last bight of the tie through the Windsor loop, he responds monosyllabically, oblivious to his daughter's consternation. Having recomposed herself, Mafalda now asks in great earnest whether the coming was worth it. We are left to wonder whether her father has an answer to so weighty a question. Nor can we know what alternative is implied in the uncomfortable possibility Mafalda raises—that her family not have come to be middle class.

This exchange is a small tragicomedy, a kind of middle-class "to be or not to be" rendered in cartoon. Tragic because, in one way or another, Mafalda's questions seem to express the worries of people who can never escape the ambivalence of their position. Comic, because it takes a pesky six-year old to make the point explicit. But Mafalda's simple query may go deeper. In framing her question—"in order to be middle class, was it worth coming?"—Quino suggests that middle-class lives be understood as an existential and ontological drama, rather than a still-life of contradictions, frustrations, and commitments. Her "was it worth coming?" hints that at the unlit core of middle-class lives coils a disquiet not only regarding whether it was worth it in some instrumental way to have become middle class but whether the entire middle-class idea as the mean between extremes can bear the weight piled atop it.

While Mafalda is asking her question *from* Buenos Aires, really she is reframing the fundamental problem of middle-class lives around the globe—which is one reason the strip came to be so widely translated. Put another way, Mafalda might be heard to ask whether the middle class is adequate to the challenge of making society from the hurly-burly of market life, in Argentina but also everywhere else people have struggled to create genuine social lives in the context of competitive economic regimes. What she seems to be asking is whether the existence of the middle class really can offset the damage of a social order premised on the stark divide between the poor-as-losers and rich-as-winners. The hope that it may do is arguably what energizes middle-class folk to seek the accouterments of class status because, from their perspective, if they can attain them, so can others. But that same hope also enables them to assert identities premised on personal freedom and to insist that morality and a politics of the good may ultimately prevail against the forces of interest and division. The fear that it may not can drive these same people to paroxysms of self-righteous envy, petty grandiosity, and political abasement in defense of what they perceive as entitlements—as happened in Latin America during the military regimes of the 1960s and 1970s. It is the play of these tendencies, and the stakes they imply, that explain why the middle class has remained so central to the imaginaries of market-oriented social regimes—in Latin America and wherever they have emerged. The essays of this volume, in all their eclecticism, are a primer in how to see modern society at large, with its fractalized contradictions, through the prism of middle-class lives.

Notes

1 Homi Kharas, "The Emerging Middle Class in Developing Countries," OECD Development Centre, Working Paper No. 285; Homi Kharas, "The Unprecedented expansion of the global middle class. An update" (2017) https://www.brookings.edu/research/the-unprecedented-expansion-of-the-global-middle-class-2/ Accessed April 5, 2021; Kharas and Kristofer Hamel, "A global tipping point: Half the world is now middle class or wealthier" (2018) https://www.brookings.edu/blog/future-development/2018/09/27/a-global-tipping-point-half-the-world-is-now-middle-class-or-wealthier/. Accessed 5 April 2021; Abhjit V. Banerjee, Esther Duflo, "What Is Middle Class About the Middle Classes Around the World," *Journal of Economic Perspectives*, 22:2 (spring 2008), 3–28.

2 Rakesh Kochnar, "A Global Middle Class Is More Promise than Reality," *Pew Research Center. Global Attitudes and Trends*. https://www.pewresearch.org/global/2015/07/08/a-global-middle-class-is-more-promise-than-reality/. Accessed April 7, 2021.
3 Sam Drabble, et al., "The rise of a global middle class. Global societal trends to 2030. Thematic report," RAND Corporation, 2015.
4 Augusto de la Torre, Jamele Rigolini, "MIC Forum: The Rise of the Middle Class," *The World Bank* https://www.worldbank.org/content/dam/Worldbank/document/MIC-Forum-Rise-of-the-Middle-Class-SM13.pdf. Accessed April 5, 2021.
5 "Latin America's Surging Middle Classes: Are They Really a Force for Change?," *Center for Global Development*, November 14, 2012. https://www.cgdev.org/event/latin-americas-surging-middle-classes-are-they-really-force-change. Accessed April 5, 2021; Torre, Rigolini, "MIC Forum," 7.
6 Raj M. Desai, "Fear and Loathing in the Global Middle Class," *Lawfare*. https://www.lawfareblog.com/fear-and-loathing-global-middle-class. Accessed April 7, 2021.
7 Rachel Heiman, Carl Freedman, Mark Liechty, eds., *The Global Middle Classes: Theorizing through Ethnography* (Santa Fe, NM: School for Advanced Research Press, 2012); A. Ricardo López and Barbara Weinstein, eds., *The Making of the Middle Class. Toward a Transnational History* (Durham, NC: Duke University Press, 2012); Cristof Dejun, David Motadel, Jürgen Osterhammel, eds., *The Global Bourgeoisie: The Rise of the Middle Classes in the Age of Empire* (Princeton University Press, 2019).
8 Hagen Koo, "The Global Middle Class: How Is It Made, What Does It Represent?," *Globalizations*, 13:4 (2016), 440–453.
9 Jess Auerbach, *From Water to Wine. Becoming Middle Class in Angola* (University of Toronto Press, 2020); John Wei, *Queer Chinese Cultures and Mobilities: Kinship, Migration, and Middle Classes* (University of Hong Kong Press, 2020); Roger Southall, *The New Black Middle Class in South Africa* (James Currey, 2016); C.J. Fuller, *Tamil Brahmans: The Making of a Middle-Class Caste* (University of Chicago Press, 2014); Li Zhang, *In Search of Paradise: Middle-Class Living in a Chinese Metropolis* (Ithaca, NY: Cornell University Press, 2010).
10 Gene Ludwig, *The Vanishing American Dream: A Frank Look at the Economic Realities Facing Middle- and Lower-Income Americans* (New York: Disruption Books, 2020); Daniel Markovits, *The Meritocracy Trap: How America's Foundational Myth Feeds Inequality, Dismantles the Middle Class, and Devours the Elite* (New York: Penguin, 2020).
11 Joel Kotkin, *The Coming Neo-Feudalism: A Warning to the Global Middle Class* (New York: Encounter Books, 2020); Bryn Rosenfeld, *The Autocratic Middle Classes: How State Dependency Reduces Demand for Democracy* (Princeton University Press, 2020); Chrystia Freeland, *Plutocrats: The Rise of the New Global Super-Rich and the Fall of Everyone Else* (New York: Penguin, 2013); Esteban Hernández, *El fin de la clase media* (Madrid: Clave Intelectual, 2013).
12 Cecilia Güemes, Ludolfo Paramio, "El porvenir de una ilusión: clases medias en América Latina," *Nueva Sociedad*, no. 285 (January–February 2020). https://nuso.org/articulo/el-porvenir-de-una-ilusion-clases-medias-en-america-latina/. Accessed April 7, 2021.
13 Sankaran Krishna, "Notes on the Dramatic Career of a Concept: The Middle Class, Democracy, and the Anthropocene," *Alternatives: Global, Local, Political* 40:1 (February 2015), 3–4.

14 Ezequiel Adamovsky, "Aristotle, Diderot, Liberalism and the Idea of 'Middle Class': A Comparison of Two Concepts of Emergence of a Metaphorical Formation," *History of Political Thought*, 26:2 (summer 2005), 303–333.
15 Jonathan Sheehan and Dror Wahrman, *Invisible Hands: Self-Organization and the Eighteenth Century* (Chicago: University of Chicago Press, 2015).
16 Karl Polanyi, *The Great Transformation. The Political and Economic Origins of Our Time* (Boston, MA: Beacon Press, 2001), 3, 136, 151, 168.
17 The image is reprinted in Rosa Aboy, "Mafalda en casa. Departamentos de clase media y vida cotidiana en los años setenta," *Anales del Instituto de Arte Americano e Investigaciones Estéticas "Mario j. Buschiazzo" (Anales del IAA)*, no. 41(2) (2011), 183. The full article may be accessed online at: http://www.iaa.fadu.uba.ar/ojs/index.php/anales/article/view/58.
18 Isabella Cosse, *Mafalda. A Social and Political History of Latin America's Global Comic* (Durham, NC: Duke University Press, 2019).
19 Claudia Stern W., *Entre el cielo y el suelo. Las identidades elásticas de las clases medias (Santiago de Chile, 1932–1962)* (Santiago: RIL Editores, 2021), 70.

Bibliography

Aboy, Rosa. "Mafalda en casa. Departamentos de clase media y vida cotidiana en los años setenta." *Anales del Instituto de Arte Americano e Investigaciones Estéticas "Mario j. Buschiazzo" (Anales del IAA)*, 41(2) (2011),179–188.

Abud, Kátia Maria. "O Sangue Intimorato e as Nobilíssimas Tradições: A Construção de um Símbolo Paulista—O Bandeirante." PhD diss., Universidade de São Paulo, 1985.

Acción Cívica Nacional. *Malos resultados del socialismo y el comunismo*. Mexico City: Acción Cívica Nacional, 1937.

Achtenberg, Emily. "Economic Growth with More Equality: Learning from Bolivia." *NACLA Report on the Americas: Rebel Currents Blog*. February 2, 2013. https://nacla.org/blog/2013/2/15/economic-growth-more-equality-learning-bolivia.

Acuña, Víctor Hugo. "Clases sociales y conflicto social en la economía cafetalera costarricense: productores contra beneficiadores (1932–1936)." *Revista de Historia*, Costa Rica (Special Issue), 1985.

Acuña, Víctor Hugo. "Historia del vocabulario político en Costa Rica: Estado, república, nación y democracia (1821–1949)." In *Identidades nacionales y Estado moderno en Centroamérica*, compiled by Jean Piel and Arturo Taracena, 141–152. San José: EUCR, 1995.

Acuña, Víctor Hugo. "La invención de la diferencia costarricense (1810–1870)." *Revista de Historia*, 45 (January–June 2002): 191–228.

Acuña, Victor Hugo. "La ideología de los pequeños y medianos productores cafetaleros costarricenses (1900–1961)." *Revista de Historia*, 16 (July–December 1987): 137–159.

Acuña, Víctor Hugo. "Patrones del conflicto social en la economía cafetalera costarricense (1900–1948)." *Revista de Ciencias Sociales*, 31, (1986): 113–122.

Acuña, Víctor Hugo and Iván Molina. *Historia económica y social de Costa Rica (1750–1950)*. San José: Porvenir, 1991.

Adamovsky, Ezequiel. "Acerca de la relación entre el Radicalismo argentino y la 'clase media' (una vez más)." *The Hispanic American Historical Review* 89, no. 2 (2009a): 209–251.

Adamovsky, Ezequiel. "Aristotle, Diderot, Liberalism, and the Idea of the Middle Class: A Comparison of Two Contexts of Emergence of a Metaphorical Formation." *History of Political Thought* 26, no. 2 (2005): 303–333.

Adamovsky, Ezequiel. "'Clase media': Reflexiones sobre los (malos) usos académicos de una categoría." *Nueva Sociedad* 247 (September–October 2013).

Adamovsky, Ezequiel. "El color de la nación argentina: Conflictos y negociaciones por la definición de un ethnos nacional, de la crisis al Bicentenario." *Jahrbuch für Geschichte Lateinamerikas* 49, no. 1 (2012): 343–364.

Adamovsky, Ezequiel. *Historia de la clase media argentina: Apogeo y decadencia de una ilusión, 1919–2003*. Buenos Aires: Planeta, 2009.

Adamovsky, Ezequiel. *Historia de la clase media en Argentina: Apogeo y decadencia de una ilusión*. Buenos Aires: Planeta, 2012.

Adamovsky, Ezequiel. Review of *The Making of the Middle Class: Toward a Transnational History*, edited by A. Ricardo López and Barbara Weinstein. *Social History* 38, no. 3 (2013): 409–411.

Adamovsky, Ezequiel, Sergio E. Visacovsky, and Patricia Vargas, eds. *Clases Medias: Nuevos enfoques desde la sociología, la historia y la antropología*. Buenos Aires: Ariel, 2014.

Aguilar Gutiérrez, Genaro. "¿Está desapareciendo la clase media en México? Análisis de la polarización del ingreso." *Revista de Ciencias Sociales* XIX, no. 1 (2013): 57–69.

Aguilar Hernández, Felipe. *Moral pública en los procesos de buen gobierno*. Mexico: Universidad Autónoma del Estado de México; Instituto de Administración Pública de Estado de México; Plaza y Valdés, 2000.

Aguilera Peña, Mario. *Contrapoder y justicia guerrillera: Fragmentación política y orden insurgente en Colombia (1952–2003)*. Bogotá: IEPRI, 2014.

Aguinis, Marcos. *Incendio de ideas: Lo que el siglo XXI tiene para aprender del siglo XX*. Buenos Aires: Sudamericana, 2017.

Albro, Robert. "The Populist Chola: Cultural Mediation and the Political Imagination in Quillacollo, Bolivia." *Journal of Latin American Anthropology* 5, no. 2 (1997): 30–88.

Alexander, Jeffrey C., and Phillip Smith. "The Discourse of American Civil Society: A New Proposal for Cultural Studies." *Theory and Society* 22, no. 2 (1993): 151–207.

Altamirano, Carlos. "José Luis Romero y la idea de la Argentina aluvial." *Prismas: Revista de historia intelectual* 5 (2001): 313–328.

De Andrade, Mário. "Guerra de São Paulo." Unpublished manuscript. Coleção Mário de Andrade, Caixa l, instituto de Estudos Brasileiros, Universidade de São Paulo, (n.d.).

Andrade, Pablo. "El imaginario democrático en el Ecuador." In *Antología. Democracia, gobernabilidad, y cultura política*, edited by Felipe Burbano de Lara, 383–405. Quito: FLACSO; Sede Ecuador, 1999.

Andrews, George Reid. *Afro-Latin America, 1800–2000*. New York: Oxford University Press USA, 2004.

Angenot, Marc. *El discurso social: Los límites históricos de lo pensable y lo decible*. Mexico City; Buenos Aires: Siglo XXI editores, 2012.

Angola, Mercedes, and Maguemati WabgouAngola Rossi, Julia Mercedes, and Maguemati Wabgou W. *Llegamos a Bogotá: Décadas 1940–1950–1960*. Bogotá: Universidad Nacional de Colombia, 2015.

Araya Espinoza, Alejandra. "¿Castas o razas?: Imaginario sociopolítico y cuerpos mezclados en la América colonial; Una propuesta desde los cuadros de castas." In *Al otro lado del cuerpo: Estudios biopolíticos en América Latina*, compiled by Hilderman Cardona and Zandra Pedraza, 53–77. Colombia: Universidad de los Andes; Universidad de Medellín, 2014.

Arboleda, Santiago. *Le han florecido nuevas estrellas al cielo: Suficiencias íntimas y clandestinización del pensamiento afrocolombiano*. Cali: Poemia, 2016.

Archetti, Eduardo. *Masculinidades: Fútbol, tango y polo en la Argentina*. Buenos Aires: Antropofagia, 2003.

Archila, Mauricio. *Idas y venidas. Vueltas y revueltas: Protestas sociales en Colombia, 1958–1990*. Bogotá: CINEP, 2003.

Archila, Mauricio, Jorge Cote, and Alvaro Guzmán Delgado. *Una Historia inconclusa: Izquierdas políticas y sociales en Colombia*. Bogotá: CINEP, 2009.

Aréchiga, Ernesto. "Lucha de clases en la ciudad: La disputa por el espacio urbano. *ca*. 1890–1930." In *Los trabajadores de la ciudad de México 1860–1950: Textos en homenaje a Clara E. Lida*, edited by Mario Barbosa and Carlos Illades. 19–50. Mexico City: El Colegio de México; UAM-Cuajimalpa, 2013.

Arenas, Jaime. *La guerrilla por dentro*. Bogotá: ICONO, 2009.

Aristóteles. *Ética a Nicómaco*. Madrid: Gredos, 2014.

Arnaud, François. *Les Barcelonnettes au Mexique*. Barcelonnette: Musée de la Vallée, 2014.

Aron, Raymond. "El Concepto de clase," *Revista Mexicana de Sociología* 1, no. 1 (1939): 97–108.

Arrom, Silvia. *The Women of Mexico City, 1790–1857*. Stanford, CA: Stanford University Press, 1983.

Asheim, Bjorn. "Differentiated Knowledge Bases and Varieties of Regional Innovation Systems." *Innovation* 20, no. 3 (2007): 223–241.

Auerbach, Jess. *From Water to Wine. Becoming Middle Class in Angola*. Toronto: University of Toronto Press, 2020.

Badiou, Alain. "Twenty-Four Notes in the Use of the Word 'People.'" In *What is a People?*, by Alain Badiou, Judith Butler, Georges Didi-Huberman, Sadri Khiari, Jacques Rancière, and Pierre Bourdieu. New York: Columbia University Press, 2016.

Ballent, Anahí. "El arte de saber vivir: Modernización del habitar doméstico y cambio urbano, 1940–1970." In *Cultura y comunicación en la ciudad de México*. vol. 1, edited by Néstor García Canclini, 65–131. Mexico City: Grijalbo; UAM-Iztapalapa, 1998.

Banerjee, Abhjit and Esther Duflo. "What Is Middle Class About the Middle Classes Around the World," *Journal of Economic Perspectives* 22, no 2 (Spring 2008), 3–28.

Barahona Streber, Óscar. *Memorias y opiniones*. San José: Editorama, 1996.

Barbosa, Mario. "Capacitación y posición social de los empleados públicos de la ciudad de México a comienzos del siglo XX." *Historia Mexicana* 68, no. 2 (2018): 747–783.

Barbosa, Mario. "Distinciones y apariencias: La clase media en la Ciudad de México entre el porfiriato y la Revolución." *Oficio: Revista de Historia e Interdisciplina* 10 (2020): 9–23.

Barbosa, Mario, "Los empleados públicos, 1903–1931," in *Los trabajadores de la ciudad de México, 1860–1950: Textos en homenaje a Clara E. Lida*, compiled by Carlos Illades and Mario Barbosa, 117–154. Mexico City: El Colegio de México, 2013.

Barbosa Cruz, Mario. "La clase media en la Ciudad de México entre el porfiriato y la Revolución." *Revista de Historia e Interdisciplina* 10 (January–June 2020): 9–23.

Barbosa Cruz, Mario. "Empleados públicos en la ciudad de México: Condiciones laborales y construcción de la administración pública (1903–1931)," in *Cuestión social, políticas sociales y construcción del Estado social en América Latina, siglo XX*, compiled by Fernando Remedi and Mario Barbosa Cruz, 137–158. Mexico City: Centro de Estudios Carlos E. Segreti; UAM Cuajimalpa, 2014.

Barbosa Cruz Mario. "Insalubres e inmorales: Alojamientos temporales en la Ciudad de México (1900–1920)." *Scripta Nova: Revista electrónica de geografía y ciencias sociales*, no. extra 7 (2003): n.p.

Barbosa Cruz, Mario. "Profesionalización, capacitación e identidades de los empleados públicos de la ciudad de México a comienzos del siglo XX." *Historia Mexicana* 270 (October–December 2018): 749–785.

Barcellos, Daisy Macedo de. "Família e ascensão social de Negros em Porto Alegre." PhD diss., Museu Nacional da Universidade Federal do Rio de Janeiro, 1996.

Bárcena, Alicia and Narcís Serra, eds. *Clases medias y desarrollo en América Latina*. Santiago de Chile: CEPAL, Santiago de Chile, 2010.

Bárcenas Olalde, Mariano. "El Estado patron: Crítica al estatuto jurídico de los trabajadores al servicio de los poderes de la Unión." Bachelor's diss., Mexico City: UNAM, 1939.

Barrionuevo Silva, Ney. *Rebelión forajida traicionada y el proceso constituyente trunco. Poder cidudadano: Poder constituyente*. Quito: Ney Barrionuevo Silva and Sur Editores, 2007.

Barr-Melej, Patrick. *Reforming Chile: Cultural Politics, Nationalism, and the Rise of the Middle Class*. Chapel Hill: University of North Carolina Press, 2001.

Barsky, Osvaldo, and Mabel Dávila. *La rebelión del campo: Historia del conflicto agrario argentino*. Buenos Aires: Sudamericana, 2012

Barros, Rodolfo. "We Were the Middle Class." In *Latin America's Middle Class: Unsettled Debates and New Histories*, edited by David S. Parker and Louise E. 197–214. Walker. Lanham, MD: Lexington Books, 2013.

Barthes, Roland. *Fragmentos de un discurso amoroso*. Mexico City: Siglo Veintiuno Editores, 1982.

Bartolucci, Mónica I. *La juventud maravillosa: La peronización y los orígenes de la violencia política, 1958–1972*. Argentina, EDUNTREF, 2018.

Bayardo, Lilia E. *Historia del consumo moderno en la ciudad de México durante los años 1909–1970 a través de las encuestas de gastos familiares y de la publicidad en prensa*. PhD diss., Mexico City: Colegio de México, 2013.

Berdejo Bravo, María del Carmen. *Regir y formar: Institucionalización jurídica y educativa de las mujeres mexicanas (1880–1884)*. México: Universidad Autónoma Metropolitana, 2011.

Berman, Marshall. *Todo lo sólido se desvanece en el aire. La experiencia de la modernidad*. Spain: Siglo XXI Editores, [1982] 1989.

Bernstein, Eduard. *Evolutionary Socialism: A Criticism and Affirmation*. New York: Schocken Books, 1961.

Bertaccini, Tiziana. *El régimen priísta frente a las clases medias, 1943–1964*. Mexico City: Consejo Nacional para la Cultura y las Artes, Dirección General de Publicaciones, 2009.

Beverley, John. "Beyond the paradigm of disillusion." In *Latin Americanism after 9/11*. Durham, NC: Duke University Press, 2011.

Biehl, João, and Peter Locke, eds. *Unfinished: The Anthropology of Becoming*. Durham, NC; London: Duke University Press, 2017.

Biernat, Carolina and Karina Ramacciotti. *Crecer y multiplicarse: La política sanitaria materno infantil argentina 1900–1960*. Buenos Aires: Editorial Biblos, 2013.

Blanksten, George I. "In Quest of the Middle Sectors." *World Politics* 12, no. 2 (1960): 323–27.

Bliss, Katherine. *Compromised Positions: Prostitution, Public Health and Gender Politics in Revolutionary Mexico City*. University Park: Pennsylvania State University Press, 2001.

Bloch, Maurice. "Why Religion Is Nothing Special but Is Central." *Philosophical Transactions of the Royal Society B: Biological Sciences* 363, no. 1499 (2008): 2055–2061.

Bobadilla Encinas, Gerardo Francisco. "Apuntes de poética narrativa. El primer costumbrismo en México (1843–1850)." In *Imágenes de México y el mexicano en dos momentos de su historia. Representaciones culturales y literarias*, coordinated by Daniel Avechuco Cabrera and Gerardo Francisco Bobadilla, Encinas, 14–36. Mexico: Universidad de Sonora, 2019.

Bolos, Silvia. "Los movimientos sociales, actores de la democratización en la ciudad." In *Democracia y exclusión: Caminos encontrados en la Ciudad de México*. Lucía Álvarez, Carlos San Juan, and Cristina Sánchez Mejorada, 73–90. Mexico City: UNAM; Plaza y Valdés; UACM; INAH, 2006).

Boltanski, Luc. *The Making of a Class: Cadres in French Society*. Cambridge; New York: Cambridge University Press, 1987.

Borchart de Moreno, Christiana. "Las tierras de comunidad de Licto, Punín y Macaxi: Factores para su disminución e intentos de restauración." *Revista Andina* 2 (December 1988).

Borges, Jorge Luis. *Evaristo Carriego*. Buenos Aires: Emecé, [1930] 1965.

Borges, Jorge Luis. *El Tango: Cuatro conferencias*. Buenos Aires: Sudamericana, 2016.

Borges, Jorge Luis. *Textos recobrados 1931–1955*, edited by S. L. del Carril and M. Rubio de Zocchi. Buenos Aires: Emecé, 2001.

Botey, Ana María. *Costa Rica entre guerras (1814–1940)*. San José: EUCR, 2007.

Botey, Ana María and Rodolfo Cisneros. *La crisis de 1929 y la fundación del Partido Comunista de Costa Rica*. San José: Ed. Costa Rica, 1984.

Bourdieu, Pierre. "Capital simbólico y clases sociales." In *Estrategias de reproducción social*, edited by P. Bourdieu, & L. Wacquant. Buenos Aires: Siglo XXI, 2011.

Bourdieu, Pierre. *La distinción: Criterio y bases sociales del gusto*. Buenos Aires: Taurus, 1998.

Bourdieu, Pierre. *Distinction: A Social Critique of the Judgment of Taste*. Abingdon: Routledge, 1984.

Bourdieu, Pierre. *Distinction: A Social Critique of the Judgment of Taste*. Cambridge, MA: Harvard University Press, 1984.

Bourdieu, Pierre. *La miseria del mundo*. Madrid: Akal, 1999.

Bourdieu, Pierre. "Los ritos de institución." In J. Pitt-Rivers, & J.G. Peristiany, *Honor y gracia*. Madrid: Alianza, 1993.

Bourdieu, Pierre. "The Social Space and the Genesis of Groups." *Theory and Society* 14, no. 6 (November 1985): 723–744.

Boyer, Richard E. *The Lives of Bigamists: Marriage, Family, and Community in Colonial Mexico*. Albuquerque: University of New Mexico Press, 1995.

Brachet-Márquez, Viviane and Mónica Uribe Gómez. *Estado y sociedad en América Latina: Acercamientos relacionales*. Mexico City: El Colegio de México, 2016.

Brading, David A. *Merchants and Miners in Bourbon Mexico 1763–1810*. Cambridge: Cambridge University Press, 1971.

Brading, David A. "Creole Nationalism and Mexican Liberalism." *Journal of Interamerican Studies and World Affairs* 15, no. 2 (May, 1973): 139–190.
Brand, Hal. *Latin American Cold War*. Cambridge, MA: Harvard University Press, 2010.
Bravo Ahúja, Víctor and Marco Antonio Michel. "Alianza de clases y dominación: México, 1930–1946," in *La democratización fundamental: El populismo en América Latina*, coordinated by Carlos M. Vilas, 309–338. Mexico City: Conaculta, 1995.
Bruner, Jerome. "Life as Narrative." *Social Research* 71, no. 3 (2004): 691–710.
Bruner, Jerome. "The Narrative Construction of Reality." *Critical Inquiry* 18, no. 1 (1991): 1–21.
Bryant, Rebecca, and Daniel M. Knight. *The Anthropology of the Future*. Cambridge: Cambridge University Press, 2019.
Bulmer-Thomas, Victor. "La crisis de la economía de agroexportación (1930–1945)." In *Historia general de Centroamérica 4: Las repúblicas agroexportadoras*, edited by Víctor Hugo Acuña Ortega. Madrid: FLACSO-Sociedad Estatal Quinto Centenario, 1993.
Bunker, Steven. *Creating Mexican Consumer Culture in the Age of Porfirio Díaz*. Albuquerque: University of New Mexico Press, 2012.
Burris, Val. "The Discovery of the New Middle Classes." In *The New Middle Classes: Life-Styles, Status Claims, and Political Orientations*, edited by Arthur J. Vidich, 15–54. London: Macmillan, 1995.
Busquets, Dante, Fernando Llanos, Guénola Capron, Martha de Alba, and Uriel Waizel, eds. *Satélite, el libro: Historias suburbanas en la ciudad de México*. Mexico City: UAM; Iztapalapa, 2011.
Bustos, Guillermo. *El culto a la nación: Escritura de la historia y rituales de la memoria en Ecuador, 1870–1950*. Quito: FCE; UASB, 2017.
Cáceres, Gonzalo. "Santiago de Chile la capital de la izquierda." In *Ciudades Sudamericanas como arenas culturales: Artes, medios, barrios de élite y villas miserias, intelectuales y urbanistas: como ciudad y cultura se activan mutuamente*, compiled by Adrián Gorelik and Fernanda Aréas Peixoto, 384–402. Buenos Aires: Siglo Veintiuno, 2016.
Caicedo Licona, Carlos Arturo. *El Chocó por dentro*. Medellín: Lealón, 1980.
Caldeira, Teresa P.R. "Imprinting and Moving Around: New Visibilities and Configurations of Public Space in São Paulo." *Public Culture* 24, no. 2 (2012): 385–419.
Callizaya Vela, Walter Ramiro, et al. *Sueños Cumplidos*. Escuela Superior de Formación de Maestros: Santiago de Huata, Bolivia, 2017. https://www.youtube.com/watch?v=oXbbJm8bUZc
Campos García, Alejandro. "Racialización, racialismo y racismo: Un discernimiento necesario." *Universidad de La Habana* 273 (January–June 2012): 184–199.
Cañas, Alberto. *80 años no es nada*. San José: EUCR, 2006.
Candina, Azun. *Clase media, Estado y sacrificio: la Agrupación Nacional de Empleados Fiscales en Chile contemporáneo (1943–1983)*. Santiago: LOM, 2013.
Candina, Azun. *Por una vida digna y decorosa: Clase media y empleados públicos en el siglo XX chileno*. Santiago: Frasis, 2009.
Candina, Azun. "Studying Other Memories: The Colegio Médico de Chile under Socialism, Dictatorship, and Democracy, 1970–1990." *Latin American Perspectives*, 43, no. 6 (2016): 75–87.

Candina, Azun. "Vivir una dictadura: historia y memoria de los profesores en Chile (1973–1990)." *Revista Historia 396* IV, no. 2 (2014): 187–216.
Cañedo, Montserrat. *Cuerpos peligrosos en el cuerpo de la ciudad: Medicina y política en el Madrid de finales del siglo XIX*. Spain: Universidad de Zaragoza, 2010.
Canessa, Andrew. "Who is Indigenous? Self-Identification, Indigeneity, and Claims to Justice in Contemporary Bolivia." *Urban Anthropology* 36, no. 3 (2007): 195–237.
Cano, Gabriela. "Ansiedades de género en México frente al ingreso de las mujeres a las profesiones de medicina y jurisprudencia." *Projeto História: Revista do Programa de Estudos Pós-Graduados de História* 45 (2012): 13–28.
Cardoso, Rafael. *Modernity in Black and White: Art and Image, Race and Identity in Brazil, 1890–1945*. Cambridge: Cambridge University Press, 2020.
Carriego, Evaristo. *La canción del barrio*. Buenos Aires: CEAL, [1913] 1967.
Castellani, Francesca, and Gwenn Parent. "Being 'Middle-Class' in Latin America." OECD Development Centre Working Paper No. 305, 2011, http://www.oecd-ilibrary.org/content/workingpaper/5kg3jcdx4jlx-en.
Castells, Manuel. *La sociedad red V1*. Madrid: Alianza, 2000.
Castro, Miguel Ángel and Guadalupe Curiel coords., *Publicaciones periódicas mexicanas del siglo XIX: 1822–1855*. Mexico: Universidad Nacional Autónoma de México, 2000.
Cavieres, Eduardo and René Salinas. *Amor, sexo y matrimonio en Chile tradicional*. Valparaíso: Universidad Católica de Valparaíso, Serie Monografías Históricas no. 5, 1991.
Ceballos Ramírez, Manuel. "El sindicalismo católico en México, 1919–1931," *Historia Mexicana* 35, no. 4 (April–June 1986): 621–673
Celag Opinión Pública. *Encuesta panorama político y social*. July 8, 2020. https://www.celag.org/encuesta-bolivia-julio-2020/.
Center for Global Development. *Latin America's Surging Middle Classes: Are They Really a Force for Change?* Washington, DC: Center for Global Development, 2012.
Cerdas, José Manuel and Gerardo Contreras Álvarez. *La política de alianzas del Partido Comunista de Costa Rica: Vanguardia Popular en los años cuarenta*. San José: Universidad de Costa Rica, 1984.
Chakrabarty, Dipesh. *Provincializing Europe: Postcolonial Thought and Historical Difference*. Princeton: Princeton University Press, 2007.
Chasteen, John Charles. *Americanos: Latin America's Struggle for Independence*. New York: Oxford University Press, 2008.
Chasteen, John Charles. *Born in Blood and Fire: A Concise History of Latin America*. New York: W.W. Norton, 2016.
Chauí, Marilena. "Uma Nova Classe Trabalhadora." In *Lula e Dilma: Dez Anos de Governos Pós-Neoliberais No Brasil*, organized by Emir Sader, 123–34. São Paulo: Boitempo, 2013.
Chávez Lomelí, Elba. *Lo público y lo privado en los impresos decimonónicos: Libertad de imprenta (1810–1882)*. México: Universidad Nacional Autónoma de México, Miguel Ángel Porrúa, 2009.
Coaracy, Vivaldo. *O Caso de São Paulo*. São Paulo: Ferraz, 1932.
Cohen, Lucy. *Colombianas en la vanguardia*. Medellín: Editorial Universidad de Antioquía, 2001.
Cohen, Stanley. *Folk Devils and Moral Panics*. Abingdon: Routledge, 2002.
Comisión Histórica del conflicto y sus victimas. *Contribucción al entendimiento del conflicto armado en Colombia*. Bogotá: Ediciones desde abajo. 2015

Connell, R. W. and Messerschmidt, James W. "Hegemonic Masculinity: Rethinking the Concept" *Gender and Society* 19, no. 6 (Dec., 2005): 829–859.

Contreras, Hugo. "Las tropas afroamericanas y mulatas durante la Guerra de Independencia de Chile. Casta, segregación y pretensions sociales, 1810–1820." *Cuaderno de Historia Militar* 15, (2019): 89–103.

Coontz, Stephanie *Historia del matrimonio: Cómo el amor conquistó el matrimonio*. Barcelona: Gedisa, 2006.

Corbin, Alain. *Historia de la vida privada: Sociedad burguesa; aspectos de la vida privada*, vol. 8. Madrid: Taurus, 1991.

Coronel, Valeria. "The Ecuadorian Left during Global Crisis: Republican Democracy, Class Struggle and State Formation (1919–1946)." In *Words of Power, the Power of Words: The Twentieth-Century Communist Discourse in International Perspective*, edited by Giulia Basi, 315–337. Trieste: EUT Edizioni, Università di Trieste, 2020.

Coronel, Valeria. *A Revolution in Stages: Subaltern Politics, Nation-State Formation, and the Origins of Social Rights in Ecuador, 1834–1943*. New York: UMI Dissertation Publishing; ProQuest, 2011.

Coronel, Valeria. *La última guerra del siglo de las luces: Partido radical, campesinos y formación del Estado nacional en Ecuador (1880–1925)*. Colección Atrio. Quito: FLACSO (forthcoming).

Corwin, Arthur. *Contemporary Mexican Attitudes toward Population, Poverty and Public Opinion*. Gainesville: University of Florida Press, 1963.

Cosse, Isabella. *Mafalda. A Social and Political History of Latin America's Global Comic*. Durham, NC: Duke University Press, 2019.

Costa, Sérgio. "¿Amores fáciles? Romanticismo y consumo en la modernidad tardía." *Revista Mexicana de Sociología* 68, no. 4 (October–December 2006): 761–782.

Costeloe, Michael P. *The Central Republic in Mexico, 1835–1846: "Hombres de bien" in the Age of Santa Anna*. Cambridge: Cambridge University Press, 1993.

Coudart, Laurence."Los orígenes de la era mediática de la prensa periódica." In *Dimensiones de la cultura literaria en México (1800–1850): Modelos de sociabilidad, materialidades, géneros y tradiciones intelectuales*, edited by Esther Martínez Luna, 21–28. Mexico: Universidad Nacional Autónoma de México, 2018.

Coudart, Laurence. "La regulación de la libertad de prensa (1863–1867)." *Historia Mexicana* 65, no. 2 (October–December 2015): 629–687.

Cowan, Benjamin A. "Holy Ghosts of Brazil's Past." *NACLA Report on the Americas* 48, no. 4 (2016): 346–52.

Crevenna, Theo. *Materiales para el estudio de la clase media en la América Latina, Vol. 1, La clase media en Argentina y Uruguay: Cuatro colaboraciones*. Washington, DC: Pan American Union, 1950a.

Crevenna, Theo. *Materiales para el estudio de la clase media en la América Latina, Vol. 2, La clase media en México y Cuba: Cuatro colaboraciones*. Washington, DC: Pan American Union, 1950b.

Crevenna, Theo. *Materiales para el estudio de la clase media en la América Latina, Vol. 3, La clase media en Bolivia, Brasil, Chile y Paraguay: Cuatro colaboraciones*. Washington, DC: Pan American Union, 1950c.

Crevenna, Theo. *Materiales para el estudio de la clase media en la América Latina, Vol. 6, La clase media en Colombia, Ecuador y la República Dominicana: Cuatro colaboraciones*. Washington, DC: Pan American Union, 1951.

Crevenna, Theo. "The Social Sciences in the Organization of American States." *UNESCO International Social Science Bulletin* IV, no. 3 (1952): 483–89.

Crossick, Geoffrey. "Formación o invención de las 'clases medias'?." In *Clases medias: Nuevos enfoques desde la sociología, la historia y la antropología*, edited by Ezequiel Adamovsky, Sergio E. Visacovsky, and Patricia Vargas. Buenos Aires: Ariel, 2014.

Cruz, María Angélica and Ramírez Camilo. "Memorias subalternas sobre la dictadura militar en Chile." *Archives de sciences sociales des religions* 170 (April–June 2015): 17–35.

Cueva, Agustín. *The Process of Political Domination in Ecuador*. New Brunswick, NJ: Transaction Books, 1982.

Dadush, Uri, and Shimelse Ali. "*In Search of the Global Middle Class: A New Index*." Washington DC: Carnegie Endowment for International Peace, 2012. http://carnegieendowment.org/2012/07/23/in-search-of-global-middle-class-new-index/cyo2#.

Daechsel, Markus. Review of *The Making of the Middle Class: Toward a Transnational History*, edited by A. Ricardo López-Pedreros and Barbara Weinstein. *Journal of Global History* 8, no. 3, (November 2013): 508–509.

Dalbosco, Hugo and Graciela Falvine. *El Estado peronista. Los planes quinquenales del peronismo: La primera experiencia argentina de planificación integral*. José C. Paz: Edunpaz, 2018.

D'Anglade, Jean-Luis. *Un gran patrón barcelonnette en México: Joseph Ollivier y su familia, 1850–1932*. Puebla: Benemérita Universidad de Puebla, 2012.

Dávalos Aguilar, Pablo. "Economia política de la Asemblea Constituyente." In *Asemblea Constituyente y Economía: Constituciones en Ecuador*, edited by Juan J. Paz y Miño Cepeda, 57–91. Quito: Ediciones ABYA-YALA, 2007.

Davis, Diane E. *El Leviatán urbano: La ciudad de México en el siglo XX*. Mexico City: Fondo de Cultura Económica, 1999.

Davis, Harold E. "Review of Materiales para el estudio de la clase media en la América Latina." *BBAA: Boletín Bibliográfico de Antropología Americana* 14, no. 2 (1951): 143–145.

De Ferranti, David, Guillermo E. Perry, Francisco H.G. Ferreira, and Michael Walton. *Inequality in Latin America: Breaking with History?* Washington, DC: World Bank, 2014.

De Garay, Graciela. *Rumores y retratos de un lugar de la modernidad: Historia oral del multifamiliar Miguel Alemán, 1949–1999*. Mexico City: Instituto Mora, 2002.

Dejung, Christof, David Motadel and Jürgen Osterhammel, "Worlds of the Bourgeoisie." In *The Global Bourgeoisie: The Rise of the Middle Classes in the Age of Empire*, edited by Christof Dejung, David Motadel and Jürgen Osterhammel, 1–39. Princeton, NJ: Princeton University Press, 2019.

de la Cadena, Marisol. *Indigenous Mestizos: The Politics of Race and Culture in Cuzco, Peru, 1919–1991*. Durham, NC: Duke University Press, 2000.

de la Cadena, Marisol. "Women are More Indian: Ethnicity and Gender in a Community Near Cuzco." In Brooke Larson, Olivia Harris, eds. *Ethnicity, Markets and Migration in the Andes: At the Crossroads of History and Anthropology*. Durham, NC: Duke University Press, 1995.

De la Calle, Luis, and Luis Rubio. *Mexico: A Middle Class Society: Poor No More, Developed Not Yet*. Mexico Institute Woodrow Wilson International Center for Scholars, 2012.

De la Pascua Sánchez, María José. "Natalie Z. Davis o la historia de las mujeres desde una historia social renovada." *Historia Social*, no. 75 (2013): 95–112.
De La Torre, Carlos. "El gobierno cayó en las calles" in *El Abril de los Forajidos*, edited by S.D. Araujo, 57–59. Quito: EDIMPRES, 2005.
De La Torre, Carlos. "The Resurgence of Radical Populism in Latin America." *Constellations* 14, no. 3 (2007): 384–397.
De La Torre, Carlos. *La seducción velasquista*. Quito: Ediciones Libri Mundi, 1993.
De la Torre, Augusto and Jamele Rigolini. *MIC Forum: The Rise of the Middle Class*. New York: The World Bank, 2016. https://www.worldbank.org/content/dam/Worldbank/document/MIC-Forum-Rise-of-the-Middle-Class-SM13.pdf.
Del Campo, Hugo. *Sindicalismo y peronismo: Los comienzos de un vínculo perdurable*. Buenos Aires: CLACSO, 1983.
Delgado, Manuel. *El espacio como ideología*. Madrid: Catarata, 2011.
de Regil y Peón, Alonso, Manuel, Sánchez Mármol, and Rubén Reyes Ramírez. *Poetas yucatecos y tabasqueños: Colección de sus mejores produccione*. Villahermosa, Tab.: Universidad Juárez Autónoma de Tabasco; Universidad Autónoma de Yucatán; Compañía Editorial de la Peninsula, S.A. de C.V., 2005.
de Santos, Martin. "Fact-Totems and the Statistical Imagination: The Public Life of a Statistic in Argentina 2001." *Sociological Theory* 27, no. 4 (2009): 466–489.
Desai, Raj M. "Fear and Loathing in the Global Middle Class," *Lawfare* October 2018. https://www.lawfareblog.com/fear-and-loathing-global-middle-class.
Devoto, Fernando J. *Historia de la inmigración en Argentina*. Buenos Aires: Sudamericana, 2003.
Díaz y de Ovando, Clementina. "Pedro Castera, novelista y minero." *Mexican Studies/ Estudios Mexicanos* 7, no. 2 (Summer 1991): 203–223.
Dickey, Sara. "Permeable Homes: Domestic Service, Household Space, and the Vulnerability of Class Boundaries in Urban India." *American Ethnologist* 27, no. 2 (2000): 462–489.
Dillingham, A.S. *Oaxaca Resurgent: Indigeneity, Development, and Inequality in Twentieth-Century Mexico*. Stanford: Stanford University Press, 2021.
Drabble, Samuel, Nora Ratzmann, Stijn Hoorens, Dmitry Khodyakov, and Ohid Yaqub, *The Rise of a Global Middle Class: Global Societal Trends to 2030: Thematic Report 6*. Santa Monica, CA: RAND Corporation, 2015. https://www.rand.org/pubs/research_reports/RR920z6.html.
Di Tella, Torcuato S. *Perón y los sindicatos: El inicio de una relación conflictiva*. Buenos Aires: Ariel, 2003.
Duhau, Emilio and Ángela Giglia. *Habitar la metrópoli*. Mexico City: Siglo XXI; UAM Azcapotzalco, 2008.
Duplat, Carlos. *Siete pecados capitales del pequeños burgués*. Bogotá: Biblioteca Nacional de Colombia, 1984.
Durán, Cecilia C. *Irrupción del sector burócrata en el Estado ecuatoriano: 1925–1944: Perspectiva a partir del análisis de la vida cotidiana de Quito*. Quito: Ediciones ABYA-YALA, 2000.
Durán, Gonzalo and Marco Kremerman. "Los bajos salarios de Chile: Análisis de la Encuesta CASEN 2017." *Fundación Sol*, 2019. http://www.fundacionsol.cl/wp-content/uploads/2019/04/Salarios-al-L%C3%ADmite-2017-NV2-1.pdf
Dussaillant, Jacqueline. *Las reinas de Estado: Consumo, grandes tiendas y mujeres en la modernización del comercio de Santiago, (1880–1930)*. Santiago: Ediciones Universidad Católica de Chile, 2011.

ECLAC, *Social Panorama of Latin America*. New York: ECLAC, 2019.

Ehrenreich, Barbara. *Fear of Falling: The Inner Life of the Middle Class*. New York: Pantheon, 1989.

Ehrenreich, Barbara, and John Ehrenreich. "The Professional-Managerial Class." In *Between Labor and Capital*, edited by Pat Walker. Boston, MA: South End Press, 1979.

Eineigel, Susanne Karin. "Distinction, Culture, and Politics in Mexico City's Middle Class, 1890–1940." PhD diss., University of Maryland, 2011.

Eley, Geoff, and Keith Neild. *El futuro de la clase en la Historia ¿Qué queda de lo social?*, translated by Mónica Burguera. Valencia: PUV, 2010.

Elías, Norbert. *El proceso de la civilización: Investigaciones sociogenéticas y psicogenéticas*. Mexico City: Fondo de Cultura Económica, 2016.

Elsey, Brenda. *Citizens and Sportsmen in Chile: Fútbol and Politics in Twentieth-century Chile*. Austin: University of Texas Press, 2011.

Epstein, Edward, and David Pion-Berlin, eds. *Broken Promises? The Argentine Crisis and Argentine Democracy*. Lanham, MD: Lexington Books, 2006.

Ervin, Michael E. "The Formation of the Revolutionary Middle Class during the Mexican Revolution" In *The Making of the Middle Class: Toward a Transnational History*, edited by A. Ricardo López and Barbara Weinstein, 196–222, Durham, NC: Duke University Press, 2012.

Esping-Andersen, Gosta. *Changing Classes: Stratification and Mobility in Post-Industrial Societies*. London: Sage Publications, 1993.

Espinoza Tamayo, Alfredo. *Psicologia y Sociologia del Pueblo Ecuatoriano*. Guayaquil: Biblioteca Ecuatoriana; Imprenta Municipal, 1918.

Esteinou, Rosario. *Familias de sectores medios: Perfiles organizativos y socioculturales*. Mexico City: CIESAS, 1996.

Esteinou, Rosario. "Intimidad y amor romántico entre 1900 y 1950 en México: Discursos y normas." *Cuicuilco Revista de Ciencias Antropológicas*, 68 (January–April 2017): 35–57.

Estrada, Margarita, coord. *1995: Familias en la crisis*. Mexico City: CIESAS, 1996.

Ezquerra Hernández, Adelaido. "El Estado patrón." Bachelor's diss., Mexico City: UNAM, 1939.

Fanon, Frantz. *Peau noire masques blancs*. Paris: Éditions du Seuil, 1952.

Farthing, Linda. "In Bolivia, the Right Returns with a Vengeance." *NACLA Report on the Americas* 52 no. 1 (2020): 5–12.

Feldman, Valentín and René Barragán. "El Problema de las Clases Medias en la U.R.S.S." *Revista Mexicana de Sociología* 2, no. 2 (1940): 15–40.

Ferguson, James. *Give a Man a Fish: Reflections on the New Politics of Distribution*. Durham, NC: Duke University Press, 2015.

Fernández, Boyoli, Manuel and Eustaquio Marrón de Angelis. *Lo que no se sabe de la rebelión cedillista*. Mexico City: Grafi-Art, 1938.

Fernández, Rueda, Sonia. *La construcción moderna de los maestros y de la infancia en el Ecuador (1925–1948): "La cuestión social," la "escuela activa" y las nuevas ciencias humanas*. PhD diss., Universidad Andina Simón Bolívar, 2013.

Ferreira, Antonio Celso. *A Epopéia Bandeirante: Letrados, Instituições, Invenção Histórica, 1870-1940*. São Paulo: Editora da UNESP, 2002.

Ferreira, Francisco H.G., Julian Messina, Jamele Rigolini, Luis-Felipe López-Calva, Maria Ana Lugo, and Renos Vakis. *Economic Mobility and the Rise of the Latin American Middle Class*. Washington, DC: World Bank, 2013a.

Ferreira, Francisco H. G., Julián Messina, Jamele Rigolini, Luis-Felipe López-Calva, María Ana Lugo, and Renos Vakis. *La movilidad económica y el crecimiento de la clase media en América Latina.* Washington, DC: Banco Internacional de Reconstrucción y Fomento; Banco Mundial, 2013b.

Ferrer, Horacio. *El tango: Su historia y evolución.* Buenos Aires: Peña Lillo, 1968.

Fiorucci, Flavia. "Fascinated by Failure: The 'Bestseller' Explanations of the Crisis." In *The Argentine Crisis at the Turn of the Millennium*, edited by Flavia Fiorucci and Marcus Kein, 150–172. Amsterdam: CEDLA, 2004.

Fischer, Edward F. *The Good Fife: Aspiration, Dignity, and the Anthropology of Wellbeing.* Stanford, CA: Stanford University Press, 2014.

Francois, Marie. "Vivir de prestado. El empeño en la Ciudad de México," in *Historia de la vida cotidiana en México.* vol. IV, coordinated by Anne Staples, 81–118. Mexico City: El Colegio de México, 2005.

Francois, Marie Eileen. *A Culture of Everyday Credit: Housekeeping, Pawnbroking, and Governance in Mexico City, 1750–1920.* Lincoln: University of Nebraska Press, 2006.

Friedman, Sam and Daniel Laurison. *The Class Ceiling: Why it Pays to be Privileged.* Bristol: Policy Press, 2019.

Freeland, Chrystia. *Plutocrats: The Rise of the New Global Super-Rich and the Fall of Everyone Else.* New York: Penguin, 2013.

French, William E. "Prostitutes and Guardian Angels: Women, Work, and the Family in Porfirian Mexico." *Hispanic American Historical Review* 72, no. 4 (1992): 529–553.

Fresneda, Oscar. "Evolución de la estructura de clases sociales en Colombia, 1938–2010: ¿Han crecido las clases medias?" *Sociedad y Economía* 33 (2017): 205–236.

Fresneda, Oscar. "Regímenes de acumulación, estructura de clases sociales y desigualdad en Colombia 1810–2010." PhD diss., Universidad Nacional de Colombia, 2016. Repositorio Institucional UN. http://bdigital.unal.edu.co/57243/.

Fromm, Eric. *El arte de amar.* México: Paidós, [1959] 1983.

Fromm, Eric. *Del tener al ser: Caminos y extravíos de la conciencia.* Edited by Rainer Funk. Barcelona: Paidós, [1991] 2016.

Frye, Northrop. *Anatomy of Criticism: Four Essays.* Princeton, NJ: Princeton University Press, 1957.

Fonseca, Claudia. *Família, Fofoca e Honra.* Porto Alegre: Editora UFRGS, 2000.

Foucault, Michel. *La arqueología del saber.* Buenos Aires: Siglo XXI, 2003.

Foucault, Michel. "Los espacios otros." *Astrágalo* (September 7, 1997): 83–91.

Foucault, Michel. *El poder psiquiátrico: Curso en el Collège de France (1973–1974).* Buenos Aires: Fondo de Cultural Económica (first edition in Spanish), 2000.

Freeman, Carla. *Entrepreneurial Selves: Neoliberal Respectability and the Making of a Caribbean Middle Class.* Durham, NC: Duke University Press, 2014.

Freyre, Gilberto. *Casa Grande e Senzala: Formação Da Família Brasileira Sob Regime Da Economia Patriarcal.* Rio de Janeiro: José Olympio, 1978.

Fuentes, Juan Francisco. "Clase." In *Diccionario político y social del siglo XIX español*, directed by Javier Fernández Sebastián and Juan Francisco Fuentes. Madrid: Alianza, 2002.

Fuller, C.J. and Tamil Brahmans. *The Making of a Middle-Class Caste.* Chicago: University of Chicago Press, 2014.

Furbank, Philip Nicholas. *Unholy Pleasure: The Idea of Social Class*. Oxford: Oxford University Press, 1985.

Galen, Joseph. "Taking Race Seriously: Whiteness in Argentina's National and Transnational Imaginary." *Identities* 7, no. 3 (2000): 333–371.

Gantús, Fausta, *Caricatura y poder politico: Crítica, censura y represión en la Ciudad de México, 1876–1888*. México: El Colegio de México; Instituto Mora, 2009.

Gantús, Fausta and Alicia Salmerón, coords. *Contribución a un diálogo abierto: Cinco ensayos de historia electoral latinoamericana*. Mexico City: Instituto de Investigaciones Dr. José María Luis Mora, 2016.

García Covarrubias, Jaime. *El Partido Radical y la clase media en Chile: La relación de intereses entre 1888–1938*. Santiago: Editorial Andres Bello, 1990.

García de Fez, Sandra. "Una escuela desconocida del exilio: La polémica en torno al Instituto Hispano Mexicano Ruiz de Alarcón." *Educació i Història: Revista d'Història de l'Educació* 17 (2011): 213–235.

Garciadiego, Javier. "La oposición conservadora y de las clases medias al cardenismo." *Istor* 25 (2006): 30–49.

García Peña, Ana Lidia. "Madres solteras, pobres y abandonadas: Ciudad de México, siglo XIX." *Historia Mexicana* 53, no. 3 (January–March 2004): 647–692.

García-Quesada, George. *Formación de la clase media en Costa Rica: Economía, sociabilidades y discursos políticos (1890–1950)*. San José, Arlekín, 2014.

García Treviño, Rodrigo. "Ejidos, 'mordidas,' hombres y clases." *Futuro* 13 (March 1937): 23–26.

Gargarella, Roberto. *La sala de máquinas de la Constitución*. Buenos Aires: Katz Editores, 2014.

Garguin, Enrique."'Los argentinos descendemos de los barcos': The Racial Articulation of Middle-Class Identity in Argentina (1920–1960)." *Latin American & Caribbean Ethnic Studies* 2, no. 2 (2007a): 161–184.

Garguin, Enrique. "'Los argentinos descendemos de los barcos': The Racial Articulation of Middle-Class Identity in Argentina, 1920–1960." In *The Making of the Middle Class: Toward a Transnational History*, edited by A. Ricardo López and Barbara Weinstein, 355–76. Durham, NC: Duke University Press, 2012.

Garguin, Enrique. "La clase media en el discurso público." *Revista Cuestiones de Sociología* 9 (2013): http://www.cuestionessociologia.fahce.unlp.edu.ar.

Garguin, Enrique. "Diferenciación e identificación de clase media en la esfera pública popular." *IX Congreso Argentino de Antropología Social*, Posadas, Misiones, 2008.

Garguin, Enrique. "Intersecciones entre clase y género en la construcción social magisterio. La Asociación de Maestros de la Provincia de Buenos Aires durante las primeras décadas del siglo XX," in *Clases medias: Nuevos enfoques desde la sociología, la historia y la antropología*, edited by Ezequiel Adamovsky, Sergio E. Visacovsky and Patricia Beatriz Vargas, 167–191. Buenos Aires: Ariel, 2014.

Garguin, Enrique. "El tardío descubrimiento de la clase media en Argentina." *Nuevo Topo* 4 (2007b): 85–108.

Gay, Peter. *La experiencia burguesa: De Victoria a Freud II; La educación de los sentidos*. Mexico City: Fondo de Cultura Económica, 1984.

Gay, Peter. *Schnitzler's Century: The Making of Middle Class Culture, 1815–1914*. New York: W.W. Norton & Company, 2002.

Germani, Gino. "La clase media en la Argentina con especial referencia a sus sectores urbanos." in *La clase media en Argentina y Uruguay: Cuatro colaboraciones*, edited and compiled by Theo R. Crevenna, 1–33. Washington, DC: Unión Panamericana, 1950.

Germani, Gino. *Estructura social de la Argentina: Análisis estadístico*. Buenos Aires: Solar, [1955] 1987.

Giddens, Anthony. *The Class Structure of the Advanced Societies*. New York: Harper & Row, 1975.

Giglia, Ángela. *El habitar y la cultura: Perspectivas teóricas y de investigación*. Barcelona; Mexico City: Anthropos; UAM-Iztapalapa, 2012.

Gilbert, Dennis. *Mexico's Middle Class in the Neoliberal Era*. Tucson: University of Arizona Press, 2007.

Gilbert, Dennis. Review of *The Making of the Middle Class: Toward a Transnational History*, edited by A. Ricardo López-Predreros and Barbara Weinstein. *Reviews in History*, review no. 1297 (August 2012).

Gilroy, Paul. *Against Race: Imagining Political Culture Beyond the Color Line*. Cambridge, MA: Harvard University Press, 2000.

Glantz, Margo. *El día de tu boda*. Mexico City: Martín Castilla editores, 1982.

Gobello, José. *Letras de tango* (3 vols.). Buenos Aires: Centro Editor, 1997.

Gobo, Giampietro. "Class: Stories of Concepts: From Ordinary Language to Scientific Language." *Social Science Information*, 32, no. 3 (1993): 467–489.

Goetschel, Ana María. *Educación de las mujeres, maestras y esferas públicas: Quito en la primera mitad del siglo XX*. Quito: FLACSO; Abya-Yala, 2007.

Goffman, Erving. *The Presentation of Self in Everyday Life*. Edinburgh: University of Edinburgh Social Sciences Research Center, 1956.

Goldstein, Jan. "Of Marksmanship and Marx: Reflections on the Linguistic Construction of Class in Some Recent Historical Scholarship." *Modern Intellectual History* 2, no. 1 (2005): 87–107.

Gómez, María Teresa. *Manuel Gómez Morin, 1915–1939*. Mexico City: Fondo de Cultura Económica, 2008.

Gómez Robleda, José and Ada D'Aloja. *La familia y la casa*. Mexico City: UNAM; IIS, 1959.

González Gangas, Yanko. *Los más ordenaditos. Fascismo y juventud en la dictadura de Pinochet*. Santiago: Hueders, 2020.

González, Fernan. *Poder y violencia en Colombia*. Bogotá: CINEP, 2014.

González Casanova, Pablo. *La democracia en México*. Mexico City: Era, 2006.

Gotkowitz, Laura. *A Revolution for Our Rights: Indigenous Struggles for Land and Justice in Bolivia, 1880–1952*. Durham, NC: Duke University Press, 2007.

Gotkowitz, Laura. "Trading Insults: Honor, Violence, and the Gendered Culture of Commerce in Cochabamba, Bolivia, 1870s–1950s." *Hispanic American Historical Review* 83, no. 1 (2003): 83–118.

Gould, Jeffrey. "Solidarity Under Siege: The Latin American Left, 1968." *The American Historical Review* 114, no. 2 (2009): 348–375.

Grandin, Greg. "Living in Revolutionary Time." In *A Century of Revolution: Insurgent and Counterinsurgent Violence during Latin America's Cold War*, edited by Greg Grandin and Gilbert Joseph. Durham, NC: Duke University Press, 2010.

Grave, Vera. *Razones de Vida*. Bogotá: Planeta, 2000.

Green, James. *We Cannot Remain Silent: Opposition to the Brazilian Military Dictatorship in the United States*. Durham, NC: Duke University Press, 2010.

Grisaffi, Thomas. *Coca Yes, Cocaine No: How Bolivia's Coca Growers Reshaped Democracy*. Durham, NC: Duke University Press, 2019.

Guano, Emanuela. "A Color for the Modern Nation: The Discourse on Class, Race and Education in the Porteño Middle Class." *The Journal of Latin American Anthropology* 8, no. 1 (2003): 148–171.

Guattari, Félix. *Chaosmosis: An Ethico-Aesthetic Paradigm*. Bloomington, Indiana University Press, 1995.

Güemes, Cecilia and Ludolfo Paramio. "El porvenir de una ilusión: clases medias en América Latina." *Nueva Sociedad* 285 (Jan.–Feb. 2020). https://nuso.org/articulo/el-porvenir-de-una-ilusion-clases-medias-en-america-latina/

Guereña, Jean Louis. "Imagen y memoria: La tarjeta postal a finales del siglo XX." *Berceo* 149 (2005): 35–58.

Guerra, Lilian. *Visions of Power in Cuba: Revolution, Redemption, and Resistance, 1959–1971*. Chapel Hill: The University of North Carolina Press, 2012.

Guerrero, Andrés. *Administración de poblaciones, ventriloquía y transescritura*. Quito: FLACSO, 2010.

Guilluy, Christophe. *No society: El fin de la clase media occidental*. Barcelona: Taurus, 2019.

Gutiérrez, Héctor. *La población de Chile*. CICRED Series World Population Year 1974. Paris: CICRED, 1975.

Gutiérrez, Leandro H. and Luis Alberto Romero. *Sectores populares, cultura y política: Buenos Aires en la entreguerra*. Buenos Aires: Sudamericana, 1995.

Gutiérrez Salazar, Raquel. *Rhythms of the Pachakuti: Indigenous Uprising and State Power in Bolivia*, translated by Stacey Alba D. Skar. Durham, NC: Duke University Press, 2014.

Gutiérrez Sanin, Fernando. *¿Lo que el viento se llevo? Partidos políticos y la democracia en Colombia, 1958–2002*. Bogotá: Grupo Editorial Norma, 2007.

Halbwachs, Maurice. "Las Características de las Clases Medias." *Revista Mexicana de Sociología* 1, no. 3 (1939): 95–109.

Hale, Charles. "Neoliberal Multiculturalism: The Remaking of Cultural Rights and Racial Dominance in Central America." *Political and Legal Anthropology Review* 28, no. 1 (2005): 10–28.

Hann, Chris, and Keith Hart. *Economic Anthropology*. Cambridge: Polity Press, 2011.

Harmer, Tanya. *Beatriz Allende: A Revolutionary Life in Cold War Latin America*. Chapel Hill: The University of North Carolina Press, 2020.

Harmer, Tanya. *Allende's Chile and the Inter-American Cold War*. Chapel Hill: University of North Carolina Press, 2011.

Harvey, David. *La condición de la posmodernidad*. Buenos Aires: Amorrortu, 1998.

Harvey, David. *The Urban Experience*. Baltimore and London: Johns Hopkins University, 1989.

Haya de la Torre, Víctor Raúl. *Por la emancipación de América Latina: Artículos, mensajes, discursos (1923–1927)*. Buenos Aires: Gleizer, 1927.

Heiman, Rachel, Carla Freeman, and Mark Liechty, eds. *The Global Middle Classes: Theorizing Through Ethnography*. Santa Fe, NM: School for Advanced Research Press, 2012.

Hernández, Esteban. *El fin de la clase media*. Madrid: Clave Intelectual, 2013.
Herrero, Fernando and Leonardo Garnier. *El desarrollo de la industria en Costa Rica*. Heredia: EUNA, 1982.
Hidrovo Quiñónez, Tatiana. *Estado, sociedad e insurgencia en Manabí 1860–1895*. Quito: UASB; Corporación Editora Nacional, 2018.
Hiner, Hillary. "'Memory Speaks from Today': Analyzing Oral Histories of Female Members of the MIR in Chile Through the Work of Luisa Passerini." *Women's History Review* 25, 3 (2016): 382–407.
Hobsbawm, Eric. *La era del imperio (1875–1914)*. Barcelona: Crítica, 1998.
Hoffmann, Odile. "Sociedades y Espacios en el Litoral Pacífico Sur Colombiano (Siglos XVIII–XX)." In *Tumaco: Haciendo ciudad; Historia, identidad y cultura*, edited by Manuela Álvarez, Michel Agier, Odile Hoffmann, and Eduardo Restrepo, 15–53. Bogotá: ICAN; IRD; Universidad del Valle, 1999. https://horizon.documentation.ird.fr/exl-doc/pleins_textes/divers17-08/010021568.pdf.
Homps-Brousse, Hélène. *L'aventure architecturale des Émigrants Barcelonnette: France-Mexique*. Barcelonnette: Musée de la Vallée, 2013.
Horowitz, Joel. *Los sindicatos, el Estado y el surgimiento de Perón, 1930–1946*. Buenos Aires: EDUNTREF, 2004.
Hubbard, Phil. "Sex Zones: Intimacy, Citizenship and Public Space." *Sexualities* 4, no. 1 (2001): 51–71.
Hurtado-Garcés, Rudy Amanda. "'Quítate de mi escalera, no me hagás oscuridad': Imágenes de lo 'negro' en la antropología colombiana 1930–1970." *Revista CS* 30 (January–April 2020): 141–172. https://doi.org/10.18046/recs.i30.3516.
Ibarra, Hernán. "Notas sobre las clases medias Ecuatorianas." *Ecuador Debate* 74 (August 2008): 40–42.
Ibarra, Hernán. "La victoria de Rafael Correa y la ola progresista en América del Sur." *Ecuador Debate* 69 (2006): 7–18.
Icaza, Xavier. "Decálogo de la clase media mexicana." *Futuro*, no. 14 (April 1937): 25–27.
Illades, Carlos. *Hacia la república del trabajo: la organización artesanal en la Ciudad de México, 1853–1876*. Mexico: El Colegio de México, 1996.
Illouz, Eva. *El Consumo de la utopía romántica: El amor y las contradicciones culturales del capitalismo*. Buenos Aires: Katz Editores, 2009.
INEGI. *Estadísticas históricas de México*. Mexico City: INEGI, 1994, CD-ROM.
Infante Vargas, Lucrecia. "De la escritura personal a la redacción de revistas femeninas: Mujeres y cultura escrita en México durante el siglo XIX." *Relaciones* 113 (Winter 2008): 69–105.
Iturriaga, Jorge E. "Proletas, limpios, cobardes y burgueses: El fútbol en 1973." In *1973: La vida cotidiana de un año crucial*, coordinated by Claudio Rolle, 297–352. Santiago: Planeta, 2003.
Iturriaga, José E. *La estructura social de México*. Mexico: Fondo de Cultura Económcia, 1951.
Iversen, Tarben and David Soskice. *Democracy and Prosperity: Reinventing Capitalism Through a Turbulent Century*. Princeton: Princeton University Press, 2020.
James, Daniel. *Doña María: Historia de vida, memoria e identidad política*. Buenos Aires: Manantial, 2014.
Jameson, Fredric. *The Political Unconscious: Narrative as a Socially Symbolic Act*. London and New York: Routledge, 1983.

Jauretche, Arturo. *El medio pelo en la sociedad argentina*. Buenos Aires: Peña Lillo, 1966.

Jessop, Bob. *The State: Past, Present, Future*. Cambridge: Polity Press, 2016.

Jiménez, Michael. "The Elision of the Middle Classes and Beyond: History, Politics and Development Studies in Latin America's 'Short Twentieth Century.'" In *Colonial Legacies: The Problem of Persistence in Latin American History*, edited by Jeremy Adelman, 199–238. Abingdon: Routledge, 1999.

Johnson, Anne. "¿Qué hay en un nombre?: Una apología del performance." *Alteridades* 24, no. 48 (2014): 9–21.

Johnson, John J. *Political Change in Latin America: The Emergence of the Middle Sectors*. Stanford, CA: Stanford University Press, 1958.

Johnston, Jake and Stephan Lefebvre. "Bolivia's Economy Under Evo in 10 Graphs." Center for Economic and Policy Research. *The Americas Blog*, October 8, 2014. http://cepr.net/blogs/the-americas-blog/bolivias-economy-under-evo-in-10-graphs.

Jokisch, Brad and Jason Pribilsky. "The Panic to Leave: Economic Crisis and the 'New Emigration' from Ecuador." *International Migration* 40, no. 4 (2002): 75–101.

Juan, Tama Marquéz. "La Clase Media en la Política Ecuatoriana, 1830–1980." In *Politica y Sociedad en Ecuador: 1830–1980*, edited by Enrique Ayala Mora, 353–362. Quito: Corporación Editora Nacional, 1980.

Karl, Rob. *Forgotten Peace. Reform, Violence, and the Making of Contemporary Colombia*. Berkeley: University of California Press, 2017.

Karush, Matthew. *Culture of Class: Radio and Cinema in the Making of a Divided Argentina, 1920–1946*. Durham, NC: Duke University Press, 2012.

Kelley, Robin D.G. *Africa Speaks, America Answers: Modern Jazz in Revolutionary Times*. Cambridge, MA: Harvard University Press, 2012.

Kessler, Gabriel. *El sentimiento de inseguridad: Sociología del temor al delito*. Buenos Aires: Siglo XXI, 2009.

Kessler, Gabriel, and María Mercedes Di Virgilio. "La nueva pobreza urbana: Dinámica global, regional y argentina en las últimas dos décadas." *Revista de la CEPAL*, no. 95 (2008): 31–50.

Kharas, Homi. "The Emerging Middle Class in Developing Countries." OECD Development Centre Working Paper No. 285, 2010. http://www.oecd.org/dev/44457738.pdf.

Kharas, Homi. "The Emerging Middle Class in Developing Countries." Washington D.C.: The World Bank, 2011.

Kharas, Homi J. *The Unprecedented Expansion of the Global Middle Class. An Update*. Washington, DC: Brookings, 2013.

Kharas, Homi J. and Kristofer Hamel. "A global tipping point: Half the world is now middle class or wealthier" (2018) https://www.brookings.edu/blog/future-development/2018/09/27/a-global-tipping-point-half-the-world-is-now-middle-class-or-wealthier/

Kim, Sung won, Kari–Elle Brown, and Vanessa L. Fong. "Chinese Individualisms: Childrearing Aspirations for the Next Generation of Middle-Class Chinese Citizens." *Ethos* 45, no. 3 (2017): 342–366.

Kingman, Eduardo. *La ciudad y los otros: Quito 1860–1940: Higienismo, ornato y policía*. Quito: FLACSO; Universitat Rovira i Virgili, 2006.

Kirk, Neville. "Decline and Fall, Resilience and Regeneration: A Review Essay on Social Class." *International Labor and Working-Class History*, 57 (Spring 2000): 88–102.
Klein, Charles H, Sean T. Mitchell, and Benjamin Junge. "Naming Brazil's Previously Poor: 'New Middle Class' as an Economic, Political, and Experiential Category." *Economic Anthropology* 5 (2018): 83–95.
Klimpel, Felícitas. *La mujer chilena: El aporte femenino al progreso de Chile, 1910–1960*. Santiago: Editorial Andrés Bello, 1962.
Knight, Alan. "Cardenismo: Juggernaut or Jalopy?" *Journal of Latin American Studies* 26, no. 1 (1994): 73–107.
Knight, Alan. "México y Estados Unidos, 1938–1940: Rumor y realidad." *Secuencia*, 34 (1996): 129–154.
Kochhar, Rakesh. *A Global Middle Class Is More Promise Than Reality*. Luxembourg: LIS, 2015.
Koo, Hagen. "The Global Middle Class: How Is It Made, What Does It Represent" *Globalizations*. 13, no. 4 (2016): 440–453.
Kopper, Moisés. "La invención de la nueva clase media Brasileña: De la antropología de los números a las políticas de movilidad social." In *Clases Medias: Nuevos Enfoques Desde La Sociología, La Historia y La Antropología*, edited by Ezequiel Adamovsky, Sergio Visacovsky, and Patricia Vargas. Buenos Aires: Ariel, 2014.
Kopper, Moisés. "Measuring the Middle: Technopolitics and the Making of Brazil's New Middle-Class." *History of Political Economy* 52, no. 3 (2020): 561–88.
Kopper, Moisés, and Arlei S. Damo. "A Emergência e Evanescência Da Nova Classe Média Brasileira." *Horizontes Antropológicos* 24, no. 50 (2018): 335–76.
Kopper, Moisés, and Matthew Richmond. "Subjetividades Periféricas: Uma Conversa Interdisciplinar." *Novos Estudos Cebrap*, 39, no. 1 (2020): 9–17.
Koselleck, Reinhart. *Futuro pasado: Para una semántica de los tiempos históricos*. Spain: Paidos, 1993 [original edition published in German, 1979].
Kozel, Andrés. "En torno a la desilusión argentina." *Varia Historia* 23, no. 38 (2007): 368–385.
Kotkin, Joel. *The Coming Neo-Feudalism: A Warning to the Global Middle Class*. New York: Encounter Books, 2020.
Kram Villarreal, Rachel. *Gladiolas for the Children of Sánchez: Ernesto P. Uruchurtu's Mexico City, 1950–1968*. PhD diss., University of Arizona, 2008.
Krishna, Sankaran. "Notes on the Dramatic Career of a Concept: The Middle Class, Democracy, and the Anthropocene." *Alternatives: Global, Local, Political* 40, no. 1 (Feb. 2015), 3–14.
Krozer, Alice. *Inequality in Perspective: Rethinking Inequality Measurement, Minimum Wages and Elites in Mexico*. PhD diss. Cambridge: Centre of Development Studies, University of Cambridge, 2018.
Labarca, Amanda. "Apuntes para estudiar la clase media en Chile." *Revista Atenea* XCIX, no. 305–306 (November-December 1950): 337–350.
Lagos, Maria L. *Autonomy and Power: The Dynamics of Class and Culture in Rural Bolivia*. Philadelphia: University of Pennsylvania Press, 1994.
Laó-Montes, Agustín. *Contrapunteos diaspóricos: Cartografías políticas de Nuestra AfroAmérica*. Bogotá: Universidad Externado de Colombia, 2020.
Lara y Pardo, Luis. *La Prostitución en México*. Mexico: Librería de la Viuda Ch. Bouret, 1908.

LaRosa, Michael and Germán Mejía P. *Colombia: A Concise Contemporary History*. Lanham, MD: Rowman & Littlefield, 2012.

Larson, Brooke. *Cochabamba 1550–1900: Colonialism and Agrarian Transformation in Bolivia*. Durham, NC: Duke University Press, 1998.

Latin American Outlook 2011: How Middle-Class is Latin America? OECD Development Centre, 2010.

Lawrence, Samuel. *American Middle Class: A Cultural History*. New York: Routledge, 2013.

Lemos, Carlos A.C. *Ramos de Azevedo e seu Escritório Técnico*. São Paulo: Editora PINI, 1998.

Lentz, Carola. *"Elites or middle classes?" Lessons from Transnational Research for the Study of Social Stratification in Africa*. Working Papers of the Department of Anthropology and African Studies of the Johannes Gutenberg University Mainz 161, 2015.

Lévi-Strauss, Claude. *El pensamiento salvaje*. Mexico City: FCE, 1970.

Liechty, Mark. "Middle-Class Déjà Vu: Conditions of Possibility, from Victorian England to Contemporary Kathmandu." In *The Global Middle Classes: Theorizing through Ethnography*, edited by Rachel Heiman, Mark Liechty, and Carla Freeman, 271–300. Santa Fe: School for Advanced Research Press, 2012.

Liechty, Mark. *Suitably Modern: Making Middle-Class Culture in a New Consumer Society*. Princeton, NJ: Princeton University Press, 2003.

Lipsett-Rivera, Sonya. *The Origins of Macho: Men and Masculinity in Colonial Mexico*. Albuquerque: University of New Mexico Press, 2019.

Loaeza, Guadalupe. *Debo, luego sufro*. Mexico City: Océano; PFC, 2000.

Loaeza, Soledad. *Clases medias y política en México: La querella escolar, 1959–1963*. Mexico City: El Colegio de México, 1988.

Loaeza, Soledad and Claudio Stern. *Las clases medias en la coyuntura actual: Seminario llevado a cabo en el Centro Tepoztlán, A.C. Tepoztlán, Mor., 26 de septiembre de 1987*. Mexico City: Cuadernos del CES 33, 1990.

López, Irene. "Morochas, milongueras y percantas. Representaciones de la mujer en las letras de tango." *Espéculo: Revista de Estudios literarios* 45 (2010): http://www.ucm.es/info/especulo/numero45/mutango.html

López Beltrán, Carlos. *Sangre y temperament: Pureza y mestizajes en las sociedades de castas americanas*. Mexico City: Directorio UNAM, electronic publication, 2008.

López-Calva, Luis, Guillermo Cruces, Samantha Lach, and Eduardo Ortiz-Juárez."Clases medias y vulnerabilidad a la pobreza: Reflexiones desde América Latina." *El Trimestre Económico* 81, no. 322 (Spring 2014): 281–307.

López-Pedreros, A. Ricardo. "'We have everything and we have nothing': Empleados and Middle-Class Identities in Bogota: 1930–1955." Master's thesis, Virginia Tech, 2001.

López-Pedreros, A. Ricardo. "'Nosotros también somos parte del pueblo': Gaitanismo, empleados y la formación histórica de la clase media en Bogotá, 1936–1948." *Revista de Estudios Sociales* 41 (2011): 84–105.

López-Pedreros, A. Ricardo. "Empleados, mujeres de oficina y la construcción de las identidades de clase media en Bogotá, 1930–1950." *Anuario Colombiano de Historia Social y de la Cultura* 30 (2003): 257–279.

López-Pedreros, A. Ricardo. *Makers of Democracy: A Transnational History of the Middle Classes in Colombia*. Durham, NC: Duke University Press, 2019.

López-Pedreros, A. Ricardo and Barbara Weinstein, eds. *The Making of the Middle Class: Toward a Transnational History*. Durham, NC: Duke University Press, 2012.

López-Pedrereros, A. Ricardo with Barbara Weinstein. "We Shall Be All: Towards a Transnational History of the Middle Class." *Introduction to The Making of the Middle Class: Toward a Transnational History*, edited by A. Ricardo López-Pedreros and Barbara Weinstein, 9–21. Durham, NC: Duke University Press, 2012.

López-Pedreros, Ricardo. "'It Is Not Something You Can Be or Come to Be Overnight': Empleados, Office Angels, and Gendered Middle Class Identifications in Bogotá, Colombia, 1930–1955." In *Latin America's Middle Class: Unsettled Debates and New Histories*, edited by David S. Parker and Louise E. Walker, 151–170. Lanham, MD: Lexington Books, 2012.

López Rosado, Diego. *La burocracia en México: México independiente*. Mexico City: Secretaría de Comercio, 1980.

Lora, Eduardo, and Johanna Fajardo. "Latin American Middle Classes: The Distance Between Perception and Reality." Inter-American Development Bank Working Paper Series No. IDB-WP-275, 2011. http://idbdocs.iadb.org/wsdocs/getdocument.aspx?docnum=36559121.

Lotman, Iuri. *La semiosfera I: Semiótica de la cultura y el texto*. Madrid: Ediciones Cátedra, 1996.

Love, Joseph L. *São Paulo in the Brazilian Federation, 1889–1937*. Stanford, CA: Stanford University Press, 1980.

Lozano, Claudio. "Contexto económico y político en la protesta social de la Argentina contemporánea." *OSAL-Observatorio Social de América Latina*, no. 5 (2001): 5–10.

Luca, Tania Regina de. *A* Revista do Brasil*: Diagnóstico para N(ação)*. São Paulo: Editora da Unesp, 1999.

Luci, Florencia. *La era de los managers: Hacer carrera en las grandes empresas*. Buenos Aires: Paidós, 2016.

Luhmann, Niklas. *El amor como pasión: hacia una codificación de la intimidad*. Barcelona: Ediciones Península, 1985.

Ludwig Gene. *The Vanishing American Dream: A Frank Look at the Economic Realities Facing Middle- and Lower-Income Americans*. New York: Disruption Books, 2020.

Luna, Sara. "Familia y retórica revolucionaria: Apuntes en torno a las reformas al Código Civil en México, 1953–1954." *Nuevo Mundo, Mundos Nuevos* [online version] (December 14, 2018). http://journals.openedition.org/nuevomundo/73760

Luna, Sara. *Modernización, género, ciudadanía, y clase media en la ciudad de México: Debates sobre la moralización y la decencia, 1952–1966*. PhD diss., Mexico City: UNAM, 2017.

Luz, Nícia Vilela. *A Luta pela Industrialização do Brasil* 2nd ed. São Paulo: Alfa-Omega, 1975.

Luzzi, Mariana, and Ariel Wilkis. "Soybean, Bricks, Dollars, and the Reality of Money: Multiple Monies During Currency Exchange Restrictions in Argentina (2011–15)." *HAU: Journal of Ethnographic Theory* 8, no. 1–2 (2018): 252–264.

Lvovich, Daniel. "Colgados de la soga: La experiencia del tránsito desde la clase media a la nueva pobreza en la ciudad de Buenos Aires." In *Desde abajo. La transformación de las identidades sociales*, edited by Maristella Svampa, 51–79. Buenos Aires: Biblos, 2000.

Mahbubani, Kishore. "Peeling Away the Western Veneer," http://www.digitalnpq.org/archive/2008_spring/02_mahbubani.html.

Mansilla, Justo and Simón Maceta, "Atrocities of the Bandeirantes." In *The Bandeirantes*, edited by Richard Morse, 39–47. New York: Alfred Knopf, 1965.

Marchesi, Aldo. "Imaginación Política del antiimplerialismo: Intelectuales y política en el Cono Sur a fines de los sesenta." *E.I.A.L* 17, no. 1 (2006): 135–159.

Marchesi, Aldo. "Southern Cone Cities as Political Laboratories of the Global Sixties: Montevideo (1962–1968); Santiago de Chile (1969–1973); Buenos Aires (1973–1976)." *E.I.A.L* 28, no. 2 (2017): 54–79.

Marchesi, Aldo. "Revolutionaries without Revolution: Regional Experiences in the Forging of a Radical Political Culture in the Southern Cone of South America (1966–1976)" In K. Young (Ed.), *Making the Revolution: Histories of the Latin American Left*. Cambridge: Cambridge University Press, 2019, 185–211.

Maqsood, Ammara. *The New Pakistani Middle Class*. Cambridge, MA: Harvard University Press, 2017.

Markovits, Daniel. *The Meritocracy Trap: How America's Foundational Myth Feeds Inequality, Dismantles the Middle Class, and Devours the Elite*. New York: Penguin, 2020.

Mariátegui, José Carlos. *Mariátegui total*, vol. II. Lima: Biblioteca Amauta, 1994.

Marx, Karl. *Capital*, vol. 1. London: Penguin, 1976.

Marx, Karl. *Capital* vol. 3. London: Penguin, 1981.

Marx, Karl. *The Class Struggles in France, 1848–1850*. New York: International Publishers, 1964.

Marx, Karl, and Friedrich Engels. *The Communist Manifesto*. New York: International Publishers, 1948.

Massolo, Alejandra. *Mujeres y ciudades: Participación social, vivienda y vida cotidiana*. Mexico City: El Colegio de México, 1982.

Matamoros, Blas. *Historia del tango*. Buenos Aires: CEAL, 1971.

Maza, Sarah. "Luxury, Morality, and Social Change: Why There Was No Middle-Class Consciousness in Prerevolutionary France." *Journal of Modern History* 69 (June 1997): 199–229.

Maza, Sarah. *The Myth of the French Bourgeoisie*. Cambridge, MA: Harvard University Press, 2003.

Mbembe, Achille. *Out of the Dark Night: Essays on Decolonization*. New York: Columbia University Press, 2021.

McCann, Bryan. "Carlos Lacerda: The Rise and Fall of a Middle-Class Populist in 1950s Brazil." *Hispanic American Historical Review* 81, no. 4 (2003): 661–696.

Meade, Teresa A. *A History of Modern Latin America*. New York: Wiley-Blackwell, 2010.

Meglio, Gabriel Di, Guzmán, Tomás, & Katz, Mariana. "Artesanos hispanoamericanos del siglo XIX: identidades, organizaciones y acción política." *Almanack* 23 (2019): 275–315.

Mehrtens, Cristina Peixoto. *Urban Space and National Identity in Early Twentieth-Century São Paulo, Brazil: Crafting Modernity*. New York: Palgrave, 2010.

Mejía, Sergio. *La Revolución en Letras: La Historia de la Revolución de Colombia de José Manuel Restrepo (1781–1863)*. Bogotá: Ceso; Ediciones Uniandes; Universidad EAFIT, 2007.

Mendieta y Núñez, Lucio. *La administración pública en México*. Mexico City: UNAM, 1942.

Mendieta y Núñez, Lucio. "La clase media en México." *Revista Mexicana de Sociología* 17, no. 2/3 (May–December 1955): 517–531.
Mentz, Brígida Von. *Movilidad social de sectores medios: Una retrospectiva histórica (siglos xvii al xx)*. México: Centro de Investigaciónes y Estudios Superiores en Antropología Social; Miguel Ángel Porrúa, 2003.
Miguel, Paula. "La estetización del espacio y la espacializacion de lo estético en Buenos Aires: Una mirada desde la producción." *Bifurcaciones: Revista de Estudios Culturales Urbanos* (December 2015): 1–16.
Minujin, Alberto. "Estrujados: La clase media en América Latina." In *Pobreza, un tema impostergable*, edited by Bernardo Kliksberg, 213–234. Mexico City: Fondo de Cultura Económica, 1997.
Minujin, Alberto, and Eduardo Anguita. *La clase media: Seducida y abandonada*. Buenos Aires: Edhasa, 2004.
Minujin, Alberto, and Gabriel Kessler. *La nueva pobreza en la Argentina*. Buenos Aires: Planeta, 1995.
Miranda P., Sergio. "La vivienda popular del milagro mexicano en la ciudad de México (1940–1970)." In *Aproximaciones a la historia del urbanismo popular: Una mirada desde México*, compiled by Héctor Quiroz, 111–125. Mexico City: UNAM, 2014.
Mitchell, Sean T. *Constellations of Inequality: Space, Race and Utopia in Brazil. Constellations of Inequality*. Chicago, IL: University of Chicago Press, 2017.
Molina Enríquez, Andrés. *Los grandes problemas nacionales*. Mexico: Imprenta de A. Carranza e hijos, 1909.
Molina Jiménez, Iván. "Clase, género y etnia van a la escuela: El alfabetismo en Costa Rica y Nicaragua (1880–1950)." In *Educando a Costa Rica: Alfabetización popular, formación docente y género (1880–1950)*, edited by Iván Molina y Steven Palmer. San José: Porvenir, 2000a
Molina Jiménez, Iván, *Costarricense por dicha: Identidad nacional y cambio cultural en Costa Rica durante los siglos XIX y XX*. San José: EUCR, 2002.
Molina Jiménez, Iván, *Demoperfectocracia: La democracia pre-reformada en Costa Rica (1885–1948)*. Heredia: EUNA, 2005.
Molina Jiménez, Iván, ed. *Ensayos políticos: Carmen Lyra y Carlos Luis Fallas*. San José: EUCR, 2000b.
Molina Jiménez, Iván, *El que quiera divertirse: Libros y sociedad en Costa Rica (1750–1914)*. San José: EUCR, 1995.
Molinares Sarmiento, Ramón. *El saxofón del cautivo*. Bogotá: College Editores, 2018.
Montaldo, Graciela. *Museo del consumo: Archivos de la cultura de masas en Argentina*. Buenos Aires: FCE, 2016.
Montaño, Jorge. *Los pobres de la ciudad en los asentamientos espontáneos: Poder y Política*. Mexico City: Siglo XXI Editores, 1976.
Monteiro, John M. *Blacks of the Land: Indian Slavery, Settler Society and the Portuguese Colonial Enterprise in South America*, edited and translated by J.P. Woodard and B. Weinstein. New York: Cambridge University Press, 2018.
Montenegro, Benedito, org. *Cruzes Paulistas: os que tombaram em 32 pela glória de servir São Paulo*. São Paulo: Campanha Pro-Monumento, 1932.
Moore, Barrington. *The Social Origins of Dictatorship and Democracy: Lord and Peasant in the Making of the Modern World*. Boston, MA: Beacon Press, 1966.

Moraga, Fabio. "'Ser joven y no ser revolucionario': La juventud y el movimiento estudiantil durante la Unidad Popular." In *Frágiles suturas: Chile a treinta años del gobierno de Salvador Allende*, compiled by Francisco Zapata, 365–411. México: El Colegio de México, 2006.

Morales, Juan Francisco. "Reflexiones Iniciales." In *Democracia Sí, Dictadura No*, edited by Ciudadanos por la Democracia. Quito: Imprenta La Union, 2005.

Morelli, Federica. "Entre el Antiguo y el Nuevo Régimen: El triunfo de los cuerpos intermedios; El caso de la Audiencia de Quito, 1765–1830." *Procesos, Revista Ecuatoriana de Historia* 21 (II semester 2004): 89–113.

Moreno, Carlos. "Lo cursi y lo grotesco: Algunos aspectos del romanticismo español." *Revista Hispánica Moderna* 48, no. 1 (1995): 7–18.

Moreno, Julio. *Yankees Don't Go Home! Mexican Nationalism, American Business Culture and the Shaping of Modern Mexico, 1920–1950*. Chapel Hill: University of North Carolina Press, 2003.

Mosquera, Sergio Antonio. *Quibdó: Un sueño en construcción*. Quibdó: Alcaldía Municipal de Quibdó, 2012.

Mosse, George L. *The Image of Man: The Creation of Modern Masculinity*. New York; Oxford: Oxford University Press, 1996.

Motatto Avalos, Efrain et al. *Los testigos M–19*. Bogotá: Presencia, 1977.

Moulier-Boutang, Yann. *Cognitive Capitalism*. Cambridge: Polity Press, 2011.

Moyano, Cristina. *MAPU o la seducción del poder y la juventud: Los años fundacionales del partido-mito de nuestra transición (1969-1973)*. Santiago: Universidad Alberto Hurtado, 2009.

Muncy, Robin. "Commentary on Part IV." In *The Making of the Middle Class: Toward a Transnational History*, edited by A. Ricardo López-Pedreros and Barbara Weinstein, 377–384. Durham, NC: Duke University Press, 2012.

Muñoz, Laura, "Agentes confidenciales y funcionarios consulares en el Golfo-Caribe: La labor de Feliciano Montenegro," *Secuencia*, no. 48 (2000): 71–80.

Nava Hernández, Eduardo and Beny Oliver Barajas Pérez. "Cooperativismo, autonomía y poder: El movimiento cooperativista en México durante el cardenismo." *Revista Cooperativismo y desarrollo* 23, no. 106 (2015): 25–34.

Navarro-Rosenblatt, Valeria, "The Untold History: Voices of Non-Affiliatd Jews in Chile, 1940–1990." In *The New Ethnic Studies: Jewish Latin Americans in a Comparative Perspective*, edited by Raanan Rein, Stefan Rinke, and Nadia Zysman, 128–147. Leiden; Boston, MA: Brill, 2017.

Neri, Marcelo. *A Nova Classe Média: O Lado Brilhante Dos Pobres*. Rio de Janeiro: CPS/FGV, 2008. http://www.cps.fgv.br/ibrecps/ncm2010/NCM_Pesquisa_FORMATADA.pdf.

No author [Luciano Kubli]. *El ejido en Yucatán*. Mexico City: Talleres Gráficos de la Nación, 1935.

Nogueira Filho, Paulo. *A Guerra Cívica 1932*, Vol. I. Rio de Janeiro: José Olympio Editora, 1965.

Nun, José. "The Middle-Class Military Coup." In *The Politics of Conformity in Latin America*, edited by Claudio Véliz, 68–118. London: Oxford University Press, 1967.

Núñez Becerra, Fernanda. *La prostitución y su represión en la ciudad de México (siglo XIX): Prácticas y representaciones*. Barcelona: Gedisa, 2002.

O'Dougherty, Maureen. *Consumption Intensified: The Politics of Middle-Class Daily Life in Brazil*. Durham, NC: Duke University Press, 2002.

OECD. *Higher Education in Mexico: Labour Market Relevance and Outcomes, Higher Education*. Paris: OECD Publishing, 2019a.

OECD. *Under Pressure: The Squeezed Middle Class*. Paris: OECD Publishing, 2019b.

Ogando, Alejandro. *Tango y misoginia: Cultura popular en América Latina*. La Plata: EdULP, 2001.

Olavarría, José. *Sobre hombres y masculinidades: "Ponerse los pantalones."* Santiago de Chile: Ediciones Universidad Academia Humanismo Cristiano, 2017.

Olguín, Jorge. "La derecha chilena y los principios legimitadores del pre y post golpe de Estado de 1973." *Izquierdas*, 38, febrero (2018): 141–163.

Olvera Serrano, Margarita. *Lucio Mendieta y Núñez y la institucionalización de la sociología en México, 1939–1965*. México: UAM-Azcapotzalco; Miguel Ángel Porrúa, 2004.

ONU-Mujeres [United Nations-Women]. *Annual Report: Bolivia*. La Paz, Bolivia: UNESCO, 2019. http://uis.unesco.org/country/BO.

Oreamuno, Yolanda, *A lo largo del corto camino*. San José: Ed. Costa Rica, 1961.

Ortiz, Renato. *Cultura Brasileira e Identidade Nacional*. São Paulo: Brasiliense, 1994.

Ospina, Omar. "¡Hay clase media!" in *El abril de los forajidos*, edited by S.D. Araujo, 128. Quito: EDIMPRES, 2005.

Otero, Mariano. *Ensayo sobre el verdadero estado de la cuestión social y política que se agita en la república*. México: Impreso por Ignacio Cumplido, 1842.

Owensby, Brian P. "Commentary on Part III." In *The Making of the Middle Class: Towards a Transnational History*, edited by A. Ricardo López-Pedreros and Barbara Weinstein, 288–295. Durham, NC: Duke University Press, 2012

Owensby, Brian P. *Intimate Ironies: Modernity and the Making of Middle-Class Lives in Brazil*. Stanford, CA: Stanford University Press, 1999.

Palacios, Guillermo, coord. *Ensayos sobre la Nueva Historia Política de América Latina, siglo XIX*. México: Colegio de México, 2007.

Palacios, Marco. *Between Legitimacy and Violence: A History of Colombia, 1875–2002*. Durham, NC: Duke University Press. 2006.

Palermo, Hernán M. *La producción de la masculinidad en el trabajo petrolero*. Buenos Aires: Editorial Biblos, 2017.

Palermo, Silvana and Jeremías Silva, "Expertos, burocracias y política de masas en Argentina." *Estudios Sociales del Estado* 2, no. 3 (2016): 6–21.

Palmer, Steven. "Adiós *laissez-faire*: La política social en Costa Rica (1880–1940)." *Revista de Historia de América*, no. 124 (January–June 1999): 99–117.

Palti, Elías J. "La Sociedad Filarmónica del Pito: Ópera, prensa y politica en la República restaurada (México, 1867–1876)." *Historia Mexicana* 52, no. 4 (April–June 2003): 941–978.

Palti, Elías J. "Tres etapas de la prensa política Mexicana del siglo XIX: El publicista y los orígenes del intelectual modern." In *Historia de los intelectuales en América Latina*, vol. 1, edited by Carlos Altamirano and Jorge Myers, 227–241. Madrid: Editorial Katz, 2008.

Palumbo, Antonino. "Liberalism." In *Understanding Democratic Politics*, edited by Roland Axtmann. London: Sage, 2003.

Pani, Erika. ¿Ciudadana y muy ciudadana?: Women and the State in Independent Mexico." *Gender and History* 18, no. 1 (2006): 5–19.

Parker, David S. "The All-Meaning Middle and the Alchemy of Class." *Estudios Interdisciplinarios de América Latina y el Caribe* 25, no. 2 (2014): 13–29.

Parker, David S. *The Idea of the Middle Class: White-Collar workers and Peruvian Society, 1900–1950*. University Park: Pennsylvania State University Press, 1998.

Parker, David S. "Asymmetric Globality and South American Narratives of Bourgeois Failure." In *The Global Bourgeoisie: The Rise of the Middle Classes in the Age of Empire*, edited by Christof Dejung, David Motadel and Jürgen Osterhammel, 275–294. Princeton, NJ: Princeton University Press, 2019.

Parker, David S. "Middle-Class Mobilization and the Language of Orders in Urban Latin America: From Caste to Category in Early Twentieth-Century Lima, Peru." *Journal of Urban History* 31, no. 3 (March 2005): 367–381.

Parker, David S. "Movilización de clase media y el lenguaje de estamentos: De "casta" a "categoría" en la Lima de principios del siglo XX." In *Moralidades, economías e identidades de clase media: Estudios históricos y etnográficos*, compiled by Sergio Eduardo Visacovsky and Enrique Garguin, 195-216. Buenos Aires: Antropofagia, 2009.

Parker, David S. and Louise E. Walker, eds. *Latin America's Middle Class: Unsettled Debates and New Histories*. Lanham, MD: Lexington Books, 2012.

Paulson, Susan. "Familias que no 'conyugan' e identidades que no conjugan: la vida en Mizque desafía nuestras categorías." In *Ser mujer indígena, chola o birlocha en la Bolivia postcolonial de los 90*, edited by Silvia Rivera, 85–154. La Paz, Bolivia: Ministerio de Desarrollo Humano, 1996.

Pécaut, Daniel. *L'Ordre et la violence: Évolution socio-politique de la Colombie entre 1930 et 1953*. Paris: Éd.de l'École des hautes études en sciences sociales, 1986.

Penner, Barbara. "A Vision of Love and Luxury: The Commercialization of Nineteenth-Century American Weddings." *Winterthur Portfolio*, 39 (2004): 1–20.

Pensado, Jaime M. *Rebel Mexico: Student Unrest and Authoritarian Political Culture During the Long Sixties*. Stanford, CA: Stanford University Press.

Pereira, Antonio Baptista. *Pelo Brasil Maior*. São Paulo: n.p., 1934.

Pérez, Janet W. and Maureen Ihrie, eds. *The Feminist Encyclopedia of Spanish Literature, N-Z*. Westport, CT: Greenwood Press, 2002.

Pérez Monfort, Ricardo. "*Por la patria y por la raza*": *La derecha secular en el sexenio de Lázaro Cárdenas*. Mexico City: Facultad de Filosofía y Letras; Universidad Nacional Autónoma de México, 1993.

Pérez Monfort, Ricardo, and Lina Odena Güemes. "*Por la patria y por la raza*": *Tres movimientos nacionalistas 1936–1940; Documentos*. Mexico City: Cuadernos de la Casa Chata; CIESAS, 1982.

Pérez Rodríguez Lara, Carolina. "La relación de servicio entre el Estado y sus trabajadores," PhD diss., Mexico City: UNAM, 1968.

Pérez Toledo, Sonia. *Los hijos del trabajo: Los artesanos de la ciudad de México*. Mexico: El Colegio de México, 1996.

Perló Cohen, M. "Historias de la Roma. Microhistoria de la Ciudad de México," *Historias*, 19 (1987–1988): 159–170.

Peugny, C. and Cecile Van de Velde. "Repenser les inégalités entre générations." *Revue Française de Sociologie* 54 (Winter 2013): 641–662.

Peukert, Detlev. *The Weimar Republic: The Crisis of Classical Modernity*. New York: Hill & Wang, 1993.
Piccato, Pablo. *La tiranía de la opinión: El honor en la construcción de la esfera pública en México*. Mexico City: El Colegio de Michoacán, Instituto Mora, 2015.
Piccato, Pablo. *The Tyranny of Opinion: Honor in the Construction of the Mexican Public Sphere*. Durham, NC: Duke University Press, 2010.
Picchia, Paulo Menotti del. *A Revolução Paulista*. São Paulo: n.p., 1932.
Pike, Fredrick B. "Aspects of Class Relations in Chile, 1850–1960." *Hispanic American Historical Review* 43, no. 1 (1963): 14–33.
Pinochet Le-Brun, Tancredo. *Un año de empleado público en Chile*. Santiago de Chile: Casa Editora Tancredo Pinochet, 1915.
Pinto, Julio y Salazar, Gabriel. *Historia Contemporánea de Chile I: Estado, legitimidad, ciudadanía*. Santiago de Chile: Ediciones LOM, 1999.
Pinto S. Francisco. *Clase media y socialismo*. Valparaíso, Chile: Imprenta Victoria, 1940.
Pírez, Pedro. "¿Qué pasó en la Argentina? Algunas piezas de un rompecabezas para intentar entender." *Estudios sociológicos* 20, no. 2 (2002): 455–467.
Pisano, Pietro. "Movilidad social e identidad 'negra' en la segunda mitad del siglo XX." *Anuario Colombiano de Historia Social y de la Cultura* 41, no. 1 (2014): 179–199.
Pisano, Pietro. "Blancos, no blancos, casi blancos: Cuerpo, color y belleza en Colombia." PhD diss., Universidad Nacional de Colombia, 2019.
Pisano, Pietro. *Liderazgo político 'negro' en Colombia, 1943–1964*. Bogotá: Universidad Nacional de Colombia, 2012.
Pochmann, Marcio. *Nova Classe Média? O Trabalho Na Base Da Pirâmide Social Brasileira*. São Paulo: Boitempo, 2012.
Polanyi, Karl. *The Great Transformation: The Political and Economic Origins of Our Time*. Boston, MA: Beacon Press, 2001.
Porta, Paula, org. *História da cidade de São Paulo: A cidade na primeira metade do século, 1890–1954*. São Paulo: Paz e Terra, 2004.
Portelli, Alessandro, *The Death of Luigi Trastulli and Other Histories: Form and Meaning in Oral History*. Albany: State University of New York Press, 1991.
Porter, Susie. "Empleadas públicas: Normas de feminidad, espacios burocráticos e identidad de la clase media en México durante la década de 1930." *Signos Históricos* 11 (January–July 2014): 40–63.
Porter, Susie S. *From Angel to Office Worker: Middle-Class Identity and Female Consciousness in Mexico, 1890–1950*. Lincoln: University of Nebraska Press, 2018.
Porter, Susie S. *Working Women in Mexico City: Public Discourses and Material Conditions, 1879–1931*. Tucson: University of Arizona Press, 2003.
Posada Carbo, Eduardo. *La nación soñada: Violencia, liberalismo y democracia en Colombia*. Bogotá: Grupo Editorial Norma, 2004.
Postero, Nancy. *The Indigenous State: Race, Politics, and Performance in Plurinational Bolivia*. Berkeley: University of California Press, 2017.
Powers, Karen. "Señores dinámicos e indios vagabundos: Riqueza migración y transformación reproductiva de los cacicazgos de Quito (1600–1700)." *Memoria*, II (November 1992).
Poweska, Radoslaw. *Indigenous Movements and Building the Plurinational State in Bolivia: Organization and Identity in the Trajectory of the CSUTCB and CONAMAQ*. Warsaw: University of Warsaw Center for Latin American Studies, 2013.

Prado, Maria Lígia Coelho. *A democracia ilustrada: O Partido Democrático de São Paulo, 1926–1934*. São Paulo: Ática, 1986.

Pujol, Sergio. *Historia del Baile: De la milonga a la disco*. Buenos Aires: Emecé, 1999.

Quadros, Waldir José. *O 'Milagre Brasileiro' e a Expansão Da Nova Classe Média*. PhD diss. Campinas: Unicamp, 1991.

Queirolo, Graciela. "Vendedoras: Género y trabajo en el sector commercial, Buenos Aires, (1910–1950)." *Estudos Feministas* 22, no. 1 (2014): 29–50.

Queirolo, Graciela. "Indemnizaciones, enfermedades y antigüedad entre los empleados de comercio: Alcances y límites de la ley 11.729 (Argentina, 1934–1945)." *Estudios Sociales* 50 (2016): 145–169.

Queirolo, Graciela Amalia. *Mujeres en las oficinas: Trabajo, género y clase en el sector administrativo, Buenos Aires, 1910–1950*. Buenos Aires: Editorial Biblos, 2018.

Quesada Pacheco, Miguel Ángel. *Diccionario histórico del español de Costa Rica*. San José: EUNED, 1995.

Quirós, Julieta. *El porqué de los que van: Peronistas y piqueteros en el Gran Buenos Aires; Una antropología de la política vivida*. Buenos Aires: Antropofagia, 2011.

Quiroz, Moisés. *Las vecindades del centro de la ciudad de México frente al crecimiento de la ciudad, 1940–1970*. PhD diss., Mexico City: Facultad de Filosofía y Letras, UNAM, 2014.

Raid, Michael. *The Forgotten Continent: A History of the New Latin America*. New Haven: Yale University Press, 2017.

Ramacciotti, Karina. "De la culpa al seguro: La Ley de Accidentes de Trabajo, Argentina (1915–1955)." *Revista Mundos do Trabalho* 3, no. 5 (2011): 266–284.

Ramírez Gallegos, Franklin. *La insurreción de abríl no fue sólo una fiesta*. Quito: Taller El Colectivo, 2005.

Ramírez Gallegos, Franklin and Ramírez, Jacques Paul. *La estampida migratoria Ecuatoriana: Crisis, redes transnacionales y repertorios de acción migratoria*. Quito: CIUDAD; ABYA YALA; UNESCO, 2005.

Ranciere, Jacques. *The Philosopher and His Poor*. Durham, NC: Duke University Press, 2003.

Rapoport, Mario, ed. *Crónicas de la Argentina sobreviviente: El presente en el espejo de la historia*. Buenos Aires: Norma, 2004.

Raphael, Lutz. *Ley y orden: Dominación mediante la administración el siglo XIX*. Madrid: Siglo XXI Ed., 2008.

Ravallion, Martin. "The Developing World's Bulging (but Vulnerable) Middle Class." *World Development* 38, no. 4 (2009): 1–31.

Ray, Raka. "'The Middle Class': Sociological Category or Proper Noun?" *Political Power and Social Theory* 21 (2010): 313–322.

Restrepo, Eduardo. "Articulaciones de negridad: Políticas y tecnologías de la diferencia en Colombia." In *Hegemonía cultural y políticas de la diferencia*, edited by Alejandro Grimson and Karina Bidaseca, 147–163. Buenos Aires: CLACSO, 2013.

Reyes-Palma, Francisco. *Pablo O'Higgins: De estética y soberanía*. Mexico City: Gobierno del Distrito Federal; Fundación Cultural María y Pablo O'Higgins, 1991.

Reyes Rodríguez, Andrés. *Clases medias y poder político en Aguascalientes*. Aguascalientes: Universidad Autónoma de Aguascalientes, 2016.

Richmond, Matthew, Moisés Kopper, Valéria Oliveira, and Jacqueline Garza. "Introdução: Espaços Periféricos, Ontem e Hoje." In *Espaços Periféricos: Política, Violência e Território Nas Bordas Da Cidade*, edited by Matthew Richmond, Moisés Kopper, Valéria Oliveira, and Jacqueline Garza. São Paulo: UFSCAR; CEM, 2020.
Rinke, Stefan. *Cultura de masas: Reforma y nacionalismo en Chile 1910–1931*. Santiago de Chile: DIBAM; Centro de Investigaciones Diego Barros Arana, 2002.
Rinke, Stefan. *Encuentros con el yanqui: norteamericanización y cambio sociocultural en Chile 1898–1990*, Santiago de Chile: DIBAM; Centro de Investigaciones Diego Barros Arana 2013.
Riquelme S. Alfredo and Joaquín Fernández. "La vida política." In *Chile: Mirando hacia adentro*, vol. 4 (1930–1960), directed by Joaquín Fermandois and coordinated by Olga Ulianova, 21–106. Madrid: Fundación Mapfre; Taurus, 2015.
Rocha, Martha Eva. "Los comportamientos amorosos en el noviazgo, 1870–1968: Historia de un proceso secular." *Historias*, no. 35 (1995): 119–139.
Rock, David. *Argentina 1516–1987: From Spanish Colonization to Alfonsín*. Berkeley: University of California Press, 1987.
Rock, David. *El radicalismo argentino, 1890–1930*. Buenos Aires: Amorrortu editores, 1977.
Rodrigues, J. *A Mulher Paulista no Movimento Pro-Constituinte*. São Paulo: Revista dos Tribunaes, 1933.
Rodríguez Albán, Cecilia Martha. *Cultura y política en Ecuador: Estudio sobre la creación de la Casa de la Cultura*. Quito: FLACSO, 2015.
Rodríguez Kuri, Ariel. *La experiencia olvidada: El Ayuntamiento de México; Política y gobierno, 1876–1912*. México: El Colegio de México; UAM-Azcapotzalco, 1996.
Rodríguez Kuri, Ariel. *Historias de desasosiego: La revolución en la ciudad de México, 1911–1922*. México: El Colegio de México, 2010.
Rodríguez Vega, Eugenio. "Clases y lucha social en Costa Rica." *Surco* 42 (December 1943).
Rodríguez Vega, Eugenio. *Voces del 43*. San José: EUCR, 1995.
Roediger, David. *The Wages of Whiteness: Race and the Making of the American Working Class*. London: Verso, 1991.
Rojas, Margarita, Flora Ovares, Carlos Santander and María Elena Carballo. *La casa paterna: Escritura y nación en Costa Rica*. San José: EUCR, 1993.
Rolle, Claudio. "La 'NO historia' de un año crucial." In *1973: La vida cotidiana de un año crucial*, coordinated by Claudio Rolle, 9–30. Santiago: Planeta, 2003.
Romero, José Luis. *Latinoamérica: Las ciudades y las ideas*. Buenos Aires: Siglo XXI, 1986.
Rosaldo, Renato. *Culture and Truth: The Remaking of Social Analysis*. Boston, MA: Beacon Press, 1989.
Rosenfeld, Bryn. *The Autocratic Middle Classes: How State Dependency Reduces Demand for Democracy*. Princeton: Princeton University Press, 2020.
Rosenweig, Fernando. "La evolución económica de México, 1870–1940." *El Trimestre económico* 56, no. 221 (January–March 1989): 11–56.
Rubenstein, Anne. *Del "Pepín" a "Los Agachados": Cómics y censura en el México posrevolucionario*. Mexico City: Fondo de Cultura Económica, 2004.

Ruckert, Arne, Laura Macdonald, and Kristina R. Proulx. "Post-Neoliberalism in Latin America: A Conceptual Review." *Third World Quarterly* 38, no. 7 (2017): 1583–1602.

Ruderer Stefan, Strassner Veit. "Recordando tiempos difíciles: La Vicaría de la Solidaridad como lugar de memoria de la Iglesia y la sociedad chilena."*Archives de sciences sociales des religions* 170 (avril-juin 2015): 37–60.

Rueschemeyer, Dietrich, Evelyn Huber Stephens and John Stephens. *Capitalist Development and Democracy*. Chicago, IL: University of Chicago Press, 1992.

Sábato, Ernesto. *Tango: Discusión y clave*. Buenos Aires: Losada, 1965.

Sader, Emir. "Dilma as Lula's Successor: The First 100 Days." *NACLA Report on the Americas* 44, no. 2 (2011): 31–33.

Sáenz, Vicente. *Obras escogidas*. San José: Editorial Costa Rica, 1985.

Safford, Frank and Marco Palacios. *Colombia: Fragmented Land. Divided Society*. Oxford: Oxford University Press, 2002.

Sahlins, Marshall. *Islands of History*. Chicago, IL: The University of Chicago Press, 1985.

Saítta, Sylvia. *Regueros de tinta: El diario Crítica en la década de 1920*. Buenos Aires: Sudamericana, 1998.

Samper, Mario. *Evolución de la estructura socio-ocupacional costarricense: Labradores, artesanos y jornaleros (1864–1935)*. San José: Universidad de Costa Rica, 1979.

Sánchez, Gonzalo. *Memorias, subjetividades y política*. Bogotá: Crítica, 2020.

Sánchez-Mejorada, Cristina. *Rezagos de la modernidad: Memorias de una ciudad presente*. México: UAM, 2005.

Sánchez Parra, J. Cristina. "'Detrás del mostrador': Espacios de trabajo y lugares de sociabilidad de los empleados de comercio en la ciudad de México a inicios del siglo XX." *Estudios del ISHiR* 26 (2020): 1–19.

Santillán, Martha. "El discurso tradicionalista sobre la maternidad: Excélsior y las madres prolíficas durante el avilacamachismo." *Secuencia: Revista de Historia y ciencias sociales*, no. 77 (May–August 2010): 91–110.

Sater, William, and Collier Simon. *Historia de Chile, 1808–2017*. Madrid: Ediciones Akal, 2018.

Savigliano, Marta. "Malevos llorones y percantas retobadas: El tango como espectáculo de razas, clases e imperialismo." *Relaciones de la Sociedad Argentina de Antropología* XIX (1993): 79–104.

Schechner, Richard. "Restauración de la conducta." In *Estudios avanzados de performance*, edited by D. Taylor, and M. Fuentes. Mexico City: FCE, 2011.

Schielke, Joska Samuli. *Egypt in the Future Tense: Hope, Frustration, and Ambivalence before and after 2011*. Bloomington: Indiana University Press, 2015.

Schielke, Samuli. "Living in the Future Tense: Aspiring for World and Class in Provincial Egypt." In *The Global Middle Classes: Theorizing through Ethnography*, edited by Rachel Heiman, Mark Liechty, and Carla Freeman. Santa Fe: School for Advanced Research Press, 2012.

Schodt, David W. *Ecuador: An Andean Enigma*. Boulder, CO: Westview Press, 1987.

Schpun, Mônica Raisa. "Carlota Pereira de Queiroz: Uma Mulher na Política." *Revista Brasileira de História* 17, no. 33 (1997): 167–200.

Schaefer, Timo H. *Liberalism as Utopia: The Rise and Fall of Legal Rule in Post-Colonial Mexico, 1820–1900*. Cambridge: Cambridge University Press, 2017.

Schmitter, Philippe C. *Interest Conflict and Political Change in Brazil*. Stanford, CA: Stanford University Press, 1971.

Schwarz, Roberto. *Misplaced Ideas: Essays on Brazilian Culture*. London: Verso, 1992.

Jonathan, Sheehan and Dror Wahrman. *Invisible Hands: Self-Organization and the Eighteenth Century*. Chicago: University of Chicago Press, 2015.

Sherman, John W. "Reassessing Cardenismo: The Mexican Right and the Failure of a Revolutionary Regime, 1934–1940." *The Americas* 54, no. 3 (1998): 357–378.

Seligmann, Linda. "To Be in Between: The Cholas as Market Women." *Comparative Studies in Society and History* 31 no. 4 (1989): 694–721.

Sémbler, Camilo, "Estratificación social y clases sociales: Una revisión analítica de los sectores medios." Santiago de Chile: CEPAL, División de Estudios, 2006.

Shakow, Miriam. *Along the Bolivian Highway: Social Mobility and Political Culture in a New Middle Class*. Philadelphia: University of Pennsylvania Press, 2014.

Shakow, Miriam. "Citizenship and Rights." In *The Andean World*, edited by Linda Seligmann and Kathleen Fine-Dare, 587–601. Abingdon: Routledge, 2018.

Shakow, Miriam. "Digital Alteration and the Law Against Racism: Conflicting Models of Citizenship Among New Bolivian Middle Classes." In *Citizenship in the Latin American Upper and Middle Classes: Ethnographic Perspectives on Culture, Politics, and Consumption*, edited by Fiorella Diaz Montero and Franka Winter. Abingdon: Routledge, 2019.

Sick, Klaus-Peter. "Le concept de classes moyennes: Notion sociologique ou slogan politique?" *Vinghtieme Siecle: Revue d'Histoire* 37 (1993): 13–34.

Sick, Klaus-Peter. "El concepto de clases medias: ¿Noción sociológica o eslogan político?." In *Clases Medias: Nuevos enfoques desde la sociología, la historia y la antropología*, edited by Ezequiel Adamovsky, Sergio E. Visacovsky, and Patricia Vargas, 21–54. Buenos Aires: Ariel, 2014.

Silva, J. Pablo. "Repensando aspectos de las relaciones de clase en el Chile del siglo XX." In *Moralidades, economías e identidades de clase media: Estudios históricos y etnográficos*, compiled by Sergio Eduardo Visacovsky, and Enrique Garguin, 123–159. Buenos Aires: Antropofagia, 2009.

Singer, André. *O lulismo em crise: Um quebra-cabeça do período Dilma, 2011–2016*. São Paulo: Companhia das Letras, 2018.

Skeggs, Beverly. *Formations of Class & Gender: Becoming Respectable*. London: Goldsmiths, University of London, 1997.

Solano D., Sergio Paolo. "Los sectores sociales medios en la historia social colombiana del siglo XIX." *Memorias: Revista digital de Historia y Arqueología desde el Caribe colombiano* 7, no. 13 (November 2010): 1–38.

Soler, Ricaurte. "El pensamiento sociológico de Mariano Otero." *Cuadernos Americanos* 1 (January–February 1960): 15–31.

Solís A. Manuel. *Costa Rica: Reformismo socialdemócrata o liberal?* San José: FLACSO, 1992.

Solís A. Manuel. *La institucionalidad ajena: Los años cuarenta y el fin de siglo*. San José: EUCR, 2006.

Somers, Margaret. "The Narrative Constitution of Identity: A Relational and Network Approach." *Theory and Society* 23, no. 5 (1994): 605–694.

Sosa-Escudero, Walter, and Sergio Petralia. "*I Can Hear the Grass Grow": The Anatomy of Distributive Changes in Argentina*. Documento de Trabajo, La Plata: Centro de Estudios Distributivos, Laborales y Sociales, 2010.

Sosenski, Susana and Sergio Miranda. "La ciudad anhelada: espacio urbano, emociones y segregación social en la publicidad inmobiliaria de la ciudad de México, 1940–1970." *Urbana* 11, no. 1(20): 172–204.

Southall, Roger. *The New Black Middle Class in South Africa*. Woodbridge: James Currey. 2020.

Souza, Laura de Mello e. "Vícios, virtudes e sentimento regional: São Paulo da lenda negra à lenda áurea." *Revista da História-USP* 142-3 (2000): 262–76.

Speckman, Elisa. "De amor y desamor: Ideas, imágenes, recetas y códigos en los impresos de Antonio Vanegas Arroyo." *Revista de Literaturas Populares*, year 1, no. 2, (July–December 2001): 68–101.

Sperber, Dan. *El simbolismo en general*. Barcelona: Anthropos, 1988.

Spivak, Gayatri. "General Introduction." Introduction to *Towards a History of the National-Popular in Bolivia*, vii–xv. By René Zavaleta Mercado. London: Seagull Books, 2018.

Stabili, Maria Rosaria. "Introducción: Los desafíos de la memoria al quehacer historiográfico." In *Entre historias y memorias: Los desafíos metodológicos del legado reciente de América Latina*, coordinated by Maria Rosaria Stabili, 7–20. Madrid: Colecciones Estudios AHILA; Iberoamericana, 2007.

Stearns, Peter. "The Middle Class: Towards a Precise Definition." *Comparative Studies in Society and History* 21, no. 3 (July 1979): 377–396.

Stedman Jones, Gareth. *Languages of Class: Studies in English Working Class History, 1832–1982*. Cambridge: Cambridge University Press, 1983.

Stern, Claudia. "Cuando Chile dejó de ser una 'copia feliz del Edén': Redefiniendo clases medias en trauma en la década del 70." *Journal of Iberian and Latin American Research* 25, no. 2 (2019): 157–176.

Stern, Claudia. *Entre el cielo y el suelo: las identidades elásticas de las clases medias (Santiago de Chile, 1932–1962)*. Santiago: RiL editores, 2021.

Stern, Claudia. "La paz neutra y el 'chileno abnegado'. Inmigrantes y sectores medios en Chile 1930–1960." *Revista de Paz y Conflictos* 9 no. 2 (2016): 125–150.

Stern, Claudia. "La sobredimensión de la educación estatal en Chile: El Liceo experimental Manuel de Salas y el 'chileno integral' (1932–1962)." *Revista Historia 396* 7, no. 1 (June 2017a): 263–299.

Stern, Claudia. "Otherness in Convergence: Arabs, Jews, and the Formation of the Chilean Middle Classes, 1930–1960" In Raanan Rein, Stefan Rinke, and Nadia Zysman, Eds., *The New Ethnic Studies: Jewish Latin Americans in a Comparative Perspective* Leiden and Boston: Brill, 2017b. 99–127.

Stern, George. "Habla la Confederación de la Clase Media." *Futuro* no. 12 (February 1937): 11–15.

Stern, Steve. *Remembering Pinochet's Chile: On the Eve of London 1998*. Durham, NC: Duke University Press, 2004.

Stern, Steve J. *Luchando por mentes y corazones: Las batallas de la memoria en el Chile de Pinochet*. Santiago de Chile: Ediciones Universidad Diego Portales, 2013.

Stoler, Ann. *Duress: Colonial Durabilities in our Times*. Durham, NC: Duke University Press, 2016.

Stoler, Ann. "Intimidation of Empire: Predicament of the Tactile and Unseen." In *Haunted by Empire: Geographies of Intimacy in North American History*, ed Ann Stoler. Durham: Duke University Press, 2006, 2–22.
Stoll, David. *Rigoberta Menchú and the Story of All Poor Guatemalans*. Boulder, CO: Westview Press, 1999.
Strassner, Veit. "La Iglesia chilena desde 1973 a 1993: De buenos samaritanos, antiguos contrahentes y nuevos aliados; Un análisis politológico." *Teología y Vida* 47, no. 1 (2006): 76–94.
Svampa, Maristella. *Los que ganaron: La vida en los countries y barrios privados*. Buenos Aires: Biblos, 2001.
Teubal, Miguel. "Rise and Collapse of Neoliberalism in Argentina. The Role of Economic Groups." *Journal of Developing Societies* 20, nos. 3–4 (2004): 173–188.
Therborn, Göran. "Dreams and Nightmares of the World's Middle Classes." *New Left Review*, 124 (July–August, 2020), 63–87.
Thompson, E. P. *La formación de la clase obrera en Inglaterra*. Barcelona: Crítica, 1989.
Thompson, E. P. *The Making of the English Working Class*. London: Victor Gollancz, 1963.
Thompson, E. P. *The Making of the English Working Class*. London: Vintage, 1964.
Thompson, E.P. *The Making of the English Working Class*. New York: Vintage, 1966.
Thorndike, Edward L. "A Constant Error in Psychological Ratings." *Journal of Applied Psychology* (1920): 25–29.
Tierno, Enrique. "Aparición y desarrollo de nuevas perspectivas de valoración social en el siglo XIX: Lo cursi." *Revista de Estudios Políticos*, no. 42 (1952): 85–106.
Tilly, Charles. *La desigualdad persistente*. Buenos Aires: Manantial, 2000.
Isabel, Torres Dujisin. "La década de los sesenta en Chile: la utopía como proyecto." *Historia Actual Online HAOL* 19 (Primavera, 2009), 139–149.
Torres Septién, V. "'Bendita sea tu pureza': Relaciones amorosas de los jóvenes católicos en México (1940–1960)." In *Tradiciones y conflictos: Historias de la vida cotidiana en México e Hispanoamérica*, edited by Pilar Gonzalbo Aizpuru and Milada Bazant, 385–413. México: El Colegio de México, El Colegio Mexiquense, 2007.
Trouillot, Michel-Rolph. *Silencing the Past: Power and Production of History*. Boston, MA: Beacon Press, 1995.
Trumper, Camilo D. *Ephemeral Histories: Public Art, Politics and the Struggle for the Streets in Chile*. Oakland: University of California Press, 2016.
Tuan, Yi-Fu. *Space and Place. The Perspective of Experience* Minneapolis: University of Minnesota Press, eighth edition, 2001.
Tuğal, Cihan. "Elusive Revolt: The Contradictory Rise of Middle-Class Politics." *Thesis Eleven* 130, no. 1 (2015): 74–95.
Turner, John Kenneth. *México bárbaro*. México: Ediciones Leyenda, 2008.
Ubidia, Abdón. "Prólogo," in *El Cojo Navarrete*, by Enrique Terán, 9–11. Quito: Campaña de Lectura Eugenio Espejo, 2009.
Ulla, Noemí. *Tango, rebelión y nostalgia*. Buenos Aires: CEAL, 1982.
Ulloa, Sergio Valerio. *Los barcelonnettes en Guadalajara, siglos XIX y XX*. Mexico City: Universidad de Guadalajara; Instituto Mora, 2015.
Urrea Giraldo, Fernando. "Dinámica de reestructuración productiva, cambios institucionales y políticos y procesos de desregulación de las relaciones asalariadas: el caso colombiano." In *Trabajo y modelos productivos en América*

Latina, edited by Enrique de la Garza Toledo and Julio César Neffa, 137–200. Buenos Aires: CLACSO, 2010.

Urrea Giraldo, Fernando. "La conformación paulatina de clases medias negras en Cali y Bogotá a lo largo del siglo XX y la primera década del XXI." *Revista de Estudios Sociales* 39 (2011): 24–41.

Urrea Giraldo, Fernando, Carlos Viáfara López, and Mara Viveros-Vigoya. "Del mestizaje blanco al multiculturalismo triétnico: Raza y etnicidad en Colombia." In *Pigmentocracias. Color, etnicidad y raza en América Latina*, edited by Edward Telles and Regina Martínez. 108–158. Mexico City: FCE, 2019.

Uzcátegui, Emilio. "Visión panorámica de la educación en el Ecuador." *Revista Ecuatoriana de Educación*, year VII (September–October 1954).

Valderrama, Carlos A. "La diferencia cultural negra en Colombia: Contrapúblicos afrocolombianos." *Revista CS* 29 (September 12, 2019): 209–242.

Valencia Sala, Gladys. *El círculo modernista ecuatoriano: Crítica y poesía*. Quito: UASB, 2007.

Valenzuela, Esteban. "El MAPU y el rol transformador de las élites iluministas: Revolución, pragmatismo y disidencia." *Revista de Ciencia Política* 31, no. 2 (2011): 187–206.

Valero, Silvia. *"Los negros se toman la palabra": Primer Congreso de la Cultura Negra de las Américas; Debates al interior de las comisiones y plenarias*. Bogotá: Editorial Pontificia Universidad Javeriana, 2020.

Valis, Noël. *The Culture of Cursilería: Bad Taste, Kitsch, and Class in Modern Spain*. Durham, NC: Duke University Press, 2002.

Vampré, Leven. *São Paulo, terra conquistada*. São Paulo: Editora Paulista, 1932.

Vanegas, Isidro. "Las Guerrillas, la democracia y el Frente Nacional." In *Ciencuenta años del regreso de la democracia. Nuevas Miradas a La relevancia histórica Del Frente Nacional*, 187–203, edited by Carlos Caballero Argáez, Mónica Pachón Buitrago and Eduardo Posada Carbó. Bogotá: Universidad de los Andes, 2012.

Vanegas, Isidro. *Todas son iguales: Estudios sobre la democracia en Colombia*. Bogotá: Universidad Externado de Colombia, 2011.

Varela, Gustavo. *Tango y política: Sexo, moral burguesa y revolución en Argentina*. Buenos Aires: Ariel, 2016.

Vargas, Concepción. "Conjunto habitacional Narciso Mendoza: Villa Coapa." In *El espacio habitacional en la arquitectura moderna*, edited by Enrique Ayala and Gerardo Álvarez, 229–233. México: UAM; CONACYT, 2013.

Velandia, Pedro J., and Eduardo Restrepo. "Estudios afrocolombianos: Balances de un campo heterogéneo." *Tabula Rasa* 27 (July–December 2017): 161–197.

Velho, Gilberto. *A Utopia Urbana: Um Estudo de Antropologia Social*. Rio de Janeiro: Jorge Zahar, 1973.

Verdery, Katherine. *The Political Lives of Dead Bodies*. New York: Columbia University, 1999.

Viales Hurtado, Ronny J. *Después del enclave (1927–1950): Un estudio de la región atlántica costarricense*. San José: EUCR, 1998.

Vidich, Arthur J., ed. *The New Middle Classes: Life-Styles, Status Claims, and Political Orientations*. London: Macmillan, 1995.

Vilar Guerra, F. *Directorio de la Colonia Española*, n.p., 1937.

Villavicencio Navarro, Víctor. "Cuando la prensa incomoda al sistema politico: La libertad de imprenta frente a la propuesta de José María Gutiérrez de Estrada de 1840." *Historia Mexicana* LXIX, no. 1 (2019): 159–204.

Visacovsky, Sergio E. "The Days Argentina Stood Still: History, Nation and Imaginable Futures in the Public Interpretations of the Argentine Crisis at the Beginning of the Twenty-First Century." *Horizontes Antropológicos* 24, no. 52 (2018): 311–341.

Visacovsky, Sergio E. "Estudios Sobre Clase Media En La Antropología Social: Una Agenda Para La Argentina." *Avá: Revista de Antropología* 13 (2008): 9–37.

Visacovsky, Sergio E. *"Hasta la próxima crisis": Historia cíclica, virtudes genealógicas y la identidad de clase media entre los afectados por la debacle financiera en la Argentina (2001–2002)*. México: CIDE, Cuadernos de trabajo, 2010.

Visacovsky, Sergio E. "Inmigración, virtudes genealógicas y los relatos de origen de la clase media argentina." In *Clases medias: Nuevos enfoques desde la sociología, la historia y la antropología*, edited by Sergio E. Visacovsky, Patricia Beatriz Vargas, and Ezequiel Adamovsky, 213–239. Buenos Aires: Ariel, 2014.

Visacovsky, Sergio E. "Intérpretes públicos, teodiceas de la nación y la creación del futuro en la crisis de inicios del siglo XXI en Argentina." In *La ilusión de la justicia transicional: Perspectivas críticas desde el Sur global*, edited by Alejandro Castillejo-Cuéllar, 373–409. Bogotá: Universidad de los Andes, 2017.

Visacovsky, Sergio and Enrique Garguin. Introduction to *Moralidades, economías e identidades de clase media: Estudios históricos y etnográficos*, 11–59. Compiled by Sergio Visacovsky and Enrique Garguin. Buenos Aires: Antropofagia, 2009.

Visacovsky, Sergio E. and Enrique Garguin, comps. *Moralidades, economías e identidades de clase media: Estudios históricos y etnográficos* Buenos Aires: Editorial Antropofagia, 2009.

Viveros Vigoya, Mara. "Social Mobility, Whiteness, and Whitening in Colombia." *The Journal of Latin American and Caribbean Anthropology* 20, no. 3 (2015): 496–512.

Viveros Vigoya, Mara and Franklin Gil Hernández. "Género y generación en las experiencias de ascenso social de personas negras en Bogotá." *Maguaré* 24 (January 1, 2010): 99–130.

Viveros Vigoya, Mara, Franklin Gil Hernández, Hernández, Pietro Pisano, and Klara Hellebrandová. "Grandes Esperanzas: Memorias de raza, género y clase en familias afrodescendientes del siglo XX." Manuscrito Convocatoria de Investigación Orlando Fals Borda – 2017 Apoyo a Proyectos de investigación docentes, 2019.

Viveros Vigoya, Mara, and Krisna Ruette-Orihuela. "Care, Aesthetic Creation, and Anti-Racist Reparations." In *Care and Care Workers: A Latin American Perspective*, edited by Nadya Araujo Guimares and Helena Hirata. New York: Springer, 2021

Viveros Vigoya, Mara *El oxímoron de las clases medias negras: Movilidad social e interseccionalidad en Colombia*, Guadalajara: CALAS, 2022

Vommaro, Gabriel and Hélène Combes. *El clientelismo político desde 1950 hasta nuestros días*. Buenos Aires: Siglo XXI Editores, 2016.

Wacquant, Löic. "Making Class: The Middle-Class(es) in Social Theory and Social Structure." In *Bringing Class Back In: Contemporary and Historical Perspectives*, edited by Scott McNall, Rhonda Levine, and Rick Fantasia. Boulder, CO: Westview Press, 1991.

Wade, Peter. *Blackness and Race Mixture: The Dynamics of Racial Identity in Colombia*. JHU, 1993a.

Wade, Peter. "La relación Chocó-Antioquia: Un caso del colonialismo interno?" In *Colombia Pacífico*, edited by Pablo Leyva, 436–453. Bogotá: Fondo para la Protección del Medio Ambiente 'José Celestino Mutis' – FEN Colombia, 1993b.

Wahrman, Dror. *Imagining the Middle Class: The Political Representation of Class in Britain, c. 1780–1840*. Cambridge: Cambridge University Press, 1995.

Walker, Louise E. *Waking from the Dream: Mexico's Middle Class after 1968*. Stanford, CA: Stanford University Press, 2013.

Wallerstein, Immanuel. "The Bourgeois(ie) as Concept and Reality." *New Left Review* I, no. /167 (1988): 91–106.

Weeks, Jeffrey. *Sex, Politics and Society: The Regulation of Society since 1800*. Abingdon: Routledge, 2012.

Wei, John. *Queer Chinese Cultures and Mobilities: Kinship, Migration, and Middle Classes*. University of Hong Kong Press, 2020.

Weinstein, Barbara. *For Social Peace in Brazil: Industrialists and the Remaking of the Working Class in São Paulo, 1920–1964*. Chapel Hill, NC: University of North Carolina Press, 1996.

Weinstein, Barbara. "The Discourse of Technical Competence: Strategies of Authority and Power in Industrializing Brazil." *Political Power and Social Theory* 12 (1998): 137–175.

Weinstein, Barbara. "Inventing the *Mulher Paulista*: Politics, Rebellion, and the Gendering of Brazilian Regional Identities." *Journal of Women's History* 18, no. 1 (Winter 2006): 22–49.

Weinstein, Barbara. *The Color of Modernity: São Paulo and the Making of Race and Nation in Brazil*. Durham, NC: Duke University Press, 2015.

Weismantel, Mary. *Cholas and Pishtacos: Stories of Race and Sex in The Andes*. Chicago, IL: University of Chicago Press, 2001.

Wilson, B. R. "Review of Crevenna, 'Materiales para el Estudio de la Clase Media en la América Latina'." *British Journal of Sociology* 2, no. 4 (1951): 375–76.

Woodard, James P. *A Place in Politics: São Paulo, Brazil, from Seigneurial Republicanism to Regionalist Revolt*. Durham, NC: Duke University Press, 2009.

Woodard, James P. *Brazil's Revolution in Commerce: Creating Consumer Capitalism in the American Century*. Chapel Hill, NC: University of North Carolina Press, 2020.

Wright, Erik Olin. *Class, Crisis, and the State*. New York: Verso, 1978.

Wright, Erik Olin. *Classes*. London: Verso, 1985.

Wright-Ríos, Edward. "La Madre Matiana: Prophetess and Nation in Mexican Satire." uilherme*The Americas* 68, no. 2 (2011): 241–274.

Xavier Sobrinho, Guilherme. "A 'Classe C' e Sua Alardeada Ascensão: Nova? Classe? Média?" *Indicadores Econômicos FEE* 38, no. 4 (2011): 67–80.

Young, Michael. *The Rise of the Meritocracy, 1870–2033: An Essay on Education and Equality*. Baltimore, MD: Penguin Books, 1961.

Zamorano, Claudia. "Los hijos de la modernidad: Movilidad social, vivienda y producción de ciudad en el México posrevolucionario." *Revista Alteridades* 17, no. 34. (2007): 75–91.

Zamorano, Claudia. *Navegando en el desierto: Estrategias residenciales en un contexto de incertidumbres; Ciudad Juárez*. México: Casa Chata, 2008.

Zamorano, Claudia. *Vivienda mínima obrera en el México Posrevolucionario: Apropiaciones de una utopía urbana, 1936–2004*. México: Casa Chata, 2013.
Zavala Díaz, Ana Laura. "La política y la discordia huyeron luego al aspecto agradable de la fraternidad: El discurso doméstico familiar en las veladas literarias de 1867–1868." In *Aproximaciones a una historia intelectual: Revistas y asociaciones literarias mexicanas del siglo XIX*, coordinated by Guadalupe Curiel Defossé and Belem Clark, 59–78 Mexico: Universidad Nacional Autónoma de México, 2016.
Zavaleta Mercado, René. *Towards a History of the National-Popular in Bolivia, 1879–1980*. London: Seagull Books, 2018.
Zermeño-Padilla, Guillermo. "Del mestizo al mestizaje: Arqueología de un concepto." *Mem.soc* 12, no. 24 (2008): 79–95.
Zhang, Li. *In Search of Paradise: Middle-Class Living in a Chinese Metropolis*. Ithaca, NY: Cornell University Press, 2010.
Zolov, Eric. "Expanding our Current Horizons." *Contracorriente* 5, no. 2 (2008): 47–73.
Zolov, Eric. *Rebeldes con causa: La contracultura mexicana y la crisis del Estado patriarcal*. Mexico City: Norma, 2003.
Zuluaga, Olga Lucía. *Pedagogía e historia: La historicidad de la pedagogía, la enseñanza, un objeto de saber*. Bogotá: Siglo del Hombre Editores, 1999.

Index

Page numbers in *italic* indicate figures and followed by n indicate notes.